DICTIONARY OF AMERICAN POP/ROCK

DICTIONARY
OF
AMERICAN POP/ROCK

Written and compiled by
ARNOLD SHAW

ROCK • POP • RHYTHM & BLUES
FOLK • COUNTRY • BLUES
GOSPEL • JAZZ • FILMS
MUSICAL THEATER • RECORDING
& MUSIC BUSINESS

SCHIRMER BOOKS
A Division of Macmillan Publishing Co., Inc.
NEW YORK

Collier Macmillan Publishers
LONDON

The Free Press
A Division of Macmillan Publishing Co., Inc.
866 Third Avenue, New York, N.Y. 10022

Collier Macmillan Canada, Inc.

Library of Congress Catalog Card Number: 82-50382

Printed in the United States of America

printing number

3   4   5   6   7   8   9   10

Library of Congress Cataloging in Publication Data

Shaw, Arnold.
    Dictionary of American pop/rock.

    1. Music, Popular (Songs, etc.)—Dictionaries.
2. Music, Popular (Songs, etc.)—Bio-bibliography.
I. Title.
ML102.P66S5 1982   780'.42'0321   82-50382
ISBN 0-02-872350-3
ISBN 0-02-872360-0 (pbk.)

Preface and Acknowledgments

This book had its beginnings in a desire to provide a concise dictionary of the terminology, the jargon, and the styles of Rock. But anyone perusing *Rolling Stone,* the Calendar section of the *Los Angeles Times,* or the Arts and Leisure Sunday supplement of *The New York Times* quickly discovers that Rock is hardly a self-contained little island. What started in 1955–1956 as an explosion of energy, musical primitivism, and youthful rebellion has through the years been transformed into an extremely complex organism. There are, and there have been, more varieties of Rock than there are Heinz products, and there are fusions of every conceivable kind. It became clear that one could not effectively describe Rockabilly without devoting attention to Rhythm & Blues; Beatles Rock without probing the modes; Soft Rock without touching aspects of Pop balladry; Soul music without considering Gospel music; and so it went.

Accordingly, the original thrust of the work had to be broadened to include the categories enumerated on the title page: Pop, R & B, C & W, Folk, Jazz, Gospel, Blues, Soul, musical theater, films, the recording and music business. In each of the enumerated fields, key figures have been included under separate listings—The Beatles, Presley, Bob Dylan, Louis Jordan, Irving Berlin, Mahalia Jackson, Richard Rodgers, Lester Young, etc. No biographical information is given in these entries. Instead, the contribution of each in the given area of artistry or expertise is described, analyzed, and evaluated. This is *not* a biographical dictionary but a style and semantic dictionary. One feature—rarely found in dictionaries—is the Index. Its function is to make the alphabetical entries accessible via the names of artists, groups, and individuals associated with given styles, forms, instruments, organizations, and awards.

My interest in the language of popular music actually antedates the rise of Rock 'n' Roll. In 1950, when I was serving as vice-president and general professional manager of Duchess Music Corporation, a Broadway music publishing company, I compiled and wrote *Lingo of Tin-Pan Alley.* This appeared first in *Notes,* a publication of the Music Library Association, and it was published later as a booklet by Broadcast Music, Inc. Linguists like Mario Pei and others praised it as a pioneering, scholarly contribution to the study of a facet of the American language. Some of the terms, including the original definitions, are to be found in this *Dictionary.* In 1967 *Cavalier* magazine published a "Glossary of

Teen-Age Rock,'' which I incorporated in augmented form in my book *The Rock Revolution* (1969). Betweentimes, I put together an unpublished manuscript, *Dictionary of Jazz Terms,* some of whose entries are also contained in the present work.

This *Dictionary of American Pop/Rock* is a product of my involvement in the music business from 1944 to 1966; my more recent work as an Adjunct Professor of Music teaching courses in rock history and black popular music at the University of Nevada at Las Vegas; and my reading, piano playing, and listening during a quarter of a century. As an executive of several Broadway music publishing companies, I had the pleasure of bringing Elvis Presley's Sun Records from Col. Tom Parker's home (where I stayed in the summer of 1955 before Elvis became nationally known) to disk jockey Bill Randle of WERE in Cleveland, whose playing of the disks led to RCA Victor's purchase of Elvis's Sun contract and to his emergence as the King of Rock 'n' Roll. Paul Simon was working as my assistant at Edward B. Marks Music Corporation when he and Art Garfunkel cut their first Columbia album, *Wednesday Morning, 3 AM.* I also published songs by Burt Bacharach and Hal David before they had their run of hits with Dionne Warwick; Jacques Brel's first American hits; and the first hit (''Tell Laura I Love Her'') of Jeff Barry, who recently wrote the score for *The Idolmaker.* Let me add that I am grateful to literally hundreds of writers on Rock and Pop and to students who have added to or challenged (and stimulated) my understanding of our contemporary music. Both insight and information were derived from such writers and critics, among others, as Whitney Balliett, Gary Giddins, Robert Hilburn, Stephen Holden, Dennis Hunt, David Marsh, Jim Miller, Robert Palmer, John Rockwell, Joel Selvin, Bill Willard, and the late Ralph J. Gleason.

I would like also to express appreciation to Jeremiah Kaplan, through whom this work became a Macmillan project; and to Ed Barry, Ken Stuart, Abigail Sterne, and Deirdre Murphy, all of whom helped bring it to fruition.

Through the years, I have known and/or interviewed artists and others in the different fields and phases of Pop and Rock covered in this *Dictionary.* Among Rock people: Paul Anka, Chuck Berry, Crew Cuts, Alan Freed, Bill Haley, Jerry Lee Lewis, Murray the K, Col. Tom Parker, and the Poni-Tails. Among Pop people: Archie Bleyer, Nat ''King'' Cole, Don Costa, Billy Daniels, Georgia Gibbs, Gordon Jenkins, Frankie Laine, Billy May, Johnny Mercer, Louis Prima, Johnnie Ray, Bill Randle, and Alec Wilder. In Black music: James Brown, Ruth Brown, Lowell Fulson, Hunter Hancock, Mahalia Jackson, Quincy Jones, Louis Jordan, Aaron ''T-Bone'' Walker, Dinah Washington, Jackie Wilson, and Jimmy Witherspoon. Among Country artists: Eddy Arnold, Tennessee Ernie Ford, Merle Haggard, Buck

Owens, Mrs. Jimmie Rodgers, and Ernest Tubb. Among Jazz people: Count Basie, Dave Brubeck, Benny Carter, Paul Desmond, Erroll Garner, Stan Getz, Dizzy Gillespie, Woody Herman, Marian McPartland, Shelly Manne, Red Norvo, Maxine Sullivan, and Mary Lou Williams. Among record producers: Ralph Bass, Joe Bihari, Ahmet Ertegun, Nesuhi Ertegun, Milt Gabler, Bob Geddins, John Hammond, Herman Lubinsky, Mitch Miller, Johnny Otis, Syd Nathan, Steve Sholes, Jerry Wexler, and Randy Wood.

ARNOLD SHAW

A

A/C   Abbreviation of "Adult Contemporary."
See also Adult Contemporary; Easy Listening; Soft Rock.

ACT   An acronym for "at the center of things," as in, "I'm getting my act together."

AGAC   *See* American Guild of Authors and Composers.

AOR   Abbreviation of "album-oriented rock." Refers to radio stations that program albums or tracks from albums instead of singles, or in addition to singles.

A & R   Abbreviation of "artists and repertoire." In the years before the rise of Rock 'n' Roll, the men who superintended record sessions were known as A & R men. Employed by the record companies, they worked at finding repertoire for the label's artists to record. While most companies still maintain A & R departments, records are generally cut today under the watchful ears of independent producers. A & R men select and contract given producers, or artists do so; then, depending on the clout of the producers, accept, reject, or ask for modification in the masters proffered by the producers. Once the A & R chieftains at eight or nine major labels—men like Mitch Miller at Columbia, Dave Kapp at Decca, Hugo and Luigi at Mercury—ruled the music business. At these high-powered labels, different A & R men administered different types of music: Capitol had Ken Nelson as A & R head of C & W, Dave Dexter on Jazz, Dave Cavanaugh on Blues and Rhythm & Blues, and Voyle Gilmore and Lee Gillette on Pop. Today, independent producers with their own production companies rule the record field.

ASCAP   *See* American Society of Composers, Authors, and Publishers.

absolute music   It has no words, and is not descriptive, illustrative, interpretative, or inspired by anything outside itself. Self-contained, it develops from its own tensions and esthetic demands. The opposite is program music.

absolute pitch   An inborn faculty through which some people can identify the precise note of any sound they hear. Most of the population operates on relative pitch, the experiential ability to distinguish higher from lower pitches, sometimes to the point of identifying intervals. Training can occasionally heighten an individual's sense of pitch so that it approaches absolute pitch.

abstract music *See* absolute music.

Academy Award songs *See* Motion Picture Academy Award (Oscar) songs.

Academy Awards Recognition of excellence in acting, directing, and other categories through the awarding of statuettes was begun by the Academy of Motion Picture Arts and Sciences on May 6, 1929. It was not until two years later that as the result of an offhand remark of Academy librarian Margaret Herrick, the statuettes became known as "Oscars"—they reminded her of her Uncle Oscar.

The first award for Best Song was made in 1934, and it went to "The Continental," music by Con Conrad and lyrics by Herb Magidson, from *The Gay Divorcee.* That same year, an award was presented to the Columbia Studio Music Department, headed by Louis Silvers, for Best Scoring of Music in the film *One Night of Love* by Victor Schertzinger and Gus Kahn.

Beginning with the annual awards in 1938, three Oscars were given in music: one for the Best Song ("Thanks for the Memory" by Ralph Rainger, music, and Leo Robin, lyrics, in *Big Broadcast of 1938*); another for the Best Scoring of Music (Alfred Newman for *Alexander's Ragtime Band*); and a third for the Best Original Score (Erich Wolfgang Korngold for *The Adventures of Robin Hood*).

Beginning in 1941 for the fourteenth annual awards, the three categories were described as follows: Best Song, Best Scoring of a Musical Picture, and Best Scoring of a Dramatic Picture, the last-mentioned being changed the following year to Best Scoring of a Dramatic or Comedy Picture.

See also Motion Picture Academy Award (Oscar) songs.

Academy of Country and Western Music Not to be confused with the Nashville-based Country Music Association, this award-granting association was founded in 1964 in Los Angeles and concerns itself with C & W music and performers in the western states. Although it made its first awards in 1964, its first official awards show was held in the Hollywood Palladium in February 1966. Top Male Vocalist that year was Merle Haggard, and Top Female Vocalist, Bonnie Guitar. Song of the Year was "Apartment # 9."

The Accurate A tabulation of the songs performed each day from 6:00 P.M. to 1:00 A.M. on the four major networks (ABC, CBS, Mutual,

NBC), The Accurate was in use during the heyday of live performances on network radio. It derived its name from that of the Brooklyn, N.Y., company that monitored the stations and delivered a mimeographed list to subscribers each morning. The subscribers were mainly the New York City music publishers, who used the list to determine the progress of a song and to check the activities of their song-pluggers. Regardless of the hour at which a song was performed, the number of stations in a network, the number of people listening to a given program, or the type of plug (vocal or instrumental, commercial or sustaining), every plug was regarded as equal in value. The Accurate merely enumerated them and carried a daily and a weekly total for each song. As large-scale evils developed in connection with payola and remote sustaining programs, the Peatman, which weighted each plug on the basis of the criteria mentioned above, came into being as a yardstick of the development of a hit.

    See also payola; The Peatman.

Accutrack turntable   A short-lived turntable, the essence of which was that it could be programmed to play bands on a disk in any preselected order. An infrared sensor located in the tone-arm head detected the space between tracks, and a digital device in the base of the turntable could be programmed to play any of the bands in any order. Although this particular model was discontinued after a short time, there are now turntables like Fisher 6360 and Optonica RP 9705 that embody the same selective feature.

"Ace"   A southern black word for "friend."

Acid Rock   Originating on the West Coast, the music sought to achieve the "mind-expanding" effects and/or disorientation of the senses produced by hallucinogenic drugs like lysergic acid diethylamide (LSD). As a music for listening rather than dancing, Acid Rock departed from the basic Rock tradition. To produce the sense distortions of the psychedelic state of mind, musicians employed synthesizers, high decibel amplification, feedback, fuzztone, and Middle Eastern and East Indian instruments like the oud and sitar. The emphasis was on languid melodies, sliding notes, an absence of chord changes, and modal sounds. Conventional and electronic instruments were also used to simulate the whining and drone sounds of the exotic instruments. Kaleidoscopic light shows were developed to intensify the psychedelic effects.

    Philosophical as well as esthetic and hedonistic concepts underlay the Acid experience: sensory disorientation could liberate the individual, expand consciousness, and transform one's outlook. The lyrics of Acid songs tended to be mystical and/or surrealistic. Concerned with musical manipulation of texture, density, tone color, and volume, Acid groups sacrificed the explosive energy, the heady buoyancy, and the sheer visceral excitement of early Rock 'n' Roll.

The first psychedelic disk was a documentary produced by Capitol Records of Los Angeles in which a group of studio musicians recorded ostensibly under the influence of LSD. Behind the narrator, one heard a weird blend of fluttering flutes and verbal moaning. Soon groups sprang up in LA with curious names like The Mushrooms and Ever-Pretending Fullness, striving to emulate the psychedelic sounds with electronic in-struments. Of greater significance in the emergence of Acid Rock were the hit singles and albums of the innovative Byrds, starting in 1965 with "Mr. Tambourine Man" (No. 1 as a single and No. 6 as an album) and continuing with "5 D" and "Eight Miles High." Although the Byrds insisted that the latter was a song about flying, their record was banned by many radio stations because of the alleged drug implications.

Despite its origin in LA and the later impact of such LA groups as the Doors and the Mothers of Invention, the center of Psychedelia quickly moved from the Sunset Strip to San Francisco's Haight-Ashbury district. Three personalities figured in this shift: novelist Ken Kesey, who began throwing "acid test" LSD parties in the Bay City in 1965; disk jockey Tom Donahue, who quit his Top 40 job and opened a psychedelic nightclub; and chemist Owsley Stanley, synthesizer of LSD, who early became a patron of the Grateful Dead.

The first of San Francisco's Acid groups to be signed to a major record company (RCA) and to attain national prominence was The Jefferson Airplane. Though it pursued a number of current trends—"flower power," Oriental mysticism, and the alternative life-style—hit singles like "White Rabbit" and "Plastic Fantastic Lover" and the album *Surrealistic Pillow* aroused interest in psychedelic music.

The Grateful Dead, who performed ear-shattering numbers at Ken Kesey's parties and whose debut album appeared in 1967, acquired a reputation for playing while stoned. Disoriented in time, they would operate in slow motion, trying the patience of audiences with the inor-dinate time it took to tune up and then to decide what song to play next. Other Acid Rock groups of the time and area included Quicksilver Messenger Service, several of whose members were busted on drug charges, and Sly & the Family Stone.

Two San Francisco ballrooms, the Fillmore and Avalon, provided platforms for local acidheads like the 13th Floor Elevators, Dr. West's Medicine Show, and Jug Band, all of whom experimented with light shows, high decibel amplification, and shock visual and aural effects.

The psychedelic syndrome was not necessarily divorced from mean-ingful lyrics, as Country Joe and the Fish demonstrated in anti-Vietnam and anti-Establishment songs; or from musical inventiveness, as Moby

Grape displayed in jams by guitarists Al Kooper (b. 1944) and Mike Bloomfield (b. circa 1942).

While San Francisco remained the City of Psychedelia, nurturing perhaps as many as 500 bands in the heyday of Haight-Ashbury (1967), LA accounted for at least two major Acid groups. Jim Morrison (1943–1971) was the intellectual and musical guru of The Doors, as Frank Zappa, (b. 1940), who coined the term "freak out," was of the Mothers of Invention. That the East Coast was not averse to mind-smashing experimentation became apparent in the work of the Fugs, Vanilla Fudge, and the Blues Magoos, the latter in their *Psychedelic Lollipop* album. Before long, a number of English groups became interested in psychedelic rock—the Yardbirds, Small Faces, Traffic, and Pink Floyd, known as the prototype psychedelic group of 1966–1967.

Some groups who were not Acid Rockers dealt with the psychedelic experience in given songs: the Beatles in "Lucy in the Sky with Diamonds," "Strawberry Fields Forever," and "A Day in the Life" in the *Sgt. Pepper* album; Bob Dylan (b. 1941), in "Rainy Day Woman #12 and #35" as well as "Mr. Tambourine Man"; the Rolling Stones in "Paint It Black"; Van Dyke Parks (b. circa 1941) in his *Song Cycle;* Jimi Hendrix (1942–1970) in "Third Stone from the Sun"; Motown's Temptations in "Cloud Nine" and "Psychedelic Shack"; and even the Beach Boys in "Good Vibrations."

During the 1970s, echoes of the psychedelic sound and style were heard in recordings of such West German groups as Kraftwerk and Tangerine Dreams.

See also feedback; *Freak Out;* fuzztone; light show; synthesizer.

"acid tests"   What Ken Kesey & his Merry Pranksters called their "social" jam sessions, run in 1965–1966 at the Fillmore and other San Francisco spots.

acoustics   The science of sound, involving both its production and reception. Refers also to the sound-projecting characteristics of a concert hall.

Roy Acuff (1903–)   A native of Maynardsville, Tenn., Acuff did not become active in music until sensitivity to the sun ruled out a career in Major League baseball. He was then 30. By 1942 he was the leading vocal star of the Grand Ole Opry. That year, he founded the first important music-publishing company in Nashville with songwriter Fred Rose, a company whose giant catalogue includes the songs of the "Hillbilly Shakespeare" Hank Williams (1923–1953). In 1942, too, he organized the Smoky Mountain Boys, with whom he recorded a vast number of hits, including "The Great Speckled Bird," "Wabash Cannonball,'' ''Precious Jewel,'' ''I Saw the Light,'' and ''Will the Circle Be Unbroken?'' He is reputed to have sold over 30 million disks in a career that in 1962 led to his being elected as the first living member of the Country Music Hall of Fame.

ad lib   Abbreviation of the Latin phrase *ad libitum,* meaning ''freely'' or ''as you desire.''

Adult Contemporary   Some trade papers use the term ''Easy Listening'' or ''MOR'' (middle of the road). *Billboard*'s most recent coinage is ''Adult Contemporary.''
    See also Easy Listening.

advance   A sum of money paid on the signing of a contract and/or the delivery of a song or score, as an advance against future earnings (royalties). When the advance is not recouped from future earnings, it is known as a bonus.

advance man   Generally a publicist who precedes the arrival of a performer in a given area and whose function it is to attract attention to the forthcoming appearance of the performer. The advance man is frequently expected to confirm hotel reservations, arrange for interviews on radio and/or TV, and make certain that the performer's working and living arrangements allow for the best performance possible.

Afro-Cuban   Music coming from Cuba and rooted in the black African tradition. The broader term ''Latin-American'' embraces dances, sounds, and rhythms developed in South America, Mexico, and the Dominican Republic as well. Rhythms comprehended under the broader term include: Bossa Nova, Cha-Cha-Cha, Cuban Bolero, Guaracha, Mambo, Merengue, Rumba, Samba, Son-Montuno, and Tango.

afterbeats   The traditional stress in 4/4 time is on the first (downbeat) and third beat of a measure. In Rhythm & Blues and Rock 'n' Roll, the stress is on the second and fourth beats, the backbeats or afterbeats: count 1, $\overset{>}{2}$, 3, $\overset{>}{4}$, and clap your hands or stamp your foot on 2 and 4.

after hours   A term that developed during the 1920s and 1930s, referring to the practice of jazz musicians performing after a gig was over. They played for their own fun and amusement, and at times for patrons who would not leave a club until dawn. A strict enforcement of union regulations and the decay of nightlife during World War II led to the eventual disappearance of the practice.

Aggie   An acronym for the highest honor awarded by the American Guild of Authors & Composers. Among the writers who have been honored with an Aggie: Harold Adamson (b. 1906), Ervin Drake (b. 1919), Sammy Fain (b. 1902), John Green (b. 1908), Johnny Mercer (1909–1976), Harry Warren (b. 1893–1981), Paul Francis Webster (b. 1907), and Meredith Willson (b.1902). The Aggie, made of transparent plastic, is a three-tiered medallion, with a center panel that gives the name of the recipient and the basis of the award, surmounted by the initials a.g.a.c.

See also American Guild of Authors & Composers.

Album of the Year, Country (CMA)

1967	*There Goes My Everything,* Jack Greene (Decca)
1968	*Johnny Cash at Folsom Prison,* Johnny Cash (Columbia)
1969	*Johnny Cash at San Quentin Prison,* Johnny Cash (Columbia)
1970	*Okie from Muskogee,* Merle Haggard (Capitol)
1971	*I Won't Mention It Again,* Ray Price (Columbia)
1972	*Let Me Tell You about a Song,* Merle Haggard (Capitol)
1973	*Behind Closed Doors,* Charlie Rich (Epic)
1974	*A Very Special Love Song,* Charlie Rich (Epic)
1975	*A Legend in My Time,* Ronnie Milsap (RCA)
1976	*Wanted—The Outlaws,* Waylon Jennings, Jessie Colter, Tompall Glaser, Willie Nelson (RCA)
1977	*Ronnie Milsap Live,* Ronnie Milsap (RCA)
1978	*It Was Almost Like a Song,* Ronnie Milsap (RCA)
1979	*The Gambler,* Kenny Rogers (United Artists)
1980	*Coal Miner's Daughter,* Original Motion Picture Soundtrack (MCA)
1981	*I Believe in You,* Don Williams (MCA)

Album of the Year, Best (NARAS Grammy Awards)

1958	*The Music from "Peter Gunn":* Henry Mancini
1959	*Come Dance with Me:* Frank Sinatra
1960	*Button-Down Mind:* Bob Newhart
1961	*Judy at Carnegie Hall:* Judy Garland
1962	*The First Family:* Vaughn Meader
1963	*The Barbra Streisand Album:* Barbara Streisand
1964	*Getz/Gilberto:* Stan Getz, João Gilberto
1965	*September of My Years:* Frank Sinatra
1966	*Sinatra: A Man & His Music:* Frank Sinatra
1967	*Sgt. Pepper's Lonely Hearts Club Band:* The Beatles
1968	*By the Time I Get to Phoenix:* Glen Campbell
1969	*Blood, Sweat & Tears:* Blood, Sweat & Tears

1970 *Bridge over Troubled Water:* Simon & Garfunkel

1971 *Tapestry:* Carole King

1972 *The Concert for Bangladesh:* George Harrison, Ravi Shankar, Bob Dylan, Leon Russell, Ringo Starr, Billy Preston, Eric Clapton, Klaus Voormann

1973 *Innervisions:* Stevie Wonder

1974 *Fulfillingness' First Finales:* Stevie Wonder

1975 *Still Crazy After All These Years:* Paul Simon

1976 *Songs in the Key of Life:* Stevie Wonder

1977 *Rumours:* Fleetwood Mac

1978 *Saturday Night Fever:* The Bee Gees, David Shire, Yvonne Elliman, Tavares, Kool & the Gang, K. C. & the Sunshine Band, MFSB, Trammps, Walter Murphy, Ralph MacDonald

1979 *52nd Street:* Billy Joel

1980 *Christopher Cross:* Christopher Cross

1981 *Double Fantasy:* John Lennon/Yoko Ono

See also National Academy of Recording Arts and Sciences.

Aleatory Rock   Long before the advent of Rock, avant-garde composers like Karlheinz Stockhausen in Europe, and Milton Babbit and, especially, John Cage in the U.S.A. experimented with chance composition. "Aleatory" derives from Latin words, *aleator* and *alea,* having to do with gambling and dice. Numbers were, in fact, used by the Russian-American Joseph Schillinger as the basis of chance patterns, while John Cage used the *I Ching* of Oriental origin. Others employed synthesizers, computers and/or taped musical sequences as the basis of random composition. The Beatles and, especially, Frank Zappa (b. 1940) experimented with this type of composing.

See also computer; synthesizer; Synth-Rock.

alla breve   A musical term indicating that a given passage, section, or movement is to be played so fast that 4/4 time sounds like 2/4 time.

The Almanac Singers   Founded late in 1940 by folk singer Pete Seeger (b. 1919), Millard Lampell, and Lee Hays (b. 1914), a former college instructor and roommate of Lampell, the Almanac Singers became a quartet with the addition of singer/songwriter Woody Guthrie (1912-1967) in June 1941. A socially conscious group, they recorded an album of labor songs (*Talking Union*) and an album supporting the war effort (*Dear Mr. President*). When they disbanded in the summer of 1942, the legendary Woody Guthrie formed the short-lived Headline Singers with legendary Leadbelly (1885-1949), Brownie McGhee (b. 1914), and Sonny Terry (b. 1911). While Millard Lampell embarked on a fulltime writing career, Pete Seeger and Lee Hays formed the highly successful Folk/Pop group The Weavers. The Almanac Singers, and especially Seeger and Guthrie, are credited with popularizing the term "hootenanny."

See also Woody Guthrie; hootenanny; Huddie Ledbetter; Pete Seeger.

Altamont   The raceway in Alameda County, CA, 60 miles from San Francisco, at which the Rolling Stones and Grateful Dead gave a free concert on December 6, 1969. It was a tragic event that involved considerable violence, including a murder, and that seemed to spell the end of the youth subculture of the sixties, including the hope of social change embodied in that subculture. With members of the Hells Angels motorcycle gang serving as security guards in return for all the beer they could consume, a number of the 300,000 attendees were beaten with cue sticks and a black youngster was stabbed to death when he tried to reach the stage. The incident is shown in the film *Gimme Shelter,* a movie made at the concert through which the culprit was identified and brought to trial. For some time after the festival, the Rolling Stones would not perform "Sympathy for the Devil," the number they were doing when the murder occurred.

See also festivals; The Rolling Stones.

Alternative Chorus–Songwriters Showcase   Patterned after *Broadside* hootenannies in Greenwich Village in which young talent could perform, the Alternative Showcase was formed in Hollywood in 1971 by John Braheny and singer/topical songwriter Len Chandler (b. 1935). First held at Ed Pearl's Ash Grove, it moved from Lincoln Center West to a Capitol Records studio, to Art Laboe's club, and back to the old Ash Grove, later known as The Improvisation.

See also Ash Grove.

alternative life-style   The 1960s were an era of alternatives for the young: an ongoing rebellion against the Organization Man and Establishment values, concepts, and traditions. It was a time of be-ins, teach-ins, love-ins, meditation, black power, tribal sex, flower power, hippie communes, and drug experimentation—all alternatives to the ways of the older generation. Before the apocalyptic bomb exploded (a real fear) and they turned 30, the young were determined to experience everything, a drive that superseded what parents, church, academia, and society required. The gurus were Timothy Leary with his slogan "Turn on, tune in, and drop out"; Ken Kesey and LSD; Aldous Huxley and mescaline. Through drugs, youth sought to unlock the doors to intensified feeling and a fresh perception of reality; to stop time and exist wholly in the here and now; to liberate the emotional and sensory self from the prison of the intellect. Young blacks moved to separate themselves from the white world and to develop ethnic alternatives; as in the youth counterculture, the emphasis was on spontaneity, a return to fundamentals, a regard for individuality, cooperation rather than competition, and a commitment to the moment and the ethnic group. For the Establishment press, the counterculture substituted posters and underground papers. In song, sex was approached directly, not metaphorically. From Establishment radio and programming, youth turned to FM. In music business, Rock groups turned away from the big, established record companies and founded their own labels; they set up their own publishing companies. The "alternative life-style" found expression in *The Whole Earth Catalog,* produced by Stewart Brand, who originated the San Francisco Trips Festival in 1966 with novelist Ken Kesey, also in such Rock musicals as *Hair* (1967), *The Last Sweet Days of Isaac* (1970), and *Pippin* (1972).

See also Acid Rock; commune; counterculture; the drug scene; flower children; *Freak Out; Hair;* hippie; Soul.

American Bandstand   The longest-lived—and, in the late 1950s, the most influential—of the Rock 'n' Roll shows, it premiered on TV on August 5, 1957, and was still visible as a Saturday TV program in 1982. Less than a year after its debut, *American Bandstand* boasted a TV network of 105 stations. With clean-cut Dick Clark as its host, it reflected and influenced the songs teenagers favored, the artists they idolized, the new dances they learned, and even the clothes they wore. Televised from Philadelphia's WFIL, the program made the city the center of Teenage and Pop Rock 'n' Roll in the 1957–1960 period, popularizing such local artists as Fabian (b. 1943), Frankie Avalon (b. 1940), Bobby Rydell (b. 1942), and others, and contributing to the rise and growth of such local record labels as Cameo-Parkway, Chancellor, Jamie, and Swan. (During the payola investigations of 1959–1960, it was revealed that genial Dick Clark was financially involved with all four labels.) In a way, *American Bandstand* embodied an era of rock, the years when the publishing and record industry, struggling to compete with the independent labels spawned by R & B and R 'n' R, invaded the rock scene with ersatz, manufactured Rock 'n' Roll. "At the Hop" by Danny & the Juniors, a song whose title was suggested by Clark, encapsulates the era with its verve, fast beat, and celebration of a typical rock phenomenon.

See also Dick Clark.

American Federation of Musicians   This is the national union that represents musicians, arrangers, and copyists in contract negotiations with employer groups in the fields of recording, television, live enter-tainment, motion pictures, and commercials. Union members pay an-nual dues to city locals, the largest being Local 802 in New York and Local 47 in Los Angeles. Employers pay the AFM money for two funds: health and welfare, and pension. Based on sales, record companies pay a royalty to the AFM's trust fund, half of which is paid to union members playing record sessions and the other half of which goes to musicians performing at free musical functions open to the public.

American Guild of Authors and Composers   AGAC was founded in 1931 when three well-known songwriters enlisted the support of fifty others in preparing a Basic Minimum Songwriters Contract. The three were Edgar Leslie (1885–1976), Billy Rose (1899–1966), and George W. Meyer (1884–1959). Within six months, the Songwriters' Protective Association, as it was then called, came into existence and achieved recognition within the music business as the legitimate spokesman of the songwriting profession. In 1958 it changed its name to the American Guild of Authors and Composers.

In working to defend and strengthen the rights of creators in their dealings with those who market their works, AGAC strives to get the best writer contract available for its members; it also collects royalties for its membership and conducts periodic audits of music publishers' books. In addition, it maintains a copyright renewal service, files ter-mination notices under revised copyright laws, administers writer-publisher catalogs (CAP), operates an estates administration service, of-fers a collaboration service, and provides song or catalog financial evaluation.

Apart from its economic functions, AGAC also has developed an educational program that includes: (1) songwriter workshops; (2) ASKAPRO rap sessions; (3) a Composers and Lyricists Education Foundation (CLEF); and (4) news bulletins with essential songwriter information.

AGAC's membership in 1981 numbered over 3,500 authors and composers whose work covered all phases of music: Pop, R & B, Rock, Folk, concert music, Country, Jazz, theater music, motion picture and TV scores, and commercials. Under its constitution, AGAC's voting members elect a council of 21 members: 14 from the East, 7 from the West. There are also 21 alternate council members. All are chosen for a period of three years. Officers are elected from the council.

See also songwriters' contract.

American Recording Studios   Located in Memphis, it was a small studio with a three-track board—a standard two-track tape recorder with another machine patched into it—run by Chips Moman and

Tommy Cogbill, who founded it in 1968. Guitarist Moman was originally a producer at Stax Records in Memphis, while Cogbill worked as a session bass player at Fame Studios in nearby Muscle Shoals, Ala. American rose to prominence, along with Fame, in the late 1960s when singers went south in an effort to revive fading record careers. Together with Stax, Fame, and Hi Records, also of Memphis, American helped form the Memphis Soul sound of the 1960s.

See also Memphis sound.

American Society of Composers, Authors, and Publishers (ASCAP). ASCAP was founded in 1914 by Nathan Burkan, a copyright lawyer; George Maxwell, an Englishman with a background in performing rights; and composer Victor Herbert (1859–1924). Its purpose was to insure, under the copyright laws of 1897 and 1909, that songwriters and publishers would receive compensation when music was publicly performed for profit in theaters, restaurants, cabarets, and other places. It made its first distribution of collected royalties in 1921. With the advent of radio, the first industry-wide agreement between ASCAP and the NAB (National Association of Broadcasters), governing use of ASCAP's catalog over the air, was made in 1932. It called for a license fee of 3 percent of all radio revenue for 1933, 4 percent for 1934, and 5 percent for 1935. A five-year extension of the 5 percent agreement brought ASCAP about $4.5 million a year.

In 1940, after a disagreement about new royalty rates, the country's radio stations boycotted ASCAP music and began operating their own publishing company, Broadcast Music Incorporated (BMI). In the settlement which brought ASCAP music back on the air, ASCAP was compelled to accept a reduced license fee. Partly because of its location in New York City, then the capital of Pop music, and largely because of the character of mainstream music in the 1930s and 1940s, ASCAP's orientation was Tin-Pan Alley and Hollywood. Not surprisingly, from 1934 until 1960 Oscars for the Motion Picture Academy Award songs all went to ASCAP songwriters; since 1960 some BMI writers have won the annual awards, but ASCAP still holds the edge by a considerable margin.

On its entry into the music scene, BMI concentrated its attention on Rhythm & Blues and Country & Western, two regional streams of music ASCAP had not cultivated at that time. As a result of its sponsorship of new publishers and writers in these areas, BMI grew rapidly and benefited greatly from the teenage turn to Rock 'n' Roll. In time, the ASCAP repertory expanded and made strides in the contemporary music scene.

Today ASCAP counts among its members distinguished writers from all branches of music: Rock, Disco, Country, Gospel, R&B, Jazz, theater, film, Latin, and so on. On its large roster are such outstanding writers of concert music and Broadway musicals as Aaron Copland, Irving Berlin, Leonard Bernstein, the Gershwins, Oscar Hammerstein, Cole Porter, Richard Rodgers, and Stephen Sondheim—to name just a few—side by side with the newer proponents of contemporary music, including the Commodores, Doobie Brothers, Blondie, Neil Diamond, Billy Joel, Earth, Wind & Fire, Kenny Rogers, Carly Simon, and Stevie Wonder. To date, ASCAP members have collectively won 110 of the 134 Oscars that have been awarded for film music; several hundred Grammys; a major share of Broadway's Tonys; numerous Emmys; and 17 Pulitzer Prizes. The organization's current president, lyricist Hal David, has garnered 20 Gold Records, an Oscar, and a Grammy, and has been elected to the Songwriters Hall of Fame.

As of May 1981, ASCAP remained the largest of the three American performing rights licensing organizations, with a writer membership of 23,273, a publisher membership of 8,987, and a gross revenue of $127,935,000 for 1979 and over $150,000,000 for 1980. In addition to its New York headquarters, the Society has 19 branch offices across the U.S.A., with membership offices in New York, Los Angeles, and Nashville.

A non-profit membership association, ASCAP distributes to its members all revenue after deducting operating costs. To become a member, a songwriter needs a musical composition which has been commercially recorded, "regularly published" (meaning that the writer has not paid someone to publish it), or performed by an ASCAP-licensed user. To become a publisher member of ASCAP, a firm should be actively engaged in the music publishing business and have a published or commercially recorded musical work. The members elect ASCAP's board of directors, which sets the Society's policies; it is the only performing rights licensing organization in the United States whose members elect a board of directors made up entirely of composers, lyricists, and music publishers. Of the 24 directors, 12 are writers elected by the writer membership and 12 are publishers elected by the publisher membership; six of the board members (three writers and three publishers) are from the "Standard" field, i.e., writers and publishers of works performed in symphony and concert halls. ASCAP's officers are elected by the board of directors. Distribution of income is made six times a year; four of these distributions cover performances in the U.S.A. and two reflect foreign performances. ASCAP has affiliations with performing rights societies in 40 foreign countries.

In addition to its regular distributions, ASCAP makes supplementary annual awards in the Pop and Standard fields to lyricist and composer members whose creative activities are not adequately reflected in surveyed performances. Since 1968 it has also made awards for literary excellence in the field of music to authors of books and magazine articles; these are known as the ASCAP-Deems Taylor Awards. Additionally, the ASCAP Symphony Orchestra Awards single out musical organizations for "adventuresome programming of contemporary music." In 1979, 27 U.S. symphony orchestras received plaques and shared in cash awards of $14,700.

The Nathan Burkan Memorial Competition for outstanding law school essays on copyright law was established in 1938 to honor the late founder, ASCAP's first general counsel and a noted copyright authority. In addition to stimulating interest in the field of copyright law, the competition has been the basis for much scholarly writing in this area. Since 1976 the ASCAP Foundation, financed primarily by the Jack and Amy Norworth Memorial Fund, has awarded grants to universities for music courses, sponsored the ASCAP Songwriters Workshop, and inaugurated a Grants to Young Composers Program.

See also Broadcast Music, Inc.; performing rights; SESAC.

amplifier   A device that ups the power, current, and/or voltage of a sound.

Androgynous Rock   There is no such thing, musically speaking. But there are a number of groups like Alice Cooper, whose leader poses as a woman although his name is Vince Furnier (b. 1948). Other sexually ambiguous individuals or groups include the British T. Rex, whose leader was the late Marc Bolan; Lou Reed (b. circa 1940) of the Velvet Underground; and David Bowie (b. 1947), who has been described as "the first space-age bisexual Deco superstar." Dyeing his hair orange and wearing heavy makeup, Bowie sometimes is said to dress like a "cross between Esther Williams and Flash Gordon." Lou Reed has dyed his hair yellow and his nails black. All of the Androgynous Rockers display a tendency toward flamboyant costuming, a trend exploited by the Village People, a group that has come forth frankly as male homosexuals, garbed as typical small-town villagers.

"angel"   One who puts up money to back a show or a record session.

"Annie Oakley"   A free pass for admission to a theater or any entertainment. Derived from the name of the pistol-packing Annie Oakley, whose countenance adorned free passes handed out by promoter Buffalo Bill for the cowboy extravaganza in which she appeared.

answer song   Songs trading on the popularity of a current song by responding to it have been a tradition in both the country and R & B fields. Sometimes the answer song will even employ the melody of the original, as in the case of the Midnighters' 1955 hit "Work with Me, Annie," to which Etta James responded with "Roll with Me, Henry," a.k.a. "The Wallflower." The latter was copied by Georgia Gibbs, with the title softened to "Dance with Me, Henry." As the writer of the original, Hank Ballard (b. circa 1930) collected royalties on all three songs. An answer to "Tell Laura I Love Her," written by the original writers as "Tell Tommy I Miss Him," did not do as well as the original. Neither did "Poor Begonia Caught Pneumonia," an answer to Brian Hyland's "Itsy Bitsy Teenie Weenie Yellow Polka Dot Bikini." When the Drifters recorded "Save the Last Dance for Me," Damita Jo replied with "I'm Saving the Last Dance for You." In another answer song of 1960, Jeanne Black countered Jim Reeve's "He'll Have to Go" with "He'll Have to Stay."

anti-drug songs   The contention by critics of Rock that it promotes the use of drugs is answered by others who point to anti-drug songs like Dion's "Your Own Back Yard," Curtis Mayfield's "Freddie's Dead," and Paul Revere & the Raiders' disk of the Barry Mann/Cynthia Weill song "Kicks."

anti-hero   The rebel as hero, really anti-hero, first apparent in modern novels and plays, suddenly appeared on the screen in the persons of James Dean as the rebel without a cause and Marlon Brando in motorcycle boots, black denim trousers, and black leather jacket, not to mention black shades. In Rock 'n' Roll, Presley sprang forth as both the visual and aural embodiment of the anti-hero with his sneering countenance, erotic pelvis, and arrogant air.
See also Elvis Presley.

Apollo Theatre   Located at 253 West 125th Street in Harlem, the Apollo was the shrine of black music and live black entertainment from 1934, when the Frank Schiffman family took it over, until 1976. Long after vaudeville had died in the 1930s, you could hear the new and the great black singers, vocal groups, and bands at the Apollo. On Wednesday evenings, when the Apollo held its all-important Amateur Night, you frequently heard up-and-coming stars. Through the R & B years and the R 'n' R years, talent hunters from every facet of show business—bookers, managers, songwriters, record men, and music publishers—all made a point of catching the Wednesday night amateurs. Those who performed inadequately before a very discerning audience were not only hooted off the stage but were literally yanked off by a long stick that was curved at one end like a shepherd's staff and that fitted around the neck of the unlucky contestant. ("Give him the hook!" as a negative reaction to a performer may well have originated in this gambit.) Winners of first prize on three consecutive Wednesdays received a one-week booking at the theater. Among the record stars who were born on the Apollo stage, one finds Billie Holiday (1915–1959), Ella Fitzgerald (b. 1918), Sarah Vaughan (b. 1924), Leslie Uggams, Joe Tex, and Varetta Dillard (b. 1928).

After singers made the big time, Harlem's audiences expected them periodically to play the Apollo as a token of their regard for their people. At Easter and Christmas, the Apollo became a black church as Gospel music took over. The Apollo did not close completely in 1976, but it stopped presenting live entertainment and discontinued its Amateur Nights, which was tantamount to closing.

Appalachian dulcimer   *See* dulcimer.

arhoolie   A cornfield holler. An inchoate, unformed, improvised bit of song, chanted either as a bit of musing by a field hand or as communication with another laborer. Arhoolies and other types of hollers anticipated the rise of the Blues. As a word, "arhoolie" is believed to derive from Gullah (a Southern African dialect), or it may be a corruption of the word "hallelujah."

Armadillo World Headquarters   A defunct National Guard armory in Austin, Tex., rechristened Armadillo World Headquarters by publicist Eddie Wilson, became the site of the first monster Country Rock concert given by Willie Nelson (b. 1933) in July 1972. It became the center of Progressive Country Music, a movement spearheaded by such anti-Nashville "outlaws" as Nelson and Waylon Jennings (b. 1937). The annual July 4 festival concerts inaugurated at the Headquarters feature a wide variety of Texas artists, including Augie Meyers' Western Head Band (Rock), Waylon Jennings (Progressive C & W), Asleep at the Wheel (Western Swing), and Jerry Jeff Walker (b. circa 1941) (Country-oriented Pop).

Louis Armstrong (1900–1971)   In a 1959 poll sponsored by *Music U.S.A.,* trumpeter/singer Daniel Louis Armstrong, widely known as "Satchmo," placed fifth in a list of greatest Jazz musicians of all time. Nevertheless, there were Jazz critics who were troubled by the transition that Armstrong made in the 1950s from Jazz to Pop and by a brand of showmanship that involved mugging, fiddling with a perspiration-soaked handkerchief, and other shenanigans.

During his early recording years in the 1920s, he accompanied some of the great Blues singers of the day, including Ma Rainey (1886–1939), Bertha "Chippie" Hill (1900[5]–1950), and the Empress of the Blues, Bessie Smith (1895–1937). With the Louis Armstrong Five and Hot

Seven, he cut records that gave him a worldwide following among Jazz fans. Accidentally or not, he developed his "scatting" style of singing, using nonsense syllables instead of words as if he were playing his horn. From the 1950s on, he achieved fame as a gravel-voiced Pop singer, recording with large orchestras and scoring top-selling hit records with "Mack the Knife" and "Hello Dolly," among others.

Despite his Pop following, he continued performing in Jazz festivals all over the world and won innumerable Jazz polls. He appeared in a number of films, some made abroad, and even played Bottom in *Swingin' the Dream,* a Broadway version of Shakespeare's *A Midsummer Night's Dream.* He had a personal charm and charisma that endeared him to people all over the world, and became known as "Satchmo" in 1932 when the editor of the British *Melody Maker,* reviewing an appearance at the London Palladium, telescoped an earlier descriptive name, "Satchelmouth." Armstrong played a melodic type of Jazz in which he used few notes but spaced them skillfully. He was the first Jazz performer to attract mass attention to Jazz and to achieve worldwide fame.

arpeggio   Derived from the Italian for harp, *arpa,* it refers to a chord whose notes are played sequentially, not simultaneously.

ARP   Trade name for a synthesizer.

arranger   The arranger is the craftsman who devises the chart, score, or sketch whereby a song or selection can be played by a group of instruments: duo, trio, quartet, quintet, band, or orchestra. The orchestrator determines which instruments are to play the different parts. The copyist takes the score and writes out each instrumental part. The symphony composer performs three functions: creating the original melody, rhythms, and harmony; arranging; and orchestrating.

Artist of the Year, Best New (NARAS Grammy Awards)

1959	Bobby Darin
1960	Bob Newhart
1961	Peter Nero
1962	Robert Goulet
1963	Swingle Singers
1964	The Beatles
1965	Tom Jones
1966	No choice
1967	Bobbie Gentry
1968	Jose Feliciano

1969   Crosby, Stills & Nash
1970   The Carpenters
1971   Carly Simon
1972   America
1973   Bette Midler
1974   Marvin Hamlisch
1975   Natalie Cole
1976   Starland Vocal Band
1977   Debby Boone
1978   A Taste of Honey
1979   Rickie Lee Jones
1980   Christopher Cross
1981   Sheena Easton

artist-owned record labels   The Beatles' Apple was among rock's first. The Rolling Stones followed with a less expansive label, Rolling Stones Records. In 1968 Curtis Mayfield organized Curtom Records, which released the disks of the Impressions, an ABC-Paramount group until then. One of the most successful artist-owned labels is Swan Song, organized by Led Zeppelin and sponsors of Bad Company, Pretty Things, and Maggie Bell, among other artists.

Art Rock   Both as a noun and an adjective, the word "art" in Rock literature tends to refer to the lyrics: their ideational content and verbal felicity. But some critics enlarge its scope to include the use of forms and devices characteristic of classical music. Art Rock does not refer to an identifiable style, as do Acid Rock and Heavy Metal Rock, but to lyrics that approach poetry and/or the allusiveness and depth of poetry. The works of a group of singer/songwriters are frequently cited as instances of Art Rock: among others, Jackson Browne (b. circa 1950), Leonard Cohen (b. 1935), Joni Mitchell (b. 1943), Randy Newman (b. 1943), Laura Nyro (b. 1947), Paul Simon (b. 1941), and Neil Young (b. 1945).

Having passed through its initial Rockabilly and Teenage stages in the late 1950s, Rock's impulse to become art began to take shape in the turbulent sixties with Bob Dylan (b. 1941) and the Beatles, the former with his lyrics and the latter with their music as well as words. As Rock became increasingly involved with the protest movements of the explosive era, the songs became freighted with analyses and criticism of life and society, frequently thereby fulfilling the role once monopolized by the novel.

From a musical standpoint, the following might be included in a list of those who have produced Art Rock albums: Todd Rundgren (*Healing*); David Bowie; Emerson, Lake & Palmer; Kansas; Moody Blues;

Styx; Talking Heads; Public Image Ltd.; and Yes. Playing in offbeat time signatures, Yes presented songs (written by founder-singer Jon Anderson) that were inspired by the Shastric Scriptures, as described in Paramhansa Yoganada's *Autobiography of a Yogi.* Jon Lord of Deep Purple wrote a *Concerto for Rock and Symphonic Orchestra,* which was premiered at the Royal Albert Hall in London on September 24, 1969, by the Royal Philharmonic Orchestra, and which received a standing ovation when it was performed at the Hollywood Bowl the following August. Lord followed this work with *The Gemini Suite,* which received its premiere in a joint performance by Deep Purple and the BBC's South Bank Pops Orchestra. Another British group, Pink Floyd, wrote several film scores in 1969, including the music for Antonioni's *Zabriskie Point,* and created a six-section tone poem, occupying an entire side of the *Atom Heart Mother* LP. In *Song Cycle* (1968), American-born Van Dyke Parks (b. circa 1941) employed a tone poem structure to develop a series of impressionistic songs about life and institutions in southern California. In *Resolution* (1976) Andy Pratt attempted a fusion of Alexander Scriabin and Bob Dylan. Some of the foregoing works could well be classified under Classical Rock.

To those who saw Rock as an explosion of energy and a youthful nose-thumbing at the older generation's hypocrisies, dullness, and pomposities, the pretensions of Art Rock were anathema.

See also Classical Rock; Punk Rock; Studio Rock.

Moe Asch   His dedication to Folk music goes back to 1939 and involves three record labels. Both Asch Records, for whom Burl Ives began recording in 1941, and Disc went bankrupt. But Folkways, which he founded with Marion Distler in 1948, remains a thriving label. His recorded catalogue includes 200 songs by Woody Guthrie (1912–1967), who inspired young Dylan; over 900 by Leadbelly (1885–1949); and more than 60 albums by Pete Seeger (b. 1919).

The Ash Grove   One of the longest-lived coffeehouses in the country, the Ash Grove was opened in July 1958 on Melrose Avenue in Los Angeles by Edward Pearl. It rapidly rose to a position of prominence in the Folk area, and over a period of time presented almost every well-known artist in the Country as well as the Folk Field, from Mother Maybelle Carter (1909–1979), to Bill Monroe (b. 1911), Brownie McGhee (b. 1914) & Sonny Terry (b. 1911), and Flatt (1914–1979) & Scruggs (b. 1924). Quite a number of Blues artists also performed in its unpretentious surroundings—Memphis Slim (b. 1915), Mance Lipscomb (1895–1976), and Joe Williams (b. 1918), among others. In the 1960s, the Ash Grove became the springboard for a number of Rock artists and groups: Chamber Brothers (1961), Canned Heat (1965), and

Ry Cooder (b. 1947), among others. Cooder has told of how he would sit in the front row night after night during his teen years and watch and learn. He made an impromptu debut at age 16 when he was pushed onstage during one of the club's "party nights." It was a debut that eventually, after appearances at the club, led to his working briefly with Jackie DeShannon (b. 1945). Because of its low-level operation, the Ash Grove was able to exist long after most coffeehouses had disappeared and to nurture young and up-and-coming artists.

See also coffeehouse.

Chet Atkins (1924–)   Born in Luttrell, Tenn., he began recording for RCA Victor in the late 1940s; became studio guitarist in its Nashville studio in 1949, and a part-time producer in 1957; has since served as vice-president and manager of the expanded Nashville studio. At the same time, he has developed an international reputation as a guitarist, making innumerable albums and appearances in a wide variety of music scenes: at the Newport Jazz Festival and the White House, and with the Boston Pops and other symphony orchestras. The Country Music Association named him Instrumentalist of the Year for three successive years, beginning in 1967. In 1971, and from 1974 through 1976, he won Grammys for Best Country Instrumental Performance. His "finger style" of playing—not picking but just touching the strings—has influenced many British Rock artists, including the Beatles (especially in *Rubber Soul*).

atonal   A term meaning without a definite tonal center, or more specifically, not in any key of the traditional major-minor key system. Twelve-tone music has sometimes been described as atonal, but not with the acquiescence of Arnold Schoenberg, who developed the system.

"A" side   The more important side of a single record, or specifically, the side being promoted by a record company as a potential hit. However, sometimes the "A" side turns out to be the "B" side, and, infrequently, both sides turn out to be "A" sides, as in the case of Elvis Presley's "Hound Dog" backed with "Don't Be Cruel," both of which went to No. 1.

attack   The initial sound of an instrument at the beginning of a piece. Also refers to a performer's style or manner on his instrument. We speak, for example, of Lester Young's smooth, relaxed attack on tenor saxophone, or of Dave Brubeck's heavy "touch" (that's what attack becomes on the piano).

Attitude Rock   An elusive category that made its appearance in the mid-1960s when Protest Rock flourished and when Bob Dylan turned from social criticism to self-analysis. Attitude Rock focused on the feelings generated by a given social or political situation. The songwriter was concerned not with criticizing, attacking, or protesting the situation but with an exploration of his own emotions or reaction.

audiophile records   A comparatively new development in the effort to attain sharper instrumental definition, greater frequency range, and better channel separation. Three technologies are currently being employed: (1) digital recording; (2) half-speed mastering; and (3) direct-to-disk recording. In digital recording, the sound is stored as a succession of pulses instead of being transformed into magnetic impulses on a tape. Half-speed mastering involves the cutting of a master at half the speed of playback time, a process that permits the placement of more input in the grooves. Artists who have used these two technologies include Neil Diamond, Pink Floyd, Billy Joel, Willie Nelson, Santana, Boz Scaggs, Bruce Springsteen, and Barbra Streisand. Half-speed masters have been reprocessed from records previously made by the Beatles, Blondie, David Bowie, Jackson Browne, Eric Clapton, the Doors, Fleetwood Mac, Steely Dan, and the Supertramps, among others. The direct-to-disk technique involves recording a performance directly on the master disk, which eliminates the use of tape and potential noise and distortion. Although audiophile records were originally released by small companies, the major record labels are now producing the high-priced platters. Curiously, the development has occurred more rapidly and more extensively in the Rock field than in classical music.

See also digital recording.

''audio spectacle''   A term used by Stony Browder, Jr., of Dr. Buzzard's Original Savannah Band to describe a style heard in the group's *James Monroe H.S. Presents Dr. Buzzard's Original Savannah Band Goes to Washington,* ostensibly a blend of discofied Swing and Modernaires-style harmonies.

audition disk   Live, in-person presentations were the accepted procedure for auditioning new songs for publishers, artists, and recording companies into the 1950s. However, by then the introduction of tape had brought down the cost and simplified the process of recording so that audition disks, or demos, rapidly replaced the live audition. Songwriters and publishers preferred the disks, since professional talent could be employed to showcase their wares. In the old days, unless a songwriter was an accomplished performer, he could bungle the sale of a new song just as a slick demonstrator could make inferior material sound attractive and saleable. The audition disk was welcomed by persons assessing new songs, since they could deal with it at their ease, and not under the probing or solicitous eyes of the songwriter or publisher.

Small studios opened in key cities, and after a time in small cities, to make audition disks, starting at first with two-track tape machines and adding equipment so that eventually they developed into operating arms of independent producers. As the demo disk became the accepted auditioning procedure, ingenuity in arranging and recording came to spell the difference in selling a new song. Some publishing companies in New York, notably Aldon Music, produced audition disks that were not only copied by recording men at the major labels but were in some instances released as commercial disks. Little Eva's record of "Locomotion" started life as a demo. The Ronald & Ruby demo of "Lollipop," made by the author of this *Dictionary,* was released commercially by RCA Victor. The song was a hit for the Chordettes, who covered Ronald & Ruby.

augmented chord   A major chord in which the fifth is raised a semitone. The augmented interval is a half-tone larger than a major or perfect interval:

Aural Exciter, Aphex

Aural Exciter, Aphex   A device developed in Los Angeles, designed to improve the clarity and presence of a sound. The device was apparently first used on the *Midnight Special* series on NBC-TV, where it was heard by Paul McCartney. His use of it at a Wings concert in San Francisco led to its being adopted by Linda Ronstadt and her record producer, Peter Asher. Since then thousands of albums have had their sound enhanced by the device, including albums by Yoko Ono, Barbra Streisand, the Bee Gees, Stevie Nicks, Kenny Rogers, Eddie Rabbitt, Fleetwood Mac, Queen, Dire Straits, Warren Zevon, Kansas, Ambrosia, Journey, and others. The Aural Exciter is now also being used by radio stations to boost and brighten their signal.

Austin High School Gang   In 1922 five youngsters, ranging in age from 14 to 17, and attending Austin High in Chicago, formed a band: Jim Lannigan (piano and later bass); Jimmy MacPartland (cornet); Dick MacPartland (banjo and guitar); Bud Freeman (C melody sax and later tenor); Frank Teschmaker (violin and later alto sax). They were inspired and influenced by the New Orleans Rhythm Kings, whom they heard (as the Friars' Inn Society Orchestra) on a local jukebox, and later by King Oliver's Creole Jazz Band and the Wolverines. Eventually, as the Wolverines fell apart, each departing member was replaced by one of the Austin Gang. In time they developed the small combo style, a fusion of black and white sounds, known as Chicago Jazz: they did not play ahead or behind but on the beat, and used a direct melodic approach. The sound is preserved on Okeh records by Red McKenzie and Eddie Condon's Chicagoans, especially the disk of "Nobody's Sweetheart."

autoharp   A chord zither whose best-known player was the late Mother Maybelle Carter (1909–1979) of the famous Carter family. It consists of 40 to 50 metal strings, which are controlled by a series of buttons (chord bars) that produce a specific chord when the strings are strummed with a finger-pick. Derived from the harp, it was ostensibly devised by Charles A. Zimmerman, later the composer of "Anchors Aweigh," the U.S. Navy song. The Appalachian autoharp, produced in the 1960s, uses only 15 chord bars. In the folk song revival after World War II, members of the famous Seeger family, especially Mike Seeger (b. 1933), used the instrument and made records with it.

availability   A concept that figures in ASCAP's distribution of royalties to writers and publishers. A catalog rates higher or lower in availability, depending on the number of recognized works or standards in it. The higher the availability, the greater the royalties.

Avalon Ballroom   Along with the Fillmore, one of the two major ballrooms in San Francisco during the 1960s. It was the ballroom in which the Family Dog first presented Rock concerts.
See also Carousel Ballroom; The Family Dog; The Fillmore; Bill Graham.

Avant-garde rock   In the 1950s, avant-garde classicism, under the influence of Karlheinz Stockhausen in Europe and Milton Babbitt and John Cage in the U.S.A., expanded from the 12-tone serialism of Arnold Schoenberg and Anton von Webern to include electronic and chance or "free form" music. Before long, the classical avant-garde embraced computer music, "minimal" or repetitive music, multimedia music (a combination of dance, art, film, and sound), and "gamelan" music played on metal and percussive instruments.
Avant-garde Rock is a loose term that might embrace Aleatory Rock, Classical Rock, Electronic Rock, Studio Rock, and even

Psychedelic Rock. It has been applied to such groups and individuals as the Mothers of Invention, the Fugs, Roxy (when Brian Eno was on synthesizer in 1971), Brian Eno, the Beatles, Pink Floyd, and others. New and bizarre sounds, instruments, and forms are important desiderata; but the crucial factor is time. When the Beatles produced *Revolver* in 1966, it was considered avant-garde; so was *Sgt. Pepper* with its super-psychedelic effects. When Pink Floyd began experimenting with electronic devices and sounds before other British groups, and later when it explored space/time concepts in *The Dark Side of the Moon,* the group was regarded as avant-garde. Brian Eno's use of synthesizers in several mid-1970s albums (e.g., *Discreet Music, Evening Star*) put him in the avant-garde. It is basically a matter of being ahead of your peers and audience—so far ahead that there is a danger of losing your audience. The Beatles were generally ahead of their time but not so far ahead that they lost touch with the mass audience, as the Fugs did. Captain Beefheart was avant-garde in 1970 with *Trout Mask Replica* and remained avant-garde in 1981 with *Doc at the Radar Station.* An innovative artist, he was still creating lyrics, rhythms, harmonies, and melodies whose complexity and originality puzzled listeners at the same time that they overwhelmed critics and served as an inspiration to groups like the Talking Heads, Pere Ubu, B-52's, and Magazine.

"axe"   In Swing and Jazz jargon, a sax, apparently because of its resemblance to an axe. The term was quickly broadened to mean any musical instrument, including even the piano.

B

BBC   British Broadcasting Corporation.

BMI   *See* Broadcast Music, Inc.

BSR   Stands for Basal Skin Resistance, a concept used in market research. It refers to the measurement of emotional responses in the automatic nervous system. To make this measurement, tiny electronic sensors are taped to the fingers. Devised by a Hollywood market research firm headed by Larry Weller, it has been used by several record companies, including A & M and ABC.

b/w   An abbreviation of "backed with," a term used by record companies and trade papers with reference to the alternative side of a disk.

Baby Grand Cafe   A famous Harlem night spot at 319 West 125th Street in New York City, best known for its introduction of the comedian Nipsey Russell, who opened for two weeks and stayed for twelve years. In existence since 1945, the Cafe played host to such black artists and groups of the 1940s and 1950s as The Ravens and Ruth Brown.

backbeats   Originally the weak beats of a four-to-the-bar measure, as in a March or Fox-trot, they were elevated to primary status by R & B and R 'n' R.
See also afterbeats.

"backdoor man"   Blues jargon for the lover of a married woman, generalized to mean someone who finds a way to skirt the rules.

background instrumental   Fees paid by motion picture companies and TV producers for the use of music in a film or on tape tend to vary, depending on whether the music is sung or just played instrumentally, and whether the performer is seen or just heard. There are four categories: (1) visual vocal, (2) background vocal, (3) visual instrumental, and (4) background instrumental. When the singer is seen on screen or on the tube (1), the fee is highest. When the music is played offstage (4), the fee is lowest.

background vocal   *See* background instrumental.

back line   The rhythm or percussion players in a Jazz group: banjo, rhythm guitar, piano, and especially bass and drums.
See also front line.

backup group   Refers to the instrumentalist accompanying a singer. Also refers to the singers behind the star or lead singer. They generally sing footballs (whole notes), sustained notes, or responses to the lead.

Joan Baez (1941-)   Making her debut at the first Newport Folk Festival in July 1959 after Bob Gibson had heard her at the Gate of Horn in Chicago, and cutting her debut album in 1960, she ascended meteorically to recognition as the Queen of Folk Music. Vanguard Record execs claim that the *Joan Baez* album, as it was titled, is the biggest-selling female folk LP in history. Together with Peter, Paul & Mary, she brought Bob Dylan and his protest songs to public notice. Throughout a distinguished career, she has integrated her art and her political convictions. In 1963 she refused to appear on ABC-TV's *Hootenanny* show unless Pete Seeger, who was then blackballed, appeared, too. (Seeger was first victimized for his views during the McCarthy era.) The following year, she began refusing to pay that portion of her taxes that was used for military purposes. Founding the Institute for the Study of Non-Violence in Carmel, Calif., she willingly went to jail in 1967 for her part in a demonstration opposing the draft and the Vietnam War. She called her autobiography, published in 1968, *Daybreak.*

"bag"   A Jazz term that became a teenage word, it meant style, conception, point of view, and by extension, mode of behavior.

Baion   A Brazilian rhythm used by the Drifters and audible on Jerry Butler's disk of "He Will Break Your Heart."

balalaika   A guitar of Russian extraction. It has a flat back, a slightly arched belly, and a narrow neck with three strings and four movable frets. Developed in the 18th century, it is now made in six sizes, with sounds varying from a high piccolo to a low contrabass.

"ball"   Among Jazz musicians in the 1930s, it meant a good time, or an exciting and easy time. After teenagers took it over, it came to refer to intercourse and was used mainly as a verb.

ballad   In folklore, the ballad was a sung story. Recent examples of this type of narrative song would include Johnny Horton's "Battle of New Orleans." In the music business and popular music, the ballad is a song dealing with love or romance. It has been and continues to be the staple of song literature, since young people date, dance, romance, and fall in love to popular music. The tempo of ballads is generally slow or dreamy.
See also rhythm ballad; torch song.

Bammy   An acronym for Bay Area Music Award, a regional "Grammy" given out in competitions in the San Francisco area.

Bandstand International Contest   An Australian contest sponsored by Philips-Mercury Records. It was won in 1966 by Helen Reddy (b. 1942) of Melbourne, Australia, whose trip to the United States led to stardom for her in the seventies.

Bangladesh, Concert for   Organized mainly by ex-Beatle George Harrison (b. 1943), the legendary concert was held on August 1, 1971, at Madison Square Garden in New York City. Many Rock artists contributed their services to help raise funds for the relief of victims of aggression. Ringo Starr (b. 1940) was a participant, marking the first time that two of the Beatles were reunited since the dissolution of the famous group. Proceeds of a three-volume recording of the concert also went for Bangladesh aid. Included were some noteworthy tracks by Bob Dylan (b. 1941), one of the participants. Harrison's single, "Bangladesh," made the Top 25 in the year of the concert.

banjo   A fretted instrument with five to nine strings, made of parchment stretched over a wooden, circular hoop. It has no back. Its sound is hard compared to that of an acoustic guitar. Possibly of Arabian origin, and known in West Africa as a *bahnjour,* it was brought here by slaves. Used extensively in minstrel shows, it has also been a favorite of folk singers, including the Weavers, Pete Seeger, and the Kingston Trio. It is one of the basic instruments of Bluegrass music.

bar   A line separating a musical composition or song into segments, based on the time signature. In 3/4 time, it would come after a count of three quarter notes, and in 4/4 time, after a count of four quarter notes. It also refers to the metrical period between two bars, being used as a synonym for "measure."
    See also double bar.

"barbershop"   A style of unaccompanied singing in harmony by male quartets that developed in the 19th century in barbershops. The style harks back in some ways to the black spirituals, not in its content but in the harmonic texture. These days, there are female quartets that imitate the improvised sound, involving square, block-chord harmony. The well-known Osmonds started out singing "barbershop."
    See also SPEBSQSA.

Baroque Rock   A style that died aborning in 1967–1968. The effort was to wed the sound of Baroque modal music to a Rock beat, a sound that was originally the product of recorders, wooden flutes, and harpsichord. Among the groups that worked at this fusion: Ars Nova, Chrysalis, New York String Ensemble, and New York Rock and Roll Ensemble. Only Procol Harum—the name presumably meant "beyond these things" in Latin—succeeded in producing a hit record, "A Whiter Shade of Pale," replete with surrealistic lyrics. Developed on a Bach cantata, *Sleepers Awake*, the piece employed two keyboard instruments, an early instance of such usage.

Barrelhouse   A barrelhouse was a low-down juice joint where the bar consisted of a plank stretched across two barrels. The rough, bluesy piano style played here took its name from the joint. To cope with the noise level of the revelers, a pianist had to have a pair of powerful mitts, with the left hand generally beating out a rocking boogie. Little Brother Montgomery (b. 1906) and Speckled Red (b. Rufus Perryman, 1892–1973) were two of the best-known practitioners of this powerhouse style. So was Count Otis Matthews, in whose Oakland, Calif., band young Johnny Otis played drums.

The Barrelhouse   Located in Los Angeles, and founded by bandleader/songwriter Johnny Otis (b. 1921), this was one of the first clubs to feature R & B entertainment exclusively. Between 1948 and 1950, Otis found such black talents as Esther Phillips (b. 1935), Mel Walker, Lady Dee Williams, and the group known as The Robins. Using these artists and others, Otis launched the Johnny Otis Rhythm & Blues Caravan. With Little Esther, as young Esther Phillips was known, and Mel Walker, Otis made a series of hits for Savoy Records: ''Double Crossing Blues'' and ''Mistrustin' Blues'' were both Top 10 on R & B charts in 1950.

See also Johnny Otis; Rhythm & Blues.

barrel organ   Also known as a street-piano or piano organ, it is a mechanical piano operated by turning a handle, which activates a barrel-and-pin mechanism like that found in a music box.

The Basement Tapes   In 1966 the Hawks, with Levon Helm (b. circa 1942) returned to perform on drums, electric bass, and mandolin, rented a large pink house in West Saugerties, N.Y., to rehearse and jam. It was just down the road from Bob Dylan's place near Woodstock. *The Basement Tapes,* originally bootlegged in part, emerged from sessions that took place between June and October 1967. Bob Dylan (b. 1941) sang lead on 16 numbers and played piano and acoustic guitar. *Music from Big Pink* was the title of the band's first album, cut in this same period and house, without Dylan.

Count Basie (1904–   )   Born in Red Bank, N.J., William Basie started as a Ragtime pianist imitating and learning from Fats Waller (1904–1943) and other Harlem 88ers. In 1928, after traveling with a vaudeville show, he was stranded in Kansas City. There, he played first with Walter Page's Blue Devils (1928–1929), and when the band broke up, with Bennie Moten (to 1935). Soon after Moten's death, Basie began an engagement with his own band at the Reno Club. Through John Hammond, who heard the band over the radio, it was brought to New York City and did its first record session for Decca in 1937. The following year, Basie's outfit became the first big band to play 52nd St., an engagement that through network radio broadcasts made it nationally known. In 1957 Basie's was the first American band ever to play a Royal Command performance for the Queen of England. That same year, the band became the first big black band to play the roof ballroom of the Waldorf-Astoria Hotel in NYC, an engagement that lasted 13 record-breaking weeks. For his appearance at the Newport Jazz Festival in July 1965, Frank Sinatra (b. 1915) chose the Basie band to accompany him. The band has made several albums with Sinatra and performed with him both here and abroad. It is one of the few big jazz bands that has kept working and recording for more than four decades.

Basin Street   The legendary street of old New Orleans, memorialized in Jazz songs of the day, that ran between the French Quarter and Storyville, the area of legalized prostitution with its elegant, high-priced mansions and low-priced "cribs."

Battle of the Bands   *See* Savoy Ballroom.

Bayou Rock   A sound developed by some natives of Louisiana, Arkansas, and Mississippi. Singer/guitarist/songwriter Tony Joe White (b. circa 1947) of Louisiana was an exponent although he is better known for such hits as "Polk Salad Annie," recorded by Presley and Tom Jones (b. 1940); "I've Got a Thing About You, Baby," recorded by Presley; "Willie and Laura Mae Jones," recorded by Dusty Springfield (b. 1939); and especially "A Rainy Night in Georgia," a bestseller for Brook Benton (b. 1931) in 1970. Despite their California background, Creedence Clearwater Revival made the most fetching use of the sound in "Bad Moon Rising" (1969), the group's second million-seller, and in *Bayou Country,* an album that sold a million and contained John Fogerty's "Born on the Bayou." The Caribbean/carnival sound did not progress beyond being regional in appeal even though the Neville Brothers of New Orleans produced *Fyo on the Bayou* in 1981.

Beach Boys   *See* Surfing music.

beach movies   These were a series of "B" films that latched onto the nationwide interest in surfing prompted by the record hits of the Beach Boys. There were *Beach Party* (1963), *Muscle Beach Party* (1964), and others. The stars were young rockers like Paul Anka (b. 1941), Frankie Avalon (b. 1940), and Fabian (b. 1943), aided and abetted by Mickey Mouseketeer Annette Funicello. Lightweight fare, these films simply exploited the fun-loving lure of surf-sand-sun-and-summer, with some Teenage Rock as accompaniment.
    See also Surfing music.

Beale Street   The 52nd St. of Memphis, whose bars and clubs contributed immensely to the growth of Jazz, Blues, and black popular music. Memphis was the home of W.C. Handy (1873–1958), regarded as the Father of the Blues, who celebrated the street in his "Beale Street Blues." He reportedly orchestrated his most famous composition, "St. Louis Blues," working at the cigar stand of Pee Wee's saloon, a musicians' hangout on Beale Street.

"Beale Street Blues Boy"   The cognomen under which B. B. King conducted his WDIA programs between 1948 and 1952. This was how Riley B. King, a pioneer and giant of Rhythm & Blues, became known as B. B. King.

"Bean"   *See* Coleman Hawkins.

Bean Blossom Bluegrass Festival   Held annually at the Jamboree Park in Bean Blossom, Indiana, owned by the Father of Blugrass, Bill Monroe (b. 1911), the event is also known as the Bill Monroe Bean Blossom Bluegrass Festival.
    See also Bluegrass.

"bear"   In black jargon, a very homely woman, as in the '49 R & B hit by Little Esther, "Double Crossing Blues."

"Bear Cat"   A nickname of showman/singer/dancer/disk jockey Rufus Thomas (b. 1917) of Station WDIA in Memphis. In the 1950s he recorded "Bear Cat" on the Sun label, a takeoff on Big Mama Thornton's "Hound Dog."

beat   Audible pulse or rhythm, produced by such instruments as drums, bass, guitar, and piano. So-called melody instruments—strings, brass, reeds—can be written for so that they maintain or stress the rhythmic pulse. Jazz singers like Ella Fitzgerald (b. 1918) deliver with a beat, as do some pop singers like Sinatra (b. 1915), Sammy Davis, Jr. (b. 1925), and Tony Bennett (b. 1926).

The Beatles   During the era of Rock, there were only two Pop Explosions—musical events that were so acutely expressive of a time, generation, and/or mood that their exponents were instantly catapulted into superstar orbit. Presley was a Pop Explosion in 1956. The Beatles were a Pop Explosion in 1964. They also remain the most influential, and the most highly publicized and acclaimed, group even up to the present. As the leading experimental group of the 1960s, they explored the technology of the recording studio, examined the validity of new philosophical concepts (Transcendental Meditation), experimented with drugs (LSD), and struck out in new directions with each new album. Rock 'n' Roll became Rock with Bob Dylan and the Beatles, who inaugurated the era of Studio Rock (700 hours to record *Sgt. Pepper*) and Rock as Art, visual as well as audible. More than any other group, they gave Rock a kind of respectability, high seriousness, and depth that elicited critical approval from the serious music world as well as the world of academe.

After commuting between Hamburg and The Cavern, a lowdown dive in their native Liverpool, the foursome was taken under the wing of Brian Epstein, a record-store owner who discovered them through their German-made recording of "My Bonnie" and who transformed them from a punkishly dressed and punkish-sounding group into the Beatles that American viewers saw on the *Ed Sullivan Show* on February 9, 1964. By then "I Wanna Hold Your Hand" was No. 1 on the Top 100 chart, and soon it was one of five records that simultaneously occupied all five top slots on *Billboard's* bestseller chart. The incredible meteoric rise of the group is apparent when one realizes that in the preceding year, Capitol Records refused to exercise its first-refusal option on the group (through its affiliation with British EMI), and three different American labels (Vee Jay, Swan, and MGM) released Beatles disks without too much of a reaction. Some historians have contended that the difference between 1963 and 1964 was the assassination in November 1963 of President John F. Kennedy, himself a youth idol. Young people, the argument goes, needed something or someone to lift them out of the doldrums and despair.

Although the Beatles made their first appearance in Hamburg under the aegis of Little Richard—Paul McCartney loved to mimic him— their roots were in Rockabilly, not R & B. At one early moment, they called themselves The Foreverlies, an appropriate testimonial to the harmonic sounds they derived from the Everly Brothers. Other Rockabilly influences included Bill Haley (b. 1925), Chet Atkins (b. 1924), Chuck Berry (b. 1926)—they covered his "Rock & Roll Music" and "Roll Over Beethoven"—and Carl Perkins (b. 1932); they recorded his "Matchbox" and "Everybody's Trying to Be My Baby."

With *Rubber Soul* (1965) the Beatles began to adventure, employing electronic devices ("Norwegian Wood") and the sitar (George Harrison). *Revolver* (1966) revealed the deepening lyrical influence of Bob Dylan (b. 1941) in analytical songs like "Eleanor Rigby." Apart from its role in promoting concept albums, *Sgt Pepper's Lonely Hearts Club Band* (1967) explored the technology, sounds, and concepts of psychedelia. Although *Sgt. Pepper* is doubtless their best-known work—it was made into a movie in the 1970s—*Abbey Road* (1969) has frequently been named as their best work. In their recording career, no Beatles album failed to make the No. 3 spot on the charts and practically all of them made No. 1.

By 1969 John Lennon (1940–1980) had formed the Plastic Ono Band with his new wife, Yoko Ono. The following year, after releasing a solo LP, Paul McCartney (b. 1942) sued to dissolve the group. Shortly thereafter, McCartney formed Wings with his new wife, Linda Eastman. Drummer Ringo Starr (b. 1940) made some albums and became a movie star. George Harrison (b. 1943) wrote and scored a hit single with "My Sweet Lord" and went on to organize the concert for Bangladesh victims, which yielded a No. 2 album in 1972. Functioning independently, each Beatle demonstrated a substantial degree of talent and creativity. But it is apparent that the whole was greater than the sum of its parts.

The contribution of George Martin, the classically trained musician who served as producer of Beatles' sessions, still remains to be fully assessed. Where the Beatles leave off and where George Martin begins, particularly as it relates to innovative studio techniques, is an unanswered question. This much is clear: that Paul McCartney, who has been the most successful on his own and has consistently placed records high on the charts through the 1970s, has retreated creatively, and much to the disappointment of critics, seems content to write bubble-gum, romantic ballads like the earliest songs of the Beatles. (As this book goes to press, the release of *Tug of War,* a new reflective album, suggests that McCartney may have taken recent criticism of his work to heart.)

See also John Lennon.

Bebop   *See* Bop.

The Beers Family   Accompanying themselves on old Folk instruments like the psaltery, fiddlesticks, and limberjacks, and concentrating on traditional Irish and Scottish ballads, the Beers Family has dedicated itself to the preservation of traditional music. In 1964 their role in this regard was honored by the National Folk Festival with the Burl Ives Award. Two years later, Bob Beers, patriarch of the family, organized the first Fox Hollow Festival, which was held on the Beers farm in the Adirondacks. Beers, who performed on psaltery, was killed in a car crash in May 1973. The work which he began has been carried on by his widow, Evelyne, now Evelyne Beers Burnstine, and by his daughter, Martha, and her husband Eric Nagler.

Beguine   A fast dance of French ancestry, originating on the Caribbean islands of Martinique and Saint Lucia. Americans became familiar with it as a result of Cole Porter's evergreen song "Begin the

Beguine,'' popularized by a 1938 hit Artie Shaw recording. As a rhythm, the beguine is notated as follows:

Leon Bismarck Beiderbecke (1903–1931)   Born in Davenport, Iowa, he was largely self-taught on piano and cornet. Star of the famous Wolverines in 1923, with whom he made his first records, he later worked with Charlie Straight's pop band, Frankie Trumbauer (1901–1956), Jean Goldkette (1899–1962), Paul Whiteman (1890–1967) and the Casa Loma Band. While playing in Chicago in 1925, he sat in with pioneer black jazzmen like King Oliver (1885–1938) and Louis Armstrong (1900–1971). After his premature death of pneumonia at 28, he became one of the first white musicians imitated by black jazzmen—Rex Stewart (1907–1967), among others. His followers included white trumpeters like Bobby Hackett (1915–1976) and Jimmy McPartland (b. 1907). One of the first jazzmen to become interested in Debussy's whole-tone harmonic concepts, he wrote a number of piano pieces (e.g., ''In a Mist'') revealing the influence. Although he was a featured player in the famous Paul Whiteman Band (1928–1930) he became a legendary figure only after his death and the publication of a bestselling novel, *Young Man with a Horn,* by Dorothy Baker, partly based on his life. Columbia released a now-hard-to-find set of three 12-inch records containing most of his best performances.

''be-in''   A mass gathering of hippies, which peaked in popularity in the 1965–1967 period. The musical *Hair* gave conventional theatergoers the first contact with a be-in. A social novelty, it shocked middle-class, middle-aged people, although participants contended that the purpose was to allow for the fullest expression of the individual in a communal setting. One of the notable be-ins, or ''gatherings of the Tribes,'' was held on Saturday, January 14, 1967, at the polo grounds of the Golden Gate Park in San Francisco: 25,000 came together to hear rock bands and celebrate the birth of the Age of Aquarius. It became a love-in, a day of such peace, love, and freedom—no drunks, no arrests, no police, and only one small incident—that the Jefferson Airplane, present as participants, was moved to write ''Saturday Afternoon.'' The Monterey Pop Festival in June 1967 was also the scene of a be-in that became a love-in.
See also Monterey Pop Festival.

Harry Belafonte (1927–   )   Known as the first Negro matinee idol, Belafonte was born in New York City but spent much of his earlier years until he was 13 in Kingston, Jamaica. After making some headway as a Pop singer in competition with the then-popular Billy Eckstine (b. 1914), he turned to Folk material and made his debut at the Village Vanguard in November 1951. He began recording for RCA Victor two years later, but made his big splash with the hit single "Day-O (The Banana Boat Song)" and the album *Harry Belafonte–Calypso* in 1957, which obviously benefited from his years in Kingston. In succeeding years, the reluctant King of Calypso was highly successful on the screen as well as in personal appearances, playing to sellout crowds in Las Vegas, Miami Beach, and Hollywood. A man of courage and a black activist, he personally broke down many racial barriers and contributed freely of his time and talents to black causes. In an earlier work, I described him as "the artist par excellence of the American era of integration."

belting   A style of Pop singing that developed in the early 1950s when a number of white singers began imitating R & B vocalists. The style was a sharp departure from the mooing balladry of crooners like Bing Crosby (1904–1979), Perry Como (b. 1912), Frank Sinatra (b. 1915), and Nat "King" Cole (1917–1969). It had drive, decibels, and a strong dance beat. The way Frankie Laine (b. 1913) handled the 1930s ballad "That's My Desire" launched the approach in 1947. The belters included young Eddie Fisher (b. 1928) ("Any Time"), Don Cornell (b. 1921) ("I'm Yours"), Guy Mitchell (b. 1925) ("Singing the Blues"), Teresa Brewer (b. 1937) ("Music, Music"), Georgia Gibbs (b. 1920), ("Kiss of Fire"), and such groups as the Four Aces ("Tell Me Why") and the McGuire Sisters ("Sincerely"). "I'm a singer who shouts," said Frankie Laine.

bend   An instrumental and a vocal device involving the flatting of a note, though not necessarily by a full semitone; in Gospel music, the addition of a note either above or below a given note. While a neighboring note on a second is quite frequent, intervals of a third or more are not uncommon. In Gospel music, the added note is like a grace note.

Irving Berlin (1888–   )   The most successful Pop songwriter from the Ragtime era until the rise of Rock 'n' Roll, he wrote more than 20 hit Broadway shows, more than 15 smash film musicals, and an amazing number (more than 130) of songs that were hits. Included among his top bestsellers: "White Christmas," "God Bless America," "Alexander's Ragtime Band," "Easter Parade," "There's No Business Like Show Business," "All Alone," "What'll I Do," "Blue Skies," "Marie." He is one of the few American songwriters who, except for the early days, wrote both words and music, and functioned as his own publisher.

Chuck Berry (1926-)   He has been called the greatest of the Rock 'n' Rollers and the greatest Rock lyricist this side of Bob Dylan. As one who gave expression to the feelings and modes of the young subculture—without himself being that young—he surely was the poet laureate of Teenage Rock. He came to Rockabilly from the black end of the color spectrum, inflecting C & W material with a bluesy sound and driving beat. With Louis Jordan (1908-1975), the Father of R & B, as his idol and model, he wrote humorous narratives about teenage life like "Roll Over Beethoven" and "Maybellene." Among the Top 10 hits that he produced between 1955 and 1959, add "Sweet Little Sixteen" (No. 1, R & B; No. 2, Pop), "Rock and Roll Music," "School Day," and "Johnny B. Goode," The sound of his rocking guitar can be heard in many of the white groups of the early 1960s, including the Beatles. Enunciating clearly and employing little or no melisma, he was able to attract a white as well as black audience. But he had to wait until 1972 before he garnered his first Gold Record: "My Ding-A-Ling" was humorously erotic.

"bicycle"   Singles-bar jargon for "bisexual." Only those in the know understood the reference in the 1978 Top 10 hit recording by Queen, "I Want to Ride My Bicycle."

"Big Apple"   A Jazz term that originated in the 1930s and is still used to mean New York City, the big town. To jazzmen raised in small towns, making it in NYC was like taking a bite from a big apple. In the 1930s there was also a dance called "The Big Apple," a swinging, square-dance version of "truckin" (*See* Truckin').

Big Ballad era   It did not come into its own until the 1930s after the formation of the radio networks—NBC in 1926 and CBS in 1927—when coast-to-coast radio superseded vaudeville as the major medium for exposing and plugging songs. Nineteen twenty-seven was also the year of *Showboat* and of *The Jazz Singer,* the former indicating that the Broadway musical had come of age, and the latter, that the era of the silent screen was at an end. Hollywood's splurge in film musicals in the thirties—together with the emergence of such stellar theater tunesmiths as Richard Rodgers (1902-1979), Vincent Youmans (1898-1946), Cole Porter (1892-1964), and George Gershwin (1898-1937), in addition to Jerome Kern (1885-1945)—all contributed to the popularity of the big, romantic ballad.

Short-lived Russ Columbo (1908-1934) and long-tenured Bing Crosby (1904-1977) were the first of a group of Big Baritones who rose to interpret the Big Ballads. They were soon followed by Perry Como (b. 1912), Vic Damone (b. 1928), Dick Haymes (1916-1980), Billy Eckstine (b. 1914), Frank Sinatra (b. 1915), Dean Martin (b. 1917),

Nat "King" Cole (1917–1969), and others, almost all of whom paid their dues as vocalists with one or another of the big Swing bands.

During its long tenure, the Big Ballad was recorded by large orchestras involving string and woodwind sections. Structurally, it consisted of 32 bars, with 8-bar segments arranged in an AABA sequence. A variant generally found in show tunes, and sometimes in film songs, consisted of 16-bar segments arranged in an ABAB sequence.

With ballads requiring an extended promotion, unlike overnight novelty hit songs, this became the era of the No. 1 plug in music business—a term signifying that a firm's entire song-plugging machinery was concentrated for a period of weeks on one ballad. When its efforts were successful, the No. 1 plug put a song on the prestigious *Your Hit Parade,* a coast-to-coast radio (and briefly TV) show sponsored by Lucky Strike cigarettes, which tabulated and presented the top songs of the week. The equivalent of today's charts, *Your Hit Parade* began a twenty-year run in 1935, terminated by the Rock Revolution.

See also No. 1 plug; Pop music; Frank Sinatra.

Big Band era   Although black bands of the late 1920s and early 1930s—Fletcher Henderson (1897–1952), Chick Webb (1909–1939), Duke Ellington (1899–1974), Count Basie (b. 1904), Jimmie Lunceford (1902–1947)—were playing in the style that became known as Swing, it was a coast-to-coast NBC radio show, *Let's Dance,* that ushered in the Swing era in 1936, helped make Benny Goodman the King of Swing, and launched an international dance craze that led to the emergence of several hundred Big Bands. These consisted, with variations, of a four- or five-piece rhythm group, four or five saxes, and four or five brasses, plus a male and female vocalist and sometimes a vocal group like Tommy Dorsey's Pied Pipers. The Big Bands were generally classified as "sweet" or "jump." Sammy Kaye (b. 1910) and Guy Lombardo (1902–1979) led sweet bands, sometimes also known as "Mickey Mouse" bands. Among the big rhythm bands, there were those of Artie Shaw (b. 1910), Glenn Miller (1904–1944), Tommy Dorsey (1905–1956), Harry James (b. 1916), Gene Krupa (1909–1973), Teddy Wilson (b. 1912), and Lionel Hampton (b. 1913)—the last four, alumni of the Benny Goodman Band.

Big Band Rock   From its beginning as Rockabilly, Rock has remained a small-combo phenomenon. By the time that the Beatles set the mold, guitar, bass, and drums, with variants, was the standard Rock instrumentation. It was not too long after the British invasion that a number of artists sought to bring horns and larger groups into the Rock framework. By 1967 there were two groups playing "Big Band" Rock: Chicago, founded that year, and Blood, Sweat & Tears, founded later but on the market with the first horn-sounding album. A spokesman for Chicago maintained that its roots were basically Rock "but we can and do play Jazz," while Blood, Sweat & Tears was Jazz-rooted but "can play Rock." Blood, Sweat & Tears was the larger group, with five horns in a nine-man lineup, while Chicago employed three horns in a seven-man group. In succeeding years, other rockers have experimented with larger formations. In an American tour in 1970, to promote their *Atom Heart Mother* album, Pink Floyd used a 10-piece orchestra behind a 20-member choir. Tower of Power, a 10-piece group from Oakland, Calif., worked with a five-man horn section and a five-piece rhythm section, including a conga drummer. On *Salisbury* (1970), the English group called Uriah Heep cut a 16-minute track with a 26-piece brass and woodwind orchestra. Critics of the Big Band groups always ask: "What happened to the Big Beat?"

Big Baritones   *See* Big Ballad era.

"The Big Bopper"   J. P. Richardson (1930–1959) was a prominent Texas disk jockey who had a No. 1 Rockabilly hit with "Chantilly Lace" in 1957–1958. He placed other songs he wrote on the charts, including "Running Bear" and "Little Red Riding Hood." Although "Chantilly Lace" was a hit again in 1972 on a new disk by Jerry Lee Lewis, the Big Bopper, as he called himself, is remembered because he was on the plane that carried Buddy Holly to his premature death on February 3, 1959.

"Big H"   Heroin.

"Big Mama"   The nickname of Willie Mae Thornton (b. 1926), the black R & B singer whose recording of "Hound Dog," an R & B hit in 1953, was the basis of Elvis Presley's '56 version, and whose song, "Ball and Chain," was both an inspiration and notable success for Janis Joplin (1943–1970).

Big Sur Festival   Held on the flat shelf of a cliff with a breathtaking view of the Pacific Ocean, 50 miles south of Carmel, Calif., and 150 miles down from San Francisco, the Big Sur Festival became the prototype of California festivals. There was a stirring camaraderie between performers and an audience limited to 5,000. Folk singer Joan Baez (b. 1941), whose family and friends were the motive force of the festival, was joined by folk singers like Judy Collins (b. 1939) and Joni Mitchell (b. 1943), folk rockers like John Sebastian (b. 1944) and Simon & Garfunkel, and others. The festival was not advertised or publicized, but grew from year to year by word-of-mouth, drawing its following from the beatniks who had settled in Big Sur in the 1950s and the hippies who emerged in the sixties. Big Sur laid the groundwork for the Pop Festival at nearby Monterey.

See also festivals; Monterey Pop Festival.

"Bird" *See* Charlie Parker.

bird groups The success of a black New York vocal group, known as The Ravens—organized in 1946 and on R & B charts in 1947 with "Ol' Man River" and in '48 with "White Christmas"—motivated other groups to adopt bird names: Orioles, Penguins, Swallows, Flamingos, Robins, Larks, Meadowlarks, Skyhawks, and so on.

Birdland A cellar Jazz club on the east side of Broadway, between 52nd and 53rd streets in New York City, originally know as The Ebony, later as the Clique, and in 1949 renamed Birdland in honor of saxist Charlie "Bird" Parker (1920–1955).

See also Charlie "Bird" Parker.

"The Birdman" Nickname of guitarist Pete Townshend (b. 1945), of the Who, because of his way of leaping in the air.

"bit" Probably a takeover of the theatrical term "a bit part," meaning a small part. Used in the late 1940s by Bop musicians synonymously with "thing"—e.g., in "doing his thing" or "bit."

"Bix" Cognomen of one of the celebrated trumpeters of the Hot Jazz era. *See* Leon Bismarck Beiderbecke.

"black and white" Before the advent of Rock 'n' Roll, music publishers distinguished between editions of new songs and songs that had become standards. The cover of a new song was printed in color, while the covers of standards used black lettering on white paper. Copies given out gratis to singers and musicians, i.e., members of the profession, were known as "professional copies," or "pros." They were also printed on white paper with black lettering, but they were not known as "black and white."

Black Country In 1962 Ray Charles (b. 1930), who established a reputation as a Jazz and Soul artist, began recording Country songs. "I Can't Stop Loving You," written and recorded in '58 by Country artist Don Gibson (b. 1928), went to No. 1 and became the biggest seller of over 100 chart songs by Charles. The album of C & W songs that followed also became a Gold Album for Charles.

Charlie Pride (b. 1938) soon followed Ray Charles in disregarding the color line in Country music, scoring 20 No. 1 hit singles between 1969 and 1978, all of them Country-oriented. O. C. Smith (b. 1936) was another black artist who turned to Country material and made the charts in 1968 with songs like "The Son of Hickory Holler's Tramp," "Honey," and "Little Green Apples," which went to No. 2.

See also Country or C & W.

"the black Elvis"   Perhaps it was the theatricality of his performances and the erotic way he handled his guitar that led critics to refer to Jimi Hendrix (1942–1970) as "the black Elvis." His hyperamplified guitar playing was shaped by an early idolization of Muddy Waters (b. 1915) and by formative stints with James Brown (b. 1928) and Little Richard (b. 1935). The Monterey Pop Festival of 1967, where he burned his guitar onstage to upstage the Who's destruction of their instruments, made a celebrity of him. In the three short years before his death from a drug overdose, he racked up four Gold albums: *Are You Experienced?, Electric Ladyland, Axis: Bold as Love,* and *Smash Hits.* Violence and eroticism marked his SRO appearances and his music.

"Black Moses"   Cognomen of Isaac Hayes (b. 1943–   ) of Memphis, who won a Grammy in 1971 for "Theme from Shaft" (Best Instrumental Arrangement) and two in 1972, one for "Shaft" (Best Original Score Written for Motion Picture), and the other for "Black Moses" (Best Pop Instrumental Performed by Arranger/Composer).

Black Pop   *See* Motown sound; Philadelphia International.

Blind Lemon Jefferson (1897–1929)   Born near Couchman, Tex., Lemon Jefferson was the prototype of the sightless, illiterate, itinerant rural bluesman who spent his days singing on street corners and in saloons, wailing about, longing for, and enjoying when he could, booze and broads. Among the 79 songs he recorded for the Paramount label (plus 2 for Okeh), many of which were fished out of the pool of Folk Blues and Texas prison songs, there were intense personal accounts of his own life, as in "Tin Cup Blues." The form of his Blues crudely followed the twelve-bar, three-line classic tradition. Singing in a high-pitched, nasal voice, he displayed an innate command of expressive figuration on the guitar. As he worked the saloons and streets of Texas tenderloins, his lead-boys included, at various times, Leadbelly (1885–1949), Lightnin' Hopkins (b. 1912), T-Bone Walker (1910–1975), and Josh White (1908–1969), all of whom he influenced in one way or another. He employed a chauffeur during the days when he recorded in Chicago, between 1927 and 1929, and one night after a late session the car failed to show up. Apparently he tried to make it on his own to a party, but was found the next morning, frozen to death, on a Chicago street. The request he made in one of his emotive Blues—"Please see that my grave is kept clean"—was hard to follow since he was buried in an overgrown field outside Wortham, Tex. Bob Dylan, who recorded Jefferson's yearning for a clean grave, is among Rock performers who have kept his memory alive. In 1967 Blind Lemon's remains were buried in Wortham's Negro cemetery, and a marker was placed there.

See also Blues; Country Blues; Delta Blues.

Martin Block (1903–1967)   Although the idea was originated by Al Jarvis, who spun records in 1932 on KFWB, Los Angeles, under the title *The World's Largest Make-Believe Ballroom,* Block became famous as the announcer of his *Make-Believe Ballroom* program on WNEW, New York City. He is said to have launched his pretense of presenting music live from a ballroom in February 1935, when as a $20 a week staff announcer he began playing records while awaiting bulletins on the Hauptmann-Lindbergh kidnapping trial. (He had to go out and purchase the records since there were none in the WNEW library.) By 1947, when he signed a deal with KFWB and moved briefly to the West Coast, he was advertised as America's No. 1 disk jockey. The first of the nationally known dee jays, he was soon said to be earning $2 million a year from combined stints on WNEW, KFWB, and CBS's *Chesterfield Supper Club.* A super-salesman—he reportedly sold 300 refrigerators for a Newark department store during the blizzard of 1938—he claimed to have originated the slogans LS/MFT (Lucky Strike Means Fine Tobacco) and ABC (Always Buy Chesterfield). With the advent of Rock 'n' Roll and Alan Freed (*see* Alan Freed), he became one of the sharpest and most outspoken critics of the new music.

block chording   A form of piano playing in which the left hand, instead of playing a bass line, moves parallel with the right, duplicating the chords and both broadening and amplifying the sound. Milt Buckner (1915–1977), pianist through the 1940s with Lionel Hampton (b. 1913), was the first to popularize the "locked-hands" piano style, as it is also called.

"blow"   Among jazz musicians, jargon for playing any musical instrument, not necessarily a wind instrument.

blow harmony   Notes are hummed rather than vocalized and then literally blown out of the mouth. An example: "Sincerely" by the Moonglows.

"blow up a storm"   To play with authority, impact, and excitement. Used as the title of a novel by Garson Kanin.

Blue-eyed Soul   The opposite of "Oreo singing": instead of black performers singing white, white performers sing black. One of the first Blue-eyed Soul groups was the Rascals of New York City, who sought to approach the intensity of expression associated with black Gospel music and consciously simulated the intonation of black singers. The Righteous Bros., who titled an album *Blue-Eyed Soul* (1963), and were produced by Phil Spector, were so successful in sounding black that they at first fooled black disc jockeys around the country. Instrumentally, the Average White Band manages to sound like a raucous R & B group.
    See also Blues Rock; "Oreo singer."

Bluegrass   A fast-two beat style that may be described as C & W Dixieland. Its locus was Kentucky, which doubtless accounts for its name; Bill Monroe (b. 1911), raised on a Kentucky farm, is its most eloquent exponent. His original Blue Grass Boys (1945–1948)—Monroe on mandolin, Chubby Wise on fiddle, Earl Scruggs on banjo, Lester Flatt on guitar, and Howard (Cedric Rainwater) Watts on bass—introduced the style. Although banjo, fiddle, mandolin, and guitar thereafter became the basic instruments of Bluegrass, Flatt & Scruggs used the dobro in their Foggy Mountain Boys Band, a Bluegrass group. Later exponents of the style include the New Lost City Ramblers, the Charles River Valley Boys, the Lovin' Spoonful, the Dillards, Clarence White of the Kentucky Colonels, and the Byrds, who recorded *Muleskinner: A Potpourri of Bluegrass* in 1973.

blue note   Traditionally, the flatted seventh and third characteristic of Blues singing and playing. But the term has been extended so that any note can, through manipulation, be made to sound blue. The true blue note is not quite a flat or a sharp.

Blue Ridge Rangers   Not a group but a name under which John Fogerty (b. 1945), founder of the Creedence Clearwater Revival, recorded after the Revival broke up in 1972. Playing all the instruments and doing all the vocals himself, Fogerty achieved two hit singles in 1973 (as the Blue Ridge Rangers) with "Hearts of Stone" and a revival of Hank Williams's "Jambalaya (On the Bayou)."

Blues   An Afro-American folk form that crystalized after the Emancipation Proclamation from centuries of the black experience in this country. Blues had its roots in work songs, hollers, arhoolies, and especially, Spiritual Sorrow songs. Black people had to become an "I," the slave had to be freed from the land and given mobility before the Blues could take shape as a form of personal expression.

In its classic form, the Blues consisted of a three-line stanza, AAB, and twelve bars of music with a chord sequence of I/IV–I/V–I, each segment made up of four bars. Some regard the three-line form as a contraction of the African call-and-response ritual since the third line serves as an answer to the preceding two lines in the way that the group responds to the leader in African choral chant.

Although Blues are recognized as songs of deprivation—people in search of food, home, sex, money, love, and work—they embody a spirit of courage in the face of defeat, hope in the face of despair, optimism in the face of suffering. This ambivalence is encompassed in a musical structure that employs blue notes with a minor sound against major chords.

The word "blues" began to appear in published songs during the second decade of the twentieth century, especially in the songs of W. C. Handy (1873–1958), Father of the Blues: "Memphis Blues" (1912), "St. Louis Blues" (1914), "Joe Turner Blues" (1915), "Beale Street Blues" (1916). As a sound and style, the Blues entered the mainstream of American Pop in the 1920s as the result of recordings made by a group of black female vaudevillians: Mamie Smith (1883[90?]–1946) ("Crazy Blues," 1920); Clara Smith (1894–1935), no relation; Alberta Hunter (b. 1897), who resurfaced recently in her eighties; Bertha "Chippie" Hill (1905–1950); Ma Rainey (1886–1939); and Bessie Smith (1894–1937), known as Empress of the Blues.

Chronologically as well as stylistically, Blues may be divided into (1) Classic Blues, (2) Country or Delta Blues, (3) Urban Blues, and (4) Rhythm & Blues. Originating in the Delta region of Mississippi, Country bluesmen were itinerants. Urban Blues developed after the Great Depression of 1929, when blacks migrated from the South to the West and Midwest and when bluesmen settled mainly in Chicago. Rhythm & Blues evolved during the 1940s as an electrified, ensemble form and became the basis of Rock 'n' Roll in the 1950s.

See also Classic Blues; Country Blues; Delta Blues; Ragtime; Rhythm & Blues; Urban Blues

Blues, British   The Blues developed into a vital sound in English pop music on the heels of the Skiffle craze of the 1950s, which itself owed a heavy debt to the ethnic music of American bluesmen. Skiffle groups went to great pains to duplicate the crude, homemade instruments used by the black pioneers of the Blues.

Although John Mayall (b. 1934) of Manchester is generally recognized as the Father of British Blues, two lesser-known British musicians antedated his dedication to the Blues revival of the sixties.

Major credit goes to Alexis Korner (b. 1928), born in Paris and raised in England, who is known as the Grandfather of British Rhythm & Blues. The title is well merited since he switched from the purity of acoustic guitar to the electric instrument in the mid-1960s. Korner's main associate in the Blues revival was harmonica player/banjoist Cyril Davies (1932–1964), whom he met at a Skiffle session and with whom he opened an R & B club (either the Roundhouse or the Blues & Barrelhouse Club) in the Soho district of London in the mid-fifties. The venture failed, but a second undertaking in 1962 with a band they called Blues Incorporated, formed in 1961, led to a long booking at the prestigious Marquee Club.

Among those who came to the Marquee and were attracted by the drive and rhythmic punch of R & B were such young musicians and future greats as Brian Jones (1944–1969) and Keith Richard (b. 1943), later of the Rolling Stones; Paul Jones (b. 1942), later of Manfred Mann; Eric Burdon (b. 1941) of the Animals and later, War; bassist Jack Bruce (b. 1943), later of Cream, who also joined Korner-Davies; and drummer Ginger Baker (b. 1940), later of Cream, who also played with Korner-Davies. A little later, when Blues Incorporated was performing at the Flamingo Club in London, Mick Jagger (b. 1944) became lead vocalist. When Davies left Korner to form the Cyril Davies Blues Band, Korner added Graham Bond to the group. (Davies, whose harmonica playing was influenced by Sonny Boy Williamson [1914–1948], Little Walter [1930–1968] and Sonny Terry (b. 1911), died at the age of 32.)

Later, Korner, whose guitar playing was modelled on Blind Lemon Jefferson (1897–1929) and Scrapper Blackwell (1903–1962), worked with CCS (Collective Consciousness Society), a British studio outfit that recorded with John Lee Hooker (b. 1917), and other American bluesmen.

Like Korner and Davies, John Mayall used Skiffle as a stepping stone to the Blues, organizing his famous Bluesbreakers in 1962. During the sixties, so many outstanding musicians played in his group that to list them is to set down a Who's Who of Rock: drummer John McVie, later of Fleetwood Mac; guitarist Eric Clapton (b. 1945), later of the Yardbirds and Cream; bassist Jack Bruce (b. 1943); guitarist Mick Taylor (b. 1949), later of the Rolling Stones; drummer Mick Fleetwood (b. 1942), drummer Aynsley Dunbar; guitarist Peter Greene—to mention but a few future stars. It is no wonder that Mayall is frequently called the Grandfather of British Rock.

Among other bands that participated in the British Blues movement were: Spencer Davis's R & B Quartet, with Stevie Winwood (b. 1948) (vocal and harmonica) and Peter York (drums), and a repertoire of material drawn from Sonny Boy Williamson, Little Walter, and

Howlin' Wolf (1910–1976); the Yardbirds, who followed the Rolling Stones into the Crawdaddy Club as house band, and included Jimmy Page (b. 1945), Jeff Beck (b. 1944), Eric Clapton (b. 1945), and John Bonham (1947–1980) at various times; the Graham Bond Organization, a fixture at the 100 Club on Oxford Street, with a personnel that included Jack Bruce and Ginger Baker; Aynsley Dunbar's Retaliation, formed by him after he left the Bluesbreakers, with Rod Stewart (b. 1945), vocals; Fleetwood Mac, also formed by Bluesbreakers alumni; the Savoy Brown Blues Band, whose raw playing was heard at the Nags Head Public House in South London; John Lee's Groundhogs, the most popular of groups backing visiting American bluesmen like Champion Jack Dupree (b. 1910), John Lee Hooker, (b. 1917), Jimmy Reed (1915–1976), and Memphis Slim (b. 1915); and Chicken Shack, a Worcestershire group whose name derived from the abandoned chicken coop in which they rehearsed and whose featured vocalist–pianist was Christine Perfect, later of Fleetwood Mac.

See also Blues Rock; Skiffle.

The Blues Foundation   A nonprofit organization, with headquarters in Memphis, which each year makes W. C. Handy Blues Awards in nine categories: (1) Male Blues Artist of the Year; (2) Female Blues Artist of the Year; (3) Blues Vocalist of the Year; (4) Blues Instrumentalist of the Year; (5) Blues Album of the Year (U.S.); (6) Blues Album of the Year (Foreign); (7) Vintage or Reissue Album of the Year (U.S.); (8) Vintage or Reissue Album of the Year (Foreign); (9) Blues Single of the Year. Nominations for the awards are made by an international panel of Blues authorities, critics, and personalities, who also vote on the winners. There are also Hall of Fame Awards, given to living or deceased individuals, a category intended to cover the entire history of the Blues, not just a given year. The Blues Foundation is at P.O. Box 161272, Memphis, TN 38116. Phone:(901) 332–6459.

Blues harp   The instrument of Blues, Folk music, and some Jazz, the Blues harmonica (''harp'' in Blues jargon) produces a single scale plus a few notes above and below in a chordal relationship to the scale. It is also known as a *diatonic* harmonica, and to play in a different diatonic scale or key, the player must change instruments. It is the instrument of such performers as Little Walter (1930–1968), Sonny Boy Williamson (1914–1948), ''Shakey'' Horton (b. 1917), and other Delta bluesmen.

By contrast, the *chromatic* harmonica spans three or four octaves and includes the sharps and flats not produced by the diatonic instrument. The chromatic harmonica is the instrument of such Pop performers as the Harmonicats, Leo Diamond, Richard Hayman (b. 1920), Eddy Lawrence Manson and Stevie Wonder (b. 1951). In 1948 the American

Federation of Musicians recognized the harmonica as a legitimate instrument.

Blues revival   The engineers of the revival, and of the renewed interest in the roots of Blues Rock, were Cream, the first of the superblues groups formed in 1967 by guitarist Eric Clapton (b. 1945). A feature of the revival that lasted through the late sixties was the reemergence of pioneer R & B figures who had been pushed into the back of the record scene by the vogue of Rock 'n' Roll, Rock, and the British Rock invasion.

See also White Blues revival.

Blues Rock   Might be called "Electric Rock" in recognition of the pioneering role of such "electricians" as B. B. King (b. 1925) and Chicago bluesmen Muddy Waters (b. 1915) and Howlin' Wolf (1910–1976) in fathering the style. Many regard Blues Rock as a British development since American proponents like Paul Butterfield (b. 1942) and the Blues Project, as well as the onset of the American Blues explosion, were all antedated by Alexis Korner's English group Blues Incorporated; Spencer Davis's group; the Yardbirds; and John Mayall's Bluesbreakers—not to mention the Animals with Eric Burdon (b. 1941), and the Rolling Stones.

As early as 1962, Korner and Cyril Davies opened an R & B club in London, later moving their group to the Marquee club, where future Rock stars like Brian Jones (1944–1969) and Keith Richards (b. 1943) of the Rolling Stones, Eric Burdon of the Animals, and others sat in; still later, working at the Flamingo, where Mick Jagger (b. 1944) became their lead vocalist. In 1962 the Bluesbreakers presented, in their title album, remakes of Blues by Ray Charles (b. 1930), Robert Johnson (1912–1938), Freddie King (1934–1976), Little Walter, and Otis Rush (b. 1934).

Functioning from 1963 to 1967, the Yardbirds nurtured Blues superstars of the late sixties: guitarists Eric Clapton (b. 1945), Jeff Beck (b. 1944), and Jimmy Page (b. 1945), among others. A most influential group and forerunners of the Heavy Metal sound, the Yardbirds revealed their sources in impact versions of Muddy Waters's "I'm a Man" and Howlin' Wolf's "Smokestack Lightnin'." When the Yardbirds fell apart, Jimmy Page formed the Led Zeppelin, Blues-oriented before it went Heavy Metal; and when Eric Clapton left the Bluesbreakers he formed Cream, frequently credited with igniting the American Blues explosion of 1968. Clapton sometimes called himself "Slow-hand" because he used B. B. King's technique of striking a note, holding it, bending it, shaking it, and then sliding to the next note, a technique that involved little hand motion. But he was also influenced by bluesmen Skip James (1902–1969), Blind Lemon Jefferson (1897–1929), and Bo Diddley (b. 1928).

By 1967 the early British Blues groups led to the rise of Fleetwood Mac, who not only recorded versions of B. B. King (b. 1925) and Elmore James (1918–1963) but wrote their own Blues. Before they disbanded and went Pop in 1970, they went to Chicago and did a series of sessions with such bluesmen as Otis Spann (1930–1970) (piano), Shakey Horton (b. 1917) (harp), and Willie Dixon (b. 1915) (bass). Among the classics they recorded: "Everyday I Have the Blues" and "Rockin' Boogie." Led Zeppelin, which soon became known as a Heavy Metal group, participated in the Blues explosion in '68 largely through Robert Plant, a big-voiced Blues shouter who had sung with Alexis Korner's group.

On the American scene, the Blues Project and the Paul Butterfield Blues Band became the first white bands to produce Electric Blues. In 1965 the former, regarded as the pioneer of American Blues Rock, also pioneered an album-only approach and the use of long, extended tracks, which led to limited underground FM exposure. While the Blues Project created its own material, Paul Butterfield covered material recorded by black bluesmen, thereby bringing Electric Rock to a white audience; his Blues harp benefited from the accompaniment of Blues guitarists Elvin Bishop and Mike Bloomfield (b. 1942).

By mid-1966 the Blues Magoos, led by singer/guitarist Emil Thielheim, had a sound that elicited a Mercury Records contract and a debut album in early '67. Although the group went through the usual reorganizations, it remained Blues-oriented into the seventies, when its repertoire still included Willie Dixon's "Heart Attack."

At the Monterey Pop Festival of June 1967, two American groups demonstrated the impact of Blues Rock. Canned Heat, organized by Bob "Bear" Hite, a Torrance, Calif., record collector who boasted over 70,000 Blues disks, made its debut at the Ash Grove in Los Angeles in 1965 and had a debut LP on the market before the festival gave it national recognition. It was guitarist Mike Bloomfield, a mid-sixties member of the Paul Butterfield Blues Band, who organized the Electric Flag in '67, an eight-piece instrumental group that included such Blues Rock devotees as drummer Buddy Miles, an Otis Redding/Wilson Pickett record-session man; organist Barry Goldberg, after he left the Steve Miller Blues Band; and Nick Gravenites, a singer/composer who was, like the others, Chicago-born and who grew up with the sound of Chicago Electric Blues in his ears.

With the Blues explosion of 1968, Blues Rock bands proliferated. Among the more important of these; Barry Goldberg Blues Band, Steve Miller Blues Band, Delaney & Bonnie, J. Geils Band, Joe Cocker's Big Blues Band, Savoy Brown, Steppenwolf, ZZ Top, and Allman Brothers

Band. There were also individual artists who favored the idiom: Bonnie Raitt (b. 1949), who learned slide guitar from Fred McDowell (1945–1972) and Blues phrasing from Sippie Wallace (b. 1898); hoarse-voiced Rod Stewart (b. 1945); and, of course, Janis Joplin (1943–1970), an erotic Blues Shouter.

See also Blues British; Blues revival; Blues Shouter.

Blues Shouter   A black style that superseded the wailing nasality of rural bluesmen like Blind Lemon Jefferson (1897–1929) and Robert Johnson (1912–1938), and Pop/Folk-inflected bluesmen like Big Bill Broonzy (1893–1958). Joe Turner (b. 1911) and Jimmy Rushing (1902–1972) were among the earliest of the shouters, followed soon by Roy Brown (b. 1925), Wynonie Harris (1915–1969), Big Mama Thornton (b. 1912), and LaVern Baker (b. 1929).

boffo   Derived from ''box office'' and means the kind of success associated with impressive ticket sales. Though generally used with reference to a performance, it can by extension refer to anything that works well.

''bofs''   A record-biz acronym for *Best Of:* i.e., an album made up of an artist's previous hits.

Bolero   An intriguing rhythm pattern that assumed the following form:

Also an exciting Spanish dance. Probably the most famous of all compositions using the idiom is the *Bolero* by Maurice Ravel, which assumed the proportions of a Pop hit in 1979 after actress Bo Derek mentioned in the film *10* that she enjoyed fornicating to it.

''bomb''   In music-biz lingo, a record or a song that fails to make it. ''Dog'' and ''flop'' are other expressions for the record or artist that misses.

bongos   *See* Latin rhythm instruments.

bonus   A sum of money paid as an incentive on the signing of a contract. Unlike an advance, the bonus is an outright payment and is not recouped from future earnings.

See also advance.

Boogaloo   A Rock 'n' Roll dance that derived from black dancing and was based on the Boogie-Woogie rhythm. One of the many teenage dancing-apart dances. Other no-touch dances include the Monkey, Frug, Hitch Hiker, Hulabaloo, Mashed Potato, Shake, Skate, and Watusi.

See also Boogie-Woogie.

Boogie-Woogie   An eight-to-the-bar piano style, employing an ostinato bass with a Blues chord structure: I/IV–I/V–I. Although it seemingly was a staple of Chicago house-rent parties in the 1920s, it was first heard on a recording by Meade Lux Lewis (1905–1964) of "Honky Tonk Train Blues" in 1927. Jimmy Yancey (1894–1951), who did not record until 1939, is recognized as the Father of Boogie-Woogie.

The sound did not enter the mainstreams of American Pop until 1938-1939, when three Boogie pianists—Meade Lux Lewis, Albert Ammons (1907–1949), and Pete Johnson (1904–1967)—played at Carnegie Hall in the famous *Spirituals to Swing* concert presented by John Hammond. The style caught on when the three toured the country as the Boogie-Woogie Trio, prompting the Big Bands of the day, white as well as black, to tackle the style. Among those who produced Boogie hit records were Tommy Dorsey (1905–1956), whose "Boogie-Woogie" (1938) was based on a 1928 disk by Clarence "Pine Top" Smith (1904–1929); Will Bradley (b. 1912), who cut a series of Boogie-oriented Pop tunes; pianists Freddie Slack (1910–1965) and Bob Zurke (1910–1944); and Bob Crosby (b. 1913), whose Bob-Cats cut "Yancey's Special," composed by Meade Lux Lewis as a tribute to the Father of Boogie.

Boogie-Woogie also invaded two other areas. A trio called The Andrews Sisters made an international reputation on disks such as "Beat Me, Daddy, Eight to the Bar" and "Boogie-Woogie Bugle Boy." Boogie also became a potent strain in C & W: Tennessee Ernie Ford (b. 1919) hit with "Shotgun Boogie"; Moon Mullican (1909–1967), with a stomping "Cherokee Boogie"; Merle Travis (b. 1917), with "Blue Smoke"; and the Delmore Brothers, with "Pan-American Boogie" and "Mobile Boogie."

Boogie as Shuffle was a staple of the work of the Tympany Five of Louis Jordan (1908–1975), the Father of R & B. An eight-to-the-bar pattern, Shuffle differs only slightly from straight boogie:

Boogie-Woogie   *Shuffle*

And here are a few of the more popular Boogie-Woogie basses:

Many of the early independent labels of R & B began with Boogie versions of standard works: e.g., by Hadda Brooks for Modern, and Hazel Scott (1920–1981) for Decca. The sound of Boogie is also prominent in Count Basie's Kansas City Jazz. In the early days of Rock, Huey (Piano) Smith & the Clowns scored a hit with "Rocking Pneumonia and the Boogie-Woogie Flu" (1957). Boogie is basic to the piano styles of Fats Domino (b. 1928) and Jerry Lee Lewis (b. 1935), among other rockers.

As black jargon, "boogie" meant the devil, and as a verb, "sexual intercourse."

See also Shuffle.

booking agent   Musicians and singers sometimes arrange for live appearances by dealing directly with the owners of clubs, bars, lounges, concert halls, theaters, arenas, showrooms, stadiums, and so on. More frequently such dates, or gigs, are arranged through a booking agent. Fees vary. Booking agents usually charge 15 to 20 percent for gigs of one to three nights, and 10 to 15 percent for 4 bookings of four nights or more.

bootleg record   A recording that is made without the permission of the copyright owner and/or artist. There are really two types, both illegal and both opening the seller to criminal prosecution. One type involves the duplication, without permission of the manufacturer, of material released commercially. The second type consists of copies of material not intended for release to the public and made illegally from a live performance or live broadcast. The former is motivated by avarice, the latter by the desire of fans and aficionados to possess something not available to others. But sometimes the latter are duplicated extensively and sold by avaricious people. Bootleg records usually have a plain white label and are packaged in a plain white sleeve, inserted in a cellophane-like jacket. Sometimes, however, bootleggers duplicate both the label and jacket of a commercially released album.

In 1967, when he was recuperating from a near-fatal motorcycle accident, Bob Dylan (b. 1941) did practice-and-relax sessions with the Band, who lived in a nearby farmhouse. Somehow, copies of the homemade tapes got out. They began to circulate so extensively, due to ardent fans as well as greedy businessmen, that the so-called *Basement Tapes* were released commercially by Dylan's record company (Columbia).

Bop   A modern Jazz style that developed in Harlem shortly after World War II and that came into the mainstream of Jazz via appearances by its innovators in the clubs of 52nd St. The main adventurers who slowly evolved the style through experimentation at Minton's included Dizzy Gillespie (b. 1917) (trumpet); Charlie "Bird" Parker (1920–1955) (alto sax); Kenny "Klook" Clarke (b. 1914) (drums); and Thelonious Monk (b. 1917) (piano). Known originally as Bebop or Rebop as the result of a characteristic two-note figure, the style eventually came to be known as Bop. The drum stopped being a time-keeper and not only soloed but dropped bombs at unexpected moments; Clarke used the top cymbal for rhythm and the bass drum for surprise punctuation. Played at whirlwind tempi, Bop was not only polyrhythmic but polyharmonic and polymodal as well. The harmonic palette was extended through the use of the flatted fifth (really the augmented fourth or eleventh), leading to the frequent use of eleventh and thirteenth chords. Turning away from the recognized repertoire of Dixieland and Pop standards, the bopsters expanded the repertoire by delving into show tunes and using the more complex chord progressions to develop new melodies. (You had to be "in" to know that Parker's "Quasimodo" was based on "Embraceable You".) "How High the Moon," played at breakneck speed, became the Bop anthem. Even the traditional triplet with its accent on the first of the three notes was upended so that the accent fell on the middle note: *eel-YA-dah.*

The tempi and surprise metrical changes took the music off the dance floor where Jazz had originally put listeners, and onto the concert stage. Since audiences consisted mostly of white people, bopster animosity, arrogance, and indifference are understandable. Bop was presumably a reflection of the resentment black musicians felt over the rewards reaped by the white Big Bands from the Swing style developed by blacks. But Bop musicians were not too friendly to other musicians, keeping them off-balance with the new repertoire, chord changes, and asymmetrical rhythms. Inevitably Bop polarized Jazz, with Dixielanders like Satchmo dismissing it as "the modern malice" while the bopsters castigated their critics as "moldy figs."

Bop at first seemed a cult development, partly perhaps because the bopsters, especially Dizzy, dressed and acted strangely. Goatees, heavy black-rimmed spectacles, and berets became a mark of the group. Turning their backs on audiences was an early mannerism, as was Diz's conducting with his rump. Stopping suddenly in what seemed the middle of a number but wasn't, and scattering off the stage, bewildered musicians as well as audiences. In time, shorn of its mannerisms, Bop came to be accepted and admired for its role in expanding the harmonic, melodic and rhythmic resources of Jazz as well as its repertoire.

See also Charlie "Bird" Parker.

"Born Again" Jesus Freaks   Rock brought with it a questioning of older-generation religious as well as other values. Of the many new religious trends, at least three appear to maintain a sizable following: Hare Krishna; the "Moonies," believers in the Rev. Sun Young Moon's Unification Church; and the New Christianity of the "born again" Christians. Among Rock artists who have embraced the new Jesus are Pat Boone, Stevie Wonder, Roger McGuinn, Donna Summer, Maria Muldaur, and Bob Dylan, who has advertised and explored his new faith in *Slow Train Coming* and *Saved*. In March 1982, *Time* reported that Dylan was turning back to his Judaic roots.

See also Jesus Rock.

Borscht Belt; Borscht Circuit   A legendary stretch of land in the Catskill and Adirondack mountains in New York State, the site of hotels, summer camps, bungalows, "kuch-a-lain"'s (do-your-own-cooking), and resorts, catering originally to a Jewish clientele and serving as the springboard for many great entertainers of the 1920s and 1930s. It became known as the Borscht Belt because one of the most popular dishes, a soup made of red beets, garnished with a boiled potato and sour cream, was called Borscht. Among the best-known resorts were Grossinger's, where Dore Schary served as social director; Camp Copake, where Moss Hart starred; White Roe Hotel, where Danny Kaye and Alan King got started; Flagler Hotel, whose playhouse was designed by Moss Hart; Green Mansions, whose entertainment staff included composer/lyricist Harold Rome; and Totem Lodge, where songwriter Henry Tobias functioned as the longtime impresario/producer. A partial list of the performers who "paid their dues" in the Borscht Belt would include comics Eddie Cantor, Milton Berle, Joey Bishop, Sam Levenson, Buddy Hackett, Jack S. Leonard, Jerry Lewis, and Sid Caesar; actors/singers/dancers John Garfield, Van Johnson, Robert Alda, Tony Curtis, Abbe Lane, Shelley Winters, and Eddie Fisher; opera stars Jan Peerce and Robert Merrill; and writers/playwrights/songwriters Clifford Odets, Herman Wouk, Lorenz Hart, Garson Kanin, and Arthur Kober. Along with Miami Beach and Las Vegas, the Borscht Belt is today one of the major bastions of live entertainment.

"boss"   It came out of Negro life, meaning someone in authority or charge, and by extension, someone at the top. When jazzmen began to use it with reference to a musician or performance, "boss" meant outstanding, superlative, authoritative.

Bossa Nova   A sound, style, and dance imported from the black ghettos of Brazil. "The Girl from Ipanema" (Ipanema is a suburb of Rio de Janeiro), a record by saxist Stan Getz (b. 1927) and guitarist Charlie Byrd (b. 1925), first acquainted Americans with this Latin-American rhythm in 1963. Written in a minor mode, the Bossa Novas conveyed a mood of great longing, emotional ennui, and gentle despair. The rhythm looked like this on paper:

"The Girl from Ipanema" was first recorded in the original Portuguese by João Gilberto (b. 1931), whose wife Astrud (b. 1940) made the first English version. The sound was popularized by jazzmen like Shorty Rogers (b. 1924) and the Brazilian Sergio Mendes (b. 1941), and Pop singers like Eydie Gorme (b. 1931)("Blame It on the Bossa Nova"); and was so infectious that Aretha Franklin (b. 1942) used it in her first hard-core Soul session ("Don't Let Me Lose This Dream").

"Boss of the Blues"   The billing of bluesman Joe Turner (b. 1911), perhaps as early as the 1930s but certainly in the mid-1950s after his career took off for a second time with "Chains of Love" (1951), "Sweet Sixteen" (1952), "Honey Love" (1953), and especially "Shake, Rattle, and Roll" (1954). Other bluesmen have used the billing, but Joe Turner was the original "Boss of the Blues."
See also Blues; Rhythm & Blues.

Boston or Bosstown Sound It was a "hype," and no one could distinguish the sound although there were groups like Ultimate Spinach, Bagatelle, Beacon Street Union, and Earth Opera who originated in the area. Apparently, it was a record company exec who maneuvered the whole thing and even sold the idea to *Newsweek*.

bottleneck guitar In an effort to approximate the whining, wailing sound of the Hawaiian guitar, fretted with a steel bar, Blues guitarists would use a flat knife, a brass ring, or a bottleneck as a slide. The bottleneck was literally the top of a bottle, broken from the body and annealed at the edge. The pinky was then inserted in the opening, converting the neck into a slide for fretting the instrument. The tuning was not the regular series of fourths and a third (e–a–d–g–b–e) but a series of notes that sounded a chord with the strings open (e–g–c–g–c–e). Thus it was possible to stop all the strings, made of steel, copper, or bronze, at the same fret position by placing a knife or a bottleneck across them. Among the best-known bottleneck guitarists, one would include Kokomo Arnold (1901–1968), Bukka White (1906–1977), Albert King (b. 1923), Ry Cooder (b. 1947), Jeremy Spencer (b. 1948) of Fleetwood Mac, and Duane Allman (1946–1971), regarded by many as the giant of the genre.
See also Hawaiian guitar; steel guitar.

Bottom Line A major showcase club for Blues, Jazz and Rock artists in Greenwich Village, New York City. Opened in 1974.
See also Greenwich Village.

bounce A musical synonym for verve or a buoyant beat.

"box" A Jazz and Swing term for piano.

bozuk, bouzouk, or bouzouki A string instrument of Eastern Aegean origin, it sounds like a mandolin with a deeper texture. The mandolin is Italian whereas the bozouk is Greek and has eight strings instead of four paired. Alexis Korner (b. 1928) played the bozouk.
See also, çaz.

"brag" form Refers to an aspect of songs by The Who, which relate to the Mod life-style. The Mods were a group of the lowest-paid members of the English working-class and lower-middle-class youth in the early 1960s. They were full of rage as a defeated, exploited, and trodden-upon group. Working long hours at dull jobs that stifled creativity, they dressed to the tens and sought to lose themselves in meaningless fun. "My Generation" by the Who is regarded as the anthem of the Mods: it embodies their underlying sense of insecurity and their outward braggadocio.

"bread"   Money in Jazz lingo.

break   In a vocal piece, a short instrumental passage. In an instrumental work, a passage by a solo instrument between ensemble segments.

Breakdown   A backwoods dance performed in rural Texas around the turn of the century. Leadbelly (1885–1949) played breakdowns.
See also Huddie Ledbetter; Sooky Jump.

"breaking out into assholes"   Rock jargon for being real scared, real terrified.

breakout   Used as a noun or adjective in music biz; refers to a town, city, or radio station which in a given period is successful in launching new record releases. At one time, especially during the heyday of the *American Bandstand,* originating on Station WFIL, the breakout city was Philadelphia. Before that it was Cleveland, where disk jockeys like Bill Randle and Alan Freed on Station KYW were able to break records open. When a new release began to take off, it was also known as a breakout.

bridge   During the Tin-Pan Alley years, 1900–1955, most popular songs consisted of 32 bars, divided into 4 segments of 8 measures each. Two melodic strains were arranged in an AABA sequence. The "B" strain, involving a change of rhythm and key, was known as the "bridge," "channel," or "release."

Brill Building   The center of Tin-Pan Alley during the 1930s and 1940s, the Brill Building is at 49th Street and Broadway in New York City.
    It was the proximity of the newly formed radio networks, CBS at 52nd Street and Madison Avenue and NBC on Fifth Avenue in the fifties, that caused Tin-Pan Alley to move uptown from its 29th Street location. During the 1930s, the Brill evolved into a throbbing beehive of music publishers, arrangers, songwriters, orchestra leaders, managers, and song-pluggers. Jerry Wexler, the well-known record producer and head of Warner Bros. Records in New York, has said of the plugger: "He was an American artifact who was replaced by an inferior surrogate—the record promoter, who in no way had his style or panache. The pluggers were sharp dressers, witty and a breed apart. They'd

target a band leader or singer and by great charm, convince him to use a song.''

Within the past few years, the owners of the Brill moved to eliminate the tall, impressive Art Deco entry to the building and to substitute offices and stores. A committee of songwriters and other interested New York citizens organized a protest so that the entry was declared a historic landmark by the Landmark Preservation Committee of the City of New York.

See also Big Ballad era; No. 1 plug; Pop music; The Sheet; Songplugger; Tin-Pan Alley; Your Hit Parade.

Brill Building Rock   A misnomer, since the Brill Building at 1619 Broadway (49th Street and Broadway) was the capital of Tin-Pan Alley in the days of the Big Bands, Big Baritones, and Big Ballads, when a Saturday-night, coast-to-coast show, *Your Hit Parade,* was the hit barometer of the business. Housing over 100 music publishers, including some of the biggest ASCAP firms, the Brill was the center of music business until the advent of Rock 'n' Roll in '56. At that point, two other Broadway buildings became important. The one at 1697 Broadway was less significant than that at 1650 Broadway. But these were the centers of Rock, not the Brill, and they housed the newer, small independent publishers, most of whom were affiliated with BMI.

If one does not take the term literally, Brill Building Rock might be understood as an evocative designation of publisher-manufactured Rock 'n' Roll. But the most successful of such firms, Aldon Music, was located not in the Brill but at 1650 Broadway. Founded in 1958 by *Al* Nevins, formerly of the Three Suns, and *Don* Kirshner, then a budding songwriter/manager, Aldon contracted teams of young songwriters, mostly youngsters who were still in high school or had just been graduated. The three most successful teams were: Neil Sedaka and Howie Greenfield, who wrote all of Sedaka's hit disks as well as songs for young artists like Connie Francis (''Stupid Cupid''); Barry Mann and Cynthia Weil, whose hits included the Righteous Brothers' ''You've Lost That Lovin' Feeling'' and ''(You're My) Soul and Inspiration;'' and Gerry Goffin and Carole King, another husband-and-wife team, who wrote No. 1 hits for the Shirelles, Bobby Vee, and Little Eva, who at one time worked as their maid.

Other songwriters whose work might be comprehended under the term Brill Building Rock or Pop would include Leiber and Stoller, the most prolific and the most consistent hit writers of the young group that came to the fore in the 1950s; Doc Pomus and Mort Shuman, who wrote hits mostly for Fabian and the Drifters; Otis Blackwell, who wrote two of Presley's biggest hits, ''Don't Be Cruel'' and ''All Shook Up,'' as well as Jerry Lee Lewis's ''Great Balls of Fire''; Ellie Greenwich and

Jeff Barry, who were then married and who wrote songs for Phil Spector's artists, including the Crystals and Ronettes, and who produced No. 1 hits for the Dixie Cups, Manfred Mann, the Shangri-Las, and Tommy James and the Shondells.

Virtually all of these Brill Building rockers shared an ability to perform as well as write—most had record releases of their own—so that the demos they made were sometimes bought as masters or used as the basis of commercial recordings. At least one of the group emerged as a superstar singer/songwriter in the 1970s. Carole King, divorced from Gerry Goffin and remarried, produced multimillion sellers in *Writer, Tapestry, Music, Rhymes & Reasons,* and other albums.

See also Leiber & Stoller.

"bringing it all together"   In teenage jargon, making it work.

British Blues   *See* Blues, British.

the British invasion   It began with the appearance of the Beatles, who came from Liverpool, on the Ed Sullivan TV show on February 9, 1964, the year that also saw the entrance of the Rolling Stones on the American Rock scene. In rapid succession, out of Merseyland—Liverpool is on the Mersey River—and manager Brian Epstein's enterprise came Gerry & the Pacemakers ("Don't Let the Sun Catch You Crying," "Ferry 'Cross the Mersey"); Swinging Blue Jeans ("Hippy, Hippy Shake"); and the Dakotas. The year 1964 saw American airwaves swamped with hits by the Kinks, the Dave Clark Five, the Searchers, Billy J. Kramer, the Bachelors, Peter & Gordon, Chad Stuart & Jeremy Clyde, Dusty Springfield, Cilla Black, the Animals (whose first single, "House of the Rising Sun," went to No. 1), Manfred Mann (who also hit No. 1 with his first single, "Do Wah Diddy Diddy"), the Nashville Teens, the Honeycombs, the Zombies, and Petula Clark (with her classic No. 1 smash "Downtown").

The following year, the tidal sweep continued with such British groups as Herman's Hermits, George Fame, Moody Blues, Freddie & the Dreamers (out of Manchester; No. 1 with "I'm Telling You Now"), Wayne Fontana & the Mindbenders (also from Manchester and No. 1 with "Game of Love"), Tom Jones (who did not make No. 1 with his first release), the Yardbirds, Donovan, Them, Silkie, Jonathan King, the Walker Brothers, the Hollies, and The Who.

The joke around the record business in those days was that all a musician had to do was wave a British passport and he would be signed to a recording contract. In truth, a Houston barber named Huey P. "Crazy Cajun" Meaux actually tried to pass off a San Antonio combo as an English group called The Sir Douglas Quintet. They scored a bestseller with their first release, "She's About a Mover" before the ruse was exposed.

Historians generally divide the British invasion into two waves, since no new groups made their appearance in 1966. The second wave came rolling in, in 1967, with the Bee Gees, followed by the Jeff Beck Group, Move, the Spencer Davis Group, Traffic, Pink Floyd, Nice, Procol Harum, and Free. These operated in the shadow of the Beatles' creativity and the rise of Psychedelic Rock. Of all the British groups that swamped the American record market from 1964 on, just the Rolling Stones, Pink Floyd, the Bee Gees, and the Who continued to be creative in the seventies.

See also The Beatles; The Rolling Stones; The Who.

Broadcast Music, Inc. (BMI)   Youngest of the three American performing rights societies, BMI was founded on October 14, 1939, following a pledge by the broadcasters of an amount of equal to 50 percent of the 1937 fees paid to ASCAP by the broadcast industry. Of this, $300,000 was for stock in the new company, and the remaining total of $1,200,000 was to be paid as initial licensee fees.

While BMI's immediate purpose was to provide an alternate source of music and thus reduce ASCAP's licensing monopoly over music performed on radio and with it the cost of airplay, its long-range effect was to establish BMI as the prime factor in broadening the character of popular music by bringing C & W and R & B into the mainstream.

The chief impetus for the formation of BMI came from ASCAP's contract demand of 15 percent of all radio revenue, increased from the 5 percent in a licensing agreement that would expire on December 31, 1940. Many stations gradually decreased their use of ASCAP repertoire, so that on January 1, 1941, they could perform non-ASCAP music with impunity. An agreement on a smaller fee was finally achieved in the early fall of 1941. During the intervening period, all of the Top 20 songs in sheet-music sales were licensed by BMI and other non-ASCAP groups—eight by newly formed publishing companies. Only one of the Top 15 Songs of the year 1941, as selected by *Variety,* was an ASCAP-licensed tune, "Shepherd Serenade," which made it after the strike was ended. ASCAP settled its contract demands by accepting 2.8 percent of radio revenues, little more than half its former rate.

Where there had been only 1,100 author/composers in 1940, and 137 music publishers, by 1980 BMI licensed the works of 37,346 songwriters and 21,130 publishers, and grossed nearly $80 million in revenues. Except for operating expenses and a limited general reserve, all BMI income, as with ASCAP, is distributed to writer and publisher affiliates. On the basis of the more than 55,000 writers and publishers it represents, together with reciprocal agreements with 39 foreign performing rights societies, BMI describes itself as "the world's largest music licensing organization."

Beginning in 1944, when the American Composers Alliance formally became associated with BMI, composers of concert music have been part of its active membership. Among the more distinguished names on its roster, one finds Elliott Carter, Norman Dello Joio, Roy Harris, Charles Ives, Ulysses Kay, Walter Piston, Walter Schuman, and Wallingford Riegger.

To assist new and promising composers, BMI sponsors a number of media. In 1951 it made its initial presentation of Awards to Student Composers. In recent years, in Los Angeles, it has sponsored the Alternative Chorus Workshop, through which new composers and authors have their works performed before audiences of publishers and record executives. Its most ambitious and productive project is the BMI Musical Theatre Workshop, which has been in operation under the direction of conductor/composer/author Lehman Engel since 1959. In the spring of each year, the best of the Workshop's output is showcased before an invited audience of theatrical producers, directors, and agents, and record and music publishing executives. Alumni of the Workshop include Carol Hall (*The Best Little Whorehouse in Texas*), Clark Gesner (*You're a Good Man, Charlie Brown*), and Ed Kleban (*A Chorus Line*).

Broadside   See *Sing Out!*

William Lee Conley Broonzy (1898–1958)   Born in Scott, Mississippi, raised in Arkansas, and making his own fiddle out of a cigar box, "Big Bill" eventually was recognized as one of this country's great Folk, Country, and Urban bluesmen. Although he arrived in Chicago in 1920, where he learned to play guitar from Papa Charlie Jackson (d. 1938) and made some records, he did not come into his own as a recording artist until after the Depression. By then, Chicago was the center of the Urban Blues development—many of the Delta bluesmen had migrated to the Windy City during the Depression—and Big Bill became the central figure as a performer in the South Side clubs and as a session man. He attained national renown to a degree when John Hammond brought him to New York in 1939 for the famous *Spirituals to Swing* concert at Carnegie Hall. Real recognition came with the Folk revival of the 1950s, when he worked with Win Stracke's Folk group *I Come for to Sing* and toured Europe. It was then that he recorded his oft-quoted song "Black, Brown, and White": "Now, if you're white/You're all right/If you're brown/Stick aroun'/But if you're black/Git back! Git back! Git back!" Despite the numerous recordings he made, Broonzy was compelled to work at various trades through most of his life. He was by turns a Pullman car porter, cook, piano mover, molder, and janitor, finding music his main source of income only during the last five years of his life. An autobiography that appeared in 1954, *Big Bill Blues: Big Bill Broonzy's Story as Told to Yannick Bruynoghe,* and an out-of-print five-record album of reminiscences that he cut for Verve with disk jockeys Bill Randle and Studs Terkel in 1957, are a gold mine of information about the Blues and black music.

See also Urban Blues.

brother duos   A Country tradition, as exemplified by the Monroe Brothers, Delmore Brothers, Blue Sky Boys, and Louvin Brothers, as well as the Everly Brothers—Don and Phil—of the Rock 'n' Roll era.

James Brown (1933–   )   Poor and a juvenile delinquent as a boy in Georgia (Macon or Augusta), by the late 1960s he owned a jet, a fleet of cars, and several radio stations. He was a super-showman who used all the resources of black thunder-and-lightning preachers. Gospel hysteria infused his first record release in 1956 with such emotion that "Please, Please, Please" became the mark of a style that earned him the cognomens Mr. Dynamite and Soul Brother No. 1. After the mid-sixties his stage shows embodied an audience-shattering routine in which he would collapse, be covered with a cape, and struggle back to the microphone, only to collapse again, be covered with a new cape, and stumble back to the microphone—an exhausting routine that reminded the more religious spectators of Christ and the Stations of the Cross.

"Pervasive as Brown's influence was during the Sixties," critic Robert Palmer has written, "he shaped the music of the Seventies even more profoundly. The chattering choke-rhythm guitars, broken bass patterns, explosive horn bursts, one-chord drones, and evangelical vocal discourses he introduced during the mid-Sixties became the *lingua franca* of contemporary black pop, the heartbeat of the discotheques, and a primary ingredient in such far-flung musical syntheses as Jamaican reggae and Nigerian Afro-beat."

It was "Papa's Got a Brand New Bag" in 1965 that set him off on a run of No. 1 R & B hits stretching into the mid-1970s: titles like "It's a Man's Man's Man's World," "Cold Sweat," "Hot Pants," "Super Bad," and "Make It Funky." Although some of these climbed into the Pop Top 10, none made No. 1, perhaps because of the "blackness" of his sound and style.

Without being involved in black nationalist movements, he produced an album in 1967 titled *Say It Loud—I'm Black and I'm Proud.* He toured Africa and entertained the troops in Vietnam but was outspoken about the second-class treatment his band received. It did not satisfy black militants. Nevertheless, his appeal was so great that during the summer riots in the late 1960s his appearance on TV prompted many blacks to remain at home to hear him urge "building instead of burning."

Musically, with Ray Charles (b. 1930), he anticipated and shaped the work of such Soul shouters as Otis Redding (1941–1967), Wilson Pickett (b. 1941), and Aretha Franklin (b. 1942).

Brownie bass   Black folk who could not afford to buy instruments, or lived far from stores where they could buy them, frequently made them out of household items: for example, a fiddle out of a cigar box. The Brownie bass consisted of an inverted metal washtub. A heavy washline was strung through a hole in the center and attached to a broom handle. By plucking the cord, a sound like that of a bass would be produced. Pitch was varied as on a regular bass by moving the left hand up and down the cord.

See also spasm band.

Brush-and-Broom guitar style   A style of guitar playing developed by Country pickers of the Tex-Mex area. It involved hitting a note (the "broom") and with the same movement brushing the fingers across a related chord (the "brush"). The ringing guitar heard on records by Buddy Holly (1938–1959), as well as on some disks of Johnny Cash (b. 1932), was a product of the technique.

See also Tex-Mex.

"B" side   *See* "A" side.

Bubble-Gum Rock   Music directed at the pre-teenage record buyer and pioneered by Buddah Records producer Neil Bogart, later a Disco impresario and the head of Casablanca Records. Among the groups that aimed their product and sound at this young market were 1910 Fruitgum Co., Ohio Express, Kasenetz-Katz Super Cirkus, Lemon Pipers, and Shadows of Knight. "Yummy, Yummy" and "Chewy, Chewy" were typical song titles. Another impresario of Bubble Gum was Don Kirshner, formerly of Aldon Music, who sponsored the Archies and Monkees. Later instances of Bubble-Gum rockers: the Partridge Family, the Osmonds, the Cowsills, Jackson 5, and Bobby Sherman (b. 1944); also Journey, who added metal to the genre.

Bugalú   Derived from the mid-sixties R & B dance, the Boogaloo, the Latin Bugalú was both a dance and a singing style of the Latin Soul movement. As a dance, the Bugalú was close to the Mambo, except that the rhythm was simpler. As a singing style, it displayed the influence of both Cuban music and R & B. In brief, the Bugalú represented a fusion of Latin and black sounds, of Cuban and R & B rhythms.

See also Mambo.

bullet   Through the years, the oversized dot • known as a "bullet" has been used in trade-paper charts to indicate a record that makes an unusual leap in popularity. *Billboard* currently uses the bullet on singles charts to designate a disk that has sold one million units or more; on the album charts, a bullet means a sale of half a million units. A triangle ▲ on singles charts means a sale of 2 million units, while on album charts it signifies a sale of one million. Stars are also used: a filled-in or black star ★ designates a disk whose airplay and sales are outstanding, while an open or outline star ☆ signifies a superstar disk, one that has made the greatest upward leap in a given week.

bull fiddle   Swing lingo for the string bass.

"bummer"   A bad acid trip. Used broadly to refer to any event or activity that does not work out.

Businessman's Bounce   A derisive term that developed during the era of the Big Bands. Young people were then doing the Lindy Hop and other uptempo dances. Middle-aged folk, who preferred the sweeter sounds and slower tempi of bands like Guy Lombardo (1902–1977) and Sammy Kaye (b. 1910), were said to be doing the Businessman's Bounce.

See also Fox-trot; Lindy Hop.

"busted"   Arrested by federal agents or the police for the possession of illegal drugs.

Jerry Butler
   See "The Iceman."

The Byrds   One of the most creative Rock groups of the sixties, they were pioneers of Folk Rock ("Turn! Turn! Turn!"), Acid Rock ("Mr. Tambourine Man"), Raga Rock ("Eight Miles High"), the use of the sitar (David Crosby), and the light show (done for the first time in New York City at the Village Gate). They were also in the vanguard of the late-sixties turn to Country Rock (*Sweetheart of the Rodeo*). Turnover in personnel doubtless played a large figure in their failure to achieve the fame that came to the more stable Beatles, who capitalized on some of their pioneering advances. By the time they did *Dr. Byrds & Mr Hyde* in 1969, hardly one of their best albums, the only original Byrd left was

Jim, later Roger, McGuinn (b. 1942). Chris Hillman (b. 1942) (bass) and Gram Parsons (b. 1945) (Country guitarist) were with the Flying Burrito Brothers, and rhythm guitarist David Crosby (b. 1941) was working with Steve Stills (b. 1945) of the Buffalo Springfield and Graham Nash (b. 1942) of the Hollies.

Jim McGuinn, who changed his name to Roger in 1968, was extremely articulate, so articulate that the group is sometimes known as the first of the Head rockers. Believing that music reflected the sounds and tensions of its time, McGuinn related Rock to jets and his music to the flight of birds. He changed the *i* to *y* in *Birds* for greater impact. Nevertheless, authorities could not be persuaded that "Eight Miles High" dealt with jet flight and not drugs—and the record was banned on many stations. No album of theirs quite matched the impact of their debut LP, *Mr. Tambourine Man,* which won a Gold Record and remains one of the watershed albums of Rock.

CBGB   A New York City club in the Bowery, which opened around 1973 as a Folk music center. After Tom Verlaine of the New Wave group Television persuaded owner Hilly Kristal to book Rock groups in 1974, CBGB became the locus of Punk, presenting groups like Patti Smith, the Ramones, Blondie, Television, Marbles, Fast, Planets and Tuff Darts. The place was lit mainly by neon beer signs.
See also New Wave; Punk Rock.

CCS   Stands for Collective Consciousness Society, a British studio recording group, assembled by producer Mickie Most and music director/composer John Cameron, both associated with Donovan (b. 1946). It numbered as many as 23 musicians—some from Alexis Korner's Blue Mink Band—and made Big Band–type disks, based on riffs, using Rock and Jazz arrangements.
See also Big Band era; riff.

CMA   *See* Country Music Association.

CW   Abbreviation of a record-biz bit of jargon, "comfortably weird," meaning someone who has achieved success without sacrificing his individuality.

C & W   Abbreviation of "Country & Western." An urban and 20th-century type of white Folk music, it developed mostly in the southeastern part of the U.S.A. Important centers were Shreveport, Louisville, and Nashville—but also Cincinnati and Chicago. The latter city was the home of the *National Barn Dance,* broadcast over Station WLS as early as 1924. In the 1940s the *Midwestern Hayride* emanated from WLW out of Cincinnati, and the *Louisiana Hayride* was heard over Station KWKH out of Shreveport. The first Country records, then known as "Hillbilly" disks, were cut in Bristol, Tenn., by the Carter Family on August 1, 1927, and by Jimmie Rodgers, the Father of Country Music, on August 4, 1927. The term "Hillbilly," in use from the 1920s on, was dropped at about the same time that "race music" gave way to R & B in the years after World War II. It was the *Grand Ole Opry* program, first heard over WSM in Nashville in 1925, that helped make Nashville the flourishing center of Country music.

The western outpost of C & W was and is centered in Bakersfield, Calif., home of Buck Owens (b. 1929) and Merle Haggard (b. 1937). The city calls itself, in signs welcoming the traveler, "Capital of Western and Country Music." It has been called "Nashville West" and "Little Nashville," and the Bakersfield music community prefers the name "Western Capital of Country Music." Cities in Texas (San Antonio, Ft. Worth, Dallas), in Oklahoma (Tulsa, Muskogee, Tioga), and Arkansas also figured prominently in the development of C & W through artists like Bob Wills (1905–1975), Ernest Tubb (b. 1914), Tex Ritter (1906–1974), Cowboy Copas (1913–1963), Gene Autry (b. 1907), and Johnny Cash (b. 1932).

See also The Carter Family; *Grand Ole Opry;* Jimmie Rodgers; Western Swing.

cabarets   During World War I, New York City saloons and cafes began to develop into cabarets, meaning places where live entertainment was added to the menu of food and liquor. Harlem saw the rise of such "dicty" cabarets as Hollywood Cabaret, Barron's Exclusive Club, Connor's Cafe, Capitol Palace, and Leroy's, which was the first to open for black patronage. Ethel Waters (1900–1977) was among the early stars appearing in some of these places. Fusing the idioms of classic Ragtime and Jazz, piano players like James P. Johnson (1891–1955) and Willie "The Lion" Smith (1897–1973) evolved the style known as Stride piano. It was these cabarets as well as booming clubs like the Cotton Club and Connie's Inn (which employed Jazz musicians who had come up from New Orleans) that were basic to the change from the Ragtime era to the Jazz age and that helped make Harlem the booming center of Manhattan nightlife during the dizzy 1920s and the Harlem Renaissance.

See also "dicty"; Hot Jazz; house-rent parties; Ragtime; Stride piano.

cabaret singers   Mabel Mercer (1900–   ), who was a cult figure of the Lost Generation in Paris during the 1920s and who, as of this writing, is still performing in one of New York City's chi-chi night spots, is the stellar example of the cabaret singer. Although Mercer was in her heyday in the 1940s at Tony's when 52nd St. was in full flower, the cabaret era flourished in NYC during the 1920s and 1930s. It produced such outstanding singers as Helen Morgan (1900–1941), who sang sitting on the top of a grand piano; Harry Richman (1895–1972), the strutting golden boy; Libby Holman (1906–1971), remembered for her singing of "Body and Soul"; Jane Froman (b. 1907); Ruth Etting (1898–1978); Ethel Waters (1900–1977); Mildred Bailey (1907–1951); and others. Many went on to achieve fame on the Broadway stage or in films. Mabel Mercer of the flawless diction and expression phrasing, whose influence is recognized in the work of singers from Frank Sinatra (b. 1915) to Barbra Streisand (b. 1942), has remained a cabaret singer.
    See also 52nd St.

cabaza   *See* Latin rhythm instruments.

cadence   Two basic types of cadences are: (1) authentic, when the V chord, or dominant, resolves to I, the tonic chord; and (2) plagal, when the IV chord, or subdominant, resolves to I.

Cadillac Jake   Nickname of harmonica player Shakey Harris (b. 1921), who also produced some of the disks of bluesman Samuel Maghett, known as Magic Sam (1937–1969).

Caesar & Cleo   The billing under which Sonny & Cher made their first single disk in 1963.

Cafe Lena (Caffe Lena)   A coffeehouse and Folk center in Saratoga Springs, N.Y., founded and run since May 1960 by Lena Spencer, who has played host to a long list of performers, including Bob Dylan (b. 1941), Jack Elliott (b. 1931), Arlo Guthrie (b. 1947), Tom Paxton (b. 1937), Dave Van Wronk (b. 1936), Jean Redpath (b. 1937), and Jim Kweskin (b. 1940). Don McLean (b. 1945), author/composer of "American Pie," is a longtime favorite, who performs traditionally at the Caffe each New Year's weekend. When he was broke in 1968, Lena Spencer arranged for him to work for New York State as the Hudson River Troubadour. Regarded by many as the Grand Lady of the Folk Circuit, Lena explains that what she does, she does "with a whole bunch of love." Performers who work at the Caffe stay there as guests of the house. In 1975 the mayor of Saratoga Springs declared one day as "Lena Spencer Day."

Cafe Society   Refers to that segment of the population that frequents supper clubs, hotel showrooms, and cafes. The implication is that they are well-heeled. But Cafe Society was a New York City nightclub that flourished on the East Side (58th Street and Lexington Avenue) in the 1930s and 1940s. Barney Josephson also ran a Cafe Society Downtown in Greenwich Village, which was more of a Jazz club. The uptown branch introduced comedian Zero Mostel and other talents considered far-out by the Broadway and midtown clubs. Along with Mostel and other entertainers, Josephson was under attack during the McCarthy witch hunts when people were smeared and victimized as "reds" for their opinions. For a number of years after he closed down his two Cafe Societies, he ran a small restaurant. Sometime in the sixties, he moved the Cookery, as he called the restaurant, down to the Village, where he has been successful in reviving the careers of Blues pioneers like Helen Humes (b. 1913), Joe Turner (b. 1911), and, especially, Alberta Hunter (b. 1897), who wrote Bessie Smith's first record hit, "Down-Hearted Blues."

John Cage (1912–   )   An avant-garde composer whose works, theoretical and creative, anticipated the development of electronic music, mixed media, "aleatory" music, unorganized sound, and the music of silence. In 1953 he presented a controversial and revolutionary work, *4′ 33″*, in which a pianist just sat silently in front of the instrument for the time indicated by the title of the work. In earlier works, he produced compositions in which he experimented with many types of "nonmusical" sounds. His *Third Construction* of 1940 employed rattles, tin cans, conch shells, and the roar of a lion. In *A Construction in Metal,* seven percussionists played on metal bars, tin sheets, bowls, pots, and gongs. After a time, he developed the "prepared piano," in which he placed all kinds of strange objects among and across the strings: bolts, nuts, pencils, strips of rubber, and so on. In the early 1950s, when he became a student of Zen Buddhism, he used *I Ching,* the ancient Tibetan book, as the basis of accidental, or "aleatory," composition. From coin tossing as the basis of abstract patterns, he turned to completely unpredictable sounds in *Imaginary Landscape No. 4,* which employed 12 portable radios and 24 players. Rock artists who were influenced by Cage include Frank Zappa & the Mothers of Invention, The Beatles, Pink Floyd, Roxy (with Brian Eno on synthesizer), Captain Beefheart, and others.

See also Aleatory Rock; Art Rock; Classical Rock.

Cajun accordion   Its keyboard looks like a piano keyboard, except that it has no black keys. There are ten treble keys and two bass keys, which are played by the left hand. Due to the absence of chromatic notes (black keys), the instrument may be played in only two keys.

Cajun music   From the Creole tradition of New Orleans, a lively dance music, played by a mix of instruments: guitars, fiddles, and rhythm instruments. In the work of Mac Rebennack (b. circa 1940), known as "Dr. John The Night Tripper" Cajun was fused with voodoo influences.

See also Zydeco.

Cakewalk   In the years of slavery, the masters would allow their slaves to dress in their finery and have a party on Sunday. The high point was a competition in which couples paraded in style. The couple that walked most elegantly and spiritedly was awarded a cake. Their stylish high-stepping, embodied today in the parading of drum majorettes, became known as the Cakewalk.

See also minstrel show; Ragtime.

California sound   Los Angeles and San Francisco were the pivots of the sound, which has many strains in it. Shortly after the invasion of the Beatles in 1964, the Byrds and the Turtles wedded Folk protest to electric Rock, producing Folk Rock. The Byrds also experimented early with Acid Rock, which became the earmark of San Francisco, home of the Jefferson Airplane and numerous other groups. The Bay City also was the locus of the sound of "flower power" and of such far-out groups as The Grateful Dead, whose LA analog was The Mothers of Invention. LA gave rise to Surfing and Hot Rod music, whose exponents were The Beach Boys and Jan & Dean. The sound also included the heady harmonies of The Mamas and the Papas, a vocal group whose "California Dreaming" (1966) articulated the mystique of laid-back, beach-front and sun-drenched living.

See also Acid Rock; The Byrds; Flower Children; Folk Rock; Hot Rod music; Surfing music.

call-and-response   A basic feature of African music, which was incorporated in the Blues and Gospel music, and earlier in spirituals and work songs: the lead voice sings or chants a line, which is repeated, echoed, or answered by the group. Blues form incorporates the device: two bars or measures are sung and a response is made by an instrument, "harp" or guitar. This pattern is followed in each of the four-bar units of the twelve-bar structure:

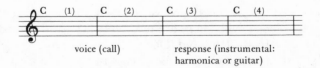

voice (call)   response (instrumental:
                      harmonica or guitar)

Instances of call-and-response are to be found in many recordings by Ray Charles (b. 1930), Aretha Franklin (b. 1942), and the Isley Brothers (''Shout'').

Calypso   A type of song, sound, and dance that originated in the West Indies, especially Trinidad. As a dance, it traces its roots back to African jungle rhythms. It is written in 2/4, with syncopation created on the timbales. All the vowel sounds are long, so that the words have a Pidgin English sound. Though markedly different in rhythm, Reggae has a Calypso sound. So does the disco-inflected music of Kid Creole and the Coconuts, an offshoot of a musical group called Dr. Buzzard's Original Savannah Band.
   See also Harry Belafonte; Reggae.

''canary''   Inside the music biz, a trade term for a female singer or vocalist.

''The Captain''   The Beach Boys' nickname for Darryl Dragon, their pianist-arranger, because he always wore a yachting cap. The cap was quite visible when Dragon and his wife emerged in 1975 as a successful duo called The Captain and Tenille. Beginning with ''Love Will Keep Us Together,'' they projected an image of young adult love in a series of middle-of-the-road ballads written by The Captain. Rock critics dismissed their work as ''Schlock.''
   See also Schlock Rock.

Captain Beefheart   Pseudonym of Don Van Vliet (b. 1941), an eccentric but extremely talented and versatile artist, who took the name Captain Beefheart from a movie he and Frank Zappa (b. 1940) planned to produce around 1963. They called the abortive undertaking *Captain Beefheart Meets the Grunt People.* Beefheart has long been an experimental, avant-garde composer/lyricist/arranger with a limited following. Rock critics have been more receptive than the public—and that includes his most recent album, *Doc at the Radar Station,* described by one critic as a ''mix of Delta Blues riffs with snippets reminding one of Stravinsky.'' Another critic, dubbing him one of the most original and radical artists America has produced, depicted his compositions as consisting of ''violent wrenches of imagery and time-signatures.''
   See also Avant-garde Rock; Experimental Rock.

car groups   Because of the success of the Ravens, a pioneer R & B group, many groups of the late 1940s and early 1950s adopted birds for their names. With the El Dorados and a burgeoning interest of teenages in automobiles, car groups became popular. Among others, there were the Cadillacs, Mark IV, the Fleetwoods, the Falcons, the Impalas and Mitch Ryder & the Detroit Wheels.

The appeal of cars to the young generation was reflected in Chuck Berry's first hit, "Maybellene," and in songs like "Teen Angel," "Last Kiss," and "Tell Laura I Love Her." The Beach Boys turned from Surfing music to an album of car songs, *Little Deuce Coupe,* which contained titles like "Little Honda," "This Car of Mine," "Car-Crazy Cutie," "Custom Machine," and "409." Jan & Dean, who had latched onto the Surfing craze, followed suit, with songs like "Drag City" and the unfortunately prophetic (for Jan) "Deadman's Curve."

See also bird groups.

Carnegie Hall   Its opening night concert was on May 5, 1891, and the Symphony Society was conducted by the eminent composer Tchaikovsky himself. The edifice was made possible by a gift of $2 million from the steel magnate Andrew Carnegie. Renowned for its remarkable acoustics, it was designed by architect William Burnet Tuthill, an amateur cellist, a friend of Carnegie, and a member of the Hall's board. Credit for the acoustical brilliance is generally also given to architect Dankmar Adler, a partner of the great architect Louis Sullivan, whose advice was sought by Tuthill. In the 1960s the venerable structure was in danger of conversion into a steel-and-glass office building when the opening of the Lincoln Center Philharmonic Hall suggested that Carnegie, with its brown Florentine facade, was outmoded. A concerted public campaign and its undeniable acoustical properties saved Carnegie from destruction. Since the 1930s the Hall has increasingly played host to Jazz and Pop artists, and in recent years, to Rock performers as well.

Carousel Ballroom   One of a group of large old halls in San Francisco—Fillmore Auditorium, Avalon Ballroom, California Hall—the Carousel Ballroom dated back to the 1930s. Situated on Market Street in the Irish section of the Bay City, it was taken over in 1967 by the Grateful Dead. Impresario Bill Graham, who had leased the Fillmore Auditorium for concerts in 1966 and was searching for a new outlet, offered to run the Carousel as a joint effort with the Dead. The group refused, but as a result of bad management, lost control of the hall. At that point in 1968, Graham took it over and renamed it Fillmore West.

See also Bill Graham.

The Carter Family   They made their first recordings for Ralph S. Peer on Victor on August 1, 1927, in Bristol, Tenn. During the next 17 years, they recorded some 300 oldtime ballads, traditional tunes, country songs, and Gospel hymns, all representative of America's southeastern folklore and heritage. The original Family consisted of Mother Maybelle Addington Carter (1909–1979), who played guitar and sang harmony; her cousin, Sara Dougherty (1898–1979), who played autoharp and sang alto lead; and Sara's husband, Alvin Pleasant (A. P.) Carter (d. 1960), who played fiddle and sang bass. They operated out of their homes in the Clinch Mountain area of Virginia until 1938, when they moved to Texas for three years, and then to Charlotte, N.C. They did their last radio show together in 1942, after which Maybelle Carter, who has been called the Queen of Country Music, continued the tradition and her career with her three daughters, Anita, Helen, and June—the last-mentioned is Mrs. Johnny Cash.

After working on WRWL Radio in Richmond, Va., from 1943 to 1946, Mother Maybelle and the Carter Sisters, as they were billed, moved first to WRVA, also in Richmond, for 18 months, and then to WNOX in Knoxville. When they were finally tapped by the *Grand Ole Opry,* Nashville became their final stop and home.

In popularizing and preserving old folk songs, the Family made accessible tunes that were later used by Pete Seeger (b. 1919), Bob Dylan (b. 1941), Odetta (b. 1930), Woody Guthrie (1912–1967), and Joan Baez (b. 1941).

"carve"   To outplay another musician.

Johnny Cash (1932–)   A unique figure in Folk, Country, and Rock music, who walked his own line and in the late sixties, saw key Rock performers like Bob Dylan (b. 1941), The Byrds (*Sweetheart of the Rodeo*), and others turn to variants of his brand of Country Rock. Initially, part of the Rockabilly development on Sun Records, he perfected a style that was enriched by his own struggle with drugs and his early immersion in Gospel music and Blues. From 1969 to 1971, he had his own TV variety show, on which he featured June Carter (b. 1929) of the famous Carter Family, whom he had married in 1968. He has had more than twenty bestselling LPs on Columbia, six of which became Gold Records: *Ring of Fire, I Walk the Line, Folsom Prison, Johnny Cash at San Quentin, Hello, I'm Johnny Cash,* and *Greatest Hits, Vol. 1.* As the titles of two of his albums indicate, he has spent much time entertaining prisoners; the feeling of kinship harks back to the days of his own incarceration. When Bob Dylan went to Music City (Nashville) in 1969 to record, Cash sang with him on one track and wrote the panegyric liner notes in verse for the album, titled *Nashville Skyline.*

castanets   A percussion instrument made of two small pieces of curved wood, hinged with a string. By pressing the two pieces together between the thumb and fingers, or palm and fingers, a clicking sound is made. Spanish dancers frequently manipulate a pair in each hand, producing trills as well as clicks.

"cat"   Lingo for a musican, but broadened to mean a male person.

"cat clothes"   A style of dressing in the early fifties, originating among black males, that affected Presley's getup. When he came to guitarist Scotty Moore's apartment in the spring of '54, Elvis wore a pink suit, white shoes, and a ducktail haircut. "I thought my wife was going out the back door," Scotty later said. Listen to the song by Carl Perkins (b. 1932) called "Put Your Cat Clothes On."

The Cavern   A dive in Liverpool near the Mersey River, which switched in the early 1960s from *Trad* to Rock, and provided a showcase for Rory Storm & the Hurricanes (Ringo Starr was their drummer), Gerry & the Pacemakers, Swinging Blue Jeans, and of course the Beatles.
   See also The Beatles; Trad.

çaz   Anglicized to *saz,* since English type fonts lack a *c* with a little tail. A string instrument of Eastern Aegean origin with 16 movable frets on a long neck, it usually has 3 strings tuned E,D,A or G,D,A. Its exotic sound derives from the melody (played on the A string) sounding simultaneously with its fifth on the low middle string, or with a single or double drone. The bouzouk, or bouzuk, used in the film *Never on Sunday,* was the first contact of Americans with a saz.
   See also Bozuk.

celesta   It looks like the keyboard of a piano, without an upright or horizontal sounding board. Instead of strings, the hammers strike metal bars, producing a bell-like sound. Most listerners know the sound from Tchaikovsky's "Dance of the Sugar-Plum Fairy" in *The Nutcracker Suite,* written shortly after the instrument was devised in 1886 by a Parisian named Mustel.

cencerro   *See* Latin rhythm instruments.

Cha-Cha   An Afro-Cuban rhythm, it has been described as a cross between the Bolero and the Danza:

A wedding of the Cha-Cha and the Rock beat produced the Rock Cha-Cha.

chair   A place in a band or orchestra.

chance music
    See Aleatory Rock.

changes   Short for "chord changes," but is also used to refer to problems or critical events in one's life.

channel   *See* bridge. Synonymous with "release."

chansonnière   Edith Piaf (1915-1963), remembered for her singing of "La vie en rose" and the autobiography "Non, je ne regrette rien," is the prime example of the theatrical type of singer known as a chansonnière. Mabel Mercer (b. 1900), more of a cabaret singer, approaches the French concept. On the contemporary scene, Judy Collins (b. 1939), who started as a folk singer, turned to theater songs and art songs in the late 1960s. While repertoire like Jacques Brel's "Song of Old Lovers" and Stephen Sondheim's "Send in the Clowns" fits in with the style, Collins is not quite dramatic and theatrical enough to be a true chansonnière.
    See also cabaret singers.

Ray Charles (1930-   )   If ever the word "genius" applied to any Pop artist, it surely is not misused with reference to the man who was born poor in Albany, Ga., and was both blinded and orphaned in his early years. Ray Charles was in turn a Jazz saxophonist, pianist/leader of a Swing trio à la Nat "King" Cole, a pioneer of Rhythm & Blues, and a hit Country singer—and he excelled in all of these disparate undertakings; in fact, he brought to each of them an intensity and expressiveness associated with great Gospel and Soul singing. He was the originator, certainly the precursor of the style that became known as Soul—a wedding of the sacred and the profane, of "devil songs" (Blues) and spiritual songs (Gospel), a bold transformation of hymns to Jesus into paeans to a loved one, as in "This Little Light (Girl) of Mine."
    Cutting his first sides for Swing Time, a small, independent Los Angeles label, he was signed by Atlantic in 1952, and found his métier when he worked with Guitar Slim (1926-1959), a Gospel-oriented singer, in New Orleans. During 1955 and '56, he cut a series of sides that embodied the volatile mixture of Gospel fervor and amatory passion: "I've Got a Woman," "Hallelujah I Love Her So," and "This Little Girl of Mine." The masterpiece of the genre is "What'd I Say?"—a No. 1 R & B hit of 1959. By 1962 he was on the charts, Country as well as R & B and Pop, with "I Can't Stop Loving You," a C & W song; he explored the genre brilliantly for several years on the ABC

label, to which he moved when he turned to Country music. He has chronicled his career and successful struggle against drug addiction in *Brother Ray*.

See also Soul.

Charleston   A fast Fox-Trot introduced by Cecil Mack and Jimmy Johnston in an all-black revue in 1923, it became one of the most popular dances of the 1920s. "Charleston" also refers to the rhythmic figure that was basic to the dance.

Charleston cymbal   *See* cymbal.

chart   A colloquialism for a musical score or arrangement. "Chart" also applies to the lists published by music trade papers, which chart the rise of records in popularity and sales.

chase chorus   A chorus in which soloists follow each other after a given number of bars or measures, each taking two or four bars as the case may be.

Cherokee Ranch   One of Hollywood's most successful recording studios, with a track record at the end of 1979 of 30 Gold Albums and close to 20 Platinums. Among Rock groups and soloists who have used its facilities on five acres of suburban Chatsworth property, or a new studio on Fairfax Avenue, previously owned by MGM Records: Steely Dan, Alice Cooper, Dr. John, David Bowie, Elton John, ELO, Rod Stewart, Cars, Journey, and Tom Petty.

Chicago Bar Blues   *See* Chicago Blues style.

Chicago Blues style   Refers to two different styles and periods. In the post-Depression 1930s when many Delta bluesmen had settled in the Windy City, Chicago Blues signified the Urban style that Country bluesmen developed as they adjusted to city life. Piano, bass, and drums were added to guitar/harmonica accompaniment by bluesmen like Big Bill Broonzy (1893–1958), Leroy Carr (1905–1935), Roosevelt Sykes (b. 1906), Lonnie Johnson (1889–1970), Tampa Red (b. 1900), and others.

Later, in the years of World War II and the postwar period, Chicago

Blues were performed by electric instruments to ensemble accompaniment. These were the Bar Blues of performers like Muddy Waters (b. 1915), Howlin' Wolf (1910–1976), Bo Diddley (b. 1928), and others who needed electricity to be heard in the rowdy clubs of the South and West sides of Chicago. Chicago's electric, ensemble Blues style was one facet of Rhythm & Blues.

See also Rhythm & Blues.

Chicago Jazz style   A derivative during the 1920s of New Orleans Jazz, heard in the Windy City when King Oliver (1885–1938) and Louis Armstrong (1900–1971) played at the Royal Garden Cafe. Young, white instrumentalists, chiefly the Austin High School Gang, developed their own style, which became known as "Dixieland Jazz." Its distinctive characteristics were a two-beat rhythm with stress on the afterbeat; tenor sax lead instead of trumpet; and choppy instead of legato phrasing.

See also Austin High School Gang; Dixieland Jazz.

"Chicago's Minstrel"   Win Stracke (1908–   ), a singer, guitarist, songwriter, and founder of Chicago's Old Town School of Folk Music and the Old Folklore Center.

Chicano Rock   Not really a category, but a descriptive term for the sound of Santana, a San Francisco Rock group with four percussionists. On a Jazz base, they superimposed a Latin beat and African rhythms.

Frances Child (1825–1896)   The Harvard professor who compiled the watershed five-volume collection *The English and Scottish Popular Ballads*. A model for all subsequent compilations of authentic Folk music, its various editions appeared between 1882 and 1898. In its completed form, it contained 305 traditional ballads, each numbered so that given ballads became identified, for example, as Child 71 or Child 105.

The Chipmunks   A so-called vocal group, created through the manipulation of tape speed. All the singing was done by David Seville (1919–1972), a cousin of author William Saroyan, with whom he wrote the Rosemary Clooney (b. 1928) fractured-English hit "Come on-a My House" (1951). Seville's real name was Ross Bagdasarian. By speeding up the voice tracks, he made himself sound like three chipmunks. In 1958 and 1959 he produced Gold Records in "Chipmunk Song," "Witch Doctor," and "Alvin's Harmonica." Imaginary Alvin was developed as the upstart of the three chipmunks.

"chirper-cleffer"   *See* singer-songwriter.

"Chitlin' Circuit"   A term first used by singer Lou Rawls (b. 1935) to describe the bars, lounges, clubs, dives, and honky-tonks, generally located in the black ghettos of big cities, at which black artists perform before a hit recording opens the door to major white outlets. These are the bread-and-butter spots where black performers pay their dues and where they sometimes return after they have passed their prime.

chocallo   *See* Latin rhythm instruments.

choke cymbal   *See* cymbal.

"chops"   Lips or any part of the mouth used in playing a wind instrument.

chordal punctuation   During an instrumental solo, the entire band or a section of it will come in at moments to emphasize or broaden a note or phrase.

chord changes   Refers to the sequence of harmonies or chords constituting a piece of music.

chord organ   An electric instrument, which, in addition to a regular piano keyboard, includes a series of buttons. When a button is depressed, a chord is sounded, making it possible for the player to accompany himself without actually playing chords.

chorus   Narrative ballads frequently consisted of verses that told the story and a repeated refrain. The form was perserved in Pop ballads of the twenties, thirties, and forties, especially in show tunes, which consisted of an introductory verse followed by the main part of the song, or chorus. The latter always embodied the title of the song.

chromatic   The chromatic scale may be heard by starting on any note and playing in succession the white and black keys on a piano; in other words, it is a scale composed entirely of semitones, or half-tones. From the standpoint of the major–minor key system, chromaticism implies the use by a composer of notes and/or chords that lie outside the prevailing key signature.

civil rights songs   During the 1960s, when young people were actively and demonstratively concerned with racism in this country, a phalanx of songwriters felt impelled to use the song as a weapon of protest. Among the writers who contributed to the creation of a literature of civil rights were Pete Seeger, Phil Ochs, and Tom Paxton. For a time,

Bob Dylan led the group with "Blowin' in the Wind," which, along with "We Shall Overcome," served as the anthem of the civil rights movement. The tendency to be drawn into the war against discrimination was so strong that Pop and Rock songwriters frequently dealt with aspects of the problem. Some instances: Paul Simon's "He Was My Brother," Wilbert Harrison's "Let's Work Together," Curtis Mayfield's "People Get Ready" and "Choice of Color" (both recorded by the Impressions), James Brown's "Say It Loud—I'm Black and I'm Proud," and Nina Simone's "Mississippi Goddam" and "Four Women."

See also Bob Dylan.

Dick Clark (1929-) One of the most influential disk jockeys of Rock 'n' Roll, with a program that has remained continually on the TV screen for more than a quarter of a century. While he was still in high school, he worked on a Rome, N.Y., radio station owned by his uncle. After graduation from Syracuse University, he served as an announcer at several upstage New York stations before coming to Philadelphia's WFIL in 1952, where he joined the staff of Bob Horn's *Bandstand.* When Horn was arrested for drunken driving in 1956 amidst rumors of his involvement with teenage girls on his program, Dick Clark took over as host. On August 5, 1957, *American Bandstand* premiered on TV, growing rapidly to a network of over 105 stations by April 1958. Concerned with giving R 'n' R a "clean" image, if not a white one, in a period when it was under severe attack by establishment authorities, it provided the new music with its first mass audience and became a model for the country's local and network teenage dance shows. It also became a prime force in shaping the dress, dances, hairstyles, and outlook of the young generation.

Powered by the impact of Clark's turntable, the Philadelphia music scene became the center of R 'n' R, with a tightly knit circle of new, local record labels, artists, songwriters, and music publishers clustering around Clark. By the time of the payola investigation of 1959–1960, his corporate holdings included interests in six music publishing companies with over 150 copyrights (most acquired without any investment), three record labels (Chancellor, Parkway, and Swan), a local record pressing plant, a record distributor, and an artist management firm. To keep his position on the *Bandstand* and to eliminate further conflicts of interest, Clark divested himself of his holdings at a substantial profit. Despite this windfall and acknowledged instances of records he had plugged after acquiring an interest in them, he came out of the congressional probe of payola with a clean bill of health. "You're not the inventor of the system or even its architect. You're a product of it. Obviously, you're a fine young man," said Chairman Oren Harris, himself involved in a conflict of interest, revealed after Clark's appearance before his House of Representatives Special Subcommitee on Legislative Oversight in April 1960.

Some historians, contrasting ABC's support of Clark with its rejection of Alan Freed, who refused to sign an affidavit that he had not taken payola, have noted that Freed brought only $200,000 a year in billings to the station, while Clark contributed $2 million.

See also American Bandstand.

Classic Blues   A twelve-bar form involving a three-line stanza (AAB) and a chord sequence of I/IV–I/V–I.

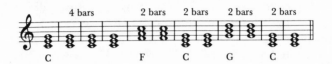

The Classic Blues singers were a group of black female vaudevillians who made records from 1920 on. Record company interest began with the startling sales of Mamie Smith's disk of ''Crazy Blues'' on OKeh. Quickly, all the active labels of the day—Paramount, Columbia, Vocalion, Perfect, Brunswick, and Victor—began recording Blues with singers like Clara, Trixie, and Bessie Smith (all unrelated); Bertha ''Chippie'' Hill (1905–1950); Ma Rainey (1886–1939) of the Rabbit Foot Minstrels; Lucille Hegamin (1894–1970); and Alberta Hunter (b. 1895).

See also Blues; Country Blues; Delta Blues; Rhythm & Blues; Bessie Smith; Urban Blues.

Classic Jazz   Originating in the late 19th century in the South—Kansas City and other cities as well as New Orleans—it was a music whose sound was the product of improvisation, solo and group; a steady pulse; and syncopation. Performers rather than composers determined the sound. Among representative groups: King Oliver's Creole Jazz Band, The New Orleans Rhythm Kings, Jelly Roll Morton's Hot Peppers, Louis Armstrong's Hot Five and Seven, and The Original Dixieland Jazz Band. The sound is Afro-American in origin.

Classical Rock   Not a stage in the development of Rock (like Rockabilly) and not a style (like Acid Rock) or a school (like Heavy Metal Rock), but an occasional fusion of disparate elements. Whether it is viewed as an aspect of Art Rock or not, Classical Rock refers to the mixing of the Big Beat with forms and/or sounds characteristic of classical music. Among the Rock groups that have experimented with the merger, there are Emerson, Lake & Palmer, who used Moussorgsky's *Pictures at an Exhibition* as the basis of a concert in 1971; Frank Zappa, whose *200 Motels* was performed by his Rock group with the L.A. Philharmonic Orchestra; Moody Blues, who recorded "Nights in White Satin" with the Lincoln Festival Orchestra; the Mothers of Invention, who used Varese's serialism in their *Freak Out* album; Yes, who recorded a classically derived "Rondo"; Electric Prunes, whose recordings included *Mass in Minor F* (1967) and *Release of an Oath: The Kol Nidre* (1968); the New York Rock Ensemble, three of whose five members were Juilliard-trained, whose first album, *Faithful Friends . . . Flattering Foe,* included a Rock version of Bach's *Trio Sonata No. 2 in G Major,* and who made appearances with several symphony orchestras, including the New York Philharmonic; Procol Harum, whose albums included *Live in Concert with the Edmonton Symphony Orchestra* of Canada; Genesis, whose "One for the Vine" in *Wind and Wuthering* embodied classical influences, including modified sonata form; Nice, whose recordings reveal the influence of Schoenberg; the classically oriented Focus, a Dutch band; and the Electric Light Orchestra before they eliminated strings and became a quartet.

Chicago's second album, named Best of the Year (1970) by *Cash Box* magazine, contained a six-movement Rock composition titled *Ballet for a Girl in Buchannon.* The group's third album also contained extended compositions: a long *Elegy,* a five-movement *Hour in the Shower,* and a six-part *Travel Suite.* A large work was also produced by Deep Purple in *The Book of Taliesyn,* which included a ten-and-a-half minute expansion of "River Deep, Mountain High," based on music in the science fiction film *2001.* In 1969 Deep Purple's Jon Lord wrote a *Concerto* for a Rock group and symphony orchestra, which was premiered by the Royal Philharmonic Orchestra and which won a standing ovation when it was performed at the Hollywood Bowl in 1970. The *Concerto* was recorded, as was his *Gemini Suite,* performed originally in 1970 over the BBC by Deep Purple and the South Bank Pop Orchestra.

In "Come," a Chopin prelude was used by Barry Manilow as the basis of the melody and harmonic sequence. Walter Murphy with his Big Apple Band made a hit single of "A Fifth of Beethoven," based on the opening theme of the *Fifth Symphony.* The Toys scored a Gold Record with "A Lover's Concerto," based on a Bach five-finger exercise. In *Journey to the Center of the Earth* and *The Myth and Legends of King Arthur,* Rick Wakeman drew extensively on his classical training as a piano student at London's Royal Academy. Borrowing from the harmonic structure of Bach's religious composition "Sleepers Awake," Procol Harum scored a worldwide hit with "A Whiter Shade of Pale." While Stevie Wonder's soundtrack for *A Journey Through the Secret Life of Plants* (1980) contains varieties of Rock and Soul, some sections have a distinctly classical sound.

claves   *See* Latin rhythm instruments.

clavichord   The strings are struck by metal tongues, or tangents, producing a cushion-like sound, softer than the piano. Unlike the hammers of a piano or the quills of a harpsichord, the tongues do not spring back but remain in contact with the vibrating string, allowing for the production of a vibrato effect.

clavinet   M. Hohner manufactures a Pianet/Clavinet electric keyboard instrument that has five full octaves and sixty standard-size keys. A foot-pedal permits switching from the pianet to the clavinet. Jazzman Chick Corea has used the instrument.

clearance   A synonym for the right to perform. Since radio and TV stations operate with catalog licenses from the performing rights societies, clearance is generally a perfunctory matter. A program director on a network broadcast sends a list of musical selections being used. Occasionally, copyright owners set down stipulations as to when a new number may be premiered; this restriction generally applies to show tunes.

Clearwater   The name of a sloop on which a group of folk singers sailed the Hudson River from South Bristol, Maine, to New York City in 1969 in an effort to arouse the public against industrial pollution of rivers. The moving spirits behind the venture were folk singer/songwriter Pete Seeger (b. 1919) and songwriter Don McLean (b. 1945), whose activities in behalf of the river as the Hudson River Troubadour prompted Seeger to enlist his aid. The cruise led to a NET-TV special, *The Sloop at Nyack,* and to a book, *Songs and Sketches of the First Clearwater Crew,* edited by McLean.

   The idea of building and using a sloop to motivate restoration of the Hudson River originated with Pete and Toshi Seeger, who presented it after the 1968 Newport Folk Festival to its governing board. A contribution of $10,000 led to a fund-raising campaign in which $10,000 was contributed each by the Rockefeller Family Fund, Lila Acheson Wallace of *Reader's Digest,* and the Boscobel Foundation. The sloop was built in South Bristol, Maine, and launched at the Goat Island Causeway in connection with the 1969 Newport Folk Festival. A permanent organization exists to fund the project: Hudson River Sloop Restoration, P.O. Box 265, Cold Spring, N.Y. 10516.

   See also Hudson River Troubadour; Pete Seeger.

"click"   A verb meaning to go over well, to register, to be accepted by an audience. Used in relation to performances by solo or group artists.

click track   A technique or device used by composers, conductors, and musicians in the film field to synchronize music with action on the screen. Originally, click tracks were made from a piece of 35-millimeter film that was punched every few frames with sprocket holes. This track was run together with the film, the clicking of the sprockets serving as a metronome for the conductor and the musicians, all of whom heard the metrical clicks through headphones. Today's click tracks are electronically contrived. They can be altered to adjust the tempo, slowing for retards and speeding up for accelerations. Click tracks, together with the timings on cue sheets to which the composer writes the background score, insure that the music will come in precisely where it should, sound for as long as it should, and cease when it should.

"clinker"   A wrong note, a mistake.

close harmony   A style of singing in which the individual notes of a chord are near each other, sometimes without attending to the harmonic progression. The Mamas and the Papas made effective use of close harmony, as Peter, Paul & Mary had done before them. The lead voice is generally a third above the harmony voice. Folk harmony usually involves the interval of a fifth, instead of a third.

"cloudville"   An old song-pluggers' term meaning a state of confusion, a lack of direction, a marked degree of ineffectiveness. Use of the suffix *ville* derived from place names, and perhaps most directly from Storyville, the New Orleans red-light district, which contributed greatly to the development of Jazz.

coda   From the Italian, meaning "tail."
    See also "tag."

coffeehouse   A facet of the Folk boom of the 1960s was the growth in numbers and popularity of the coffeehouse. The prototype was the Cafe Reggio, established in Greenwich Village in 1935 and followed by the opening of the nearby Cafe Rienzi. Apparently, proprietors at first prohibited singing and playing, largely because they installed high fidelity record players. But the folk song revival changed this, so that coffeehouses, usually located in the environs of colleges and universities, became the launching pads of new songs and singers. In some establishments, like Gerde's Folk City, where Bob Dylan (b. 1941) first performed, and the Bitter End. Folk music rather than exotic coffees, checkerboards, and conversation were the attraction. Joan Baez made her first public appearance at a Boston coffeehouse. But as Folk music developed a mass following, the coffeehouses lost out to concert halls and large clubs. By the mid-1970s, Caffe Lena, which had opened in

1960 in Saratoga Springs, N.Y., was regarded as the oldest continuously running coffeehouse in the country. Bob Dylan performed here before he became known, as did Arlo Guthrie (b. 1947) of "Alice's Restaurant" and Don McLean (b. 1945) of "American Pie" fame.

See also The Ash Grove.

color organ   In this era of mixed media, it is interesting to note that as far back as 1911 the composer Alexander Scriabin used a light-projecting instrument in *Prometheus.*

combo   Short for "combination," meaning a small group of musicians or a small band.

commercial   As a noun, (1) the sales pitch for a product or service on TV and/or radio; (2) the performance of a song on a sponsored radio or TV show—it commanded a higher fee than a performance on a sustaining show. As an adjective with regard to a literary or musical work, the quality of appealing to a mass audience.

commune   A group of people, generally residing in a rural area, who share belongings, facilities, produce, property, and partners, and who function as a large family. Probably the best-known commune of recent times was the notorious Manson family. In the rock musical *Hair,* the communal group is referred to as a "tribe."

See also *Hair.*

"comp"   Shortened form of "accompany," used originally by jazzmen.

Compo Direct   Haitian Calypso music that's been updated. More generally, Carribbean music with a modern, electric, driving feel.

concept album   An album with a central idea, theme, or subject to which all or most of the songs in it relate. Although the Beatles' *Sgt. Pepper* LP (1967) is generally cited as the first concept album, it was actually anticipated by *Freak Out* (1966) a Mothers of Invention album, which Paul McCartney unhesitatingly named as a key inspiration for the *Sgt. Pepper* work. The Rolling Stones quickly took up the Beatles' challenge and produced *Their Satanic Majesties Request* (1967). Not to be outclassed, The Who entered the competition with *The Who Sell Out* (1968), an album in which obnoxious commercials and hard-sell jingles appeared between songs. In 1968, too, Bob Dylan presented *John Wesley Harding,* an album that dealt with loners and social outcasts: hoboes, drifters, outlaws, immigrants, and saints. Laura Nyro's *Eli and the Thirteenth Con-*

fession (1968) depicted a young girl's growth from childhood to maturity. In 1969 the Kinks' *Arthur* examined the problems and frustrations of a middle-aged British workman; a TV presentation preceded the release of the album.

While the years 1967–1969 seemed a peak period for the concept album, groups periodically released LPs with a unifying theme all through the seventies. In 1971 Laura Nyro produced a chart LP in *Christmas and the Beads of Sweat,* an album that suggested the irony of trying to enjoy the season of peace in a world torn by war. In *Aqualung* (1971) Jethro Tull explored the misuses of religion and the search for God; Gothic lettering on the cover served to emphasize the religious tenor of the album. In *The Rise and Fall of Ziggy Stardust and the Spiders from Mars* (1972), gifted David Bowie (b. 1947) narrated the rise and fall of a rock star, with the final track fixing on "Rock 'n' Roll Suicide."

"Story" albums were the work also of Rick Wakeman, keyboardist of Yes, who soloed on two of his own creation: *The Six Wives of Henry VIII* (1973) and *Voyage to the Center of the Earth* (1974). Rush's "*2112*" of 1976 was based on Ayn Rand's novel *Anthem.* In the late 1970s, "Country Outlaw" Willie Nelson (b. 1933) produced three engaging concept albums: *Red-Headed Stranger* was a "story" dealing with love and death in the old West; *Yesterday's Wine* pursued the stages in a man's life from birth to death; and *Phases and Stages* concerned itself with the breakup of a marriage, one side presenting the woman's point of view and the other, the man's outlook. In *Gaucho* (1981) Steely Dan composed seven interrelated tales, all dealing with would-be hipsters.

See also Space Rock.

concert band   Composed of woodwinds, brasses, and percussion instruments, it consists of as many as 100 players. Most Americans know it as a result of watching the halftime entertainment at football games. Also known as a marching band.

concert pitch   The pitch sounded rather than the pitch notated for a transposing instrument. Thus, for a tenor $B^{\flat}$ sax, written C is $B^{\flat}$ concert, and for an $E^{\flat}$ alto sax, written C is $E^{\flat}$ concert.

Concrete Music   A composition and/or type of music made up entirely of sounds, musical and natural (like thunder or traffic), recorded and then assembled into a coherent structure. The recorded sound is sometimes distorted electronically for effect, through the use of filters, echo, and speed variations. Another approach is to take natural or instrumental sounds, not electronically generated sounds, and combine them electronically. Pierre Schaeffer, who worked in a Paris radio station in 1948 and 1949, is credited with originating this type of quasi-musical organization of recorded sound. A Rock use of Concrete Music is heard in the Beatles' *Sgt. Pepper* album at the end of "A Day in the Life"; also in *Ceremony*, an album in which the British Hard Rock group, Spooky Tooth, collaborated with Pierre Henry, an electronic pioneer who had worked with Schaeffer.

Conga   A Cuban carnival dance whose basic beat is:

Introduced to American dancers by Desi Arnaz, it became popular around 1937. It's the syncopation in the second measure that gives the dance its characteristic rhythm.

conga drum   *See* Latin rhythm instruments.

Connie's Inn   Located at 165 West 131st Street in New York City but using a 7th Avenue address (2221), Connie's Inn was one of the big three night spots of the Harlem Renaissance (1926-1933). The other two major shrines of Harlem nightlife were the Cotton Club and Ed Smalls' Paradise. This was the era when celebrities of the stage, national figures, and members of high society all hurried to Harlem at sunset and frequently remained until sunrise. Originally known as Shuffle Inn after the Broadway black hit, Noble Sissle and Eubie Blake's *Shuffle Along,* it became Connie's Inn when it was bought by George and Connie Immerman, who were then (June 1923) in the delicatessen business and employed Fats Waller (1904-1943) as their delivery boy.

It was Fats and his collaborator, Andy Razaf (1895-1973), who brought renown to Connie's Inn in 1929 with *Hot Chocolates,* the floorshow revue that included "Ain't Misbehavin'," "Can't We Get Together?" and "Black and Blue." From 1929 to 1931, the Fletcher Henderson Band was the big attraction, followed by lesser bands of the day like Luis Russell's and Don Redman's. When the rush to Harlem petered out around 1933, Connie's Inn was moved by its owners downtown. The old place was later reopened as the Harlem Club and then as the Ubangi Club.

See also Cotton Club; Harlem Renaissance; Ed Smalls' Paradise (under S).

console   *See* upright.

contact man   He was to the music publisher during the 1920s, 1930s, 1940s and early 1950s what the record promotion man is today to the recording company. His job was to cajole those who could bring a new song to the ears of the public into performing it. He was known as a song-plugger before he came to be called a contact man, being a member of the Music Publishers Contact Employees Union. But he was a vital figure even before he was known as a song-plugger or contact man, or as a professional man. At the beginning of the music publishing industry in New York City in the 1890s, when publishers' offices were located in the Union Square area, he worked at bringing a new song to the ears of the public: by singing it in cabarets; singing from the box of a vaudeville theater; and performing on a piano in the window of a five-and-ten-cents store, aiming thereby at actually promoting immediate sheet-music sales. During the vaudeville era, song-pluggers gave major attention to performers who played the major circuits of the time: Keith-Albee, Loews, etc. With the advent of radio, attention shifted to the bands and singers on the air, especially those featured on the prime-time, sponsored, network shows. By then, there was a hierarchy, with the professional manager at the top, then the day men and night men, and finally, the counter boys who handed out and carried professional copies to performers. As recordings became important, a new position was added to the hierarchy: the general professional manager, whose job was to get songs recorded through contact with record executives and recording artists. As records superseded live performances in making hits, and plays by disk jockeys became the crux of the business, contact men carried disks in their attaché cases instead of leadsheets and professional copies in the back pockets of their pants. They had become record promoters.
See also Big Ballad Era; *Your Hit Parade.*

contact microphone   A microphone that transforms vibrations into electrical impulses as a result of being in contact with a vibrating medium—violin, bass, or guitar string.

Continental Baths   A Turkish-bath house in New York City, catering to homosexuals, where Bette Midler (b. circa 1945) performed in 1970; it served as her lauching pad to singing and acting fame.
See also The Divine Miss M.

continuous loop   A record pattern developed by Holland–Dozier–Holland, a team of writer-producers on the Motown label. Instead of cadencing a chorus with the normal harmonic change (V–I,

IV–I), the harmony remains suspended so that the melody returns to the beginning. Thus, instead of a series of choruses, there is a continuous loop—exemplified by recordings of the Supremes, like "I Hear a Symphony," and the Temptations' "My Girl."

contrapuntal   Refers to an interplay between two or more melodies, each acting independently but in relation to each other.

"cook"   Like water coming to a boil, to heat up in playing—a jazz term.

"cool"   From Negro slang usage, meaning to be relaxed, calm, restrained, and in control, it was taken over in the Bop era as a term of high praise—and is still used in that way by the Rock generation.

Cool Jazz   A development of the early fifties whose high priest was Lester "Prez" Young (1909–1959). He was dubbed "Prez" by singer Billie Holiday (1915–1959) in honor of Franklin Delano Roosevelt. Young developed a non-vibrato, lag-along style, which was at the opposite end of Bop in the Jazz spectrum. Prez's followers included tenorman Stan Getz (b. 1927) and the purveyors of what became known as West Coast Jazz.

copyist   *See* arranger.

copyright   Under the Constitution, a grant by the federal government of certain rights to composers and authors, the purpose of which is to encourage the creation of musical and intellectual works for the public good and financially to reward the creators of such works.

February 3, 1981, marked the 150th anniversary of President Andrew Jackson's signing into law the first formal provision of federal copyright protection for American music. The 1831 law represented an amendment of the original Copyright Act of 1790, in which books, maps, and charts were protected but not music. In addition to extending protection to music, the 1831 bill also extended the term of copyright from 14 to 28 years.

In 1976 the Copyright Act of 1909 was amended by Public Law 94–553 to extend the period of protection from 56 years (an initial period of 28 years could be extended by renewal for an additional 28) to the life of the composer/author plus 50 years. Copyright protection is secured by filing a published or unpublished copy of a work and paying a fee to the Register of Copyrights at the Library of Congress in Washington, D. C.

Five basic rights are embraced under the copyright law: (1) right of reproduction; (2) "adaptation right," which includes the right of synchronization; (3) publication right; (4) "public performance right," now defined as transmission by any medium; and (5) the right of public display, which concerns mainly works of art. The definition of "public performance" has been broadened to refer to a performance not only in any place open to the public but in any place where a substantial number of people are present beyond the family or an ordinary circle of friends. On the expiration of copyright, a work falls into the "public domain" (PD), and the protection of all rights disappears, making it possible for anyone to exercise those rights without the payment of fees or royalties.

See also synchronization.

"corny"   Lacking freshness; cliché; banal; painfully obvious or saccharine. The contemporary equivalent is "plastic."

Elizabeth Cotten (1893–   )   As there is a "Carter Scratch," named after Mother Maybelle Carter's guitar style, so there is a "Cotten Style" of guitar playing. Libba Cotten, being left-handed and self-taught, held her instrument upside down and played with two fingers and "banjo styling." Her reputation, which led to her receiving the Burl Ives Award from the National Folk Festival Association in 1972, was based on her original composition "Freight Train," long a Folk favorite. Written when she was about 12, in 1905, it did not become her copyright until 52 years later, after a long-drawn-out court suit. Libba might never have achieved musical renown had she not worked as a domestic in her middle years for Ruth Crawford Seeger and ethnomusicologist Charles Seeger, the parents of Pete (b. 1919) and Mike Seeger (1933), all of whom helped in bringing her musical recognition. (Libba became associated with the Seegers as a result of finding Peggy Seeger [b. 1935], who was lost in a department store.)

Cotton Club   A famous New York City nightclub at 644 Lenox Avenue in Harlem that flourished from 1921 to 1936. It was owned by a group of well-known gangsters, including Owney Madden, "Big Frenchy" De Mange, and others. In its heyday, *Cotton Club Parades,* as the floor shows were called, were so opulent that opening nights were as glamorous as Broadway openings. The producers included men like Walter Brooks, who put *Shuffle Along* on Broadway; Lew Leslie, later producer of the *Blackbird* shows; and Dan Healy, the well-known showman. Musical scores were written by hit songwriters like Jimmy McHugh and Dorothy Fields ("I Can't Give You Anything But Love, Baby") and Harold Arlen and Ted Koehler ("Get Happy," "Stormy Weather"). Among the bands that added luster: Duke Ellington's, which had become known at the midtown Kentucky Club and was ordered by "the boys" to play the Cotton; Cab Calloway's (b. 1907), who attained renown with "Minnie the Moocher"; and the band of the redoubtable Jimmie Lunceford (1902–1947). The performers, all black, though no blacks were admitted to the club, included stars like dancer Bill Robinson (1878–1949), comedian Dusty Fletcher ("Open the Door, Richard"), and singer Ethel Waters.

When the club was padlocked in spring 1925 by the Feds for violating Prohibition, it remained closed for only a brief period and reopened opulent as ever. When Lena Horne (b. 1917), who scored in a duet with Avon Long of "As Long as I Live," wanted to leave to join Noble Sissle's Band as featured vocalist, the racketeer owners manhandled her father for requesting her release. The club closed on February 15, 1936, and moved downtown to the spot later occupied by the Latin Quarter, on 47th Street between Broadway and 7th Avenue. Three years after it shuttered, the Golden Gate Ballroom was opened in the auditorium above the street-level floor occupied by the Cotton.

Incidentally, before the gangsters took over the spot in 1921, it had been occupied by the Douglas Theatre (1918–1920) and the Club Deluxe, run by heavyweight champ Jack Johnson. Around 1930, a rival gang of racketeers opened the Plantation on West 126th Street near Lenox Avenue, and hired Cab Calloway away from the Cotton. After two nights, one of the Plantation's backers was found dead and the club's bar was discovered in pieces in the gutter.

See also Connie's Inn; Ed Small's Paradise (under S).

"The Count"   *See* Count Basie.

counterculture   It took many forms, all of them a search for an alternative to the culture of the older generation. There were religious deviants like the Hare Krishnas, the Moonies, the Jesus Freaks, and the transcendental meditators. There were political insurgents like the Yippies and the Weathermen. And then there were the hippies, who longed for a new order, an alternative society dedicated to love and peace and organic vegetables. The peak of the counterculture syndrome came with the Woodstock Art & Music Festival of August 19, 1969, when half a million kids "sat, ate, slept, crapped, and fornicated through three days of Rock music and muddy fields." Short-lived as it was, the occasion was suffused with good vibes, love, and peace.

See also "Be-in"; Flower Children; *Hair; Woodstock Nation.*

counterfeit record   A pirate record that not only sounds like the legitimate disk from which it is copied but is packaged so that it looks like the original, including the label and jacket. Since label and jacket are reproduced through a photographic process, the colors are not always true and the printing is sometimes fuzzy, as the sound itself is inferior.

Country, or C & W   Once the music of the southeastern U.S.A., centered around Nashville but including Louisiana and reaching as far north as Cincinnati, was known as "Hillbilly." Around World War II, when people became sensitive to the pejorative overtones of the designation, "Hillbilly" became known as "Country & Western." In the 1970s the term was contracted to "Country." In a real sense, the changes in terminology also represent changes in the sound, and today there is even the sound of the Country Outlaws, the anti-Nashville contingent.
See also Nashville Outlaws.

Country Album of the Year   *See* Album of the Year, Country (CMA)

Country Blues   The earliest form of the Blues was developed by men who came from the Delta area of Mississippi and parts of Texas and Arkansas, men like Blind Lemon Jefferson (1897–1929), Robert Johnson (1912–1938), Charley Patton (1887–1934), Bukka White (1906–1977), Mance Lipscomb (1895–1976), and others. They played acoustic guitar, sometimes using the harmonica ("harp") as a responsorial voice, and sang with a high-pitched nasal twang. Although they antedated the Classic Blues singers, all of whom were women, they were recorded later when record companies like OKeh, Paramount, Vocalion, Brunswick, and Victor began making field trips into the South.
See also Blues; Blues, British; Delta Blues; Rhythm & Blues; Bessie Smith; Urban Blues.

Country Entertainer of the Year (CMA awards)

1967	Eddy Arnold
1968	Glen Campbell
1969	Johnny Cash
1970	Merle Haggard
1971	Charley Pride
1972	Loretta Lynn
1973	Roy Clark
1974	Charlie Rich
1975	John Denver
1976	Mel Tillis
1977	Ronnie Milsap
1978	Dolly Parton

1979   Willie Nelson
1980   Barbara Mandrell
1981   Barbara Mandrell

See also Country Music Association.

Country Music Association (CMA)   A trade association that was organized in November 1958 and that grew out of the Country Music Disc Jockeys' Association, organized in 1954. Headquartered in Nashville, Tenn., the CMA at first concerned itself with getting more airplay for Country Music and more extensive media recognition. Its efforts bore fruit so that 81 fulltime Country radio stations in 1961 rose to 328 by 1966. By then there were well over 2,000 stations that included Country music in their regular programming. In 1961 the CMA elected the first members to the newly established Country Music Hall of Fame, and in 1967 it opened the doors of a million-dollar structure, the Country Music Hall of Fame and Museum, situated in the heart of Nashville. Annually, it accords recognition to the top Country performers, songs, and records through awards voted by its membership. As with the Oscars and Grammys, the CMA awards ceremony is televised—in this instance, from the stage of Opryland.
See also Opryland.

Country Music Hall of Fame   Modeled on the Baseball Hall of Fame at Cooperstown, N.Y., the Country Music Hall of Fame acquired its first members in 1961 with the election of Jimmie Rodgers (1897–1933), Fred Rose (1897–1954), and Hank Williams (1923–1953). The following year, the CMA altered its original plan of honoring only deceased figures and elected Roy Acuff (b. 1903) as the first living member. The plaques bearing the names and likenesses of honorees are now housed in the million-dollar Country Music Hall of Fame and Museum, opened on March 31, 1967.
See also Hall of Fame, Country (CMA).

Country Music Shows

1924   *National Barn Dance:* WLS Radio, Chicago. Sponsored by Sears, Roebuck and regarded as the first Country music jamboree.
1924   *Tennessee Barn Dance:* WNOX Radio, Knoxville.
1925   *Grand Ole Opry:* WSM Radio, Nashville. NBC Radio network in 1939, and broadcast live from the Ryman Auditorium from 1941 on.
1926   *World's Original WWVA Jamboree:* WWVA Radio, Wheeling, W. Va. CBS Radio.
1937   *Renfro Valley Barn Dance:* WLW Radio, Cincinnati. In 1939 moved to WHAS Radio, Louisville, Ky., and NBC network.

1937 *Midwestern Hayride:* WLW Radio and WLW-TV, Cincinnati.

1946 *Old Dominion Barn Dance:* WRVA Radio, Richmond, Va.

1947 *Big D Jamboree:* KRLD Radio, Dallas, and CBS Radio network. Performers included Carl Perkins, Gene Vincent, and Elvis Presley.

1948 *Louisiana Hayride:* KWKH Radio, Shereveport, La., and KTHS Radio, Little Rock, Ark. In 1954, after the release of his first Sun disk, Presley appeared regularly until Col. Parker eased him out of a year's contract.

1954 *Jubilee, U.S.A.:* KWTO-TV, Springfield, Mo., and ABC–TV. Carl Perkins performed on this show, which starred Red Foley, father-in-law of Pat Boone.

1957 *Town Hall Party:* TV Channel 11, Compton, Calif.

Country Outlaws   *See* Armadillo World Headquarters; Nashville Outlaws.

Country Pop   An elusive category that would include Country artists who sing Pop songs and/or Country artists whose records cross over into Pop. Eddy Arnold (b. 1918) is the progenitor of the development, a Country singer who started as "the Tennessee Plowboy" and moved into Pop with "Bouquet of Roses" in 1947. Since then his sound and material have mixed Country and Pop but apparently in such a way that Country people objected to his election to the Country Music Hall of Fame in 1966. The list of Country Pop singers is a long one and would include such contemporaries as Crystal Gayle("Miss the Mississippi"), Kenny Rogers (b. 1941) (*The Gambler*), and Willie Nelson (b. 1933), whose recorded repertoire includes Irving Berlin ballads and Fats Waller's "Honeysuckle Rose."

Country Record of the Year, Single (CMA awards)

1967 "There Goes My Everything," Jack Greene (Decca)

1968 "Harper Valley PTA," Jeannie C. Riley (Plantation).

1969 "A Boy Named Sue," Johnny Cash (Columbia)

1970 "Okie from Muskogee," Merle Haggard (Capitol)

1971 "Help Me Make It Through the Night," Sammi Smith (Mega)

1972 "Happiest Girl in the Whole U.S.A.," Donna Fargo (Dot)

1973 "Behind Closed Doors," Charlie Rich (Epic)

1974 "Country Bumpkin," Cal Smith (MCA)

1975 "Before the Next Teardrop Falls," Freddy Fender (ABC-Dot)

1976 "Good Hearted Woman," Waylon Jennings and Willie Nelson (RCA)

1977 "Lucille," Kenny Rogers (United Artists)

1978 "Heaven's Just a Sin Away," Kendalls (Ovation)

1979   "The Devil Went Down to Georgia," Charlie Daniels Band (Epic)
1980   "He Stopped Loving Her Today," George Jones (Epic)
1981   "Elvira," Oak Ridge Boys (MCA)

See also Country Music Association (CMA)

Country Rock   Some regard it as compromise, others as escape. As the protest movements of the 1960s reached dead ends, hippies and radicals alike began to retreat from the city, to embrace the simple life of the country, and to seek out grass-rooted fundamentals of living. Bob Dylan (b. 1941) took the lead with his *John Wesley Harding* album (1968) and pursued the vision in *Nashville Skyline* (1969), for which Johnny Cash (b. 1932) with whom he dueted, wrote the laudatory liner note. Also in 1969 John Sebastian (b. 1944) of the Lovin' Spoonful sang of "Nashville Cats"; Buffy Sainte-Marie (b. 1941) asserted, "I'm a Country Girl Again"; and Joan Baez (b. 1941) filled *David's Album* (1969) and *One Day at a Time* (1970) with references to the Blue Ridge Mountains, hickory wood, the sunny South, and the "Green, Green Grass of Home."

But there were Country rockers among the teenage artists of the late 1950s and early sixties: the Everly Brothers, Don (b. 1937) and Phil (b. 1939); Roy Orbison (b. 1936), who scored with "Only the Lonely" and with whom Bobby Goldsboro (b. 1941) toured and developed a Country Rock sound of his own; Bobbie Gentry (b. 1944), who rode to fame on "Ode to Billy Joe"; and Rick Nelson (b. 1940), who was part of the Teenage Rock development and turned to Country Rock in the late sixties when he recorded with a group called Stone Canyon.

Between 1971 and 1975, the outstanding Country Rock band was the Eagles, remembered for "Desperado," "Saturday Night," "Out of Control," and their first big single, Jackson Browne's "Take It Easy." Others in the genre include the Byrds, whose *Sweetheart of the Rodeo* (1968) was instrumental in launching the trend; Buffalo Springfield; Poco, a spinoff from the Springfield, which featured the Country Rock harmonies of rhythm guitarist Richie Furay (b. 1944) and bass guitarist Jim Messina (b. 1947); New Riders of the Purple Sage; The Band; the Youngbloods; and Crosby, Stills, Nash & Young. For some years, Linda Ronstadt (b. 1946) was known as the Queen of Country Rock.

The turn of the Byrds, from their earlier Acid Rock, Folk Rock, and Electronic Rock explorations, to Country Rock was largely as a result of the influence of vocalist/rhythm guitarist Gram Parsons (b. 1945), later the motive power of the Flying Burritos. A Byrd from 1967–1969, Parsons made Country Rock albums under his own name until his death in 1973.

Despite its brief existence in 1967, the Buffalo Springfield exerted considerable influence through the caliber of its members: Richie Furay (b. 1944), Steve Stills (b. 1945), Neil Young (b. 1945), and Jim Messina (b. 1947). All later made their mark with other groups.

The Band, out of Canada with the exception of drummer Levon Helm (b. circa 1942) of Alabama, came to prominence when Dylan went electric in 1965. The first of many piano-organ groups, they used the wah-wah pedal to produce the sound of the Country-styled steel guitar, modeling some of their songs on sentimental ballads of the late 19th century. Among their best-known hits: "The Night They Drove Old Dixie Down" and "King Harvest." The first album of Crosby, Stills, & Nash, employing unamplified guitars, included three songs by Judy Collins (b. 1939) and Stephen Stills's (b. 1945) seven-minute "Suite Judy Blue Eyes." Issued in 1969, it became a Gold Record the following year.

The soft style in which the Country sound is energized by a Rock beat continues to attract adherents. In 1979 Country Music Association Awards went to the Charlie Daniels Band for "The Devil Went Down to Georgia," an upbeat Country rocker.

By 1981 Country music was sweeping into the mainstream with the same gusto as back in the days of Hank Williams (1923–1953), partly as a result of the impact of the film *Urban Cowboy,* but also because of the rise of artists like Dolly Parton (b. 1946), Willie Nelson (b. 1933), and Kenny Rogers (b. 1941). In 1980–1981 Dolly Parton scored a No. 1 single and album with *9 to 5,* the theme of the film of the same name. When she played the Riviera in Las Vega, she received $350,000 for a week, the highest sum ever paid to a headliner. But by then, the Las Vegas Strip seemed like an outpost of booming Nashville, with artists like Mickey Gilley, Johnny Lee, Eddie Rabbit (b. 1941), Dottie West (b. 1932), Crystal Gayle (b. 1951), Mel Tillis (b. 1932), Loretta Lynn (b. 1935), and Waylon Jennings (b. 1937), as well as Kenny Rogers and Willie Nelson—all headlining at the top "casinotels."

See also Gilley's; Nashville Outlaws; Urban Cowboy.

Country Song, Best (NARAS Grammy Awards) (songwriter awards)

1964 "Dang Me": Roger Miller
1965 "King of the Road": Roger Miller
1966 "Almost Persuaded": Billy Sherrill, Glen Sutton
1967 "Gentle on My Mind": John Hartford
1968 "Little Green Apples": Bobby Russell
1969 "A Boy Named Sue": Shel Silverstein
1970 "My Woman, My Woman, My Wife": Marty Robbins
1971 "Help Me Make It Through the Night": Kris Kristofferson
1972 "Kiss an Angel Good Mornin'": Ben Peters
1973 "Behind Closed Doors": Kenny O'Dell
1974 "A Very Special Love Song": Norris Wilson and Billy Sherrill
1975 "(Hey Won't You Play) Another Somebody Done Somebody Wrong Song": Chips Moman and Larry Butler

1976 "Broken Lady": Larry Gatlin
1977 "Don't It Make My Brown Eyes Blue": Richard Leigh
1978 "The Gambler": Don Schlitz
1979 "You Decorated My Life": Bob Morrison and Debbie Hupp
1980 "On the Road Again": Willie Nelson
1981 "9 to 5": Dolly Parton

See also National Academy of Recording Arts and Sciences (NARAS).

Country Song of the Year (CMA awards)

1967 "There Goes My Everything": Dallas Frazier
1968 "Honey": Bobby Russell
1969 "Caroll County Accident": Bob Ferguson
1970 "Sunday Morning Coming Down": Kris Kristofferson
1971 "Easy Loving": Freddie Hart
1972 "Easy Loving": Freddie Hart
1973 "Behind Closed Doors": Kenny O'Dell
1974 "Country Bumpkin": Don Wayne
1975 "Back Home Again": John Denver
1976 "Rhinestone Cowboy": Larry Weiss
1977 "Lucille": Roger Bowling, Hal Bynum
1978 "Don't It Make My Brown Eyes Blue": Richard Leigh
1979 "The Gambler": Don Schlitz
1980 "He Stopped Loving Her Today": Bobby Braddock and Curley Putnam
1981 "He Stopped Loving Her Today": Bobby Braddock and Curley Putnam

See also Country Music Association (CMA).

Country Vocal Duo of the Year (CMA awards)

1970 Porter Wagoner and Dolly Parton
1971 Porter Wagoner and Dolly Parton
1972 Conway Twitty and Loretta Lynn
1973 Conway Twitty and Loretta Lynn
1974 Conway Twitty and Loretta Lynn
1975 Conway Twitty and Loretta Lynn
1976 Waylon Jennings and Willie Nelson
1977 Jim Ed Brown and Helen Cornelius
1978 Kenny Rogers and Dottie West
1979 Kenny Rogers and Dottie West

1980   Moe Bandy and Joe Stampley
1981   David Frizzell and Shelly West

See also Country Music Association (CMA).

Country Vocal Group of the Year (CMA awards)

1967   Stoneman Family
1968   Porter Wagoner and Dolly Parton
1969   Johnny Cash and June Carter
1970   Glaser Brothers
1971   Osborne Brothers
1972   Statler Brothers
1973   Statler Brothers
1974   Statler Brothers
1975   Statler Brothers
1976   Statler Brothers
1977   Statler Brothers
1978   Oak Ridge Boys
1979   Statler Brothers
1980   Statler Brothers
1981   Alabama

See also Country Music Association (CMA).

Country Vocalist of the Year, Female (CMA awards)

1967   Loretta Lynn
1968   Tammy Wynette
1969   Tammy Wynette
1970   Tammy Wynette
1971   Lynn Anderson
1972   Loretta Lynn
1973   Loretta Lynn
1974   Olivia Newton-John
1975   Dolly Parton
1976   Dolly Parton
1977   Crystal Gayle
1978   Crystal Gayle
1979   Barbara Mandrell
1980   Emmylou Harris
1981   Barbara Mandrell

See also Country Music Association (CMA).

Country Vocalist of the Year, Male (CMA awards)

1967	Jack Greene
1968	Glen Campbell
1969	Johnny Cash
1970	Ronnie Milsap
1971	Charley Pride
1972	Charley Pride
1973	Charley Pride
1974	Ronnie Milsap
1975	Waylon Jennings
1976	Ronnie Milsap
1977	Ronnie Milsap
1978	Don Williams
1979	Kenny Rogers
1980	George Jones
1981	George Jones

See also Country Music Association (CMA).

Country Vocal Performance, Best—Duo or Group (NARAS Grammy Awards)

1967	Johnny Cash and June Carter: "Jackson"
1969	Waylon Jennings and the Kimberlys: "MacArthur Park"
1970	Johnny Cash and June Carter: "If I Were a Carpenter"
1971	Conway Twitty and Loretta Lynn: "After the Fire is Gone"
1972	The Statler Brothers: "Class of '57"
1973	Kris Kristofferson and Rita Coolidge: "From the Bottom to the Bottom"
1974	The Pointer Sisters: "Fairy Tale"
1975	Kris Kristofferson and Rita Coolidge: "Lover Please"
1976	Amazing Rhythm Aces: "The End Is Not in Sight" (The Cowboy Tune)
1977	The Kendalls: "Heaven's Just a Sin Away"
1978	Waylon Jennings and Willie Nelson: "Mama Don't Let Your Babies Grow Up to Be Cowboys"
1979	Charlie Daniels Band: "The Devil Went Down to Georgia"
1980	Roy Orbison and Emmylou Harris: "That Lovin' You Feelin' Again"
1981	Oak Ridge Boys: "Elvira"

See also National Academy of Recording Arts and Sciences.

Country Vocal Performance, Best—Female (NARAS Grammy Awards)

1964   Dottie West: "Here Comes My Baby"
1965   Jody Miller: "Queen of the House"
1966   Jeannie Seely: "Don't Touch Me"
1967   Tammy Wynette: "I Don't Wanna Play House"
1968   Jeannie C. Riley: "Harper Valley P.T.A."
1969   Tammy Wynette: "Stand By Your Man"
1970   Lynn Anderson: "Rose Garden"
1971   Sammi Smith: "Help Me Make It Through the Night"
1972   Donna Fargo: "Happiest Girl in the Whole USA"
1973   Olivia Newton-John: "Let Me Be There"
1974   Anne Murray: "Love Song"
1975   Linda Ronstadt: "I Can't Help It"
1976   Emmylou Harris: "Elite Hotel"
1977   Crystal Gayle: "Don't It Make My Brown Eyes Blue"
1978   Dolly Parton: "Here You Come Again"
1979   Emmylou Harris: "Blue Kentucky Girl"
1980   Anne Murray: "Could I Have This Dance"
1981   Dolly Parton: "9 to 5"

See also National Academy of Recording Arts and Sciences (NARAS).

Country Vocal Performance, Best—Male (NARAS Grammy Awards)

1964   Roger Miller: "Dang Me"
1965   Roger Miller: "King of the Road"
1966   David Houston: "Almost Persuaded"
1967   Glen Campbell: "Gentle on My Mind"
1968   Johnny Cash: "Folsom Prison Blues"
1969   Johnny Cash: "A Boy Named Sue"
1970   Ray Price: "For the Good Times"
1971   Jerry Reed: "When You're Hot, You're Hot"
1972   Charley Pride: *Charley Pride Sings Heart Songs*
1973   Charlie Rich: "Behind Closed Doors"
1974   Ronnie Milsap: "Please Don't Tell Me How the Story Ends"
1975   Willie Nelson: "Blue Eyes Crying in the Rain"
1976   Ronnie Milsap: "Stand by My Woman Man"
1977   Kenny Rogers: "Lucille"

1978   Willie Nelson: "Georgia on My Mind"
1979   Kenny Rogers: "The Gambler"
1980   George Jones: "He Stopped Loving Her Today"
1981   Ronnie Milsap: "(There's) No Gettin' Over Me"

See also National Academy of Recording Arts and Sciences (NARAS).

cover record   Originally, a cover record was simply a disk other than the first version of a song. All through the era of the No. 1 plug in the music business, it was customary for a publisher to seek different versions of a plug song. Each of these was done by an artist in his own identifiable style. In the early 1950s, Mitch Miller, A & R chief of Columbia Records, frequently covered Country songs with Pop artists. Tony Bennett (b. 1926) made a Pop hit of Hank Williams's "Cold, Cold Heart," Jo Stafford (b. 1920) covered his "Jambalaya," and Rosemary Clooney (b. 1928) put his "Half as Much" on Pop bestseller charts. None of these artists attempted to copy or model their versions on Williams's original Country versions.

In the mid-1950s, just before the emergence of Rock 'n' Roll, cover records assumed a different character. When an A & R man at a major label learned of a black disk on an "indie" label that showed signs of turning into a hit, he would quickly cover the song with a white artist, making a record that extracted the catchy elements from the black disk but was polished and sweetened for white ears. Because the country's big 50,000-watt stations would not, in that period, play disks with a black sound (R & B), the white artist would achieve the mainstream bestseller and steal the hit from the black artist. Although many white artists indulged in this practice, including Perry Como (b. 1912) who covered Gene & Eunice's "Ko Ko Mo," two record companies built their catalogs on white covers: Dot with Pat Boone (b. 1934) and Coral with the McGuire Sisters. Mercury Records developed the Crew Cuts, a new group out of Canada, into a hit quartet with covers of black groups. The most notorious covers of the period were Georgia Gibbs's copies for Mercury of LaVern Baker's "Tweedle Dee" (Atlantic) and Etta James's "Dance with Me, Henry" (Argo).

While the major labels watched the black R & B labels for songs they could cover, they were frequently apprised of potential bestsellers by the R & B labels themselves. What these small labels lost in record revenues, they recaptured in royalties derived from ownership of the copyright. Black artists were the basic losers, although they enjoyed increased fees for personal appearances as a result of their association with a big hit. Not all white covers knocked the black originals out of the box. Fats Domino was generally able to cross over into Pop charts, despite competition from a white cover.

Song	Black Artist	White Cover
1954		
"Earth Angel"	Penguins (Dootone)	The Crew Cuts (Mercury)
"Goodnight, Well It's Time to Go"	Spaniels (Vee Jay)	McGuire Sisters (Coral)
"Hearts of Stone"	The Charms (De Luxe)	Fontane Sisters (Dot)
"Shake, Rattle and Roll"	Joe Turner (Atlantic)	Bill Haley & the Comets (Decca)
"Sh-Boom"	The Chords (Cat)	The Crew Cuts (Mercury)
"Sincerely"	Moonglows (Chess)	McGuire Sisters (Coral)
"Two Hearts"	The Charms (De Luxe)	Pat Boone (Dot)
"Tweedle Dee"	LaVern Baker (Atlantic)	Georgie Gibbs (Mercury)
1955		
"Ain't That a Shame"	Fats Domino (Imperial)	Pat Boone (Dot)
"Dance with Me, Henry"	Etta James (Modern): a reply to "Work with Me, Annie" by The Midnighters (Federal)	Georgia Gibbs (Mercury)
"Don't Be Angry"	Nappy Brown (Savoy)	The Crew Cuts (Mercury)
"Gum Drop"	The Charms (De Luxe)	The Crew Cuts (Mercury)
"I Hear You Knocking"	Smiley Lewis (Imperial)	Gale Storm (Dot)
"Ko Ko Mo, I Love You So"	Gene & Eunice (Combo)	Perry Como (RCA Victor)
"Piddily Patter Patter"	Nappy Brown (Savoy)	Patti Page (Mercury)
"Rollin' Stone"	The Marigolds (Excello)	Fontane Sisters (Dot)
"Tutti Frutti"	Little Richard (Specialty)	Pat Boone (Dot)
1956		
"Eddie My Love"	The Teen Queens (RPM)	Fontane Sisters (Dot)
"Fever"	Little Willie John (King)	Peggy Lee (Capitol)
"Good Rockin' Tonight"	Roy Brown (De Luxe)	Pat Boone (Dot)

"I Almost Lost My Mind"	Ivory Joe Hunter (MGM)	Pat Boone (Dot)
"I'll Be Home"	Flamingos (Checker)	Pat Boone (Dot)
"Hound Dog"	Big Mama Thornton (Peacock)	Elvis Presley (RCA Victor)
"Ivory Tower"	Otis Williams (De Luxe)	Cathy Carr (Fraternity)
"Seven Days"	The Drifters (Atlantic)	Dorothy Collins (Coral)
"Why Do Fools Fall in Love?"	The Teenagers (Gee)	Gale Storm (Dot)
1957		
"I'm Walkin'"	Fats Domino (Imperial)	Ricky Nelson (Imperial)
"Jim Dandy"	LaVern Baker (Atlantic)	Georgia Gibbs (Mercury)
"Little Darlin'"	The Gladiolas (Excello)	The Diamonds (Mercury)

Cow Jazz   The designation used by Jerry Jeff Walker (b. 1942) for his brand of the Austin outlaw-country sound. Originally an upstate New Yorker, Walker is the author/composer of "Mr. Bojangles," a chart disk for the Nitty Gritty Dirt Band, one of Sammy Davis' most effective in-person numbers, and a song recorded by a large number of artists, including Nina Simone (b. 1933).

See also Nashville Outlaws.

Crawdaddy Club   A rock club in London where the Rolling Stones worked as the house band and were succeeded in mid-1965 by the Yardbirds.

See also the Rolling Stones.

"Crazy Cajun"   Cognomen for Huey P. Meaux, a record producer who worked out of his barbershop in Houston, Tex., beginning in 1959. His early disks, cut in Ville Platte, La., or in Cosimo Matassa's New Orleans studio, were seldom heard outside the Texas-Louisiana area. After the British invasion wiped him out, he promoted a San Antonio group he called the Sir Douglas Quintet as a new English combo. The exposure of the sham did not daunt him. Although he was indicted after the 1966 Country Music Disc Jockey convention in Nashville for conspiracy to violate the Mann Act and served 14 months in jail, he made a comeback in 1975 with Chicago singer Freddy Fender (b. 1937) ("Before the Last Teardrop Falls").

croon   A style of singing prevalent in the 1930s and 1940s whose major proponents were Bing Crosby (1904–1977), Frank Sinatra (b. 1915), Rudy Vallee (b. 1901), Perry Como (b. 1912), and Dean Martin (b. 1917). Whether the sound was sent through the nose or not, it was soft and cowlike. The singers required a microphone to project. Sinatra was frequently characterized as "The Crooner," a misnomer to a careful student of his style.

See also Big Ballad era; Big Band era; No. 1 plug.

Bing Crosby (1903–1977)   Harry Lillis Crosby made his mark initially singing with the Rhythm Boys, a vocal trio (Crosby plus Al Rinker and Harry Barris) with the Paul Whiteman Orchestra. Although he became one of the most potent creators of hits during the Big Ballad era (1930-1950), he was always admired, like Sinatra, for the jazzy undertones and overtones of his style. That style was one of singing as though he were speaking, a relaxed, easy delivery as if he were standing near your piano and sing/talking to you. With him, the microphone became the singers' instrument. The first of the great romantic crooners, he made his network radio debut on CBS on September 2, 1931, singing "Just One More Time." In no time at all, his starring career spanned all the media—films, records, TV, as well as radio. In his fifty-one-year recording career, he cut more than 1,600 songs. He made his first solo record in March 1927 while he was still a member of The Rhythm Boys and working with Paul Whiteman (1891-1967); the song was "Muddy Water."

On August 8, 1934, he recorded "I Love You Truly" for Decca. It was not only the first disk he cut for the label, but also the first record made and released by the newly formed company. Other well-known hit disks include "San Antonio Rose" (1940); "White Christmas" (1942), regarded as the biggest-selling disk of all time; "I'll Be Home for Christmas" (1943); "South America, Take It Away" (1946); "Now Is the Hour" (1948); and "True Love," a duet with Grace Kelly (1956).

"crossed note" tuning   A type of tuning a guitar by Blues singers in which the standard tuning e–b–g–d–a–e is altered to make a chord by raising and/or lowering strings. Different artists used different names for such retunings: e.g., Spanish, Sebastopol, Crossed E, Hi-wanna (for Hawaiian).

crossovers   Records intended for one market (R & B, C & W, Jazz) that succeed in selling in another market, mainly Pop, are known as crossovers. During the 1930s and 1940s, disks by the Mills Brothers, Louis Jordan (1908-1975), and the Ink Spots, ostensibly cut for black consumption, frequently were bought by white recordbuyers and became mainstream hits. Had there been trade paper charts in the 1920s, there is good reason to believe that Bessie Smith's Blues disks would have found a place on Pop charts. In the early years of the R & B era, songs like "(I Love You) for Sentimental Reasons," "I Wonder," and "Open the Door, Richard" started with black audiences and became white favorites. In the early fifties, Lloyd Price's "Lawdy, Miss Clawdy" was a crossover, as were most of Fats Domino's recordings. From November 1963 until January 1965, *Billboard* did not publish R & B charts because the crossovers had become so numerous that Pop and R & B charts looked alike.

Arthur Crudup   *See* "Father of Rock 'n' Roll."

Crusading Rock   In 1978–1979 a number of groups took names that pinpointed specific causes they were espousing. Health Insurance, for example, was a band concerned with compulsory national health insurance. Gunplay opted for the constitutional right to bear arms. Johnny & the Empiricists raised their voices for the funding of basic scientific research. The aim of the English Preservation Rock Band was to perserve the purity of the English language. Democracy termed its music "anti-Marxist disco."

cuatro   *See* Latin rhythm instruments.

cue   A signal by a conductor's stick, indicated by notation in a score, for an instrumentalist to begin playing or a singer to begin singing.

"cues"   Jargon for headphones worn by recording musicians when they overdub a tape. Previously recorded material, played by the engineer in the booth, is heard through the earphones, cueing the musicians on when they are to play.

cue sheet   A log of the musical selections played on a radio or TV show, or in a film. Supplied by producers to performing rights societies, which use such logs in calculating writer/publisher credits.

"curlicues"   *See* melisma.

cut   Although virtually all recording is done today with tape passing over a magnetic head, record masters were originally made by a needle cutting grooves in a metal disk. "Cut" is also used as a verb meaning to outplay or best another player. As a noun, "cut" is used for "take" or track.

cut-in   Refers to the practice of allowing someone to share in the credits, royalties, and/or revenues of a song to whose writing that person did not contribute. A cut-in is either a performer or someone else (e.g., a disk jockey) who can bring a song to the ears of the public. The practice goes back at least to the minstrel era, when an entrepreneur like E. P. Christy could be cut in to insure the use of a new song in a show. Al Jolson (1886–1950) had his name on many songs, including "Sonny Boy," to which his contribution was a sensational performance. Although disk jockey Alan Freed (1922–1965) was a capable songwriter, his credit as a cowriter of Chuck Berry's "Maybelline," in whose success he otherwise played a significant role, is not genuine. The proprietors of small record companies, like Don Robey at Peacock and J. Taub at Modern, frequently cut into original songs recorded by their artists, thereby reducing the royalties owing to such artists.

cutting contest   In the days of New Orleans Jazz, the pioneers frequently participated in competitions designed to establish the superiority of one band over another. These competitions were known as cutting contests. In Harlem in the 1930s, they were called "battles of the bands."
    See also Savoy Ballroom.

cyclical structure   A type of song structure in which the song's hook is repeated again and again: ABABCAC. It was developed by the Motown songwriting team of Holland–Dozier–Holland, who wrote and produced hits by the Supremes, Martha & the Vandellas, and others.
    See also continuous loop; hook; Motown sound.

cymbal   A percussion instrument made of a round metal plate, played by being struck either with a drumstick, or another cymbal, or a fanlike wire brush. The high-hat cymbal consists of two metal plates, one mounted above the other on a tall metal pole; the upper plate is stationary while the lower makes contact with it through the use of a foot pedal. The choke cymbal is a single plate mounted on a metal pole that is struck with a mallet or drumstick; the plate is immediately seized by a hand to choke the vibratory sound. The Charleston cymbal is just a variant of the choke cymbal, acquiring its title during the period when the dance known as the Charleston was popular.

"DA"   *See* ducktail haircut.

Dada Rock   An allusive rather than an exact term that takes its meaning from an avant-garde literary movement of the 1920s. The

Dadaists took their name from the first sound uttered by a newborn child and were concerned with recapturing the sense of childlike wonder and innocence. Among Rock groups, Alice Cooper (b. 1948) and his band of ruffians, with their childish pranks and destructive antics—tearing up pillows and scattering feathers over the audience or engaging in a mock battle with inflated toys—were the progenitors of the style. A celebrated proponent was Captain Beefheart (b. 1941) and His Magic Band, who produced a far-out mixture of sounds—Free Jazz, Delta Blues, and Avant-garde Rock—with weird, underground titles like *Lick My Decals Off, Baby* and *Trout Mask Replica.*

See also Captain Beefheart.

"daddy-o"   Black jargon for pal, buddy, friend. In "Charlie Brown" by the Coasters, Charlie gets into trouble by getting too familiar with his English teacher, whom he calls "daddy-o."

"Daddy of Western Swing"   Bob Wills (1906–1979), who led a band, The Texas Playboys, organized in 1932.

dance songs   Through the years, there have always been songs about new dances. Back in the 1920s, songs describing the Black Bottom and the Charleston were extremely popular. The thirties gave us "Beer Barrel Polka," "The Continental," "The Dipsey Doodle," and other songs about dances. In the R & B era, "The Hucklebuck" was a big hit. The Rock years were no exception. "The Twist" and "The Hustle" quickly come to mind. There were dozens of others. Having scored with "Walking the Dog," Rufus Thomas of Memphis followed with "Do the Funky Chicken," "(Do the) Push and Pull," "The Breakdown," and "Do the Funky Penguin." Cameo/Parkway Records of Philadelphia came up with a new dance with almost every new release: "The Wah Watusi" and "Shimmy Shimmy" by the Orlons; "The Cha-Cha-Cha" by Bobby Rydell (b. 1942); "Mashed Potato Time" by Dee Dee Sharp (b. 1945); and "Bristol Stomp" by the Dovells. Apart from descriptions of the steps on a record, new dances had to be demonstrated—and Cameo/Parkway was fortunate in having easy access to *American Bandstand,* whose host had a piece of the company's action. In Chubby Checker (1941), the label found an artist who not only delivered a Gold Record with his version of "The Twist" but was a superlative dancer. No sooner had "The Twist" taken off than Parkway issued a disk by Chubby called "The Hucklebuck." This was followed by "Pony Time," "Dance the Mess Around," "La Paloma Twist," Limbo Rock," and "Let's Do the Freddie." Checker's disk of "The Twist" twice went to No. 1, once in 1960 and again in 1962. No other artist and no other label was quite as successful in exploiting the younger generation's penchant for new Rock dances.

See also The Twist.

"The Day the Music Stopped"   The reference is to February 3, 1959, the day that a private plane carrying Buddy Holly (1936–1959) and other rock 'n' roll artists crashed in the midwest, killing all the occupants.

See also the Big Bopper; Buddy Holly.

"dead heads"   That's what fans of the Grateful Dead called themselves. One of the earliest Psychedelic and Electronic Rock bands out of San Francisco, the Dead were sponsored by LSD chemist Stanley Owsley and participated in novelist Ken Kesey's "acid test" parties, frequently playing never-ending variations on "In the Midnight Hour" while they were stoned.

See also Acid Rock.

decibel   The basic unit of loudness.

"dee jay"   Abbreviation of "disk jockey."

Delta Blues   If any one region may be said to be the birthplace of the Blues, the Delta area of Mississippi is the most likely place. A D-shaped lowland lying between the Yazoo and Mississippi rivers, it is south of Memphis and north of Vicksburg. Out of this area came an enormous number of influential pioneer bluesmen. Among others: Charley Patton (b. circa 1885 near Edwards, Miss.); Son House (b. 1902 near Lyon, Miss.); Skip James (b. 1902 near Bentonia, Miss.); Bukka White (b. 1909 in Houston, Miss.); Sunnyland Slim (b. 1907 in Vance, Miss.); Howlin' Wolf (b. 1920 in Aberdeen, Miss.); James Cotton (b. 1935 in Tunica, Miss.); Robert Johnson (b. 1912 in Hazlehurst, Miss.); Elmore James (b. 1918 in Canton, Miss.); Muddy Waters (b. 1915 in Rolling Fork, Miss.).

See also Country Blues.

"demo"   Short for "demonstration record," meaning a disk made for auditioning a song, singer, style, or all three.

"denim discos"   A succession of western-oriented films—*Electric Horseman, Bronco Billy, The Long Riders,* and *Coal Miner's Daughter*— capped by the impact of *Urban Cowboy,* led not only to the popularization of western garb but to the rise of Country music discos. In Los Angeles, the Crescendo, a well-known discotheque, changed its name to The

Cowboy. In a short time, there were more than two dozen denim discos in the LA area, with names like Sh__ Kickers, Georgia Round-Up, and Cowboy Cantina. Instead of spiked heels, slit skirts, and shiny disco pants, dancers came in jeans, western boots and skirts, and the sculptured cowboy hats seen in *Urban Cowboy.* Instead of the Hustle and other disco dances, they did such down-home dances as Cotton-Eye Joe, Cowboy Polka, or the Freeze, and such Country line-dances as the Backwalk, Texas Twist, and Four Corners.

See also Disco; discotheque.

Destruction Rock   A number of groups indulged in destructive antics onstage. Members of Alice Cooper pulverized watermelons, ripped pillows apart, and even decapitated chickens. At the Monterey Pop Festival in 1967, guitarist Jimi Hendrix (1942–1970) set his instrument on fire. He did this in an effort to outdo The Who, who pioneered the antic and were doubtless the most persistent auto-destruct group. Apparently, the gambit started quite accidentally when the group was performing at a local London pub, the Railway Tavern, and Peter Townshend broke the neck of his guitar by sticking it through the low ceiling. In a fury, he smashed the instrument to pieces, garnering so much publicity that thereafter it became a calculated bit of showmanship. The Who did not confine their destructive antics to the stage; they wrecked so many hotel rooms that paying for the damage became a drain on their earnings. In 1981 the Plasmatics were destroying guitars, TV sets, and Cadillacs(!) onstage.

See also Glitter Rock.

Detroit sound   Although much ink has been used in an effort to specify the Detroit sound—the afterbeat tinkle of tambourines, call-and-response vocals, continuous loops, etc.—it is not an identifiable sound. But it is identified with the recordings produced on the many record labels established by Berry Gordy (1929) (Tamla, Motown, Gordy, Soul) and by such groups as the Miracles, Marvelettes, Contours, Supremes, Temptations, Four Tops, Spinners, and Martha & the Vandellas. Individual artists involved in the Detroit sound include Mary Wells (b. 1943), Marvin Gaye (b. circa 1939), Eddie Holland (b. 1939), Tammi Terrell (1946–1970), and Stevie Wonder (b. 1951). While the Detroit sound is black-based and rooted in Gospel music, it has enough melody and rhythm to be a crossover sound. It has been described as Pop Soul.

See also Pop Soul.

"Devil's music"   Among religious blacks, the Blues have frequently been condemned as music of the Devil, contrasting with Gospel song, the music of the Lord.

diatonic   Our major-minor system of scales involving a set sequence of eight tones without chromatic deviation within the octave.

"dicty"   Snobbish, high-falutin', stuck-up—in black slang.

digital recording   An advanced recording procedure in which musical sounds are transformed into "bits" in a storage medium in the same way that a computer operates. The resulting sound is purer, and without surface noises and other distortions. 3M, which manufactures the 32-track digital recording and mastering system, prices it at $100,000. At least four "A" Hollywood studios—A & M, Record Plant, Warner Bros., and Westlake Audio—were renting the system, at last writing, at $4,000 a month, $300 for a three-minute tape, and a $10,000 deposit in front.

In the process of recording, a computer picks up each audio impulse from a microphone and assigns it a numerical value, which is then called back and reassembled precisely as it was originally produced. Devoid of hiss and irregularities of speed found on records produced from conventional tapes, records produced from digital tapes are called "hybrids" and retail in this period of limited digital recording at $15. It is expected that digital systems and playback machines will become available for home use in the mid-1980s, at which time the digital playback will employ a tiny laser to read a digital recording on a disk the size of a three-by-five-inch index card. Such disks will be impervious to dust, fingerprints, and scratches.

diminished chord   A major chord consists of the first, third, and fifth note of a major scale. When both the third and the fifth are flatted, a diminished chord results:

G major   G minor   G dim.

"Dirty Dozens"   An erotic song recorded by such bluesmen as Tampa Red (b. 1900), Leroy Carr (1905–1935), Kokomo Arnold (1901–1968), and Speckled Red (Rufus Perryman, 1892–1973), who had a bestselling disk in 1929. The "Dirty Dozens" is a gambit of black origin in which insults are traded until one contender is accused of having sex with his mother (mother-fucker), at which point physical violence supersedes verbal abuse. Curiously, the gambit is supposed to have originated in a patter song of a religious nature whose purpose was to teach the young Biblical lore. In time, the content was transformed into the erotic and sacrilegious classic of Blues literature.

"dirty" tone   An alteration in the texture of a note played by the brasses or reeds that gives it an erotic sound or quality.

Disco   A distinction must be made between *disco,* an abbreviation of "discotheque," and *Disco,* a musical style that began to take shape in 1975 and became the rage in 1977–1979. Discos as dancehalls existed all through the 1960s, developing as hangouts for gays because of the privacy they afforded. In 1975 two things happened that initiated the craze. Soul producer/songwriter/arranger Van McCoy (1940–1979) wrote and recorded "The Hustle"; it became a Gold Record and the biggest dance record of the seventies, establishing the Hustle and its variants as the basic dance of Disco. In time, there were the California Hustle (a.k.a. Bus Stop), New York Hustle, Latin Hustle, Tango Hustle, and American Hustle as well as the Detroit Shuffle, Bump, and Time Warp. In 1975, too, a Boston gal who had spent much of her time in Europe, Donna Summer (b. 1950), co-wrote and recorded "Love to Love You, Baby." In its original version, a record of normal length, it was, at the suggestion of the record company to whom the disk was offered, extended to 16 minutes and 50 seconds, during most of which Ms. Summer moaned, panted, and sounded as if she were having orgasms, as she kept repeating, over and over, "Love to love you, baby." The disk set the pattern for future Disco records; after a time, record companies released 12-inch singles, with a Disco song on each side, songs that generally consisted of little more than one or two lines of lyrics. It was the beat that counted on Disco records, a steady four-to-the-bar beat in which the thump-thump-thump-thump of the drum was way out in front. Disco records tended to be sensual, bluesy, and emotively soulful.

It was the film *Saturday Night Fever,* starring John Travolta as a macho discotheque king, that ignited the explosion and turned Disco into a worldwide craze in 1977–1979. The soundtrack album, with songs by the Bee Gees ("Staying Alive," "Night Fever," etc.), reportedly sold over 12 million copies. The craze brought to the fore Soul singers like Gloria Gaynor ("I Will Survive"), Chic ("Le Freak"), and a new Peaches & Herb ("Reunited"), as well as the very gay Village People ("In the Navy," "YMCA").

As the fever rose, everybody made Disco records, including oldtime Broadway star Ethel Merman (b. 1909), Boston Pops conductor Arthur Fiedler (*Saturday Night Fiedler*), and Easy Listening–ballad singer Barbra Streisand (b. 1942), who recorded "Enough is Enough," a Top 10 seller, with Donna Summer (b. 1950). There was even a *Mickey Mouse Disco* album, directed at the teenyboppers who were frequenting after-school discotheques. Small radio stations climbed overnight in popularity and ratings by substituting the extended-play format of Disco for

Top 40 Rock. By 1979 a backlash was in evidence, stirred by those who found Disco lyrics puerile and devoid of meaning, and the music, despite the use of big bands, monotonous. As the U.S.A. moved into the 1980s, Disco was on the decline, although discotheques continued to flourish.

See also denim discos; discotheque.

discotheque   This type of dancehall had its start in France in the 1960s when cabaret owners replaced live talent with disk jockeys spinning records for dancing. The economy of the setup, and the scope of the records that could be played in an evening, made it very attractive to club owners. During the 1960s and early 1970s, the discotheque was largely an underground development in the U.S.A., cultivated by the jet set and especially by gays, who favored them as private places where they could meet, dine, and dance without being harassed by the hoi polloi or the authorities. With the impact of the film *Saturday Night Fever*, discotheques for the masses began springing up all over the country, some built at a cost of over $1 million, others converted from defunct barns, halls, and ballrooms. The more opulent exploited every resource of light, sound, and lasers, overwhelming the ears, eyes, and other sense organs and providing exhibitionists an ego dance trip with a kaleidoscopic scene of color, motion, rhythms, and high decibels. The most publicized of discos, Studio 54 in New York City, was rumored to make cocaine and other drugs available to its special patrons. At the height of the Disco craze, there were reportedly over 10,000 discotheques in North America, with over 200 to 300 in NYC alone.

See also denim discos; Disco.

"The Divine Miss M."   Her name is Bette Midler (b. circa 1945), and the title of her first LP was *The Divine Miss M* (1972). "There's nothing she can't sing," wrote a *New York Times* reviewer. "Rock, Blues, Songs from the forties, fifties, sixties . . . Shangri Las' songs, Dixie Cups, Andrews Sisters." She rated kudos on her first starring role in the film *The Rose*, based loosely on the career of Janis Joplin.

See also Continental Baths.

"The Divine Sarah"   Sarah Vaughan (b. 1924), the noted Jazz singer.

Dixieland Jazz   A happy, peppy two-beat or two-to-the bar Jazz style, developed by white musicians in the 1920s under the influence of New Orleans pioneers like King Oliver (1885–1938), Louis Armstrong (1900–1971), the New Orleans Rhythm Kings, and especially the Original Dixieland Jazz Band. Among the best-known Dixieland exponents, one finds members of the so-called Austin High School Gang, of Chicago. In the heyday of 52nd Street, Jimmy Ryan's was a bastion of Dixieland Jazz, and some of the performers may still be heard today in the club at its West 54th Street location. Various combos led by Eddie Condon (1905–1973) on 52nd St., at Nick's in Greenwich Village, and later on East 56th Street in the Hotel Sutton were strong Dixieland proponents. The style may be heard in New Orleans these days, where trumpeter Al Hirt (b. 1922) and clarinetist Pete Fountain (b. 1930) each lead their own combos in their own clubs.

See also Austin High School Gang; 52nd St.

"Diz"   Nickname of John Birks "Dizzy" Gillespie (b. 1917), the world-famous trumpeter and Bop pioneer. As bandleader, composer, and instrumentalist, he has earned an international reputation; his name is imbedded in 52nd St.'s newly established Jazzwalk. Before forming his own band in 1945, he was a featured performer in the bands of Cab Calloway (b. 1907), Charlie Barnet (b. 1913), Les Hite (b. 1903), and Billy Eckstine (b. 1914). When Bop moved downtown from its experimental sessions at Minton's in Harlem, Diz fronted the first Bop combo on 52nd St. at the Three Deuces. Beginning with the *Esquire* New Star Award in 1945, he has won innumerable polls run by *Down Beat, Metronome,* and *Playboy.* An autobiographical tome titled *To Be—or To Bop* appeared in 1979.

dobro   Introduced by Flatt & Scruggs in their Foggy Mountain Boys band in 1955, the dobro is a guitar with raised strings and a resonator cone that causes it to produce a whining sound like the Hawaiian guitar. The name of the instrument is derived from the family name of its inventors: *Do*pera *Bro*thers. Initially its sole manufacturers during the late twenties, the Dopera Brothers sold the rights to the instrument to National Music Co. in 1932, from which they were bought in 1954 by the Valco Co. Of the two types of dobros now on the market, one retains the ringing sound of the Hawaiian guitar and the other is preferred by Bluegrass bands. Red Rhodes of Mike Nesmith & the First National Band plays the dobro. The instrument was used in *The Buffalo Springfield Again.*

"Dr. Demento"   A California disk jockey whose real name is Barry Hansen and who began his show during FM radio's "underground" days in the late sixties. His emphasis is on "demented" or funny material, something which is suggested by the cackling voice in which he speaks and the black top hat and tails in which he works. Locally, the madman's show is heard on KMET–FM, but he also does a syndicated show that is heard on 125 stations.

"Dr. John the Night Tripper"   Pseudonym of Malcolm John Rebennack (b. circa 1940), songwriter, guitarist, bassist, and record producer, originally of New Orleans, where he developed an interest in voodoo. The first album in which he mixed Soul and voodoo, recorded in Los Angeles, appeared under the credit of "Dr. John and the Night Tripper."
See also Voodoo Rock.

"dog"   A music-biz colloquialism for a song or disk that does not make it. Also known as a "bomb."

Dolby   A synonym for noiseless music reproduction, it is derived from Ray Dolby, who invented a device for eliminating the tape hiss that plagued the record industry from the introduction of tape recording in the 1940s. Since 1966 major recording studios have used a series of brushed aluminum boxes, labeled "Dolby Sytem: A Tape Noise Reduction," containing 520 resistors, transistors, and capacitors. Home tape recorders began using Dolby B in 1968. Radio stations and film companies are also now using the device, which works hardest during low-frequency passages. Founded in London in 1965 and now located in San Francisco, Dolby Laboratories, Inc., advertises the device with the slogan "The Sound of Silence." There are now competitive noise-reduction systems in High-Com II and Super-D, both manufactured by Japanese companies.

dominant   The fifth note of any major or minor scale. It is the pivotal note, since the chord on the dominant demands resolution to the first, or tonic, chord. That sequence, V–I, is known as an authentic cadence, contrasting with the IV–I sequence, or plagal cadence.

Doobie Brothers   The name of the well-known Rock group is derived from a slang term for a marijuana cigarette. Once a Hard Rock, leather-jacketed, motorcycle kind of group, it moved in 1975 with the introduction of Michael McDonald into Pop Funk, Pop Jazz, and a banner tenth anniversary: three Top 10 singles, six Grammy nominations, and four wins.

"doo-wop"   One of the many nonsense syllables used by *a capella* vocal groups of the forties and fifties, "doo-wop" served to develop rhythm patterns and was used as a rhythmic fill under held notes. The doo-wop groups, as they came to be known, emerged mostly from the country's black ghettos—e.g., Harlem and Bedford-Stuyvesant in New York City, Watts in Los Angeles—rehearsing without instrumental accompaniment on street-corners and in schoolyards, tenement hallways, and subways. The bass opening of the Teenagers' disk of "Why Do Fools Fall in Love?" boomed "eh toom-ah-ta toom-ah-ta toom-ah-toh-doh." In "Come Go with Me," the Del-Vikings employed "dum-dum-dum-dum-dum, dum-be-oo-bee." "Sh-Boom" gave its name to a hit disk by the Chords and Crew Cuts. In addition to the groups mentioned, the following started as doo-wop or street-corner groups: Orioles, Harptones, Crows, Belmonts, Flamingos, Imperials, Dells, Spaniels, and David Peel & the Lower East Side.

Thomas A. Dorsey (1899-   )   Mahalia Jackson, the great Gospel singer (1911-1972), called him "our Irving Berlin." His long list of classic Gospel songs includes "Peace in the Valley," a hit for both Red Foley (1910-1968) and Elvis Presley; "If You See My Saviour"; and "Precious Lord," the song requested by Dr. Martin Luther King, Jr., the night of his death. Although he was inspired by C. H. Tindley, founder of Tindley Methodist Church in Philadelphia and a great writer of hymns, Dorsey wrote neither hymns nor spirituals; he wrote pop-religiosos (religious songs with a popular rather than a sacred orientation) for which he coined the designation "gospel songs."

Yet he started as a blues singer/writer/accompanist, who wrote the erotic hit "Tight Like That"; was known variously as Georgia Tom, Smokehouse Charley, and Texas Tommy; and served as accompanist to Ma Rainey (1886-1939) and Bessie Smith (1894-1937), Empress of the Blues. He turned to religious music during the Great Depression when he formed the Thomas A. Dorsey Gospel Songs Music Publishing Co. of Chicago and sought to combine "the good news of Gospel with the bad news of the Blues." From 1932 to 1937 he performed on Station WLFL with his own University Gospel Singers. In 1932-1933 he and the famous Sallie Martin founded the National Convention of Gospel Choirs and Choruses, and worked with it and its annual festivals into the 1970s. He traveled with the great Mahalia Jackson from 1939-1944, seeking to uplift the spirit of the poor with songs of hope.

dotted note   A note whose duration is lengthened by half through the addition of a dot. A quarter-note, ♩ when dotted, becomes ♩., equivalent to three eighth-notes; and a half-note, ♩, when dotted, becomes ♩., equivalent to three quarter-notes.

double bar   Two perpendicular lines, which mark either the end of a main division of a composition or the end of it. When the double bar is preceded by two dots, it signifies that the preceding segment is to be repeated.

end   repeat

"Double Dynamite"   Nickname of the Soul duo, Sam & Dave, on Stax Records, one of whose major hits was "Hold On, I'm Coming" (1966).

double time   In 4/4 time, playing eight notes during the count of 4 instead of just four notes.

down beat   The first beat of a measure, so-called because of the downward motion of a conductor's hand or stick in signaling the initial beat of a bar. *Down Beat* is also the name of a Jazz magazine still published monthly out of Chicago.

Downer Rock   A limited category based on the morbidity of the message and the lugubriousness of the mood. Chief exponents would include Black Sabbath, Bloodrod (with "D.O.A."), and MC 5. All groups indulge in superamplified sounds.

"down home"   Initially the term had geographical import—"down home" was the South—but after Jazz moved north it acquired psychological and musical significance. "Down home" had reference to the black man's ethnic roots and referred musically to playing with an earthiness that came from the soil and an emotion that came from within.

dreadlocks   Stringy, uncombed hair, favored by the Rastafarian religious sect of Jamaica, who do not believe in cutting the hair and whose ideas and sentiments are reflected in Reggae music.
    See also Reggae.

"Drifting Cowboy"   *See* Hank Williams.

drive   Refers to playing with a propulsive quality or singing with thrust.

drone   Associated with the extended sound of the bagpipe in Western music—the continuing sound of a fixed pitch. In Indian music, popularized in this country by Ravi Shankar, a drone is the continuing sound of one of the strings of the sitar, vibrating sympathetically to the oscillation of another string.

drop-off   An effect produced by brass instruments in which a written note is sounded and, through relaxed lip pressure, there is a downward slide of four or five notes. The volume is generally diminished at the same time. The opposite effect is a "rip," in which the brass player starts four or five notes below the written note and glisses up to it, hitting the written note hard and staccato.

The rip is written: The drop-off is written:

the drug scene   LSD was in an experimental stage at the beginning of the sixties. But by the mid-sixties, Timothy Leary, who had been fired from Harvard University's psychology department, was promulgating the slogan "Turn On, Tune In, and Drop Out!" The counterculture took the advice to heart and eagerly welcomed drugs not merely as a kick but as a means of liberation—liberation of the senses, the mind, and one's outlook on the world. The Jefferson Airplane said it in "White Rabbit."

Bob Dylan was among the early explorers of the drug experience in song: "Mr. Tambourine Man" and "Rainy Day Women #12 and 35." So were the Byrds in "Eight Miles High" and "5-D," and the Beatles in "Lucy in the Sky with Diamonds"—the "diamond sky" was an image in "Mr. Tambourine Man"—and "A Day in the Life," both in the *Sgt. Pepper* album. Despite the L/S/D imbedded in the "Lucy" title, the Beatles denied the drug connection just as the Byrds did, denials made necessary by Federal Communications Commission surveillance that would have barred the records from the airwaves.

Yet some artists openly dealt with the drug experience if they did not celebrate it: Strawberry Alarm Clock in "Incense and Peppermints"; Steppenwolf in "Faster Than the Speed of Life"; Country Joe McDonald in "Acid Commercial" and "Bass Strings," the latter about pot. Other rockers used personification or imagery to shroud their design. Drugs were personified by women in the Association's "Along Comes Mary," Creedence Clearwater Revival's "Proud Mary," the Jefferson Airplane's "Plastic Fantastic Lover," and the Rolling Stones' "Lady Jane." Donovan fell back on sunshine in "Mellow Yellow," "Sunny Goodge Street," and "Sunshine Superman." Those in the know recognized that when the Rolling Stones sang "Jumpin' Jack Flash is a gas, gas, gas," they were chanting about Methedrine.

The prevalence of drugs led artists to protest the inequity and severity of drug laws: Phil Ochs in "Miranda" and Graham Nash in "Prison Song." Others expressed their concern about addiction: Joni Mitchell in "Cold Blue Steel and Sweet Fire" and the Rolling Stones in "Sister Morphine." Their concern was well-grounded. Among the groups that faced problems generated by the addiction of a member, there were the Association, the Byrds, Canned Heat, the Flying Burrito Brothers, Little Feat, Led Zeppelin, the New York Dolls, the Rolling Stones, and the Who, among others. The Lovin' Spoonful broke up shortly after members were busted on drug possession charges. From 1967 to 1981, no fewer than 25 Rock people perished from overdoses or drug-related (or alcohol-related) maladies or accidents. Here is a list of the fatalities:

1967	Brian Epstein, 32, manager of the Beatles
1968	Frankie Lymon, 26, of the Teenagers
1969	Brian Jones, 27, of the Rolling Stones
1970	Alan Wilson, 27, of Canned Heat
	Janis Joplin, 27
	Jimi Hendrix, 27
1972	Danny Whitten, of Crazy Horse
	Brian Cole, 28, of the Association
	Clyde McPhatter, 39
	Billy Murcia, of the New York Dolls
1973	Gram Parsons, 26, of the Byrds
1974	Robbie McIntosh, 28, of the Average White Band
	Nick Drake, 26
1975	Tim Buckley, 28
	Tommy Bolin, 25, of Deep Purple
1976	Florence Ballard, 33, of the Supremes
1977	Elvis Presley, 42
1978	Keith Moon, 32, of the Who
1979	Sid Vicious, 21, of Sex Pistols
	Jimmy McCullogh, 26
	Lowell George, 34, of Little Feat
1980	John Bonham, 32, of Led Zeppelin
	Bon Scott, 33, of AC/DC
1981	Tim Hardin, 39,
	Michael Bloomfield, 37

dub   A trial copy made on disk from a master tape. "To dub off" is to make such a copy or duplicate.

Dub   A form of Reggae, pioneered in Jamaica by a trio of producer/engineers (Coxson Dodd, Lee Perry, and King Tubby) in the early seventies. They dropped out the instruments on a completed recording, except for bass guitar and drums, added echo to each instrument, and faded the voices in and out, producing a ghostly kind of effect. The most influential figure in the Dub scene is Horace Swaby of Kingston, better known as Augustus Pablo, who performs on the melodica and whose disk "Selassie I Chant" cogently presents the weird sound. A number of New Wave Rock bands, including Clash,

Gang of Four, and Public Image, Ltd., have reacted strongly to Dub. Like other Reggae performers, Pablo is a Rastafarian and venerates Ethiopia's last emperor, Haile Selassie, as the divinity of an African redemption of Jamaica's dispossessed.

See also melodica; Reggae.

ducktail haircut   The hairstyle boys favored in the late 1950s—the hair, relatively short, combed back on each side into a DA or ducktail, and held in place with oily lotion. Celebrated in *Grease,* the nostalgic Rock 'n' Roll musical about the 1950s.

"dues"   The sacrifices and concessions an apprentice has to make, and the indignities and frustrations he has to endure, while working for meager pay at third-class joints. That's "paying one's dues."

"Duke"   *See* Edward Kennedy Ellington.

dulcimer   Unlike the European dulcimer of Persian or Arabian origin, regarded as a forerunner of the piano, the American dulcimer is not played by being struck with wooden or cork mallets. Descendant of the German folk zither, the American dulcimer was developed in the southern Appalachian mountains. Traditionally, it has three strings— one melody and two drone—with the melody string positioned over fixed frets. Strummed with a small stick or a turkey or goose quill, it is placed across the knees of a player or on a table. The fretboard is not chromatic but diatonic, and is tuned to various modes. Such Folk artists as the late Richard Farina (1937–1966), Jean Ritchie (b. 1922), and Taj Mahal (b. 1942) have used the instrument; also Joni Mitchell (b. 1943).

See also drone.

Durrell synthesizer   Used by Joe Byrd & the Field Hippies in *The American Metaphysical Circus* and by United States of America in their first album.

See also synthesizer.

Bob Dylan (1941-)   One of the most gifted, influential, and highly publicized figures in the history of Rock. With him, Rock 'n' Roll lyrics took on the trappings of poetry and expanded from a concern with teenage problems to controversial social issues. Born Robert Allen Zimmerman in Duluth and raised in the Jewish faith in Hibbing, Minnesota, he came to New York City in the early sixties to visit an ailing Woody Guthrie whose "talking" folk songs inspired his first album. With "Blowing in the Wind," popularized by Peter, Paul & Mary and Joan Baez (b. 1941), then the reigning Queen of Folk Music, he became the spokesman of the civil rights movement. His wedding of protest material to Rock and electric instruments caused him to be hooted off the stage at the Newport Folk Festival of 1964, where a year earlier he had been lionized. After the assassination of John F. Kennedy, which made him fearful for his own life, he turned from Protest Rock to personal problems. By 1965, when the Byrds made a hit of "Mr. Tambourine Man," he was involved in the drug scene, a subject that concerned him in his own hit, "Rainy Day Women #12 and 35." After a motorcycle accident, which almost took his life, his writing assumed a Country flavor in albums like *John Wesley Harding,* No. 2 in 1968, and *Nashville Skyline,* No. 3 in 1969, for which Johnny Cash (b. 1932) wrote the adulatory liner. He dealt with his marital situation and divorce in albums of the seventies, especially *Blood on the Tracks,* No. 1 in 1975, and *Desire,* No 1 in 1976. As the seventies closed, he forsook his Jewish origins and became a born-again Christian, a conversion that figured prominently in *Slow Train Coming* and *Saved.* Among the creators of Rock, he exhibited the keenest understanding of the times, a sense that made him seem visionary in anticipating changes in the public frame of mind and opportunistic in exploiting it. In March 1982 there were reports that he was returning to Judaism.

See also Jesus Rock; message songs.

E

Easy Listening   A trade-paper term loosely covering non-Rock, non-Disco, and non-Soul songs, records, and artists. Refers generally to ballads recorded by middle-generation artists like Frank Sinatra (b. 1915) and Barbra Streisand (b. 1942). But there is an overlap, and disks by younger artists like Barry Manilow (b. 1947) sometimes find their way into Easy Listening or MOR charts.

See also Adult Contemporary; MOR.

"easy rider"   Blues jargon for a pimp or inconstant peripatetic lover, as in "C. C. Rider," the famous Blues. Also "low rider."

echo   A sound effect produced naturally when a sound is reflected back from a barrier of some type. In recording, echo was first produced in that way: Columbia Records used a stairwell at 799 7th Avenue to bring the sound back. Leonard Chess of Chess Records used the toilet of their street-level office and studio as an echo chamber. In time, echo was produced through the use of a tape, which would delay the return of the signal. The volume, depth, and character of the echo always depended on the time elapsed between the original and the reflected sound, the size of the area in which the delay occurred, and the texture of the barrier. For some years, echo has been produced electronically, permitting a very precise control of the depth, volume, and character of the sound.

See also tape reverb.

editing   Basically involves mixing down 24 or more tracks to the 2 or 4 that are used as masters for stereo or quadraphonic reproduction. Developing the proper "mix" has become a high craft, posing such problems as: what instruments to emphasize, what "highs" to reduce, what "lows" to modulate, whether to slow or accelerate the tape, how to delete obvious mistakes. While engineers generally participate in the editing process, its control is vested in the record producer—men like Tom Dowd, Phil Spector, Arif Mardin, Jerry Wexler, and Phil Ramone—and, not infrequently, in the Rock artists themselves.

John Edwards Memorial Foundation   Chartered in 1962 as an educational, nonprofit corporation in California, it supports an archive of American Folk music in the Folklore and Mythology Center of UCLA. The basis of the archive was a collection of material gathered by the late John Edwards, an Australian who was killed in a car crash in 1960 and who had dedicated his life to a compilation of material on American Folk music. The original collection has been expanded to include C & W, Hillbilly, Bluegrass, Cowboy, Sacred, and contemporary Folk. In addition to housing a huge collection of recordings, it includes magazines, vertical files, and taped interviews. The Foundation also publishes a quarterly journal.

eel-YA-dah   The Bop drive to turn things around and upside down found expression in a triplet that broke with tradition. Instead of the accent falling on the first note of the three

the accent in the Bop triplet was on the middle note,

eel-YA-dah in nonsense syllables. The transference was achieved by sounding a note that was an octave above the first note:

Eight-to-the-bar   A rhythmic pattern in which there are 8 eighth notes in a measure:

It's basic to Boogie-woogie and Rock.
See also shuffle.

"eighty-eighter"   Swing term for a pianist, based on the fact that a piano keyboard includes 88 keys, counting black and white.

Roy Eldridge (1911–   )   A giant of the jazz trumpet, David Roy Eldridge may still be heard at Jimmy Ryan's, the 52nd St. Dixieland club, relocated on West 54th near 7th Avenue. After working with such well-known bands as Teddy Hill's, McKinney's Cotton Pickers, Mal Hallett's, and Fletcher Henderson's, he became nationally known in 1941–1943 during his sojourn with Gene Krupa (1909–1973) when he sang and played "Let Me Off Uptown" and other Pop-Jazz hits. The *Encyclopedia of Jazz* notes that he was "as vital a figure in the development of trumpet jazz during the thirties as Armstrong had been in the twenties and as Gillespie was to be in the forties and Miles Davis in the fifties." In 1980 he was chosen for a Prez Award and his name was imbedded in the pavement of the Jazzwalk on 52nd St.
See also Jazzwalk.

Electric Blues   Refers to the style developed by Muddy Waters (b. 1915) and other Delta bluesmen after they settled in the Windy City and began using electric guitars and basses. Also known as Chicago Blues.

Electric Flag   An integrated Blues group, formed by guitarist Mike Bloomfield (b. circa 1942) of the Paul Butterfield Blues Band, which took its name from the device that uses an electrically activated blower to keep a flag waving.

electric guitar   It is said that the electric guitar was developed in the U.S.A. around 1936. But as early as 1933 or 1934, Bob Dunn, who recorded with Milton Brown & His Musical Brownies, raised the strings on his Martin guitar, magnetized them, attached an electric pickup, and plugged into an amplifier. The solid-body electric guitar, developed by Leo Fender, did not come into being until 1948. The guitarist who is generally cited as the pioneer of the electric type is Eddie Durham (b. 1906), who recorded a series of solos in 1938 with the Kansas City

Five and Six, recruited by him from the Count Basie Band. The following year, Charlie Christian (1916–1942), a bluesman from Oklahoma, used the electric guitar in recordings with the Benny Goodman Band. Christian, who played hornlike, single-string melodies in a bluesy vein, had worked with Aaron "T-Bone" Walker (1909–1975), the innovator who influenced all the R & B guitar players, including B. B. King (b. 1925), as well as British rockers like Eric Clapton (b. 1945).

R & B was born when the electric guitar and the tenor sax superseded the acoustic guitar and harmonica as accompaniment for the Blues. The Chicago electric Blues of Muddy Waters (b. 1915), Howlin' Wolf (1910–1976) and Bo Diddley (b. 1928) was a small-combo, rhythmic blues in which the electric guitar was basic. The instrument was basic, too, to Rock 'n' Roll into which R & B evolved.

A composer/performer named Glenn Branca (b. 1948) wrote a *Second Symphony* (1982) in which he employs 11 electric guitarists. To achieve "the massive sonic grandeur," as John Rockwell characterized it in *The New York Times,* Mr. Branca builds his own instruments. Instead of strapping them to the performer's body, he mounts three sets of strings on a single table so that each player can simultaneously strum, pluck, or bow more than one guitar. Although Branca worked with several experimental rock groups in the late 70s, and at first aimed his "guitar armies" at rock clubs and audiences, his music now defies classification.

See also Louis Jordan; R & B; Muddy Waters.

electric piano   The tone is produced when a string, reed, or metal bar is struck or plucked as a key is depressed. The tone is picked up and amplified electronically. The sound, except for a middle octave of the keyboard, is quite different from that of a regular piano.

Electric Sky Church   An experimental group that Jimi Hendrix (1942–1970) gathered around himself during the summer of 1969 when he hid out in upstate New York. The musicians included avant-garde classical composers as well as old bluesmen. Part of the group appeared with him at Woodstock in the summer of 1969 and can be heard in the apocalyptic version of "The Star-Spangled Banner" in the *Woodstock* album.

electronic instruments   There are two types: (1) the sound is produced by electronic means (vacuum tubes, transistors, etc.), as in the Hammond organ; or (2) the sound is produced in traditional ways (blowing, scraping, beating) and is then amplified electronically, as in the electric guitar. In addition to instruments, the electronic family now includes synthesizers like the Moog, Mellotron, Echoplex, and Arp, which manufacture or synthesize sounds from the different components of sound waves. According to Robert Moog, who developed the instruments that bear his name: "Electronic music consists of electronically generated sounds and natural sounds that are modified electronically, assembled into music by magnetic tape manipulation or performed live."

See also Mellotron; Moog; synthesizer.

Electronic Rock   The first album to be promoted as Electronic Rock appeared in March 1968, the product of an extremely sophisticated classical group of musicians out of California and avant-garde composer John Cage. Headed by Joseph Byrd, an experimental composer/conductor/arranger, United States of America employed a battery of electric instruments, including even an electronically adapted violin; also gadgets that became part of the synthesizer syndrome like ring modulators, tape reverb units, and distortion amplifiers. Another Joseph Byrd group, the Field Hippies, produced *The American Metaphysical Circus,* also on Columbia Records.

But almost a year before the United States of America's debut album, that innovative rock group The Byrds (no relation to Joseph) used a Theremin, oscillator, and other electronic gadgets in "C.T.A.-102" (*Younger Than Yesterday*) in an effort to suggest spaceflight. Electronics also figured in "Space Odyssey" in *The Notorious Byrd Brothers,* released in the same month as the United States of America album. However, it is the Beatles and *Sgt. Pepper* that are most frequently credited with initiating Electronic Rock. Effects used in "A Day in the Life" are cited as an esthetic rather than an experimental use of electronics. *Sgt. Pepper,* released in June 1967, was followed that year by *Magical Mystery Tour,* in which "Flying," "Blue Jay Way," and "I Am the Walrus" all manipulated vocal fragments, reversed tape passages, and used electronic distortion. Another group that early experimented with electronic effects was Lothar & the Hand People, a Connecticut Rock combo. Although its debut album appeared in 1968, it was known around New York City in the fall of 1966. However, it took time to discover that Lothar was the nickname not of John Emelin, the group's leader, but of the Theremin he played by waving his hands over an electronic box out of which jutted an upright pole.

The year 1967 saw the release of the Cyrkle's *Neon* album, the debut album of Velvet Underground & Nico, and Van Dyke Parks's *Song Cycle*—all involving forays into electronic sounds. Soon the Mothers of Invention, piloted by Frank Zappa (b. 1940), produced *We're Only in It for the Money* and *Lumpy Gravy.* Other examples of Electronic Rock are to be found in *Plugged-in Pop* by the Copper-Plated Integrated Circuit; *Electric Love* and *Moog Groove* by Electronic Concept Orchestra; *The Jimi Hendrix Experience,* especially "Third Stone from the Sun"; *Tubular Bells,* with Mike Oldfield; *Ummagumma* by Pink Floyd ("Do ya dig it, Edgar Varèse?"); *Moog España* arranged and conducted by Sid Bass; *Ceremony* by Spooky Tooth/Pierre Henry; *Country Moog Switched-On Nashville* by Gilbert Trythall; *The Six Wives of Henry VIII* and *Voyage to the Center of the Earth* by keyboardist Rick Wakeman.

See also Moog; synthesizer; Theremin; Edgard Varèse.

Electro-Pop   A style and sound of the 1980s in which human performers are reduced to a minimum and the music is produced by synthesizers, computers, and microchip technology. The development has gained momentum in England and Europe with such British "bands" as Soft Cell, Dépêche Mode, Human League, Pete Shelley, Orchestral Manoeuvres in the Dark, and others. Soft Cell consists of Marc Almond, a singer, and David Ball, an electronics expert. Dépêche Mode is just a vocalist plus a group of synthesizers. Soft Cell's first album, *Non-Stop Erotic Cabaret,* and Dépêche Mode's *Speak & Spell* have both been released in this country, as have *Pace,* an album by the Human League, which went to No. 1 in Great Britain, and *Architecture and Morality* by the Orchestral Manoeuvres in the Dark. Although these albums have become favorites on American dance floors because of their rhythmic quality, their appeal has yet to manifest itself on the charts. Critics contend that the Electro-Pop "bands" fail to achieve the drive of the first-rate drummer and that their disks have an inescapable synthetic sound. (By summer 1982 Soft Cell's "Tainted Love" was a Top Ten single.)

See also Electronic Rock.

Edward Kennedy Ellington (1899–1974)   Acquiring the cognomen "Duke" in his youth, apparently because of his sartorial elegance and regal manner, he studied art and music but gravitated to the latter field, despite an offer of a scholarship to Pratt Institute. Imitating the Ragtime and Stride pianists he heard around Washington, D. C., his birthplace, he began booking bands. Returning to New York City at Fats Waller's urging, after an unsuccessful visit, he formed the Washingtonians and got his first important engagement at the Hollywood, later known as the Kentucky Club. In December 1929, he began a five-year stand that brought him renown at the Cotton Club in Harlem, scoring his first Pop hit with "Mood Indigo" in 1931. Other Pop hits followed: "Solitude" (1933), "Sophisticated Lady" (1933), "In a Sentimental Mood" (1935). In the Jazz field, his reputation grew partly because of the caliber of his sidemen but also because of his unique talents as an orchestrator. With the addition of Billy Strayhorn as arranger/pianist/co-composer in 1939, the Ellington band climbed to new heights in the recording field.

From 1943 to 1950 Ellington played a series of annual concerts at Carnegie Hall at which he introduced the longer works that established his reputation as a serious composer: *Black, Brown, and Beige; Deep South Suite; Liberian Suite; New World A-Comin'*, and others. In 1959 he wrote his first film score for *Anatomy of a Murder*. With fewer changes in personnel than most bands, the Ellington band remained a working/touring/recording organization for almost 50 years. At his death in 1974, the band was taken over by his son, Mercer Kennedy Ellington, who co-authored an award-winning book with Jazz critic Stanley Dance about his father.

"Empress of the Blues"   The cognomen of Bessie Smith (1894–1937), regarded by many as the greatest of all the Blues singers and, in impresario/recording executive John Hammond's words, "the greatest artist American Jazz ever produced." Cutting her first record in 1923, she reportedly sold over 2 million disks in her first year.
See also Bessie Smith.

"the end"   Unsurpassed or unsurpassable. Can be said of a performer or a performance.

enharmonic   A flatted or a sharped note may be viewed in two ways, depending on the scale or chord to which one relates it. A♭ may be seen as G♯; F♯ as G♭, etc. On the piano, F♯ and G♭ are the same black key. The difference is a matter of notation. But on other instruments—strings, reeds, and brasses—there may be a slight difference in pitch.

Environmental Studio   The Air Montserrat Studios in the British West Indies, opened by ex–Beatles producer George Martin.

equalizer (equalization)   A device for increasing or decreasing the highs and lows of a note. As a process, to modify the tonal response by reducing or increasing the highs and/or lows.

Ethnic or Traditional Recording, Best (NARAS Grammy Awards)

1970   T-Bone Walker: "Good Feelin;"
1971   Muddy Waters: *They Call Me Muddy Waters*
1972   Muddy Waters: *The London Muddy Waters Session*
1973   Doc Watson: *Then and Now*
1974   Doc & Merle Watson: *Two Days in November*
1975   Muddy Waters: *The Muddy Waters Woodstock Album*
1976   John Hartford: *Mark Twang*
1977   Muddy Waters: *Hard Again*

1978   Muddy Waters: *I'm Ready*
1979   Muddy Waters: *Muddy 'Mississipi' Waters Live*
1980   Dr. Isaiah Ross, Maxwell Street Jimmy, Big Joe Williams, Son House, Reverend Robert Wilkins, Little Brother Montgomery, Sunnyland Slim: *Rare Blues*
1981   B. B. King: *There Must Be a Better World Somewhere*

See also National Academy of Recording Arts and Sciences (NARAS).

executive producer   A title or function in the motion picture and TV worlds, now frequently seen on record albums. The executive producer exercises overall control and veto power, but the actual supervision of work in the studio is in the hands of the producer.

Experimental Rock   An omnibus term, rather than a style or category, comprehending Aleatory Rock, Avant-garde Rock, Classical Rock, and Electronic Rock.

The Exploding Plastic Inevitable   Andy Warhol's mixed-media, traveling circus of 1966–1967. The experimental group known as the Velvet Underground appeared in it.

extended composition
    See Classical Rock.

F

FMQB Album Report   An album-oriented tipsheet, sister publication of the *Friday Morning Quarterback,* tipsheet on record singles issued by Kal Rudman of Philadelphia.

"The Fab Four"   Refers to the Beatles.

fade   The end of a recording in which a phrase is repeated over and over as the volume is reduced until it finally fades away. The fade is accomplished by an engineer slowly turning down the input from the microphones.

fake   To play by ear.

Fake Book   Although faking is done without music, the Fake Book is a collection of leadsheets of hundreds of standards, printed generally without the permission of the copyright owners. The printers and sellers of such books are subject to prosecution.

falsetto   A high-pitched voice; more specifically, a male voice simulating a female sound. The quartet known as The Ink Spots, popular during the 1930s and 1940s, featured a high tenor falsetto lead. Among Rock groups, the Orioles and the Four Seasons both include falsetto lead singers, and all three of the Bee Gees sing and harmonize in falsetto.

Fame Studio   Founded in 1961 at Muscle Shoals, Ala., by Rick Hall, Fame's full-time session musicians included legendary guitarist Duane Allman (1946–1971), later of the Allman Brothers band. Among the artists who recorded at the studio, there were Aretha Franklin (b. 1942), Wilson Pickett (b. 1941), Etta James (b. circa 1930), Joe Tex (b. circa 1940), Otis Rush (b. 1934), and Irma Thomas (b. 1941). Toward the end of the sixties, various Rock performers did sessions at Fame—among others, Boz Scaggs (b. 1944) and Cher (b. 1946). From 1962 to 1967, Atlantic Records served as distributor for Fame; thereafter, Capitol Records assumed the role.

The Family Dog   Not a Rock group but four people who adopted the name for the purpose of presenting Rock dances in San Francisco. For their first presentation, on October 16, 1965, they rented the Longshore Hall near Fisherman's Wharf and employed as emcee Russ Syracuse, the disk jockey in charge of the surrealistic *All Night Flyer* program on KYA. Titling the evening "A Tribute to Dr. Strange," they featured The Great Society, The Charlatans, and The Jefferson Airplane. Later they ran dances at the Avalon Ballroom. Chet Helm headed the group.

Famous Door   A famous New York City Jazz club on 52nd St., (Swing Street, or just The Street, as it was known among Jazz musicians and fans) in its heyday. Initially a cooperative venture, the Door was opened by a group of musicians, each of whom contributed a sum of money and each of whom signed a door that was kept near the bar—that's why it was called the Famous Door. As time passed, many celebrities signed the door. Like most of the music clubs on The Street, it changed ownership and locations a number of times. Located like all the clubs in what were originally step-down or street-level basements of five-story brownstones, the Door was too small to accommodate a big band. But in return for an air-conditioning unit, the two men who owned the club in the summer of 1938 booked the Count Basie Band. It

was the Count's (b. 1904) first date at a midtown Manhattan club and marked his debut over coast-to-coast radio, a development that brought him national renown. It was at the Door, too, that trumpeter Louis Prima (1911–1978) made his New York debut and the great Billie Holiday (1915–1959) made her Street debut.
See also 52nd St.

"far-out"   In the Swing era, "hot" was the term of critical approval, while "cool" was the accolade for excellence among the bopsters. In the mid-fifties, when you had to be "hip," not "hep," the expression for something outstanding was "far-out."

Fast Western   An early designation of the piano style that became known as Boogie-Woogie.

"Fatha"   Nickname of Jazz pianist Earl "Fatha" Hines (b. 1903), noted for his development of a one-finger melody style.

"Father of Bluegrass Music"   Bill Monroe, born in 1911 in Rosine, Kentucky, and founder of the famous Blue Grass Boys.
See also Bill Monroe.

"Father of the Blues"   *See* William Christopher Handy.

"Father of Boogie-Woogie"   *See* Jimmy Yancey.

"Father of British Blues"   John Mayall (1934–   ), born in Manchester, England, and founder of the Bluesbreakers.

"Father of the British Blues Revival"   Alexis Korner.
See Blues, British.

"Father of Country music"   *See* Jimmie Rodgers.

"Father of Folk Rock"   *See* Bob Dylan. Consider also the Byrds.

"Father of Gospel music"   *See* Thomas A. Dorsey.

"Father of Rhythm & Blues"   *See* Louis Jordan.

"Father of Rock 'n' Roll"   By virtue of his influence on Elvis Presley (1935–1977), Arthur "Big Boy" Crudup (1905–1974) of Mississippi is regarded as the Father of Rock 'n' Roll, a title conferred upon him in an RCA Victor compilation of his recordings. Presley's first disk release on Sun Records in 1954 was a remake of Crudup's song "That's All Right, Mama," recorded several years earlier by the pioneer Rhythm & Blues artist. Presley acknowledged his indebtedness on a number of occasions. In one interview, he said that in an early session he had cut a Western song "and it sounded terrible. But the second idea Sam Phillips (owner of Sun) had, was the one that jelled.

"'You want to make some Blues?' he suggested over the phone, knowing I'd always been a sucker for that kind of jive. He mentioned Big Boy Crudup's name and maybe others, too. All I know is, I hung up and ran 15 blocks to Mr. Phillips's office before he'd gotten off the line —or so he tells me. We talked about the Crudup records I knew—"Cool Disposition," "Rock Me, Mama," "Hey, Mama" "Everyone's All Right," and others, but settled for "That's All Right," one of my top favorites."

In the same interview, Presley also said: "I'd play guitar along with the radio or phonograph, and taught myself the chord positions. We were a religious family, going around together to sing at camp meetings and revivals, and I'd take my guitar with us when I could. I also dug the real low-down Mississippi singers, mostly Big Bill Broonzy and Big Boy Crudup, although they would scold me at home for listening to them. 'Sinful music,' the townsfolk of Memphis said it was. Which never bothered me, I guess." [*Hit Parade* (Britain), January 1957]

After singing with several Gospel quartets, Crudup (pronounced "Crood-up") made his first recordings for Bluebird in Chicago in 1941–1942 and cut additional sides for the label in Chicago in 1944–1945. From 1945 until 1951, he recorded for the Victor label and also performed on occasion on the *King Biscuit Time* program over KFFA Radio in Helena, Ark. During 1952–1954, he made records in Atlanta and in Jackson, Miss., cutting for Victor and Groove in the former city, and for Trumpet/Checker, Champion, and Ace in the latter. After Presley's rise, he recorded for the Fire label in Nashville in 1959; for Delmark in Chicago in 1967; and for Liberty in London in 1970.

He made appearances at various festivals: University of Chicago R & B Festival in 1967; Central Park Music Festival in New York City in 1967; Philadelphia Folk Festival at Schweksville, Pa., in 1967; Ann Arbor Blues Festival in Ann Arbor, Mich., in 1969; Festival of American Folk Life in Washington, D.C., in 1970; Washington Blues Festival at Howard University in Washington, D.C., in 1970; and Newport Jazz Festival at Philharmonic Hall in NYC in 1973.

Despite Crudup's influence and recording activity, he never derived enough income from music to take him away from his Mississippi farm and sawmill, to which he returned after recording sessions and live appearances. In 1959 Presley reportedly put up the money for the recording of an LP that was cut by Fireball Records of Nashville and released by Fire Records. But it was the publishing firm owned jointly by Presley and his publishers, Hill & Range Songs, that was charged in 1970 by the American Guild of Authors and Composers with not paying royalties due Crudup on songs of his acquired by them. Legal action was also instituted against Crudup's first manager, Lester Melrose, who arranged the Chicago Bluebird sessions, for nonpayment of royalties

Before either claim was settled, Crudup died. "I was born poor," he said shortly before his death, "I lived poor and I'm going to die poor." And so he did.

"You hear Elvis Presley," Big Bill Broonzy said shortly before he died, "you hearin' Big Boy Crudup." Crudup's influence extended beyond Presley. Creedence Clearwater Revival recorded his Blues "My Baby Left Me," as did Elvis. Other contemporary rockers who have recorded Crudup's songs include Elton John (b. 1947), Rod Stewart (b. 1945), Johnny Winter (b. 1944), Paul Butterfield (b. 1942), Buffy Sainte-Marie (b. 1941), Tina Turner, (b. 1938), Canned Heat, and B. B. King (b. 1925), who scored a hit with Crudup's "Rock Me, Mama."

"Father of Soul"   *See* Ray Charles.

Fats Domino (1928–   )   A seminal figure in the transformation of R & B into Rock 'n' Roll, Fats began making the charts in the early 1950s, first in R & B and then in Pop as well as R & B, as Pat Boone (b. 1934) and other Teenage Rock 'n' Rollers tried to rip off his hits ("Ain't It a Shame," et al.). Although he was born and grew up in New Orleans, and his constant collaborator/conductor/co-writer was ex-Ellington trumpeter and bandleader Dave Bartholomew, the basis of his style was not Jazz but Boogie-Woogie, as was also true of Louis Jordan. In fact, Jordan's Jump Blues found its vocal expression in Fats, who played a jaunty eight-to-the-bar piano style, sang in a high-pitched nasal tenor with a bubbling Cajun accent, and projected Jordan's good-humored ebullience. "Blueberry Hill," a revival of a C & W standard, was his biggest hit, going to No. 1 on R & B charts and No. 4 in Pop in 1956. In 20 years, he is said to have sold over 65 million disks and to have earned more Gold Records than any artist of the fifties and sixties, except Elvis and the Beatles.

See also cover records; Louis Jordan.

"fay"   Colloquialism for homosexual. Did it come from Pha Terrell, Andy Kirk's vocalist, who made a hit of "Until the Real Thing Comes Along" singing in a high-pitched falsetto?

feedback   A shrill, high-pitched sound, produced when a microphone (input mechanism) is placed so close to a speaker (output mechanism) that the electric signal loops back and forth, resulting in a high, ear-shattering squeal. Originally a sound to be avoided, it was used as a "musical" effect by Rock performers like the Yardbirds ("I'm a Man"), Mothers of Invention, Blues Magoos, Rolling Stones ("I Can't Get No Satisfaction"), Jimi Hendrix, and Jefferson Airplane. When Decca received the first album of The Who (*My Generation*), it almost refused to press records on the ground that it had been sent a defective master. For some time, it has been possible to produce feedback electronically.

See also fuzztone; reverb; wah-wah pedal.

Fender bass   Leo Fender invented the solid-body electric guitar in 1948. The Fender bass looks like another electric guitar, but it is tuned like a string bass and produces the deep, low, throbbing notes of a bass. It is played with a plectrum instead of being plucked. CBS now owns the Fender company, which manufactures the instrument.

Fender Rhodes   An electric piano, widely used on Rock records and by Rock groups.

festivals   Festivals were a way of life for the Rock generation in the 1960s, spawned by the granddaddy of the form, the Newport Jazz Festival, and an expression of the alternate culture espoused by the generation of which the civil rights and antiwar movements, the Freedom Riders and the Freedom Singers, the seizure and occupation of college buildings, Bob Dylan and the Beatles, were integral parts. Until the catastrophic Altamont Festival of 1969, such occasions were heightened expressions of a sense of community, of the hippie espousal of love and flowers to mold a world of peace. Like "be-ins" in the prevalence of drugs and the presence of feelings of collective frolic, they were not meant to involve confrontations or to be "events."

The archetype was the festival, mostly of Folk music and Folk-oriented Rock, held at Big Sur on the Pacific coast in the early sixties. Most notable was the sensationally successful Monterey Pop Festival of 1967. The climax came with three festivals in 1969, one in Great Britain at the Isle of Wight, and two in the U.S.A. The Woodstock Festival in August '69 overwhelmed and challenged the world with its show of peacefulness, love, and good vibes under the most trying conditions. The Altamont Festival at the year's end upset the Rock world with ugliness and violence, including a murder. There were many other Rock festivals, some held in baseball stadiums, on raceways, in volcanoes, on farmland pastures, in parks, and on fairgrounds, some lasting a day, others for a long weekend. In retrospect, Monterey, Isle of Wight, Woodstock, and Altamont seem to be a summation of one of the striking phenomena of the explosive sixties.

See also Altamont; Big Sur Festival; Isle of Wight Festival; Monterey Pop Festival; Newport Folk Festival; *Woodstock Nation*.

festival seating   First come, first served. Rock promoters recognize the danger in this method of handling seating. Riots have resulted in the rush for seats. The most flagrant and tragic instance of what can happen were the 11 deaths in 1978 at a Who concert in Cincinnati.

52nd St.   The legendary Manhattan street of the thirties, forties, and fifties, between 5th and 6th avenues, "52nd St." also included the block to the west of 6th Avenue. Crowded into small cellar or street-level clubs—originally, the so-called English basements of the five-story brownstone townhouses—musical activities on The Street (as the area was known to Jazz musicians and fans) made it the Mecca of Jazz people all over the world between 1935 and 1955. The Onyx, an upstairs speakeasy for musicians during Prohibition, became the first club on the street after Repeal. In time, there were the Famous Door, Tony's, Jimmy Ryan's, the Yacht Club, Hickory House, Kelly's Stable, Downbeat, Spotlite, Samoa, Three Deuces, and others. A list of the performers who played these "upholstered sewers" would include all the best-known jazzmen of the day: pianist Art Tatum, tenor saxist Coleman Hawkins, trumpeter Roy Eldridge, alto saxist Charlie Parker, trumpeter Dizzy Gillespie, tenor saxist Lester Young, pianist Erroll Garner, pianist/comic Fats Waller, xylophonist Red Norvo, pianist Johnny Guarnieri, the bands of Count Basie and Charlie Barnet, and vocalist Mildred Bailey, Sarah Vaughan, Lee Wiley, Mabel Mercer, and Billie Holiday, among others. The Street embodied changes in Jazz styles from Dixieland and Swing to Bop and Cool Jazz, and after World War II it was split into warring factions: adherents of Bop ("the modern malice," in Louis Armstrong's phrase) versus supporters of Dixieland ("the moldy figs"). The demise of The Street came as G strings (strippers) increasingly replaced G chords. In 1962 *The New York Times* headlined one of its real estate sections: "Skyscrapers Overwhelm 52nd St."

In 1977, after an extended campaign by this writer and others, 52nd St. was given historical status by the City as Swing Street, and the sidewalks between 5th and 6th Avenues became a Jazzwalk into which the names of its great performers were to be imbedded. As of this writing, the names of 12 Jazz performers have been memorialized on medallions imbedded in the pavement in front of the CBS Building.

See also The Jazzwalk.

The Fillmore   A San Francisco ballroom at which promoter Bill Graham ran Rock concerts, it became nationally known during the psychedelic era when it pioneered light shows by the Haight-Ashbury acid groups. It was an old hall at the corner of Geary and Fillmore streets, on the edge of the black ghetto known as "the Fillmore" and just a short walk from the low-rental, free-form hippie area, Haight-Ashbury. Quite a number of albums have been recorded live at the ballroom. After a time, Graham launched a Fillmore East in a defunct Loew's Theatre on 2nd Avenue in lower Manhattan. In 1968 he took over the Carousel on San Francisco's Market Street and renamed it Fillmore West.

films   *See* Rock films.

"finger popper"   A player with outstanding technique or a tune that requires finger popping. By extension, someone who not only snaps his fingers excitedly but is overcome by the music. Hank Ballard, leader of the Midnighters and author of "The Twist," followed it with a hit tune titled "Finger-Poppin' Time."

"The First Tycoon of Teen"   What Phil Spector (b. 1940) was called in a famous article by Tom Wolfe because he had made over $1 million producing records by the age of 21.
   See also Wall-of-Sound.

"flag waver"   Refers to a song, an instrumental, or even a single chorus of a tune that builds to such a climactic pitch it brings an audience to its feet.

flatted fifth   The Blues used a scale that contained a flatted third and seventh. Bop made extensive use of the flatted fifth, technically a sharped fourth or eleventh. During the controversy that developed between Dixieland and Bop performers, splitting Jazz into warring camps, guitarist Eddie Condon (1905–1973), a leading exponent of the two-beat Dixieland style, said: "We don't flat our fifths; we drink them."

flip one's lid   To react with tremendous enthusiasm and excitement.

flip side   Either side of a record can be the flip side. But it generally refers to the so-called "B" side rather than the "A" side of a disk.
   See also "A" side.

Flower Children   They were the proponents of an idea that caught fire for a brief moment in the years 1967–1968. The idea was that love would change the world, and flowers were the symbols of that conviction. Scott McKenzie's (b. 1944) song "San Francisco (Wear Some Flowers in Your Hair)" sounded the theme. Donovan (b. 1946), from Glasgow, Scotland, echoed the idea in his album *Gift from a Flower to a Garden,* Part 1: *Wear Your Love Like Heaven,* and appeared at a Lincoln Center concert on a stage filled to overflowing with flowers. At the Monterey Pop Festival in 1967, it was reported that even the police succumbed to the feeling and wore flowers in their helmets. But like many visionary concepts, Flower Power died aborning.

See also "be-in"; The Love Generation; "love-in."

fluff   A mistake. As a nonmusical verb, "to fluff" is to be disregarded, avoided, or brushed off.

See also "clinker"; "goof off."

folio   An anthology of songs.

Folk Music   Folk music, in the traditional sense, consists of songs written by that prolific author/composer—anonymous, i.e., the folk. It is a music that is transmitted orally for long periods of time before it is written down or recorded. The Puritan settlers brought with them a copious collection of British and Scottish ballads as well as religious songs. Through several centuries, black people created a rich musical literature of Spirituals, Blues, work songs, hollers, prison songs, and love ballads. Adapting the ballads they brought from Great Britain, Appalachian mountain people sang of their working and emotional experiences just as Westerners developed a tuneful cowboy folklore. Add to these the songs that came out of the labor movement, the songs of social protest, and the marching songs that came out of various wars.

In recent years, starting with The Weavers in the early fifties and their record of Leadbelly's "Good Night Irene" (No. 1 in 1950) as well as their popularization of Appalachian ballads and songs by Woody Guthrie, there have been several waves of folk song revivals. Toward the end of the fifties, The Kingston Trio, adapting a Civil War ballad, "Tom Dooley" (No. 1 in 1958), brought a new stream of folk ballads into the Pop mainstream.

In the R & B era and the sixties, black singers almost invariably started by singing religious and gospel music in church. White groups, especially those on the West Coast, invariably started by singing folk songs before they moved into various styles of Rock.

See also Acid Rock; Almanac Singers; Arhoolies; Francis Child; Bob Dylan; Folk Rock; The Kingston Trio; Huddie Ledbetter; Mariposa Folk Festival; Newport Folk Festival; The Weavers; Woody Guthrie.

Folk Performance, Best (NARAS Grammy Awards)

1959 The Kingston Trio: *The Kingston Trio at Large*
1960 Harry Belafonte: "Swing Dat Hammer"
1961 Belafonte Folk Singers: *Belafonte Folk Singers at Home and Abroad*
1962 Peter, Paul & Mary: "If I Had a Hammer"
1963 Peter, Paul & Mary: "Blowin' in the Wind"
1964 Gale Garnett: "We'll Sing in the Sunshine"
1965 Harry Belafonte/Miriam Makeba: *An Evening with Belafonte/Makeba*
1966 Cortelia Clark: *Blues in the Street*
1967 John Hartford: "Gentle on My Mind"
1968 Judy Collins: "Both Sides Now"
1969 Joni Mitchell: *Clouds*

See also National Academy of Recording Arts and Sciences (NARAS).

Folk Rock   Unlike other Rock styles, Folk Rock has a birthday. It is the summer of 1965, when to the dismay and anger of Folk fans, Bob Dylan (b. 1941) added the sound of the electric guitar (in place of the acoustic instrument) and the big beat to his performance. At the Newport Folk Festival where this occurred, Dylan was booed offstage. In actuality, Dylan had already made and released a Folk Rock record: "Subterranean Homesick Blues" was on the charts as of May 1965. It was the first of Dylan's disks to make the Pop charts. The awareness of Dylan's shift, however, did not come until his summer appearances, and that's when Folk purists, including Joan Baez, condemned his embrace of Rock.

The shift from Folk to Folk Rock had also preceded Dylan's Newport appearance with the Byrds' recording of Dylan's "Mr. Tambourine Man," which made No. 1 in June 1965 and became the first of the Folk Rock hits. The impact of the stylistic change made by two influential forces like Dylan and the Byrds moved other groups in Folk Rock direction. Among the first "converts" were The Mamas and The Papas and the Lovin' Spoonful, as well as the Buffalo Springfield and the Turtles of Los Angeles. To name all the groups and artists that delivered a message with a beat—a quick definition of Folk Rock— would be difficult. A partial list would include the Youngbloods, Joy of Cooking, James Taylor (b. 1948), Hot Tuna, T. Rex, Loggins & Messina, New Seekers, Simon & Garfunkel, Neil Young and Crazy Horse. Most or all of these viewed songs as a vehicle for examining the world and voicing their outlook. In their lyrics, they aimed for the authenticity of experience, the immediacy of feeling, and the probing commentary of ethnic song. Their music was a gentle or soft type of Rock.

See also The Byrds; Bob Dylan.

Harry Fox   *See* Harry Fox Agency.

Fox-Trot   Still danced today by older-generation folks, the Fox-Trot originated in the days before World War I, when apparently America went dance-mad. According to reports, from 1912 to 1914 as many as 100 new dances found their way in and out of fashionable ballrooms. Many of these dances had animals in their names: e.g., the Grizzly Bear, Bunny Hug, Monkey Glide, and Turkey-Trot. Key entertainers of the era were Vernon and Irene Castle, ballroom dancers whose popularity peaked with their appearance in a Broadway show, *The Sunshine Girl* (1913), in which they danced the Turkey-Trot and took New York by storm. By the following year, they had opened Castle House, a classy dance instruction studio, in which, responding to pressures from genteel society, the Castles rejected the Turkey-Trot and other dances as "ugly, ungraceful, and out of fashion." Not too long after, they introduced the Fox-Trot, for whose invention they are sometimes credited. But Irene Castle credited the famous black bandleader James Reese Europe (1881–1919) with bringing the dance to their attention, and perhaps devising it. Slower and simpler than the Castle Walk and fast one-steps like the animal dances, the Fox-Trot has outlasted all the dances of the era. These days, bands playing for weddings, confirmations, barmitzvahs, engagement parties, and related social affairs play Rock and Disco for the younger generation and Fox-Trots and Waltzes for the older one.

See also The Hustle; The Twist.

Aretha Franklin (1942–   )   In her peak period (1967–1969), she became known as "Lady Soul," an appropriate cognomen for an artist whose singing was the epitome of unbridled emotion. There were raucous Blues shouters before her like Big Mama Thornton (b. 1926) and awesome Gospel voices like Mahalia Jackson (1911–1972). She grew up, in fact, singing Gospel as a protégé of Mahalia Jackson, Clara Ward (1924–1973), and James Cleveland (b. 1932), the last of whom taught her the Gospel piano style she played on some of her great recordings. The major influence during her early years was Clara Ward, two of whose company-singers mothered her when her own mother deserted the family. When she cut her first sides "live" in the New Bethel Baptist Church in Detroit as a 14-year-old, she included three Clara Ward favorites, modeling her delivery on Clara's moaning style. Singing with Columbia Records in 1960, she spent six years trying unsuccessfully to establish herself in a groove that was part Jazz, part Pop, and part Gospel. Her affiliation in 1966 with Atlantic Records and producer Jerry Wexler led to her putting on records an intensity of impassioned feeling seldom heard until then. She covered the gamut of a woman's search for love, frustration at its elusiveness, joy at its possible rebirth, ecstasy at its possession—pouring her feelings with a Gospel-like fervor onto wax and opening the door for emotional extremists and screamers like Janis Joplin (1943–1970).

"I Never Loved a Man," her first Atlantic disk, recorded in Muscle Shoals, Ala., became No. 1 on R & B charts (No. 9 on Pop) in 1967 and was immediately followed by Otis Redding's extraordinary ballad "Respect" (No. 1 on Pop as well as R & B). She scored Gold Records also on "Baby, I Love You," "Chain of Fools," "Since You've Been Gone," "Think," "I Say a Little Prayer," and "See-Saw," also with the albums *Lady Soul, Aretha Now, Aretha Live at Fillmore West,* and, in collaboration with James Cleveland, *Amazing Grace* (1972). In addition to Grammy Awards, she was named Top Female Vocalist of 1967 in a *Billboard* poll and Top Female Vocalist of 1971 in a *Record World* poll.

"freak"   A user of "acid" (LSD). After a time, the term came to mean any liberated individual associated with the youth subculture or counterculture, and "doing his own thing." The "freak" found meaning by rebelling against conventional life and society, by maintaining a position of defiance and opposition to what he regarded as a plastic world. "Eco-freaks" were concerned with preserving and purifying the natural environment.

See also alternative life-style.

Freak Out   The title of the first album by Frank Zappa and the Mothers of Invention (1966), *Freak Out* referred to a disorientation of the senses associated with the consumption of LSD but produced through music or multimedia. "Withough using the bad stuff," Zappa explained, "we get the same effect as from taking acid [LSD]." The effect was to be achieved through the use of echo, feedback, fuzztone, tape reverb, and anything else that amplified and distorted the original musical impulse. For live audiences, light shows were employed for added effect. Among other groups that experimented with the mode, there were the Byrds, Doors, Grateful Dead, and Jefferson Airplane as well as the Beatles. "Freak" was the word for someone who took LSD.

See also echo; feedback; fuzztone; light show; tape reverb.

Freak Rock   Refers to the oddball costumes, outrageous props, and crazy makeup used by some rock groups in their personal appearances.

See also Glitter Rock; Shock Rock; Theater Rock.

The Freddie   A variation of the Twist introduced in 1965 on American TV by Manchester-born Freddie & the Dreamers. The dance enjoyed a short-lived vogue, mainly among teenyboppers.

See also The Twist.

Alan Freed (1921–1965)   He was not the first white disk jockey to program R & B records and interest white youngsters in the black sound. But he quickly attracted nationwide attention, introduced a raucous style into radio announcing, named the new teenage music ''Rock 'n' Roll,'' became the center of juvenile-delinquency controversies over Rock, and was the major casualty of the payola probes of 1959–1960, dying at 43 on the day that Lyndon B. Johnson was inaugurated as president. Beginning his career as a classical disk jockey in New Castle, Pa.—he was born in Johnstown, Pa., and grew up in Salem, Ohio—he launched *The Moon Dog House Rock 'n' Roll Party* in June 1952 on indie station WJW of Cleveland. By 1954 he was shaking up New York City broadcast circles with his big-beat show on WINS, announcing records with a hoarse, rapid-fire delivery, pounding a phonebook on the afterbeat, and ringing a cowbell as he brought R & B into the mainstream. Even before the advent of Presley, he ran Rock 'n' Roll dances, featuring black artists, that were riotous sellouts. His '56 Easter Week show at the Brooklyn Paramount was likened by *Variety* to ''having an aisle seat for the San Francisco earthquake.'' He appeared in three films: *Don't Knock the Rock* (1956), *Mister Rock 'n' Roll* (1957), and *Go, Johnny, Go* (1959). In 1958 he left WINS when the station would not support him in his fight against a trumped-up charge of inciting to riot after a Boston concert. In November 1959 he was dropped by WABC when he refused ''on principle'' to sign an affidavit averring he had never received funds or gifts to play records. Two days later, WNEW–TV canceled his video disk show. On May 20, 1960, he was indicted together with six others for receiving $30,650 from six record companies; in 1962 he received a suspended six-month sentence and a $300 fine. Shortly before his death, he was indicted for evading $47,920 in income taxes, a charge that never came to trial. In the eyes of music-business cognoscenti, he took the fall for an industry-wide problem, becoming the target because of his antagonism toward the major record companies, his sponsorship of black artists, and his limited advertising billings as compared with Dick Clark, whom WABC stood by.

See also Dick Clark; ''payola.''

Freedom Singers   The name of several different vocal groups. The original Freedom Singers consisted of four field secretaries associated with the Student Non-Violent Coordinating Committee. Although they were concerned with raising funds for SNCC, they used song also as a means of uniting blacks in the integration struggle. Perhaps their most memorable appearance occurred at the Newport Folk Festival in 1963, when Bob Dylan and his "Blowin' in the Wind" proved the high point of the week's concerts. The Freedom Singers were closely associated with "We Shall Overcome," the "official" theme of the civil rights movement of the 1960s, originally a religious folk song converted into a Baptist hymn by the Rev. C. H. Tindley in 1901, which was then transformed into the integration anthem by a quartet of songwriters, including Pete Seeger. (Dr. Tindley was the founder of Tindley Methodist Church in Philadelphia, where Bessie Smith (1894–1937) was buried.)

Free Jazz   A style developed in the 1960s by performers like saxists John Coltrane (1926–1967), Archie Shepp (b. 1937), and Ornette Coleman (b. 1930); pianist Cecil Taylor (b. 1933); trumpeter Don Cherry (b. 1936); and others. The Five Spot in Greenwich Village is said to have launched the movement with a booking of Ornette Coleman around 1960, at which time Coleman recorded an album titled *Free Jazz* with a double quartet. The Jazz Gallery in the Village was also hospitable to the movement, which most listeners found too difficult to accept because of the emphasis on random expression of feeling—a freedom which violated traditional structures, tonalities, forms, chord sequences, modes of improvisation, rhythms, and even the tempered scale. To many, "the new thing," as it was called, was an incomprehensible mishmash of grunts, groans, cries, and shouts—total disorder. Nonetheless, Free Jazz prospered so that there were concerts of it in Berlin in 1965 and in London in 1966. Listen to John Coltrane's "India" in *Impressions,* cut in 1961, or Cecil Taylor's "Unit Structure/As of Now/Section."

"Frogman"   Clarence Henry (b. 1937) of Louisiana, influenced by Fats Domino (b. 1928) and "Professor Longhair" (1918–1980), was known as "Frogman" because of his use of trick vocal effects.
    See also Fats Domino; "Professor Longhair."

front line   The melody-playing instruments in a Jazz or Rock combo. The rhythm instruments—piano, bass, drums, etc.—generally, though not always, are seated or standing behind.

fugal   Suggestive of the fugue, in which a number of instruments or voices enter a composition successively, not simultaneously, in imitation of each other.

"funk(y)"   In Negro slang, "funk" is an odor produced during sexual excitement. The adjective, "funky," is used with reference to Blues, Jazz, or Rock of a sensual character. In the 1960s James Brown was a pioneer of soulful funk. George Clinton, now regarded as the godfather of funk, has said: "It deals with sexual urges and taboo rhythms. Funk is raw. It's straight from the jungle and the streets." Clinton is main composer, producer, and lead singer of Parliament-Funkadelic, the band recording under different names for different labels: Parliament (Casablanca Records) and Funkadelic (Warner Brothers Records). Its brand of funk involves a multiplicity of rhythms, analogous to the African use of layers of rhythms. In the 1950s, pianist Horace Silver (b. 1928) and drummer Art Blakey (b. 1919) regarded "funky" as a fusion of hard Bop with Blues and Gospel. In the late seventies, Rock pianist Leon Russell (b. 1941) led a southwestern funk movement, a laid-back funk emanating from the Texas-Oklahoma area that included Doug Sahm (b. 1943), Kinky Friedman (b. 1944), and Steve Miller (b. circa 1945). Listen also to "Funky Street" by Arthur Conley (b. circa 1946), *Injoy* by the Bar-Kays, the punk funk of Rick James on *Fire It Up,* and the soulful funk of Kool and the Gang (*Celebration*) and Rufus, with Chaka Khan as a lead singer (*Camouflage*).

Fusion Rock   An umbrella term that refers to the experimentation of the 1970s when Jazz groups tried to Rock and Rock groups played with Jazz. Others attempted to mix Rock and Latin rhythms.
   See also Jazz Rock; Latin Rock.

fuzzbox   Somebody said, "It makes a guitar sound as though it were being played through the back end of an elephant." This device for altering the texture of the guitar sound presumably made its debut on the Rolling Stones' "Satisfaction," and it has since been widely used by Rock groups. Jimi Hendrix (1942–1970) made extensive use of the sound. In the late fifties, Link Wray (b. 1930) produced the blurred, rasping, dirty sound by punching holes in his speakers. Fuzztone is now produced electrically by adding overtones and increasing vibrations, thereby literally smearing the original impulse or tone. Someone has suggested that the beards and long hair of the sixties are symbolic of a generation that prefers "fuzz" to clarity.
   See also feedback; tape reverb; wah-wah pedal.

fuzztone   The blurred sound, devoid of peaks and troughs, produced on a guitar through the use of the fuzzbox; also, a distortion of the normal guitar tone through electrical means.
   See also feedback; fuzzbox; tape reverb; wah-wah pedal.

G

gain   In recording, a quantity expressing the degree of amplification of a signal.

Gamble & Huff   *See* Philadelphia International.

gandy dancer   In American Folk music, a railroad worker who lays the wooden ties on which the rails are mounted.

garage bands   Vocal groups that started in school or in neighborhoods and developed without musical instruction into viable performing and recording groups are known as "doo-wop," or street-corner, groups. In the instrumental area, amateurs that came together to make music and developed into professional combos—they also sang—are known as "garage bands." Probably the best example is the Beach Boys, a quintet composed of the three Wilson brothers of Hawthorne, Calif., a cousin, and a school chum, who got together at first just to listen to records and sing for their own pleasure. They cut their first record as a demo at a small local studio, all five singing to a single guitar accompaniment. They paid for the session themselves. When "Surfin'" came out on a small local label (Candix), it led to a Capitol recording contract and launched the Surfing music craze.

"gas"   As a verb, to overwhelm: "It gassed me!" As an adjective, superb: "His playing was a gas!"
    See also "the end."

"Gatemouth"   While "gate" was used during the Swing era to mean a man, "gatemouth" referred to a big, wide mouth. Louis Armstrong (1900–1971) came from New Orleans with the nickname "Gatemouth" before he became known as "Satchmo." Among bluesmen, there are Clarence "Gatemouth" Brown (b. 1924) and Dwight "Gatemouth" Moore (b. 1913).

Gen. Prof. Mgr. (General Professional Manager)   The head of a Tin-Pan Alley music firm's song-plugging department was known as the professional manager during the 1920s and 1930s when live performances accounted for the hits. As records became the sine qua non of music business, a new executive position emerged: general professional manager. While he superintended all phases of the promotion and development of a hit song, his major functions were (1) to accept or reject songs submitted to a firm, and (2) to get recordings of accepted songs.

Georgy Awards   Established in 1979, the Georgy Awards are given by the Georgia Hall of Fame. The awards were designed and contributed by Tiffany and Co., with the Rev. Thomas A Dorsey (b. 1899), Joe South (b. 1942), and the late Otis Redding (1941–1967) being cited at ceremonies in October 1981.

Georgia Sea Island Singers   A group organized in the 1920s on St. Simon Island off the Georgia coast by musicologist Mrs. Maxfield Parrish. Singing without instrumental accompaniment, they created rhythmic patterns by hand-clapping and stamping the floor with their feet or a broomstick. They danced as they sang. With a repertoire of shouts and old-time work, play, and gospel songs, they were dedicated to the preservation of their African heritage.

George Gershwin (1898–1937)   Gershwin and his brother Ira (b. 1896), of the superb lyrics, were part of the golden group of supremely talented composer/lyricists who filled the Broadway theater of the twenties, thirties, and forties with musicals and songs that have become an imperishable lode of our Pop repertoire. Like their confreres, they produced many hits: evergreens like "The Man I Love," "Embraceable You," "Someone to Watch Over Me," "I Got Rhythm," "Fascinating Rhythm," "'S Wonderful," "Lady Be Good," "My One and Only," "That Certain Feeling," and a score of others. With *Strike Up the Band* (1930) and *Of Thee I Sing* (1931), they helped give the musical comedy a new dimension. Both were path-breaking political satires, and *Of Thee I Sing* became the first musical to win a Pulitzer Prize and to have its book published without the music.

However, Gershwin's name looms large in American music because of a series of works in which he took classical forms like the rhapsody, concerto, and opera and filled them with the dynamic rhythms and modern sounds of Jazz and Pop. Beginning with the one-act Negro opera *Blue Monday,* which he wrote for the *Scandals* of 1922 and which became well known in a later version as *135th Street,* he compelled the world of concert and symphonic music to recognize the validity and esthetic appeal of Jazz and Pop.

A high point in this conscious undertaking was the Lincoln's Birthday concert of 1924 at Aeolian Hall in New York City, when Paul Whiteman, a proponent of symphonic Jazz, introduced Gershwin's *Rhapsody in Blue*, with Gershwin at the piano. *Concerto in F,* introduced by the New York Symphony Society, followed in 1925; *An American in Paris,* with a first performance by the New York Philharmonic, in 1928; and *Second Rhapsody*, premiered by the Boston Symphony, in 1932. The climax of this invasion of the larger forms by Gershwin came in 1935 with the presentation of the folk opera *Porgy and Bess*. From a slow beginning, the work progressed steadily in time to receive worldwide critical and audience acclaim—also recognition as America's most performed and popular operatic work.

As a product of Tin-Pan Alley and the Broadway stage, Gershwin's journey to greatness was a challenge to other songsmiths. Ferde Grofe (1892–1972), Whiteman's adroit arranger, produced a number of larger works, notably *Grand Canyon Suite* (1931). So did Jerome Kern (1885–1945) and Broadway show orchestrator Robert Russell Bennett (b. 1894). Impressed by Gershwin's use of Jazz and Pop rhythms and sounds, symphonic composers like Aaron Copland (b. 1900), Leonard Bernstein (b. 1918), George Antheil (1900–1959), and Louis Gruenberg (1884–1964), among others, availed themselves of resources once shunned by serious composers.

See also Musical, Tony Awards for Best; Richard Rodgers.

gig   A job at a club, theater, showroom, or private party. The word is not generally used with regard to a record session.

"Dizzy" Gillespie.   *See* "Diz."

Gilley's   A modern-day honky-tonk in Pasadena, Tex., ten miles south of Houston, which is listed as the largest nightclub in the world in the *Guinness Book of World Records*. With a hall measuring 48,000 square feet and a capacity of 5,500 drugstore cowboys and gals, it boasts bars, bands, a ballroom-size dance floor, pinball machines, pool tables, a mechanical punching bag, and most important of all, a bogus, mechanical bull. It is on the last-mentioned that urban cowboys mimic the macho mannerisms of their real-life counterparts and sometimes end up with broken bones. When they are not testing themselves on the mechanical punching bag or bull, young men who work in nearby refineries, grain elevators, and shipyards dance the Cotton-eye Joe or Two-Step with waitresses and clerks, some of whom come to be picked up. Gilley's was used as the setting for the film *Urban Cowboy*, igniting a craze for sculptured cowboy Stetson hats among urban people, women as well as men. It also helped spark a surge of C & W music into the mainstream. Starring John Travolta, the film brought national recognition to Mickey Gilley, the singing nightclub owner, whose record of "That's All That Matters" became a bestseller; to his Urban Cowboy Band; and to Johnny Lee ("Lookin' for Love"), who has also become a headliner at the MGM Grand in Las Vegas.

See also C & W; honky-tonk; mechanical bull; Nashville Outlaws; Urban Cowboys.

gimmick   Any device—printed circular, commodity, commercial, etc.—that is useful in plugging, selling, advertising, or promoting a record, song, or artist. To promote the Pink Floyd album of *The Wall,* Columbia supplied record stores with a giant-sized replica of a brick wall as a display piece. Give-aways and tie-ins are frequently useful gimmicks.

Girl Group Rock   Not a style or a school. But since Rock, like Jazz, is largely a male phenomenon, the appearance of a considerable number of girl groups in the late fifties and early sixties warrants a separate classification. The earliest groups, like the Chordettes from Sheboygan, Wisc. ("Mr. Sandman," 1954, and "Lollipop," 1958), Patience & Prudence from Los Angeles ("Tonight You Belong to Me," 1956), and the Poni-Tails from Cleveland ("Born Too Late," 1958), were white, although the Teen Queens from Los Angeles, who hit with "Eddie, My Love" in 1956, were a black duo.

The first major black group was the Chantels, who came from the Bronx, and who scored their biggest hits with their first release, "Maybe" (1958) and "Look in My Eyes" (1961). In 1958 the Shirelles came from Passaic, N.J., to capture No. 1 with their second release, "Will You Love Me Tomorrow?" (1960), and with "Soldier Boy" (1962). Although the Paris Sisters from San Francisco ("I Love How You Love Me," 1961), and the Angels from Orange N.J. ("Till," 1961, and "My Boyfriend's Back," No. 1 in 1963) were white, the early sixties brought a proliferation of mostly black groups. The Marvelettes were the first of three big Motown/Berry Gordy girl groups, who hit No. 1 with their first release ("Please, Mr. Postman," 1961). The Crystals (No. 1 with "He's a Rebel," 1962, followed by "Da Doo Ron Ron," 1963) were the first of Phil Spector's three major girl groups.

The Cookies, three black girls from Brooklyn, made No. 17 with "Chains," their debut disk in 1962, and climbed to No. 7 the following year with "Don't Say Nothin' Bad (About My Baby)." Although the Orlons, three girls and a boy from Philadelphia, began recording in 1960, they did not garner a national hit until 1962 with "The Wah-Watusi," which started the dance craze of the same name. In 1962 the most successful of all the girl groups, the Supremes, made their bid for fame but scored their first No. 1 with "Where Did Our Love Go?" in 1964, after which they racked up a record-breaking succession of a dozen No. 1's. The Chiffons, four Bronx blacks, appeared with a No. 1 hit "He's So Fine" (1963). Phil Spector's Ronettes, one of whose members became Mrs. Spector in 1968, made No. 2 with "Be My

Baby'' in 1963, the year that the Bronx Jaynettes also scored No. 2 with ''Sally, Go Round the Roses.'' Martha & the Vandellas, another Motown star group, made its disk debut in 1963, the year in which ''Heat Wave'' went to No. 4 on Pop charts and No. 1 on R & B charts. The year 1964 brought chart makers to the Dixie Cups (No. 1 with ''Chapel of Love''), the Jelly Beans (No. 4 with ''I Wanna Love Him So Bad''), and especially, the Shangri-Las, who made No. 1 with ''Leader of the Pack'' and enjoyed bestsellers in ''Give Him a Great Big Kiss'' (1964) and ''I Can Never Go Home Anymore'' (1965).

Since virtually all of these groups came to the recording studio with little or no professional background, they had to rely on producers like George Goldner (End, Gone, and Gee Records), Phil Spector (Philles), Leiber & Stoller (Red Bird), Florence Greenberg (Scepter and Wand), Berry Gordy (Tamla, Gordy, Motown) and their staffs for advice on the choice of material, styling, and other considerations. There was something basically plaintive not only in the shrill sounds of the groups, sometimes innocent, sometimes soulful, but in the substance of their songs—a heartfelt plea for a lasting and fulfilling love.

Women gained a new foothold in Rock with the rise in the seventies of singers like Helen Reddy (''I Am Woman'') in 1972, and Donna Summer (''Enough Is Enough'') and Gloria Gaynor (''I Will Survive''), all of whom enunciated sentiments of women's lib. In 1982 a new girl quintet, The Go-Go's, who had started as a punk rock group, made the top of the album charts with *Beauty and the Beat*.

give-away   A prize given to consumers, disk jockeys, or retailers in an effort to hype sales.

gliss   An abbreviation of *glissando,* a rapid sliding over a series of notes. The nature of the sound is most easily demonstrated on the piano by running a finger in a sweeping motion across the black keys or the white keys.

Glitter Rock   Took its name from an Englishman whose given name was Paul Gadd (b. 1944, Banbury, Oxfordshire) but who took the name Gary Glitter in the early seventies; he was a forerunner of rockers who made spectacle part of their onstage appearances. Odd and outrageous costumes, makeup, hairdos, props, and antics all figure in the effort to add a visual dimension to a musical program. When the artist goes beyond visual appeal into the viscera, and, through the use of violence and sex, goes beyond mere entertainment and amusement, we have Shock Rock. An umbrella term for these different types of spectacular presentations is Theater Rock.

See also Shock Rock; Theater Rock.

glottis   The elongated space between the vocal chords and surrounding flesh. The glottal stop was an effect produced by closing the glottis, thereby interrupting the breath. Elvis and Buddy Holly used the effect, which sounded like a hiccup.

go "bananas" or "ape"   To be upset, worn-out, out of control; to go out of one's mind.

God Rock   Refers to compositions with a religious orientation. In 1967 the Electric Prunes recorded *Mass in F minor,* following it with *Release of an Oath: The Kol Nidre,* which was based on the Hebrew litany. Another group, the Association, recorded a *Requiem for the Masses.* Bob Dylan's albums *Slow Train Coming* (1979) and *Saved* (1980), both of which dealt with his new ideas as a Born-Again Christian, might be included under this heading, although some may feel that they should be classified as Jesus Rock rather than God Rock. At best, it is a limited category, since the Rock generations tend to turn from traditional religions to Eastern faiths.
    See also Jesus Rock.

"goes"   In conversation, the word "says" has almost completely disappeared from the vocabulary of the Rock generation and "goes" has taken its place.

Go-Go   An English derivative of the French colloquialism *agogo,* meaning "full of" or "loaded with." However, it is believed that the American usage, as in the name of a Hollywood club, Whiskey-A-Go-Go, came about because of the exhortation "Go, man, go!"—which connoted excitement.

Gold Record   A single record is certified Gold by the Recording Industry Association of America (RIAA) after it has sold 1 million copies. Under a recent change in rules, a Gold Album is one which has sold 500,000 copies. The emphasis in each instance is on *sold,* not just shipped.
    See also Platinum Record; Titanium Album.

"gone"   Together with "something else," "out of this world," "boss," and "the end," an exclamation of excited admiration, approval, praise.

Benny Goodman (1909–   )   He became the King of Swing in 1935, much to the annoyance of Jazz aficionados, who felt that the title properly belonged to bandleaders like Count Basie (b. 1904), Duke Ellington

(1899–1974), Jimmy Lunceford (1902–1947) or to Fletcher Henderson (1898–1952) whose arrangements were instrumental in bringing fame to the Goodman band, and all of whom had been playing in the style that became known as Swing. Goodman's ascent to the throne began with his band being featured in 1934 on NBC's network radio show *Let's Dance.* A subsequent cross-country tour proved unsuccessful until the band appeared at the Palomar Ballroom in Los Angeles. Performances of the Fletcher Henderson arrangements brought such a roar of approval on the evening of August 21, 1935, that the date is generally accepted as inaugurating the Swing era. During the nine years in which the band functioned as the most successful of the commercial Big Bands, Goodman broke the taboo against bands of mixed color. He used pianist Teddy Wilson (b. 1912) and vibraharpist Lionel Hampton (b. 1909) not only on record dates but in personal appearances. As a clarinetist, Goodman rated accolades not only from Jazz fans but from classical audiences as well; from 1938 on, he recorded and performed with groups like the Budapest String Quartet. He appeared in two Broadway shows (*Swingin' the Dream,* 1939, and *Seven Lively Arts,* 1944) and many motion pictures, left a large legacy of recorded music, and won awards from *Metronome, Down Beat, Esquire,* and *Playboy.* Steve Allen played Goodman in *The Benny Goodman Story* (1955).

See also Swing.

"goof off"   To be irresponsible, to fail to perform one's duties. Originally, a "goof" was synonymous with a "clinker," a wrong note.

"gorilla"   A new record and music biz term meaning a monster of a bestseller.

Gospel music   A form of demonstrative religious music that developed in black Baptist churches, especially among the Sanctified, Holiness, and Pentecostal sects, during the Depression years. By 1942 Gospel supported a number of publishing houses, the largest of which was built by Thomas A. Dorsey (originally "Georgia Tom," a songwriter/singer of Blues, b. 1899), Sallie Martin, and their discovery, Roberta Martin, who died in 1969. Even earlier, by 1940 three radio networks were presenting a "secularized" version of Gospel, as sung by the Golden Gate Quartet, Charioteers, and Deep River Boys; and Sallie Martin hired a teenager named Ruth Jones (later known as Dinah Washington, (1924–1963) as her accompanist.

As R & B developed into R 'n' R, Gospel, which shaped R & B, developed into Soul. An enormous number of R & B singers began by singing Gospel in church—Aretha Franklin (b. 1943), Sam Cooke (1935–1964) (Soul Stirrers), LaVern Baker (b. 1929), Della Reese

(b. 1932) (Meditation Singers), Dionne Warwick (b. 1940) (Drinkard Singers), Lou Rawls (b. 1936) (Pilgrim Travellers), Clyde McPhatter (1931-1972), Wilson Pickett (b. 1940) (Violinaires)—and many R & B groups began as Gospel groups: Billy Ward & the Dominoes, the Drifters, and the Royales, among others.

Although a deep chasm separated Gospel from the Blues—one was the music of the Lord, as the other was of the Devil, and Mahalia Jackson (1911-1972) would not sing a Blues—Ray Charles (b. 1930) audaciously took several Gospel songs and transformed them into R & B shouts. "This Little Light of Mine" became "This Little Love of Mine," "How Jesus Died" became "Lonely Avenue," and "My Jesus Is All the World to Me" became "I Got a Woman." After a time, out of the hand-clapping, foot-stamping, ringing tambourines, "curlicues, flowers and frills," and frenzy came the Soul music of James Brown (b. 1928), Otis Redding (1941-1967), Ray Charles, and Aretha Franklin.

Gospel music is today a road with two forks. James Cleveland, Alberta Walker, Andrae Crouch, Shirley Caesar, and others sing in church, for church people and for religious purposes, in sacred devotion. The "secular" wing performs in clubs and theaters, to entertain, and is represented by the Dixie Hummingbirds, Mighty Clouds of Joy, and Violinaires, among others. Rosetta Tharpe (1915-1973), who began recording for Decca in 1948, is generally recognized as the first national Gospel singer—the first to take the music out of the church to the general public. She actually scored a Pop hit in 1939 with a recording of Thomas Dorsey's "Rock Me," cut with the Lucky Millinder Band. After Sister Tharpe came Clara Ward (1924-1973) with the first Gospel-originated song, "Our God is Able," which sold over 1 million copies in 1950. Mahalia Jackson (1911-1972) sold over 2 million copies of "Move On Up a Little Higher," which she recorded in 1947.

See also Thomas A. Dorsey.

Gospel or Other Religious Recording, Best (NARAS Grammy Awards)

1961   Mahalia Jackson: "Every Time I Feel the Spirit"

1962   Mahalia Jackson: *Great Songs of Love and Faith*

1963   Soeur Sourire: "Dominique"

1964   Tennessee Ernie Ford: *Great Gospel Songs*

1965   George Beverly Shea and the Anita Kerr Singers: *Southland Favorites*

[Gospel] Sacred Performance, Best (NARAS Grammy Award)

This category was substituted for Best Gospel in 1966 when Porter Wagoner and the Blackwood Brothers won with *Grand Old Gospel*.

In 1967 Grammys were awarded in two classifications:

1967	Best Gospel Performance	Porter Wagoner and the Blackwood Brothers Quartet: *More Grand Ole Gospel*
	Best Sacred Performance	Elvis Presley: "How Great Thou Art"

From 1968 through 1971, a third category was added:

1968	Best Gospel Performance	Happy Goodman Family: *The Happy Gospel of the Happy Goodmans*
	Best Sacred Performance	Jake Hess: "Beautiful Isle of Somewhere"
	Best Soul Gospel Performance	Dottie Rambo: *The Soul of Me*
1969	Best Gospel Performance	Porter Wagoner and the Blackwood Brothers: *In Gospel Country*
	Best Sacred Performance	Jake Hess: *Ain't That Beautiful Singing*
	Best Soul Gospel Performance	Edwin Hawkins Singers: *Oh Happy Day*
1970	Best Gospel Performance	Oak Ridge Boys: *Talk About the Good Times*
	Best Sacred Performance	Jake Hess: *Everything Is Beautiful*
	Best Soul Gospel Performance	Edwin Hawkins Singers: *Every Man Wants to Be Free*
1971	Best Gospel Performance	Charley Pride: *Let Me Live*
	Best Sacred Performance	Charley Pride: *Did You Think to Pray*
	Best Soul Gospel Performance	Shirley Caesar: *Put Your Hand in the Hand of the Man from Galilee*

From 1972 through 1976, Best Gospel and Best Soul Gospel were retained, but Best Inspirational Performance was substituted for Best Sacred.

1972	Best Gospel Performance	Blackwood Brothers: "L–O–V–E"
	Best Soul Gospel Performance	Aretha Franklin: *Amazing Grace*
	Best Inspirational Performance	Elvis Presley: *He Touched Me*
1973	Best Gospel Performance	Blackwood Brothers: *Release Me (From My Sin)*
	Best Soul Gospel Performance	Dixie Hummingbirds: "Loves Me Like a Rock"

	Best Inspirational Performance	Bill Gaither Trio: *Let's Just Praise the Lord*
1974	Best Gospel Performance	Oak Ridge Boys: "The Baptism of Jesse Taylor"
	Best Soul Gospel Performance	James Cleveland and the Southern California Community Choir: *In the Ghetto*
	Best Inspiration Performance	Elvis Presley: "How Great Thou Art"
1975	Best Gospel Performance	Imperials: *No Shortage*
	Best Soul Gospel Performance	Andrae Crouch and the Disciples: *Take Me Back*
	Best Inspirational Performance	The Bill Gaither Trio: *Jesus, We Just Want to Thank You*
1976	Best Gospel Performance	Oak Ridge Boys: "Where the Soul Never Dies"
	Best Soul Gospel Performance	Mahalia Jackson: *How I Got Over*
	Best Inspirational Performance	Gary S. Paxton: *The Astonishing, Outrageous, Amazing, Incredible, Unbelievable, Different World of Gary S. Paxton*

From 1977, awards were made in five classifications

1977	Best Gospel Performance, Contemporary or Inspirational	Imperials: *Sail On*
	Best Gospel Performance	Oak Ridge Boys: "Just a Talk with Jesus"
	Best Soul Gospel Performance, Contemporary	Edwin Hawkins and the Edwin Hawkins Singers: *Wonderful!*
	Best Soul Gospel Performance, Traditional	James Cleveland: *James Cleveland Live at Carnegie Hall*
	Best Inspirational Performance	B. J. Thomas: *Home Where I Belong*
1978	Best Gospel Performance, Contemporary or Inspirational	Imperials: *Sail On*
	Best Gospel Performance, Traditional	Oak Ridge Boys: "Just a Little Talk with Jesus"
	Best Soul Gospel Performance, Contemporary	Edwin Hawkins and the Edwin Hawkins Singers: *Wonderful!*
	Best Soul Gospel Performance, Traditional	James Cleveland: *James Cleveland at Carnegie Hall*

	Best Inspirational Performance	B. J. Thomas: *Home Is Where I Belong*
1979	Best Gospel Performance, Contemporary or Inspirational	Larry Hart: "What a Friend"
	Best Gospel Performance, Traditional	The Happy Goodman Family: *Refreshing*
	Best Soul Gospel Performance, Contemporary	Andrea Crouch and the Disciples: *Live in London*
	Best Soul Gospel Performance, Traditional	Mighty Clouds of Joy: *Live and Direct*
	Best Inspirational Performance	B. J. Thomas: *Happy Man*
1980	Best Gospel Performance, Contemporary or Traditional	Imperials: *Heed the Call*
	Best Gospel Performance, Traditional	The Blackwood Brothers: *Lift up the Name of Jesus*
	Best Soul Gospel Performance, Contemporary	Andrae Crouch: *I'll Be Thinking of You*
	Best of Soul Gospel Performance, Traditional	Mighty Clouds of Joy: *Changing Times*
	Best Inspirational Performance	B. J. Thomas: *You Gave Me Love (When Nobody Gave Me a Prayer)*
1981	Best Contemporary or Inspirational Gospel Performance	Reba Rambo, Dony McGuire, B. J. Thomas, Andrae Crouch, The Archers, Walter and Tremaine Hawkins, Cynthia Clawson: *The Lord's Prayer*
	Best Traditional Gospel Performance	Blackwood Brothers: *We Come to Worship*
	Best Contemporary Soul Gospel Performance	Shirley Caesar: *Rejoice*
	Best Traditional Soul Gospel Performance	James Cleveland and the Charles Ford Singers: *Lord, Let Me Be an Instrument*
	Best Inspirational Performance	Debby Boone: *With My Song I Will Praise Him*
1982	Best Contemporary or Inspirational Gospel Performance	The Imperials: *Priority*
	Best Traditional Gospel Performance	J. D. Sumner, James Blackwood, Hovie Lister, Rosie Rozell, Jake Hess: *The Masters V*

Best Contemporary Soul Gospel Performance	Andrae Crouch: *Don't Give Up*
Best Traditional Soul Gospel Performance	Al Green: *The Lord Will Make a Way*
Best Inspirational Performance	B. J. Thomas: *Amazing Grace*

Gospel-Pop fusion   A style inaugurated by Berry Gordy and his Motown complex with singer Marv Johnson (b. 1938), using a female chorus for Gospel call-and-response exchanges and a rhythmic tambourine ("Come to Me"). Employing a swinging four-to-the-bar rhythm, Gordy had tambourines ringing on the afterbeat while strings, played on many occasions by members of the Detroit Symphony Orchestra, swirled in the background. The Temptations, a group that included singers from the deep South, was regarded as most Gospel-oriented of the Motown groups, while the Supremes were the most Pop-oriented.

Bill Graham (1931–   )   Born Wolfgang Grajonca in Berlin, promoter/manager/booker Bill Graham suffered through the nightmare of Hitler's brutalization of Germany and France before he escaped to New York, graduated from City College with a B.B.A., and moved to San Francisco. Business manager of the San Francisco Mime Troupe, a group whose productions were banned by local censors, he leased a run-down skating rink in the black ghetto and renamed it The Fillmore. A succession of successful Rock concerts led to his leasing a second auditorium—an old dancehall named the Carousel Ballroom—which he renamed Fillmore West. Many Rock groups rose to national prominence through appearances in his halls, including the Jefferson Airplane, Grateful Dead, Quicksilver Messenger Service, and Big Brother & the Holding Company, featuring Janis Joplin. In 1968 he opened a theater in New York City, converting a defunct Loew's on 2nd Avenue below 14th Street into Fillmore East. Here he repeated his West Coast successes in presenting concerts that drew sellout audiences. Although he closed down the Fillmores in 1971, he has continued active on the Rock scene, arranging such events as the "Summer Jam" in Watkins Glen, N. Y., in July 1973, and Bob Dylan's concert tour in 1974, etc.

Grammy   The National Academy of Recording Arts and Sciences' equivalent for the Oscar. It takes the shape of an old-fashioned phonograph with the angled horn. The first Grammy Awards, then limited to 28 categories, were announced on May 4, 1959. The membership of NARAS votes annually as to who shall receive Grammys in different classifications, now grown to 58 categories. Presentation of the Grammys is televised nationally.

See also Album of the Year (NARAS); National Academy of Recording Arts and Sciences; Producer of the Year (NARAS); Song of the Year (NARAS).

"Grandfather of British Rock"   John Mayall (b. Manchester, England, 1934). From 1956 to 1966, his band included a long list of later superstars of Rock, including guitarist Eric Clapton (b. 1945) and bassist Jack Bruce (b. 1943), both of the Cream; also bassist John McVie (b. 1945) and drummer Mick Fleetwood (b. 1942) of Fleetwood Mac; and Mick Taylor (b. 1949) of the Rolling Stones.

See also Blues, British; British Invasion.

Grand Ole Opry   It was originally known as *WSM Barn Dance,* and its inaugural broadcast was made from that station's small fifth-floor Studio A on November 28, 1925. Uncle Jimmy Thompson, who claimed he could "fiddle the bugs off a 'tater vine,'" was the initial performer, and the cast included Dr. Humphrey Bate and his daughter Alcyone, the Crook Brothers, and Kirk McGee, who still perform on the *Opry.* By the time the show was moved to Studio B of WSM, still in the National Life & Accident Insurance Building at 7th Avenue North and Union Street, its name had been changed from *WSM Barn Dance* to the *Grand Ole Opry.* The change reportedly came about in an accidental way, the result of an ad lib by announcer George D. Hay, who called himself "The Solemn Old Judge" and who had originated the *National Barn Dance* on WLS in Chicago in 1924. Apparently, the *WSM Barn Dance* came on the air immediately after a broadcast of the *NBC Music Appreciation Hour,* conducted by Dr. Walter Damrosch. Hay opened the program by saying: "For the past hour, you have been listening to Grand Opera. Now we will present Grand Ole Opry!" The name stuck, and in succeeding years, as the live audience grew, the program moved, first to a newly built studio that accommodated about 500, then to the Hillsboro Theatre, an East Nashville tabernacle, and later to the auditorium of the War Memorial, which seated about 1,200. Two years after the *Opry* became a network show, with a half-hour broadcast coast to coast (1939), it moved to the famous Ryan Auditorium, where it remained until 1974. With the opening of Opryland, U.S.A., a $41 million amusement park dedicated by President Nixon on March 16, 1974, the *Opry* moved into a new $15 million theater, the largest broadcasting studio in the world, with a seating capacity of 4,400. Here, on October 15, 1975, it celebrated its golden anniversary. Needless to say, there is no Country singer who has not appeared before *Opry* audiences.

See also Ryman Auditorium.

"grass"   Marijuana.

Grease   A nostalgic musical about the 1950s, with book, music, and lyrics by Jim Jacobs and Warren Casey, that opened off-Broadway on February 12, 1972, and after 128 performances moved to the Broadhurst Theatre on June 7, 1972. It ran continuously until April 13, 1980, racking up 3,388 performances to become the longest-running show in Broadway history. (The previous record holder was *Fiddler on the Roof,* which ran for 3,242 performances before it closed.) The title of the Rock 'n' Roll tale of high school life in the fifties was derived from the boys' hairstyle of the period: the DA, or ducktail cut, as it was known, was held in place with oily preparations. Produced at a nominal cost of $150,000, *Grease* grossed more than $8 million from ticket sales, a cast album, and a hit movie, starring John Travolta and Olivia Newton-John.

"green"   Money. Another jazz colloquialism is "bread."

Greenwich Village   An area of irregular streets below 14th Street, mostly on Manhattan's West Side, which, because of its low rentals, early became a haven of indigent and up-and-coming writers and artists. Low rentals disappeared in the inflationary seventies. But during the early years of Rock, Greenwich Village was a center of the counter-culture, and in music, a center of Jazz and Folk. When Bob Dylan (b. 1941) came to NYC in the early sixties, it was to Greenwich Village, and it was at Gerde's Folk City, one of the many coffeehouses and clubs, that he made his debut. The Folk boom of the early sixties brought many future stars to the Village, but even before then, John Sebastian (b. 1944), who grew up in the Village and later founded the Lovin' Spoonful, performed in Village coffeehouses, joined first the Even Dozen Jug Band and then in '62, the Mugwumps, another Village group, which included Cass Elliot (1943–1974) and Dennis Doherty (b. 1941), later of The Mamas and the Papas. Roger McGuinn (b. 1942 in Chicago) worked Village coffeehouses in the late fifties, where he met and wrote arrangements for folk singer Judy Collins (b. 1939), became lead guitarist for Bobby Darin (1936–1973), and joined the Chad Mitchell Trio, with whom he toured for two years. Around 1957, John Phillips, born in South Carolina in 1935, lived in the Village, where he met Holly Michelle Gilliam (who was born in California in 1944) and Cass Elliot (then working with a Village group called the Big Three) all of whom, with Dennis Doherty, comprised The Mamas and The Papas.

In the early sixties, Richie Havens (b. 1941) settled in the Village, where he eeked out a living by drawing portraits of tourists, and where, as a result of listening to Paul Stookey (b. 1937, later of Peter, Paul and

Mary), Len Chandler (b. 1935), and other coffeehouse folk singers, he turned to singing and songwriting as a career. The Village was the launching pad for Bob Dylan and Jose Feliciano (b. circa 1945), both of whom were plucked out of Gerde's Folk City by record companies, and for Felix Pappalardi (b. 1939), whose Village friendships led to his producing the debut album of the Youngbloods in 1966. The Cafe Bizarre in the Village led also to the association of the Velvet Underground with Andy Warhol's Exploding Plastic Inevitable.

In the late 1960s, Davie Peel & the Lower East Side, a group that paid its dues singing in the Washington Square area of the Village, garnered a recording contract when they were heard by a record exec at a Village "happening." They recorded their first album (*Have a Marijuana*) in the Square on four successive Sundays in 1969.

Bleecker and MacDougal (two Village streets) was the title of an early album by Fred Neil (b. circa 1938), who wrote the theme of *Midnight Cowboy,* sung by Harry Nilsson. Backing Neil on some of his original songs were two Villagers, John Sebastian on harmonica and Felix Pappalardi on guitar. One of Paul Simon's earliest songs, appearing on the first Simon & Garfunkel album, *Wednesday Morning, 3 AM,* was titled "Bleecker Street." (The author of this *Dictionary* worked with Simon on the original demo of the song.)

The best-known and the oldest club in the area is Art D'Lugoff's Village Gate on Bleecker Street, located in what once was the laundry-basement area of the Mills Hotel, later the down-at-the-heels Greenwich Hotel, and now an elegant apartment house called The Atrium. The Gate celebrated its 22nd anniversary in 1980, having opened its doors in 1958 with funds derived partly from royalties accruing to brother Burt D'Lugoff as the co-writer of "Cindy, Oh Cindy," introduced by Vince Martin and a late hit for Eddie Fisher. There is hardly a Jazz or Folk performer who has not played at the Gate, which also offered an unknown and then unsuccessful Aretha Franklin (b. 1942) to the public. D'Lugoff has been phenomenally successful in presenting shows like *Jacques Brel Is Alive and Well and Living in Paris,* which ran for five years; the controversial *Let My People Come,* his biggest money-maker, which briefly resulted in the cancelation of his liquor license; *Scrambled Feet,* the show which featured a duck; and *One Mo' Time,* which D'Lugoff brought north from New Orleans.

The role of Greenwich Village, also of the east Village, warrants a full volume.

"The Groaner"   *See* Bing Crosby.

"groovy"   "In the groove" or "groovy" generally refers to the appealing rhythmic quality of a performance or recording. The meaning has been extended to describe a pleasant, relaxed, carefree state of feeling, as in Paul Simon's "59th St. Bridge Song," subtitled "Feelin' Groovy."

groupies   Girls who follow Rock groups about and casually offer sex to the musicians. Brian Jones (1944-1969) of the Rolling Stones used to find girls in his closets, his bed, and his bathroom. In one month, a box score he kept revealed that he had bedded down with 64 chicks.

gruppetto   A decorative cluster of notes executed in rapid succession; they can go up or down, or both ways, and neighboring or separated notes can be employed. In Gospel, the singer can take more liberties than in classical music.

Guaracha   The most popular of Cuban social dances, it is faster than the Bolero and slower than the Rumba. Its basic beat, as played by the bass drum:

guiro   *See* Latin rhythm instruments.

guitar   The most popular of stringed instruments in the 20th century, the guitar was apparently introduced into America by early Spanish explorers. The 19th century brought to these shores Johann Georg Martin and his son Christian, the latter founding the C. F. Martin Co., which still manufactures guitars today. In the latter part of the century, a shoe clerk named Orville Gibson, who liked to build musical instruments, applied the violin idea of construction (carved top and back, and arching) to develop a still-popular model of the instrument. In the early 1950s, guitarist Les Paul added features to the electric guitar that make a model named after him attractive to many performers. Whether it is a Martin, Gibson, or Les Paul, the guitar is played by strumming or plucking its strings, which can be of gut, nylon, or metal (steel, copper, or bronze).

With the advent of Rock 'n' Roll in the 1950s, the guitar superseded the piano as the basic instrument for accompanying singers. Until then, it had in its acoustic form been associated with Blues, Country, and Folk music. Blues pioneer Blind Lemon Jefferson (1897-1929), Jimmie Rodgers, the Father of Country Music (1897-1933), and folk singer Woody Guthrie (1912-1967) all accompanied themselves on the guitar. B. B. King attributes the popularity of the instrument among bluesmen to its low cost and the simplicity of building it, not to a musical or ethnic factor. Although a few performers used an electrically amplified instrument in the 1930s, notably Charlie Christian (1919–1942) of the Benny Goodman Band, the electric guitar did not come to the fore until the R & B years (1945–1955), with the T-Bone Walker (1913–1975) acting as the main proponent.

Coming out of a Country tradition, it is not surprising that the King of Rock 'n' Roll played guitar and was accompanied by a trio that included another guitar. As a folk singer in the Woody Guthrie tradition, Bob Dylan (b. 1941) accompanied himself on acoustic guitar (cum harmonica); he stirred a furor among his Folk followers when he substituted the electric instrument as he turned to Rock. The popularity of the Beatles established the quartet setup involving two guitars, melody and rhythm, as the accepted format for a large number of Rock groups. Advances in the use of electricity and electronics have made it possible to manipulate the texture, volume, and quality of the guitar tone through the use of the fuzzbox, wah-wah pedals, and other devices.

See also Bluegrass; "crossed-note" tuning; dobro; fuzztone; wahwah pedal.

"Guitar Man"   Nickname of Jerry Reed (b. 1937), as a result of Presley's recording of his song "Guitar Man," a hit in 1968.

gut-bucket   The gut-bucket, in the post–Civil War period, was a container that caught the drippings, or "guttering," of the reclining barrels from which gin was sold. The low-down music played in the honky-tonks dispensing the gin well caught the spirit of the surroundings, and quite naturally, the music took its name from the scene.

Woody Guthrie (1912–1967)   A legendary folk singer and prolific songwriter/folk poet, he influenced Folk and Rock music through such venerators of his creativity and artistry as Pete Seeger (b. 1919), Judy Collins (b. 1939), Odetta (b. 1930), Tom Paxton (b. 1937), Peter LaFarge (1931–1965), Phil Ochs (1940–1976), and Bob Dylan (b. 1941). (In his first album, Dylan not only imitated Guthrie's "talking" style but included a dedicatory song, "Talking Woody Guthrie." The title of Dylan's album *Slow Train Coming,* 1979, which deals with his conversion as a Born-Again Christian, seems to echo Guthrie's songbook title *On a Slow Train Through California.*)

In a dedicated career of writing—Woody religiously wrote two songs a day from 1934 until Huntington's chorea hospitalized him in the early fifties—he produced over a thousand published compositions. Among his well-loved songs are such popular numbers as "This Land Is Your

Land'' (written in response to Irving Berlin's ''God Bless America''), ''So Long, It's Been Good to Know You,'' ''Pastures of Plenty,'' ''This Train Is Bound for Glory,'' and numerous others, including a classic collection of children's songs.

Born of pioneering American stock in the Indian country of Oklahoma, he grew up surrounded by Folk music—songs sung by his grandparents, his father (who had played guitar and banjo with cowboy bands), and his black and Indian neighbors. Leaving home in his teens after family tragedies terminated his schooling in tenth grade, he became a migratory worker and wandering minstrel, filling inspired songs with the life and experiences he endured during the Depression, the Dust Bowl days, the unionization of labor, and World War II. By the time he settled in California, performing on Los Angeles radio, he was interested in unions and left-wing organizations. When he moved to New York City in the thirties, he began writing a column for the Communist *Daily Worker* and the West Coast *People's World,* selections of which have been published in *Woody Sez* (1974). At this time, folklorist Alan Lomax brought him to Washington, D.C., where he recorded twelve records of *Dust Bowl Ballads* for the Archives of American Folk Song. Returning to the West Coast in 1938, Guthrie traveled through California with singer Cisco Houston (1918–1961) and actor Will Geer entertaining migratory workers. Thereafter, he traveled extensively with Houston, playing a guitar that boldly proclaimed: ''This Machine Kills Fascists.''

In the early forties, having met folk singer Pete Seeger, he became part of the Alamanac Singers, a quartet including Lee Hays and Millard Lampell (later the well-known screenwriter), which sang at union and radical meetings and recorded *Union Maid, Talking Union,* and *Union Train a-Comin'.''* In 1943 Guthrie's autobiography, *Bound for Glory,* was published. It became the title of the United Artists' biographical film in which David Carradine portrayed Woody.

After World War II—he anc Cisco Houston joined the merchant marine in 1943, surviving torpedo attacks, and he was later briefly drafted—Woody began recording for Moe Asch's Folkways label, eventually cutting over a hundred songs and helping the label avoid possible bankruptcy. His artistry is also to be heard on Elektra, RCA Victor, and Stinson Records. Several of his songs, notably ''So Long, It's Been Good to Know You'' and ''This Land Is Your Land,'' yielded hit records for the Weavers, a Decca Records Folk group whose members included Pete Seeger (b. 1919) and Lee Hays (1914–1981).

Guthrie fought the debilitating muscular disease to which he succumbed in October 1967 for fifteen years. A posthumous tribute at Carnegie Hall in January 1968, with actors Will Geer and Robert Ryan as narrators, brought song testimonials from Bob Dylan (b. 1941), Judy

Collins (b. 1939), Jack Elliott (b. 1931), Richie Havens (b. 1941), Odetta (b. 1930), Tom Paxton (b. 1937), and Woody's son Arlo Guthrie (b. 1947). It was followed by a tribute, scripted by Millard Lampell, in September 1970 at the Hollywood Bowl. The luminaries who paid homage to the legendary folk poet included Joan Baez (b. 1941), Country Joe McDonald, Earl Robinson (composer of *Ballad for Americans*), Pete Seeger (b. 1919), and actors Will Geer and Peter Fonda. Critic Clifton Fadiman has described Guthrie's songs as a national treasure "like Yellowstone or Yosemite."

"The Guv-nor"   This is how the top English rockers referred to Alexis Korner (b. 1928), the Parisian who was the Father of British Blues groups and, in turn, of British Rock. He was also known as the Grandfather of British R & B.
      See also Blues, British.

"H"   Heroin. Also known as "horse."

H–D–H   The initials of Motown's most successful writing/producing team: Eddie Holland, Lamont Dozier, and Brian Holland. They contributed song hits to the repertoire of many of Motown's groups: the Temptations' "My Girl" (1965), Martha & the Vandellas' "Heat Wave" (1963), and the Miracles' "Mickey's Monkey" (1963). But they played *the* critical role in making superstars of the Four Tops and the Supremes. For the former group's disk hits, they devised "Baby, I Need Your Loving" (1964), the hand-clapping "I Can't Help Myself" (1965), "Reach Out, I'll Be There (1966), and "Standing in the Shadows of Love" (1966)—all of which sold a million or more copies. H–D–H were even more effective in their handling of the Supremes. In the first year (1964) of writing/producing for the Diana Ross trio, they developed three hits: "Where Did Our Love Go?" "Baby Love," and "Come See About Me," all of which sold a million or more copies. 1965 was an even better year, the H–D–H/Supremes collaboration resulting in four disk hits "Stop in the Name of Love," "Back in My Arms Again," "Nothing but Heartaches," and "I Hear a Symphony." In 1966, H–D–H once again delivered three hit disks for the group: "My World Is Empty Without You," "You Can't Hurry Love," and "You

Keep Me Hangin' On.'' But 1967 was the final year of H–D–H's association not only with the Supremes but with Motown. For the Supremes, H–D–H produced ''Love Is Here and Now You're Gone'' and ''This Happening,'' both million sellers. Then, in the midst of negotiations for a new contract, H–D–H requested an accounting of royalties. Berry Gordy, the owner of Motown, responded by firing the team. H–D–H thereupon filed a lawsuit and proceeded to form their own label and production company. The separation proved advantageous neither to Motown nor to the trio. While at Motown, H–D–H developed a cyclical song structure, which many believe was the source of their phenomenal succession of hits. Instead of cadencing a chorus, they would return directly to the opening, repeating the song's ''hook'' again and again. Tension increased as the listener waited for the ''release'' that never came; in its absence, the listener was hooked for the duration of the disk.

See also Motown sound.

HIP   Record-biz acronym for ''high-intent priority,'' a record slated for an all-out promotional, publicity, and advertising push.

HN   Abbreviation of ''house nigger,'' the latest black term for an Uncle Tom, someone who has sold out to Mr. Charley.

Habanera   Derived from Havana (Habana), Cuba, the Habanera is a Cuban dance that has some similarity to the Argentinian Tango. W. C. Handy (1873–1958) used the rhythm in ''St. Louis Blues.''

Haight-Ashbury   The district in San Francisco that was the center of hippie subculture in the 1960s. Its heyday was 1967, when, it is estimated, there were over 500 psychedelic bands rehearsing at and working the acid/hippie scene. One of the places where young, aspiring musicians hung out was in the apartment of Chet Helm at 1090 Page Street. Helm both managed and played with some of the groups. Among those who came by to jam, meet other musicians, or arrange playing dates were the three singer/guitarists who formed Big Brother & the Holding Company in 1965. It was Chet Helm who suggested that Janis Joplin (1943–1970) be added to the group, which made a show-stopping appearance at the Monterey Pop Festival in 1967—and introduced Janis to the world.

See also Acid Rock; alternative life-style; Monterey Pop Festival.

Hair   Billed as America's ''tribal love-Rock musical,'' it was the first Broadway show in the Rock idiom. The question of whether the main character should accept the draft provided the framework for what was a series of scenes depicting the new life-style of the hippie subculture.

Hair, with music by Galt MacDermot, who had earned a Grammy in 1961 for "African Waltz," and book and lyrics by actors Gerome Ragni and James Rado, started as an off-Broadway presentation at Joseph Papp's partly subsidized Public Theatre on October 29, 1967. A sellout during an eight-week run, it garnered an Original Cast Album (OCA), recorded by RCA Victor. After a short, unsuccessful stand at the Cheetah, a Broadway dancehall, its sponsorship was assumed by millionaire Michael Butler, who brought the show to Broadway after extensive revisions. Opening at the Biltmore Theatre on April 29, 1968, it ran for 1,729 performances, closing on July 1, 1972. A new Original Cast Album, released in June 1968, became a Gold Album, received a Grammy Award for the Best Score from an OCA (1968), and reportedly went on to sell over 5 million copies by mid-1971. An album of the score by the Cowsills, released in March 1969, went Gold.

A two-sided disk by the Fifth Dimension ("Aquarius" b/w "Let the Sunshine in") shot up to No. 1, where it stayed for six weeks, becoming a Gold Record, and eventually selling over 3 million copies by the end of 1969. A third song "Good Morning, Starshine," stepped out as a single and yielded a Gold Record for the pop singer Oliver. As of October 1970, it was reported that more than 800 recordings had been made worldwide from the score. *Hair*'s success in this country was duplicated when the show opened in countries around the world, including Israel, Japan, Sweden, Holland, and Australia, with Original Cast Albums being released in each country. On the basis of the number of recordings released worldwide, it has been claimed that *Hair* was the most successful score in history as well as the most performed score ever written for Broadway.

Bill Haley (1925–1981)   Part of the first school of rockers playing what is known as Rockabilly, he started out as a Country & Western singer, traveling through the Midwest with a Country band he called The Saddlemen. He claims that "way back in 1947, 1948, and 1949" he was playing "a combination of Country & Western, Dixieland, and the old-style Rhythm and Blues." But his earliest imitative approach to R & B came in 1951, when he covered Jackie Brenston's Chess recording of "Rocket 88" b/w a cover of Jimmy Preston's '49 R & B hit "Rock the Joint." In 1954 he covered the blue-penciled Joe Turner's R & B smash "Shake, Rattle, and Roll," racking up a million seller for his Comets. That year Decca Records, which had just dropped the Father of R & B, Louis Jordan (1908–1975), from its roster, signed Haley. Though Haley will not admit that he was consciously influenced by Jordan, Milt Gabler, Jordan's record producer, became his producer, and Gabler has stated that he consciously sought to introduce the Jordan beat into Haley's style. On April 12, 1954, Haley waxed "Rock Around the

Clock,'' again covering a previously recorded black version of the song. The record, generally recognized as the disk that helped make a world-wide phenomenon of Rock 'n' Roll, looked like a dud until it became the theme of the film *Blackboard Jungle*. Then it became a runaway hit, racking up sales all over the world as the film opened in different countries (where it frequently stirred riots). In England it became the first record to sell over a million copies—and its worldwide sales have been estimated at over 22 million. Despite the phenomenal success of the disk, Haley was apparently too old and too lacking in charisma to ascend to the Rock throne soon occupied by Elvis Presley (1956). Nevertheless, Haley became a worldwide figure, maintaining a hold on European audiences that Presley and others quickly usurped in this country. In fact, in 1979 English Rock fans enjoyed a revival of Rockabilly that put Haley once again at the top of British Rock.

Hall of Fame, Blues   Awards made annually under the aegis of the Blues Foundation of Memphis for general contributions to the Blues. Recipients may be alive or deceased and are accorded recognition for their contribution to the entire history of the Blues, and not for any one year. Those elected thus far by the votes of an international panel of Blues authorities, critics, and personalities are:

Muddy Waters (b. 1915)

Howlin' Wolf (1910-1976)

B. B. King (b. 1925)

Elmore James (1918-1963)

Robert Johnson (c 1912-1938)

Little Walter (1930-1968)

Bessie Smith (1894-1937)

T-Bone Walker (1910-1975)

Sonny Boy Williamson, No. 2
  (Rice Miller, 1899-1965)

John Lee Hooker (b. 1917)

Willie Dixon (b. 1915)

Lightnin' Hopkins (1912-1982)

Big Bill Broonzy (1893-1958)

Blind Lemon Jefferson (1897-1929)

Son House (b. 1902)

Otis Spann (1930-1970)

Jimmy Reed (1925-1976)

Charley Patton (1887-1934)

Sonny Boy Williamson, No. 1
  (John Lee Williamson, 1914-1948)

Memphis Minnie (1897-1973)

Professor Longhair (Roy Bird)
  (1918-1980)

Roy Brown (1925-1981)

Bobby ''Blue'' Bland (b. 1930)

Blind Willie McTell
  (1901-1959)

Tampa Red (1900-1982)

Hall of Fame, Country (CMA)

1961 (limited to deceased)
  Jimmie Rodgers (1897-1933)
  Fred Rose (1897-1954)
  Hank Williams (1923-1953)
1962   Roy Acuff (1903-   )

1963   No addition

1964   Tex Ritter (1906–1974)

1965   Ernest Tubb (1914–   )

1966   Eddy Arnold (1918–   )
James R. (Jim) Denny (1911–1963)
Judge George Dewey Hay (1895–1968)
Uncle Dave Macon (1870–1952)

1967   Red Foley (1910–1968)
J. R. L. (Joe) Frank (1900–1952)
Jim Reeves (1924–1964)
Steve Sholes (1911–1968)

1968   Bob Wills (1905–1975)

1969   Gene Autry (1907–   )
Bill Monroe (1911–   )

1970   Original Carter Family:
A. P. Carter (1891–1960)
Maybelle Carter (1909–1978)
Sara Carter (1899–1979)

1971   Arthur Edward Satherley (1889–   )

1972   Jimmie H. Davis (1904–   )

1973   Chet Atkins (1924–   )
Patsy Cline (1932–1963)

1974   Owen Bradley (1915–   )
Frank "Pee Wee" King (1914–   )

1975   Minnie Pearl (1912–   )

1976   Paul Cohen (1908–1971)
Kitty Wells (1919–   )

1977   Merle Travis (1917–   )

1978   Grandpa Jones (1913–   )

1979   Hank Snow (1914–   )
Hubert Long (1923–1972)

1980   Connie B. Gay (1914–   )
Original Sons of the Pioneers:
Hugh Farr (1903–1980)
Karl Farr (1909–1961)
Bob Nolan (1908–1980)
Lloyd Perryman (1917–1977)
Roy Rogers (1911–   )
Tim Spencer (1908–1974)
Johnny Cash (1932–   )

Hall of Fame, Performers (Playboy), in alphabetical order

Duane Allman   Jimi Hendrix
Herb Alpert   Mick Jagger

Louis Armstrong
Count Basie
Dave Brubeck
Ray Charles
Eric Clapton
John Coltrane
Miles Davis
Bob Dylan
Duke Ellington
Ella Fitzgerald
Benny Goodman
George Harrison

Elton John
Janis Joplin
John Lennon
Paul McCartney
Wes Montgomery
Keith Moon
Jim Morrison
Elvis Presley
Linda Ronstadt
Frank Sinatra
Ringo Starr
Stevie Wonder

Hall of Fame Recordings (NARAS)   Since 1974 when these awards were established, the following Pop and Jazz historic recordings have been elected to the Hall of Fame by the members of the National Academy of Recording Arts and Sciences:

"Begin the Beguine": Artie Shaw (Bluebird, 1938)

Birth of the Cool: Miles Davis (Capitol, 1930)

Black and Tan Fantasy: Duke Ellington (Victor, 1928)

"Body and Soul": Coleman Hawkins (Bluebird, 1939)

Carnegie Hall Jazz Concert: Benny Goodman (Columbia, 1950)

"Christmas Song": Nat "King" Cole (Capitol, 1946)

The Genuis of Art Tatum (Vols. 1–13): Art Tatum (Verve, 1954–1955)

Gershwin: Porgy & Bess: Lehman Engel, conductor; Lawrence Winters, Camilla Williams and others (Columbia, 1951)

Gershwin: Rhapsody in Blue: Paul Whiteman with George Gershwin (RCA Victor, 1927)

"God Bless America": Kate Smith (Victor, 1939)

"God Bless the Child": Billie Holiday (OKeh, 1941)

"How High the Moon": Les Paul and Mary Ford (Capitol, 1951)

"I Can't Get Started": Bunny Berigan (Victor, 1937)

"In a Mist": Bix Beiderbecke (OKeh, 1927)

I'll Never Smile Again": Tommy Dorsey with Frank Sinatra and the Pied Pipers (Victor, 1940)

Jelly Roll Morton: The Saga of Mr. Jelly Lord (12 albums): Ferdinand "Jelly Roll" Morton (Circle Sound, 1949–1950)

"Mood Indigo": Duke Ellington (Brunswick, 1931)

"My Blue Heaven": Gene Austin (Victor, 1928)

My Fair Lady: original Broadway cast with Rex Harrison and Julie Andrews (Columbia, 1956)

Oklahoma: original Broadway cast with Alfred Drake, orchestra, and chorus, directed by Jay Blackton (Decca, 1943)

"One O'Clock Jump": Count Basie (Decca, 1937)

"Over the Rainbow": Judy Garland (Decca, 1939)

"Rock Around the Clock": Bill Haley and the Comets (Decca, 1955)

"Singin' in the Rain": Frankie Trumbauer and his orchestra, featuring Bix Beiderbecke on cornet (OKeh, 1927)

"Sing, Sing, Sing": Benny Goodman and his orchestra (Victor, 1936)

"Strange Fruit": Billie Holiday (Commodore, 1939)

"Take the 'A' Train": Duke Ellington and his orchestra (Victor, 1941)

"West End Blues": Louis Armstrong (OKeh, 1928)

"White Christmas": Bing Crosby (Decca, 1942)

Hall of Fame, Songwriters' (NAPM)   An adjunct activity of the National Academy of Popular Music, the Songwriters' Hall of Fame (and Museum) honors living and deceased writers, chosen by a vote of the membership of the Academy. Each year, an Awards Commitee selects candidates to be memorialized, eligibility being limited to those who have engaged in the profession of writing popular music for over 20 years. The paid membership then votes on the candidates. Since the balloting began in 1969, 177 living and deceased songwriters have been inducted into the Hall of Fame: They are:

Living Writers

Harold Arlen	Howard Dietz	Frederick Loewe
Burt Bacharach	Edward Eliscu	Herb Magidson
Alan Bergman	Ray Evans	Johnny Marks
Marilyn Bergman	Sammy Fain	Joseph Meyer
Irving Berlin	Ira Gershwin	Mitchell Parish
Leonard Bernstein	Adolph Green	Leo Robin
Jerry Bock	Bud Green	Arthur Schwartz
Irving Caesar	John Green	Pete Seeger
Sammy Cahn	E.Y. Harburg	Carl Sigman
Hoagy Carmichael	Sheldon Harnick	Stephen Sondheim
Cy Coleman	Edward Heyman	Jule Styne
Betty Comden	Burton Lane	Jimmy Van Heusen
J. Fred Coots	Jack Lawrence	Harry Warren
Sam Coslow	Alan Jay Lerner	Paul Francis Webster
Hal David	Jay Livingston	Jack Yellen
Mack David	Jerry Livingston	

Deceased Writers

Harold Adamson	Patrick S. Gilmore	J. S. Pierpont
Milton Ager	Mack Gordon	Lou Pollack

Fred Ahlert
Louis Alter
Ernest Ball
Katherine Lee Bates
William Becket
William Billings
James Bland
Carrie Jacobs Bond
James Brockman
Lew Brown
Nacio Herb Brown
Alfred Bryan
Joe Burke
Johnny Burke
Anne Caldwell
Harry Carroll
Sidney Clare
Will D. Cobb
George M. Cohan
Con Conrad
Hart P. Danks
Benny Davis
Reginald De Koven
Peter De Rose
Buddy De Sylva
Mort Dixon
Walter Donaldson
Paul Dresser
Dave Dreyer
Al Dubin
Vernon Duke
Gus Edwards
Raymond B. Egan
Duke Ellington
Daniel Decatur Emmet
Dorothy Fields
Ted Fiorito
Fred Fisher
Stephen Foster
Arthur Freed
Rudolf Friml

Ferde Grofe
Woody Guthrie
Oscar Hammerstein II
Lou Handman
W. C. Handy
James F. Hanley
Otto Harbach
Charles K. Harris
Lorenz Hart
Ray Henderson
Victor Herbert
William J. (Billy) Hill
Joseph E. (Joe) Howard
Julia Ward Howe
Howard Johnson
James P. Johnson
James Weldon Johnson
Arthur Johnston
Isham Jones
Scott Joplin
Irving Kahal
Gus Kahn
Bert Kalmar
Jerome Kern
Francis Scott Key
Ted Koehler
Huddie Ledbetter
Edgar Leslie
Sam Lewis
Frank Loesser
Ballard MacDonald
Edward Madden
Joseph McCarthy
Jimmy McHugh
Johnny Mercer
George W. Meyer
Jimmy Monaco
Neil Moret
Theodore Morse
Lewis F. Muir
Ethelbert Nevin

Cole Porter
Ralph Rainger
Andy Razaf
Harry Revel
Eben E. Rexford
Jimmie Rodgers
Richard Rodgers
Sigmund Romberg
George F. Root
Billy Rose
Vincent Rose
Harry Ruby
Bob Russell
Jean Schwartz
Seymour Simons
Harry B. Smith
Samuel Francis Smith
Ted Snyder
John Philip Sousa
Andrew B. Sterling
Harry A. Tierney
Charles Tobias
Roy Turk
Egbert Van Alstyne
Albert Von Tilzer
Harry Von Tilzer
Fats Waller
Samuel A. Ward
Ned Washington
Mabel Wayne
Kurt Weill
Percy Wenrich
Richard Whiting
Clarence Williams
Hank Williams
Spencer Williams
Septimus Winner
Harry MacGregor Woods
Henry C. Work
Allie Wrubel
Vincent Youmans

George Gershwin   Jack Norworth   Joe Young

L. Wolfe Gilbert   Chauncey Olcott   Rida Johnson Young

Haven Gillespie   John Howard Payne   Victor Young

Hammond organ   Invented in 1934 by the man after whom it is named, the Hammond organ was the earliest of the electronic organs. While the sound was produced by electrical instead of traditional means, it was close to that of the pipeorgan. In 1959 Yamaha developed a transistorized electronic organ.

See also chord organ; Solovox.

William Christopher Handy (1873–1958)   He called himself *Father of the Blues* in titling his autobiography (1941), and many historians preserve the designation. But Blues purists would argue that the title more properly belongs to men like Blind Lemon Jefferson (1897–1929), Charley Patton (1887–1934), whose rural blues he knew, or Leadbelly (1889–1949), true pioneers of the form. Nevertheless, he wrote four of the best-known, most-recorded and most-performed blues: "Memphis Blues" (1912), "St. Louis Blues" (1914), "Beale Street Blues" (1917), and "Harlem Blues" (1923), all of which helped propel the Blues as a fresh, new sound and form into the mainstream of popular music. In 1926 he compiled *Blues: An Anthology,* a watershed work that led to the vogue of Blues in Tin-Pan Alley and contributed to the rise of the "torch song," a derivative white form of Blues concerned with unfulfilled love. Handy was a cornetist and bandmaster—he led the band of the famous minstrel troupe know as Mahara's Minstrels—before he became a celebrated songwriter and music publisher. The firm he launched with Harry Pace in 1913 to publish "St. Louis Blues" continues today as W. C. Handy Music Co. In 1931 a park and a square were named after him in Memphis, where he began his songwriting career with "Mister Crump," written during the mayoralty campaign of 1909 and later published as "Memphis Blues." In 1947, his name went up on the marquee of a Memphis theater. In Florence, Ala., where he was born, a school has been named after him, and in Henderson, Ky., where he worked as a bandmaster from 1896 to 1900, a public swimming pool bears his name. The premiere of *St. Louis Blues,* a Paramount film based on his life, was held in St. Louis ten days after his death in New York City on March 28, 1958.

W. C. Handy Blues Awards   A series of annual awards given by the Blues Foundation of Memphis in nine categories. Nominations are made by an international panel of Blues authorities, critics, and personalities. The winners are presented at an annual gathering in the Peabody Hotel in Memphis.

The first awards were made in 1981:

Male, Contemporary, Albert Collins
Female, Contemporary: Koko Taylor
Male, Traditional: Lightnin' Hopkins
Female, Traditional: Alberta Hunter
Contemporary Blues Album: Professor Longhair, *Crawfish Fiesta,* Alligator 4718
Traditional Blues Album: Robert Lockwood, Jr., and Johnny Shines, *Hangin' On,* Rounder 2023
Vintage or Reissue Album: Robert Nighthawk, *Live on Maxwell Street—1964,* Rounder 2022
Blues Single of the Year: Jimmy Johnson, "I Need Some Easy Money"/ "Ashes in My Ashtray," Delmark 4503

The 1982 awards were as follows:

Male Blues Artist: Albert Collins
Female Blues Artist: Koko Taylor
Blues Vocalist: Bobby "Blue" Bland
Blues Instrumentalist: Albert Collins
Blues Album (U.S.): Johnny Copeland, *Copeland Special,* Rounder 2025
Blues Album (Foreign): Professor Longhair, *The London Concert,* JSP 1025 (U.K.)
Vintage or Reissue Album (U.S.): Professor Longhair, *Mardi Gras in New Orleans 1949–1957,* Nighthawk 108
Vintage or Reissue Album (Foreign): Champion Jack Dupree, *Blues from the Gutter,* Atlantic P-6183 (Japan)
Blues Single of the Year: Magic Slim & the Teardrops, "Teardrops"/ "Wonder Why You Need Me," Rooster Blues 707

See also Blues Foundation; Hall of Fame, Blues.

The Hangar   A worldwide symbol for the San Francisco Rock scene, The Hangar, as it came to be known, was a huge old airplane hangar in Marin County above Sausalito, terminus of the helicopter service that ferried people to San Francisco airport and served as a rehearsal hall for local Rock groups.

"hangup"   In counterculture argot, that part of the self which, because of social conventions, personal inhibitions, or fears, prevents the individual from functioning freely and effectively.

"happening"   A planned or unplanned event—artistic, cultural, or just spectacular—which becomes a memorable experience for participants. As a verb: "That's where it's happening" means "That's where you'll find the excitement." Also, when a record does not sell, people in the biz say: "It's not happening." There was a Rock group that called itself The Happenings. Unfortunately, they never did.

Hard Rock   The dividing line between Hard Rock and Heavy Metal seems rather thin since both involve loud volume, pounding rhythm, and a driving beat. But chronologically, Hard Rock antedated Heavy Metal, taking off directly from Rhythm & Blues. To partisans of the style, Hard Rock is Elvis (1935-1977) in "Hound Dog," Jerry Lee Lewis (b. 1935) in "Whole Lotta Shakin' Going On" and "Great Balls of Fire," Eddie Cochran (1938-1960) in "Summertime Blues," Little Richard (b. 1935) in "Tutti Frutti"—a rip-it-up, raucous, rocking sound. To such fans, the electronic gadgetry that carried Hard Rock to the outer limits of Heavy Metal after the mid-sixties only served to weaken the impact, subverting lyrics and even the vibrant rhythm. Of the sixties groups that teeter on the boundary line between Hard Rock and Heavy Metal, the Rolling Stones and Cream stand out for their strong allegiance to the Blues tradition. Mick Jagger (b.1944) was a rasping shouter in the Big Mama Thornton (b. 1926) vein and the music of his group was sensual, menacing, and brutally powerful. Yet even in an early work like "Satisfaction (I Can't Get No)," they traded on distortions characteristic of the Heavy Metal contingent. Then again, *Beggar's Banquet,* released in the year (1968) that saw the upsurge of Heavy Metal, was an unabashed return to the simple Hard Rock of the fifties. As for Cream, formed in 1966 by three musicians—guitarist Eric Clapton (b. 1945), bassist Jack Bruce (b. 1943), and drummer Ginger Baker (b. 1940)—who regarded themselves as the cream of English Rock, they came from Blues-oriented English groups like Mayall's Bluesbreakers and specialized in remakes of Blues classics of the fifties. However, they were concerned with albums, not hit singles, and since each operated as a soloist they produced extended tracks of interest to FM rather than AM radio. Clapton's debt to the guitarists of R & B as well as Delta Blues was unmistakable, nor did the group make any secret of its roots: R & B men like Muddy Waters (b. 1915), Howlin' Wolf (1910-1976), B. B. King (b. 1925), and others were constantly mentioned in live performances as their idols. Many historians name Cream as the group most responsible for the Blues revival of the late 1960s.

In the seventies Punk Rock emerged as an apparent effort to revive the simple Hard Rock of the early days of Rock 'n' Roll. But the social attitudes and stage manners of groups like the Sex Pistols stirred so much controversy that the nostalgic return to the past had to find a new label and became known as the New Wave.

See also Blues revival; Heavy Metal Rock; New Wave; Punk Rock.

Harlem   The black ghetto of Manhattan, which originally was bounded by 110th Street on the south and 155th Street on the north, with Lenox and 7th avenues as its main arteries. By the time that Ben E.

King was singing "Spanish Harlem," the boundaries of the area had been stretched and it included a large influx of Spanish-speaking people. In its heyday in the 1920s and 1930s, Harlem was the cultural capital of black America. It was also the major center of nightlife in NYC, with its ballrooms (Alhambra, Renaissance, Rose Danceland, Savoy), cabarets (Connie's Inn, Cotton Club, Ed Smalls' Paradise), and theaters (Alhambra, Apollo, Harlem Opera House, Lafayette, Lincoln). The first black-owned record company, Black Swan Records, was started by Harry Pace, W. C. Handy's music publishing partner, in the basement of his Seventh Avenue home in 1920–1921.

See also Apollo Theatre; Connie's Inn; Cotton Club; Harlem Renaissance; Savoy Ballroom; Ed Smalls' Paradise.

Harlem Renaissance   The designation of the artistic and intellectual ferment in black culture that originated in Harlem during the 1920s. Black poetry flourished with Langston Hughes and Countee Cullen. Black novelists like Jean Toomer and Zora Neale Hurston achieved national prominence. Musically, Jazz and the Blues swept into the mainstream. Stride piano, evolving from Ragtime, flowered as a style with James P. Johnson (1891–1955), Charles Luckeyeth Roberts (1887–1968), Willie "The Lion" Smith (1897–1973), and Art Tatum (1910–1956). The popularity of "Crazy Blues," recorded in 1920 by Mamie Smith (1883–1946) on OKeh Records, led to the rise of the Classic Blues singers, among whom Bessie Smith (1894–1937) was soon recognized as the Empress. Nightlife flourished, attracting white crowds from the worlds of sport, show business, and high society to the many cabarets and cafes—especially Connie's Inn, the Cotton Club, and Ed Smalls' Paradise. For the dancing crowd, there was the Savoy Ballroom, which featured the top bands of Jazz, and later Swing. Out of Harlem came Noble Sissle (1889–1975) and Eubie Blake (b. 1883) with the first all-black musical, *Shuffle Along,* the daddy of all-black shows that made Broadway in the twenties. Ethel Waters (1900–1977), Paul Robeson (1888–1976), and Duke Ellington (1899–1974) were three giants, among others, who gave musical stature to the Harlem Renaissance. The development attracted the patronage, support and interplay of such white creative luminaries as actress Tallulah Bankhead, actor John Barrymore, composer George Gershwin, novelist Fannie Hurst, playwright Eugene O'Neill, poet Edna St. Vincent Millay, poet Vachel Lindsay, actress Pola Negri, critic Alexander Woollcott, and H.L. Mencken of the *American Mercury.*

See also Connie's Inn; Cotton Club; Duke Ellington; Paul Robeson; Savoy Ballroom; Stride piano.

harmonic series   Only a tuning fork produces a "pure'" tone. When a note is struck on the piano or produced by a vibrating string or air-column, the resultant tone is a blend of the vibrations of the whole string or air-column (fundamental) plus the vibrations of portions of the string or air-column. The harmonic series consists of all the tones, fundamental and partials, that blend in the resultant tone:

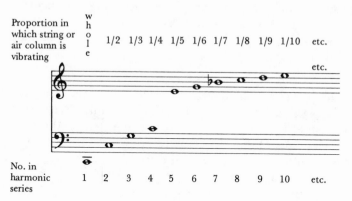

harmonica   *See* Blues harp; mouth organ.

"harp"   Blues lingo for the harmonica. Abbreviated from "mouth harp."
See also Blues harp; mouth organ.

The Harry Fox Agency   In operation since 1927, the Agency was established by NMPA, then known as the Music Publishers Protective Association, on the introduction of talking pictures, as a vehicle through which movie producers could secure rights for the use of music and music publishers could negotiate such licenses. In 1936 the service was extended to include the licensing of electrical transcriptions. Two years later, when Harry Fox became head of the agency later to bear his name, it undertook the licensing of recordings, the collection of mechanical royalties from record companies, the distribution of such royalties to music publishers, and the periodic audit of record company books. With the introduction recently of new media, the Agency's scope has once again been expanded, this time to embrace TV films and videotapes.

Serving over 3,500 music publishers, the Agency charges a basic fee of 3½ percent for its services. Mechanical royalties are distributed shortly after they are received from the record companies, which generally make quarterly accountings. When a publisher has not made arrangements for sub-publication of his copyrights in a foreign country, the Agency can collect mechanical royalties direct from foreign licensing societies. In addition to negotiating synchronization rights on behalf of its clients, the Agency also will handle motion picture theatrical performing rights, which film producers generally request, and the charge for which is added to the synchronization fee. For this service, the Agency charges a commission of 10 percent.

In 1969, on the death of Harry Fox, the agency was incorporated as a wholly owned subsidiary of NMPA.

See also mechanicals; National Music Publishers Association; synchronization.

Hawaiian guitar   The instrument is held flat on the lap and fretted with a metal slide. It has a ringing, whining sound. Because the metal slide, known as a "steel," goes across all the strings, thirds are easily sounded and glissandos are a natural device. The tuning of the Hawaiian is different from that of the acoustic instrument. In an effort to produce the sliding, whining quality, rural bluesmen employed a flat knife or a bottleneck.

See also bottleneck guitar; dobro; electric guitar; guitar.

"Hawk"   *See* Coleman Hawkins.

Coleman Hawkins (1904–1969)   He was known as "Bean" as well as "Hawk"—"Bean" because of his appetite for every type of bean (and popcorn). He is credited with raising the status of the tenor sax to a major solo instrument as the result of a ten-year stint with the Fletcher Henderson Band (1923–1933), with whom he also made his very first recording. He achieved national renown during a gig with a small combo at Kelly's Stable on 52nd Street in New York City, where his after-hours version of "Body and Soul," introduced by Libby Holman in the revue *Three's a Crowd* (1930), became a crowd spellbinder. It led to a recording of the song on October 11, 1939, which sold over a million copies and became a Jazz classic. Although he was a child of the Swing era, he swung with changes in Jazz, and in February 1944 assembled an all-star band for a Bop record session. With his big-toned, lush sound and rhythmic buoyancy, he was then at the peak of his popularity. Through the years, he was recognized as the top tenor saxist of his time in *Esquire, Playboy, Metronome* and *Down Beat* polls. His name was among the first five names imbedded in the Jazzwalk on 52nd St.

See also 52nd Street; Jazzwalk.

"head"   The sixties term for anyone involved in the counterculture now generally refers to a drug user. "Heads" are characterized on the basis of the drugs they trip on: "A" head, LSD; "B" head, barbiturates; "C" head, cocaine; "hop head," opium; "juice head," alcohol; "shit head," heroin; "garbage head," anything goes.

"head arrangement"   An arrangement worked out by a group of musicians in the process of playing or recording. It's not on paper but comes out of the head.

Head Music   A synonym for Acid Rock, or what Frank Zappa (b. 1940) termed a "freak out": music that produced the state of mind generated by LSD, but without taking the drug. Others see Head Music in relation to marijuana rather than LSD, producing the same relaxed state as marijuana or heightening the impact of the drug. Among the compositions frequently cited as Head Music, one finds the Byrds' "Eight Miles High" and "Mr. Tambourine Man," the Beatles' "Norwegian Wood" and their "A Day in the Life" from *Sgt. Pepper,* the Rolling Stones' "Paint It Black," and the Beach Boys' "Good Vibrations." The whine of the sitar or the Theremin is heard on these selections, instruments whose drone strings and glissandos supposedly have a hypnotic effect.

See also Acid Rock; *Freak Out;* sitar; Theremin.

"heavy"   A colloquialism meaning "weighty" or "ponderous" when used with regard to the meaning of something; and "unusual," "sophisticated," or "complex" with regard to a performance.

Heavy Metal Rock   Jimi Hendrix (1942–1970) was the Heavy Metallurgist par excellence. The sound engineer who handled his equipment said at one point: "He plays both amplifiers full up at Volume 10. . . . He destroys at least two speakers whenever he plays. . . . Most people just touch the wah-wah pedal with their foot. Jimi jumps on it with his full weight. . . . He ruins a lot of tremolo bars, too. He bends the strings with the bar, and they get bent way past the distortion level. That starts the feedback. . . . The pickups in the guitar amplify all the strings bending. That's how he gets that terrifying roar. . . . He also burns up a lot of tubes because of the great volume. . . . One night he burned out four amplifiers. You see, his amplifiers are turned up full and pushing what they're supposed to, but then all the speakers are pushing plus fuzz and the wah-wah, so there's more power than the amplifiers can take." After one tour he stated: "I think I've gone deaf . . . I'm going home to Scotland for two weeks to see if my hearing comes back to normal."

    Hendrix came thundering onto the scene just before the Heavy Metal explosion of 1968, when Blue Cheer, Iron Butterfly (*Heavy*),

Velvet Underground (*White Light/White Heat*), and Deep Purple came booming out of the telephonebooth amplifiers, their very names and song titles suggesting the ear-shattering power of their music. By '69 Black Pearl, MC 5 (*Kick Out the Jams*), The Stooges, Mountain, Grand Funk Railroad, and Led Zeppelin were adding their distortions, screaming highs, explosive lows, and clamorous decibels to the charts.

One should not forget that when Decca Records received the British Who's "My Generation" in 1966, the feedback distortion was so grating that executives feared they had received a defective master. Whether the Who antedated the Yardbirds or not in the pioneering of feedback, their "I Can See for Miles" was a masterpiece of artistic distortion. Yet the Yardbirds are generally cited as the oldest of the Heavy Metal groups, remembered for their "Rave-ups," as they typed their long, free-form instrumental breaks. But it was really the Led Zeppelin into which four Yardbirds modulated in '68 that became the longest-lived of the power bands. Transforming distortion, reverb, echo, feedback, fuzztone, wah-wah pedaling, and amplification into an overwhelming experience, the Zeppelin produced seven consecutive Gold and Platinum albums from 1969 through the *Physical Graffiti* LP of 1975 and *Presence* of 1976; nor did their *In Through the Out Door* of 1979 display any lessening of their hard impact or audience appeal.

According to the *Guiness Book of World Records,* Deep Purple, which made its debut in 1968, holds the title of the "world's loudest rock band." Quite a number of groups would dispute this, the Los Angeles–based Iron Butterfly and Michigan-based Grand Funk Railroad, among others. Both were among the first of the American Heavy Metallurgists, as Steppenwolf was among the first of the Canadian electronic screamers. Iron Butterfly has not been forgotten for its 17-minute '69 thunderer, "In-a-Gadda-da-Vida," which without distortion would read "In the Garden of Eden." Grand Funk Railroad, which made its debut with a free appearance at the Atlanta International Pop Festival in 1969, matched the size of its billboard advertising to the volume of its sound. In the summer of 1960, New Yorkers were treated to 60-foot portraits of the trio appearing on the largest billboard in the world, one that stretched across two Broadway blocks. Although hip critics disparaged the group, its first four albums in 1969–1970 were all million dollar sellers.

Taking its name from the famous novel by Hermann Hesse, Steppenwolf has been described as a group that "pins their listeners to their seats by their eardrums." "Born to be Wild" and "Magic Carpet Ride," both released in 1968 after the quintet was discovered in a Venice Beach, Calif., coffeehouse, were both Gold Records and tough examples of pure power and driving rhythms. "Born to Be Wild" was used as the motorbike theme in the film *Easy Rider,* and "Rock Me"

(1969) in the film *Candy*. The latter was described as a "supercharged disk with pulverizing vocal performance and intense rhythmic underpinning."

The 1970s saw the emergence of such power groups as ZZ Top, a Texas Blues Rock trio who perform in cowboy hats and garnered a Platinum Album for *Tres Hombres* (1973) and a Gold Record for *Fandango* (1975); Aerosmith, a high-voltage New England quintet with Gold Records in 1973, 1974, and 1975; Kiss; and Queen, all four of whom made their debut in 1973. Kiss has made the most imaginative use of makeup, as Queen has done with the electronics of Heavy Metal.

Termed "America's masters of outrage and arrogance," Kiss has hidden its members behind painted faces which give one the visage of a vampire or demon; another, that of a cat-man; the third, that of a star-man; and the fourth, of a spaceman. Appearing in costumes as spectacular as their makeup is bizarre, Rock's most explosive and incendiary group had its fifteenth album release in *Dynasty* in 1979. As for the British group Queen, with two members who possess degrees in physics or electronics, its *A Night at the Opera* offered a most innovative use of overdubbing and engineering. The high-decibel group moved into 1980 with a hit album, *The Game,* and a hit single, "Another One Bites the Dust," that masterfully exploited a studio's electronic resources to simulate war effects.

Heavy Metal is supposed to have enjoyed its heyday between 1968 and 1975. But a look at recent charts reveals the presence of such thunder-and-lightning groups as Rush, a Canadian trio that took a critical shellacking for six years until its *Permanent Waves* album of 1980 leaped into the Top 10; AC/DC, a feisty group out of Australia, which, despite the absence of media exposure and a hit single, sold over 3 million copies of *Back in Black* in the U.S.A.; and Plasmatics, a Shock-Rock New York group that developed a large live audience without a hit record. Other Heavy Metallurgist groups that emerged or peaked in the 1980s included Judas Priest, UFO, Scorpions, Foreigner, Journey, Van Halen (from the Netherlands), Pat Benatar, Triumph, and especially, Reo Speedwagon. The last-mentioned zoomed to the top of the charts in '81 with *Hi Infidelity,* their eleventh album, after a ten-year struggle. Their rise was as much a testimonial to the resurgence of Heavy Metal as the film of the same title, which featured an unabating stream of thundering groups, including veteran Visigoths like Cheap Trick, Blue Oyster Cult, Sammy Hagar, Devo, Black Sabbath, and a reconstituted Grand Funk Railroad, as well as the newer high-decibel exponents: Trust, Riggs, Journey, et al.

Against those who condemn Heavy Metal as mindless, proponents argue that the power chording, macho singing, and ear-shattering decibels provide listeners with a deafening and uproarious escape from drudgery, monotony, and futility. They point to shows when the bellowing of the audience vies with the roar of the band and the two streams of sound merge into one thunderous explosion of ecstasy. One critic has suggested that no music "more accurately conveys the screaming nerves of pubescent frustration than Heavy Metal." San Francisco promoter Bill Graham contends: "Heavy Metal may not be fashionable with critics and sponsors; but teenagers want that sound." Jimi Hendrix once said: "Man, the world's a bring-down. If we play loud enough, maybe we can drown it out."

See also Hard Rock; Shock Rock.

hemiola   The principle of alternating rhythmic patterns of three and two pulses while maintaining a constant pulse value:

Jimi Hendrix.   *See* "the black Elvis"; Heavy Metal Rock.

"hep cat"   *Hep* was superseded by *hip* as a term for an accomplished musician or a knowledgeable fan. *Square* was the opposite of *hep*.

"hide-beater"   Swing term for drummer.

high hat cymbal   *See* cymbal.

"high place"   To be in a "high place" is Rock jargon meaning to be happy, contented, or flying in spirit.

"High Priestess of Soul"   A designation of Nina Simone (b. 1933), singer, pianist, songwriter, whose performing style spans the gamut from Jazz to Soul.

See also Soul.

The "Hillbilly Cat"   An early cognomen for Elvis Presley (1935–1977) before he came to national renown early in 1956.

Hillbilly music   Although "Hillbilly" was in general use from the turn of the century onward as a designation of inhabitants of the southeastern section of the U.S.A., especially its backwoods and mountainous areas, it did not become a music term until 1925. Ralph Peer

(1892–1960), recording director of OKeh Records, is credited with the coinage. In January 1925 when he was recording a Carolina band, he heard a member refer to his associates as North Carolina hillbillies, with the result that Peer named them The Hillbillies. The group played white Country music, as distinguished from black Country music, which Peer dubbed Race music. Apparently the term used by Peer to describe rural white southern folk music actually appeared on a Vocalion label before 1925. One side of a disk by Uncle Dave Mason, an early performer on the *Grand Ole Opry,* was called "Hill Billie Blues." After World War II, the term was dropped in favor of "Country & Western."

See also Country & Western; *Grand Ole Opry;* Race music.

hippie   While a "hipster," derived from "hip," is a sophisticate who really knows and truly feels, a "hippie" is, in its original pejorative sense, a pretender, one who affects sophistication. But in the 1960s "hippies," with their long hair and oddball dress, were a significant part of the counterculture. San Francisco's Haight-Ashbury district was a hippie gathering place, as was Manhattan's Greenwich Village and the SoHo area. Among groups that emerged from the hippie turbulence, there were The Jefferson Airplane, The Mamas & The Papas, The Grateful Dead, Big Brother & the Holding Company, Sonny & Cher, and other San Francisco groups. The hippie outlook and life-style were the basis of the well-known rock musical *Hair.* Country singer Merle Haggard (b. 1937) attacked the hippie view of life in his song "Okie from Muskogee."

See also Haight-Ashbury; *Hair;* Acid Rock.

hit   A hit is a hit—a song, record, or artist that garners widespread acceptance or popularity as reflected in sales. From the turn of the century into the 1950s, a song hit was measured by the number of sheets or copies a song sold. Million-copy sellers were not unusual. By World War II, the sheet-music market had dwindled so that million-copy songs were rare, and a song was a hit if it sold 250,000 copies. In the years of the Lucky Strike network radio and TV show *Your Hit Parade* (1935–1958), making the Top 10 was also the token of a hit. Songs that made the Saturday night *Parade* received a "rack" order, which meant that in addition to music stores, sheets were sold in outlets such as five-and-ten-cents stores and supermarkets where the racks were displayed.

By the late fifties, a hit was determined not by sheet-music sales but by record sales. When a record received extensive air-play but the exposure was not reflected in sales, it was known in the business as a "turntable hit," which meant that it really did not make it.

See also Gold Record; Platinum Record; *Your Hit Parade.*

"hit on"   To ask somebody for something, and, doubtless, to press for it.

Hit Parade   See *Your Hit Parade.*

Hitsville, U.S.A.   What founder-owner Berry Gordy called the headquarters of Motown Records at 2648 West Grand Boulevard, in Detroit. The slogan appeared on a large sign over the two-story white bungalow.

Hoedown   A rural dance to celebrate the planting or picking of crops. Some of the early Country shows on the radio were known as Barn Dances and a few were known as Hoedowns.
    See also Country music shows.

Billie Holiday (1915–1959)   Still revered by many as the greatest of female Jazz singers almost a quarter of a century after her death, Billie turned Pop singing from a form of entertainment to an expressive art. The disciple of her transformation was Frank Sinatra (b. 1915), who sat at her feet on 52nd St. in New York City, where she became the highest-paid of all the club performers. "With few exceptions," Sinatra later said, "every major Pop singer in the U.S.A. during her generation has been touched in some way by her genius." As for himself: "It is Billie whom I first heard in the 52nd St. clubs in the early thirties, who was and still remains the greatest single musical influence on me." He could have added that the qualities of intensity and immediacy, self and sex, which became earmarks of Pop singing after his emergence, were a Blues heritage transmitted via Billie.
    For Billie, as for Sinatra later, Pop songs and singing were a form of autobiography: self-examination and self-expression. Scarred by a traumatic and sordid childhood, outraged by white prejudice, hounded by the police as a junkie, hurt by bad choices of husbands and friends, she brought to song a bitterness and sweetness, and a depth of feeling, never heard before. She said at one point: "I've been told that nobody sings the word 'hunger' like I do, or the word 'love.'"
    As for her style, Billie said: "I don't think I'm singing. I feel like I'm playing a horn. I try to improvise like Lester Young, like Louis Armstrong, or someone else I admire. What comes out is what I feel. I have to change a tune to my own way of doing it."
    Through the indefatigable John Hammond of Columbia Records, she began a recording career in 1933, cutting two sides with Benny Goodman, a career that yielded some of the great classics of Jazz and Pop: "God Bless the Child," a song she co-wrote and that was revived during the 1960s; "Strange Fruit," an angry song about lynching;

"Lover Man," "I Cover the Waterfront," "Mean to Me," "He's Funny That Way," "More Than You Know," "I'm Gonna Lock My Heart and Throw Away the Key," and many, many others.

In 1937 she sang with Count Basie, suffering the indignity of being told that her skin was too white; the following year, she became the first black vocalist to work with a white band, Artie Shaw's, and was told to use the freight entrance at the Hotel Edison where the band played.

Over 50 albums of her recordings have been reissued by various companies since her death in 1959. In 1972 Diana Ross played Billie Holiday in a film based on *Lady Sings the Blues,* Billie's autobiography. Hers was among the first five names of Jazz greats imbedded in the 52nd St. Jazzwalk.

holler   *See* arhoolie.

Buddy Holly (1936–1959)   Some type him Tex-Mex, a rather elusive sound. Others place him with Rockabilly singers like Elvis (b. 1935), Carl Perkins, (b. 1932), and Jerry Lee Lewis (b. 1935). Regardless, he was one of the early giants of Rock 'n' Roll, emerging in the year after Presley broke into the national limelight. He came to Rock as did the other Rockabilly singers, starting as a Country singer from Lubbock, Tex.; in fact, while he was in high school, he formed a group known as the Western and Bop Band, one of whose members was songwriter/vocalist Bob Montgomery, today a prominent Nashville record producer/publisher/songwriter ("Misty Blue" and other hits). Holly's short-lived career went into orbit when he became associated with Norman Petty, owner of a recording studio in Clovis, N. Mex. A disk of "That'll Be the Day," previously recorded for Decca and then unreleased, was re-recorded under Petty's aegis with the group that became known as the Crickets. It went to No. 1 both in England and the U.S.A. With the Crickets recording on the Brunswick label, and Holly soloing on Coral, his first solo hit was "Peggy Sue," followed immediately by "Rave On." These marked the beginning of a two-year run of hits during which he produced seven Top 40 songs. Energized by his ringing guitar, sock glottal stops, and an expansion of the vocal line ("uh-uh-uh-uh" instead of "oh"), Holly's disks possess an animal vitality and rhythmic drive that many associate with the golden years of Rock 'n' Roll. Early in 1959 he was on tour with J. P. Richardson (1930–1959), the Big Bopper of "Chantilly Lace," and Richie Valens (1941–1959), remembered for "Donna," when they charted a plane to take them from Clear Lake, Iowa, to Fargo, N.D. The four-passenger Beechcraft Bonanza N3749N crashed immediately after takeoff in Mason City, Iowa, killing all occupants. (Waylon Jennings [b. 1937], then playing bass with Holly's backup group, The Crickets, would have been a fatality, had he not given up his seat to the Big Bopper, who was suffering from the flu.) February 3, 1959, has become known as "The Day the Music Died." Of Holly, who was then 23, Bob Dylan has said: "Buddy Holly and Johnny Ace are just as valid to me today as they were in the late fifties." Holly's influence has been detected not only in the Beatles but in singers as varied as Bobby Vee (b. 1943), Tom Paxton (b. 1937), the Everly Brothers (Don, b. 1937; Phil, b. 1939), Creedence Clearwater Revival, and Dylan himself. The impact of his sudden and early death found expression in Don McLean's classic "American Pie."

Hollywood Palladium   The famous ballroom that was built by the Big Bands of the Swing era, opened in 1940. In 1980 it kicked off its fortieth anniversary week with a tribute to Tommy Dorsey (1905–1956), followed by a tribute to Artie Shaw (b. 1910). During the week of the celebration, many of the great bands of the thirties and forties were heard, including those of Les Brown (b. 1912), Benny Carter (b. 1907), Freddy Martin (b. 1906), Bob Crosby (b. 1913), and Tex Beneke (b. 1914).
See also Palomar Ballroom; Swing.

Home of Happy Feet   *See* Savoy Ballroom.

"honking"   Playing a note with force in the lower register of the tenor sax. Honking was a sociological as well as a musical phenomenon in the years after World War II—an expression of the anger and frustration blacks felt over their promised liberation from second-class citizenship. Musically, it was an attempt to dissociate the sax sound from the sweet, mooing sound of white Swing saxophonists. The honker produced a loud, rasping, throbbing sound, sometimes emphasizing his furious feelings by repeating one grating note over and over. Texan Illinois Jacquet (b. 1922), regarded as the first of the honkers, showcased the raucous, shrieking sound on Lionel Hampton's hit disk of "Flying Home" (1942). Other well-known honkers include Eddie "Lockjaw" Davis (b. 1921), Sam "The Man" Taylor (b. 1926), Eddie "Mr. Cleanhead" Vinson (b. 1917), King Curtis (mid- 1930s–1971), and Cecil "Big Jay" McNeely (b. 1928).

honky-tonk   Said to be black slang for a gin mill. Texas was a rich breeding-ground for Country music stars: Ernest Tubb (b. 1914), Bob Wills (1905–1979), Ray Price (b. 1926), George Jones (b. 1931), Johnny Horton (1929–1960), Buck Owens (b. 1929), and Hank Thompson (b. 1925), among others. During an oil boom in the 1930s, wide-open taverns sprang up, selling illicit liquor and providing a postage-stamp dance floor. Generally located on the outskirts of towns, they became known as "honky-tonks." The style of music that developed in these places was high-spirited, rhythmic, and amplified (to cope with the noise and revelry). Among the songs that caught the spirit of these joints: "Stompin' at the Honky-Tonk," "I Ain't Goin' Honky-Tonkin' Anymore," "Headin' Down the Wrong Highway." One of the earliest recorded Boogie-Woogie numbers, written and waxed by Meade "Lux" Lewis (1905–1964) in 1929 for Paramount, was titled "Honky-Tonk Train." It later became a best-selling number for Bob Crosby (b. 1913) and his orchestra, with Bob Zurke (1910–1944) at the piano. Country songwriter/singer/guitarist Hank Williams (1923–1953) evoked the "hell-raising" style in "Honky-Tonk Blues" and "Honky-Tonkin'" (1948). Ernest Tubb (b. 1914), who tried to walk in the footsteps of the Father of Country Music, Jimmie Rodgers (1897–1933), and who was one of the first Country singers to use an electric guitar, is regarded as the pioneer of the Honky-Tonk style. A strong revival of the style occurred in the sixties with singers like Ray Price (b. 1926) of Perryville, Tex., and Johnny Horton (1929–1960) of Tyler, Tex., the latter remembered for "The Battle of New Orleans," a worldwide hit in 1957. But the fifties saw a proliferation of songs trading on the style and spirit: "Honky-Tonk Girl," recorded by Hank Thompson in '54; "Honky-Tonk Man," recorded by Johnny Horton (1929–1960) in '56; "Honky-Tonk Song," recorded by Webb Pierce (b. 1926) in '57. And into the 1960s: "Honky-Tonk Troubles," recorded by "Little" Jimmy Dickens (b. 1925) in '62 and "Honky Tonk Women," recorded by the Rolling Stones (1969). A two-sided record released by King Records in 1956–1957 and titled simply "Honky-Tonk," by Bill Doggett (b. 1916)—who worked at various times as arranger/pianist/organist with the Ink Spots, Lucky Millinder (b. 1900), Lionel Hampton (b. 1913), Louis Armstrong (1900–1971), Count Basie (b. 1904), and Louis Jordan (1908–1975)—became the biggest-selling disk of its time, reportedly passing the 4 million mark.

"hook"   An appealing musical sequence or phrase, a bit of harmony or sound, or a rhythmic figure that grabs or hooks a listener. It can also be a lyric phrase or a group of words. But virtually no hit record is without a bit of music or words so compelling that it worms its way into one's memory and won't go away.

hootennany   A folk singer's word, it was popularized by the Almanac Singers, especially Pete Seeger (b. 1919) and Woody Guthrie (1912–1967). According to Seeger, the word came from the Midwest, where it meant an informal party, "like wingding or shindig," and may be of French origin. Seeger adds: "In 1941 Woody and I found them using the term in Seattle for a monthly fund-raising party, where they had some singing and dancing, a little bit of everything, food. We took it to New York and used it for our weekly rent parties. . . . Leadbelly [1885–1949], Burl Ives [b. 1909], Josh White [1908–1969], and many other people used to drop into Almanac House and sing with us on a Sunday afternoon. Then after World War II, we used the word for the fund-raising songfests of the organization called People's Songs.'' In short, the hootenanny was an informal gathering of folk singers who sang, swapped stories, and invited audience participation and who used the event to raise needed funds. In the fall of 1962 ABC–TV instituted a weekly show titled *Hootenanny* in which it used the idea of the "hoots" presented by folk artist Ed McCurdy (b. 1919) on Tuesday nights at the Bitter End in Greenwich Village. The show was videotaped on college campuses with a well-known performer as host and headliner. Seeger objected to the equating of a TV variety show with the hootenanny. "It was a phony program," he said. "It wasn't a real hootenanny. The word almost got ruined and I almost stopped using it."

See also Woody Guthrie; Pete Seeger.

"hops"   Once they were known as dances, balls, or just shows. But in the early years of Rock 'n' Roll, they became known as hops, partly because a hit record by Danny & the Juniors was called "At the Hop" (1957–1958). Apparently, the song was first known as "Doin' the Bop," but its title was changed at the suggestion of Philadelphia disk jockey Dick Clark (b. 1929), who was instrumental in making it into a hit and who was given part of the copyright by the writers. Like other dee jays, Clark ran record hops at which popular artists of the day appeared live and the kids danced. Admission was charged, although the artists, anxious to secure airplay of their disks, appeared gratis. For the young people, it was an exciting evening of doing all the current dances and hearing and seeing current record stars live. For the disk jockeys, record hops were moneymakers.

"horse"   Lingo for heroin.

Hot Rod music   Chuck Berry (b. 1926), who was approaching 30 when he made his big record debut with "Maybelline," sensed the fascination of young people with speeding cars when he described the triumph of a souped-up V–8 Ford over a Coup-de-Ville Cadillac. Many of the early Rock 'n' Roll groups named themselves after birds, hoping to imitate the success of the Ravens. But after a short time, car names became popular, and there were the Cadillacs, Edsels, El Dorados, The Essex, Falcons, Fleetwoods, Impalas, Valiants, and others. Hot Rod music really peaked with two groups, the Beach Boys and Jan & Dean.

Both started by writing and recording Surfing songs. Soon the lure of the big waves yielded to the spell of the open road. In '63 the Beach Boys dealt with "Little Deuce Coupe," followed by "Little Honda" and others. Jan & Dean (b. 1941) sang of "Drag City" and "Dead Man's Curve," the latter becoming a real life-size drama when Jan (b. 1941) emerged paralyzed from an auto crash that almost cost him his life.

Hot Jazz   Used with reference to sounds of the so-called Jazz Age, the 1920s of F. Scott Fitzgerald and the Lost Generation; the era of flappers, speakeasies, sex in the backseat of flivvers, and bootleg booze. The sounds stemmed from the New Orleans pioneers of Jazz, modified by the two-beat Dixielanders out of Chicago. Among the best-known Hot Jazz combos of the time: the Original Memphis Five, the Wolverines with Bix Beiderbecke, Red Nichols & the Five Pennies, Louis Armstrong's Hot Five, King Oliver's Creole Jazz Band, Red McKenzie & his Blue Blowers, Miff Mole's Stompers, Jelly Roll Morton & his Red Hot Peppers. Swing was played by fairly large aggregations of 12 men or more, with a brass choir, woodwind and sax choir, rhythm section, and sometimes even a string section. Hot Jazz, a more freely improvised sound, was the work of combos of five to seven men, with a lineup like that of the New Orleans pioneers of Jazz: a front line of trumpet, trombone, clarinet and/or tenor sax plus a rhythm section of drums, bass, and possibly guitar and piano.
See also Dixieland Jazz

"hot stove"   A music-biz colloquialism of the Tin-Pan Alley era of live plugs. Contact men (song-pluggers, that is) offered all kinds of rewards to artists and bandleaders in their efforts to secure radio performances of their songs. When an artist solicited or accepted outright cash, he was said to take a "hot stove."

house-rent parties   Parties run generally in black ghettos to raise the rent; known as Boogie parties in Chicago; also known as "buffet flats." Under whatever name, they were a feature of black life in the Depression era, with free entertainment being provided by Stride piano-players like J. P. Johnson (1891–1955), Willie "The Lion" Smith (1897–1973), Fats Waller (1904–1943), Duke Ellington (1899–1974), and others.
See also Stride piano.

Hudson River Troubadour   The billing of Don McLean (b. 1945), later of "American Pie" fame, when he worked for New York State, performing in communities along the Hudson River.
See also *Clearwater.*

Hullabaloo   A TV show of the 1960s that featured Rock artists and groups.

hurdy-gurdy   Street or barrel organs used by organ grinders were once called "hurdy-gurdies." The reason may have been because the hurdy-gurdy is activated by a rotating crank. But in actuality the hurdy-gurdy is a stringed folk instrument resembling the dulcimer in design and tuning; the crank turns a wheel that rubs a group of strings to produce a kind of bagpipe sound. Once the hurdy gurdy was so long that is required two men to operate it in the churches and monasteries where it was used; it was superseded by the organ. In time, the size and the number of strings were reduced, making it portable. At the same time, drone strings were added. In 1968 Donovan (b. 1946), the Scottish singer/songwriter/guitarist whose albums include *Sunshine Superman* (1966), *Mellow Yellow* (1967), and *Gift from a Flower to a Garden* (1968), and who was part of the Flower Power movement, recorded "Hurdy-Gurdy Man," which became the title song of a bestselling album. It aroused interest in the European instrument.

Hurrah   In the 1980s, the major New Wave disco in New York City.
See also New Wave.

Hustle   The biggest dance record of the 1970s—it became a Gold Record two months after its release in May 1975; it also was the most popular of all the Disco dances. "The Hustle" was written and recorded by Van McCoy (1940–1979), who worked while a high school student with the Starlighters, then the Heartbeats, and eventually the Shirelles. As a staff writer for the famous producer/songwriters Leiber & Stoller, and later, for a publishing affiliate of Columbia Records, he wrote songs for Gladys Knight & the Pips, Aretha Franklin (b. 1943), Bobby Vinton (b. 1941), and Peter & Gordon. After the Hustle became the basic dance of Disco, variants developed, including the Latin Hustle, California Hustle, and New York Hustle. Doing the last-mentioned, partners dance face-to-face, holding hands at arm's length and moving or pointing to a count of six. In the Los Angeles Hustle, also known as the Pasadena Line Walk, they dance in the long-line tradition of the Conga and the Stroll.

"hybrid"   A record produced from digital tapes.
See also digital recording.

hype   Apparently derived from "hypodermic," it refers to an excited, enthusiastic superdrive to promote a record, song, or artist. Both as a noun and a verb, "hype" generally connotes that the enthusiasm is calculated if not fabricated. But ''hypes'' sometimes work, which then means that the thing hyped had enough appeal and quality to warrant the outlay of time, effort, and budget.

I

''The Iceman''   Nickname of Jerry Butler (b. 1939), who acquired it partly because he studied to be a chef in ice sculptor, and partly, it seems, because of his cool temperament. He served as lead voice for the Impressions' recording of ''For Your Precious Love'' (1958). Then he stepped out as a solo singer, scoring in 1960 with ''He Will Break Your Heart,'' which he co-wrote; with ''Only the Strong Survive'' in 1969; and with ''Ain't Misunderstanding Mellow,'' a Gold Record in 1972, made as a duet with Brenda Lee Eager (b. 1948).

Impressionism   A musical, literary, and art style. Composers like Ravel and Debussy sought to suggest the impressions experienced by an observer of a scene. The concept originated with French painters in the nineteenth century, men like Degas, Monet, Gaugin, Van Gogh, et al. Impressionism differs from Romanticism, which concerns itself with the drama, emotion, and tension in a situation or relationship. Perhaps the best example of Impressionism in Rock is *Song Cycle* (1967) of Van Dyke Parks (b. circa 1941), who tried to paint pictures in sound of Hollywood: ''Vine Street,'' ''Laurel Canyon Boulevard,'' etc. Rick Wakeman's *Six Wives of Henry VIII* also stands forth as an impressionistic projection of images through the keyboard.

improvisation   Spontaneous performance in which the player, operating with a known or unknown selection, invents variations on the spur of the moment. Variations include alterations of melody, rhythmic patterns, harmonic structures and sequences, inspired by the way a performer feels during the performance. The character of improvisation changes, depending on the person's technical resources and the sounds of the time. What was regarded as fresh by the Dixieland crowd sounded stale to the boppers, just as some of the sounds of R & B sound lifeless to the Soul crowd.
See also Dixieland Jazz, New Orleans Jazz.

independent producer   Before the mid-1950s, record companies employed A & R men to select repertoire for their artists, to superintend the recording process, and with the assistance of company audio engineers, to mix the results for commercial release. For some time now, these functions have been in the hands of producers who operate independently under short-term or long-term contracts, or on specific assignment. The first such arrangement was made in 1956 when Atlantic Records, impressed by a Spark record by the West Coast Robins (''Riot in Cell Block # 9'' b/w ''Smokey Joe's Cafe''), signed the two young men who wrote the songs, owned the label, and produced the regional hit. For several years, Jerry Leiber and Mike Stoller wrote and produced disks made by the Coasters as well as other Atlantic groups. After a time, the entire industry followed suit. Thus, where once a small group of A & R men ruled the music business, there are now several hundred independent producers who exercise their responsibilities and power. All records today carry the name of a producer, and sometimes an executive producer as well. Depending on their track record, such people generally are paid a fee for their services as well as a royalty based on sales. Following on the heels of Leiber and Stoller, young Phil Spector (b. 1940), who served an apprenticeship with them, produced 28 records between 1962 and 1966, of which 18 sold more than a million copies. In the same period, George Martin attained renown as the producer of the Beatles, and Andrew Loog Oldham as the producer of the Rolling Stones. A number of groups (the Beach Boys, among others) supervised their own production. During the years of her rise to fame when she had one hit after another, Dionne Warwick (b. 1941) was produced by Burt Bacharach (b. 1928) and Hal David (b. 1921), who wrote her songs. Today the list of independent producers would fill several pages of this book; readers will find the names in annual directories published by *Billboard* and other music trade papers.

Indian influence in Rock During the 1960s, largely as a result of Beatle George Harrison (b. 1943), quite a number of groups developed an interest in Indian music and Indian instruments. Not long after Beatlemania swept the USA in 1964, Harrison was attracted to the sitar, an ancient Indian instrument, and began studying with India's master sitarist, Ravi Shankar. The impact of that study became apparent in the *Rubber Soul* album when Harrison performed on the sitar in ''Norwegian Wood.'' So much interest was stirred in the instrument among rock performers that Ravi Shankar began giving classes. Soon musicians were talking about ragas, tablas, and the sarod, another Indian instrument. The Beatles moved from Indian music into Indian religion and philosophy and made a trip to India to study Transcendental Meditation with Maharishi Mahesh Yogi.

One of the groups influenced by the Beatles' interest in Indian music was the Incredible String Band out of Scotland. In their second album,

The 5,000 Spirits of the Layers of the Onion, "Mad Hatter's Song" was composed of five movements, three of which employed Indian themes, and "You Know What You Could Be" was a fusion of C & W and Indian raga elements. The Indian influence persisted into the 1970s when John McLaughlin (b. Yorkshire, England, 1942) underwent a religious conversion and assumed the name of Mahavishnu. In describing the direction of the Mahavishnu Orchestra, he said: "Through the grace of Sri Chinmoy, my spiritual musician, I've become more aware of the presence of God. God is the supreme musician, the soul of music, and the spirit of music. I'm trying to reach him by allowing myself to become his instrument."

Harrison's interest in Indian religion found expression in a recording he produced in 1969 of "Hare Krishna Mantra" by the Hare Krishna Temple.

See also Sarod; Sitar; Transcendental Rock.

Ink Spots   A hit singing group of the 1940s whose success as one of the first black groups to cross the color line inspired the early R & B and "doo-wop" groups like the Ravens and Orioles. Originally porters at the New York City Paramount Theatre, they scored their first big hit with "If I Didn't Care" in 1939. Their first million seller was "Into Each Life Some Rain Must Fall," a 1944 duet with Ella Fitzgerald (b. 1918). Their second and third million-copy sellers were "To Each His Own," a song discarded from the film of the same title; and "The Gypsy," both 1946 releases. The quartet consisted of Billy Kenny, tenor; Ivory "Deek" Watson, tenor; Charlie Fuqua, bass and guitar; and Orville "Hoppy" Jones, bass and cello. The Ink Spots became quite famous for their use of a talking chorus, one that featured a low bass voice contrasting with a chorus sung in a high tenor, almost falsetto voice. Billy Kenny was usually the tenor, and the talking bass was Orville "Happy" Jones. The major friendly competitors of the Ink Spots were the Mills Brothers, who pursued a swinging style (whereas the Spots leaned toward slow ballads) and who celebrated their fiftieth year in show business in 1980.

instrumental   A composition without words, or rendition of a song without a vocal.

Instrumental Group or Band of the Year, Best Country (CMA awards)

1967   Buckaroos

1968   Buckaroos

1969   Danny Davis and the Nashville Brass

1970	Danny Davis and the Nashville Brass
1971	Danny Davis and the Nashville Brass
1972	Danny Davis and the Nashville Brass
1973	Danny Davis and the Nashville Brass
1974	Danny Davis and the Nashville Brass
1975	Roy Clark and Buck Trent
1976	Roy Clark and Buck Trent
1977	Original Texas Playboys
1978	Oak Ridge Boys Band
1979	Charlie Daniels Band
1980	The Charlie Daniels Band
1981	Alabama

Instrumentalist of the Year, Best Country (CMA awards)

1967	Chet Atkins
1968	Chet Atkins
1969	Chet Atkins
1970	Jerry Reed
1971	Jerry Reed
1972	Charlie McCoy
1973	Charlie McCoy
1974	Don Rich
1975	Johnny Gimble
1976	Hargus "Pig" Robbins
1978	Roy Clark
1979	Charlie Daniels
1980	Roy Clark
1981	Chet Atkins

Instrumental Performance, Best (NARAS Grammy Awards)

1958	Billy May: *Billy May's Big Fat Brass* Count Basie: *Basie*
1959	David Rose & Orchestra with Andre Previn: *Like Young* Duke Ellington: *Anatomy of a Murder*
1960	Henry Mancini: *Mr. Lucky* Count Basie: *Dance with Basie*
1961	Henry Mancini: *Breakfast at Tiffany's* Si Zentner: *Up a Lazy River*
1962	Peter Nero: *The Colorful Peter Nero* Joe Harnell: "Fly Me to the Moon Bossa Nova"

1963   Al Hirt: "Java"
       Count Basie: *This Time by Basie! Hits of the 50s and 60s*
1964   Henry Mancini: *The Pink Panther*
1965   Herb Alpert & the Tijuana Brass: "A Taste of Honey"
1966   Herb Alpert & the Tijuana Brass: "What Now, My Love?"
1967   Chet Atkins: *Chet Atkins Picks the Best*
1968   Mason Williams: *Classical Gas*
1969   Blood, Sweat & Tears: "Variations on a Theme by Erik Satie"
1970   Henry Mancini: *Theme from "Z" and Other Film Music*
1971   Quincy Jones: *Smackwater Jack*
1972   Billy Preston: *Outa-Space* (pure instrumental)
       Isaac Hayes: *Black Moses* (vocal coloring)
1973   Eumir Deodata: "Also Sprach Zarathustra" (*2001*)
1974   Marvin Hamlisch: "The Entertainer"
1975   Van McCoy & the Soul City Symphony: "The Hustle"
1976   George Benson: "Breezin'"
1977   John Williams conducting the London Symphony Orchestra: *Star Wars*
1978   Chuck Mangione Group: *Children of Sanchez*
1979   Herb Alpert: "Rise"
1980   Bob James and Earl Klugh: "One on One"
1981   Mike Post, featuring Larry Carlton: "The Theme from Hill Street Blues"

See also National Academy of Recording Arts and Sciences.

Instrumental Performance, Best Country (NARAS Grammy Awards)

1968   Flatt & Scruggs: "Foggy Mountain Breakdown"
1969   Danny Davis & the Nashville Brass: *The Nashville Brass featuring Danny Davis/Play More Nashville Sounds*
1970   Chet Atkins & Jerry Reed: *Me and Jerry*
1971   Chet Atkins: "Snow Bird"
1972   Charlie McCoy: *Charlie McCoy/The Real McCoy*
1973   Eric Weissberg and Steve Mandell: *Dueling Banjos*
1974   Chet Atkins & Merle Travis: *The Atkins-Travis Traveling Show*
1975   Chet Atkins: "The Entertainer"
1976   Chet Atkins & Les Paul: *Chester & Lester*
1977   Hargus "Pig" Robbins: *Country Instrumentalist of the Year*
1978   Asleep at the Wheel: "One O'Clock Jump"
1979   Doc & Merle Watson: "Big Sandy/Leather Britches"

1980   Gilley's "Urban Cowboy" Band: "Orange Blossom Special/ Hoedown"

1981   Chet Atkins: *Country—After All These Years*

See also National Academy of Recording Arts and Sciences.

Instrumental Rock   Rock without vocals peaked in the period from 1959 to 1963, with interest centered in the electric organ, electric guitar, and tenor sax. Regardless of the novelty of the sound, these records were basically dance records. The original inspiration of the trend might have come from Bill Doggett's two-sided disk of "Honky-Tonk," an R & B instrumental featuring tenor saxist Clifford Scott that went to No. 2 on Pop charts and reportedly sold over 4 million copies in 1956–1957. In '58 a Los Angeles Latin Rock group went to No. 1 with "Tequila." The trend gained ascendancy with two guitarists who began using electricity imaginatively. Duane Eddy (b. 1938), assisted by his producer, Lee Hazlewood, who was an audio expert, developed a "twangy" guitar sound by loosening the strings on his instrument. The loud, echoing sound of "Mr. Twangy," as he became known, produced hits in tough-titled instrumentals: "Rebel Rouser" (1958), "Ramrod" (1958), "Cannonball" (1958), "Forty Miles of Bad Road" (1959), and "Some Kind-a Earthquake" (1959). The other guitarist was Link Wray (b. 1935), who also opted for explosive titles like "Rumble" (1958) and "Rawhide" (1959), and whose work is said to have influenced British guitarists like Eric Clapton (b. 1945) and Peter Townshend (b. 1945) of The Who.

Soon instrumental groups began calling themselves by names with raunchy, violent, and aggressive connotations: Fireballs, Ramrods, Routers, Rebels, Busters, Johnny & the Hurricanes. Starting with "Crossfire" (1959), the last-mentioned group was extremely successful with Hard Rock transformations of "Red River Valley" (titled "Red River Rock," 1959); "Blue Tail Fly" (titled "Beatnik Fly," 1960); and a "Reveille Rock" (1959). By contrast, Santo & Johnny had a dream-like No. 1 hit in "Sleep Walk" (1959). Out of Tacoma, Washington, a group consisting of three driving guitars and drums, the Ventures, had a run of instrumental hits, starting with "Walk, Don't Run" (1960). From Memphis, Tenn., Booker T. & the MG's (Memphis Group), an integrated group consisting of organ, guitar, bass and drums, hit No. 3 with "Green Onions" (1962). That year, hot tenor saxist King Curtis (1935–1971) turned the Twist into a remunerative disk with "Soul Twist." Bill Black, who played bass in Elvis Presley's Sun group, organized a combo in '59, which cut a bestseller in "Smokie—Part 2" that year and did even better the following year with "White Silver

Sands" and an instrumental version of Elvis's hit "Don't Be Cruel."

The electric organ came to the fore not only with Booker T. but even earlier with Dave Cortez Clowney (b. 1939) of Detroit, who became known as Baby Cortez and racked up a No. 1 hit in "The Happy Organ" (1959). Although the Twist was launched by two vocal records, by Chubby Checker (b. 1941) and Hank Ballard (b. 1936) & the Midnighters, it elicited a large number of instrumental records. With the arrival of Bob Dylan and meaningful lyrics in 1962, Rock veered away from instrumental records to vocals, largely by groups.

integrated album   An album whose tracks all relate to a central theme, subject, situation, or problem. The Beatles' *Sgt. Pepper* album (1967) is generally regarded as a pioneering effort. Another type of continuity was attempted in *The Notorious Byrd Brothers* when the tracks were cross-faced into one another.

See also Art Rock; Classical Rock; concept album.

Isle of Wight Festival   The festival on the island in the English Channel was held in September 1969 just after the legendary Woodstock festival. It presented the accepted array of well-known Rock artists, including Creedence Clearwater Revival, Joni Mitchell (b. 1943), and The Who, whose Rock opera, *Tommy,* had been released in April '69 and who performed selections from it (*The New York Times* hailed *Tommy* as "the first pop masterpiece"). But the artist for whom the Isle of Wight Festival proved a triumph was Bob Dylan (b. 1941). It was his first festival appearance after his near-fatal motorcycle accident; he reportedly was paid a fee of $50,000; and he manipulated publicity with the savvy of a Sinatra, flying in several days in advance and holing up in an isolated villa, accessible only to other legendary figures like the Beatles and the Rolling Stones. Although his performance received mixed notices, he was the talk of the festival, as once he had been at the Newport Folk Festival of 1963. The Isle of Wight Festival of summer 1970 gave prominence to the Allman Brothers Band, Eric Burdon & War, and Canned Heat, among other groups.

See also Festivals.

Italo-American Rock   Not a style or category but just a way of noting that a number of groups came out of the Italian sections of New Jersey and the Bronx: the Crests, Dion & the Belmonts, Frankie Valli & the Four Seasons, the Young Rascals. Later there were the Blues Magoos, Vanilla Fudge, and Jay & the Americans, among others.

Burl Ives Award   A series of cash prizes established by folk artist Burl Ives (b. 1909) and awarded annually by the National Folk Festival Association to those "who have made outstanding contributions in the authentic music field and have helped spread and preserve the folk heritage in everyday life."

J

JATP   The initials stand for "Jazz at the Philharmonic," the umbrella for Jazz concerts sponsored here and abroad by Norman Granz (b. 1918). The name is derived from concerts that Los Angeles–born Granz ran at the LA Philharmonic Auditorium in 1944. That year he produced a short film, *Jammin' the Blues,* which won an Academy Award for the Best Short Feature of the Year. Granz also produced Jazz records, at first for other labels and then for his own: Clef, Norgran, and later Pablo, named in honor of Pablo Picasso, with whom he had become quite friendly. He conceived and produced a series of *Songbooks,* as he called comprehensive albums (five LPs in the case of George Gershwin [1898–1937] and Ira Gershwin [b. 1896], devoted to music of some of the great show composers. Ella Fitzgerald (b. 1918) sang, in addition to the Gershwin music, the songs of Cole Porter (1892–1964), Irving Berlin (b. 1888), Duke Ellington (1899–1974), and Richard Rodgers (1902–1979) and Lorenz Hart (1895–1943). Granz is credited with initiating the practice of recording Jazz live at concerts, and not just in a recording studio.

J.D.'s   Located in Phoenix, Ariz., it was one of the largest nightclubs in the Southwest. Waylon Jennings (b. 1937) & the Waylors starred here in the early sixties and landed an RCA Victor recording contract while performing at the club.
See also Armadillo World Headquarters.

Mahalia Jackson (1911–1972)   Although she was born in New Orleans and grew up with the sound of Bessie Smith (1889–1937), Ma Rainey (1886–1939), Ragtime, and Jazz in her ears, she turned exclusively to Gospel singing during the Depression—she had sung in church from the age of five. After she moved to Chicago when she was 16, she rejected an offer to sing with the Earl Hines Band and instead joined the choir of the Great Salem Baptist Church. Singing with the

Johnson Gospel Singers eventually led to solo work. She made her first Gospel recordings in 1935. In 1947 she recorded "Move On Up a Little Higher" for a small Harlem label, a disk that subsequently sold over 2 million copies. Public recognition came to her through appearances on the Ed Sullivan show, at the National Baptist Convention as official soloist, and on her own radio and TV program out of Chicago. A close friend of Dr. Martin Luther King, Jr., she participated actively in the civil rights movement of the sixties. Dr. King delivered his famous "I have a dream," speech, on the steps of the Lincoln Memorial in 1963, following her singing of "I Been 'Buked and I Been Scorned." Her many recordings on Columbia helped her earn the title "Queen of Gospel Singers." In the film *Jazz on a Summer's Day* (1960), she may be heard singing "The Lord's Prayer."

See also Gospel music.

jam session   A scheduled or unscheduled convocation of jazzmen, who improvise for the sheer fun of it—no set program, no leader, no music. Jam sessions were a regular feature on 52nd Street clubs during the Street's heyday. Among the most successful, if not the longest-lived series were jams run at Jimmy Ryan's by Milt Gabler, owner of the Commodore Record Shop and founder of Commodore Records, starting in 1939. Gabler usually had two mobs on stage, one consisting of the Eddie Condon (1904–1973) Dixieland crowd, and the other of a Harlem-type band, built around trumpeter Henry "Red" Allen (1908–1967), tenor saxist Ben Webster (1909–1973), or another black jazzman. By the time the evening was coming to a close with the playing either of "Bugle Call Rag" or just the Blues, every musician in the club was onstage.

About the same time, two producers, Monte Kay and Pete Kameron, began running jams at Nick's in Greenwich Village, a Dixieland outpost; later, around 1942, they moved uptown and began running jams with more modern jazzmen at Kelly's Stable. Perhaps the earliest jams on 52nd Street were those run at the Hickory House (now the home of Joe's Pier 52) under the aegis of clarinetist Joe Marsala (b. 1907). About the time that Kelly's Stable settled across the Street from Hickory House in 1940, trumpeter Frankie Newton (1906–1954) launched a series of jams at the Stable. Jam sessions disappeared from the music scene as Jazz and its audience splintered into warring groups, and also because the Musicians Union was opposed to providing clubs with music without adequate compensation.

"Jimmy James"   The name under which Jimi Hendrix (1942–1970) led a band, the Blue Flames, when he worked in Greenwich Village in early 1966.

See also "the black Elvis"; Heavy Metal Rock.

Al Jarvis (1909–1970)   The Los Angeles disk jockey who originated the "Make-believe ballroom" framework of programming records, popularized by disk jockey Martin Block (1903–1967), to whom it brought both fame and fortune. Jarvis called his program *The World's Largest Make-Believe Ballroom.* The gimmick devised by Jarvis in 1932 was to pretend that he was on the spot where a given performer or band was playing rather than to indicate that he was spinning a record. Jarvis originated the idea on Station KFWB, which retained Block when Jarvis left the station in 1946 after fourteen years. Initially, Block appeared live on KFWB but was heard over WNEW in New York, where he soon settled for a long run.

Jazz   Since its emergence toward the end of the nineteenth century, Jazz has developed so many different styles that it is difficult to find a common denominator in Ragtime, New Orleans Jazz, Boogie-Woogie, Blues, Dixieland, Swing, Bop, Third Stream, Free Jazz, and other recent avant-garde forms. Once, rhythm and a beat would have been regarded as a common element. But since the advent of Bop, rhythm in terms of dance meter has largely disappeared from Jazz. Pulse as a more subtle aspect of rhythm might be acceptable. Another common element might be syncopation, i.e., the displacement, anticipation, and delay of regular accents. Perhaps, the only irrefutable element one finds in all Jazz is spontaneity, improvisation, or instant creation. (Whitney Balliett, veteran jazz critic of *The New Yorker,* titled one of his collections *The Sound of Surprise.*)

Jazz Performance, Best—Large Group or Soloist with Large Group/Big Band (NARAS Grammy Awards)

Large Group or Soloist with Large Group

1960   Henry Mancini: *Blues and the Beat*
1961   Stan Kenton: *West Side Story*
1962   Stan Kenton: *Adventures in Jazz*
1963   Woody Herman Band: *Encore: Woody Herman, 1963*
1964   Laurindo Almeida: *Guitar from Ipanema*
1965   Duke Ellington Orchestra: *Ellington '66*
1966   (No award)
1967   Duke Ellington: *Far East Suite*
1968   Duke Ellington: *And His Mother Called Him Bill*
1969   Quincy Jones: *Walking in Space*
1970   Miles Davis: *Bitches Brew*

Big Band (New Heading)

1971   Duke Ellington: *New Orleans Suite*
1972   Duke Ellington: *Togo Brava Suite*

1973   Woody Herman: *Giant Steps*
1974   Woody Herman: *Thundering Herd*
1975   Phil Woods with Michel Legrand and His Orchestra: *Images*
1976   Duke Ellington: *The Ellington Suites*
1977   Count Basie and His Orchestra: *Prime Time*
1978   Thad Jones and Mel Lewis: *Live in Munich*
1979   Duke Ellington: *At Fargo, 1940 Live*
1980   Count Basie and Orchestra: *On the Road*
1981   Gerry Mulligan and his Orchestra: *Walk on the Water*

Jazz Performance, Best—Soloist or Group (NARAS Grammy Awards)

1958   Ella Fitzgerald: *Ella Fitzgerald Sings the Duke Ellington Songbook* (soloist)
        Count Basie: *Basie* (group)
1959   Ella Fitzgerald: *Ella Swings Lightly* (soloist)
        Jonah Jones: *I Dig Chicks* (group)
1960   Andre Previn: *West Side Story*
1961   Andre Previn: *Andre Previn Plays Harold Arlen*
1962   Stan Getz: "Desafinado"
1963   Bill Evans: *Conversations with Myself*
1964   Stan Getz: *Getz/Gilberto*
1965   Ramsey Lewis Trio: *The "In" Crowd*
1966   Wes Montgomery: *Goin' Out of My Head*
1967   Cannonball Adderley Quintet: "Mercy, Mercy, Mercy"
1968   Bill Evans Trio: *Bill Evans of the Montreaux Jazz Festival*
1969   Wes Montgomery: "Willow Weep for Me"
1970   Bill Evans: "Alone"
1971   Bill Evans: *The Bill Evans Album*
1972   Gary Burton: *Alone at Last* (soloist)
        Freddie Hubbard: "First Light" (group)
1973   Art Tatum: *God Is in the House* (soloist)
        Supersax: *Supersax Plays the Bird* (group)
1974   Charlie Parker: *First Recordings* (soloist)
        Oscar Peterson, Joe Pass, Niels Pedersen: *The Trio* (group)
1975   Dizzy Gillespie: *Oscar Peterson & Dizzy Gillespie* (soloist)
        Chick Corea & Return to Forever: *No Mystery* (group)
1976   Count Basie: *Basie & Zoot* (soloist)
        Chick Corea: *The Leprechaun* (group)
1977   Oscar Peterson: *The Giants* (soloist)
        Phil Woods: *The Phil Woods Six—Live from the Showboat* (group)
1978   Oscar Peterson: *Montreux '77—Oscar Peterson Jam* (soloist)
        Chick Corea: *Friends* (group)

1979   Oscar Peterson: *Jousts* (soloist)
        Gary Burton and Chick Corea: *Duet* (group)
1980   Bill Evans: *I Will Say Goodbye* (soloist)
        Bill Evans: *We Will Meet Again* (group)
1981   John Coltrane: *Bye Bye Blackbird* (soloist)
        Chick Corea and Gary Burton: *Chick Corea and Gary Burton in Concert, Zurich, October 28, 1979* (group)

Jazz-Rock fusion   The experimental spirit that led the Beatles to produce their *Sgt. Pepper* album in 1967 also moved other groups to strike out in new directions. Three groups, all formed about the same time, sought to fuse Rock and Jazz through the addition of horns to the typical Rock quartet. Two of the three were organized by Blues guitarists. Mike Bloomfield (1944–1981), former lead guitarist of the Paul Butterfield Blues Band, launched the Electric Flag while Al Kooper (b. 1944) of the Blues Project formed Blood, Sweat & Tears. The Flag was an eleven-piece group, established in 1967, that included, in addition to the typical four-man Rock lineup, trumpet, alto sax, tenor sax, a baritone sax who doubled on soprano sax and flute, piano, and organ. After three albums, all released in 1968 and including the sound track of the film *The Trip,* the Flag tore apart. Blood, Sweat & Tears, a more sophisticated group whose two albums included variations on themes by the neoclassic European composer Erik Satie, was longer-lived. Its nine-man group included a front line of four horns: a brass choir of two trumpets and trombone plus an alto sax. Their title album *B S & T,* which followed their debut LP, *The Child Is Father to the Man,* made No. 1 on Pop charts, became a Gold Album, and won a Grammy for Album of the Year (1969) and another for Best Instrumental Performance for the Erik Satie variations. From the title album, three singles were released: "You've Made Me So Very Happy," a song on which Berry Gordy collaborated; "Spinning Wheel," a song by lead singer David Clayton-Thomas, which won a Grammy (1969) for Best Arrangement Accompanying a Vocalist; and "And When I Die," a song by Laura Nyro (b. 1947), which was a Gold Record. All three singles sold over a million records each. With a lineup of men who were graduates of the Juilliard, Manhattan, and Eastman Schools of music, the group scored a giant seller in 1970 of *B S & T 3,* an album that shipped more than a million copies in its first week and that went to No. 1. *B S & T 4* was one of Columbia Records' fastest-moving LPs, with a sellout within 24 hours of its release and a sale that made it a Gold Album.

The third group that participated in the Jazz-Rock fusion was Chicago, who racked up million sellers every year from 1969 into 1975 with albums that were simply titled *Chicago I, Chicago 2,* etc. With a seven-man lineup that included three horns—trumpet, trombone, and woodwinds—they began as the Big Thing in 1967 but became the *Chicago Transit Authority* in their first double-album release in 1969. In the early days, they were at pains to note that they came into being before Blood, Sweat & Tears, although their first album appeared after B S & T's. They contrasted themselves with this competing group by saying "Our roots are basically Rock but we can and do play Jazz. Blood, Sweat & Tears is basically a Jazz-rooted combo that can play a lot of Rock." In 1978 guitarist/vocalist Terry Kath, then 31, accidentally shot himself to death. However, Chicago continued to function into the 1980s, moving in a Pop Rock direction.

From the jazz side of the tracks, trumpeter Miles Davis (b. 1926) crossed into Rock, if only briefly, in 1969 with *Bitches Brew,* an album in which he used Rock rhythms, an electric guitar, and electric keyboards. British guitarist John McLaughlin (b. 1942), who worked with Davis on *Bitches Brew,* formed his own group in 1971, which became the Mahavishnu Orchestra after his religious conversion through Sri Chinmoy (*see also* Indian influence in Rock). The four musicians who collaborated with him all had Jazz backgrounds; he had previously worked with Rock as well as Jazz groups. Signed by Columbia Records in '71, he produced three Jazz Rock albums (*Inner Mounting Flame; Birds of Devotion; Love, Devotion, Surrender*), which became bestsellers. The last-mentioned involved another musician who had also become a follower of Sri Chinmoy: Carlos Santana, whose group blended Latin-American, African, and Blues rhythms.

Avant-garde jazz was the métier of the Soft Machine, a British three-man group with a lead vocalist in Robert Wyatt, who played many instruments including trumpet and cello. Although their music embodied the influences of jazzmen like saxist Ornette Coleman (b. 1930) and pianist Cecil Taylor (b. 1933) and of avant-garde composers like Karlheinz Stockhausen and John Cage, their longhair and light shows suggest a Rock orientation. Termed the "futuristic Beatles" by some critics, they exerted more influence than their sales would indicate.

In 1976 Ornette Coleman, the enfant terrible of free-association improvisation and a personalized sound that some rejected as out-of-tune playing, organized a group that included two electric guitars, an electric bass, and drums. Prime Time, as he called the group, produced two albums of Jazz Rock (*Dancing In Your Head* and *Body Meta*) and faded from the scene. But in 1981 it gave a series of live performances, and hoped for the release of an unreleased digitally recorded album (*Fashion Faces*) and a new recording contract.

Other groups that must be considered in a survey of Jazz Rock include: Weather Report, influenced by the Soft Machine; Chick Corea with *Return to Forever*; and Herbie Hancock, two of whose albums, *Head Hunters* and *Thrust,* both 1974 issues, made the Top 20.

Jazzwalk   The sidewalks of New York City's 52nd Street, between 5th and 6th avenues, into the pavement of which medallions are being placed with the names of the Jazz performers who helped make the area known as Swing Street famous throughout the world. Since 1979, when the first medallions were imbedded in the pavement in front of the CBS Building, the following names have been memorialized: saxist Charlie "Bird" Parker, trumpeter Dizzy Gillespie, singer Billie Holiday, saxist Lester Young, saxist Coleman Hawkins, trumpeter Roy Eldridge, pianist Art Tatum, violinist Stuff Smith, drummer Kenny Clarke, singer Sarah Vaughan, pianist Thelonious Monk, and trumpeter Miles Davis. The recipients of the Prez Awards, named in honor of tenor saxist Lester "Prez" Young, which resulted in their names being inscribed on imbedded medallions, were selected by an ad hoc committee composed of Jazz performers, critics, and historians. The idea of the Jazzwalk was generated by Jazz critic Leonard Feather in reviewing a history of 52nd Street, *The Street That Never Slept* (now known as *52nd St.: The Street of Jazz*), written by this author. In 1972 this author broached the project to representatives of Mayor John Lindsay. It was not until six years later that the needed finances were secured. An approach to Bruce Lundvall, President of CBS Records, led to the company's footing the bills for the initial ceremonies and medallions. New names will be added in years to come.

See also 52nd St.

"Jefferson airplane"   A "roach clip" made by splitting a match down the middle so that it can hold the remnants of a marijuana "joint." It is said that the well-known Rock group took its name from this makeshift joint holder.

Starting as a Folk Rock group, the Jefferson Airplane, founded by Marty Balin (b. 1943), became an outstanding Acid Rock group with their debut album, *Jefferson Airplane Takes Off.* The album went Gold and was followed by *Surrealistic Pillow,* which contained "White Rabbit," a song in which the characters of *Alice in Wonderland* were viewed psychedelically. "White Rabbit" was the work of Grace Slick (b. 1943), who quickly became the major competitor of Janis Joplin (1943–1970) on the San Francisco and the national scene. The Airplane was one of the first groups to play the Fillmore in San Francisco; was managed by Bill Graham, impresario of the Fillmore; and was the first San Francisco group to land a recording contract with a major company, RCA Victor.

See also Acid Rock; California sound; Fillmore; Bill Graham.

"jelly roll"   Black jargon for vagina. Refers also to a sexual partner, and, as a verb, to fornication.

Jesus Rock   The 1970s witnessed a marked rise of religious feeling in Rock. At the beginning of the decade, British rocker Cliff Richard (b. India, 1940) produced an album titled *About the Man* in which he read the life of Christ in the New Testament Bible and recorded four especially written religious songs. The following year, Linda Ronstadt (b. 1946) sang: "We need a lot more of Jesus and a lot less of Rock and Roll." The shift from Now Rock to Rock of Ages found expression that year in Norman Greenbaum's "Spirit in the Sky," Judy Collins's, "Amazing Grace," Bob Dylan's "Three Angels," and ex-Beatle George Harrison's "My Sweet Lord," a Top 10 hit. In 1971, too, *Godspell,* a musical based on the Gospel according to St. Matthew, opened at the off-Broadway Cherry Lane Theatre, later moving to Broadway. Its religious theme had been anticipated in *Salvation,* a 1969 off-Broadway musical, which was cast in the looser framework of an old-fashioned revival meeting and which ran at the Jan Hus Playhouse for 239 performances. The most ambitious and most provocative of the religious musicals, *Jesus Christ Superstar,* began as a widely acclaimed Rock opera recording and then ran for 720 performances at the Mark Hellinger Theatre after an October '71 opening.

As the seventies progressed, more and more established Rock and Folk artists became born-again Christians. Barry McGuire (b. 1935), whose antiwar disk, "Eve of Destruction," had become a Gold Record in 1965, early dedicated his life to Jesus, thereafter devoting his talents as a self-taught composer, poet, and storyteller to the writing of such devout songs as "Anyone but Jesus," "Love Is" and "I Love You, Lord." Among others who embraced Christianity, there were B. J. Thomas (b. 1946), who had a series of million-copy hits, starting with Hank Williams's song "I'm So Lonesome I Could Cry" and including the Oscar song "Raindrops Falling on My Head"; Disco queen Donna Summer (b. 1950); Dion Dimucci (b. 1939) of Dion & the Belmonts; Richie Furay (b. 1944), formerly of the Buffalo Springfield and the spark of Poco; Joe English, formerly of Paul McCartney's Wings; Bonnie Bramlett (b. circa 1940) of Delaney & Bonnie; Leon Patillo, formerly of Santana; Billy Preston (b. 1946), who became internationally famous through his organ performance on the Beatles' "Get Back" (1969); Arlo Guthrie (b. 1947), famed son of the legendary Woody Guthrie; and Van Morrison (b. 1945).

The year 1979 brought the climactic news of the turn to Christianity of Bob Dylan (b. 1941), the sixties prophet of social change and born a Jew. Dylan's conversion was suggested in his album *Slow Train Coming.* Although his fans booed and walked out of concerts devoid of his "Blowin' in the Wind" songs, Dylan confirmed his conversion as a born-again Christian in *Saved,* his 1980 album. In interviews that year, he said he had accepted Jesus Christ in his heart in 1978 after a "vision and feeling" during which the room in which he sat moved. "There was a presence in that room," he said, "that couldn't have been anybody but Jesus." (In 1982 there were reports that Dylan was turning back to Judaism.)

Within the record industry, there had been other signs of the growing impact of Jesus Rock. In 1974 the ABC television network bought Word Records of Waco, Tex., one of Jesus music's premier labels. Arista Records, with artists like Barry Manilow (b. 1947), Dionne Warwick (b. 1941), and Air Supply, purchased Savoy Records, a 30-year-old black Gospel label. In 1979, MCA Records established Songbird Records as its own Christian label.

By 1980 the Gospel Music Association, located in Nashville, was offering the following statistics on the growth of Jesus music, including Jesus Rock: (1) Christian record companies gross $100 million a year in sales of records and tapes; (2) time-sales revenues on 1,400 Christian radio stations top $40 million a year; (3) 500 Christian artists, performing live, gross $50 million in concert gates and offerings. To which should be added a Gallup Poll survey that found 19 percent of Americans identifying themselves as born-again Christians—a total of 41 million people.

At the beginning of the eighties, the Jesus music industry was split into two camps. One favored a concerted move to advance the crossover of religious records into the mainstream; the other questioned or opposed it. Those who favored it were fully aware that as early as 1967 Elvis Presley had produced an album of Gospel songs and hymns, *How Great Thou Art,* which had made the Top 20 and had been certified Gold ($1 million or more in retail sales) by the RIAA. But Edwin Hawkins (b. 1942) whose recording of "Oh Happy Day" was a 1969 crossover, took the position: "My music is my ministry as a Gospel artist. I will not compromise. If something crosses over, fine. If it doesn't, fine. My first duty is my ministry." This position is strongly seconded by Ralph Carmichael, president of the San Fernando Valley–based Light Records, an exclusive Christian label. Nevertheless, Andrae Crouch, sometimes called the "Stevie Wonder of Gospel music," who is Light Records' most celebrated artist, has made appearances on *Saturday Night Live* and recorded an album of non-Christian songs for a non-Christian label.

B. J. Thomas (b. 1946), who "came to the Lord" in the mid-seventies after a bout with drugs and who concentrated solely on Jesus music for three years, has returned to Pop. "I want to praise the Lord," he has said, "and I'm gonna live right. But if I'm gonna make records, I want them to sell. I'm not a Christian entertainer. I'm an entertainer who's a Christian."

An opposing view is taken by Dallas Holm (born 1949), who has two single records, "Alleluia" and "Rise Again," that have been at the top of Gospel charts and approach Gold certification. His position is that Christian artists should set moral examples for non-Christian performers and not copy their excesses and commercial ploys. "With what little experience I have had in Rock," he says, "I just can't put that together with Christianity."

The contending views found expression at a Gospel music conference sponsored in November 1980 by *Billboard* magazine, which issued a special supplement titled: "Gospel Music: Bridging the Secular Waters."

See also Gospel music.

Jew's harp   Though the origin of the instrument's name is unknown, it is apparently a misnomer. Corruption of "jaw harp"? Sold by Jews in England? Resemblance to the biblical lyre? An ancient folk instrument, it does consist of a horseshoe-shaped metal frame to which a flexible metal tongue is attached. It is played by holding the instrument to the mouth and striking the vibrating metal tongue with the fingers of the free hand. The mouth cavity serves as a resonator, with the size and shape of the cavity determining the pitch.

Jitterbug   A dance of the Depression era and the Swing era, which was known in some cities (e.g., Detroit and Pittsburgh) as the "Lindy Hop." There were Jitterbug Jamborees at the Randall's Island Jazz Festival in 1938 and at the World's Fair in 1940. The kids who danced the Jitterbug or Lindy were themselves known as "jitterbugs." The girls generally wore saddle shoes, full, pleated skirts, and bulky sweaters, while the boys wore their hair cut long and one-button, rolled-lapel suits with peg-leg trousers.

"jive"   Black talk meaning to flatter, not with sincerity but with the purpose of gaining something. Also to doubletalk or kid.

Robert Johnson (1912-1938)   Born in Robinsonville, Miss., he was the archetype of the restless, wandering bluesman, sensual, paranoid, and self-destructive. "He'll say 'Hey, I'm going out and take a leak,'" bluesman Johnny Shines (b. 1915) has said of the Delta bluesman with whom he worked for several years, "then that would be the last you'd see of him for two weeks." And bluesman Son House (b. 1902), who most influenced him and from whom he derived some of his Blues, said: "He'd go up to a gal he saw at one of those dances and try to take her off, no matter who was around, her husband or boyfriend." For some years it was thought that Johnson, who never saw his twenty-sixth birthday, had been poisoned by a jealous girlfriend. Recent research has established that he was killed by a jealous husband.

In his short life, Johnson tried to engulf a world of sensation, so much so that he has been called the Shelley, Keats, and Rimbaud of the Blues. The sensuality was accompanied by a constant and inescapable paranoid feeling that there was "a hellhound on my trail," as one of his famous songs is titled. He was such an abysmally lonesome man ("Terraplane Blues") that he had to keep continually on the move ("Stones in My Passway"). Illiterate though he was, he found words that gave expression to an amazing depth of feeling. His mastery of the guitar was so great that Johnny Shines claimed he never had to learn the instrument. "They don't talk about a duck learning to swim," Shines said.

Johnson's power as a bottleneck bluesman is evident in the influence he exerted on Elmore James (1918–1963) and Muddy Waters (b. 1915), two giants of Chicago Electric Blues. James called his group the Broomdusters, using as a theme Johnson's famous Blues "I Believe I'll Dust My Broom." Muddy's first recorded single included "Walking Blues," modeled on Johnson's 1936 disk of the song.

Johnson's impact speared into the Rock generation. "Walking Blues" was adapted by Paul Butterfield. The Rolling Stones' *Let It Bleed* album contains a version of Johnson's "Love in Vain." Cream's "Crossroads" is an adaptation of "Crossroad Blues." In *Layla* by Derek and the Dominoes, Eric Clapton (b. 1945), who founded the group, employed a Robert Johnson melody to express his anguish over the rupture of his affair with the wife of Beatle George Harrison (b. 1943). Taj Mahal (b. 1942) has recorded Johnson's "Sweet Home Chicago" and Bonnie Raitt (b. 1949) has made many of his Blues a part of her onstage repertoire.

See also Delta Blues; Muddy Waters.

"joint"   Refers either to (1) a low-down dive or club; or (2) a stick of marijuana. Also known as a reefer or roach at different times.

Al Jolson (1886–1950)   A seminal figure in the history of popular singing and pop song. The son of a rabbi, he gave up the career of a Jewish cantor to become a pop singer and brought the influence of minstrelsy into popular singing. He was a singer who moved, danced, emoted. From 1909 to 1911 he worked in blackface as an endman in Lew Dockstader's Minstrels. This led to a 10-year stint on Broadway in Shubert shows. He made his screen debut in the pioneering film *The Jazz Singer*—recently a starring vehicle for Neil Diamond (b. 1941)—the first motion picture (1927) with dialogue. After World War II, in which he spent untold hours entertaining the troops overseas, his career seemed at an end. But a film executive who heard him at a benefit at the Hillcrest Country Club in Beverly Hills (when he came at the end of a long line of luminaries) got the idea of *The Jolson Story* (1947) and *Jolson Sings Again* (1950), which led to a second gigantic career. In these films, Jolson sang the songs while actor Larry Parks played his role; the first film grossed $8 million, and the second $5 million.

Starting with "Ragging the Baby to Sleep" in 1912, Jolson had million-copy sellers in "Sonny Boy" b/w "There's a Rainbow Round My Shoulder" (1928), which he sang in *The Singing Fool;* "April Showers" b/w "Swanee," the song with which he introduced George Gershwin to the music world in 1919, and which was part of the two-sided hit in 1945; "Rockabye Your Baby" b/w "California, Here I Come," "You Made Me Love You" b/w "Ma Blushin' Rosie," "Sonny Boy" b/w "My Mammy," and "Anniversary Song" b/w "Avalon"—all songs that he sang either in *The Jolson Story* or *Jolson Sings Again,* but that were released on disks in 1946. Jolson's imprint on these songs was so unique that no one has been able to sing them without sounding like him. Together with the black singers of the R & B era, he was a major influence in bringing muscle, excitement, and drive back into pop singing with belters like Frankie Laine (b. 1913), Eddie Fisher (b. 1928), and Rosemary Clooney (b. 1928), the transition group of the late forties and early fifties that led from the crooners to Rock 'n' Roll. Jolson's imitators and idolizers are almost as numerous as Presley's, and include Eddie Fisher, Steve Lawrence (b. 1933), Vicki Carr (b. 1938), Debbie Reynolds (b. 1932), and many others.

About Jolson, pioneer rocker Jerry Lee Lewis (b. 1935) had the following to say (in an interview with the author of this book): "When I was about 12, I walked into a theater in Ferriday, La., where I was born. Before the picture went on, they played a record. I never stayed for the picture. That record hit me so hard I rushed out, ran all the way home, sat down at the piano, and tried to sing 'Down Among the Sheltering Pines' exactly as Al Jolson had done it. And would you believe it? Although I heard the song just once, I knew every word. The way Jolson did it, each word stood out like an electrified stop sign. I've never forgotten those words—and I've never stopped admiring Al Jolson.

"Jolson is still the No. 1 showman-singer to me. . . . I would gladly follow Presley onstage and I'd hold my own. I respect Johnny Cash, Merle Haggard, and Tom Jones. But they don't bother me. Now, Al Jolson is a different story. If he were alive today, he could take tonight's audience and make them beg and beg for more. I wouldn't want to follow him."

Scott Joplin (1868-1917)   The most famous and most influential of the Ragtime composers, to whose music America two-stepped, turkey-trotted, and cakewalked into the twentieth century. Until the film *The Sting,* starring Paul Newman and Robert Redford, appeared in 1974, Joplin's "Maple Leaf Rag" (1899) was the best-known Ragtime piece. *The Sting* attracted attention to "The Entertainer," which he wrote in 1902, and brought two Academy Awards to composer Marvin Hamlisch (b. 1944) for adapting and scoring Joplin's music. Although Ragtime roguishly expressed the jaunty spirit of America between the Spanish-American War and World War I and though it has been heard through the years in western barroom scenes on film and on TV, Joplin regarded his compositions as classic American piano pieces, to be viewed in the same vein as Chopin's piano music. He used the Ragtime sound and form in writing two operas, one of which, *A Guest of Honor,* has been lost. *Treemonisha,* the other, was Joplin's all-encompassing interest during the latter years of his life; the frustrations he suffered in not being able to get it published or produced doubtless contributed to his death. *Treemonisha* was first presented in full at Atlanta, Georgia, in January 1972 in a Katherine Dunham production. In the preceding year, the New York Public Library published *Collected Works of Scott Joplin* in two facsimile volumes, while an album of his rags by Joshua Rifkin appeared on *Billboard*'s chart of Best-Selling Classical LPs. Both these developments seemed to vindicate Joplin's assessment of his music, since the *Collected Works* as well as the Rifkin album were the work of people not in the Pop field but in concert music. But it was the popularity of *The Sting* that generated such interest in Joplin's music and Ragtime that more than 50 albums of Ragtime music, played and sung by every conceivable instrument and type of combo, were released by record companies. Productions of *Treemonisha* were presented in Houston and at the Kennedy Center for the Performing Arts in Washington, D.C., culminating in a Broadway presentation on October 21, 1975, that earned for Joplin a "special" posthumous Pulitzer Prize in 1976.

Louis Jordan (1908-1975)   The Father of Rhythm & Blues came out of the Blues world of Brinkley, Ark., to play in Chick Webb's swing band from 1932 to 1938; he played alto sax and participated in comedy routines. He began recording for Decca in '38 with his own Tympany Five, remaining on the label until 1953. He had his first million-seller in 1944 with "Is You Is, Or Is You Ain't Ma Baby?"—having previously attracted attention with "Knock Me a Kiss" and "I'm Gonna Move to the Outskirts of Town," the latter a classic Blues. He sang "Is You Is" in the film *Follow the Boys.* His second million-seller was "Caldonia (What Makes Your Big Head So Hard?)," followed in '46 by two million-sellers, "Beware, Brother, Beware" and "Choo Choo Ch'Boogie," the biggest seller of all. His last big hit was "Saturday Night Fish Fry," a song that dealt humorously with an aspect of Negro life. In all of these, he pursued a basic rhythm of Shuffle Boogie, later taken over by early Rock 'n' Roll. As he said, he "made the Blues jump," and in so doing, influenced B. B. King (b. 1925), Chuck Berry (b. 1926), and Bill Haley (b. 1925), who joined Decca the year that Jordan left and was produced by the same A & R man, Milt Gabler. Showman/talent scout/drummer Johnny Otis (b. 1922) has said: "Whenever we played shows with Louis Jordan, all the members of my group would stand in the wings and watch the master showman at work." Ace guitarist T-Bone Walker (1910–1975) has said: "Louis Jordan plays good Blues, and he sings them like they were originally sung, too." And Chuck Berry, the Poet Laureate of Rock 'n' Roll, has said: "I identify myself with Louis Jordan more than any other artist. I have a lot of flighty things like Louis, comical things and natural things and not too heavy. . . . If I had only one artist to listen to through eternity, it would be Nat Cole. And if I had to work through eternity, it would be Louis Jordan."

See also Rhythm & Blues.

jubilee   The jubilee was originally a slave plantation celebration, usually accompanied by the distribution of prizes, cakes, and even clothes. A pageant of music, dance, and comedy developed in connection with such celebrations. Spirituals were at first called "jubilee songs." The reference doubtless was not to the so-called Sorrow songs but to the jubilant expressions of religious ecstasy—not "Nobody Knows the Trouble I've Seen" but "Little David, Play on Your Harp."

See also Spirituals.

jug band   Although it was a folk string-band that included guitar, fiddle, perhaps a mandolin, and even a piano at times, it derived its name from the ordinary jug. A gallon glass bottle or an earthenware demijohn was used by players who half-vocalized and half-blew across the opening, producing a tuba-like sound. Some of the better-known jug bands included the Memphis Jug Band, Mississippi Jug Band, and Gus Cannon's Stompers. In 1927 Ma Rainey recorded "Black Cat, Hoot Owl Blues," accompanied by the Tub Jug Washboard Band. The sound may be heard on albums released by Origin, Riverside, Blues Classics, and RCA Victor Records. Among Rock performers, Bob "Bear" Hite (b. 1945) of Canned Heat plays the jug, and the Nitty Gritty Dirt Band called itself at first the Illegitimate Jug Band because it played jug band music without a jug player. However, it did use homemade instruments like washtub bass, kazoo, tissue-paper combs, sandblocks, and a bubble machine.

See also spasm band.

jukebox   A mechanical record machine, activated by coins, and introduced in the late thirties. Jukeboxes were installed in every cafe, honky-tonk, joint, roadside booth, and beanery, replacing live performers in many of these places. By 1942, because of the growth of jukebox usage, the president of the American Federation of Musicians labeled the record "the No. 1 scab" of music and established a ban on recording. While live performances on the radio made hits in the Pop field before the rise of the disk jockey in the early fifties, jukeboxes played an enormous role in developing hits in the R & B and C & W fields. In fact, in 1943 a small West Coast company that planned to make records by black artists called itself Juke Box Records. In 1942 Glenn Miller and His Orchestra (vocal by Tex Beneke, Marion Hutton, and the Modernaires) made a hit of a song titled "Juke Box Saturday Night." And in 1956 Perry Como recorded a song titled "Juke Box Baby." Both of these suggest that Pop artists were also not unconcerned about record plays in the jukeboxes.

See also juke joint.

juke joint   Little more than a shack, and sometimes just a tent, in deep South towns and rural areas where liquor could be bought and drunk, and the crowd could dance and live it up. It was these little joints that gave their name to the mechanical, coin-operated record-players that came into vogue in the late thirties.

Jump Blues   "With my little band," Louis Jordan said, "I did everything they did with a big band. I made the Blues jump." In other words, Jordan & his Tympany Five added rhythm to the Blues, thereby entitling him to be called Father of Rhythm & Blues.

See also Louis Jordan; Rhythm & Blues.

Juno Awards   Annual awards, voted in categories like those used by NARAS, made by the Association of Canadian Television and Radio Artists. In 1971, the year after she became nationally known in the U.S.A. for "Snowbird," Anne Murray (b. 1945) was voted Best Female Artist of the year.

See also National Academy of Recording Arts and Sciences.

K

KC style   Kansas City is today recognized as one of the launching or landmark areas in the development of Jazz, especially of Big Band Swing. Among the better-known bands that emerged from its free-wheeling clubs were Bennie Moten's, Jay McShann's, and of course Count Basie's. To distinguish a KC style presents difficulties. But a few characteristics might be enumerated: (1) frequent use of riffs against which soloists improvised; (2) light rhythm and controlled percussion: (3) emphasis on brass.
    See also Swing.

Kiddie Rock   *See* Bubble-Gum Rock.

"The Killer"   Jerry Lee Lewis's nickname for himself.
    See also Rockabilly.

"King Freak of New York"   Cognomen of Lou Reed (b. circa 1940), because of his shocking performances with the Velvet Underground.

"King of Calypso"   *See* Harry Belanfonte.

"King of the Crooners"   *See* Bing Crosby; Frank Sinatra.

"King of Delta Blues Singers"   *See* Robert Johnson.

"King of Hillbilly Piano Players"   Moon Mullican (1909–1967), Texas singer, organist, pianist, and songwriter.

"King of Jazz"   *See* Paul Whiteman.

"King of the Mambo"   Two different Latin bandleaders have carried this appellation. Since the dance and the beat come from Cuba, Perez Prado (b. 1918 in Cuba) doubtless bore it first. The dance made its mark in the U.S.A. in 1954 through disks by Perry Como ("Papa Loves Mambo") and Rosemary Clooney ("Mambo Italiano."). Prado's version was first heard the following year when he and his orchestra performed in the film *Underwater,* which used as its theme "Cherry Pink and Apple Blossom White," originally recorded by Prado in 1951. The other bandleader who also was known as King of the

Mambo was Tito Puente, born in New York of Puerto Rican parents. Puente (b. in 1920s), who was an arranger and virtuoso timbales player, achieved recognition through his handling of the big band Mambo style in the fifties and sixties.

See also Mambo; timbales (*under* Latin rhythm instruments).

"King of Mountain Music"   *See* Roy Acuff.

"King of Progressive Country"   *See* Willie Nelson (*under* Nashville Outlaws).

"King of Ragtime"   *See* Irving Berlin; Scott Joplin.

"King of the Road"   *See* Roger Miller.

"King of Rock 'n' Soul"   A title conferred on Solomon Burke (b. circa 1940) by disk jockey Rockin' Robin of Station WEBB in Baltimore.

"King of the Stroll"   Chuck Willis (1928–1958), who became the king of the Rock dance by virtue of his recording of "C. C. Rider" (1957), whose tempo and rhythm just fitted the dance.

"King of the Surf"   A title given to folk singer Trini Lopez (b. 1937) as the result of a Rock dance, The Surf, which he introduced in 1964 during a tour of Europe.

"King of Swing"   *See* Benny Goodman.

"King of Twelve-String Guitar Players"   *See* Huddie Ledbetter ("Leadbelly").

"King of Western Pop"   *See* Elvis Presley.

"King of Western Swing"   Spade Cooley, the Oklahoma bandleader, who died in 1972.

Kings of Rhythm   That's what Ike Turner's band was called, which later was the backup band for Ike (b. circa 1933) & Tina Turner (b. Anne Mae Bullock, circa 1938).

"Kings of Rock Comedy"   The comedy duo of Cheech & Chong, the former born Cheech Marin in Los Angeles and the latter born Tommy Chong in Edmonton, Canada.

Kingston Trio   Their recording of "Tom Dooley," a mainstream hit in 1958–1959—No. 1 in November 1958—is recognized as the spark that ignited the Urban Folk boom of the sixties. Among the groups that participated in the Folk explosion, there were the Brothers Four ("Greenfields," 1960), Peter, Paul & Mary (debut album, 1962), New Christy Minstrels ("Green, Green," 1963), Rooftop Singers ("Walk Right In," 1963), as well as the Journeymen, Limeliters, and New Lost City Ramblers. The Kingston Trio was formed in 1957 when Nick Reynolds (b. 1933) (guitar) met Bob Shane (b. 1934) (guitar) at Menlo Park School of Business Administration and they were joined by Dave Guard (b. 1934) (banjo), who made most of their arrangements. The Trio made its debut at the Purple Onion in San Francisco in '57. Before it finally disbanded in 1968, it made over 30 albums and had sold close to 20 million LPs. The Trio won a Grammy for Best Folk Recording of 1959 for *The Kingston Trio at Large*.

"kinky"   Current slang for "strange," "bizarre," "perverted"— all having to do with sex, but by extension, with conduct in general.

"kitsch"   Pseudo-art; the appearance of art without its substance or form. In the sixties, a number of new art forms emerged: light shows, album covers, street theater, posters, beads, belt buckles, the underground press, et al. Generally, these were unpretentious and un-self-conscious attempts at expression and adornment: the work of primitives, of unprofessional artists, of people concerned with saying something right, not necessarily artistically. To Establishment artists, patrons of the arts, and critics of the fine arts, all of this was "kitsch."
    See also alternative life-style.

Klezmer music   A high-spirited, folk-dance idiom, generally with a minor sound, that originated among Polish and Russian Jews. The Klezmorim or Klezmerin were bands of itinerant, unschooled musicians who roamed Eastern Europe during the eighteenth and nineteenth centuries, playing homemade and secondhand instruments by ear. Their improvised music, performed at fairs, weddings, dances, and celebrations of any kind, is analogous to the music of Appalachian spasm bands and jug bands. They performed for Gentiles or Jews—anybody who would give them a handout of food, liquor, and/or money. The music has recently been revived by informal instrumental groups in Jewish sections of New York City, and can be heard on records released by Arhoolie and Folklyric.

L

L 7   If you move the 7 close to the L, it will make a square. Saying, "L7," usually accompanied with a two-hand representation of a square, was used to typify someone who was not with it—in the fifties.

"Lady Day"   Legend has it that they started calling Billie Holiday "Lady" when she refused, during her days as a waitress in Harlem, to pick up coins from tables without the use of her hands; the other scantily attired girls did. If saxist Lester Young (1909–1959) did not give her the nickname, he surely helped popularize it. Billie gave him the nickname "Prez" (after President Franklin Delano Roosevelt) because he was the leading tenor saxist of the day.
   See also Billie Holiday.

"Lady Soul"   *See* Aretha Franklin.

La Honda   The headquarters of Ken Kesey, exponent of LSD and the man who called his affairs "acid tests." The Grateful Dead jammed and juiced here.
   See also Acid Rock.

"laid back"   To "lay back" in accompanying a featured performer is to give him or her full headway by means of the low dynamics and simplicity of one's playing. "Laid back" has come to mean a relaxed, understated, lag-along style of expression. Some trace the development to the easygoing life of California with its sundrenched beaches and equable climate, giving rise to a laid-back type of Rock, as in the music of the Eagles or the Country Rock of Linda Ronstadt (b. 1946). The Mamas and the Papas described the life-style in "California Dreamin'."
   See also California sound.

large-note editions   Simplified arrangements of music that are printed with over-sized notes. This type of edition is intended for children and beginning students, especially of the piano.

laser   Acronym for "light amplification by stimulated emission of radiation." Lasers were developed in the late fifties, just about the time that Chuck Berry and Elvis were turning the music scene around. By the early seventies, lasers had been improved to the point where a narrow beam could be used as a replacement for conventional stage lighting.

206

Among the Rock acts that have used lasers in their onstage appearances are Todd Rundgren and the Electric Light Orchestra.

laser phonograph   Target dates for the introduction of this sophisticated digital machine are 1982 in Europe and 1983 in the U.S.A. It represents the ultimate in the development of digital disks, which at this writing involve a digital master but a conventional, nondigital LP record. The advanced technology, making possible a digital disk (only four and a half inches in diameter but containing an hour of music), employs a small laser. In digital recording, sound is stored and processed in the form of electrical impulses, represented by numbers. The laser shines a beam on the numbers, contained in microscopic pits, and counts them, thereby translating them into the original sound. Since the musical signal, translated into numbers, is immune to noise and distortion, and nothing but the laser beam touches the record, the ultimate in fidelity is attained. It is expected that the new digital system and the traditional phonograph will coexist in the same way that cassettes and LP records coexist.

See also digital recording.

"later"   Jazz argot for saying goodbye, for leaving.

Latin Jazz   Guitarist Carlos Santana's forte is Latin Rock. But after he became a follower of Sri Chinmoy in 1972, he became involved with a number of converts who were jazzmen, notably John McLaughlin of the Mahavishnu Orchestra, and he made three albums that were a fusion of his Latin background and Jazz. The more extensive and expansive blending of the two sounds came with the Bossa Nova explosion ignited by guitarist Charlie Byrd (b. 1925) and tenor saxist Stan Getz (b. 1927) with their hit album *Jazz Samba* and the hit single from it, "Desafinado" (slightly out of tune), both million-copy sellers in 1962. Among the jazzmen who essayed the union, there were guitarist Laurindo Almeida (b. 1917), singer Chris Connor (b. 1927), clarinetist Buddy De Franco (b. 1923), tenor saxist Coleman Hawkins (1904–1969), vibraharpist Milt Jackson (b. 1923), pianist/trumpeter/composer Quincy Jones (b. 1933), pianist Ramsey Lewis (b. 1935), flutist Herbie Mann (b. 1930), pianist/composer Lalo Schifrin (b. 1932), and saxist Bud Shank (b. 1926). Apart from the Bossa Nova, a number of jazzmen explored Latin sounds in their ruminations: Bud Shank in five albums of Brazilian music; pianist George Shearing (b. 1919) in four albums with titles like *Latin Escapade;* saxist Sonny Stitt (b. 1924) in *Goes Latin;* vibes player Cal Tjader (b. 1925) in three Mambo albums and eight others in a Latin style.

Although the marriage seemed mainly the idea of U.S. jazzmen, there were instances in which Latins attempted the wedding—like Tito Puente's *Puente Goes Jazz* (1956) and *Dancemania* (1958). Some regard Havana-born Machito (Frank Grillo) (b. 1912) as the key figure in inaugurating the Latin Jazz movement. As early as 1940 he played at New York City's Club Cuba, and then at the midtown La Conga, where he employed such jazzmen as trumpeter Dizzy Gillespie (b. 1917), saxist Cannonball Adderley (1928–1975), and trumpeter Howard McGhee (b. 1918). In 1950 Machito & His Afro-Cubans recorded *Afro-Cuban Jazz Suite,* composed on a Norman Granz commission by Cuban Chico O'Farrill (b. 1921), using saxist Charlie "Bird" Parker (1920–1955), tenorist Flip Phillips (b. 1915), and drummer Buddy Rich (b. 1917) as soloists.

As Blues Image was a forerunner of Santana, Malo was a successor. In 1980 John McLaughlin cut a live album. *Friday Night in San Francisco,* with two Latin guitarists, Al Di Meola and Paco De Lucia.

Yet trumpeter Dizzy Gillespie could well claim priority. In the winter of 1947, Gillespie played a Big Band concert in NYC's Town Hall, featuring Cuban conga player Chano Pozo (1915–1948), and through the forties into the fifties, he recorded Latin Jazz works like "Manteca," "Guachi Guara," "Algo Bueno" (a.k.a. "Woody'n You"), and a two-part work by composer/drummer George Russell (b. 1923).

Latin rhythm instruments   To produce their intricate polyrhythms, the musicians of Mexico, South America, Puerto Rico, and especially Cuba use a variety of rhythm instruments. Brief descriptions of those most frequently found in *conjuntos* (combos) and *charangas* (Cuban dance bands consisting of a flute, several fiddles, piano, bass, timbales, et al.) follow:

1. bongos: two small drums that are fastened together. They are held between the knees, resting on the calves of the seated musician. They are played with the index finger of the right hand, initiating the beat, and the thumb and index finger of the left hand, complementing it.

2. cabaza: a large, dried calabash, surrounded by a loose net of beads and fitted with a stem, which is held by the right hand so that the head rests on the palm of the left hand. It is played by half-rotating the head with a twisting movement of the wrist. Used mostly in Brazilian music.

3. cencerro: a large, hand-held cowbell, played with a stick. Two notes are produced, depending upon where it is struck. Played by the bongo-man, it is used in Cuban music and Salsa to add drive and excitement in the contrapuntal instrumental section, known as the mambo section.

4. chocallo: a closed metal cylinder filled with seeds. Held at the center by one hand for soft passages and at the ends with both hands for louder and faster segments, it makes a high, swishing sound when shaken. Used mainly in Brazilian Sambas, Maxixes, and Marches.

5. claves: two sticks of resonant wood, one of which rests on the palm and fingertips of the left hand and is struck by the other, held in the right hand.

6. conga: a drum that is played by the cupped right hand while the left hand either lies flat on the head to muffle it or to bring out the sound. Congas come in several sizes: the small quinto, for improvised soloing; the mid-sized conga, which stands about three feet high; and the large tumbadora. All have slightly tapered heads and play a major role in Salsa rhythm sections.

7. cuatro: a small, 10-stringed guitar, it is a major instrument in Puerto Rican *jibaro*, or country music, emanating from the mountain farmers.

8. guiro: a gourd, resembling a large, dried squash, with ribbed cuts along its body and sound holes in the base. Usually played by a singer in the group, it is held with the thumb and one or more fingers of the left hand, which are stuck into the sound holes. The sound is produced by rubbing a stick (in Puerto Rico) or metal probe (in the Dominican Republic) over the ribbed cuts. A characteristic sound of the Merengue.

9. maracas: two small gourds, filled with seeds, tuned, and to which handles are attached. Known as "shakers," they are held in each hand and shaken alternately. They are of American Indian derivation. The famous Cuban bandleader Machito was a masterful maracas player.

10. quija: a cleaned donkey's jaw, it is held with the left hand near the front teeth, with the large open end extending upward. The sound is produced by striking the top of the jaw with the right fist so that it slams against the other side.

11. shekere: Unlike the maracas, this large gourd has beads in a net-like bag on the outside. It is an African-derived rattle.

12. timbales: two drum heads mounted on a stand and tuned a fourth apart, with two cowbells also tuned a fourth apart. Sometimes a cymbal is added. The percussion group is played with sticks, the player striking heads, rims, and in the Bolero, the sides of the metal drums, known as the *paila*.

13. tres: a nine-stringed guitar out of Cuba whose sound became familiar through Salsa.

Latin Rock   The key figure in this fusion is Mexican-born Carlos Santana, founder of the Santana Sextet, a group whose debut album, released in 1969, sold 2 million copies in 12 months. Known originally as the Santana Blues Band when it started in San Francisco circa 1966—it blended the Blues with Afro-Cuban rhythms—the group developed a huge following in San Francisco's Spanish Mission District and through appearances at Fillmore West. Its sensational appearance at the Woodstock Festival in 1969 led to the release of its first album, which turned Gold before the end of the year. Pursuing its style of limited vocals, the group scored with a million-selling album in 1971, including the hit single "No One to Depend on Me." Unlike Latin Jazz, where the incentive for the fusion emanates from jazzmen, the initiative in Latin Rock comes from Latin groups, among whom one finds lesser-known combos like El Chicano, Chango, and Seguida.

Some critics regard the recordings of Herb Alpert (b. 1937) & His Tijuana Brass as exemplary of Latin Rock. He made his first hit, "The Lonely Bull," originally titled "Twinkle Star," by adding the *ole*s of a bullfight crowd and the sounds of a mariachi band to the beginning and end of his record. He also worked at getting the "Spanish flair" of trumpets in the bull ring by overdubbing the harmony part, which he also played. For a time, his sound was known as Ameriachi ("American" plus "Mariachi"), but Rock as well as Jazz inflections are audible in the Mexican brew. *The Lonely Bull* album launched not only a phenomenal career for trumpeter Alpert but a thriving record label, A & M, a partnership of Herb Alpert and Jerry Moss. Between 1962 and 1968, Alpert & His Tijuana Brass racked up 10 million–copy albums. A number of them preserved the south-of-the-border motive in individual titles, e.g., "A Quiet Tear (*Lagrima Quieta*)," as well as in album titles, e.g., *South of the Border* (1965). The last-mentioned was in best-selling charts for 163 weeks, over three years. *What Now My Love* (1966), with an initial order of almost a million, received the first "Gold Cartridge" award (an award given by International Tape Cartridge Company for a sale of over 250,000 tape cartridges). *Whipped Cream & Other Delights* (1965) sold 4.5 million copies by the end of its second year. *S.R.O.* (1966) had a fantastic advance order of 1,700,000 copies, and in the first 10 months of the year Alpert and his group reportedly sold more than twice the number of LPs as the Beatles. In 1979, after an absence of almost 10 years from recording, Alpert made a comeback with "Rise," a Latin Rock Jazz instrumental.

Latin Soul   Known also as Latin Bugalú, this sound was first heard around 1966 when Joe Cuba's disk of "Bang Bang" sold a million records. It was followed in '67 by Hector Rivera's "At the Party." A fusion of R & B and Afro-Cuban rhythms, the sound was apparently first heard on a Ricardo Ray album, *Se Soltó*. The style is exemplified also by Pete Rodriguez's "I Like It Like That," originally a hit for Chris Kenner in 1961; Johnny Colon's "Boogaloo Blues," and three albums by the Afro-Filipino Joe Bataan (*Gypsy Lady, Subway Joe,* and *Riot,* 1967–1968). The Latin Soul or bugalú conjuntos (combos) apparently favored a deep, gutsy sound produced by a two-trombone frontline, originally used by bandleader Eddie Palmieri of Salsa fame.

"Leadbelly"   *See* Huddie Ledbetter.

leadsheet   An outline of a song containing the lyrics, the melody, and chord indications—no accompaniment or fills.

Huddie Ledbetter (1885–1949)   He was known as "Leadbelly," probably a corruption of his surname; but several legendary stories have been told about his great strength or great laziness, both of which involved "lead" and may also have contributed to the nickname. A supremely talented Blues singer and folk singer, he had a violent temper that brought him prison sentences for murder, attempted homicide, and assault. He managed to maneuver his way out of several jails; in one instance, a singing appeal is supposed to have elicited a pardon from the governor. Billing himself "King of the 12-String Guitar," he recorded extensively and performed in concert halls and on college campuses. His first tour of colleges was arranged in late 1934 by John A. and Alan Lomax, who became acquainted with him when they visited the Louisiana State Farm prison at Angola on a folk song–collecting trip. The following year, he began recording for American Record Company, later Columbia Records. In 1940 he participated in benefits for the migratory workers of California, together with Burl Ives (b. 1909), Pete Seeger (b. 1919), Josh White (b. 1908), and the legendary Woody Guthrie (1912–1967). During the forties, he was part of the Headline Singers, a group that included Woody Guthrie, Brownie McGhee (b. 1915), and Sonny Terry (b. 1911). A year after Leadbelly died of the same muscular disease that killed baseball giant Lou Gehrig, his ballad "Goodnight, Irene" was a Pop smash as the result of a recording by the Weavers and the Gordon Jenkins Orchestra. A Leadbelly Memorial Concert, held that year, brought out the Weavers, Sonny Terry, Brownie McGhee, Woody Guthrie, Jean Ritchie (b. 1922), Rev. Gary Davis (1896–1972), Count Basie (b. 1904), and others. In 1976 Paramount Pictures released a biofilm *Leadbelly,* starring Roger E. Mosley in the title role and directed by the late Gordon Parks. In addition to "Goodnight, Irene," Leadbelly is well remembered for such Blues as "Boll Weevil," "Old Cottonfields at Home," "Rock Island Line," and "Midnight Special" (the last-mentioned is the title of a very popular late-night TV show devoted to Rock 'n' Roll).

"leerics"   A term coined by *Variety* editor Abel Green in the 1950s in an Establishment attack against suggestive or erotic lyrics in Rock 'n' Roll. Among the records singled out were "Work with Me, Annie" by the Midnighters (1954), "Sixty Minute Man" by the Dominoes (1951), "Honey Love" by the Drifters (1954), "I Got a Woman" by Ray Charles (1954), and others—all of them by black artists. Green argued that "dirty postcards have been translated into songs." Responding to the charge of "leerics," a top songwriter (Al Stillman, b. 1906), who had written some of Johnny Mathis's biggest hits, said: "As far as I can remember, practically all lyrics, except *Barney Google,* have been dirty—with the carriage trade practitioners, Cole Porter, Larry Hart, etc., contributing their share." Citing songs like "You Took Advantage of Me" and "All of You," Stillman added: "Actually, the object of all leericists, outside of W. S. Gilbert, has always been to get as close [as possible] to the Main Subject without stating it and/or 'cleaning it up' by marrying them in the last line. The current Rock 'n' Rollers are not beating around the bush. But without condoning 'em, it's at least a less hypocritical approach."

Leiber & Stoller (1933–   )   Jerry Leiber, born in Baltimore, and Mike Stoller, born in New York City, are perhaps the most successful songwriting team in Rock 'n' Roll, even if you compare them with John Lennon and Paul McCartney of the Beatles, Goffin & King, Mann & Weil, Greenfield & Sedaka, Elton John & Bernie Taupin. They began writing hits in the heyday of Rhythm & Blues, turning out songs that have become classics for such black artists as Amos Milburn (b. 1927), Charles Brown (b. 1920), Little Willie Littlefield (b. 1931)—"Kansas City" was a smash for Wilbert Harrison in 1959—and Willie Mae "Big Mama" Thornton (b. 1926), whose disk of "Hound Dog" was No. 1 on R & B charts three years before Elvis became associated with it.

In 1955 two West Coast groups that Leiber & Stoller formed produced hits for them. The Cheers, whom they placed on Capitol Records, scored with "Black Denim Trousers and Motorcycle Boots," a raunchy song that Edith Piaf helped make internationally famous. The Robins, with whom they produced "Smoky Joe's Cafe" for their own record label, not only gave them an R & B hit, but led to their becoming associated with Atlantic Records in the capacity of independent producers, then an unusual setup. In that capacity, they produced hits for many Atlantic artists, including Ben E. King, LaVern Baker, and especially the Coasters and the Drifters. For the Coasters, formed when two of the Robins elected to come east, they wrote and produced a series of comic playlets, which have become classics: "Young Blood" (1957), "Yakety Yak" (1958), "Charlie Brown" (1959), "Poison Ivy" (1959), and others. For the Drifters, they produced such hits as "There

Goes My Baby'' (1959), ''Save the Last Dance for Me'' (1960), and ''Up on the Roof'' (1962), introducing strings as an innovative move on R & B disks.

From 1962 to 1965, they ran their own record label, Red Bird, and in the early seventies, they became part of the managerial team that took over the catalogs of Starday and King Records, two of the pioneer labels of R & B. But what gives them a supreme position in the creative pantheon of Rock is their unflagging writing of hit songs. For Elvis Presley, they created such evergreens as ''Loving You,'' ''Treat Me Nice,'' and ''Jailhouse Rock,'' all million sellers of 1957. Their Presley hits include ''Don't'' (1958), ''She's Not You'' (1962), and ''Bossa Nova Baby'' (1963).

The scope of Leiber & Stoller's creativity as songwriters is greater than their prominence and large achievement on the Rock scene would suggest. In the late sixties and early seventies, they wrote a number of songs that frame the European cabaret tune and art song in a uniquely American context, bridging the gap between popular and art music. Perhaps the best known of these is the existential ballad ''Is That All There Is?'' which proved a chart song for Peggy Lee (b. 1920).

See also Elvis Presley.

John Lennon (1940-1980)   The murder of ex-Beatle John Lennon on December 8, 1980, and the outpour of fan grief and critical adulation, made the world at large cognizant of the high esteem in which he was held by the Rock world. People generally had had some awareness of Lennon's iconoclastic outlook as a result of the years in which he fought the U.S. Immigration Service's efforts to deport him, ostensibly because of a drug bust. Fans knew the legitimacy of Lennon's claim that he was being penalized for his antiwar and antidiscrimination activities. The documentation of his radical views was to be found in the songs he wrote and recorded on his own with the Plastic Ono Band.

Even before the dissolution of the Beatles was announced in 1970, Lennon had written and recorded ''Give Peace a Chance'' (1969). This was followed in succeeding years by ''Instant Karma (We All Shine On),'' ''Power to the People,'' ''Imagine,'' ''Woman Is the Nigger of the World,'' and other socially conscious songs. In the full-page advertisement in which Yoko Ono, his widow, thanked the world for its anger over his murder, she described their outlook as a belief ''in brotherhood and sisterhood that goes beyond race, color and creed'' and an abiding conviction that ''love breeds love.''

Of all Lennon's message songs, ''Imagine'' was most often quoted in the days of worldwide mourning: ''Imagine all the people living in peace,'' he had written in a song that went to No. 3 on 1971's charts. ''Imagine there's no countries. . . . Nothing to kill or die for, and no religions too. . . . Imagine no possessions . . . a brotherhood of man. . . . Imagine all the people sharing all the world. . . ."

From the early days of the Beatles, Lennon had been the most outspoken, evincing a sardonic wit that marked many of the songs he and Paul McCartney wrote in the sixties. He early had also displayed talents as a caricaturist and a writer of light verse in the vein of Lewis Carroll's art of the absurd: *In His Own Write* and *A Spaniard in the Works,* two published volumes. His involvement with drugs became quite apparent in the famous *Sgt. Pepper* album, as his later successful struggle against drugs was explored in "Cold Turkey" and "Whatever Gets You Through the Night," the latter the most popular song of his post-Beatles career. The change that came about in his life-style and outlook after the divorce from his first wife and subsequent marriage to Yoko Ono in 1969 eventually led to his retirement from the music scene in 1975 and a five-year hiatus as a "house-husband," devoted to the raising of his young son, Sean.

It was just after he had returned to recording in 1980 and was enjoying the acceptance of his first album in five years, *Double Fantasy,* that his murder occurred. The album went to No. 1, remaining there for many weeks, as some of its tracks, "Starting All Over" and "Woman," climbed the singles charts to No. 1.

Although Lennon had said in interviews less than three months before his death that there was no chance for a reunion of the Beatles—"the four guys who used to be that group can never be that group again even if they wanted to be"—many for whom the Beatles produced the soundtrack of the sixties, and whose lives were affected by them, kept hoping for a reunion. Lennon's murder wrote an irreversible end to an era.

Although many tributes were paid to Lennon in song (by George Harrison, Elton John, and other artists), Paul McCartney did not express his feelings until his *Tug of War* (1982) album, regarded as McCartney's best solo LP since the breakup of The Beatles. In "Here Today" McCartney leaps the gap that developed between him and Lennon during the post-Beatles years to express his abiding love for the man who was his longtime songwriting collaborator.

See also The Beatles.

"Let the Good Times Roll"   In the 1930s they sang "Happy Days Are Here Again," and Franklin Delano Roosevelt adopted it as his presidential campaign song in 1932. The song is still used as a theme by the Democratic party at its presidential nominating conventions. But in the forties, the expression changed to "Let the Good Times Roll," a song first recorded in 1946 by Louis Jordan (1908–1975) & His Tympany Five. Another song with the same title became a million-copy seller for Shirley & Lee, a Rock 'n' Roll duo who wrote it, in 1956. Ray Charles revived the Louis Jordan tune in 1960, garnering a Grammy for the Best Rhythm & Blues Recording of the year. In the seventies the expression was used for presentations featuring artists and songs of the early Rock 'n' Roll days.

"lick" A musical phrase that is distinctive and appealing enough to hold interest beyond another phrase. Technically, a lick is an identifiable sequence within a chord; it differs from a "run," which is a sequence linking chords in a progression.

"licorice stick" Swing term for the clarinet.

light show An original Rock art form: painting with light and using it to enhance the impact of music. Colored transparencies and film slides are manipulated so as to synchronize with, punctuate and/or contrast with the rhythm, pulse, or tempo of a selection. Use is also made of subliminal flashes of faces, nudes, signs, structures, shapes, or images. Magnification and reduction are alternated, and the ceiling as well as four walls are used for projection.

As San Francisco was the locus of Acid Rock, it apparently was the area in which light shows were first seen. The concept of Acid rockers like Frank Zappa & the Mothers of Invention as well as the Jefferson Airplane was to produce through visual as well as aural means the expansion and disorientation of the senses motivated by acid. Both these groups made their debut in '67. But the Byrds, a Los Angeles group who had their first hit in '65 ("Mr. Tambourine Man"), apparently used a light show during a '66 appearance in Greenwich Village at the Village Gate. According to reports, both the audience and some critics were nonplussed, feeling that the visual display distracted from rather than heightened the impact of the music. Nevertheless, light shows quickly became a standard part of every Rock group appearance at San Francisco's two dancehalls, the Fillmore West and Avalon. By the time that Bill Graham opened Fillmore East in 1968, no Rock group could appear without a light show—and multimedia were in.

See also Acid Rock; Haight-Ashbury.

Lindy Hop It was called "the Hop" before Charles Lindbergh made his phenomenal hop across the Atlantic in 1927. Dancer Ray Bolger has claimed that he invented the Lindy Hop in '27 at the Hotel Coronado in St. Louis. On the other hand, George "Shorty" Snowden, all-time champion dancer of the Savoy Ballroom in Harlem, contends that by inventing the "breakaway" portion of the dance, he gave the Lindy Hop its unique character; and Shorty Snowden remembers the place and the date: a dance marathon at the Manhattan Casino on June 17, 1928. Ethel Williams, who with Johnny Peters introduced the Texas Tommy in the *Darktown Follies* of 1913, feels that the Lindy Hop originated in the Texas Tommy and points out that the two dances have an identical breakaway. Marshall and Jean Stearns, who state that the Lindy became a recognized part of the American scene in 1936 (with the rise of Swing), describe it as "a syncopated two step or box step, accenting the off-beat." Ethel Williams describes the basic step of the Texas Tommy as "a kick and hop three times on each foot."

A Harlem fringe-hood named Herbert White, who was head bouncer at the Savoy Ballroom, cornered the market on Lindy hoppers when they became in great demand in vaudeville, nightclubs, movies, and Broadway musicals in the 1930s. He apparently had a dozen troupes who appeared under such names as The Savoy Hoppers, The Jive-A-Dears, and Whitey's Lindy Hoppers. In 1939, for example, White supplied Mike Todd's production of *The Hot Mikado* with seven teams of Lindy hoppers. (The champion Lindy hopper at Roseland ballroom in midtown Manhattan, according to the Stearnses in *The Jazz Dance,* was a white boy named Lou Levy, who later managed the Andrews Sisters and founded Leeds Music Corporation, the publishing complex now known as MCA Music.)

According to the Stearnses, the Lindy is not an isolated step but a fundamental approach used in later dances such as the Afro-Cuban Mambo as well as the Rock 'n' Roll Chicken. In certain cities, e.g., Detroit, the Lindy was known as the "Jitterbug."

See also Jitterbug; Savoy Ballroom.

liner note   Information appearing on the back of a record album as to the songs, songwriters, musicians, producers, and the recording session. Although many artists and record companies have dispensed with liner notes, preferring photographs and abstract designs, NARAS still gives a Grammy each year to the writer of the best liner note.

See also Grammy.

lip-sync   Abbreviation of "lip synchronization." The singers do not vocalize, but they move their lips as if they were singing—and the sound comes from a record, cassette, or reel of tape. From a musical standpoint, lip-sync may have stemmed from the inability to duplicate the sound on a record in a TV studio, including the sound of the accompanying band. But lip-sync also has an economic origin: The cost of bringing a live combo into a studio could be prohibitive; moreover, if the singer(s) do not sing, their appearance might be regarded as a promotional interview rather than entertainment and they might not be paid a fee.

"**Little Jazz**"   *See* Roy Eldridge.

"**Little Miss Sharecropper**"   A billing used by R & B singer LaVern Baker (b. 1928) in the early 1940s.

Little Richard (1935-   )   One of the great pioneers of Rock 'n' Roll and an outstanding Rhythm & Bluesman, Richard Penniman sang Gospel and learned piano in a Macon, Ga., church. He recorded for RCA Victor and Peacock Records before he exhibited the burst of energy, the wild abandon and sexual excitement of "Tutti-Frutti" in late 1955 on Specialty Records of Los Angeles. Recorded almost as an afterthought on September 14, 1955, in the J & M Studios in New Orleans, it became a crossover: No. 2 on R & B charts and No. 21 on Pop. Between 1955 and 1958, he had a score of bestsellers, producing No. 1 and No. 2 R & B hits in "Long Tall Sally" b/w "Slippin' and Slidin'," "Rip It Up" b/w "Ready Teddy," "Lucille" b/w "Send Me Some Lovin'," and "Jenny, Jenny" b/w "Miss Ann." During those years, he appeared in three films: *Don't Knock the Rock* (1956), *The Girl Can't Help It* (1956) and *Mister Rock and Roll* (1957). At the peak of his career, he suddenly withdrew into the world of religion and began studying to be a preacher. He reemerged after a seven-year hiatus and attempted a comeback on records, cutting first for Vee Jay and then for OKeh. But those were the years of the British invasion, and he made no headway in a market dominated by the Beatles, who had made their first appearance outside of Liverpool (in Hamburg) under his aegis. Once again, he disappeared from the record scene, emerging in the late seventies as a fulltime evangelical preacher. Little Richard left an indelible mark on Rock 'n' Roll, influencing a long line of singers from Jerry Lee Lewis (b. 1935), who imitated all his stage shticks, to the most recent proponents of Hard Rock, Punk Rock, and New Wave. He remains a towering figure to those who think of Rock as an explosion of energy and unbuttoned excitement.

"**The Lizard King**"   Cognomen of Jim Morrison (1943–1971) of the Doors. Based partly on a hit song, partly on the skin-tight, imitation-leather pants he wore, and partly on his squirming stage behavior.

"**locked-hands**" **style**   *See* block chording.

John A. Lomax (1875-1948)   Journeying on horseback and on foot, by car and rail, and lugging an Ediphone cylinder recording machine, Lomax established himself as the prime folklore collector of the twentieth century. His pioneering collection of *Cowboy Songs and Other Frontier Ballads* appeared in 1910, *Songs of the Cattle Trail and Cow Camp* in 1917, and his monumental *American Ballads and Folk Songs* (coauthored with his son Alan) in 1934. From 1934 to 1942 he served as honorary consultant to the Archives of Folk Song at the Library of Congress, contributing with his son over 3,000 recordings of folk material. He was instrumental in bringing Leadbelly (1885–1949) before the concert and college world.

See also Huddie Ledbetter (''Leadbelly'').

Liverpool sound   *See* Mersey sound.

Guy Lombardo Orchestra   When the Guy Lombardo Orchestra performed on New Year's Eve 1980 in a Sparks, Nev., casino, it was the first time in 50 years that the famous Royal Canadians had not rung in the New Year in New York City with a broadcast or telecast of ''Auld Lang Syne.''

From 1929 until 1962, Lombardo (1902–1977) played the nostalgic tune from the bandstand of the Hotel Roosevelt in Manhattan. From 1962 until his death in November 1977, he and ''the sweetest music this side of Heaven'' welcomed the New Year on a nationwide telecast from a showroom of the Waldorf-Astoria Hotel on NYC's Park Avenue. The band struck up ''Auld Lang Syne'' as home viewers watched a ball descend from the top of the Times Square Tower at a minute before midnight. After Guy Lombardo's death, the Waldorf continued the tradition, with the band being led first by brother Lebert Lombardo, and in '78–'79 by Lebert's son, Bill. The breakup of the band in '80 led the Waldorf to turn to new and contemporary faces for the 1980 New Year's program.

The Lombardo Orchestra that appeared in Sparks did not include a single musician from Guy's last band. But it apparently had the sanction of the Lombardo estate and used the arrangements played by the Royal Canadians under Guy's baton.

London sound   Some critics who were partial to the Rolling Stones as against the Beatles started writing about the London sound as contrasted with the Mersey sound. It was, of course, a heavier and blacker sound, emphasizing guitar riffs that served as an ostinato throughout a song plus drone drumming. In actuality, the London sound had even less identity than the Mersey sound, which lacked definition.

See also Mersey sound.

''long-hair''   A vague term that is used with reference to those who play, sing, compose, or write about classical, concert, or ''serious,'' music.

Long Island sound   The Rascals, or Young Rascals, as they were known at the outset, were not born on the Island. But they did work as the regular band at the Barge, a floating nightclub in Westhampton, L.I.—whence the Long Island sound, a contrived category. The Rascals were R & B–oriented and might well be regarded as "blue-eyed soul" performers.

Los Angeles sound   What do The Doors, The Beach Boys, The Mamas & the Papas, Jackson Browne, The Byrds, Sonny & Cher, Jan & Dean, The Turtles, and Linda Ronstadt have in common? Although he wrote mystical/surrealist poetry, Jim Morrison (1943–1971) led a Hard Rock group in The Doors. The Byrds and Jan & Dean were in the Surfing thing. The Mamas & the Papas were hippie Modernaires, singing Pop Rock. I guess the point must be coming clear: it is quite difficult to find a common denominator. But for some unaccountable reason, except possibly the life-style in the California sunshine and the languorous mood celebrated in The Mamas & the Papas' "California Dreaming," the Los Angeles sound came to mean a laid-back, Country Folk kind of sound. Now, it is true that Sonny & Cher ("I Got You, Babe," 1965), The Turtles, Jackson Browne, and the early Byrds were Folk rockers, at least at the outset. But Linda Ronstadt (b. 1946) started out as a middle-of-the-road rocker (with the Stone Poneys), and as a soloist veered in the direction of Nashville-style Country. Nevertheless, the Los Angeles sound meant a commercial, if not slick type of easygoing, relaxed, studio-styled, Pop-sounding Country music.
See also Country Rock.

Louisiana Hayride   One of the post–World War II radio shows devoted to Country music, the *Hayride* was first broadcast on Saturday night, April 3, 1948, from Shreveport, La. The immortal Hank Williams (1923–1953), an early cast member, performed on the show for over a year. Unlike the *Grand Ole Opry,* which booked only established Country stars, the *Hayride* welcomed newcomers, calling itself "The Cradle of the Stars." Prior to his emergence as the King of Rock 'n' Roll, Elvis Presley performed regularly over an 18-month period. Reduced to a monthly program with only guest artists in the sixties, the *Hayride* returned as a regular Saturday night feature over KWKH in 1974. At that time, the show moved across the river from Shreveport to Bossier City, La., where it is broadcast from a $750,000 auditorium-restaurant complex.

The Love Generation   Along with Flower Power, it was a visionary concept of the sixties that generated excitement, stirred deep feelings, sold posters, T-shirts, and bumper-stickers—and then went up in smoke like Puff the Magic Dragon. Like Flower Power, its center was San Francisco, where early in 1966 cars carried bumper-stickers reading "Jefferson Airplane Loves You." The year 1967 brought the Summer of Love to San Francisco, with the Jefferson Airplane urging everybody, "Let's Get Together." It all seemed to come to a climactic peak in 1969 at Woodstock: the three-day, rain-soaked festival of love and peace. But before 1969 was torn from the calendar, the Rolling Stones gave a free concert at Altamont Speedway that ended in a disastrous murder. The Love Generation had come to a dead end.

See also Flower Children; *Woodstock Nation.*

"Love-In"   A gathering of young people in the sixties, a counter-cultural phenomenon in which good vibes made for a feeling of peace, serenity, affection, and love, not excluding communal sex. Singer/song-writer/record producer Kim Fowley (b. 1942), who was a pioneer of the flower-love movement, gained notoriety as an organizer of West coast "love-ins." In 1967 he produced an album of "flower-power" material, titled *Love Is Alive and Well.* The well-known rock musical *Hair* contains a "love-in."

See also "Be-in"; Flower children; *Hair.*

"low-down"   The term started with the Blues—Blues emanating from the deepest suffering and expressive of the deepest emotions. Used to characterize singing and even instrumental solos that are suffused with feeling.

"Luke the Drifter"   *See* Hank Williams.

lute   An ancient instrument that fathered the guitar and was superseded by it in popularity. Until the end of the eighteenth century, it was well loved as an accompaniment of folk songs.

M

MFSB   The house band of Philadelphia International Records, which can be heard on Cliff Nobles & Co.'s chart-maker "The Horse" (1968). MFSB is credited with helping define the Disco style through such recordings as "Love Train," "I'll Always Love My Mama," "Bad Luck," and "TSOP." (MFSB presumably stands for *mother/father/sister/brother.*)

The MG's   The initials stand for Memphis Group, a combo led by Booker T. Jones (b. 1944) on piano and organ, and consisting of Steve

Cropper (b. 1942), guitar; Donald "Duck" Dunn (b. 1941), bass; and Al Jackson (1934–1975), drums. An integrated group, they operated out of Stax Records studio in Memphis, functioning as the house combo for most Stax artists and recording on their own. They can be heard on virtually all of soulman Otis Redding's (1941–1967) disks and on Wilson Pickett's (b. 1941) hit disk of "In the Midnight Hour" (1966). Their own instrumental hits include "Green Onions," their first release, which made No. 1 on R & B charts and No. 3 on Pop in 1962; "Boot Leg" in 1965; "My Sweet Potato" in 1966; "Hip Hug-Her" in 1967; "Soul-Limbo" in 1968; and "Time Is Tight" (1969), which came closest in popularity to their debut disk.

See also Memphis Sound; Soul.

MOR   Acronym for "middle of the road," also known as "Easy Listening" on trade-paper charts. Generally refers to older-generation artists like Barbra Streisand (b. 1942), Frank Sinatra (b. 1915), and Engelbert Humperdinck (b. 1936)—Pop artists whose style is pre-Rock. Naturally, it also refers to a style that is closer to that of the Big Ballad and Big Baritone of the 1940s than it is to contemporary Rock, although few MOR records today are entirely devoid of Rock features. As a category, Pop Rock occupies the thin line between Rock and MOR. Barry Manilow (b. 1947), Melissa Manchester (b. 1951), Neil Diamond (b. 1945), Billy Joel (b. 1949), The Captain & Tenille, Bread, Three Dog Night, Rupert Holmes, Boz Scaggs (b. 1944), et al. walk this line. MOR sometimes also refers to the audience: middle-aged, middle-class, and middle-American.

See also Big Ballad era; Pop Rock.

MPA   *See* National Music Publishers Association.

"Magic Sam"   A Grenada, Miss., bluesman whose baptismal name was Sam Maghett (1937–1969), who often performed at Sylvio's and Alex's on Chicago's West Side, who was influenced by the guitar style of B. B. King (b. 1925), and who played for a time with the kingpin of Chicago Electric Blues, Muddy Waters (b. 1915).

See also Muddy Waters.

magnetic tape   Plastic tape coated with iron oxide and used in recording. Standard widths are one-quarter, one-half, and one inch.

"mainstream"   Once the designation of a type of Jazz that sounded neither traditional nor modern, the term has come to mean music that makes the widest possible appeal, commanding the largest audience. It's a question, obviously, of quantity, not quality.

major record company   Before the advent of Rock 'n' Roll, the record scene was dominated by a group of seven companies, not counting their subsidiaries: Capitol, Columbia, Decca, London, Mercury, MGM, and RCA Victor. They were major companies because they simultaneously released disks throughout the country through their own distribution outlets, which they either owned outright or leased. In addition, most owned their own manufacturing and pressing plants. It was these plants, through custom-service departments, that made possible the proliferation of labels during the R & B era. They pressed records for anyone who paid the cost, and they were delighted to take outside orders that kept their plants humming day and night.

A few of the R & B labels—King of Cincinnati and Modern/RPM of Los Angeles—built their own pressing and manufacturing plants, which doubtless helped account for the growth and expansion of these two labels.

Today, with the worldwide market for Rock, it is possible for labels to become major overnight, regardless of whether they own their own processing plants. In the late seventies, RSO became major because of the phenomenal sales of the Bee Gees. So did Arista, through the sales of Barry Manilow (b. 1947), Melissa Manchester (b. 1951), and other new artists. Casablanca emerged as a new power on the record scene with Donna Summer (b. 1949), Kiss, and the Disco explosion.

Make-Believe Ballroom   *See* Martin Block; Al Jarvis.

"make it"   A teenage colloquialism meaning to have sex.

Mambo   An Afro-Cuban form and dance that peaked in the 1950s. The name of Perez Prado (b. 1918), a Cuban bandleader, immediately comes to mind because of such instrumental hits as "Cherry Pink and Apple Blossom White" (1955) and "Patricia" (1958), which was not a Mambo but a Cha-Cha-Cha. Prado actually recorded "Cherry Pink" in 1951 shortly after English words were written to a French tune, published in 1950. Nothing happened to the record until RKO films selected the tune as the theme of *Underwater,* a 1955 film starring Jane Russell. Prado, whose orchestra performed the tune in the film, then rerecorded it and produced a disk that went to No. 1. Although interest in the Mambo intensified, the dance had been around for a time. In truth, in 1954 the recordings of two Pop stars testify to its popularity: Rosemary Clooney's "Mambo Italiano," a million seller, as was Perry Como's "Papa Loves Mambo."

But Latin-American scholars track the presence of the sound and the dance back to 1946 in performances by the Big Band of José Curbelo and popular recordings of "El Rey de Mambo" and "Rumba

Gallego.'' The Curbelo band included two Puerto Rican musicians who figured prominently in the rise of the Mambo during the fifties. Tito Rodriguez (1923–1973), who served Xavier Cugat (b.1900) as a vocalist/bongo player, formed the Mambo Devils in 1947, a combo he soon expanded to a Big Band. That same year, Tito Puente (b. 1923), a virtuoso timbales player and a man who was to record over 120 albums of Latin dance music, also formed his own combo, later billing himself as King of the Mambo.

As the Mambo developed into a craze during the early fifties, the small combos (conjuntos) expanded into Big Bands, taking over some of the devices of Big Band Swing. What soon became known as the Mambo section of Afro-Cuban performances involved a back-and-forth play between the brass and sax sections of the bands. These developments—the work of Curbelo, Rodriguez, and Puente—were East Coast phenomena. Aficionados regarded the West Coast Mambo as less authentic Afro-Cuban music. The work mainly of Perez Prado, who disputed Puente's claim to the title King of Mambo, it was seen as too commercial and catering to non-Latin audiences. Prado's famous grunt, ''Unh,'' during breaks was dismissed as ersatz. Nevertheless, some scholars saw the Mambo as a marriage of Swing and Latin-American rhythms.

See also Afro-Cuban; Latin rhythm instruments; Swing.

mandolin   A pear-shaped stringed instrument of Italian origin with four to six pairs of strings, tuned in fifths, played with a plectrum. The eight-stringed mandolin, with a two-and-a-half-octave range, is a basic instrument of Bluegrass music, and was played in the famous Bluegrass Boys band by its founder, Bill Monroe (b. 1911).

''map''   Like ''chart,'' jargon for an arrangement or score.

maracas   *See* Latin rhythm instruments.

mariachi   Strolling bands of players in Mexico, which originally earned their bread by playing for weddings. The word *mariachi* is supposedly related to ''marriage.'' Consisting usually of two trumpets and several string instruments (guitars and bass), the bands played a happy-sounding type of Latin music. The sound of Herb Alpert's Tijuana Brass is an American adaptation of mariachi.

See also Latin Rock.

marimba   Devised by an African princess, after whom it is named, it much resembles the xylophone, except that it has tuned resonators. Its sound is less percussive than the xylophone is and has a floating quality.

It was used on the hit version of "The Stroll" by Chuck Willis (1928–1958).

Mariposa Folk Festival   An annual daytime festival of Folk music, dance, and crafts, held since 1961 on the Toronto Islands, Ontario, Canada. The event has been called "a multinational smorgasbord" because of its concern with the interrelationship of all music traditions: Blues, Gospel, work songs, and so on. But the emphasis is on traditional folklore and a conscious effort is made to avoid stars among the performers. Leonard Cohen (b. 1935) made an appearance before he was signed by Columbia Records.
   See also festivals.

The Marquee Club   A major Rock club in London, where The Who made their debut in 1964. In 1962 the Rolling Stones more or less coalesced at the Marquee when Mick Jagger (b. 1944) joined members of Blues Incorporated for a BBC broadcast. Blues Incorporated, the band formed in '61 by Alexis Korner (b. 1928) and Cyril Davies (1932–1964), was the rage of the Marquee in 1962. Through the sixties, the Marquee also booked such American bluesmen as John Lee Hooker (b. 1917).
   See also Blues, British.

master   The finished tape from which saleable records, cassettes, or tapes are made. "Mastering" is the process of taking different "takes," tracks, and overdubs of a selection, picking the most desirable features of each, and putting them together to produce a finished master. Mastering is also the process whereby a disk-engraving machine transfers the electronic information from a stereo master tape to a master lacquer, which is forwarded to a pressing plant for duplication and production of saleable disks.

The Matrix   A San Francisco club, operated by musicians and artists, where the Jefferson Airplane got its start. Marty Balin (b. 1943), founder of the group, took over the club in the spring 1965, decorated the walls with his paintings and collages—and the Airplane took flight there in August 1965.

Maxixe   An old Brazilian dance related to the Tango. Briefly popular around World War I, it never really caught on.

Maxwell Street Market   Located in an area of vacant lots at Halstead, Peoria, and Sangamon streets on the South Side of Chicago, this open-air street market was a hangout of struggling bluesmen in the thirties and forties and into the sixties. In order to perform on electric guitars, the bluesmen picked up current by stringing lines from adjacent houses. Big Bill Broonzy (1893–1958) first heard harmonica player Little Walter Jacobs (1930–1968) in the Market and began using him on record dates. Guitarist Charles Thomas (b. 1925) came from Clarksdale, Miss., to work on Maxwell Street for tips, and adopted the name of Maxwell Street Jimmie Davis. Robert Nighthawk (1909–1967) celebrated the Market in an album titled *Live on Maxwell Street.* Among others who used the Market as a training ground and played for handouts were Blind James Brewer (b. 1921); Blind Arvella Gray (b. 1906); Johnny Watson (1867–1963), who played guitar, harmonica, jug, and kazoo, and became known as "Daddy Stovepipe"; and harpist Walter "Shakey" Horton (b. 1917). During the R & B era, a number of small labels made disks with some of the street players. Little Walter cut his first sides on Ora Nelle, an in-and-out Maxwell Street label.

See also Rhythm & Blues.

mechanical(s)   "Mechanical" refers to sound that is reproduced by a record, cassette, tape, transcription, film track, videotape, or even a piano roll: in short, any means except the original live performance. The word "mechanicals" refers to revenues derived from the sale of mechanical reproduction: records, cassettes, etc. Revenues collected from mechanicals are split fifty-fifty between publishers and songwriters or composers. Such mechanicals are collected from record companies and others for music publishers by the Harry Fox Agency. The publishers in turn pay the 50 percent share to the writers. Under the present copyright law, which became operative on January 1, 1978, record companies must pay 2.75 cents for each disk sold, or half a cent per minute or fraction thereof, whichever is larger: on songs of 5:01 minutes of longer a royalty of 3 cents plus is to be paid, depending on duration. Mechanicals are one of the three major sources of income from a song or composition. The other sources are performing rights and synchronization.

See also Harry Fox Agency.

mechanical bull   A rodeo-training device, devised by a Corrales, N.M., man and patented in 1975, the mechanical bull achieved national renown as a result of its use in *Urban Cowboy,* starring John Travolta. The character played by Travolta recaptured the heart of his wife by outlasting competitors on the headless, legless, lifeless animal, which can buck 80 times a minute while making 35 revolutions in either direction. Run by an operator, who controls its motions, the mechanical bull first became known by its presence, from 1977 on, at Gilley's, the giant honky-tonk Texas nightclub used as the setting of *Urban Cowboy.*

In 1979 Gilley's bought the rights to the device (El Toro) from its inventor. In less than two years, it sold 400 El Toros at $7,500 a bull, the sales energized by the popularity of the film. In 1980, the device became the subject of a lawsuit when Gilley's charged infringement by three companies manufacturing and selling versions of the mechanical bull.

See also Gilley's; Urban Cowboy.

medicine show   A feature of life in the rural, mountain, and backwoods areas of the U.S.A., the so-called "physick" wagon was a familiar sight as late as the 1930s. Many a black and Country performer served his apprenticeship working to help a quack sell his medicines to unsuspecting people. The "doctor" used song and dance men to attract and hold a crowd; in addition, some of the performers helped mix the "medicines" and sell them. When Jimmie Rodgers (1897–1933), the Father of Country Music, decided on a full-time music career in 1935, he signed on as a blackface entertainer with a medicine show that toured the mountain and hill country of the upper South. Roy Acuff (b. 1903), the singer/fiddler who was elected to the Country Music Hall of Fame in 1962, entered show business in the early thirties by joining Doc Hower's Medicine Show, which toured eastern Tennessee. Other Country performers who worked in medicine shows include Dave Macon (1870–1952), Clarence Ashley (b. 1895), and Hank Williams (1923–1953). In the absence of medical facilities and doctors, rural black folk were the prey of the "physick" wagons. Sonny Terry (b. 1911), the harmonica player who lost his sight as a boy, worked medicine shows touring North Carolina in the thirties. Joe Lee Williams (b. 1903), a Mississippi bluesman, drew crowds to Doc Bennett's Medicine Show in 1918 around Mobile, Ala., playing accordion, guitar, harmonica, and kazoo.

melisma   In singing, the stretching of a syllable over several notes. A decorative or expressive device like appogiatura instrumentally. Characteristic especially of Gospel and Soul singing. The gospel term is "curlicues" and the Blues term is "worryin' a word."

mellophone   An instrument played by Oran (Hot Lips) Page (1908–1954), who toured with Walter Page's Blue Devils (1927–1930) and Bennie Moten (1931–1935), and played and recorded with Artie Shaw.

Mellotron   Trade name for a synthesizer that uses tapes of recorded sounds. It was used by the Beatles and the Rolling Stones. It may be heard in *Days of Future Passed* by the Moody Blues, where it sounds like a mutative organ. In fact, the instrument is sometimes described as a mutant organ capable of reproducing the sounds of the stringed instruments of an orchestra: violins, violas, cellos. Robert Fripp (b. 1946) and Ian MacDonald (b. 1946), both of King Crimson, played the Mellotron, as did Les Holroyd (b. 1948) of Barclay James Harvest.

"mellow"   Being "mellow" was the relaxed state of quietly enjoying the simple, natural pleasures of life, as in the disk and album by Olivia Newton-John (b. 1949), *Have You Never Been Mellow?* (1975). Although the concept is supposed to have originated with the Woodstock Festival of love and peace in August 1969, it was severely challenged by the debacle of the Altamont concert later that year. "Mellow speak" was the jargon spoken by the Rock generation following Woodstock. "Mellow" is also a drug term used with regard to the effect produced by quaaludes and other "downers."

melodica   A toy-sized wind instrument that looks and sounds like a crew-cut accordion. The short keyboard has two octaves. The best known performer is Horace Swaby of Kingston, Jamaica, who is better known as Augustus Pablo and is the foremost exponent of Dub, a popular form of Reggae.
    See also Dub; Reggae.

"memory's little helper"   A derisive phrase used by Rock musicians with reference to the computers that invaded recording studios in the 1970s.

Memphis Horns   Originally the house band at Stax Records in Memphis in the 1960s was known as the Mar-Keys. After a time, Booker T. & the MG's emerged as a separate entity with hits like "Green Onions" (1962). Trumpeter Wayne Jackson and saxophonists Andrew Love and Floyd Newman took over the Mar-Keys' name, eventually incorporating as the Memphis Horns. They worked not only at Stax but at Chip Moman's American Recording Studios, where Dusty Springfield (b. 1939), King Curtis (b. circa 1935–1971), and other Atlantic artists recorded.

"Memphis Slim"   Nickname of Blues singer/songwriter Peter Chatman (b. 1915), who accompanied Big Bill Broonzy (1893–1958) in the 1940s and worked with bassist Willie Dixon (b. 1915) in the fifties. His songs include the classic "Every Day I Have the Blues," used as a theme by B. B. King (b. 1925), and the Joe Williams (b. 1918) favorite, "The Comeback."
    See also Rhythm & Blues.

Memphis sound   The sound of Memphis changed through the years. In the period when the Father of the Blues, W. C. Handy

(1873–1958), was composing "The Memphis Blues" (1912), "St. Louis Blues" (1914), and "Beale Street Blues" (1917), the sound of Memphis was basically the sound of the Blues: Country Blues and Delta Blues. Handy was a popularizer, arranging and jazzing the Blues.

In the 1950s the sound of Memphis became the sound of Rockabilly, the earliest stage of Rock 'n' Roll. Out of the Sun studios of Sam Phillips (b. 1925) emerged Elvis Presley (1935–1977), Jerry Lee Lewis (b. 1935), Carl Perkins (b. 1932), Roy Orbison (b. 1936), and Johnny Cash (b. 1932), Mississippi, Arkansas, Louisiana, and Tennessee boys imitating black R & B singers, blending their C & W backgrounds with R & B material and textures.

In the 1960s the sound of Memphis was darker, deeper, more bluesy, more soulful. It had a shrieking electric organ, the bark and bite of funky horns, and the black vocals of such Stax artists as Sam & Dave ("Hold on, I'm Coming," 1966), Carla Thomas ("Gee Whiz," 1961), Rufus Thomas ("Walking the Dog," 1963), Wilson Pickett ("In the Midnight Hour," 1965), Eddie Floyd ("Knock on Wood," 1966), Johnnie Taylor ("Who's Making Love," 1968), Arthur Conley ("Funky Street," 1968), and Otis Redding (*Dictionary of Soul,* 1966). Add the funk of such instrumental artists as King Curtis ("Memphis Soul Stew," 1967), Booker T. & the MG's ("Green Onions," 1962), and the Mar-Keys ("Last Night," 1961), as well as the electric Soul of Isaac Hayes's "Theme from Shaft," 1971). The Memphis sound was more soulful, bluesy, and funky than the sound of Detroit, emanating in the same period from the studios of Motown Records.

See also Blues; Delta Blues; Motown Sound.

Mento   An indigenous dance of Jamaica. The beat is heard in recordings by Toots & the Maytalls. Harry Belafonte's "Jamaica Farewell" was originally a Mento folk song.

See also Reggae.

Merengue   A fast dance in 2/4 rhythm that originated in the Dominican Republic, perhaps as far back as the early nineteenth century. The combos still playing it in the Republic generally consist of accordion, metal scraper, tambora drum, voice, and sax. The dancers keep one leg stiff in memory, legend has it, of a Dominican general who returned from the wars with a leg he could not bend; in order not to embarrass him on the dance floor, others danced with one leg stiff. The basic rhythm consists of an accented quarter note, followed by a tap and five eighth notes. Americans first heard the authentic Merengue in the early 1950s when a musician named Angel Viloria organized a group that captured the basic accordion cum sax sound. In the seventies Big Bands led by Felix del Rosario and Johnny Ventura came from the

Dominican Republic to play Merengues *con salsa* ("with spicy sauce").
See also Salsa.

Mersey sound   The term derives from the Mersey River, on which
the grimy city of Liverpool is situated. In the early sixties, a dive called
The Cavern switched from Trad Jazz to Rock and began booking bands
that imitated Little Richard (b. 1935), Buddy Holly (1936–1959), and
the girl groups of the day like the Shirelles and the Ronettes. Among the
bands were Rory Storm & the Hurricanes (drummer, Ringo Starr),
Freddie & the Dreamers, Billy J. Kramer & the Dakotas, Gerry & the
Pacemakers, Swinging Blue Jeans, and, of course, the Beatles. The emphasis of all these groups was on the big afterbeat, with a sound that was
closer to Rockabilly than to R & B.
See also The Beatles.

message songs   If Bob Dylan's "Blowin' in the Wind" (1963) was
not the first, it surely was the song that awakened the Rock generation to
the power of music to stir the feelings of people on social issues and,
perhaps, to provoke action. Dylan's albums of 1963 and 1964, especially
Free Wheelin' Bob Dylan, displayed a deep concern with such topical matters as the danger of a thermonuclear war ("A Hard Rain's Gonna
Fall," "Talking World War III"); the ordeal of James Meredith, the
first black to enter the University of Mississippi ("Oxford Town"); and
other social problems. It came as a great shock to Dylan's followers
when he turned away from protest songs in the aftermath of the
assassination of President John F. Kennedy.

But by then a school of message/protest writers had emerged—a list
that included Phil Ochs (1940–1976), who wrote the anti-Vietnam War
song "I Ain't Marching Anymore"; Tom Paxton (b. 1937), whose
dozen albums include *Peace Will Come;* Peter La Farge (1931–1965), who
was concerned with the plight of the American Indian and scored a
chart-climber in "Ballad of Ira Hayes," recorded by Johnny Cash;
Malvina Reynolds, author of a satiric commentary on tract housing,
"Little Boxes," a bestseller for Pete Seeger (b. 1919); and others. Two
small journals, *Sing Out!* and *Broadside,* published their topical and protest songs even before they were recorded. In 1964 *Broadside* sponsored
the first topical workshop at the Village Gate in Greenwich Village,
which attracted the following participants: Tom Paxton, Eric Andersen
(b. 1943), Len Chandler (b. 1935), Phil Ochs, Bernice Johnson Reagon
(one of the original Freedom Singers), Buffy Sainte-Marie (b. 1941),
and Pete Seeger, among others. Their message songs were sung and
recorded by artists like Joan Baez (b. 1941), and Judy Collins (b. 1939)
and by Folk groups like Peter, Paul & Mary, the Limeliters, and the
Chad Mitchell Trio.

Apart from the songwriters who saw songs as a weapon in the struggle for social justice, numerous uncommitted Rock artists were moved by the temper of the time to deal with social questions. In "He Was My Brother" Paul Simon spoke out against the murder of Freedom Riders in Mississippi; he also wrote a bitterly ironic commentary on the singing of "Silent Night" in a world overwhelmed by violence and murder. (Freedom Riders were civil rights workers who rode through the South to check on desegregation of public facilities). Spanky & Our Gang recorded "Give a Damn" on ghetto life, which was banned on the radio. Laura Nyro (b. 1947) included a plea, "Save the Country," in her *New York Tendaberry* album. The Youngbloods produced a million seller in "Get Together" (1969), a plea for brotherhood and love. In "Eleanor Rigby," The Beatles dealt provocatively with loneliness and the lack of communication between people—a theme also of Paul Simon's "Sounds of Silence"—and in *Sgt. Pepper* they presented an indictment of the emotional emptiness and dullness of middleclass existence ("A Day in the Life" and "She's Leaving Home").

The war in Vietnam, which split the country into bitterly opposed factions, was a target of many writers. In 1965 Barry McGuire (b. 1935), who had worked with the New Christy Minstrels, recorded "Eve of Destruction," an antiwar song by 19-year-old P. F. Sloan and Steve Barri. Although the disk was banned by some American stations, it became a Gold Record. When the BBC in England refused to clear it for broadcasting, pirate radio stations programmed it so that it sold nearly 2 million copies globally. Edwin Starr (b. 1942) made No. 1 with "War" and No. 4 with "Stop the War." Country Joe (McDonald, b. 1942) wrote, and Country Joe & the Fish recorded, "I-Feel-Like-I'm-Fixin'-to-Die Rag," which contained the mordant line "Be the first on your block to have your boy come home in a box." Donovan (b. 1946) voiced his protest in "Universal Soldier." A group calling itself C Company stirred much controversy with "Battle Hymn of Lt. Calley." Ex-Beatle John Lennon (1940–1980) made peace-and-love the core of his work after the breakup of the Fab Four, pouring his feelings into incisive and memorable songs like "Imagine," "Give Peace a Chance," and "Happy Christmas (War Is Over)."

Lennon's concern and outlook were shared by the Staple Singers. "Our message is peace," said Mavis Staples after the group had turned from Gospel to secular song. "Our message is wider than racial injustice. It could affect anyone. There are many people in the world being mistreated, many at war. Our message just calls for love and peace." But racial injustice was a topic to which many black artists addressed themselves, as others dealt with the new sense of pride in being black.

"Be What You Are" sang the Staple Singers, a follow-up to their album *Attitude/Respect Yourself*. James Brown (b. 1928) importuned his brethren to *Say It Loud—I'm Black and I'm Proud;* they responded by making the disk No. 1 on R & B charts and No. 10 on Pop charts. Nancy Wilson (b. 1937) made an even stronger assertion: "Black Is Beautiful." Turning to the prejudices and indignities black people suffered, the Temptations sang "Ball of Confusion (That's What the World Is Today)" and followed with a plea: *"Ungena Za Ulimwengu* (Unite the World)." Reviving a song of brotherhood written in 1956 by David Arkin and Earl Robinson, "Black and White"—"A child is black, a child is white . . . a beautiful sight"—Three Dog Night took it to No. 1 in 1972. Junior Walker (b. Autry DeWalt, circa 1942) hoped for "Peace and Understanding," while Joe South (b. 1942) pleaded for tolerance in "Walk a Mile in My Shoes."

Reacting to the rise of black nationalism, Curtis Mayfield (b. 1942) urged "People, Get Ready," while the Isley Brothers cried "Fight the Power," a thought underscored by the Chi-Lites in "(For God's Sake) Give More Power to the People." Some blacks were angry. Nina Simone (b. 1933), a brilliant Jazz pianist and Soul singer, responded to the bombing of black churches in the South with the furious "Mississippi Goddamn," a disk that was banned on radio, as was her searing study of skin color, "Four Women." Earlier, in a vindictive mood, the Long Beach Creators sang, just before the riots in Watts, "Burn, Baby, Burn." Dionne Warwick (b. 1941) countered: "What the World Needs Now Is Love."

The 1960s were an embattled era, rife with contention and confrontations, not to mention assassinations. To do justice to the Rock literature generated by the high emotions of the time would require a volume. Message, topical, and protest songs did not die with the sixties. In 1981 the Clash, a seminal Punk Rock group, devoted much of a three-record set, *Sandinista!*, to problems of oppression.

In 1982 the New Orleans-based Red Rockers wrote and recorded singles with a militant point of view, songs like "Voice of America," an angry denunciation of American involvement in El Salvador.

meter   As in poetry, a clear distinction must be made between meter and rhythm. Meter is the regular sequence of accented and unaccented syllables, while rhythm is the possible variations which may occur within the parameters of a given meter. In poetry, iambic pentameter means a sequence of five short/long feet: ˘/˘/˘/˘/˘/: "No longer mourn for me when I am dead." This line of a Shakespearean sonnet has an identical meter and rhythm. But two lines later, the Bard writes: "Give warning to the world that I am fled." Now, while the meter is still iambic pentameter, a variant anapest, "to the world," yields a different rhythm for the line. The same concept applies to music; but in place of pentameters and hexameters, we have 3/4 time in which the meter involves measures with three beats, the accent falling on the first; also 8-bar or 12-bar sequences in which regular meters appear and rhythmic variants may develop.

metronome Like the second-hand on a watch, it ticks out the beats. Operating mechanically or electrically, it can be set so as to vary the number of clicks in a minute. It is calibrated from 40 to 208 clicks per minute. Although it was invented by a man named Winkel early in the nineteenth century, it was patented by a man named Maelzel, who began manufacturing it in 1816. When a number appears next to a quarter or eighth note at the head of a piece with the letters M. M. before it, the reference is to Maelzel's Metronome. The metronome provides a more exact way of setting the tempo of a selection than directions like *Adante, Presto, Allegro,* and so on.

Mickey Mouse band A derisive term arising from Walt Disney's famous cartoon mouse with the squeaky voice. It is used to characterize small combos and bands that have a corny sound.

microtone An interval smaller than a semitone, which is the distance between two adjacent notes on the piano (two white notes with no black note between them or a white and a black note). Microtones cannot be notated, but they are heard in the Blues constantly when singers or instruments (brasses, woodwinds, and strings) bend their notes. Many of the Blues-oriented Rock groups likewise use microtones.

"Midnight Idol" The billing of Wayne Newton (b. 1943), one of the most popular of the regular entertainers on the Las Vegas Strip. Singer Bobby Darin (1936–1973), who had hits himself in 1958 with "Splish, Splash" and "Queen of the Hop," and won two Grammys for his "Mack the Knife" in 1959, produced Newton's first recording, "Heart," in 1963. Later that year, Newton scored with "Danke Schoen." Nine years elapsed before he achieved a Gold Record in "Daddy Don't You Walk So Fast" (1972). Playing virtually every musical instrument and possessed of a voice with a three octave range, Newton is a superstar in showroom appearances. Until he became a co-owner of the Aladdin Hotel and Casino on the Vegas Strip, he worked for the several Howard Hughes hotels in Vegas under a $13 million deal.
See also Schlock Rock.

The Midnight Special Currently the name of a late-hour TV show (on the NBC network) that features Rock performers; originally the title of a famous prison Blues, popularized by Leadbelly (1885–1949). It is based on a legend, popular among convicts of the prison known as Central Unit No. 2, at Sugarland, Tex. The belief was that if the midnight express, a passing train, shone its headlight into a prisoner's cell as it went roaring by, that prisoner would soon be released. As a TV program, *The Midnight Special* bowed in 1973.

Roger Miller (1936–   )   Influenced by Hank Williams (1923–1953) and working first with Ray Price (b. 1926) and then with Faron Young (b. 1932), he reached a peak in his career with his song "King of the Road." It sold over 2 million copies and won Miller six Grammys in 1965: Best Contemporary (R & R) Recording; Best Contemporary (R & R) Vocal Performance, Male; Best Country & Western Recording (two awards, one for the single and one for the album); Best Country & Western Vocal Performance, Male; and Best Country & Western Song. Prior to "King of the Road," Miller had two million-sellers in C & W novelty songs: "Dang Me" and "Chug-a-Lug" (both 1964).

minimalism   Viewed by many as a minimalist art form because of its abundant use of repetition, Rock nevertheless developed a complexity in the wake of the Beatles that brought outcries of anger and protest from the "true" aficionados of the form. The feeling was that the extensive use of electronic gadgetry—amplification, synthesizers, electrified instruments, 24-track recording boards, textural manipulation, over-dubbing, and distortion devices like feedback, reverb, and wah-wah pedals—vitiated the simple explosion of energy, excitement, and rebellion that were at the heart of Rock. Critics of complexity wanted an elimination of drums and horns, complex chord lines, sophisticated harmonies, and cultivated singing styles. Thus, Punk and New Wave were welcomed as a return to minimalism. Some of the smaller labels also explored a reduction of instrumentation below the level of Rockabilly. Linton Kwesi Johnson, a Briton of Jamaican origin, declaimed his poetry over a Reggae background. A group called Suicide consisted simply of a singer and an electronic keyboard player. Young Marble Giants from England offered a singer backed by a bass player and a second musician on guitar and organ. All three of these exemplified a rare degree of minimalism on disk.

On the concert or classical front, minimalism also found exponents. Philip Glass and Steve Reich indulged in a repetition and juxtaposition of short melodic and/or rhythmic patterns that were regarded by some as hypnotic and by others as simplistic. Like that of the Rock minimalists, their music was dubbed "trance music" or "pulse music." Turning back to the R & B scene of the 1950s, one hears in a song like "Smokestack Lightning" by Howlin' Wolf (1910–1976) a set of words projected over a two-bar melodic phrase, repeated innumerable times from the beginning to the end of the track. An early instance of minimalism?

See also New Wave; Punk Rock; Rockabilly.

minipiano   Literally, a small piano both in size and range. Instead of 88 notes, it has a range of only five octaves (62 notes).

minstrel show   A unique form of entertainment that evolved before the Civil War, based on plantation life, in which white men (later black) worked in blackface. A combination of singing, dancing, playing, and comedy, it popularized the Cakewalk as a dance, the olio, the walk-around, banjo playing, and the black humor of Mr. Tambo and Mr. Bones. These were the endmen of a semicircle in which the performers sat onstage before doing their bits: Mr. Tambo played the tambourine and Mr. Bones played the bones in addition to exchanging humorous routines with the Interlocutor, who sat in the middle of the semicircle. The best-known minstrel groups included the Virginia Minstrels of Dan Emmett (1815–1904), generally recognized as the first of the minstrel groups; Bryant's Minstrels, with whom Emmett worked from 1858 to 1866 and for whom he wrote "Dixie" as a walkaround; Ma Rainey's Rabbit Foot Minstrels, with whom the Empress of the Blues, Bessie Smith (1895–1937), served an apprenticeship; and Mahara's Minstrels, with whom the Father of the Blues, W. C. Handy (1873–1958), worked for seven years.

Three of America's earliest and foremost songwriters emerged from minstrelsy. Dan Emmett wrote, in addition to "Dixie" (1859), "Turkey in de Straw" (1861), "Old Dan Tucker" (1840), and many other banjo and minstrel songs. James A. Bland (1854–1911) wrote "Carry Me Back to Old Virginia" (1878), which was introduced by the George Primrose Minstrels and became the official song of the State of Virginia in 1940. Bland also wrote "In the Evening by the Moonlight" (1879), which was introduced by Bland and Callender's Original Georgia Minstrels. The third outstanding songwriter was Stephen Foster (1826–1864), whose song "My Old Kentucky Home" (1853) is the official state song of Kentucky and the anthem of the annual Kentucky Derby at Churchill Downs. It was originally introduced by the Christy Minstrels. In fact, E. P. Christy's name appeared as the writer and composer of "Old Folks at Home" when it first appeared in print because the prejudice of "refined people" was so strong against "Ethiopian" melodies that Foster was ashamed to be associated with it. There is little need to list all of the evergreen melodies that Foster wrote, some of which were introduced to the world by the Christy Minstrels. But mention should be made of "Oh, Susannah" (1848), "Camptown

Races'' (1850), ''Massa's in de Cold, Cold Ground'' (1852), ''Jeanie with the Light Brown Hair'' (1854), ''Old Black Joe'' (1860), and ''Beautiful Dreamer'' (1863).

Al Jolson (1886–1950), one of the giant figures in American popular song, served an apprenticeship working in blackface with Lew Dockstader's Minstrels. Eddie Cantor (1892–1964), singer and comedian, began his career as a blackface comic. After the turn of the century, vaudeville, which evolved from the olio (varied acts) of minstrelsy, superseded the minstrel show as America's major form of live entertainment and became the medium for popularizing songs.

See also Cakewalk; Al Jolson; minstrel show; vaudeville; walkaround.

''Mr. C.''   Perry Como (b. 1912), record and TV singing star of the Big Ballad era in the fifties.

''Mr. Dynamite''   *See* James Brown.

''Mr. Guitar''   A sometime nickname for country guitarist Chet Atkins.
See also Chet Atkins.

''Mr. Personality''   Cognomen of R & B singer Lloyd Price (b. 1933), who was able to cross over in 1959 with a succession of hits, including ''Stagger Lee,'' ''Personality'' (whence the nickname), and ''I'm Gonna Get Married.''
See also Rhythm & Blues.

''Mr. Pitiful''   *See* Otis Redding.

mix (mix down)   To put together or mix down all the tracks cut for a record. The process involves an array of electronic equipment. The aim is to get the best and most appealing sound by manipulating such elements as volume, dynamics, textures, levels, highs and lows, and echoes. Since as many as 24 tracks (or more) are used today in cutting a record, it becomes necessary to mix down the initial number to the 2 or 4 tracks that make up the final record sent out to the market. As a noun, the ''mix'' is the resulting combination of sounds.

mixed media   The combination of different art forms, as, for example, music and light shows. Among the earliest users of light shows were the Byrds in performances at New York City's Village Gate late in 1966. San Francisco's dancehalls and Acid bands are generally credited with popularizing the use of mixed media starting in the mid-1960s.
See also Acid Rock; light shows.

modes   Unlike our major and minor scales, whose notes follow a set sequence of intervals—whole step (c–d), whole step (d–e), half step (e–f), whole step (f–g), whole step (g–a), whole step (a–b), half step (b–c) in major—the modes varied in their structure. The sequence of whole and half steps change, depending on the starting note. Rock music brought a return of modal forms, which anticipated our major–minor system and were evolved in the Middle Ages.

By playing the white keys of the piano in sequence and starting on a different note each time, one can approximate the various church modes, the four authentic church modes being the Dorian, Phrygian, Lydian, and Mixolydian.

		In terms of half steps
c–d–e–f–g–a–b–c	Ionian or Hypolydian	2 + 2 + 1 + 2 + 2 + 2 + 1
d–e–f–g–a–b–c–d	Dorian	2 + 1 + 2 + 2 + 2 + 1 + 2
e–f–g–a–b–c–d–e	Phrygian	1 + 2 + 2 + 2 + 1 + 2 + 2
f–g–a–b–c–d–e–f	Lydian	2 + 2 + 2 + 1 + 2 + 2 + 1
g–a–b–c–d–e–f–g	Mixolydian	2 + 2 + 1 + 2 + 2 + 1 + 2
a–b–c–d–e–f–g–a	Aeolian or Hypodorian	2 + 1 + 2 + 2 + 1 + 2 + 2
b–c–d–e–f–g–a–b	Locrian or Hypophrygian	1 + 2 + 2 + 1 + 2 + 2 + 2

The names of the various modes suggest that they date back to the days of the Greeks and Romans, which they do, except that they then consisted of a series of only five notes: that is, they were pentatonic. It is believed that the modes derived from the natural acoustics of the human voice and that they therefore predominate in Folk music. This may help explain their prominence in Rock music. It should, perhaps, be noted that the mode that starts on the note c is identical in the sequence of intervals with the major scale on c.

Mods   The Mods were British working-class and lower-middle-class youths who dressed to kill. Laboring at dull, low-paying jobs, disaffected by their inability to enjoy the expensive things so seductively presented by advertisers, especially on TV, they vented their frustration in foppish dress. Their anger and alienation were ventilated in songs by the Who, Rolling Stones, Small Faces, and other groups who were their idols. The Mods warred with the Teddy Boys, teenage reactionaries who contended that nothing good had happened in Rock 'n' Roll after Little Richard (b. 1935).

modulation   A procedure in the diatonic major–minor system of moving from one key to another through the use of common tones and an approach via the dominant or V^7 chord of the new key. Like Folk music, Rock 'n' Roll generally eschewed this type of modulation and tended to move directly from one key to another without the use of modulatory chords.

Mohawk haircut   A hairdo, apparently adapted from that of the Mohawk Indians, in which both sides of the scalp are shaved clean and a row of hair is left sticking up on the top of the head from the forehead to the nape of the neck. Favored by Punk Rock fans, along with the Skinhead haircut.
   See also Punk Rock; Skinhead haircut.

"moldy fig"   A vituperative term applied by bopsters and Bop fans to those who favored Dixieland Jazz. In turn, the two-beat adherents castigated Bop, in Louis Armstrong's words, as "the modern malice." The conflict between the two schools peaked in the post–World War II years and found expression on 52nd Street. Jimmy Ryan's club favored and booked the Dixielanders, while the Three Deuces, Onyx, and other clubs tended to favor the music and followers of saxophonist Charlie "Bird" Parker (1920–1955) and trumpeter Dizzy Gillespie (b. 1917).

Bill Monroe (b. 1911)   In 1938 he named his band the Blue Grass Boys in honor of his home state (Kentucky), and their distinctive brand of music came to identify a style, of which Bill Monroe is the father. Although he played several string instruments, the mandolin became his primary vehicle and a basic sound of Bluegrass. To its piercing metallic sound was added the five-string melodic banjo of Earl Scruggs—also acoustic guitar, Country fiddlin', and bass. The Blue Grass Boys made their first appearance in October 1939 on WSM's *Grand Ole Opry* after Bill had attained prominence as part of the Monroe Brothers. He and brother Charlie (1903–1975) recorded 60 songs for Bluebird Records between 1936 and 1938, including "Kentucky Waltz," which he wrote. It was not until after World War II, sometime between 1945 and 1948, that the Bluegrass sound was perfected. In that period Bill Monroe had guitarist Lester Flatt (b. 1914) and banjoist Earl Scruggs (b. 1924) working with him. When Flatt and Scruggs left Monroe in 1948 and formed the Foggy Mountain Boys, Bluegrass acquired a second distinguished medium of expression. In general, the Bluegrass sound is a jaunty, uptempo, rhythmic style, which may be described as Country-sounding Dixieland with strings (fiddle, banjo, guitar, mandolin), not horns.

Monterey Jazz Festival   Dating back to 1958, the Festival has been held annually for three days late in September at Monterey, Calif. It has provided a showcase for new as well as established talent, and on occasion, for significant developments. In 1964 bassist Charles Mingus (1922–1979) presented one of the first concerts of atonal orchestral Jazz with a Big Band. In 1966 trumpeter Don Ellis (b. 1934) scored a sensation when he introduced his new Big Band. At one of the Festivals, Dizzy Gillespie (b. 1917) premiered "Perceptions," a work he commissioned from trombonist J. J. Johnson (b. 1924), which he described as "the most difficult piece I'd ever played." An all-year-round contact point is maintained at Jazz Festival, Box JAZZ, Monterey, CA 93940.

Monterey Pop Festival (1967)   Organized by Hollywood record producer/promoter Lou Adler and John Phillips of The Mamas & The Papas, the Monterey Pop Festival brought together the most impressive array of talent, new as well as established, ever gathered at a three-day set of concerts. The Who and Jimi Hendrix (1942–1970) came from London. Sitarist Ravi Shankar, who would not appear with any other artist and had Sunday afternoon to himself, flew in from India. Guitarists Paul Butterfield (b. 1942) and Mike Bloomfield (b. circa 1942) came from the world of Chicago Blues. And from San Francisco came the first wave of Bay City bands: Jefferson Airplane, Big Brother & the Holding Co., the Grateful Dead, the Steve Miller Band, Quicksilver Messenger Service, Country Joe & the Fish. The Festival proved the launching pad for such future "greats" as Otis Redding (1941–1967), Hendrix, The Who, Canned Heat, Electric Flag, and above all Janis Joplin (1943–1970), whose afternoon appearance was such a sensation that she was brought back for the evening concert. American Rock fans and media had their first encounter with the instrument-smashing show-tactics of The Who, whose spectacle of destruction was challenged by Jimi Hendrix when he doused his guitar with lighter fluid and set it on fire. Since over 30,000 people flocked into an area whose fairground accommodated only 10,000, a number of the San Francisco bands, pursuant to a Bay City tradition, put on a free show that lasted for 12 hours on the football field of the Monterey Peninsula College. The Monterey chief of police later said: "The long-haired hippies proved flowers and love are a symbol of what they really believe in." The Festival was not only peaceful and filled with a sense of community, but was an explosion of talent—and $160,000 was taken in at the box office.
    See also "be-in"; festivals.

Moog   A synthesizer developed in 1964 by Robert A. Moog (rhymes with "rogue") who holds a degree in electronic engineering from Columbia and a Ph.D. in engineering physics from Cornell. Moog's originality lay in combining significant features of a number of electronic devices dating back to 1896. That year, Thaddeus Cahill developed the Telharmonium, a music synthesizer that reportedly weighed over 200 tons and required several railroad flatcars to move. The Telharmonium led to the invention in 1920 of the Theremin, a device named after its Russian creator; a squealing sound like that of a saw was generated when hands were waved near a pole jutting out of an electronic box. The Theremin's sound was first heard by audiences in the film *Spellbound* (1945), an Alfred Hitchcock production. Starting with elements of the Theremin, and working with a musician friend, Herbert Deutsch, Moog adapted features of three other devices: (1) the Novachord, developed by Laurens Hammond, who developed the electric organ in 1935; (2) the Ondes Martenot, a device invented by Maurice Martenot in 1929; and (3) the RCA synthesizer Mark II. Capable of producing a vast variety of sounds, including animal noises and other natural sounds, speech, sound effects, and virtually any musical instrument, the Moog ranges in size from that of a portable TV set to the size of a pickup truck. Activated by a keyboard or programmed by computer, it has been used by such Rock groups, among others, as the Byrds, Electric Flag, Beatles, Rolling Stones, God Squad, Bread, and Emerson, Lake & Palmer.

Although Moog developed his instrument for use basically by experimental composers, the idea that synthesizers were useful only for avant-garde music and sound effects was shattered by the success of Walter Carlos's 1968 LP *Switched-on Bach*. The album was not only on bestselling Classical charts but on national mainstream charts. Aggregating an unbelievable sale of over a million, it went on to win three Grammy awards for 1969: Best Performance by an Instrumental Soloist; Best Classical Album of the Year; and Best Engineered Recording Classical Album.

Soon there was a flock of albums on the market, employing the Moog: *Moog Power* by Hugo Montenegro; *Music to Moog By* by Gershon Kingsley; *Switched-On Bacharach* by Christopher Scott; *electro-vibrations* by John Eaton; *The Copper Plated Integrated Circuit* by Sear Electronic Music Productions; *Moog: The Electric Eclectics of Dick Hyman,* Original Compositions and Improvisations by Dick Hyman; and others.

In 1970 Rock groups became much interested in the instrument when showy Keith Emerson of Emerson, Lake & Palmer used the synthesizer on their debut album. As more and more Progressive Rock groups began using the instrument, a backlash developed so that Queen, for example, announced on an LP cover that it did NOT use a synthesizer. This phase, intensified by the rise of Punk Rock, did not last too long. During a 1976 tour, David Bowie provoked new interest in the Moog when he collaborated with Brian Eno on two LPs, *Low* and

Heroes. Demonstrating that the synthesizer could be used in a more challenging and creative way, Bowie sparked English bands like Ultravox, Cabaret Voltaire, and Human League (also American bands like Suicide, Units, and Wall of Voodoo) to build their sound around synthesizers. By 1978 Gary Numan made bestselling Pop charts with his synthesized single, "Cars." During the Disco craze, synthesizers figured heavily on most disks. Among other groups and individuals that have made significant uses of the instrument, are Jeff Beck ("Star Cycle"), Weather Report ("Rockin' in Rhythm"), and Funkadelic ("Knee Deep"). In 1977 Moog sold out his interest in Moog Music to the Norlin Corporation.

See also synthesizer.

Moondog Matinee   He called himself "King of the Moondoggers"; his logo on his stationery was "Moondog House"; and his daily show, on Station WSU of Cleveland, Monday through Friday from 5:00 to 6:00 P.M., was called *Moondog Matinee.* In 1952 Alan Freed (1922–1965) who used Todd Rhodes's disk "Blues for Moondog" as his theme, also was on the air Monday through Friday from 11:15 P.M. until 2:00 A.M., and on Saturday night from 11:15 P.M. until 3:00 A.M.— programming R & B records, or "Blues and Rhythm" as it was called on his "Moondog House" stationery. That year, Freed ran a Moondog Coronation Ball at the Cleveland Arena, which required 30 extra firemen and 40 extra police "to disperse a crushing mob of 25,000," according to the *Cleveland Press.* After "turnstiles totaled 10,091 admissions and still more ticket holders began to storm the entrance," the *Cleveland News* reported, "the doors were closed." The *Cleveland Plain Dealer* reported that "people came from as far as Toledo." Station WJW put out a flyer boasting that "Radio Alone Pulled 25,000." Freed made the nation's press not only because of the enormous crowd his program of black artists drew but because he and several associates were indicted for overselling tickets; the charge was dismissed. In November 1954 Freed was enjoined from use of the Moondog label—he was then on Station WINS in New York City—when a Supreme Court Justice ruled that a blind, colorful street-musician named Louis "Moondog" Hardin had been using the name since 1947 whereas Freed had used it only since 1951. Freed, whose phenomenal career was brought to a dismal end by the payola investigations of 1959–1960, was the focus of a 1978 Paramount film, *American Hot Wax.* In 1973, The Band released an album titled *Moondog Matinee* as a tribute to Freed's WJW radio show.

McKinley Morganfield   *See* Muddy Waters.

"mother" or "mother fucker"   "Mother" is short for "mother fucker," meaning someone or something that is extraordinary or outstanding. Mostly an accolade today, it started as the worst insult one man could levy against another. It was popularized by a song titled "The Dirty Dozens," in which men traded insults, building toward the accusation of incest with one's mother. The accusation of incest with one's father took the form of "poppa-stoppa." Pronounced "mutha" in black and Rock circles, "mother fucker" can be used in either a friendly or an aggressive way, as a greeting or a challenge.

Mother Station of the Negroes   Station WDIA of Memphis, Tenn., on which B. B. King (b. 1925), Rufus Thomas (b. 1918), and other outstanding Rhythm & Blues entertainers performed or served as disk jockeys. Riley B. King was known as the Beale Street Blues Boy in the four years (1948–1952) that he worked at WDIA, which yielded the name by which he is known, B. B. King.

Motion Picture Academy Award (Oscar) songs   Since the Academy began awarding Oscars for songs, only one songwriter, lyricist Sammy Cahn (b. 1913), has won four of the statuettes. Four songwriters have each won three Oscars: composers Harry Warren (1893–1981) and Jimmy Van Heusen (b. 1913) and lyricists Johnny Mercer (1909–1976) and Paul Francis Webster (b. 1907). The complete list of Oscar winners for best songs follows:

1934	"The Continental": Con Conrad/Herb Magidson (*Gay Divorcee*)
1935	"Lullaby of Broadway": Harry Warren/Al Dubin (*Gold Diggers 1935*)
1936	"The Way You Look Tonight": Jerome Kern/Dorothy Fields (*Swingtime*)
1937	"Sweet Leilani": Harry Owens (*Waikiki Wedding*)
1938	"Thanks for the Memory": Leo Robin/Ralph Rainger (*Big B'D Cast 1938*)
1939	"Over the Rainbow": E. Y. Harburg/Harold Arlen (*Wizard of Oz*)
1940	"When You Wish Upon A Star": Ned Washington/Leigh Harline (*Pinocchio*)
1941	"The Last Time I Saw Paris": Oscar Hammerstein/Jerome Kern (*Lady be Good*)
1942	"White Christmas": Irving Berlin (*Holiday Inn*)
1943	"You'll Never Know": Mack Gordon/Harry Warren (*Hello Frisco, Hello*)
1944	"Swinging on a Star:" Johnny Burke/Jimmy Van Heusen (*Going my Way*)
1945	"It Might as Well Be Spring" Richard Rodgers/Oscar Hammerstein (*State Fair*)

1946   "On the Atchison Topeka & the Santa Fe": Johnny Mercer/Harry Warren (*Harvey Girls*)

1947   "Zip A Dee Do Dah": Allie Wrubel/Ray Gilbert (*Song of the South*)

1948   "Buttons & Bows": Ray Evans/Jay Livingston (*Paleface*)

1949   "Baby, It's Cold Outside": Frank Loesser (*Neptune's Daughter*)

1950   "Mona Lisa": Ray Evans/Jay Livingston (*Capt. Carey, U.S.A.*)

1951   "In the Cool Cool of the Evening": Hoagy Carmichael/Johnny Mercer (*Here Comes the Groom*)

1952   "High Noon (Do Not Forsake Me, Oh My Darling)": Dimitri Tiomkin/Ned Washington (*High Noon*)

1953   "Secret Love": Sammy Fain/Paul Francis Webster (*Calamity Jane*)

1954   "Three Coins in the Fountain": Sammy Cahn/Jule Styne (*Three Coins in the Fountain*)

1955   "Love is a Many Splendored Thing": Sammy Fain/Paul Francis Webster (*Love is a Many Splendored Thing*)

1956   "Que Sera Sera": Ray Evans/Jay Livingston (*The Man Who Knew Too Much*)

1957   "All The Way": Sammy Cahn/James Van Heusen (*The Joker is Wild*)

1958   "Gigi": Frederick Loewe/Alan Jay Lerner (*Gigi*)

1959   "High Hopes": Sammy Cahn/James Van Heusen (*Hole in the Head*)

1960   "Never on Sunday": Manos Hadjidakis (*Never on Sunday*)

1961   "Moon River": Henry Mancini (*Breakfast at Tiffany's*)

1962   "Days of Wine and Roses": Johnny Mercer/Henry Mancini (*Days of Wine and Roses*)

1963   "Call Me Irresponsible": Sammy Cahn/James Van Heusen (*Pappa's Delicate Condition*)

1964   "Chim Chim Cher-ee": Richard M. Sherman/Robert B. Sherman (*Mary Poppins*)

1965   "The Shadow of Your Smile": Paul Francis Webster/Johnny Mandel (*Sandpiper*)

1966   "Born Free": John Barry/Don Black (*Born Free*)

1967   "Talk to the Animals": Leslie Bricusse (*Doctor Doolittle*)

1968   "The Windmills of Your Mind": Alan and Marilyn Bergman/Michel LeGrand (*The Thomas Crown Affair*)

1969   "Raindrops Keep Falling on My Head": Hal David/Burt Bacharach (*Butch Cassidy & the Sundance Kid*)

1970   "For All We Know": Fred Karlin, Robb Royer, and James Griffin, a.k.a. Robb Wilson and Arthur James (*Lovers and Other Strangers*)

1971   "Theme from Shaft": Isaac Hayes (*Shaft*)

1972   "The Morning After": Al Kasha and Joel Hirschhorn (*The Poseidon Adventure*)

1973   "The Way We Were": Marvin Hamlisch/Alan and Marilyn Bergman (*The Way We Were*)

1974   "We May Never Love Like This Again": Al Kasha and Joel Hirschhorn (*The Towering Inferno*)

1975   "I'm Easy": Keith Carradine (*Nashville*)

1976   "Evergreen": Barbra Streisand/Paul Williams (*A Star Is Born*)

1977   "You Light Up My Life": Joseph Brooks (*You Light Up My Life*)

1978   "Last Dance": Paul Jabara (*Thank God It's Friday*)

1979   "It Goes Like It Goes": David Shire/Norman Gimbel (*Norma Rae*)

1980   "Fame" Michael Gore (*Fame*)

1981   "Arthur's Theme (Best That You Can Do)": Peter Allen, Burt Bacharach, Christopher Cross, and Carol Bayer Sager (*Arthur*)

motorcycle songs   The first of a series of bike songs was "Black Denim Trousers and Motorcycle Boots" (1955), written by Leiber & Stoller. It appeared about the same time as "Maybellene," in which Chuck Berry (b. 1926) dealt with a chase between two cars. The feeling for fast motion, drag racing, daredevil antics like speeding toward the edge of a cliff—all this had something to do with the sense of power and bravado they connoted, as well as the defiance of disaster and death.

During the sixties, the Beach Boys and Jan & Dean turned from Surfing songs to car songs: "Little Deuce Coupe" (1963), "Dead Man's Curve" (1964), "Drag City" (1964), and others. Among other bike and car songs: "Tell Laura I Love Her" (1960), which dealt with death in a stock-car race; "Hey Little Cobra" (1964), by the Rip Cords; "Little Honda," (1964) by the Hondells (assembled by Mike Curb to record a jingle, "You Meet the Nicest People on a Honda"); and "Leader of the Pack" (1964), by the Shangri-Las, which featured the roar of a motorbike on the disk.

Motown sound   The brainchild of Berry Gordy (b. 1929), an erstwhile Detroit boxer, songwriter, and Ford Motors mechanic who turned to record production around 1959 and launched Tamla Records (originally named "Tammie" after the hit picture of that time). Before Tamla got off the ground in 1961 with "Shop Around" by the Miracles, Gordy leased R & B recordings he made with singer Marv Johnson (b. 1938) and the Miracles to other labels. By 1962 Gordy had added two other labels—Motown and Gordy—to his complex and was on the way to defining the Motown sound. ("Motown was a contraction of "Motor town."). It was a product of a number of groups—Miracles, Temptations, Supremes, Martha & the Vandellas; a number of solo singers—

Eddie Holland (b. 1939), Mary Wells (b. 1943), Marvin Gaye (b. 1939), Little Stevie Wonder (b. 1951); and a number of producers —Smokey Robinson (b. 1940), Holland-Dozier-Holland, Norman Whitfield, Nicholas Ashford, and Valerie Simpson. In essence, the Motown Sound was black Pop, Pop Gospel and Pop Soul. On most of the records, Gospel elements were present in the use of tambourines and call-and-response. Horns had the bite of R & B records. But the strings were played by members of the Detroit Symphony Orchestra. In short, although Gordy's artists did not forsake their black roots, their records were not as black as Stax recordings and not so black that they would alienate white listeners. They had the makings of crossovers—and cross over they did, so much so that in one year (1964) *Billboard* discontinued its R & B charts because they were practically identical with the Pop charts. In 1966, Motown's hit ratio was close to 75 percent: i.e., three-quarters of all the records released by the Motown labels made national Pop charts. By then, V.I.P. and Soul had been added to the other active labels. Situated originally in a series of bungalows in a run-down section of Detroit's Grand Avenue, Motown moved in the 1970s to Hollywood, where it soon embarked on the production of films. By then, Motown was grossing over $10 million a year, and Diana Ross (b. 1944) had embarked on a grandiose solo career and was starred in *Lady Sings the Blues,* based on the life of Billie Holiday (1915–1959), Gordy's first film venture.

See also Hitsville, U.S.A.; Soul.

mouth bow   Developed by the bushmen of Africa and played by some Country and Folk performers, the mouth bow is strung like a regular bow that shoots arrows. Banjo or guitar string is sometimes used instead of an ordinary piece of string, its tightness determining the bow's pitch and range. In performance, the flat side of the bow is pressed against the cheek near the player's mouth, which acts as the resonator. Varying the size of the mouth opening yields different pitches. Buffy Sainte-Marie (b. 1941) and Jimmy Driftwood (b. 1917), the writer/performer of "Tennessee Stud" (1958) and "Battle of New Orleans" (1957), are performers who have used the mouth bow.

mouth organ (harmonica)   A wind instrument used by Blues, Folk, and C & W performers, played by blowing the breath into and sucking the breath from apertures containing metal reeds. Some harmonicas, or "harps" (in Blues jargon), have a lever that is operated by a finger and that makes sharps, flats, and key changes possible. Singers frequently have a harmonica positioned on a metal stand attached to their neck or guitar so that they can strum and blow at the same time. Young Bob Dylan (b. 1941) accompanied himself in this way on his first recording.

Outstanding performers on the instrument include bluesmen like Sonny Terry (b. 1911), Howlin' Wolf (1910–1976), Robert Johnson (1914– 1938), Muddy Waters (b. 1915), John Lee (Sonny Boy) Williamson (1914–1948), Willie "Rice" Miller—Sonny Boy Williamson II (1899– 1965), Walter "Shakey" Horton (b. 1917), Willie Mae "Big Mama" Thornton (b. 1926), Little Junior Parker (b. 1927), Little Walter (1930–1968), James Cotten (b. 1935), and De Ford Bailey, the first performer on the *Grand Ole Opry;* and also Pop artists like Borrah Minnevitch, Jerry Murad & the Harmonicats—their "Peg o' My Heart" (1913) sold a million records between 1947 and 1950—and John Benson Sebastian (b. 1944) of the Lovin' Spoonful.

Muddy Waters (b. 1915)   The Delta bluesman from one of whose recorded songs the Rolling Stones took their name was McKinley Morganfield (b. 1915, Rolling Fork, Miss.), better known as Muddy Waters. Settling in Chicago in 1943, Waters played the South Side clubs with such impact that a generation of white Blues rockers sat at his feet: Mike Bloomfield (b. 1942), Nick Gravenites (b. 1938), and Paul Butterfield (b. 1942), among others. In 1969 Muddy recorded an album with these young followers appropriately titled *Fathers and Sons.*

The most influential exponent of Chicago's electric, ensemble Blues style, Muddy began playing mouth organ and bottleneck guitar in Clarksdale, Miss., where he was reared by his grandmother, and bought his first electric instrument in 1945 after he had settled in Chicago. "Rolling Stone" was on the first date he did for the Chess Records original label, Aristocrat, in 1946. Up until then he had worked in a paper factory, having given up driving a tractor in Clarksdale. Sales of his first recordings were quickly reflected in the demand for live appearances in the South Side black clubs, a demand which had not abated even in 1981.

Praising Paul Butterfield and Mike Bloomfield as "good white musicians," Muddy adds: "But, of course, they can't *sing* the Blues the way we can. We are the best Blues singers in the world—I mean, the black man." Muddy's explanation is that having worked for as little as 50 cents a day from sunup to sundown, the Blues early became part of him. As for the Rolling Stones and the Beatles, he says: "They love the Blues in England and they woke up our white kids over here. They got them listening to the Blues."

The seminal influence in the stylization of Chicago Electric Blues, Muddy also early helped shape the new macho image of the black man after World War II. In records like "I've Got My Mojo Working," "I'm Your Hootchie-Coochie Man," "I'm Ready," and "I'm a Man," he gave full-bodied expression to the black man as a potent, self-satisfied, if not boastful, sexual figure. Unlike his fellow Chess artist,

Chuck Berry, or Fats Domino or Sam Cooke, Muddy's records were too bluesy, too black, and too tough to cross over. But many of the songs he recorded have been recorded by British Rock groups: e.g., "Mannish Boy" by the Rolling Stones, "I'm a Man" by the Yardbirds, "I Just Had to Make Love to You" by the Rolling Stones, and "I'm Your Hootchie-Coochie Man" by John Mayall's Bluesbreakers and Manfred Mann.

See also Chicago Blues style; Rhythm & Blues.

"mulatto music"   The term used by Dr. Buzzard's Original Savannah Band to describe their brand of Latinized Disco/Swing. The sound was heard in a local New York City record hit, "Cherchez la Femme."

Muscle Shoals sound   Fame Studios were established in Muscle Shoals, Ala., in 1961 by producer Rick Hall. Muscle Shoals soon became recognized as the center of Funk and Soul. In 1965 Joe Tex (b.1936) cut "Hold What You've Got," which became the first southern Soul song to make the Pop charts. The following year, Percy Sledge (b. 1941), who comes from Muscle Shoals, scored a No. 1 Pop hit with "When a Man Loves a Woman." From 1966 on, Wilson Pickett (b. 1941) cut many of his hits at Muscle Shoals, including the classic "In the Midnight Hour." In a sense, the Muscle Shoals explosion came in 1967 when Aretha Franklin (b. 1942), after years of so-so recordings on Columbia, journeyed to the Rick Hall Studios and made "I Never Loved a Man" and "Respect," Gold Records that established her as the preeminent exponent of Soul and caused her to be named the Top Female Vocalist of 1967 by *Billboard*. Now white singers began to make the trek south to freshen their work. In 1969 Boz Scaggs cut disks, coproduced by Duane Allman (1946–1971), who worked as a session guitarist at Muscle Shoals until he and his brother, Greg, formed the famous Allman Brothers Band. Bob Seger (b. 1945) used the Muscle Shoals rhythm section on his *Night Moves* hit album in '76, and again in 1980, on *Against the Wind*. In 1974 Willie Nelson (b. 1933), leader of the anti-Nashville, "outlaw" movement in Country music, cut *Phases and Stages* at Muscle Shoals. As in Aretha Franklin's famous sessions, the recordings were produced by Jerry Wexler, formerly of Atlantic Records and now with Warner Bros. Records.

Muse   An antinuclear organization, Musicians United for Safe Energy, formed by Rock artists, with a board including Jackson Browne (b. circa 1949), Graham Nash (b. 1942), Bonnie Raitt (b. 1949), and John Hall. In September 1979, Muse sponsored a series of antinuclear concerts at Madison Square Garden in New York City and an outdoor rally at Battery Park on the day of the last concert. A documentary film and an album titled *No Nukes* were released. The participants, in addition to the board members mentioned, included Crosby, Stills & Nash, Doobie Brothers, Gil Scott-Heron, Carly Simon (b. 1945), Bruce Springsteen (b. 1949), James Taylor (b. 1948), and Jesse Colin Young (b. 1941).

In June 1982, 90,000 fans gathered at Peace Sunday in Pasadena's Rose Bowl to raise $250,000 for nuclear disarmament. Among the rock artists who participated in the day-long benefit: Jackson Browne; Linda Ronstadt; Bette Midler, Stevie Wonder; Crosby, Stills & Nash; Joan Baez and Bob Dylan, who harmonized in Dylan's Civil Rights anthem of the sixties "Blowin' in the Wind." The benefit ended with the crowd joining in a sing-along rendition of John Lennon's "Give Peace a Chance."

Musical, Tony Awards for Best   The beginnings of the American musical are generally traced to an extravanganza, *The Black Crook,* that was presented in 1866 at Niblo's Gardens in New York City and had a continuous run of 16 months and 474 performances. (The circumstances surrounding this production became the basis of *The Girl in the Pink Tights,* 1954, the last musical score of Sigmund Romberg, 1887–1951). The early years of the American musical were years in which scores and stories both owed a heavy debt to Viennese operatta. It was not until after the turn of the century, with the musicals of George M. Cohan (1878–1942), that the American musical comedy—American in characters, theme, and sound—was born. And it was not until 1931 that any musical received the recognition that the form deserved. That year's production of *Of Thee I Sing,* with music and lyrics by the Gershwins and a book by Morrie Ryskind and George S. Kaufman, became the first musical in theater history to receive the Pulitzer Prize. It was also the first American musical comedy to have its book published as a separate entity without the songs.

In 1936 the New York Drama Critics Awards were established. They did not find a worthy musical recipient until *Carousel,* a 1945 musical play with book and lyrics by Oscar Hammerstein II (1895–1960) and music by Richard Rodgers (1902–1979). The Donaldson Award, founded in 1944 in memory of the founder of *Billboard* magazine (W. H. Donaldson), was first given in the musical theater that year to *Carmen Jones,* a black adaptation of Bizet's opera *Carmen* by Oscar Hammerstein II.

The Tony Awards (a colloquialism for the Antoinette Perry Awards) did not come into existence until 1947. The awards were established by the American Theater Wing in honor of its chairman of th board during World War II, Ms. Antoinette Perry. The first musical to receive the Tony was *Kiss Me, Kate* in 1949.

Here is a list of the musicals, composers, and lyricists that have won Tonys:

Musical	Composer and Lyricist
1949 *Kiss Me, Kate*	Cole Porter, *Kiss Me Kate* (m & l)
1950 *South Pacific*	Richard Rodgers, *South Pacific* (no lyricist category in 1950)
1951 *Guys and Dolls*	Frank Loesser, *Guys and Dolls* (m & l)
1952 *The King and I*	————
1953 *Wonderful Town*	Leonard Bernstein, *Wonderful Town* (no lyricist category in 1953)
1954 *Kismet*	Alexander Borodin, *Kismet* (no lyricist category in 1954)
1955 *The Pajama Game*	Richard Adler and Jerry Ross, *The Pajama Game* (m & l)
1956 *Damn Yankees*	Richard Adler and Jerry Ross, *Damn Yankess* (m & l)
1957 *My Fair Lady*	Frederick Loewe, *My Fair Lady* (no lyricist category in 1957)
1958 *The Music Man*	Meredith Willson, *The Music Man* (m & l)
1959 *Redhead*	Albert Hague *Redhead* (no lyricist category in 1959)
1960 *Fiorello!*	Jerry Bock, *Fiorello!* (no lyricist category in 1960)
1961 *Bye, Bye, Birdie*	————
1962 *How to Succeed in Business Without Really Trying*	Richard Rodgers, *No Strings* (m & l)
1963 *A Funny Thing Happened on the Way to the Forum*	Lionel Bart, *Oliver!* (m & l)
1964 *Hello, Dolly!*	Jerry Herman, *Hello, Dolly!* (m & l)
1965 *Fiddler on the Roof*	Jerry Bock and Sheldon Harnick, *Fiddler on the Roof* (m & l)
1966 *Man of La Mancha*	Mitch Leigh and Joe Darion, *Man of La Mancha* (m & l)
1967 *Cabaret*	John Kander and Fred Ebb, *Cabaret* (m & l)
1968 *Hallelujah, Baby!*	Jule Styne, Betty Comden and Adolph Green, *Hallelujah, Baby!* (m & l)

1969	*1776*	————
1970	*Applause*	————
1971	*Company*	Stephen Sondheim, *Company* (m & l)
1972	*Two Gentleman of Verona*	Stephen Sondheim, *Follies* (m & l)
1973	*A Little Night Music*	Stephen Sondheim, *A Little Night Music* (m & l)
1974	*Raisin*	Frederick Loewe (music) and Alan Jay Lerner (lyrics), *Gigi*
1975	*The Wiz*	Charlie Smalls, *The Wiz* (m & l)
1976	*A Chorus Line*	Marvin Hamlisch (music) and Ed Kleban (lyrics) *A Chorus Line*
1977	*Annie*	Charles Strouse and Martin Charnin, *Annie* (music and lyrics)
1978	*Ain't Misbehavin'*	Fats Waller (music)
1979	*Sweeney Todd*	Stephen Sondheim, *Sweeney Todd* (m & l)
1980	*Evita*	Andrew Lloyd Webber and Tim Rice
1981	*42nd Street*	Harry Warren and Al Dubin

The composer with the most awards (four) was Stephen Sondheim (b. 1930), followed closely by Richard Rodgers (1902–1979), who had three awards.

Music City, U.S.A.   A cognomen of Nashville, Tenn. But it really refers to the section in the city around 16th and 17th Avenues, North and South, now known as Music Row. In this area are to be found the big record company studios (RCA Victor, Columbia, etc.), the Country Music Hall of Fame, the Nashville regional offices of ASCAP and BMI, and literally hundreds of other music-related enterprises.
    See also Nashville sound.

Musique Concrète   *See* Concrete Music.

mute   A device for altering the sound and/or the tonal character of an instrument. Mutes for trumpet and trombone, placed in or near the bell, include the bucket mute, cup mute, harmon mute, plunger mute, and straight mute. Each of these has a different shape, resulting in different sound transformations.

Muzak   Has become a generic term for canned music heard in banks, factories, supermarkets, restaurants, elevators, and other public places. Muzak is the name of the organization that originated the practice. When it did in the 1930s, establishments paid a fee to receive the performance of a live orchestra via telephone lines. Vinylite disks and tape eventually superseded live performance. Muzak's biggest competitor is Minnesota Mining, which sells a machine operated on a tape loop. Many restaurants and other enterprises also use an internal arrangement of speakers, connected to their own tape deck or local FM station. In a recent survey, only 7 of the 150 largest corporations in the U.S.A. were not availing themselves of Muzak's music. The survey also revealed that programmed music, vended by several other companies as well as Muzak, reaches 100 million people daily in 25 countries. Minnesota Mining's 3M Corporation accounts for 25 percent of programmed music business.

As an adjective, Muzak has come to mean dull music that has no impact.

N

NAB   National Association of Broadcasters.

NARAS   *See* National Academy of Recording Arts and Sciences.

NARM   *See* National Association of Record Merchants.

NMC   *See* National Music Council.

NMPA   *See* National Music Publishers Association.

NOPE   Acronym for "no promotion," which is what the majority of record releases receive.

N.O.R.K.   The New Orleans Rhythm Kings, a pioneer white Jazz band, formed in 1919 or 1920 when trumpeter Paul Mares (1900–1949) was invited to form a New Orleans–style band—something like the Original Dixieland Jazz Band. For about two years, they played the Friars' Inn in Chicago, a cabaret supposedly frequented by Al Capone and other gangsters. They recorded about 30 sides, which greatly impressed and influenced the members of the Austin High School group of Chicago. The 1922–1923 sides were made for Gennett, while the 1925 sides, cut shortly before they broke up, were produced on OKeh and

Victor. Known also as the Friars Society Orchestra because of their association with the cabaret of the same name, the Kings included, besides Mares, Leon Rappolo (1902–1943) on clarinet and George Brunies (1900–1974) on trombone.

Nashville Outlaws   There was nothing in the traditional backgrounds of Willie Nelson (b. 1933 in Fort Worth, Tex.), Waylon Jennings (b. 1937 in Littlefield, Tex.), and Tompall Glaser (b. 1933 in Spaulding, Neb.) to prepare them for the "outlaw" roles they espoused in the 1970s. Waylon Jennings was a precocious disk jockey in his hometown at the age of 12, played electric bass with Buddy Holly (1936–1959) during his short-lived career, became a star attraction in Phoenix with his Waylors in the early sixties, and made hit Country records for RCA Victor from 1965 on. Tompall & the Glaser Brothers, a highly successful vocal and instrumental trio, worked with Arthur Godfrey in the late fifties, along with Marty Robbins (b. 1925) and Johnny Cash (b. 1932); became regulars on the *Grand Ole Opry* in 1962, having begun recording for Decca in the late fifties; and wrote hits for Jimmy Dean (b. 1928), Bobby Bare (b. 1935), Jimmy Newman (b. 1927), and other Country artists of the sixties. Willie Nelson began his career as a songwriter and a disk jockey. For seven years, starting in the mid-1950s, his chores as a DJ kept him busy on stations in Texas, Oregon, and California. Starting with a Patsy Cline hit ("Crazy") in the early sixties, he wrote hit songs for Faron Young (b. 1932) and other Country artists. He himself began recording in 1962 and became a regular on the *Grand Ole Opry* in 1964.

Over a five-year period, Nelson found that he could not break through the strictures of the Nashville enclave. Although he did not like the way he sounded, the material he had to record, or the way his music sounded on his records, he could not budge record executives or booking agents. They had the creative as well as business control. Finally, in 1969 he left Nashville and returned to Texas, where he soon cut out of his conservative clothes and short hair-style, began wearing faded T-shirts and jeans, grew his hair long and pigtailed it, and even put an earring in his ear. Moving from RCA Records to Atlantic and then to Columbia, he finally gained creative control of the record process. By the time he recorded an "outlaw" sampler with Waylon Jennings, he had crossed over into Pop and was a recognized superstar in Country. Departing completely from Nashville strictures, he recorded a Gospel album, an LP with rocker Leon Russell (b. 1941), tribute albums to songwriter Kris Kristofferson (b. 1936) and honky-tonk singer/songwriter Lefty Frizzell (1928–1975), and a Pop album titled *Stardust.* The last-mentioned included ballads like Irving Berlin's "Blue Skies" and Pop standards like "All of Me" (1931).

Of the *Stardust* album, which has sold over 2 million copies, he said: "I recorded those songs because I believed in them. I've been singing those songs in Texas for years. It wasn't until I got to Nashville that people started talking about this being a 'Pop' song and that being a Country song. Back home, it was all just music, and I figured that's the way it was most places."

In describing his singing style, Nelson has said: "It's phrasing . . . Sinatra's been phrasing for years. A lot of Pop singers do. It's just that nobody in Country music in those days was doing it. But I couldn't imitate anybody else."

Diversity is the name of Nelson's game. And individuality is the name of the "outlaw" game. Following the two concepts has brought fame and fortune to Nelson, Waylon Jennings, Jerry Jeff Walker (who wrote "Mr. Bojangles"), and the other "outlaws," who have made Austin, Tex., their operational base and Armadillo World Headquarters, a defunct National Guard armory in Austin, the site of their most celebrated Country/Rock concerts.

See also Armadillo World Headquarters.

Nashville sound   Depending on the era, the Nashville sound went through several changes. Going back to the days of the Carter Family, Roy Acuff (b. 1903), Ernest Tubb (b. 1914), and the Father of Country Music, Jimmie Rodgers (1897–1933), Nashville meant the sound of acoustic guitars, whining slide guitars, nasal baritones, head arrangements—and no drums. In the 1950s, the decorative thirds of Floyd Cramer's (b. 1933) piano and Chet Atkins's (b. 1924) schooled guitar were added. In the 1960s drums, electricity, and Rock rhythms invaded Nashville. But its Country roots gave it a sound that brought Bob Dylan (b. 1941), the Byrds, Buffy Saint-Marie (b. 1941), and other Folk and Rock stars to Nashville in an effort to freshen their work. After a time, extensive studio work and high living—more Cadillacs were sold in Nashville per capita than in any other city of comparable size—gave the sound a fabricated gloss, a slick commercialism, and an emotional emptiness that led to the rise of the so-called "outlaws." Even New York producers like Jerry Wexler of Atlantic Records began talking of "the Nashville stink" and sought out studios in Memphis, Tenn., Muscle Shoals, Ala., Austin, Tex., and other, less sophisticated Blues and Country musical communities. In 1974 the *Grand Ole Opry* moved from its home in Nashville's Ryman Auditorium, a historic converted tabernacle, to a 4,400-seat air-conditioned theater in the million-dollar Opryland, U.S.A., complex. Now, the Nashville sound was the sound of Music City, indeed: an urban community whose Music Row comprised an estimated 120 record production outlets, 80 record manufacturing companies, 80 booking agencies, 10 music organizations and unions, 20 radio commercial and jingle companies, 20 album cover photographers, 2 radio stations, several music-oriented newspapers and magazines, and the Country Music Hall of Fame. When the Bradley brothers, Owen and Harold, remodeled a house in 1955 on what is now Music Row, using a Quonset hut as the shell of the first recording studio in Nashville, they paid $7,500 for a lot that today tops the $100,000 mark.

See also Chet Atkins; *Grand Ole Opry;* Music City, U.S.A.; Nashville Outlaws; Jimmie Rodgers.

National Academy of Popular Music (NAPM)   Three men were instrumental in the founding of the Academy in 1967: the late song-writer Johnny Mercer (1909–1976) longtime music executive Abe Olman, and publisher Howard Richmond. To be eligible for member-ship, a songwriter must be affiliated with one of the three recognized American performing-rights societies: ASCAP, BMI, or SESAC. On January 18, 1977, the Academy formally launched the Songwriters' Hall of Fame and Museum. Its permanent location is on the eighth floor of One Times Square in the heart of New York City's celebrated theatrical district and in the center of what was the city's Tin-Pan Alley from World War I until after World War II. The museum's present col-lection includes original manuscripts of famous songs, rare sheet music, books about the country's songwriters, musical instruments, and such priceless memorabilia as George Gershwin's writing desk, instruments on which Duke Ellington and Fats Waller wrote some of their composi-sions, Johnny Mercer's typewriter, Woody Guthrie's drawings, and Fred Astaire's hat. Admission to the museum, six days a week, is free. The museum's present curator is folk singer/songwriter/author Oscar Brand (b. 1920).

See also American Society of Composers, Authors, and Publishers; Broadcast Music, Inc.; Hall of Fame, Songwriters'; Tin-Pan Alley; SESAC.

National Academy of Recording Arts & Sciences (NARAS)   The Academy came into existence in 1957 when the Hollywood Beautifica-tion Committee turned to a group of West Coast record executives for help in choosing entertainment greats whose names would be placed in stars imbedded in the sidewalks of downtown Hollywood. The ex-ecutives whom they consulted became the nucleus of the Academy. They were Lloyd Dunn of Capitol, Paul Weston of Columbia, Sonny Burke of Decca, Jesse Kay of MGM, and Dennis Farnon of RCA Vic-tor. The five chose as temporary chairman of the organization-to-be Jim Conkling, then the recently retired President of Columbia Records.

By 1958, a New York chapter had come into existence, with bandleader Guy Lombardo serving briefly as the first President, followed by veteran talent scout/record executive John Hammond. In this period, the offices of a New York music business attorney, Dick Jablow, served as headquarters for the fledgling organization. Soon, a miniature replica of an oldtime phonograph, the gramophone, was chosen as the Academy's emblem, and a nationwide contest to "name-that-statuette" resulted in its being called the Grammy, short for gramophone.

The first Grammy Awards dinner was held in May 1958 in the Grand Ballroom of the Beverly Hilton Hotel, with Frank Sinatra, Dean Martin, Sammy Davis, Jr., Peggy Lee, and others serving as presenters. The following year, the Academy aired its first TV show. In 1964, after a four-year gap, NBC began running an annual taped show, *Best on Record,* which featured award-winning performances. The first live telecast of *The Grammy Awards Show* came in 1971.

By 1974 the Academy consisted of seven chapters. In addition to those in Los Angeles and New York, there was a Nashville chapter (formed in 1959), Chicago chapter (1961), Atlanta chapter (1969), Memphis chapter (1972), and San Francisco chapter (1974). As the chapters grew, so did the categories of awards, increasing from 28 at the beginning, to 51 in 1978, and to 61 in 1982. In addition, five recordings are inducted annually into the Academy's Hall of Fame, which was established in 1973.

The Grammy Awards are chosen by a vote of the Academy's membership after a determination of eligible records and nominations have been made by the membership and, in certain categories, by National Special committees and Craft committees. Before the final vote is taken by mailed, secret ballot, the nominations are narrowed to the top five in each category. All members vote for the Grammys in four general categories: Record of the Year, Album of the Year, Song of the Year, and Best New Artist. As for the other categories, which are arranged in 13 Specialized Fields, members select a limited number of fields in which to cast votes.

The national headquarters of NARAS is on the West Coast in Burbank, Calif., where it was established in 1971 by a vote of the National Trustees, who serve on a strictly voluntary basis as do all local and national officers of the Academy.

See also the Grammy Awards listed under various categories —Album of the Year, Instrumental Performance, Record of the Year, Song of the Year, Vocal Performances, Female and Male, etc.; Hall of Fame Awards.

National Barn Dance   A pioneer country program that was sired by Station WLS of Chicago from 1924 until 1960. Originated by George D.

Hay, who was later responsible for giving the *Grand Ole Opry* its name, it played a vital role in bringing Country music into the mainstream. It was the rise of the *Opry* out of Nashville, particularly after World War II, that reduced the *Barn Dance* from its position of national prominence in the 1930s to a local Midwest program and led to its eventual demise. Bluegrass pioneer Bill Monroe (b. 1911) appeared for several years with his brother in the late twenties when the show was known in its initial stage as the *WLS Barn Dance*. WLS took its initials from "World's Largest Store," as Sears Roebuck, the original station owner from 1924–1928, typed itself. From 1930 to 1934 Gene Autry (b. 1907) was a regular on the *National Barn Dance*.

See also *Grand Ole Opry;* Bill Monroe.

National Educational Conference (NEC)   An organization of the program staffs of colleges and universities, founded to enable students and faculties to share information about entertainment programming, to establish training programs, and to arrange for cooperative programming. It publishes the NEC *Newsletter* eight times a year out of Columbia, S.C. Full membership is restricted to institutions of higher learning. Associate membership is restricted to firms whose products or services are directly related to college entertainment.

National Music Council (NMC)   Chartered by an act of Congress, the National Music Council is constituted of 60 music organizations, representing the entire world of American music and totaling over 1.5 million individual members.

National Music Publishers Association (NMPA)   Formed in May 1917 as the Music Publishers Protective Association, the NMPA, as it became known in 1966, stated its objectives as follows: "To maintain high standards of commercial honor and integrity among its members; to promote and inculcate just and equitable principles of trade and business; and to foster and encourage the art of music and songwriting." With vaudeville as the main medium through which songs were then popularized, the Association struggled heroically to create an equitable balance in the dealings of its members with vaudeville performers. (Although the word "payola" did not surface in the media until the congressional investigation of 1959–1960, it was trade vernacular inside music business as far back as the 1920s.) In time, as the Association undertook the common objectives of any trade association—to protect and advance the interests of the industry—it became deeply concerned with problems arising in connection with the federal copyright law, copyright being the foundation of the music business. Working with other organizations in the music and literary worlds for revision of the outmoded copyright law of 1909, it finally saw the passage of a new law in 1976, which went into effect as of January 1, 1978. Among the positive changes effected by the new law was an increase of the statutory royalty rate on recordings from 2 cents a side to 2.75 cents, or half a cent per minute or fraction thereof of playing time, whichever is greater; a provision requiring coin-machine operators, exempt under the 1909 law, to secure and exhibit performance licenses at $8.00 per jukebox per year; also, an increase of the term of copyright from 56 years to the life of the author/composer plus 50 years.

Infringement of copyrights has long been an Association concern. In 1971, working with the record industry, it succeeded in securing the passage of a law which, for the first time, made unauthorized duplication of records and tapes illegal. Pirates faced criminal penalties and a minimum of $250 in statutory damage claims.

With the advent of talking pictures in 1927, NMPA moved to create an instrument through which film producers could negotiate rights to music and music publishers could license these rights. In 1936, the licensing service was extended to electrical transcriptions. Finally, in 1938 the licensing of recordings and the collection of mechanical royalties was undertaken under Harry Fox, who had assumed the role of agent in that year. (Before Fox, E. Claude Mills and John Paine, both of whom went on to become general managers of ASCAP, served as agents.) The agency did not become known as the Harry Fox Agency until several years after Fox's appointment as agent. On Fox's death in 1969, Albert Berman, his longtime associate, was appointed managing director, and the agency was incorporated as a wholly owned subsidiary of NMPA.

Membership in the NMPA, a nonstock membership corporation, is open to anyone ''actively engaged in the business of publishing music in the U.S.A. for a period of at least one year, whose musical publications have been used or distributed on a commercial scale, or who assumes the financial risk involved in the normal publication of musical works.'' Members are elected by a majority vote of the board of directors, which consists of 18 members elected every two years. The officers of the NMPA are elected by the board, all of whom are members of the industry, with the exception of the chief executive officer, the president.

In 1980, the Association instituted a series of annual awards, to be given to a Song of the Year and also to a winning song in each of eight different categories.

In December 1980 the Copyright Royalty Tribunal, established by the revised Copyright Law of 1976, voted to increase the mechanical royalty rate to 4 cents per song, or three-quarters of a cent per minute of playing time or fraction thereof, whichever is greater. The new rate became effective July 1, 1981. At the discretion of the Tribunal, the new rate was to be further adjusted on January 1, 1982, and on an annual basis thereafter.

See also copyright; The Harry Fox Agency; mechanicals; payola; pirate record; synchronization; Song of the Year awards; vaudeville.

Willie Nelson   *See* Nashville Outlaws.

Newgrass   A play on the word "Bluegrass," suggesting an updating of the style. Newgrass apparently equals Bluegrass plus Rock rhythms and modern lyrics. Among other groups, one might include the Kentucky Colonels and some of the recordings of the Flying Burrito Brothers, who led a short but distinguished existence in 1969.

See also Bluegrass.

New Orleans Dance Blues style   The source of the Jump Blues developed by the Father of Rhythm & Blues, Louis Jordan (1908–1975), and his Tympany Five. The New Orleans purveyors of the style were similar combos: rhythm section (piano, bass, drums, guitar) plus one or two hot saxes, tenor or alto. Led either by saxist Lee Allen or former Ellington trumpeter Dave Bartholomew, they supplied the buoyant Boogie beat or the hoppity Shuffle heard behind singers like Fats Domino (b. 1928), Lloyd Price (b. 1933), and Smiley Lewis (1920–1966). The last-mentioned was the least successful of the three, scoring a near hit with "I Hear You Knockin'" (1955), co-written by Bartholomew. Lloyd Price, who was born in New Orleans, as was Fats Domino, hit a bull's-eye with his first record: "Lawdy, Miss Clawdy" not only sold a million but was an early crossover. Price had a smile in his voice, and his best year was 1959, when he put three songs on the charts: "Personality," the happy "I'm Gonna Get Married," and the million seller "Stagger Lee," a bouncy rewrite of the old Blues. The triumphal figure of the three was, of course, Fats Domino, who started as an R & B artist but easily crossed over into Rock 'n' Roll. Collaborating with Dave Bartholomew on the originals he wrote and using Bartholomew as his conductor, arranger, and record producer, Fats was consistently on bestselling charts from 1950 into 1968, reportedly selling in excess of 60 million records. Whereas Smiley Lewis was unable to compete with a Gale Storm cover of "I Hear You Knockin'," Fats was more than a match even for Pat Boone, who covered "Ain't That a Shame." Singing with a pronounced Louisiana accent, Fats possessed a verve, buoyancy, and youthful sound that won him a wide audience among teenagers. Playing a bouncing Boogie piano, Fats was able even to score hits with Jump versions of Pop standards like "Blueberry Hill" (1940) and "My Blue Heaven" (1927). Another New Orleans musician who is mentioned in connection with the Jump dance style popularized by Fats is the man who recorded under the name of Professor Longhair and His Shuffling Hungarians. Christened Henry Roeland Byrd (1918-1980), he is remembered for "Bald Head" (1950), "Tipitina" (1953), and "Go to the Mardi Gras" (1958), the last-mentioned a regular musical feature of the annual Mardi Gras in New Orleans. Professor Longhair's piano style was a curious fusion of Blues and "offbeat Spanish beats and Calypso downbeats," to use his own description. As I have written in *Honkers and Shouters,* "When you hear Longhair's piano styling, you hear Fats Domino," and the fact is that the Professor was a direct influence in shaping Fats's style.

See also New Orleans Rhythm & Blues.

New Orleans Jazz   Even though no records exist of the sound of Jazz as it was made by the original pioneers, there is little disagreement about it. However, there is controversy about New Orleans as the birthplace of Jazz. Ross Russell in *Jazz Style in Kansas City and the Southwest* (1971) well represents the present majority, who maintain that Jazz developed at about the same time from the black subculture in a number of cities—Kansas City, St. Louis, and Chicago, among others. James Lincoln Collier in *The Making of Jazz* (1978) takes what is now the minority position: namely, that Jazz was born in New Orleans and traveled from there by Mississippi riverboat and by other means, establishing early outposts in Memphis, Kansas City, St. Louis, and Chicago. No one questions that the style crystallized around the turn of the century as an improvised, syncopated form of playing by black musicians. Although African, European, and native Folk influences are recognized, it would appear that the most immediate source was marching-band music. It is not irrelevant to recall that when the well-known "When the Saints Go Marching In" was performed at burial services in New Orleans, it was played first as a slow march to accompany the casket to the cemetery, and, after burial, when the combo was returning, as a bright, freewheeling "Jazz" piece.

The first Jazz record was made on February 26, 1917, by five New Orleans musicians who called themselves the Original Dixieland Jazz Band. They spelled Jazz "Jass"—and they were white, a fact that is disturbing, considering the black origin of the music. Jazz recordings were made around 1923 by the black New Orleans musicians of Oliver's Creole Jazz Band, in which Louis Armstrong played. From these and the records of the white New Orleans Rhythm Kings, we know that New Orleans Jazz combos consisted of a front line of clarinet, cornet, and trombone (basic instruments of marching bands) with a varying complement of rhythm instruments: drums, piano, bass, guitar. Although there was some solo playing, collective improvisation was the mark of New Orleans Jazz.

See also Austin High School Gang; Dixieland Jazz.

New Orleans Jazz and Heritage Festival   Launched in 1970 with a conclave of performers (200) in Congo Square, the Festival attracted so few paying customers that its Board of Directors was on the verge of abandoning it. But George Wein, its executive producer, persuaded the group that the heritage was too significant not to be preserved and vitalized. In April 1982, the Festival attracted so large a complement of performers (390) and listeners (over 84,000) that it was held on the New Orleans Fair Grounds and Race Track. Rooted strongly in the local music of Louisiana, Cajun and Jazz, the Festival also heard a vast variety of black performers, including amateur and professional performers of Ragtime, Boogie Woogie, Blues, R & B, Texas Swing, Bluegrass, Gospel, and Zydeco.

See also Cajun music; Jazz; Zydeco.

New Orleans Rhythm & Blues   A number of other sounds and artists, in addition to those described under the New Orleans Dance Blues style, figured in the sound of that city's R & B. There was Clarence "Frogman" Henry (b. 1937), who came from Algiers, La., and sang in three different voices, the lowest sounding like a frog. He recorded for a Chess subsidiary and made Top 10 R & B charts briefly, starting with "Ain't Got No Home" in 1956. There was Guitar Slim (b. Eddie Jones, 1926–1959), who came from a church choir in Mississippi but worked around New Orleans and made a hit of "The Things I Used to Do" (No. 1 on R & B charts in 1954) for Specialty Records; Ray Charles (b. 1930) arranged and played piano. There was Huey "Piano" Smith (b. 1924), with whom Guitar Slim formed a trio, and who was deeply indebted to Professor Longhair's shuffling piano style. Huey & His Clowns made the Top 10 in R & B with the funny novelty "Rocking Pneumonia & the Boogie-Woogie Flu" in 1957, and again in 1958 with "Don't You Just Know It," both cut for Ace Records, a local Mississippi label. There was the group called the Spiders, who were discovered at New Orleans's Pelican Club and who recorded slow Blues ballads for Imperial Records, Fats Domino's label. They placed three records in the Top 10 of R & B: "I Didn't Want to Do It" (1954), "You're the One," which became a hit in '54 when the initial side was turned over), and "Witchcraft" (1955). There was the duo Shirley & Lee (b. 1937 and 1935 respectively), who were named the Sweethearts of the Blues, partly because of their youth but also as a promotional gimmick—they were just friends. Recording for another of the early Los Angeles R & B labels, Aladdin, they put "I'm Gone" on the charts in '52, "Feel So Good" in '55, and "I Feel Good" in '56—all in the Top 10. Their biggest seller was the classic "Let the Good Times Roll," written by Leonard Lee, a record that went to No. 2. The Blues, Boogie, and Gospel sounds struck by these artists in the R & B and early R 'n' R years were shaped in part by Cosimo Matassa's J & M Studios, where Fats recorded most of his sides.

In 1960 Minit Records was founded in New Orleans, with Allen Toussaint (b. 1938) as producer, pianist, and session bandleader. Toussaint was an extremely talented songwriter, a major figure on the New Orleans scene who has largely remained in the background. For Minit, he produced modest hits with Jessie Hill ("Ooh Poo Pha Doo," 1960, No. 3 on the charts) and with Aaron Neville ("Over You," 1960). The following year, a song he wrote with Chris Kenner, "I Like It Like That," was an Instant Records bestseller for Kenner, and it was later recorded by the British Dave Clark Five. In 1965 Toussaint formed a new label called Tou Sea Sansu, one of whose artists was Lee Dorsey, an ex-prizefighter out of Portland, Ore., known as "Kid Chocolate." In 1961 Toussaint had produced "Ya Ya" (No. 1, R & B) with Dorsey. In 1966 Toussaint wrote and produced three R & B chartmakers with Dorsey: "Get Out of My life, Woman," "Working in the Coal Mine," and "Holy Cow." That same year, Toussaint's production talent put Aaron Neville, a singer with limited vocal control, on the R & B charts with "Tell It Like It Is," again a No. 1 disk. New Orleans R & B was largely a product of small indie labels like Fury/Fire, Amy, Parlo, and Minit, and it lacked the crossover potential of the R & B turned out by the bigger indie labels like Atlantic and Chess. This is to say that it had a deeper Gospel and Blues sound.

See also New Orleans Dance Blues style.

New Orleans Rhythm Kings　*See* N.O.R.K.

Newport Folk Festival　It started as a commercial venture in 1959, coproduced by Jazz pianist aficionado George Wein of Boston and manager Albert Grossman. At the suggestion of folk singer/writer Pete Seeger (b. 1919), seconded by singer/actor Theodore Bikel (b. 1924), the Festival became a nonprofit venture in 1963, run by a rotating committee of seven Folk performers. That year, more than 40,000 attended the Festival in Rhode Island, rising to 70,000 in 1964 and a record 80,000 in 1965. As the numbers rose and problems developed with rowdy elements, the Newport City Council became disaffected—causing cancellation of the Festival in 1970 and finally rescinding its license at the last minute in 1971.

In the 1964 Festival program, in an article called "The Year of the Topical Song," folk singer/writer Phil Ochs (1940–1976) hailed Bob Dylan's success as unparalleled in folk song history, named Tom Paxton (b. 1937) as the best craftsman of the topical writers, and praised Buffy Sainte-Marie (b. 1941), who had emerged that year, as "the finest female writing talent on the scene." In the following year's Festival program, Bob Shelton, the Folk and Country music Critic of *The New York Times,* announced his conversion from Folk to Folk Rock. It was the year also of Dylan's conversion, a move that brought catcalls and boos when he appeared on the stage with an electric guitar. In his article, Bob Shelton admitted that he was at first blinded to the big beat by loud-mouthed disk jockeys and the hysteria created by publicists. He added: "Middle-class college audiences of Folk music are only a part of the music scene. The tastes, interests, and social attitudes of the high school student or drop-out, the working class kids, must also be appreciated and understood."

During the sixties, the Festival was not only the largest and most widely publicized Folk event, but it supported a Foundation that sponsored performances by authentic unknowns as well as current stars like Joan Baez (b. 1941) and Peter, Paul & Mary. Foundation resources were also available to promote and finance research in and studies of Folk music.

Newport Jazz Festival   The first was held in July 1954 at an open-air casino in Newport, Rhode Island. A two-day affair, it was produced by George Theodore Wein (b. 1925), a Boston Jazz pianist and owner of the Storyville Jazz nightclub in Boston. Among those who appeared on the first evening were Eddie Condon (1905–1973) and his Dixieland cohorts, Dizzy Gillespie (b. 1917) and his bop quintet, Oscar Peterson (b. 1925) and his trio, Gerry Mulligan (b. 1927) and his piano-less combo, and a 20-man jam session. Pianists were featured on the following evening: George Shearing (b. 1919), Erroll Garner (1921–1977), and Lennie Tristano (1919–1980). In between, a forum was held on the origin and meaning of Jazz. The following year (1955), the Festival was moved at the behest of the city fathers to Freebody Park, where it was held annually until the summer of 1971, when a scheduled four-day Festival was terminated after the first day, due to disturbances. Since 1972 the Newport Jazz Festival has been held each summer in New York City, where the event stretches over a week and more, with concerts being heard in, on, and at Lincoln Center, Carnegie Hall, Radio City Music Hall, the Staten Island ferry, Hudson River day-liners, the Brooklyn Museum, Yankee Stadium, and elsewhere. The Festivals continue to be produced by George Wein.

See also festivals.

New Romantics   A Rock trend of the early 1980s in Great Britain, which was anti-Reggae, anti–Rock 'n' Roll, and mostly anti-Punk. For Punk's emphasis on working-class struggle, egalitarianism, and anarchy, the New Romantics substituted elitism, escapism, money, glamour, and Art. Their musical influences came from European synthesizer music, New Wave Funk, and Pop melodies. As with other turns in Britain's Rock culture, this one was accompanied also by a sharp shift in fashion. The Who came in with the fashion cult of British "mod." The New Romantics stressed variety and flamboyance in dress, with David Bowie as their closest model. The two best-known groups of the New Romantics are Spandau Ballet and Adam & the Ants. The followers of the trend are also known as the New Narcissists, the New Dandies, the Futurists, and the Modernes.

See also New Wave; Punk Rock.

New Wave   There are at least two possible approaches to this style. One sees New Wave as an American offshoot of British Punk Rock, a subtler but uncontrolled style, devoid of the gruesome posturings that alienated American audiences—the masochistic practices like safety-pins in the flesh, the outrageous militaristic garb, the bizarre hair coloring, and the violence. Another concept of New Wave is that it is just another name for Punk, adopted to evade the criticism and censure visited upon that style. Regardless, New Wave is a musical movement against the established order, an attack on blandness, complacency, and lack of emotion that tends toward the grotesque, outrageous, and off-beat. It is aggressive, defiant, and prizes intensity of emotion over talent and technical virtuosity.

Nineteen seventy-eight was the year that drew a line, if there is any, between Punk and New Wave. The group that drew the line, by its disastrous American appearance, was the highly publicized Sex Pistols. Following on the heels of outrageous Elvis Costello, the Pistols outraged British society by using four-letter words on TV, indulged in widely publicized sadomasochistic behavior, and played what has been described as a "blend of Heavy Metal and crazed chaos," energized by the bellowing voice of Johnny Rotten (b. 1956). Despite the heavy advance barrage of publicity, the Pistols misfired badly on their American appearance and folded shortly thereafter. (The Punk label took an even more severe lambasting when the group's Sid Vicious (b. 1957) murdered his sweetheart and then died of an overdose at the age of twenty-one.) In 1978, too, Television, a well-received Punk group led by Tom Verlaine (b. 1950), also disbanded.

The setback to the movement was temporary as the New Wave label superseded the Punk designation—and the Cars found a million purchasers for their debut album. By the following year (1979), the record-buying public accepted Blondie, Devo, and Cheap Trick, as well as such British groups as Joe Jackson, Boomtown Rats, Police, and Clash. Other New Wave groups include Damned, Weirdos, Gang of Four, Shoes, Tom Robinson Band, Dictators, Pere Uba, XTC, Dead Kennedys, Adam & the Ants, Vibrators, Skids, Stranglers, MC 5, and Plasmatics.

New Wave has won the approval of some Rock critics as an antidote to the thump-thump-thump of Disco and the overload of Heavy Metal, as a music that possesses emotional intensity even if it lacks technical virtuosity, and as a style that sometimes recaptures the excitement of the early unsophisticated days of Rock 'n' Roll. Not long before he was shot to death, John Lennon (1940–1980) said: ''I love the music of today. It's the best period since the 1960s, the Pretenders, B 52's, Madness, the Clash. . . .''

See also Punk Rock; Synth-Rock.

New Year's Eve   For years, NBC reporter/announcer Ben Grauer described the crowds gathered in New York City's Times Square to welcome the New Year and to watch the ball descend from the top of the Times Square Tower in the climactic moment before midnight. After his death in 1977, Dick Clark of *American Bandstand* fame took over the assignment.

See also Guy Lombardo Orchestra.

ninth chord   A major chord consists of three notes; a seventh chord, of four notes; and a ninth, of five notes. Each note in the vertical structure is a third apart:

Maj. chord   7th   9th

''nitty gritty''   The title of a hit R & B song of the 1960s, it became the ''in'' word for the essence, the bottom line, or the heart of the matter.

nocturne   A dreamy, romantic composition.

Novachord   An electronic instrument with a six-octave keyboard like a piano, manual controls for varying the tone, and pedals for sustaining notes and varying the volume.

See also synthesizer.

novelty song   One of the mainstays of Pop music during the Tin-Pan Alley era, the novelty song still exists, though the term seems passé, but not as a distinct category. In the era of *Your Hit Parade,* inaugurated in 1935 and the fulcrum of music business into the fifties, music publishers divided songs into three classifications: (1) ballads, (2) rhythm ballads, and (3) novelty songs. The last-mentioned included cute kiddie tunes like "How Much Is That Doggie in the Window?" and "Who's Afraid of the Big, Bad Wolf"; nonsense ditties like "Mairzy Doats" and "Flat Foot Floogie (with the Floy Floy)"; comedy songs like "Yes, We Have No Bananas"; and songs based on sound effects like "Open the Door, Richard" (knocking) and "Deep in the Heart of Texas" (clapping). In the *Hit Parade* era, novelty songs were seldom given a concentrated plug, as was the case with ballads. They either happened—broke open fast as sleeper hits—or bombed. Since the rise of Rock 'n' Roll, there have been comedy songs like "Yakety Yak" and "Charlie Brown," both hits for the Coasters. More recently, Paul Simon registered a hit with "Fifty Ways to Leave Your Lover"; Rupert Holmes, with "Escape (the Piña Colada song)"; and Charlie Daniels, with "The Devil Went Down to Georgia"—all novelty songs.

See also "bomb"; "happening"; No. 1 Plug; *Your Hit Parade.*

No Wave Rock   An offshoot of Punk and New Wave, which carries the process to its noncommercial extreme and involves the making of music by non-musicians. For obvious reasons, what is available on disk is the product of small, alternative labels.

See also New Wave; Punk Rock.

No. 1 plug   In the era (1930s and 1940s) when live plugs on the radio determined the fate of a song and were the crux of the hit-making process, a No. 1 plug was what potential hit ballads received and songwriters sought for their product. What it involved was: (1) a substantial budget for promotion, advertising, and, most of all, plugging; (2) a period of 6 to 12 weeks; and (3) the concentration of a publisher's song-plugging staff on the particular song. After professional copies and a stock orchestration were printed, the company's top song-plugger, the professional manager, would contact bandleaders and/or vocalists on the big commercial network shows to find someone to introduce the new song. When he had what looked like a firm date, the other members of the plugging staff, the day-men and the night-men, would try to add plugs to build the total for the given week. Weekly tallies played a decisive role in moving a song onto *Your Hit Parade,* with other areas like jukebox plays and sheet-music sales adding their impact. Subsequently, other "drive" weeks were set. By the twelfth week or so, the song had become a hit or had been dropped as a bomb. Potential No. 1 plug songs garnered the biggest advances, between $1,000 and $5,000, depending on the songwriter's track record. Naturally, more No. 1 plugs were promised by publishers than they delivered, and not every No. 1 plug produced a hit.

See also Big Ballad era; Big Baritones; *Your Hit Parade.*

"obscene"   In the 1920s the expression, à la Cole Porter (1892–1964), was "the top." Later, it was "out of this world." Still later, it was "the end," "out of sight," or just "obscene."

"ofay"   From "pig-Latin"; "foe is converted into "ofay." It's black jargon for a white person, especially an unfriendly white.

"offbeat"   Outside the normal, traditional, or expected. Weird, bizarre, grotesque.

Oi   The word means "hey" in London cockney slang. It refers to a British social and sound movement that has been characterized as "music to riot by." Among the best-known Oi groups are the 4-Skins, Infa-Riot, Splodge, and Blitz.
See also Skinheads; Two-Tone movement.

"Ol' Blue Eyes"   What Frank Sinatra (b. 1915) called himself, when he emerged from a near two-year retirement (1971–1973), in a TV Special, *Ol' Blues Eyes Is Back*. It also became the title of an album released shortly thereafter in 1973.
See also Frank Sinatra.

"oldies but goodies"   Refers to records and songs of the initial years of Rock 'n' Roll, the 1950s, not excluding Rhythm & Blues. Most of the disks were made by small, independent labels that emerged during the 1940s and 1950s. The origin of the term is shrouded in mystery, but it was used in 1961 on a record by Little Caesar & The Romans, "These Oldies but Goodies Remind Me of You." The New York group Sha Na Na specializes in recreating visually and aurally the era of the "oldies but goodies." The records, songs, and labels are well covered in a book titled *Those Oldies but Goodies: A Guide to 50s Record Collecting* by Steve Propes.

olio   A segment of the minstrel show in which different members of the troupe performed their specialties—a mixture of song and dance. It was generally preceded by a humorous interchange between the Interlocutor, who sat in the middle of the semicircle of performers, and Mr. Tambo and Mr. Bones, the endmen. The olio developed into what later became known as "variety" or "vaudeville." Possible origin of

265

the term: a modification of the Spanish word *olla*, meaning a miscellaneous mixture or hodgepodge.

See also minstrel show.

one-hit wonders   During the early days of Rock 'n' Roll when spontaneity if not crudeness were prized, amateurs were welcomed by the record companies and occasionally produced hits. Inside the business, they became known as "one-hit wonders." Although they sometimes came up with more than one best-seller, it was only one that really made it big. Some of the artists to whom the term seems applicable include: 1954 The Penguins: "Earth Angel"; 1958 The Teddy Bears: "To Know Him Is to Love Him"; 1960 Hollywood Argyles: "Alley Oop"; 1960 Zodiacs: "Stay"; 1962 The Tornados: "Telstar."

See also "one-shots."

one-nighter   A booking in which an artist or group plays only a single night in a given club, theater, stadium, showroom, or arena and moves on to another place for the next night's engagement. It's a money-making syndrome but physically debilitating since it involves playing into the late hours of the night, traveling through the day, and then performing again in another locale. Sleeping tends to be catch-as-catch can; ditto, eating. Even laundry becomes a hangup. The problems are somewhat reduced when an artist or a group travels in their own private plane, bus, or other means of transportation.

one-shot   A record distributor that handles many different labels. The one-shot developed with the emergence of many independent record labels, which did not have their own distribution outlets, as the major companies did. The one-shot makes it possible for the record dealer and jukebox operator to get an overview of the new releases of many labels. It also centralizes the purchase of records by dealers and jukebox operators.

See also Jukebox.

"one-shots"   A term sometimes used with reference to artists and groups, especially those of the 1950s, who achieved only a single hit record. Among others: the Cadillacs ("Speedo"), the Monotones ("Book of Love"), the Nutmegs ("Story Untold"), and the Silhouettes ("Get a Job").

onion skin   Like the transparent paper sometimes used for typewriter carbon copies, the onion skin is used as a master sheet from which to reproduce handwritten music.

"on the nose"   A colloquial musical term meaning "at or from the beginning." It also refers to the first beat of a measure.

"open up"   A record is said to "open up" when it begins to appear on charts and to receive widespread play. The reference here is to regional rather than national charts. A record "breaks open" when it displays signs of moving into the Top 40.

Opryland   An amusement park opened in 1974 in Nashville, Tenn., as the new theater and broadcasting studio of the *Grand Ole Opry*. The $41 million entertainment complex was dedicated by the President of the United States himself on March, 16, 1974. It houses a $15 million theater with a seating capacity of 4,400, making it the largest broadcasting studio in the world.
  See also *Grand Ole Opry;* Ryman Auditorium.

orchestrate   To score for orchestra a work originally written for a solo instrument, trio, quartet, or quintet.
  See also arranger.

"Oreo singer"   A term based on the Oreo cookie, which is black on the outside and has a white filling. It refers to black singers who temper their sound and style so as to attract white followers and listeners. The term did not come into vogue until the 1960s, probably as a pejorative one in the period when black nationalism in various forms was polarizing the black community. Two of the groups to whom it was applied were the Fifth Dimension and the Impressions. It was also applied to singers like Brook Benton (b. 1931), Dionne Warwick (b. 1940), Sammy Davis, Jr. (b. 1925), and others.
  See also Blue-eyed soul.

organ and piano   A sonic combination that seemingly started with Gospel music and was explored by Rock performers after the mid 1960s. It was used effectively by Procol Harum on their record hit "A Whiter Shade of Pale" and by The Band, originally Bob Dylan's backup group when he moved from Folk to Folk Rock. Other masters of the combination included Brian Auger (b. 1939), Al Kooper (b. 1944), and Felix Cavaliere of the Rascals (b. 1944).

"originals"   It sounds like a musical term but refers to clothes that have never been washed—not new clothes, but old clothes. The usage presumably originated with the Hell's Angels, and it was taken over by teenagers who pride themselves on their coarse and dirty appearance.

Original Cast Album (ORC)   The recording of the score of a musical by the cast that first presented the work on Broadway or off-Broadway. If the world premiere—not trial runs, run-throughs, or pre-opening performances—occurs elsewhere, as in Los Angeles, San Francisco, or London, the Original Cast Album may be cut there. Some shows like *Hair* have an ORC made by the off-Broadway cast and another made by the Broadway cast; some shows have an ORC for the American (world) premiere and another for an English production. The recording of the ORC is generally done a week after the opening or at any point when it seems apparent that the musical will have a run of some length. (In New York, ORC albums are generally cut on a Sunday, since that is the only day when the cast is free for sessions that may well run into the evening.)

Producers generally audition a new musical for record companies in the hope of getting a monetary advance for rights to the ORC. The advance can be sizable, or it can be in the form of participation in the financing of the show. Decca's recording of Rodgers and Hammerstein's *Oklahoma* in March 1943 was the first instance of an Original Cast Album.

See also George Gershwin; Musical, Tony Awards for Best; Richard Rodgers.

Original Dixieland Jazz Band (O. D. J. B.)   Coming from New Orleans by way of Chicago, the O. D. J. B. opened in 1917 at Reisenweber's Cafe, near Columbus Circle in Manhattan, where it was billed as the Original Dixieland Jass Band. With its Victor recordings, made in February 1917, it became the first band to play Jazz on disk. A white band, it consisted of Nick La Rocca (cornet), Larry Shields (clarinet), Eddie "Daddy" Edwards (trombone), Henry Ragas (piano), and Tony Sbarbaro (drums). It popularized tunes learned and played when its members were part of "Papa" Laurie's Reliance Brass Band and other New Orleans marching bands. Historians tend to characterize its style as Ragtime rather than Jazz. No black Jazz combo was heard on a label with national distribution until King Oliver's Creole Jazz Band recorded in 1923. Kid Ory's Original Creole Jazz Band did record in 1921 for a small Los Angeles label.

See also New Orleans Jazz; Ragtime.

"ork"   Abbreviated form of "orchestration" and "orchestra."

"Oscar" song   *See also* Academy Awards; Motown Picture Academy Award songs.

oscilloscope   An instrument that produces a graphic representation of electric signals through the use of a cathode-ray tube. It allows for the determination of amplitude (maximum value of power or voltage), frequency (vibrations per second), and other wave-form characteristics.

ostinato   The extended repetition of a musical phrase, sequence of chords, or rhythmic figure. The eight-to-the-bar pattern of Boogie-Woogie is a good instance of ostinato. In Swing, the word is "riff."
See also riff.

Johnny Otis (b. 1921)   A versatile musician, a pioneer of R & B, and a man who has made a distinguished contribution to contemporary music as a bandleader, songwriter, talent scout, record producer, and recording artist. He was so intimately involved with black artists and their music that he has frequently been thought to be black, although he is of Greek-American extraction. He was inspired to become a drummer after he watched Jo Jones (b. 1911) in the Count Basie Band in 1939. Before he formed his own band in 1945 as the house combo at the Club Alabam in Los Angeles, he worked with the bands of barrelhouse pianist Count Otis Matthews, George Morrison, Lloyd Hunter, Harlan Leonard, Jack McVea, and Bardu Ali. In 1948 he opened with an R & B combo at the Barrel House in Watts, LA's black ghetto, where, through the Johnny Otis Rhythm & Blues Caravan, he discovered such R & B artists as the Robins, Mel Walker, and Little Esther (whom he spotted in an amateur show at the Largo Theatre, burned down during the Watts riot of 1965). In 1950 he produced a series of records for the Savoy label of Newark, N.J., which rated as the No. 2, No. 5, and No. 10 R & B hits of the year. All were made with Little Esther, Mel Walker, and himself. In succeeding years, Otis's talent discoveries included Little Willie John (1937–1968), Jackie Wilson (b. 1934), Hank Ballard (b. 1936) and the Midnighters, and Big Mama Thornton (b. 1926), with whom he recorded "Hound Dog," later copied by Elvis Presley. In 1958 he made a hit record on his own of his own song "Willie and the Hand Jive." In 1961 Gladys Knight & the Pips produced their first hit in a recording of "Every Beat of My Heart," a song he had originally written for Jackie Wilson.

When the British wave engulfed American Rock and R & B in the mid-1960s, Otis went into politics as a deputy for State Senator Mervyn Dymally of California, later writing a brilliant book, *Listen to the Lambs* (1968), that was triggered by the Watts riot of 1965. He has been called the "Godfather of Rhythm & Blues"—and is that rare human being, a man who has chosen to live in and belong to the black world because of its atmosphere and exuberance, if not as a persistent protest against the white world's treatment of blacks.
See also Rhythm & Blues.

oud   A lute originating in the Near or Middle East, the oud has a bulging belly, a curved fretboard, four to six pairs of strings, and three sound-holes and is heard in places like Algeria, Morocco, and Tunisia. It was used by the Devil's Anvil, a Rock group of the sixties, composed of two Arabians and two Americans. Jazz flutist Herbie Mann (b. 1930) used the oud on a late-sixties album, as did The Incredible String Band.

See also sarod; sitar; viña.

"outlaws"   *See* Nashville Outlaws.

outtake   The recording (take) of a song or instrumental, rejected for commercial release because of errors, inadequacies in the performance, or faulty engineering.

overdub   In the days before the rise of Rock and the development of synthesizers and other sophisticated electronic devices, the entire complement of musicians went into a studio and cut a record. If somebody goofed, the master had to be scrapped, and the selection had to be cut again from the beginning. With the development of tape in place of metal masters, it became possible to correct errors by splicing. In time, as different instruments were recorded on separate tracks—today, as many as 24 or 30—it became possible to alter sound levels, dynamics, textures, and other elements on each separate track before mixing them. Today all Rock recording is done in a series of stages. Generally a rhythm track is laid down first. Then horns and/or strings are overdubbed. Finally, a vocal is overdubbed. The word "overdub" is also used as a noun to refer to a track that is recorded over a previously cut track.

overtone   Vibrations of portions of a string or column of air produce tones other than the tone sounded when the entire string or air column vibrates. These are overtones. Any note heard on a musical instrument is a combination of the fundamental tone, sounded by the full string or air column, and the partials—vibrations of parts of a string or air column—overtones, or overtone series.

See also harmonic series.

"owsley"   Derived from the name of the chemist (Augustus Owsley) who concocted LSD, it has come to mean the best acid. Operating in the Haight-Ashbury district of San Francisco from 1967–1969, he was a sponsor of the Grateful Dead, who were said to perform while they were stoned on acid.

See also Acid Rock; Freak Out; Haight-Ashbury.

P

PD   Abbreviation of "public domain." It refers to that period when the copyright on a work has expired and the work now belongs to the public. According to the copyright law now in force (enacted in 1976), a musical work can be protected for the life of the composer/author plus 50 years. After that, it can be printed, recorded, and performed without royalty being payable either to the songwriter(s) or publisher.

See also copyright.

paila   *See under* timbales *in* Latin rhythm instruments.

Pachanga   A fast Latin dance that was briefly the rage among Spanish teenagers around 1961. It was played by Cuban dance orchestras, known as *charangas,* whose instrumentation consisted of several fiddles, piano, bass, and timbales. Apparently, the fast, syncopated tempo limited the dance's popularity.

Palladium   There is a Hollywood Palladium, a ballroom on Sunset Boulevard in Los Angeles that dates back to the era of the Big Bands and is still in existence today. In New York City, the Palladium was located at 53rd Street and Broadway. Originally called the Alma Dance Studio, it was renamed the Palladium in the late 1940s and became Latin NYC's answer to the Savoy Ballroom in Harlem.

See also Hollywood Palladium.

Palomar Ballroom   Regarded as the most famous of West Coast ballrooms, Hollywood's Palomar played host to all the big Swing bands of the thirties and forties. In a sense, Swing, or at least the Swing era, was born here on the evening of August 21, 1935. The new Benny Goodman band opened that night after a dismal cross-country tour in which dancers at Elitch's Garden in Denver demanded their money back until the band began playing waltzes. But opening night at the Palomar brought a wildly enthusiastic reception and the engagement was a sensation. From the Palomar, the band went to Chicago's Congress Hotel, where a three-week engagement turned into an eight-month stand. The Goodman band was "in" and so was Swing.

See also Hollywood Palladium; Swing.

"pals"   Rock jargon for hired studio musicians, used to enhance the sound of a Rock group on records. The term is apparently an abbreviation of "Paladin," the main character of *Have Gun, Will Travel,* whose name was derived from medieval knights who roamed the countryside doing noble deeds.

"Paris's Black Pearl"   A cognomen for Dionne Warwick (b. 1941), pinned on her by a Paris journalist during a period of performances in Paris.

partial   *See* overtone.

Charlie "Bird" Parker (1920–1955)   A creator of Bop, he was one of the great figures in modern Jazz. A narcotics addict from his teen years in Kansas City, he worked with the bands of Jay McShann, Noble Sissle, Earl Hines, and Billy Eckstine. Early in 1945, he recorded seven tunes with Dizzy Gillespie (issued under Dizzy's name) that became definitive in their evocation of the new sound known as Bop. His originality and improvisational genius were such that pianist Lennie Tristano (b. 1919) once said: "If Charlie wanted to invoke plagiarism laws, he could sue almost everybody who's made a record in the last ten years." Bird was also an effective composer, one of whose pieces, "Now's the Time," became the basis of the R & B and Pop hit "The Hucklebuck." Starting in 1946 with *Esquire's* New Star poll, he won innumerable *Down Beat* and *Metronome* polls. In 1980 the Newport Jazz Festival memorialized the twenty-fifth anniversary of his death by dedicating its entire proceedings to his memory.
     See also Bop.

"patting Juba"   Forbidden to use drums, slaves devised a method of accompanying dance steps with rhythm patterns sounded through the use of hands, feet, and thighs—clapping hands, stamping feet, and slapping thighs. The procedure was carried into Gospel music and the minstrel shows.
     See also Gospel music; minstrel show.

"payola"   A word that the media and the general public did not know until the congressional probe of 1959–1960, when a certain number of disk jockeys were fired or forced to resign for accepting money to spin given records on their turntables. A spurious attempt was made to connect payola with Rock 'n' Roll and thereby to destroy the new style. It did not work. And it was spurious because "payola" as a word and as a problem had long been a music industry headache. It simply took different forms as the media for exposing and promoting songs changed. In the period of World War I and the 1920s, the recipients of payola were the vaudeville singers, whose bills for costumes, scenery, travel, and other performing expenses were paid by publishers. As radio became the main vehicle for making hits, bandleaders and singers were given free arrangements and other emoluments to perform songs. Through the years, organizations of publishers and of song-pluggers had tried to limit and curb payola. When the record became king, and the disk jockey the hit maker, payola became a nexus between record distributors and/or record manufacturers and the knights of the turntable.

The hearings in Washington of the House of Representatives Special Subcommittee on Legislative Oversight began on February 8, 1960, with appearances of disk jockeys from Cleveland and Boston. But the focus of the probe was Alan Freed (1922–1965), the man who had labeled the new music Rock 'n' Roll, and Dick Clark (b. 1929), host of *American Bandstand* of the ABC network, out of Philadelphia. Freed had already lost his radio and TV shows, having "on principle" refused to sign an affidavit stating that he had not taken payola for playing records. Freed did not appear before the House investigating committee. On May 19, 1960, a grand jury sitting in New York City issued an information, charging eight disk jockeys with having received $116,580 in payola. When Freed was subpoenaed to testify, he took the Fifth Amendment and was soon indicted on 26 counts of bribery. At the trial, held in December 1962, he pleaded guilty to two counts of bribery and was fined $300 and given a six months' suspended sentence. His troubles were not over. On March 16, 1964, he was indicted for having evaded taxes on an unreported income, between 1957 and 1959, of $56,562. The indictment never came to trial, for he died on January 20, 1965, apparently of uremia. The general opinion in the music industry was that he was the scapegoat for the scandal.

Dick Clark did appear before the House committee. On May 2, 1960, he testified, the committee's records revealed, that he had an interest in 27 percent of the songs and/or records he had spun on *Bandstand* in a 28-month period and that he had a part or whole interest in 33 music-related businesses: publishing companies, record labels, a record-pressing plant, etc. He had divested himself of all these before his appearance in the House, when the ABC network made this a condition of his remaining on *Bandstand.* At the conclusion of the hearing, Chairman Oren Harris said: "You are obviously a fine young man . . . I do not think that you are the inventor of the system; I do not think that you are even the architect of it, apparently. I think you are the product that has taken advantage of a unique opportunity."

Later, it was learned that Chairman Harris had himself been involved in a bit of payola. Station KRBB in El Dorado, Ark., had been having some difficulty getting its license renewed until Harris became a 25 percent owner; Harris had been forced to relinquish his share when the fact was exposed. Almost at the start of the hearings, another Washington figure was exposed as the recipient of payola. The chairman of the Federal Communications Commission could not deny that he had enjoyed a six-day junket in Florida, with all expenses being paid by the Storer Broadcasting Company; at President Eisenhower's request, he submitted his resignation.

On September 13, 1960, Congress enacted a law, at the suggestion of the FCC, making payola a criminal offense punishable by a $10,000 fine and/or a year in jail.

In 1975 a new series of payola investigations resulted in charges against Kenny Gamble and Leon Huff of Philadelphia International Records. The charge against Huff was dismissed, but Gamble was fined $2,500.

See also Dick Clark; Alan Freed.

"Pearl"   Nickname of Janis Joplin (1943–1970) and the title of a posthumous album.

See also Blued-eyed soul; Blues Rock.

The Peatman   A weekly listing of the 50 songs with the largest listening audience, the Peatman was produced by a professor at New York's City College during the 1940s and early 1950s. Unlike the Accurate, which was just a listing of every song performed on the major networks during the hours of 6:00 P.M. to 1:00 A.M., the Peatman weighted each performance or plug on the basis of the Hooper (pre-Neilsen) ratings of the show. A point value was arrived at, with each point signifying 20,000 listeners. This was known as the ACI, or Audience Coverage Index, and the top 50 songs were listed weekly in the order of the point value. By averaging three successive weeks, the Peatman arrived at the ATI, or Audience Trend Index. While Peatman reports were confidential to paid subscribers, the trade papers were permitted to print an alphabetical listing (sans the ratings), with the top 30 songs appearing in one group and the succeeding 20 in a second group. Producers of radio shows were among Peatman subscribers; it was believed that to be programmed by the big, sponsored network shows, a song had to be up among the first 30 for several weeks.

In the very late 1940s, bandleader Richard Himber (1907–1966) began selling a report that was known as the Himber sheet. Like the Peatman, it weighted performances. Instead of using the size of the audience as its yardstick, it assigned points on the basis of whether a plug was vocal or instrumental, and the show was commercial (sponsored) or sustaining. Vocal commercials rated the highest point value, and sustaining instrumentals the lowest. The Peatman and the Himber were the first attempts to bring the weight of statistics into song-plugging, in order to provide performers and producers with a somewhat objective yardstick for evaluating the hit potential of a new song.

See also The Accurate; No. 1 plug; *Your Hit Parade.*

Peckin'   A popular dance in the Swing era.

See also Savoy Ballroom.

Pee Wee's   A saloon in Memphis at the turn of the century. Located at 317 Beale Street, it became, in W. C. Handy's words, "almost a landmark and a legend. Moreover, it was a headquarters for musicians." A side room was dedicated to billiards and pool, and another to crap games and cards. In a back room, musicians stored their instruments and received calls over phone number 2893. Just inside the entrance to the saloon, there was a cigar stand. In the fall of 1909, Handy used this cigar stand "to write out copies of the following lyrics for visiting bands: "Mr. Crump won't 'low no easy riders here. . . . We don't care what Mr. Crump don't 'low/We gon' to bar'l-house anyhow. . .'" Handy had composed the tune for "Mr. Crump" without words, which he added during the campaign to elect him mayor. Although Crump was running on a reform platform, Handy's band was hired to help put over his campaign. Later, in 1912, Handy published the tune without words under the title "Memphis Blues." It was not "the first published Blues," as Handy claims, although it was one of the earliest. This honor belongs to a little-known song titled "Dallas Blues" by Hart Wand, also published in 1912. Another Blues that antedated Handy's song was Arthur Seals' "Baby Seals' Blues", published one month before his. However, "Memphis Blues" is, of the earliest Blues, unquestionably the most popular and most recorded.

See also Blues; W. C. Handy.

pentatonic   A five-note scale, especially the five-note modes represented by the black notes on the piano keyboard: C♯, D♯, F♯, G♯, A♯. Because these notes derive directly from the harmonic series, they are said to form the basis of primitive music. Children brought up on the equal-tempered scale of our music nevertheless improvise pentatonic tunes naturally. Many Rock groups, including the Beatles, used pentatonic scales. A hit tune of 1922, "Stumbling," by the Ragtime pianist Zez Confrey (1895–1972), opened with three repeats of the pentatonic scale on the five black keys of the piano.

People's Songs   Founded in 1946 as an organization concerned with topical songwriting, it published a *People's Songs Bulletin,* which grew from 6 mimeographed pages to 12 printed pages. It went bankrupt in 1949 after it supported Henry A. Wallace in his third-party bid for the presidency. The following year, some of the performers and songwriters associated with People's Songs launched the publication *Sing Out!*

See also *Sing Out!*

Peppermint Lounge   A defunct, nondescript club in New York City's West 40s that became the center of the Twist dance craze in the early 1960s, just as Studio 54 was the center of the Disco craze in the 1970s. At the height of the excitement about the new dance, long lines formed outside the Lounge, which somehow attracted stars of stage, screen, and TV as well as social celebrities and political bigwigs. A little-known five-piece vocal/instrumental/dance combo called Joey Dee & the Starlighters (after the Starlight Amusement Park on the Jersey Palisades above the Hudson River) became famous as a result of the Twist. "Peppermint Twist," written by Joey Dee and record exec Henry Glover, became a hit single, garnering a Gold Record in 1961. The Starlighters were also responsible for an album, *Doing the Twist at the Peppermint Lounge.* Curiously, the doorman of the Lounge in the Twist days was Gilbert J. Pincus, who had been the doorman at Jimmy Ryan's on 52nd St. during the heyday of The Street and later served as the doorman of Jimmy Ryan's on 54th Street.

See also The Twist.

performing rights   Among the rights inherent in the copyright are (1) right of publication; (2) synchronization right; (3) right to record; and (4) the performing right. The last-mentioned involves the right to license and collect fees from anyone performing a composition in any medium for profit. Three societies exist in this country to effectuate this right: ASCAP, BMI, and SESAC. Their function is to collect fees for authors, composers, and publishers from users of music. The major sources of revenue are TV and radio. But theaters, nightclubs, restaurants, skating rinks, football stadiums, and every place of business that uses music for public profit must obtain a license. The three organizations grant blanket licenses, which permit the user access to the entire catalog for a stipulated annual fee. The networks pay a percentage of their gross advertising income. Fees for places of business relate to the size of the establishment and the number of people it can accommodate. In order to determine the share of each author, composer, and publisher, the three societies monitor the selections performed on each network. Major network shows provide each society with a list of the musical selections they use. As for local performances, each society logs a different set of stations each month and employs a statistical formula to determine writers' and publishers' shares. After each society deducts a sum of money for running expenses, overhead, taxes, and insurance, the income available for distribution is split evenly, 50 percent to writers, 50 percent to publishers.

See also American Society of Authors, Composers, and Publishers; Broadcast Music, Inc.; copyright; SESAC.

Peter, Paul & Mary   One of the major influences in widening the audience for Folk material, Peter, Paul & Mary came together in New York City's Greenwich Village when Noel Stookey (b. 1937) met Mary Travers (b. 1937) at the Gaslight cafe. Mary brought Peter Yarrow (b. 1938) into the trio, at which juncture Noel changed his name to Paul. Albert Grossman, who had built Chicago's first Folk music club (Gate of Horn) and produced the 1959 and 1960 Newport Folk Festivals, became their manager. Signed to Warner Brothers Records, they debuted on disk in 1962 with an album and a hit single, "If I Were a Hammer" b/w "Lemon Tree." The following year, their "Blowin' in the Wind" brought fame to Bob Dylan (b. 1941) and a Grammy Award to the trio. The three worked together for nine years, during which they were among the first entertainers to become involved in anti–Vietnam War and civil rights movements. They disbanded in 1970, having garnered Gold Albums with three of their ten releases and Platinum Albums with five. After a hiatus of nine years, they reunited in 1979 and cut a new album. It was well received but hardly a bestseller; but the trio was warmly welcomed in concert performances.

See also Bob Dylan; message songs; Urban Folk.

Philadelphia International   It has been said that Kenny Gamble (b. 1944), Leon Huff (b. 1942), and Thom Bell, the creative spirits behind Philadelphia International, are to the 1970s what Holland-Dozier-Holland plus Smokey Robinson (b. 1940) were to the sixties—the most important source of black music and the outstanding Soul producers of the decade. All three had their beginnings during the heyday of *American Bandstand* in Philadelphia, with Leon Huff participating in the development of the million-copy hit "At the Hop" by Danny & the Juniors (1957), and later in "1,2,3," the hit by Len Barry (b. 1942), who was formerly with the Dovells. In 1967 Kenny Gamble and Leon Huff wrote and produced "Expressway to Your Heart," a million-copy seller for the Soul Survivors. By 1968 the Gamble label was in existence and "Cowboys to Girls," a song written by the two and produced by Huff, became a Gold Record for the Intruders, an R & B quartet, and the label's first million seller. The following year Jerry Butler (b. 1939), formerly of the Impressions and dead-ended as a solo artist, came to them. With Gamble and Huff, Jerry wrote and they produced "Only the Strong Survive," a Gold Record for Butler.

Philadelphia International was formed in 1971 after Gamble and Huff had used Chess and Atlantic to distribute their records. Using the distribution facilities of Columbia Records, PI began producing a flow of hits by the O'Jays, Melvin & the Blue Notes, and Billy Paul (b. 1939). "Me and Mrs. Jones," co-written by Gamble and Huff and released by PI, won a Grammy for Paul as Best Male Vocal R & B Performer of 1972. Although the disco-oriented Trammps and the Stylistics were released on other labels, their records were produced in the Sigma Sound Studios of PI. Thom Bell, who co-wrote and produced "La La (Means I Love You)," a million seller by the Delfonics in 1968, handled the production of the Stylistics. Beginning in 1971 with "You're a Big Girl Now," the group had a succession of million-copy sellers for five consecutive years, virtually all of them co-written by Thom Bell. All of these had the sound of Soul, sweetened by string-orchestral backing. After Motown, Philadelphia International established itself as the most successful black-owned record label. In 1974 the three dominated *Billboard*'s year-end producer awards: Bell charted 11 hit singles that year and Gamble and Huff accounted for 10.

See also Motown sound; payola.

Philadelphia "Mafia"   Speaking of Philadelphia in the heyday of Dick Clark and the *American Bandstand,* writer/producer/record owner Phil Spector (b. 1940) said: "Philadelphia was just the most insane, most dynamic, the most beautiful city in the history of rock and roll. . . . Everyone you met was raging and racing 24 hours a day, seven days a week, and existed for nothing but the hype. . . . Money was a lot of it, of course, but there was something else as well: a purist's love of hustle for its own sake." Out of that hustle came a tightly knit complex of record labels, managers, record promoters, and singers, all revolving around Dick Clark, which has been called the Philadelphia "Mafia." Trading on the powerful, cross-country impact of exposure on *American Bandstand*'s over 100 TV stations, they made Philadelphia the hub of music business and of Rock 'n' Roll from 1957 into the early 1960s. Among the record labels that were part of the inner circle, there were Chancellor, Swan, and Cameo Parkway, in all of whose profits Dick Clark participated. There was also Mallard Pressing and a group of music publishing companies, all partly or wholly owned by Clark. Among the artists who emerged from the Philadelphia scene were Charlie Gracie (b. 1936), Danny & the Juniors, Frankie Avalon (b. 1940), Freddy Cannon (b. 1940), Fabian (b. 1943), Duane Eddy (b. 1938), the Dovells, and Chubby Checker (b. 1941).

See also *American Bandstand;* Dick Clark; payola.

Phonolog   Initiating publication in 1948, Phonolog is a looseleaf listing of all currently available records, which is kept up-to-date for subscribers with weekly reports of new releases. Available in record stores and in many public libraries, Phonolog is indexed, with records being classified under a series of headings. The major section of the looseleaf setup is devoted to Pop Titles, Pop Artists and Pop Albums; the word "Pop" is used here to include Country, R & B, Rock, and Soul, as well as Pop. Records are thereafter listed under the following classifications: Children, Christmas, Hawaiian, Latin-American, Motion Pictures, Sacred, Show Tunes, Specialties, and Theme Songs. The final segment of the compendium is devoted to Classical material under three headings: Titles, Composers, Artists. Subscribers to Phonolog, now published in San Diego, Calif., also receive a weekly tabulation of the top singles and albums.

pianissimo (*pp.*)   A term meaning "very or exceedingly soft," as distinguished from *piano* (*p.*), "soft," and *mezzo piano* (*mp.*), "moderately soft."

pianoforte   The full and actual name of the piano, meaning "soft and loud," at its origin. The harpsichord, which was the pianoforte's predecessor, lacked its flexibility in dynamics.
   See also minipiano; upright.

Pianola   A device patented by Votey in the U.S.A. in 1897. During the next decade, it was developed into the player piano, an instrument that became very popular in the 1920s and that has recently undergone something of a revival. In player pianos, the keys are activated by perforations in a paper roll, moved by foot pedals, as they pass over a metal tube mounted above the keyboard. The tube has holes in it that correspond with the piano keys. The perforated rolls were cut by pianists, including George Gershwin (1898–1937), mounted on rollers, and packaged in rectangular boxes manufactured by QRS and other companies.

piano roll   *See* Pianola.

"pimple music"   A pejorative term for Teenage Rock 'n' Roll, the music of the late fifties and early sixties, so-called because of its amateurish sound, its concern with adolescent subjects and themes, and the youth of singers like Paul Anka (b. 1941), Neil Sedaka (b. 1939), Fabian (b. 1943), and Frankie Avalon (b. 1940), most of whom were still in their teens.

pirate record   A recording whose sounds have been lifted from a commercial record through electronic techniques; it is sold as if it were the original. Though most sellers and buyers are aware that it is not the original, they traffic in the pirate because of reduced cost (which is partly the result of the failure to pay royalties to artists, songwriters, and publishers).

"plastic"   In subculture argot, a term for anything—an event, place, person, or activity—that is meretricious, pretentious, phony, corrupted by the Establishment, just conventional, or "system-oriented."

Platinum Record   Singles are certified "Platinum" by the Recording Industry Association of America (RIAA) when they have sold 2 million or more copies. Albums or their counterparts on prerecorded tapes are certified "Platinum" after selling 1 million copies or more.
   See also Gold Record; Titanium Album.

platter   Trade papers' and reviewers' term for a record.

playback   At a recording session, to "play back" is to listen to what has been recorded in order to check for clinkers, incorrect tempi, rhythmic imbalance, and other problems. The term is also used as a noun.

player piano   The trade name of this instrument was Pianola. In addition to QRS, the W. W. Kimball Co. of Chicago, Universal Music, and Columbia all manufactured piano rolls.
   See also Pianola.

playlets   The word Mike Stoller (b. 1933) used to describe the narrative ballads that he and Jerry Leiber (b. 1933) wrote mainly for recordings by the Coasters. Teenage life and problems were the subject of such songs as "Young Blood" (1957), "Yakety Yak" (1958), "Charlie Brown" (1959), and other narratives. But they also dealt with more general situations in "Poison Ivy" (1959), "Along Came Jones" (1959), and "Smokey Joe's Cafe" (1955). The disks, which they produced themselves, were a triumphant integration of music, story, and group delivery.
   See also Leiber & Stoller.

plectrum   A device made of wood, ivory, metal, tortoiseshell, or quill, and used for plucking strings. It may be held in the hand or worn around a finger. The device is used on instruments like the banjo, mandolin, and guitar. The term is also used with reference to that part of the mechanism of the harpsichord that activates the strings.

Poetic Rock   In the 1960s Rock lyrics acquired, with Bob Dylan (b. 1941) and the Beatles, depth in subject matter, freshness in imagery, and elegance of expression. These qualities, associated with poetry, are to be found in varying degrees in the songs of Joni Mitchell (b. 1943), Neil Young (b. 1945), Laura Nyro (b. 1947), Jackson Browne (b. circa 1949), James Taylor (b. 1948), Carole King (b. 1942), Randy Newman (b. 1943), Paul Simon (b. 1942), Cat Stevens (b. 1948), Donald Fagen and Walter Becker of Steeley Dan, and Leonard Cohen (b. 1935). The last-mentioned was, in fact, a recognized novelist and poet before he became a Rock singer and songwriter in 1968. There are Rock critics and groups who feel strongly that poetry is too heavy a burden for Rock 'n' Roll to carry.

See also New Wave; Punk Rock; singer-songwriter.

Pogo   A dance of the 1970s consisting mainly of bouncing up and down, favored by Punk Rock fans.

Polka   Originating in Bohemia (now part of Czechoslovakia) in the nineteenth century; a lively dance in 2/4 time for couples. The best-known proponent of the dance today is Lawrence Welk (b. 1903), who plays and dances Polkas on his TV show.

polymodal   Characterized by a simultaneous use of several different modes.

See also modes.

polyphonic   The opposite of homophonic. The simultaneous sounding of different notes. In this sense, any chord is an example of polyphony. However, "polyphonic" generally refers to the sounding of several chords at the same time. Depending on the proximity of the chords or of their tonic notes, there may be much or little discordance.

polyrhythmic   The sounding of two or more different rhythm patterns at the same time. African music is noted for the interplay of different rhythms, sounded on different drums.

See also hemiola.

polytonal   The simultaneous use of the notes of two or more different scales.

See also polyphonic.

Pop Explosion   In our time, there have been three Pop Explosions: one when Sinatra emerged in 1944, another with the appearance of Presley in 1956, and still another with the arrival of the Beatles in 1964.

In all three instances the artists involved became superstars overnight, eliciting from fans such hysterical adulation as occurs only in a Pop Explosion. The musical aspect of each event was merely an index of a deeper-seated change that was taking place, a change in outlook, manners, speech, dress, dancing, and psychology. In some periods of history, a younger generation will treasure the security of walking in the parent generation's footsteps. But in a Pop Explosion, a sharp cleavage develops between the two generations, with the younger operating to create a culture of its own.

See also Alternative life-style; The Beatles; Elvis Presley; Frank Sinatra.

"poppa-stoppa"   Black slang for a man who has intercourse with his own father.

Pop music   Mainstream American Pop music had an identity of sound and structure from the early twenties into the mid-fifties that was completely shattered by the Rock Revolution. In form, most Pop songs, emanating from Tin-Pan Alley, were 32 bars long, divided into a series of 8-bar sections structured as AABA. The "B" segment, which involved a change of key and rhythm pattern, was known as the "bridge" or "release." The vocabulary was simple, veering away from polysyllabic words. Lorenz Hart (1895–1943), of the famous team of Rodgers & Hart and a writer who created some of the most sophisticated and intricately rhymed lyrics, once poked fun at Tin-Pan Alley and demonstrated what he could do with monosyllables in "My Heart Stood Still" (1927) from the musical A Connecticut Yankee. The words were: "I took one look at you/That's all I meant to do/And then my heart stood still...." Rhyming was considered essential in Pop tunes as well as show songs. Most songs were romantic ballads; there were also novelty songs like "Three Little Fishes (Itty Bitty Poo)" (1939) and "Mairzy Doats" (1943). Passion and sex were approached via delicate imagery, never realistically or naturalistically. The songwriter's drive was to create simple melodies that made a strong, fast appeal and were quickly remembered. (In the Rock era, such appealing melodic strains became known as "hooks.") Harmonically, most songs had a major sound—although there were some minor-sounding melodies—with triad chords expanding in time into sevenths, ninths, and elevenths.

Show tunes frequently used a variant of the AABA form in which the 32 bars were structured into two units of 16 bars each (ABAB)—and were more complex harmonically and rhythmically. The two most successful writers of Pop in the 30-plus years of its dominance were Irving Berlin (b. 1888) of Tin-Pan Alley and Richard Rodgers (1902–1979) in the show field.

During the summer of '81, *The New York Times Magazine* ran a long, provocative article whose title, together with a life-sized head of Sinatra, was blazoned on the cover: "Outlasting Rock: Sophisticated Melody and Lyrics Make a Comeback." The writer's contention was that the old tunes and Pop style of the pre-Rock era were returning to the music scene. The evidence consisted mainly of a number of nostalgic Broadway shows with standards by Duke Ellington (*Sophisticated Ladies*), Jimmy McHugh (*Sugar Babies*), Harry Warren (*42nd Street*), and Fats Waller (*Ain't Misbehavin'*). But a survey of the recording scene yielded little evidence to support the writer's contention. To be sure, there were two albums by Willie Nelson with songs of the Irving Berlin era, another by Carly Simon of torch songs of the Judy Garland days, and an album of Jazz ballads by Linda Ronstadt, which eventually was not released. On the other hand, there was a growing trend toward melody in the works of some of the top Rock groups, including the Electric Light Orchestra, Foreigner, and others.

See also Irving Berlin; Big Ballad era; 52nd St.; No. 1 plug; The Peatman; Pop Rock; Richard Rodgers; Tin-Pan Alley; The Sheet; *Your Hit Parade.*

Pop Rock   With the rise of *American Bandstand* in 1957 as the propulsive force in its spread, Rock 'n' Roll "ceased to be an uncontrolled natural force," as *Rolling Stone* reported, "and turned into a product understood and exploitable." The year 1957 saw the awakening of the music industry to the appeal that R 'n' R made to the record-buying generation—and the major record labels and Broadway publishers moved to invade the teenage market. Of the new music publishers, Aldon Music (a partnership of Al Nevins, formerly of the Three Suns, and Don Kirshner) set the pace in developing Pop Rock, Teenage Rock, or Brill Building Rock. All three terms refer to the same development, with the last term being a misnomer since the Brill Building was the hub of music business during the Tin-Pan Alley era and the new R & B and R 'n' R publishers, including Aldon, operated out of 1650 Broadway, not 1619 Broadway. Aldon established an assembly line of young songwriters—Goffin & King, Mann & Weil, Sedaka & Greenfield, among others—who vied with each other in producing songs and demos for the record market. Whereas Rockabilly had been a spontaneous expression of Presley and other Sun artists—Jerry Lee Lewis, Carl Perkins, Johnny Cash, et al.—now songs were tailored to meet a growing demand and taste for teenage sounds, themes, and singers. The explosive energy and fire of a Little Richard or Elvis Presley were now being simulated, and the natural alienation from society of Buddy Holly, Eddie Cochran, and Elvis was being intellectualized into a definition of teenage culture.

Jerry Leiber and Mike Stoller, who wrote and produced the original record of the challenging "Black Denim Trousers and Motorcycle Boots," are sometimes regarded as the Fathers of Pop Rock because of their work with two Atlantic Record groups. Producing the records of the Coasters, they wrote songs for them like "Yakety Yak," "Charlie Brown," and "Young Blood"—all slanted toward the teenage market. With the Drifters, many of whose songs were written by the Aldon song manufacturers, Leiber and Stoller used string backing as well as charts written by schooled studio arrangers who had worked with the Big Baritones of the 1940s.

In the early sixties, before the appearance of Bob Dylan and the Beatles, Pop Rock took the shape of the Twist and the Surfing music of the Beach Boys. The sixties quickly turned into an embittered and embattled decade in which the polarization of the public over the Vietnam War and civil rights issues was reflected deeply in the songs. At the end of the decade, just about the time that the Woodstock Generation fell apart at Altamont, Creedence Clearwater Revival emerged as a Pop Rock group with seven two-sided hit singles and five hit albums.

In the seventies, as the concern with social issues diminished and songs increasingly dealt with personal problems, Pop Rock grew as a trend, vying with Disco, Punk Rock, and New Wave. By the end of the seventies, Rock had grown softer, more melodic, nostalgic. Among the groups and artists involved in varying degrees with Pop Rock were the Eagles, Pablo Cruise, Electric Light Orchestra, Chicago, Elton John, Billy Joel, Fleetwood Mac (*Rumors*), Three Dog Night, Bread, Boston, Foreigner, Airplay, Rupert Holmes, Rick Springfield, and Asia. Although the sounds of these artists and groups varied greatly, involving synthesizers, heavy metal textures, and touches of New Wave in different degrees, all were concerned with pop "hooks" that would give them access to the airwaves and retail sales.

In the summer of 1982, bespectacled Elvis Costello (b. 1945) shed his image of the angry, abrasive young man. In *Imperial Bedroom,* he produced an album that emphasized "melody rather than energy," in his words, and that brought critical comparisons with sophisticated pre-Rock songwriters like Cole Porter. At the same time, Warren Zevon (b. 1947), classically trained and blues-oriented, with a backlog of songs of chaos and conflict, produced *The Envoy,* an album containing tender, melodic songs like "It's Never Too Late for Love."

See also Altamont; *American Bandstand;* Brill Building Rock; "hook"; Leiber & Stoller; Surfing Music; Teenage Rock; The Twist; *Woodstock Nation.*

Pop Schlock   *See* Schlock Rock.

Pop Soul   As the most intense, most exhibitionist, and most Gospel-oriented of black styles, Soul had limited crossover potential. Of the best-known Soul artists, James Brown (b. 1928), Bobby Bland (b. 1930), and Jackie Wilson (b. circa 1932) never had a No. 1 Pop record, and while Soul Brother No. 1, as Brown called himself, hit the Top 10 with 6 out of 92 singles and Wilson scored 6 Top 10s out of 54, Bland never made the Top 10 once with 37 singles. However, Lady Soul (Aretha Franklin) made the Top 10 with 14 disks and hit No. 1 with "Respect."

But it was Motown Records of Detroit that made mainstream music out of Soul. Although the tambourines, hand-clapping, and call-and-response vocals typical of Gospel were still quite audible, various devices were used to sweeten and soften the sound, including use of the mellifluous strings of the Detroit Symphony Orchestra. Accordingly, virtually all Motown artists were able to cross over. Mary Wells (b. 1943), the Miracles, the Temptations, Marvin Gaye (b. circa 1939), Stevie Wonder (b. 1951), and the Supremes all hit the top of the Pop charts, with Stevie scoring six No. 1 hits and the Supremes registering twelve consecutive No. 1's.

Taking a leaf from the Motown book, Philadelphia International proceeded to duplicate, though not equal, its Detroit competitor's success in giving mainstream appeal to Soul. Among the artists produced by Thom Bell, Kenny Gamble, and Leon Huff, the O'Jays, Melvin & the Blue Notes, Billy Paul, the Stylistics, and the Trammps all fused Soul and Pop.

Other black artists who might be included under the Pop Soul designation are Sam Cooke (b. 1964), Fifth Dimension, Dionne Warwick (b. 1941), Lou Rawls (b. 1936), Diana Ross (b. 1944), Michael Jackson (b. circa 1960) and the Commodores.

See also Gospel Music; Motown sound; Philadelphia International.

portamento   A slur, slide, or "scoop," executed in Gospel music by sounding all the intermediate pitches between two notes. A slur is used to indicate the device. It is used by instrumentalists as well as singers, especially ballad singers like Barbra Streisand and Sinatra. There is no break in the sound as the artist moves from one note to the next.

power chording   A style of playing the guitar, especially in Heavy Metal groups, in which a full-bodied, high-decibel tone is accompanied by feedback and other distortions.

See also feedback; Heavy Metal Rock.

Power Pop   Introduced by the music business as a euphemism for Punk Rock in a calculated attempt to avoid the bad reactions stirred by

Punk; Power Pop developed an identifiable personality of its own in the late seventies. In brief, it was Punk without the mannerisms and ideology of Punk; Rock with the energy and force of Punk but with a cynical feeling about radio listeners and the Top 40. Emphasizing guitars rather than keyboards, Power Pop seeks to recreate Rock 'n' Roll of the early 1960s, before Dylan and the Beatles, without nostalgia or revisionism. Unlike the Punk groups, Power Pop groups are concerned about their craft and freshness. A number of Power Pop groups come from Los Angeles: The Motels, 20/20, and The Beat, among others. Other American representatives include The Pop from San Francisco, and The Shoes from Illinois. From England come The Yachts, and also The Members; and from Australia, The Sports.

See also New Wave; Punk Rock.

prepared piano   Although avant-garde composer John Cage (b. 1912) is credited with originating the idea of altering ("preparing") the sound of the piano by doctoring it with various objects, Pop pianists have frequently laced pieces of paper through the strings to produce a ricky-tick effect, making it sound almost like a harpsichord.

Prepubescent Rock   Also known as Bubble-Gum Rock. The appeal of the Monkees was largely to a pre-teen audience.

See also Bubble-Gum Rock.

Elvis Aron Presley (1935–1977)   Born in Tupelo, Miss., and raised in Memphis, Tenn., he absorbed three musical influences: (1) white Gospel music from the Assembly of God church his family attended; (2) white Country music; and (3) black Rhythm & Blues from listening to Big Bill Broonzy, Arthur "Big Boy" Crudup, and other bluesmen. "*Sinful music*, the townsfolk in Memphis said it was," he later said of the attitude toward R & B. "They would scold me at home for listening to them. Which never bothered me, I guess." When he began bucking to make some records for Sun, he encountered a man in Sam Phillips, the owner, who was looking for white men who could sing black. Each of the five disks released by Sun in 1954–55 contained a Country song on one side and a Blues on the other; he had learned the latter genre from listening to and trying to imitate Big Boy Crudup (1905–1974), Roy Brown (b. 1925), Little Junior Parker (1932–1971), Sleepy John Estes (1899–1977), and Arthur Gunter (1926–1976). Rockabilly, the style with which he became identified—along with other Sun singers like Jerry Lee Lewis (b. 1935), Johnny Cash (b. 1932), and Carl Perkins (b. 1932)—was a fusion of C & W and R & B, sung with Gospel fervor and excitement. The Rock Revolution was made, in short, by white southern teenagers trying to sing black.

The author of this book was directly involved in the transformation of Presley from a regional Country artist into a national Rock figure. A stay by the author at the home of Presley's manager, Col. Tom Parker, in the summer of 1955 led to his taking Presley's five Sun records and bringing them to the attention of disk jockey Bill Randle of Station WERE in Cleveland. Up until then, Presley's records had been heard only south of the Mason-Dixon line. Randle's spinning of the Sun disks elicited such an explosive response that many of the country's major record companies began bidding for Presley's Sun contract. RCA Victor came up the winner in the competitive bidding with an offer of $25,000, expanded to $40,000 when Hill & Range, a publishing company, bought the Presley-recorded songs which were owned by Sun Records. Later, the author of this book learned that Parker had been trying to interest RCA Victor in Presley for almost a year but had been unable to negotiate a deal until Randle's spinning of the disks provoked such widespread interest in the singer.

When Presley's Sun contract was purchased by RCA Victor and he emerged on the national music scene with ''Heartbreak Hotel'' in 1956, it was a Pop Explosion. Presley represented not only a new sound but a new look (sideburns and ducktail haircut), new dress (blue suedes), new sensibility (the sneer), new mores (a more sensual approach to love), new speech (''all shook up''), and new dances. His hysterical acceptance was the expression of a young generation in conflict with and in rebellion against the older generation. Rock 'n' Roll, with Presley as its flamboyant King, was the symbol of a new youth subculture. The older generation, civil and religious authorities as well as the music establishment, mounted a counterrevolution, which had its peak in the payola investigations of 1959-1960. But Rock 'n' Roll could not be destroyed.

Under the astute management of Col. Tom Parker, Presley began making movies the very first year of his stardom. Between 1956 and 1972, he appeared in 33 films, earning as much as a $1 million per film. He cut few records that were not bestsellers, and 48 sold more than a million copies each—a fantastic achievement. In a weighted survey of records released between 1955 and 1977, he scored No. 1 for the 1950s, No. 2 for the 1960s, and No. 4 for the 1970s, emerging as the No. 1 figure of the Rock era, with double the number of points scored by the Beatles, who were No. 2.

His death in 1977 came as an overpowering shock to Rock fans all over the world. It was not that much of a surprise to the people who worked closely with him, a number of whom have written books dealing with his extensive involvement with drugs (Presley's personal physician was accused of providing prescriptions for 12,000 stimulants, sedatives, and painkillers in the 20 months before Presley's death). The Shelby County medical examiner ruled shortly after the death that it had been due to heart failure. Unquestionably, drugs and a weakened heart led to Presley's demise. But viewed analytically, the death was perhaps brought about by a more elusive ailment: the failure to grow as an artist and to mature as a person. Presley may have developed this ailment as a result of the limited vision of his manager, his father, his entourage of boyhood friends—and himself. Despite his innate talent, his charisma, his achievements, and his influence, he became another statistic in the necrology of premature and senseless Rock deaths.

But the scope of his impact remains unassailable. Mick Fleetwood of Fleetwood Mac said on Elvis's death: "I was a real little toddler when I first heard *Hound Dog.* I learned to play drums listening to him—beating on tin cans to his records. I'm sure his measurable effect on culture and music was even greater in England than in the States. People there are still really, really fanatical about Elvis. The news came over like a ton of bricks." Paul Simon, who writes and sings in an entirely different vein than Elvis, admitted that at one time "I grew my hair like him, imitated his stage act—once I went all over New York looking for a lavender shirt like the one he wore on one of his albums."

To Jim Miller of *Rolling Stone* and *Newsweek,* as to millions of members of the Rock generation, "Elvis Presley remains the quintessential American Pop star: gaudy, garish, compromised in his middle age by commercial considerations, yet gifted with an enormous talent and a charismatic appeal beyond mere nostalgia. Presley remains a true American artist—one of the greatest in American Popular music, a singer of native brilliance and a performer of magnetic dimensions."

Between 1956 and the year of his death (1977), he placed almost 150 disks on single charts. Of these, 38 were in the Top 10:

No. 1 hits: "All Shook Up"; "Don't Be Cruel"; "Heartbreak Hotel"; "Hound Dog"; "Jailhouse Rock"; "Let Me Be Your Teddy Bear"; "Are You Lonesome Tonight?"; "Love Me Tender"; "It's Now or Never"; "Don't"; "Stuck on You"; "Too Much"; "Hard-headed Woman"; "A Big Hunk O' Love"; "Good Luck Charm"; "Surrender"; "I Want You, I Need You, I Love You"; "Suspicious Minds."

No. 2 hits: "Return to Sender"; "Love Me"; "Burning Love"; "Wear My Ring Around Your Neck"; "(Now and Then There's) A Fool Such As I"; "Can't Help Falling in Love."

No. 3 hits: "Crying in the Chapel"; "In the Ghetto"; "(You're the) Devil in Disguise."

No. 4 hits: "One Night"; "I Need Your Love Tonight"; "Marie's the Name of His Latest Flame."

No. 5 hits: "Little Sister"; "She's Not You"; "I Feel So Bad."

No. 6, 7, 8 and 9 hits: "Don't Cry, Daddy"; "I Got Stung"; "I Beg of You"; "Bossa Nova Baby"; "The Wonder of You."

From 1956 through 1972, Elvis starred in 33 films. He was paid as much as $1 million per film, a dozen of which were produced by Hal Wallis. They were formula films, emphasizing song and sex. Hungering for a more challenging role, one that would give him an opportunity to act, Elvis was offered the Kris Kristofferson role opposite Barbra Streisand in the remake of *A Star is Born*. Elvis ostensibly lost the part because of Col. Parker's fiscal demands; but it was also reported that Parker had opposed straight acting roles for Presley on the ground that it would hurt his image.

Among the films in which he starred: *Love Me Tender; Loving You; Jailhouse Rock; King Creole; G.I. Blues; Flaming Star; Wild in the Country; Blue Hawaii; Kid Galahad;* and *Girls! Girls! Girls!*

See also payola; Pop Explosion; Rockabilly; Sun Records.

press roll   A swift, agitated drum roll on the snare drum, employing both sticks. It was developed and used by drummers during the Dixieland era. Accents and time-keeping became the province of cymbals and the bass drum during the Bop era.

"prewashers"   A derisive music-biz term for less-than-knowledgeable, less-than-sharp executives who *dress* sharp (in prewashed denims, as it were).

"Prez"   Nickname given to tenor saxist Lester Young (1909–1959).
See also Lester "Prez" Young.

Prez Awards   *See* Jazzwalk.

Procol Harum   The name of a Rock group of the 1960s, derived from garbled Latin for "far from these things." The group made a hit of "A Whiter Shade of Pale," the music being derived from Bach's "Sleepers Awake."
See also Classical Rock.

producer   Public awareness of the producer as a creative personality in the recording process came after, it not with, the Beatles' *Sgt Pepper* album. This occurred partly because of the number of hours the group spent in recording the album. In a larger sense, it was a development that had to come as tape recorders, sound-mixing boards, and studio technology became more complex and opened new possibilities for the manipulation of sound on tape. The studio had, in fact, become an instrument, and the producer became in a sense an added performer. Now there is no album and no trade-paper chart that does not credit the producer of the work. Among the most successful producers of the sixties and seventies, there were: Brian Holland, Lamont Dozier, Bob

Crewe, Norman Whitfield, Lou Adler, Micky Most, Snuff Garrett, Phil Spector, Barry Gibb, James William Guercio, George Martin, and Richard Perry.

Producer of the Year, Best (NARAS Grammy Awards)   Although NARAS began giving Grammys in 1959, it was not until the 17th Annual Awards for 1974, announced on March 1, 1975, that the category of "Best Producer" was included. The annual winners are as follows:

1974	Thom Bell
1975	Arif Mardin
1976	Stevie Wonder
1977	Peter Asher
1978	Bee Gees, Albhy Galuten and Karl Richardson
1979	Larry Butler
1980	Phil Ramone
1981	Quincy Jones

production song   A song written especially for a TV variety show; an in-person appearance in a showroom; or a scene in a Broadway musical or Hollywood motion picture. Such songs deal with a situation, event, problem, theme, or circumstance; they do not follow any of the traditional forms of the Pop song; and they are almost never romantic ballads.

professional copy   In the era of the Big Baritones and Big Bands (1936–1945), music publishers printed, in addition to saleable copies of a song, black and white copies, which were given out gratis to performers. They were known as "pro copies" and sometimes as "black and whites."

professional man   A song-plugger in the days when live performances on radio made the hits.
See also contact man; No. 1 plug; *Your Hit Parade.*

"Professor Longhair"   Performing name of Roy Byrd (1918–1980), a seminal influence on Fats Domino (b. 1928), Huey "Piano" Smith (b. 1924), and Clarence "Frogman" Henry (b. 1937).
See also New Orleans Rhythm & Blues.

program music   The opposite of absolute music, it is music written to dramatize, describe, develop, or interpret sonically a stated program, story, or picture: e.g., Moussorgsky's *Pictures at an Exhibition.* Other instances in Classical Music include Vivaldi's *Four Seasons,* Berlioz's *Fan-*

tastic Symphony and *Harold in Italy* (based on Byron's poem), Liszt's *Faust Symphony* (based on Goethe's poem) and Richard Strauss's *Don Quixote.* The Rock analogue would be the concept album.

See also concept album.

Progressive Country Music   *See* Armadillo World Headquarters; Nashville Outlaws.

Progressive Jazz   A development of the 1940s involving a limited number of Big Bands—that of Stan Kenton (1912–1979) for one—that sought to develop a concert style in exploring radical harmonic concepts, unexpected changes of tempo, and startling orchestral timbres. In a sense, Progressive Jazz involved an effort to adapt aspects of European music to Jazz. Kenton's "Artistry in Rhythm" (1943), was based on a theme from Ravel's *Daphnis and Chloe,* included out-of-tempo sections and a Classical-styled piano solo.

Progressive Radio   Refers to FM radio, which has been more flexible than AM radio in programming albums and tracks that exceed the traditional three- to four-minute disk length.

See also Underground Radio.

Progressive Rock   Not so much a category as a trend in the sixties after the emergence of the Beatles in 1964. With all the new recording gadgetry available, Rock groups moved to use various distortion devices, new electrified instruments, synthesizers, and other innovations. Early examples were the Byrds' "Eight Miles High," the Beach Boys' "Good Vibrations," and the Beatles' "Norwegian Wood." The trend away from the minimalist instrumentation and sounds of early Rock 'n' Roll led eventually to the complexities of Studio Rock.

Protest Rock   As Progressive Rock was largely a matter of the music, so Protest Rock involved the lyrics: subject matter, attitude, outlook. It developed in the 1960s as part of the protest movements against the Vietnam War, prejudicial treatment of blacks, nuclear energy, and so on. Bob Dylan (b. 1941) became the spearhead of a style that was represented in the songs of Phil Ochs (1940–1976), Tom Paxton (b. 1937), Pete Seeger (b. 1919), and others. In a sense, it was Dylan's "Blowin' in the Wind," a No. 2 Pop hit, that awakened and energized the movement. The songwriters of Protest Rock tended also to be activists. But many Rock songwriters who were not activists were moved by events and the temper of the times to write protest songs. "Spanish Harlem" (1961) by Leiber, Stoller, and Spector; "He's a Rebel" (1962) by Gene Pitney, a hit for the Crystals; "Eve of Destruction" by

Barry McGuire (No. 1 in 1965); "Mr. Soul" by Neil Young (1967); and "American Pie" by Don McLean (1972) are all instances of such protest songs.

See also message songs; topical songs.

psaltery   An ancient instrument related to both the harpsichord and spinet. However, it has no keyboard like either of these relatives and its sound is produced by plucking the strings.

See also The Beers Family.

psychedelia   Although the first psychedelic disk was made in Los Angeles, and the Byrds, one of the earliest Acid groups, operated out of Los Angeles, the focus of psychedelic music quickly shifted to San Francisco—and the Haight-Ashbury area became the center of psychedelia.

See also Acid Rock; Haight-Ashbury.

Psychedelic Rock   *See* Acid Rock.

Pub Rock   British precursor of Punk, the term being derived from the bars and clubs (pubs) in which the groups played. Their names are not too well known: Ducks Deluxe, Brinsley Schwarz, Bees Make Honey, Kilburn & the High Roads, among others. They played a louder, more aggressive, and tougher Rock 'n' Roll than was then being heard in mainstream Rock. Some of the members of these groups later surfaced in New Wave groups.

See also Punk Rock.

Pumping Piano style   A driving, fast Boogie-Woogie piano style, full of glissandos, and popularized by Jerry Lee Lewis (b. 1935). The originator of the style was Little Richard (b. 1935). It can be heard on certain records made by Chuck Berry (b. 1926).

punctuation   Analogous to the use of commas, semicolons, and periods in prose, musical punctuation involves the use of hesitations and pauses in performing a work, to give emphasis or to indicate the end of a phrase or passage.

Punk Rock   A development of the 1970s, it represented a two-pronged rebellion: (1) against middle-class society and the upper classes; and (2) against the Rock establishment. An expression of frustrated rage, it tried to be outrageous and to provoke outraged reactions. Socially, it was a kind of nihilistic, lumpen-proletariat revolt by dispossessed, dislocated, unemployed, and underprivileged youth, who vented their anger at an affluent society with violent, disruptive, and abusive behavior, and expressed their frustration in self-abusive conduct. This aspect of Punk was largely a British manifestation. Onstage, a group like the Sex Pistols appeared in dirty clothes, Nazi regalia, and torn T-shirts, their hair dyed in streaks of orange, purple, and what-have-you, with safety pins stuck through their noses. They expressed their hostility in spitting, vomiting, and using foul language, even on TV. James Chance went about slapping people in his audience. Iggy & the Stooges, who came from Detroit and played loud, sloppy music devoid of melody and structure, performed acts of sadistic violence and masochistic self-mutilation; at Max's Kansas City in Manhattan in July 1973, Iggy slit open his chest with a broken glass.

Musically, the proponents of Punk contended that they were returning to the real basis of Rock: i.e., its explosive energy, high spirited spontaneity, and driving excitement. Detractors rejected the music as raw, primitive, and amateurishly crude. Some of the Punk rockers did claim that any kid could pick up an instrument and without training or experience become a Rock star. And the short-lived New York Dolls, five non-musicians, did get a recording contract!

The Rolling Stones are sometimes mentioned as the original Punk rockers. In an interview, guitarist/writer Keith Richard (b. 1943) of the Stones agreed that "there was a certain spirit in Punk rock" but added: "I don't think there was anything new musically, or even from the PR point of view, image-wise. There was too much image . . . and the music seemed to be the least important thing. It was more important if you puked over somebody. But that's a legacy from us. After all, we're still the only Rock & Roll band arrested for peeing on a wall."

Regardless of the Stones, the earliest exponents of Punk were American: Patti Smith (b. 1946); the Ramones, who performed in sneakers and black leather jackets at CBGB in Manhattan, where Johnny Rotten (b. 1956) of the Sex Pistols later hung out; and, earliest of all, Lou Reed (b. circa 1940) & the Velvet Underground, whose songs (1966) dealt with smack, speed, homosexuality, lesbianism, transvestitism, sadomasochism, misogyny, murder, suicide, and death. The screeching music played by these groups was a reaction against Soft Rock, Studio Rock, Art Rock, Avant-garde Rock—all the forms of experimental, sophisticated, or electronic rock that had developed in the wake of the adventuring Beatles.

In England similarly disaffected groups began to emerge about the same time. They had little impact until the debut of Dr. Feelgood in 1975, followed by Eddie & the Hot Rods, whose followers frequently wrecked the halls in which they appeared. The music soon became freighted with social overtones as the alienated, economically deprived, and unemployed youth made it a rallying point of rebellion against authority and aggression against respectable society. Although Graham

Parker's band made its debut in 1976, it was not until Patti Smith toured England in May of that year and the Ramones appeared in July that the British Punk movement developed impetus. By 1977 when Elvis Costello erupted on the scene, the apotheosis of the amateur was in full operation.

Among the many groups of the seventies who started as Punk rockers or who have risen or died with the style are the following (some of the names themselves suggest the nihilism of the trend); Kiss, Television, Aerosmith, Dictators, Weirdos, Zeroes, Void-Oids, Motels, 999, B–52s, and Elvis Costello. With these groups, synthesizers are out, horns are out; instrumentation and sound are minimalist. Although the Clash were in the forefront of English Punk, along with the Sex Pistols, they have managed to remain productive. *London Calling* (1980) harks back to Presley not only in its Rockabilly sound but in the design of the cover. For the nihilism of the Sex Pistols, the Clash substituted a militant anti-Fascist and anti-racist outlook. In ''Spanish Bombs'' (*London Calling*), they celebrate those who fought Franco as ''freedom fighters,'' and in ''The Guns of Brixton'' they urge a forceful stand against oppression in a black ghetto. Similar attitudes mark the work of the Gang of Four, who are greatly concerned with the Irish fight for freedom. Still another Punk rocker who has sought to merge Rock and politics, making his raw music a vehicle of social conscience, is Tom Robinson. A gay political activist, Robinson took the position ''You can't have liberation for homosexuals while women and blacks are oppressed.'' Of the Sex Pistols, he said: ''After ten years of bland, brilliant music, we were back to what Rock 'n' Roll should be—nasty, crude, rebellious people's music.''

That rarity in Rock, a successful girl's group, The Go-Go's, began as five punk rockers in Los Angeles but were motivated by their record producer, Richard Gottehrer, who produced Blondie's first album, to candy-coat their sound. The best-selling *Beauty and the Beat,* their debut album, held the promise of a new superstar group.

With the failure of the Sex Pistols' initial tour of the U.S.A. in 1978, Punk took on such a negative connotation that the term New Wave was substituted for it. Nevertheless, Punk (or New Wave) clubs continued to operate in New York City (C.B.G.B.); in Los Angeles (Troubadour); and in San Francisco, where Hole Street, a cross between Hollywood Boulevard and Haight-Ashbury, housed a number of them. The favorite dance at these establishments was Pogo, which consisted of bouncing up and down to the beat of the drums.

See also New Wave; Rockabilly.

pyramid   A musical device, usually employed in an introduction, break, transition, or ending, in which instruments climb on the notes of a chord, using each succeeding third as a starting note. The steadily ascending sound on the one chord creates tension and anticipation. The device may be heard in the introduction to "At the Hop" by Danny & the Juniors.

quadraphonic sound   A sound system involving four channels, it was introduced in the early 1970s. The first Pop LPs designed for playing on four speakers—placed in the four corners of a room so that the listener would be completely surrounded by the sound—were produced for RCA in 1972 by screen composer Hugo Montenegro (b. 1925). *Neil's Diamonds* and *Hugo in Wonder-Land* (composed of songs by Stevie Wonder) were well received. But the system died aborning due to the high cost of equipment and the competition between several incompatable systems.

Quadrille   A type of square dance that was popular in New Orleans during the early years of Jazz. It involved four segments of 32 bars each plus a finale, and was danced by four couples. A sequence of five or six formations was performed in 2/4 or 6/8 time.

quartet   In Gospel music, a vocal group was called a "quartet," regardless of how many singers were actually in the group. The Dixie Hummingbirds, Pilgrim Travellers, and Soul Stirrers, well-known Gospel groups of the fifties, were all known as quartets.

"quartet singing"   Referred originally to a type of Gospel group: the *a capella* male group, which used barbershop harmony, and slapped their thighs for rhythm. "Gospel singing" referred to the other prevalent type of Gospel group: the female group, which was accompanied by piano, and clapped their hands for rhythmic effect. The Jackson Southernaires, Nightingales, and Violinaires were instances of quartet singing, while the Sallie Martin Singers and Clara Ward Singers were instances of Gospel singing.

"Queen of the Blues"   The billing of Dinah Washington (1924–1963, born Ruth Jones), who was the leading female R & B singer of the 1950s and who crossed over into Pop with a 1959 remake of "What a

Difference a Day Makes,'' a ballad of 1934. She continued on Pop charts with a series of duets with Brook Benton (b. 1931)—''Baby (You Got What It Takes)'' and ''A Rockin' Good Way''—climaxing her career with ''This Bitter Earth'' and a 1963 remake of ''September in the Rain,'' a film ballad of 1937. Dinah also was known as ''Queen of the Jukeboxes.''

See also Rhythm & Blues.

"Queen of Country Music"   Mother Maybelle Carter.
See The Carter Family.

"Queen of Folk Music"   *See* Joan Baez.

"Queen of Gospel Singers"   *See* Mahalia Jackson.

"Queen of the Jukeboxes"   *See* "Queen of the Blues."

"Queen of the Ragtime Pianists"   Del Wood (b. 1920) was also known as the "Down Yonder Girl" because of the success of her piano record of the song of the same name.

"Queen of Rock"   An informal title frequently conferred upon Janis Joplin (1943–1970), after whose death the contenders included Rita Coolidge (b. 1944), Carly Simon (b. 1945), and Carole King (b. 1942).
See also Blues Rock.

quija   *See* Latin rhythm instruments.

quills   Also known among bluesmen as Pan pipes. The quills were a groups of cane reed pipes of varying lengths—the pitch being determined by length. The sound was produced by blowing across the openings at the top. Henry Thomas (b. 1894) tuned his to a local folk scale: e/f♯/a/b/c♯/e but also used the diatonic scale. The light piping sound of the quills, alternating with his voice, may be heard on "Cottonfield Blues" and other Vocalion Records. He was known as "Ragtime Texas" and apparently recorded "After the Ball (Is Over)," a pop hit of 1892.

R

RAP   Acronym for "radio air play." A record that is RAPed is receiving substantial airplay.

R & B   Abbreviation for "Rhythm & Blues," a designation for black Pop music that replaced "race" in 1949. *Billboard* magazine led the music business, which had become sensitive to the pejorative overtones of "race" during World War II, in switching the headings of several charts in the issue of June 25, 1949.

See also race records; Rhythm & Blues.

RIAA   *See* Record Industry Association of America.

"Rabbit"   Nickname of alto saxist Johnny Hodges (1907–1970), who attained renown for his playing with the Duke Ellington Band from 1928–1951 and from 1955 until his fatal heart attack in 1970.

race records   A trade term for records made by black artists and addressed to black listeners. The term was apparently introduced by Ralph Peer (1892–1960) when he was recording director of OKeh Records and shortly after he recorded Mamie Smith (1883–1946) singing "Crazy Blues." Made in 1920, this was the record whose phenomenal sales prompted all the other record companies to cut Blues by the so-called Classic Blues singers and thereby ignited the blues explosion of the 1920s.

See also Classic Blues; Bessie Smith.

Radio Caroline   One of the offshore "pirate" Rock stations operating near Great Britain. One of its programs, *Zowie One,* broadcast from the Brighton Tower Ballroom outside Liverpool, introduced some of the new Rock groups, who appeared for no fee in return for promotional plugs. The Yardbirds were one of the groups who took advantage of this arrangement.

Radio City Music Hall   The famous Art Deco movie palace on Avenue of the Americas and 50th Street in New York City, seating 5,882 customers, opened its doors on December 27, 1932, as a vaudeville house. As vaudeville died, it became one of the seven "cathedrals of the cinema"—along with the 6,000-seat Roxy, the 4,000-seat Capitol, and the Paramount, Palace, Loew's State, and Warner's Strand—that presented a format of stage-show and first-run film. By the 1950s the Music Hall was the sole theater in NYC, and possibly in the world, that continued a film/stage-show policy. In addition, it was the only movie palace that boasted a chorus line (the famous Rockettes, of 72 high-kicking legs), a corps de ballet, and a symphony orchestra, plus an annual pageant, "The Glory of Easter," and a Christmas spectacular. All went well for the Hall, whose operating weekly budget was over $150,000, until 1969, when it began losing money. By 1977 the annual deficit had reached $2.3 million. Even before '77, the management began instituting such economies as dropping its corps de ballet and reducing the number of Rockettes. At the same time, it began experimenting with more contemporary forms of entertainment. In September 1975 the Ice Follies was followed by appearances of twister Chubby Checker (b. 1941) and Rock pioneer Little Richard (b. 1935). In 1978 Rockefeller Center and the Rockefeller Brothers Fund, which had been making up the annual losses, decided to close the Hall. The closing was scheduled for April immediately following the final show of the forty-sixth annual Easter pageant.

But there was such an outcry of protest from New Yorkers and theatergoers nationwide that the Landmark Preservation Commission of the City of New York was moved to designate the interior of the Hall a landmark. This meant that all the public areas of the theater, including carpets, drapes, wall coverings, furnishings, and ornamentation, had to be restored in their original design, fabric, color, and style. Because everything in the Hall was an original design, replacement involved a countrywide search over a period of more than a year for materials and manufacturers. Restoration was finally begun on April 26, 1979, and completed for the gala opening of the Radio City Music Hall Entertainment Center, as it was now called, on May 31, 1979.

Since then, in addition to presenting eight music spectaculars and touring the Rockettes from San Francisco to London, Radio City Music Hall Productions, Inc., has presented concerts by such current artists as Linda Ronstadt (b. 1946), Diana Ross (b. 1944), Sammy Davis, Jr. (b. 1925), and Kris Kristofferson (b. 1937). At a benefit concert in 1980 Frank Sinatra (b. 1915) raised over $1 million for the Memorial Sloan-Kettering Cancer Research Center. In February 1981, the Grammy Awards ceremony of NARAS was televised nationally from the Hall—a first in its forty-nine year history.

In an effort to raise the income of the Hall, its Art Deco public areas, including the Grand Foyer, Grand Lounge, and Mezzanine, are being rented for private parties, cocktail or sit-down, when the house is dark.

See also Vaudeville.

Radio Luxembourg   The airwaves in Great Britain are government-controlled and there is no commercial radio. When artists or records were turned down by the BBC (British Broadcasting Corporation), the only outlet was Radio Luxembourg, a station under independent sponsorship operating outside England. The BBC did not add Rock programming to its network, despite the royal recognition of the Beatles, until October 4, 1971.

Raga Rock   For a time in the mid 1960s various Rock groups, especially the Byrds and the Beatles, became interested in East Indian instruments like the sitar, and in East Indian ''scales,'' known as "ragas" (of which there are 72, as against 36 in the diatonic system). More complex sequences than diatonic scales, the ragas have been described as a unique combination of notes expressing a specific mood. The raga concept entered Rock through the work of George Harrison (b. 1943) of the Beatles, who spent time studying the sitar with the famed Indian sitarist Ravi Shankar. After the Beatles used the instrument on their *Rubber Soul* album (1965), so many other groups became interested in it that a Broadway publisher printed a how-to book about it.

So-called Raga Rock is modal, uses instruments like the sarod and sitar, and pursues rhythm patterns comprehended under such complex time signatures as 10/8 and 7/4. In 1968 the Incredible String Band used raga elements in "You Know What You Could Be" in their album *The 5,000 Spirits or the Layers of the Onion*.

See also sarod; sitar; viña.

Ragtime   A piano style that developed and became popular between the Spanish-American War and World War I. As a form, Ragtime followed the March, being written in 2/4 time and including a trio section. Although it was syncopated like Jazz, it was unlike Jazz in that it was written, not improvised, music. The bass or left hand performed a regular oom-pah, oom-pah rhythm (which readily developed into Stride piano) against which the right hand performed syncopated figures. The right hand played broken chords, which could have been derived from banjo or guitar figurations. Although it became the dance music of an era, the prime exponent of Ragtime, Scott Joplin (1868–1917), viewed it as a Classical American piano style, akin to the style of Mozart or Chopin. Unlike Jazz, Ragtime evolved in Missouri, giving rise to two schools: Sedalia, the original locus of Joplin, where his playing at the Maple Leaf club led to the famous Ragtime piece "Maple Leaf Rag" (1899); and St. Louis, where he moved and where Tom Turpin (c. 1873–1922), a bar owner, and other Ragtime pianist composers operated. Toward the end of the Ragtime era, between 1910 and 1917, a New York school involving Luckeyeth Roberts (1887–1968) and others worked and composed.

Ragtime became a craze through its popularization by Tin-Pan Alley. A series of Pop rags was written, like "Alexander's Ragtime Band" (1911) by Irving Berlin (b. 1888), and rag piano solos like "Nola" (1916), "Ragging the Scale" (1915), and "Bugle Call Rag" (1916). The Original Dixieland Jazz Band introduced "Tiger Rag" in 1917. The first hit of George Gershwin (1898–1937) was a rag-influenced song, "Swanee," sung by Al Jolson (1886–1950) in the Broadway extravaganza *Sinbad* (1919).

Although *Musical Courier* chided the fashionable folk of high society for their shocking interest in "degenerate music" (meaning Ragtime, which it also condemned with epithets like "vulgar," "filthy," "suggestive," and "nigger music"), a tour by the band of John Philip Sousa (1854–1932) through Europe turned Ragtime into an international craze. It also aroused the interest of Classical composers. In 1918–1919 Stravinsky wrote "Ragtime" and "Piano Rag Music." Debussy's "Golliwog's Cakewalk" in *Children's Corner* employed Ragtime rhythms and syncopation. Darius Milhaud wrote "Three Rag Caprices," and Paul Hindemith, "Shimmy-Ragtime."

As an expression of the jangling optimism and bouncy muscular spirit of pre–World War I America, Ragtime seemed to go out of style around 1917, the year that America entered World War I and Scott Joplin died. But its impact was still felt in the twenties when Zez Confrey (1895–1971) produced hits in "Kitten on the Keys," a piano solo, and the song "Stumbling"; also in the classic ballad "Star Dust" (1929), which appeared originally as a Ragtime piano solo. Of course, the sound of Ragtime never really disappeared since virtually every western film or TV show has employed it, with the help of a ricky-tick piano, as an identification of pioneer days. In 1974 the use of Scott Joplin's "The Entertainer" as the theme of a hit film, *The Sting*—coming on the heels of the publication by the New York Public Library of the *Collected Works of Scott Joplin* in two facsimile volumes (1971) and the appearance that year on *Billboard*'s Classical chart of a Joshua Rifkin LP of *Joplin Rags*—resulted in a sweeping Scott Joplin revival. Almost 100 albums of Ragtime music, by every conceivable artist and in every conceivable instrumental combination, were released in a three-year resurgence. Two Academy Awards went to Joplin's music, though they were collected by the composer/arranger who adapted his rags for the screen.

The following chart suggests the contrasts between Ragtime, Jazz, and the Blues:

Ragtime	Jazz	Blues
1. Written	1. Improvised	1. Oral transmission
2. Piano	2. Instrumental	2. Vocal
3. Solo	3. Combo	3. Guitar/harmonica accompaniment
4. Missouri (Sedalia; St. Louis)	4. Louisiana (New Orleans) Kansas City, Mo., etc.	4. Mississippi Delta

Among Rock groups that used Ragtime figures and rhythms, one finds the early Youngbloods, the Grateful Dead ("Everybody's Doing That Rag"), and the Kaleidoscope. During the sixties, Country Joe &

the Fish made use of Ragtime in "I-Feel-Like-I'm-Fixin'-to-Die-Rag" (1967).

See also Scott Joplin.

rapping   Originating in the black subculture, it surfaced as a mainstream phenomenon with the hit recording of "Rapper's Delight" by the Sugarhill Gang of New Jersey in 1979. In 1980 Kurtis Blow of Harlem and the Bronx, whose real name is Kurt Walker (b. 1960), also made the charts with a fast-talking disk titled "The Breaks." Rapping is a style of delivery in which the performer does not sing but talks rapidly over a rudimentary musical background. In "Rapper's Delight," the musical accompaniment was a simple percussive ostinato, with an occasional guitar chord for punctuation. The style has its antecedents in operatic recitative and in beatnik poets chanting verse to a Jazz background. But rapping as a black style involves the use of rhymed street slang delivered at breakneck speed. Black disk jockeys through the years have resorted to a fast delivery, sometimes involving rhyme. It is not surprising, then, that Kurt Walker functioned for a period as a Disco disk jockey, many of whom helped popularize the rapping style. Among the more popular rappers, there are Grandmaster Flash & the Furious Five (*Grandmaster Flash on the Wheels of Steel*), The Funky Four Plus One (*That's the Joint*), Count Coolout (*Rhythm Rap Rock*), The Treacherous Three ("Body Rock"), and the erotic female trio, called Sequence ("The Monster Jam"). Popularizers of the style include Blondie ("Rapture") and Lakeside ("Fantastic Voyage").

See also Disco; Alan Freed.

raunchy   The word served as the title of a guitar instrumental in 1957 by Bill Justis. It had a dirty, sexy sound, which linked up with the dictionary meaning of the word: slovenly, dirty, obscene, smutty. "Raunchy" is used to describe records that have an abrasive but insinuating sound, and behavior that is challenging, aggressive, and rough.

"rave-up"   A term that originated with the Yardbirds and referred to a long instrumental guitar break they developed as a show-stopper in 1964. The break would sometimes last for as long as 30 minutes. But apparently it was not long or frequent enough for guitarist Eric Clapton (b. 1945), who left the group to join John Mayall's Bluesbreakers. The "rave-up" continued as a Yardbirds tradition until the group disbanded in 1967.

Ready, Steady, Go   England's No. 1 Rock TV program in the 1960s. Its theme was "54321," a disk by Manfred Mann (b. Johannesburg, S. Africa, 1940) and the Manfreds.

recitative   Although it is written in regular musical notation, performers half-talk, half-sing the recitative, taking certain freedoms in the delivery. A recent instance in black pop music on disk: "Rapper's Delight" by the Sugar Hill Gang.

See also rapping.

Recombinant Rock   *See* Crusading Rock.

recorder   A woodwind instrument without a reed; the predecessor of the flute. It is made of wood and blown at the tip, and held in front of the player like a clarinet, not crosswise like a flute.

record hop   *See* "hop."

Recording Industry Association of America (RIAA)   A trade association made up of the companies that manufacture and release records, it was formed in 1951 by a group of record executives, including Milton Rackmil and Leonard Schneider of Decca, Glenn Wallichs of Capitol, and Frank Buckley Walker of MGM Records. From the standpoint of artists, songwriters, publishers, and the public, its most important function is to certify records that sell enough copies to be labeled Gold or Platinum.

See also Gold Record; Platinum Record.

recording studio   No instrument played in a Rock group is as important as the recording studio, which is really the group's basic instrument. Studios have reputations, based on the hit records that have been cut there, with the result that groups record all over the country and the world. Carole King's album, *Pearls,* for example, was recorded and mixed at Pecan Street Studios in Austin, Tex., but mastered at Warner Brothers Recording Studios in North Hollywood. The Beatles inaugurated the creative use of the studio with their *Sgt. Pepper* album, accompanying its release in 1967 with the announcement that it had taken 700 hours to record. In 1978, Village Recorder of Los Angeles built a new and special Studio D for the exclusive use of Fleetwood Mac, which worked in it for an entire year to produce *Tusk.*

In New York City in 1980, there were at least seven studios that stood out because of the eminence of the groups that used them and the hit records that they produced:

1. A & R: co-owner Phil Ramone was renowned for his success with Paul Simon and Billy Joel.
2. Atlantic Studios: celebrated for engineer/producer Tom Dowd's work with Ray Charles and other R & B/Soul artists.

3. Electric Lady: built in Greenwich Village in 1969 by guitar great Jimi Hendrix and an associate. One of the first to use 24 tracks and 2-track digital machines. The early Rolling Stones, Led Zeppelin, Aerosmith, and Kiss used it successfully.

4. Hit Factory: changes its carpets to blend with groups recording at the time, which have included Talking Heads, Village People, Meat Loaf, and Patti Smith.

5. Media Sound: located in a defunct Baptist Church on West 57th Street. Used by Barry Manilow, Blondie, Barbra Streisand.

6. Power Station: in its own building on West 53rd Street, it produced Chic's Disco hits. Other clients include the Kinks, Bruce Springsteen, and Foghat.

7. Soundmixers: boasting four studios, all automated and with MCI 24-track boards; a favorite of Kenny Loggins, Average White Band, Peter Tosh.

Los Angeles was the site of the following outstanding studios:

1. A & M Recording Studio: the leading major-label, in-house studio, built by Herb Alpert's hits with the Tijuana Brass. One of the few studios with 32-track digital 3M machines, it has been used by the Village People, Chicago, Kris Kristofferson, Dolly Parton, and Gladys Knight.

2. Cherokee Studios: exclusive, with no staff engineers and tight security. Most of Rod Stewart's recordings are made here; also used by David Bowie and Barbra Streisand.

3. Filmways/Heider: known as the largest independent recording complex in the country, with ten studios in Hollywood and four in San Francisco. One of its studios is a former aircraft hangar that can accommodate the 150 members of the Los Angeles Philharmonic. Started in 1964, its work with Crosby, Stills, Nash & Young, the Rolling Stones, and Cream opened the door to its enormous growth. A favorite of John Denver; used also by Paul McCartney & Wings, Peter Frampton, and for the *Grease* soundtrack.

5. Record Plant: has four studios in LA, two in Sausalito, Calif., and five in New York. Gary Kelgun, who started the studio in the sixties with Tom Wilson of Columbia Records (who drowned in his swimming pool in 1977), is credited with bringing the concept of the "living room" to the recording field. Used by Donna Summer, Blues Brothers, Eagles, the Moody Blues, Fleetwood Mac (*Rumours*), and Paul McCartney (*London Town*).

6. Village Recorder: the first studio to use 16-track Dolby, it is considered the last word in elegant studio design. In addition to Fleetwood Mac, for whom it built a $1.5 million studio, it has been used by Neil Diamond (*Beautiful Noise*), Band (*Last Waltz*), Steely Dan (*Aja* and *Royal Scam*), Frank Zappa (*Sheik Yer Bouti*), and Supertramp (*Breakfast in America*).

Miami has become an important link in the recording industry chain as a result of Criteria Recording Studio, founded in 1954 and a resounding success since the Bee Gees cut nine Gold singles in the late seventies. Since then, the studio has produced the Allman Brothers Band (*Enlightened Rogues*), the Eagles (*Hotel California*), Andy Gibb (*Shadow Dancing*), and Crosby, Stills & Nash (*CSN*), as well as the Bee Gees' *Saturday Night Fever*. Beachfront mansions and a yacht are part of the complex.

Other cities with studios that have achieved prominence include:

1. Chicago—Universal Recorders: the Midwest's leading studio and one of the country's foremost advertising studios. The punchy sound perfected for advertising jingles has brought Aerosmith, Shirley Bassey, Tower of Power, Blues Brothers, and Ramsey Lewis to its doors.

2. Minneapolis—Sound 80: its proximity to the 3M company has made it the testing ground for digital equipment. The Doobie Brothers, Cat Stevens, and Bob Dylan have recorded here.

3. Nashville—Woodland Sound Studio: a standout in an area with over 100 studios. Its simplicity attracts Kansas (*Point of No Return*), Neil Young (*Comes the Time*), and Charlie Daniels (*Million-Mile Reflections*).

4. Nederland, Colorado—Caribou Ranch: opened as the alternative to the LA/NYC urban style. Originally a horse ranch on 3,000 acres; its studio is a converted barn. Favored by Chicago, Waylon Jennings, Elton John, and Tony Orlando.

5. Orange, N.J.—House of Music: another country-type studio, with a barn, pond, and river. Blind Faith put it on the map in 1971. A favorite of Patti Smith, Stuff, and Kool & the Gang.

6. Philadelphia—Sigma Sound: expanded rapidly with the rise of the Sound of Philadelphia and Gamble/Huff/Thom Bell from 1971 on. Opened a NYC studio in 1976. Deejay producer Tom Moulton raised its standing with the pioneer editing of Pop hits into long Disco versions. Hit records have come out of here by Ashford & Simpson, the O'Jays, Teddy Pendergrass, McFadden & Whitehead, and the Village People.

7. Sheffield, Ala.—Muscle Shoals Sound Studios: started as Fame Studios & Publishing in 1958 by Richard Hall, who was joined by men who became part owners and made up the famous Muscle Shoals Rhythm Section. Present location, a 31,000-square-foot building on the Tennessee River. Among those who have recorded here: the Rolling Stones, the Allman Brothers, Lynyrd Skynyrd (*The Jukes, First and Last*), Dr. Hook, Joan Baez, and Bob Dylan (*Slow Train Coming*).
   See also Muscle Shoals sound.

Record of the Year, Country Single (CMA awards)

1967	"There Goes My Everything": Jack Greene
1968	"Harper Valley PTA": Jeannie C. Riley
1969	"A Boy Named Sue": Johnny Cash

1970 "Okie from Muskogee": Merle Haggard
1971 "Help Me Make It Through the Night": Sammi Smith
1972 "Happiest Girl in the Whole U.S.A.": Donna Fargo
1973 "Behind Closed Doors": Charlie Rich
1974 "Country Bumpkin": Cal Smith
1975 "Before the Next Teardrop Falls": Freddy Fender
1976 "Good-Hearted Woman": Waylon Jennings and Willie Nelson
1977 "Lucille": Kenny Rogers
1978 "Heaven's Just a Sin Away": Kendalls
1979 "The Devil Went Down to Georgia": Charlie Daniels Band
1980 "He Stopped Loving Her Today": George Jones
1981 "Elvira": Oak Ridge Boys

See also Country Music Association (CMA).

Record of the Year (NARAS Grammy Awards)

1958 "Nel Blu Dipinto Di Blu" (Volare): Domenico Modugno
1959 "Mack the Knife": Bobby Darin
1960 "Theme from a Summer Place": Percy Faith
1961 "Moon River": Henry Mancini
1962 "I Left My Heart in San Francisco": Tony Bennett
1963 "The Days of Wine and Roses": Henry Mancini
1964 "The Girl from Ipanema": Stan Getz and Astrud Gilberto
1965 "A Taste of Honey": Herb Alpert & the Tijuana Brass
1966 "Strangers in the Night": Frank Sinatra
1967 "Up, Up and Away": 5th Dimension
1968 "Mrs. Robinson": Simon & Garfunkel
1969 "Aquarius/Let the Sunshine In": 5th Dimension
1970 "Bridge Over Troubled Water": Simon & Garfunkel
1971 "It's Too Late": Carole King
1972 "The First Time Ever I Saw Your Face": Roberta Flack
1973 "Killing Me Softly with His Song": Robert Flack
1974 "I Honestly Love You": Olivia Newton-John
1975 "Love Will Keep Us Together": The Captain & Tenille
1976 "This Masquerade": George Benson
1977 "Hotel California": The Eagles
1978 "Just the Way You Are": Billy Joel
1979 "What a Fool Believes": The Doobie Brothers
1980 "Sailing": Christopher Cross
1981 "Bette Davis Eyes": Kim Carnes

See also National Academy of Recording Arts and Sciences.

Otis Redding (1941–1967)   He was first known as Mr. Pitiful as the result of records he made between 1962 and 1964 in which he dealt with lovers begging forgiveness or the return of a loved one; "Mr. Pitiful" was the title of one wailer. By 1965 he had stepped forth as a Soul performer with his driving demand for "Respect," a hit for Aretha Franklin (b. 1942). In 1966 he created the intense, Gospel-oriented *Dictionary of Soul.* He exploded as a dynamic performer at the Monterey Pop Festival in 1967. By then he was making plans to launch an entertainment complex that would embrace recording, publishing, booking, and managing. But that year he perished in a plane crash about which there has been speculation as to whether it was an accident or sabotage. He did not live to enjoy his biggest hit, "(Sittin' on) The Dock of the Bay." In October 1981 he was posthumously elected and inducted into the Georgia Music Hall of Fame.

Redneck Rock   Another descriptive term for Outlaw Country music, whose locale is Austin, Tex., and whose proponents include Willie Nelson (b. 1933), Leon Russell (b. 1941), Kinky Friedman (b. 1944), and Waylon Jennings (b. 1937).
See also Nashville Outlaws.

reeds   Instruments like the saxophone, clarinet, oboe, and bassoon, which use a single or a double reed. During the Big Band era, the reed section of major bands consisted of as many as five saxes (two altos, tenor, baritone, and bass, or variants of this setup), most of whom doubled on clarinet and/or flute, and sometimes oboe.

reel   According to bluesman Big Bill Broonzy, who was born of ex-slaves in Scott, Miss., in 1893, Blues were known as "reels" back in his youth.
See also Blues.

Reeperbahn   A red-light district in Hamburg, Germany, that provided a jumping-off place for Liverpool groups like the Beatles. It was a rowdy area that featured all-night entertainment—loud, fast, raw music. No one really listened, since booze and broads were the main attraction, and Liverpudlian groups could be as amateurish, wild, and outrageous as they pleased. The first time the Beatles played the Reeperbahn, in the early sixties, they were part of a Little Richard troupe.

refrain   Characteristic of folk songs but also of many Rock songs—a segment, including words and music, repeated at the end of each verse or stanza. A recent example: "Escape (The Piña Colada Song)."

Reggae   A style that originated in Jamaica in the mid-1960s, evolving from Ska and Rock Steady. The Ska sound was developed by Jamaican musicians as a result of their contact with American Rhythm & Blues, which they heard over the radio via Miami's Station WIZZ and stations in New Orleans. The word "ska" is said to come from "skat," a simulation of the scratching sound made by strumming a guitar. Just about the time that Presley emerged on the American scene in 1956, Ska began to be heard in Jamaica, a product of horns (trombones, trumpets, tenor saxes), Jazz riffs, and a chug-a-lug tempo. It spread to London, whch has a West Indian population, so that Britain's outstanding R & B artist, Georgie Fame (b. 1943), performed Ska numbers with his Blue Flames at the Flamingo Club. By 1964 American charts carried "My Boy Lollipop," a Ska novelty, as a hit for Millie Small. (Rod Stewart, b. 1945, played harmonica on the disk.)

What R & B was to Ska, Soul proved to a new Jamaican sound, Rock Steady. Under the impact of James Brown (b. circa 1928), the tempo became upbeat, and electric bass and guitar superseded the chug-a-lug horn sound. In 1966 Alton Ellis set the pattern with "Rock Steady." By then, two of Reggae's future stars had made records and scored their first hits: Jimmy Cliff with "Daisy Got Me Crazy" and Bob Marley & the Wailers with "Judge Not" (1961) and "Simmer Down" (1964), the later a "rude boy" classic, released in England on Chris Blackwell's Island label. (In 1980 Blondie revived "The Tide Is High," a mid-sixties Rock Steady single by the Paragons.)

The first appearance of the word "Reggae" on a record occurred presumably in 1968, on a disk by the Maytals, "Do the Reggay." The first authentic U.S.A. Reggae hit was heard the following year: Desmond Dekker's "Israelites," a bestseller that eventually sold less than Dekker's "It Mek" (which means "That's Why" in West Indian parlance). With Reggae, Ska's shuffle became syncopated, and the electric bass and guitar remained prominent as on Rock Steady disks. Reggae rhythm dropped the backbeat, and put the downbeat where the backbeat was, creating an upside-down feeling.

Reggae musicians reflected the outlook of dispossessed Jamaicans who embraced Rastafarianism, a faith which revered the late emperor of Ethiopia, Haile Selassie, whose common name was Ras Tafari. Subscribing also to the late Marcus Garvey's "back to Africa" movement, Rastafarians venerated Selassie as the black God who would lead deprived Jamaican blacks out of white captivity back to their natural homeland, Africa. Like his fans, Bob Marley (b. 1945), who became the poet laureate of Reggae and died prematurely of cancer in 1981, wore his hair in long, unruly "dreadlocks" and smoked "spliffs," even on the stage.

From 1972 on, a number of American and British Rock artists cut records with a Reggae beat. These included Johnny Nash (b. 1940), "I Can See Clearly," (1972); Paul Simon, "Mother and Child Reunion" and "Take Me to the Mardi Gras"; Led Zeppelin, *House of the Holy;* and the Staple Singers, "I'll Take You There," (1972). Two years later, Stevie Wonder (b. 1950) produced "Boogie on Reggae Woman," while Eric Clapton (b. 1945) grossed a Gold Record with "I Shot the Sheriff," a revival of Bob Marley's original disk. That year, Americans saw *The Harder They Come,* a film starring Jimmy Cliff that dealt with a Reggae singer who became a Caribbean folk hero. Even wider recognition came to Reggae when Bob Marley & the Wailers played Madison Square Garden in 1978. Among Reggae-derived songs, there are: "Stir It Up" by Johnny Nash; "Watching the Detectives" by Elvis Costello; "Movin' On" by Taj Mahal; "Why Can't We Be Friends" by War; "Protection" by Graham Parker; "Hotel California" by the Eagles; "Police and Thieves" by the Clash; "Dreadlock Holiday" by 10cc; "The Tide is High" by Blondie; the songs in McCartney's *Wings Wild Life;* "Don't Stand So Close to Me" by the Police; Johnny Rivers' *L.A. Reggae;* and Grace Jones' *Warm Leatherette* and *Nightclubbing.*

In 1980, an adaptation of the film *The Harder They Come* appeared as a novel by Jamaican writer Michael Thelwell, just about the time that Stevie Wonder produced his "Master Blaster (Jammin')."

With the death of Bob Marley, Peter Tosh, who founded the Wailers with him but split away in 1974, seemed heir apparent to the throne of Reggae. But Tosh points out that he goes "in my own direction, not Bob Marley's" (with whom he disagreed musically and politically). Belonging to the more radical wing of the Rastafarians, he states: "I am a musical messenger . . . and I want to educate people through music." Even though he has been befriended by Mick Jagger and Keith Richard of the Rolling Stones and signed to their own label, his records have limited sales. In 1982 Rita Marley, who inherited her husband's music empire, scored a hit single with "One Draw" and was regarded as a potential "Queen of Reggae."

See also Dub; Mento; Skinheads; Sound System; Two-Tone movement.

rehearsal pianist   In the heyday of vaudeville and in the early days of radio, the song-plugger or professional man was frequently a pianist who helped singers learn new songs. George Gershwin (1898–1937), Jerome Kern (1885–1945), and Jimmy McHugh (1894–1969) were all employed as rehearsal pianists by Broadway music publishers before they embarked on their illustrious careers as writers of hit songs.

release   *See* bridge.

relief band   A band that performs on nights when the regular band is off.

renewal   Before the revision of the copyright law that has been in effect since 1976 (when the original copyright term of 28 years expired), it was possible to file a supplementary application and renew the copyright for another 28 years. Since the renewal could be given to a new publisher, either by the writer or his heirs, the original publisher and a possible new publisher were very much concerned about a renewal. Under the copyright law now in force, there are no renewals. A work is protected by copyright for the life of the composer or author plus 50 years.

See also copyright.

reprise   In Pop music, and specifically in a musical, the repetition of a song. In the Golden Age of the American musical theater (1920s–1940s), reprises were used in an effort to embed a potential hit song in the consciousness of the audience. The hope was that the spectators would go out whistling the hit. As character, pace, and plot became increasingly important and songs were regarded as adjuncts to advance the story, reprises were sacrificed. Over a period of years, few hit songs have emerged even from the biggest and longest-run musicals.

restricted   Before a song, particularly a song from a musical, is performed for the first time on radio or TV, it is possible through ASCAP or BMI to restrict the song: that is, to delay or prevent a performance.

reverb   Echo can be produced mechanically by sending sound through a large space, as Columbia Records once did when it used the five-story stairwell at 799 7th Avenue New York City. When it is produced electronically, echo is called "reverb," derived from "reverberation," a vibrancy of sound like that produced by the loud pedal on a piano. Tape is also used to produce echo effects through delaying the return of the signal. Electronic echo can be controlled in relation to the size and depth of the reverberations. As the spacing in time of the repetition of a sound is narrowed, distinctions in pitch disappear.

See also fuzztone; Moog; tape reverb; wah-wah pedal.

Rhinestone Cowboy   Like the Urban Cowboy, the Rhinestone Cowboy (cf. Glen Campbell's hit recording of that title) never got any closer to a cow than the T-bone on his plate.

See also Urban Cowboy.

"Rhubarb Red"   Nickname of guitarist Les Paul (b. 1916 in Waukesha, Wisc.). With Mary Ford, he created a series of hit records, employing a self-devised multiple dubbing technique: "How High the Moon," "Mockin' Bird Hill," "The World Is Waiting for the Sunrise"—all million sellers in 1951—"Vaya con Dios" (1954), and others. Leslie Polfuss (as he was christened) was a brilliant, self-taught electronics wizard who designed one of the earliest electric guitars, which is still in use.

Rhythm & Blues   In the 1940s, the Blues acquired a strong dance beat, the rhythm emanating from Boogie-Woogie and Shuffle. "With my little band," said Louis Jordan (1908–1975), regarded as the Father of R & B, "I did everything they did with a big band. I made the blues jump" (R & B is sometimes known as Jump Blues). Several other elements entered into the mix that became R & B: (1) the electric guitar, (2) the honking tenor sax, and (3) Gospel emotion and excitement. R & B came roaring out of the segregated ghettos of big cities, the street-front churches of black America, and the black bands of the Swing era. Economically, it was a product of the shortage of black disks, the rising purchasing power of black people during and after World War II, and the reduced cost of recording made possible with the introduction of tape. Flourishing from 1945 to 1960, R & B was good-time music, black ghetto music, entertainment created by a people who were still excluded from white clubs, theaters, showrooms, and even first-run-movie houses, and who turned to records, whether played at home or on juke-boxes in bars and clubs. To supply the demand in a period when the major record companies, restricted by wartime shortages, stopped recording black artists, large numbers of small, independent record-makers began producing disks for black listeners. Although there were in the early 1940s a group of "race" labels, as they were then known, in the New York area (Varsity, Beacon, Savoy, De Luxe, Apollo, and National), the R & B explosion came in Los Angeles at the end of World War II.

"R & B started here in LA," record producer Johnny Otis (b. 1921) has said. "Roy Milton was here, Joe Liggins was here, T-Bone Walker was here, Charles Brown was here. I was here, and others, too. By '48 or '49 it was set—we had an art form, though we didn't know it then." There were quite a number of R & B record labels, too: Black & White, Atlas, Jukebox, Specialty, Modern/RPM, Aladdin, Gilt Edge, Excelsior, Swing Time, Imperial, and others. Only one of these, Modern/RPM, continues to operate into the present. Other long-lived giants that emerged from this era include: Chess/Checker of Chicago; Peacock/Duke of Houston; King/Federal of Cincinnati; and Atlantic/Atco of New York. All of these are now under different ownership.

R & B fathered R 'n' R, and some of the giant artists of R & B were able to flourish in the Presley years: e.g., Fats Domino (b. 1928), Little Richard (b. 1932), B. B. King (b. 1925), Dinah Washington (1924–1963), Lloyd Price (b. 1933), and Chuck Berry (b. 1926), who was really a Rockabilly artist from the start. Big Mama Thornton (b. 1926), whose R & B hit "Hound Dog" (1953) was the source of

Presley's imitative version (1956), continues to be a potent in-person performer but her record impact was short-lived.

R & B was the source of the muscular ballad style of Frankie Laine (b. 1913) ("That's My Desire," 1947), as it was the basis of hits by Bill Haley (b. 1925). "See You Later, Alligator," "Shake, Rattle, and Roll," and "Rock Around the Clock" (1955) were all covers of records previously cut by R & B artists. In the two or three years before Presley's appearance on the national record scene, Pop artists and groups scored hits by covering R & B disks.

See also belting; cover record; Elvis Presley; Rockabilly.

Rhythm & Blues Caravan   The full title was *The Johnny Otis Rhythm & Blues Caravan,* and it was a show organized by Johnny (b. 1921) for a nightclub he opened in the Watts district of Los Angeles called the Barrel House. Between 1948 and 1950, he found such black artists as Little Esther (b. 1935), later known as Esther Phillips; Mel Walker, who was featured on disks with Little Esther; and the Robins. Later Johnny discovered Little Willie John (1937–1968), Jackie Wilson (b. circa 1932), the Midnighters, and Big Mama Thornton (b. 1926). The *Caravan* was a traveling show and it included amateur nights wherever it appeared. Although Johnny discontinued the show in 1955 when he became an LA disk jockey, he has revived it periodically for appearances during the seventies not only in this country but abroad.

See also Johnny Otis; Rhythm & Blues.

Rhythm & Blues Instrumental Performance, Best (NARAS Grammy Awards)

1969	King Curtis: "Games People Play"
1972	The Temptations: "Papa Was a Rolling Stone"
1973	Ramsey Lewis: "Hang On, Sloopy"
1974	MFSB: "TSOP (The Sound of Philadelphia)"
1975	Silver Convention: "Fly, Robin, Fly"
1976	George Benson: "Theme from the Good King Bad"
1977	The Brothers Johnson: "Q"
1978	Earth, Wind & Fire, "Runnin'"
1979	Earth, Wind & Fire: "Boogie Wonderland"
1980	George Benson: "Off Broadway"
1981	David Sanborn: "All I Need Is You"

Rhythm & Blues Performance by a Duo or Group, Best (NARAS Grammy Awards)

1966	Ramsey Lewis: "Hold It Right There"
1967	Sam & Dave: "Soul Man"

1968   The Isley Brothers: "It's Your Thing"
King Curtis: "Games People Play" (instrumental)
1969   The Temptations: "Cloud Nine"
1970   The Delfonics: "Didn't I (Blow Your Mind This Time)"
1971   Ike & Tina Turner: "Proud Mary"
1972   The Temptations: "Papa Was a Rolling Stone"
The Temptations: "Papa Was a Rolling Stone" (instrumental)
1973   Gladys Knight & the Pips: "Midnight Train to Georgia"
1974   Rufus: "Tell Me Something Good"
1975   Earth, Wind & Fire: "Shining Star"
1976   Marilyn McCoo & Billy Davis, Jr.: "You Don't Have to Be a Star (To Be in My Show)"
1977   Emotions: "Best of My Love"
1978   Earth, Wind, & Fire: *All 'n All*
1979   Earth, Wind, & Fire: "After the Love Has Gone"
1980   Manhattans: "Shining Star"
1981   Quincy Jones: "The Dude"

Rhythm & Blues Recording, Best (NARAS Grammy Awards)

1958   "Tequila": The Champs
1959   "What a Difference a Day Makes": Dinah Washington
1960   "Let the Good Times Roll": Ray Charles
1961   "Hit the Road, Jack": Ray Charles
1962   "I Can't Stop Loving You": Ray Charles
1963   "Busted": Ray Charles
1964   "How Glad I Am": Nancy Wilson
1965   "Papa's Got a Brand New Bag": James Brown
1966   "Crying Time": Ray Charles
1967   "Respect": Aretha Franklin

After 1967 the category was eliminated and Grammys were awarded in five R & B classifications: Best Female Vocal, Best Male Vocal, Best Duo or Group performance, Best Instrumental Performance and Best Song.

Rhythm & Blues Song, Best (NARAS Grammy Awards)

1968   "(Sittin' on) The Dock of the Bay": Otis Redding and Steve Cropper
1969   "Color Him Father": Richard Spencer
1970   "Patches": Ronald Dunbar and General Johnson
1971   "Ain't No Sunshine": Bill Withers

1972   "Papa Was a Rolling Stone": Barrett Strong and Norman Whit-field

1973   "Superstition": Stevie Wonder

1974   "Living for the City": Stevie Wonder

1975   "Where Is the Love": Harry Wayne Casey, Richard Finch, Willie Clarke, Betty Wright

1976   "Lowdown": Boz Scaggs, David Paich

1977   "You Make Me Feel Like Dancing": Leo Sayer and Vini Poncia

1978   "Last Dance": Paul Jabara

1979   "After the Love Has Gone": David Foster, Jay Graydon, Bill Champlin

1980   "Never Knew Love Like This Before": Reggie Lucas and James Mtume

1981   "Just the Two of Us": Bill Withers, William Salter, Ralph McDonald

Rhythm & Blues Vocal Performance, Best—Female (NARAS Grammy Awards)

1967   Aretha Franklin: "Respect"

1968   Aretha Franklin: "Chain of Fools"

1969   Aretha Franklin: "Share Your Love with Me"

1970   Aretha Franklin: "Don't Play That Song"

1971   Aretha Franklin: "Bridge Over Troubled Water"

1972   Aretha Franklin: "Young, Gifted, and Black"

1973   Aretha Franklin: "Master of Eyes"

1974   Aretha Franklin: "Ain't Nothing Like the Real Thing"

1975   Natalie Cole: "This Will Be"

1975   Natalie Cole: "Sophisticated Lady (She's a Different Lady)"

1977   Thelma Houston: "Don't Leave Me This Way"

1978   Donna Summer: "Last Dance"

1979   Dionne Warwick: "Déjà Vu"

1980   Stephanie Mills: "Never Knew Love Like This Before"

1981   Aretha Franklin: "Hold On I'm Comin'"

See also National Academy of Recording Arts and Sciences.

Rhythm & Blues Vocal Performance, Best—Male (NARAS Grammy Awards)

1966   Ray Charles: "Crying Time"

1967   Lou Rawls: "Dead End Street"

1968   Otis Redding: "(Sittin' on) The Dock of the Bay"

1969   Joe Simon: "The Chokin' Kind"

1970   B. B. King: "The Thrill Is Gone"
1971   Lou Rawls: "A Natural Man"
1972   Billy Paul: "Me and Mrs. Jones"
1973   Stevie Wonder: "Superstition"
1974   Stevie Wonder: "Boogie on Reggae Woman"
1975   Ray Charles: "Living for the City"
1976   Stevie Wonder: "I Wish"
1977   Lou Rawls: *Unmistakably Lou*
1978   George Benson: "On Broadway"
1979   Michael Jackson "Don't Stop 'Til You Get Enough"
1980   George Benson: *Give Me The Night*
1981   James Ingram: "One Hundred Ways" from Quincy Jones' *The Dude*

See also National Academy of Recording Arts and Sciences

Rhythm & Blues revival   In the wake of the Beatles and the British invasion of the American record scene, R & B enjoyed a revival after the mid-1960s. Although R & B groups like the Coasters, Drifters, Shirelles, and others managed to keep afloat during the high tides of Teenage Rock, Folk Rock, and Protest Rock, and even during the British tidal wave, the pioneer R & B performers were temporarily beached for lack of airplay. However, the devotion of the Beatles and other British groups to the work of the pioneers—they used some of them on their tours—brought a reawakening of R & B in the late 1960s. In the seventies, despite the vogue of Soul, Reggae, and Disco, all black-oriented styles, R & B continued to be heard on the records of Kool & the Gang, Daryl Hall & John Oates, Joan Armatrading (b. 1950), the Commodores, Michael Jackson (b. 1958), and others.
   See also Rhythm & Blues.

Rhythm & Gospel   A descriptive term, rather than a category or style, used with reference to recordings made in the early fifties by black groups with Gospel backgrounds who fused Blues with Gospel. In some instances, as, for example, "Have Mercy, Baby," a group took a Gospel hymn and gave it romantic overtones by changing "Lord" to "Baby." Ray Charles (b. 1930) did this with "This Little Light of Mine," which became "This Little Girl of Mine" (1955), "Hallelujah, I Love Her So," and other Gospel songs, thereby pioneering the Gospel/Blues sound that became later known as Soul. Clyde McPhatter (1931–1972), who started as a Gospel singer; the Dominoes, who started as a Gospel group; and Billy Ward (b. 1921), who brought a Gospel background to leadership of the group—all imparted the high-level emotion of Gospel singing to their Blues-styled material. When

McPhatter brought the Drifters together, they sang with the same sense of deep feeling. The Five Royales, headed by gospeleer/songwriter Lowman Pauling, likewise infused the Blues with a Gospel excitement in "Dedicated to the One I Love" and other R & B hits.

rhythm ballad   *See* ballad.

rhythm section   During the Big Band era, the rhythm section generally consisted of piano, bass (string or tuba), drums, and guitar. In the minimalist combos of early R 'n' R and even the Beatles, rhythm was laid down by drums, electric bass, and rhythm guitar.

ride cymbal   A single cymbal mounted on the rim of the bass drum and struck with a drumstick.

riff   A musical phrase that is repeated or imitated over a changing chord pattern. It can be a melodic phrase or a rhythmic figure. The underlying changes can be either harmonic or melodic, depending on whether the riff itself is melodic or rhythmic. In time, the term moved into general usage to mean something irrelevant introduced into a conversation. In this sense, as well as the musical one, it could be used as a verb as well as a noun. The classical equivalent of *riff* is *ostinato*.

rim shot   The drummer striking the metal rim of his snare drum with one of his sticks.

ring-shout   Back in slavery days, the "shout" was an orgiastic outburst of religious ecstasy, exemplified by such spirituals as "This Old Time Religion" or "Little David, Play on Your Harp." The "ringshout" was a combination of dance and song in which the group, arranged in a ring, moved ever faster in a circle, and sang and chanted. As James Weldon Johnson described it in *The Book of American Negro Spirituals:* "Around and around, the ring moves on shuffling feet. The music is supplemented by the clapping of hands. As the ring goes around, it begins to take on signs of frenzy.... The same musical phrase is repeated over and over, one, two, three, four, five hours.... The very monotony of sound and motion produces an ecstatic state. Women, screaming, fall to the ground.... Men, exhausted, drop out of the Shout. But the ring closes up and moves around and around." John Lomax and his son, Alan, recorded a ring-shout in a small rural church in 1934 for the Library of Congress, released as "Run, Old Jeremiah."

rip   *See* drop-off.

Jean Ritchie (b. 1922)   One of the foremost performers, writers, and recording artists of Appalachian music, she has brought national attention to the dulcimer, on which she is a master performer. The Ritchie family, descendants of English settlers as far back as 1768, has been such an authentic source of traditional folk material that John A. Lomax and his son made field recordings of their singing for the Library of Congress Archives of Folk Song.

road manager   When an artist or group is on tour, the road manager takes care of transportation and hotel arrangements. He may also operate as an advance man, arriving before the performer(s) and arranging for newspaper interviews and promotional appearances on radio and TV and in stores. The road manager may also be involved in such matters as laundry, equipment, and food. Depending on the fees commanded by an artist, the road manager may simply serve as the man in charge of the tour, parceling out the various functions to subordinates.

Paul Robeson (1898–1976)   A towering and unyielding figure in the struggle for black rights, he was a folk singer in the classic connotation of the calling, a dramatic actor, motion picture star, and one of the great voices of our time. His premier concert in 1925 was devoted to spirituals. Three years later, he became widely known for his singing of ''Ol' Man River'' in the path-breaking musical *Showboat*. In 1939 he achieved even wider renown with his radio performance of *Ballad for Americans*. Throughout his life, he suffered from racist harassment and political discrimination. But starting with his distinguished career at Rutgers University, where he was an All-American football star and graduated with a Phi Beta Kappa key, he rose steadily to a pinnacle of recognition as a creative artist.
    See also spirituals.

Rock   As a term, it did not come into existence until the 1960s when Rock 'n' Roll became more sophisticated and innovative. As of this writing, it has become a catch-all term, a generic term for the sounds and rhythms that came crashing into Pop music after the mid-1950s and that continue, with many changes, to be the Pop music of the world. The contrast between Rock and Pop may be generalized as follows: (1) the form of Rock is modeled on 12-bar Blues, whereas Pop was built on 8-bar and 16-bar formations and the 32-bar song; (2) rhythmically, Rock is modeled on the 8-to-the-bar meter of Boogie-Woogie, and it stresses the afterbeat and relies on the bass rather than the drum; (3) harmonically, Rock tends to be modal rather than diatonic and to work with direct modulation instead of the circle of sevenths; (4) while Pop was concerned with attractive and appealing melody, Rock emphasizes energy and sensory overload, boldly exploiting various types of distortion (feedback, fuzztone, reverb, wah-wah pedal, etc.) ''to expand the consciousness, liberate the self, and rediscover the world.''

See also Blues; Boogie-Woogie; feedback; fuzztone; Pop music; reverb; sensory overload; wah-wah pedal.

Rockabilly   The first stage of Rock 'n' Roll, a music of high energy and youthful rebelliousness, produced mainly by white southern teenagers who were attracted by the exuberance, excitement, and beat of Rhythm & Blues and who adapted the black sound. As the prime, charismatic exponent, Elvis Presley (1935–1977) popularized the sound with recordings modeled on disks by Arthur ''Big Boy'' Crudup (1905–1974), Willia Mae ''Big Mama'' Thornton (b. 1926), Little Richard (b. 1935), and other black R & B singers. Rockabilly is thus defined by some as a mix of R & B and C & W, and by others, as a merger of Jump Blues and rural Country music. Carl Perkins (b. 1930), who wrote ''Blue Suede Shoes'' and was a leading Rockabilly artist, termed it ''Blues with a Country beat.'' Charlie Feathers, who was at Sun Records when Presley made his first recordings and who co-wrote ''I Forgot to Remember to Forget,'' one of the songs Elvis recorded for Sun, has described Rockabilly as ''a merger of Bluegrass, the music of white hill country, and Cottonpatch Blues, the music of the southern black fieldhand.'' Rockabilly has also been defined simply as a ''union of Blues and Bluegrass.''

Presley's Rockabilly combo consisted of electric guitar, rhythm guitar, and string bass. In keeping with Country tradition, the bass acted as time-keeper instead of a drum. (During the thirties and forties, drums were anathema to the *Grand Ole Opry* because of their association with blacks, and when some Country combos began using them in the fifties, the drummer could not be seen onstage; he performed behind a curtain.) The Rockbilly bass player slapped the strings instead of plucking them. The rhythm guitar played 8-to-the-bar figures derived from Boogie-Woogie. Musically, Rockbilly had the uptempo gusto of Bluegrass. It was a 4-to-the-bar sound with a triple beat, modified by R & B's accented afterbeat. The echo used on the recordings was contrived, not electronic, involving a delayed tape sound (''slapback''). Rockabilly singers, including Buddy Holly as well as Elvis, used melisma, double glottis, stuttering, and hiccups—black-derived devices designed to add tension and intensity.

Most Rockabilly artists emerged from the Sun label of Memphis. Owner Sam Phillips recorded many R & B singers before he encouraged Presley and other southern whites to sing black. In addition to Presley and Perkins, Sun rockabillies included: Johnny Cash (b. 1932) of Arkansas; Jerry Lee Lewis (b. 1933) of Louisiana; Conway Twitty (b. 1935) of Arkansas; and Roy Orbison (b. 1936) of Texas.

Other purveyors of the sound: Bill Haley (b. 1925) of Michigan, who anticipated Presley and recorded for Essex Records of Philadelphia; Gene Vincent (1935–1971) of Virginia, who recorded for Capitol; Johnny Burnette (1934–1964) of Tennessee, who recorded for Liberty; Ricky Nelson (b. 1940) of New Jersey and California, who recorded for Verve and Imperial; Buddy Holly (1938–1959) of Texas and New Mexico, who recorded for Brunswick and Coral; Eddie Cochran (1938–1960) of Oklahoma, who recorded for Liberty; and coming from the other end of the color spectrum, Chuck Berry (b. 1931) of California and Missouri, who recorded for Chess Records. Except for Bill Haley, Presley and the Sun rockabillies anticipated the others by two years or more.

See also Bluegrass; Blues; Boogie-Woogie; glottis; Jump Blues; Rhythm & Blues.

Rockers   The title of a Jamaican film along the lines of *The Harder They Come,* it was developed as another term for Reggae music (whose origins are explained in the film).

See also Reggae.

Rock festivals   Spawned by the highly successful Monterey Pop Festival in June 1967, festivals began to multiply in 1968, and by the summer of '69 the sky was the limit. The Monterey Festival used as its slogan ''Music, Love and Flowers,'' and with its gate receipts (the artists were paid for expenses only) and the proceeds from a film documentary it was able to contribute $200,000 to charity. Although some attribute the rising popularity of festivals in '68 and '69 to the rise of the Yippie movement, the Black Panthers, and the SDS (Students for a Democratic Society), the festivals were huge, profit-oriented promotions, from the standpoint of both the producers and the performers. The year 1969 represented the peak and the trough of the festival scene, with Woodstock symbolizing a remarkable feeling of youthful peace-and-love sentiments, and Altamont becoming a nightmare of violence. But there were a number of festivals preceding Altamont that were hardly emblems of idealism. An Easter festival at Palm Springs erupted into a riot in which 250 were arrested and 2 were wounded. At Newport in '69, there were 300 injuries, 76 arrests, and $50,000 in property damage. A festival at Denver closed in showers of tear gas. And yet there was Woodstock at White Lake near Bethel, N.Y., where 300,000 suffered through three days of rain, mud, and inadequate facilities—without police, arrests, or casualties; there was just music and good feeling. The high hopes of the Woodstock Nation, as young people started calling themselves, exploded in less than six months. The free concert at Altamont by the Rolling Stones, with members of Hell's Angels acting as security, brought death to four from drugs and injuries, and the murder of a black. It seemed to mark the end of the youth counterculture as well as monster festivals.

See also Altamont; festivals; Isle of Wight Festival; Watkins Glen "Summer Jam"; *Woodstock Nation.*

Rock films   Among the films that use Rock music, deal with Rock artists, or are Rock-related (*see* Elvis Presley for a list of his starring films):

1955   *The Blackboard Jungle:* Bill Haley and "Rock Around the Clock" behind the credits

1956   *The Girl Can't Help It:* features Little Richard
Rock Around the Clock: Bill Haley
Rock, Rock, Rock: features Frankie Lymon, Alan Freed
Love Me Tender: Elvis Presley's first starring film
Shake, Rattle, and Roll: Fats Domino

1957   *Don't Knock the Rock:* Bill Haley, Alan Freed, Alan Dale
Mister Rock and Roll: features Alan Freed, Lionel Hampton
Rock Around the World: Tommy Steele
Rock, Pretty Baby: Sal Mineo

1958   *Go, Johnny, Go:* features Chuck Berry, Jimmy Clanton, Alan Freed, Eddie Cochran, Ritchie Valens, and the Platters
High School Confidential: Jerry Lee Lewis on the title tune
Hot Rod Gang
Let's Rock: Julius La Rosa

1960   *Take a Giant Step:* Johnny Nash

1962   *Don't Knock the Twist:* features Chubby Checker

1963   *Beach Party:* Frankie Avalon, Annette Funicello

1964   *A Hard Day's Night:* stars the Beatles; their first film
Around the Beatles: film for TV
Scorpio Rising: Rock 'n' Roll records used as soundtrack (a first), including "He's a Rebel" by the Crystals
What's Happening! The Beatles in the U.S.A.: a documentary
Lonely Boy: story of Paul Anka

1965   *Beach Blanket Bingo:* Frankie Avalon, Annete Funicello
Ferry Across the Mersey: Gerry & the Pacemakers, Cilla Black
Having a Wild Weekend: Dave Clark 5, the Animals
Help!: the Beatles
How to Stuff a Wild Bikini: Frankie Avalon, Annette Funicello
The T.A.M.I. Show: Chuck Berry, Leslie Gore, Jan & Dean, Billy J. Kramer & the Dakotas, Gerry & the Pacemakers, Marvin

Gaye, the Miracles, the Supremes, the Rolling Stones, Diana Ross, James Brown.

Charlie Is My Darling: Rolling Stones documentary

1966   *Blow-Up:* included live performance by the Yardbirds

The Big T.N.T. Show: the Ronettes, Ike & Tina Turner, the Byrds, the Lovin' Spoonful, Joan Baez, Ray Charles, Donovan, Bo Diddley, Phil Spector

You Know Something Is Happening: Bob Dylan tour with the Hawks, Johnny Cash, John Lennon. Never released, but footage used in *Eat the Document:* Bob Dylan and The Band

1967   *Don't Look Back:* Bob Dylan

Good Times: Sonny & Cher

Magical Mystery Tour: a TV film with the Beatles

Privilege

The Monkees

1968   *Elvis :* his TV comeback special

Head: Frank Zappa, the Monkees, Annette Funicello

Monterey Pop: Janis Joplin, Jimi Hendrix, the Mamas & the Papas, The Who, Otis Redding

Who's That Knocking at My Door? Rock 'n' Roll records used to comment on action

Yellow Submarine: a Beatles cartoon

The Graduate: Paul Simon songs

Wild in the Streets

1969   *Easy Rider:* scored with Rock records

Farewell of the Cream

One Plus One: the Rolling Stones

1970   *Gimme Shelter:* American tour of the Rolling Stones, including the murder of Meredith Hunter at Altamont

Let It Be: the Beatles

Performance: stars Mick Jagger

That's the Way It Is: Elvis Presley

Zabriskie Point: scored with Rock records by Kaleidoscope, Rolling Stones, The Youngbloods, The Grateful Dead, and with original music by Pink Floyd.

Woodstock: Jimi Hendrix, The Who, Santana, Ten Years After, Sly & the Family Stone, and others

1971   *Mad Dogs and Englishmen:* Joe Cocker

Soul to Soul stars Wilson Pickett, Ike and Tina Turner, Millie Bobo, Roberta Flack, Eddie Harris, The Staple Singers, The Voices of East Harlem, The Isley Brothers

Zachariah: Country Joe and the Fish, Doug Kershaw, The James Gang, New York Rock and Roll Ensemble, Elvin Jones.

1972   *Cocksucker Blues:* the Rolling Stones (unreleased)
        Concert for Bangladesh stars George Harrison, Bob Dylan, Eric Clapton, Ravi Shankar, Ringo Starr, Leon Russell.
        Elvis on Tour
        Ladies and Gentlemen: the Rolling Stones
        Super Fly: Curtis Mayfield soundtrack
1973   *American Graffiti:* Rock records soundtrack
        Godspell
        The Harder They Come: Reggae singer Jimmy Cliff, the Maytalls
        Jesus Christ Superstar
        Jonathan Livingston Seagull: score by Neil Diamond
        Let the Good Times Roll
        Live and Let Die: score by Paul McCartney
        Mean Streets: uses recordings by Marvelettes ("Please, Mr. Postman") and Johnny Ace ("Pledging My Love")
        The Naked Ape: score by Jimmy Webb
        Pat Garrett and Billy the Kid: songs and background music by Bob Dylan
        Super Fly: score by Curtis Mayfield
        Wattstax
1974   *That'll Be the Day* stars Keith Moon, Ringo Starr, and others
1975   *Stardust* stars Adam Faith, Keith Moon, and others
1976   *The Song Remains the Same:* a concert by Led Zeppelin
        Car Wash: features The Pointer Sisters
1977   *Saturday Night Fever:* music by the Bee Gees
        Americathon features Elvis Costello, Meat Loaf.
1978   *American Hot Wax:* portrayal of Rock music in 1959 and Alan Freed's contribution
        The Buddy Holly Story: his career and his songs
        Dead Man's Curve: The Story of Jan & Dean: a TV film
        FM: Linda Ronstadt, Jimmy Buffet, Steely Dan
        Grease: the film version of the Broadway hit show, with Olivia Newton-John
        I Wanna Hold Your Hand: deals with hysteria accompanying Beatles' arrival
        The Last Waltz: The Band is stage center but there are performances by Bob Dylan, Van Morrison, Eric Clapton, Neil Young, and others
        Renaldo and Clara: Bob Dylan stars and there are performances by Joan Baez, Roger McGuinn, Arlo Guthrie, Roberta Flack, Jack Elliott, and others
        Sgt. Pepper's Lonely Hearts Club Band: the Bee Gees, Peter Frampton, Aerosmith, Earth, Wind & Fire

Thank God It's Friday: Donna Summer, the Commodores, and Disco

The Wiz: the hit musical on the screen with Diana Ross and Michael Jackson

1979   *The Kids Are Alright:* a Who documentary

Quadrophenia: Peter Townshend's second opera

Rock 'n' Roll High School: the Ramones

The Rose: the Janis Joplin story starring Bette Midler

Hair: screen adaptation of Broadway "tribal love-rock musical"

1980   *The Blues Borthers:* starring the Blues Brothers, with appearances by Ray Charles, James Brown, and Aretha Franklin

Fame: Irene Cara

The Jazz Singer: starring, and songs by, Neil Diamond

One-Trick Pony: starring Paul Simon, with songs by Paul Simon

Roadie: starring Meat Loaf

Rockers: Reggae music

Urban Cowboy: songs by Jimmy Buffett, the Charlie Daniels Band, the Eagles, Dan Fogelberg, Mickey Gilley, Johnny Lee, Anne Murray, Bonnie Raitt, Linda Ronstadt/J. D. Souther, Kenny Rogers, Boz Scaggs, Bob Seger, Joe Walsh

1981   *American Pop:* an animated film by Ralph Bakshi, with the music of Bob Seger, Jim Morrison, Jimi Hendrix, Janis Joplin, and others.

Heavy Metal: an animated feature film, with the music of Black Sabbath, Blue Oyster Cult, and others.

This Is Elvis: written, produced, and directed by Andrew Solt and Malcolm Leo.

The Idolmaker: based on the career of Bob Marcucci, who managed Fabian and Frankie Avalon.

The Decline of Western Civilization: Penelope Spheeris' documentary about Los Angeles' Punk Rock scene.

Breaking Glass: a Punk Rock musical.

rocking chair hit   An out-of-date, colorful song-pluggers' term for a hit that happens by itself, permitting the publisher and his staff to sit back in their chairs and rock.

Rock Musicals and Operas

| 1967 | ***You're A Good Man Charlie Brown*** | Music and lyrics by Clark Gesner. Book by John Gordon, based on the comic strip "Peanuts" by Charles Schulz. Opened at Theatre 80 St. Marks 3/7/67. |

		Reopened at Golden Theater (1,897 performances). Original Cast album: MGM ISE 90 CX. New Original TV Cast album: Atlantic SD 7252.
1967	*Hair*	Book and lyrics by Gerome Ragni and James Rado. Music by Galt MacDermot. Off-Broadway opening: 10/29/67, Public Theater. Broadway opening: 4/28/68, Biltmore (1729 performances). Broadway Original Cast album: RCA LSO-1150; ABDI-2045, (Q); 08S-1038; OK-1038. Off-Broadway album: RCA ANL1-0986; ANS1-9086.
1968	*Your Own Thing*	Music and lyrics by Hal Hester and Danny Apolinar. Book by Donald Driver, based loosely on William Shakespeare's *Twelfth Night*. Opened at Orpheum Theater 1/13/68 (933 performances). Voted Best Musical of 1967–68 season by N.Y. Drama Critics Circle. Original Cast album:
1968	*Tommy*	Rock opera by Peter Townshend (The Who), with some material by John Entwistle, Keith Moon, Sonny Boy Williamson. First performed and released as 2-record LP by Decca in 1968. Presented at the Metropolitan Opera, New York City, in April 1970. 2 Pol. 9502; 8F-9502; CF-9502.
1968	*Catch My Soul*	A Rock version of Shakespeare's *Othello*, with Jerry Lee Lewis as Iago. Presented at the Los Angeles Music Center.
1969	*Salvation*	Music, book, and lyrics by Peter Link and C. C. Courtney. First presentation in concert form at Village Gate, spring 1969. Formal opening (off-Broadway), Jan Hus Playhouse, 9/23/69 (239 performances).

Original Cast album: Capitol Records.

1970 *The Last Sweet Days of Isaac*

Book and lyrics by Gretchen Cryer. Music by Nancy Ford.
Off-Broadway opening: 1/26/70, Eastside Playhouse (465 performances).
Original Cast recording: RCA LSO–1169.

1970 *Touch*

Music by Kenn Long and Jim Crozier. Lyrics by Kenn Long.
Book by Kenn Long in collaboration with Amy Saltz. The Country Rock musical.
Opened off-Broadway 11/8/70.
Original Cast album: Ampex records A 50102.

1971 *Godspell*

Music and lyrics by Stephen Schwartz. Book by John-Michael Tebelak. First presentation, Carnegie-Mellon Institute, Pittsburgh, Pa. New York debut, Cafe La Mama.
Formal opening (off-Broadway): Cherry Lane Theatre 5/17/71.
Original Cast album: Arista 4001; 8301–4001H; 5301–4001H.
Soundtrack album: Arista 4005; 8301–4005H; 5301–4005H.
Studio Cast album: Pickwick 3343; P8–1185.

1971 *Jesus Christ, Superstar*

Lyrics by Tim Rice.
Music by Andrew Lloyd Webber.
New York opening: 10/20/71, Mark Hellinger Theatre (720 performances).
Original Cast album: MCA 5000; T–5000; C–5000.
Soundtrack album: 2–MCA 11000; T–11000; C–11000.
Soul version Sup: M 1610.
Studio Cast album: Pickwick 3262; P 8–1124.

1971 *The Wedding of Iphigenia*

Lyrics by Gretchen Cryer.
Music by Peter Link.
Book adapted from Euripedes by Doug Dyer, Gretchen Cryer, and Peter Link.

Opened at the New York Public Theater 11/4/71 (139 performances).

1971   *Two Gentlemen of Verona*

Music by Galt MacDermot.
Lyrics by John Guare.
Adapted from the play by William Shakespeare by John Guare and Mel Shapiro.
Opened at St. James Theatre 12/1/71.
Original Cast album: ABC Records BCSY-1001 (2-record set).

1971   *Inner City*

Lyrics by Eve Merriam.
Music by Helen Miller.
Based on the book *Inner City Mother Goose* by Eve Merriam.
New York opening: Ethel Barrymore Theatre, 1971. (97 performances).
Original Cast album: RCA Victor LSO 1171.

1972*   *Grease*

Book, music and lyrics by Jim Jacobs and Warren Casey.
Off-Broadway opening: 2/14/72, Martin Eden Theatre (128 performances).
Broadway opening: 6/2/72, Broadhurst Theater.
Original Cast album: MGM 1SE-34 OC; M8H-34; M5H-34.

1972   *Don't Bother Me, I Can't Cope*

A new musical entertainment by Micki Grant.
Opened at Playhouse Theater 4/19/72.
Voted Best Musical of 1972 by Outer Circle Critics; Obie Award.
Original Cast album: Polydor PD 6013.

1972   *Pippin*

Music and lyrics by Stephen Schwartz.
Book by Roger O. Hirson.
Opened at J. F Kennedy Center, Washington, D.C., 9/20/72; Imperial Theater 10/23/72.
Original Cast album: Motown M76OL.

*When *Grease* closed on April 14, 1980, it became the longest-running show in Broadway history, with 3,388 performances. The previous title-holder was *Fiddler on the Roof,* which ran for 3,243 performances.

1975	*The Wiz*	Music and lyrics by Charles Smalls. Book by William F. Brown. Opened at Majestic Theater 1/5/75. Original Cast album: Atlantic SD 18137. Soundtrack album: MCA Records CA 2-14000.
1977	*Nightclub Cantana*	Conceived, composed, and directed by Elizabeth Swados. Opened at Top of Gate 1/9/77.
1977	*Beatlemania*	Songs written by John Lennon and Paul McCartney. Opened at Winter Garden Theater 6/16/77. Original Cast album: Arista AL 8501.
1978	*Runaways*	Written, composed, and directed by Elizabeth Swados. Opened at the New York Public Theater Cabaret 3/9/78. Original Cast album: Columbia Records 35410.
1978	*Working*	Songs by Craig Carnelia, Micki Grant, Mary Rodgers, Susan Birkenhead, Stephen Schwartz, James Taylor. Adapted by Stephen Schwartz from the book of the same name by Studs Terkel. Opened at 46th St. Theater 5/14/78. Original Cast album: Columbia Records 35411.
1978	*Evita*	An opera based on the life story of Eva Perón. Music by Andrew Lloyd Webber. Lyrics by Tim Rice. Opened in London 6/78; at Broadway Theater in New York 4/25/79. Original Cast album: MCA 2-11003.
1978	*I'm Getting My Act Together and Taking It on the Road*	Music by Nancy Ford. Book and Lyrics by Gretchen Cryer. Opened at the Public/Anspacter Theater 6/14/78.
1979	*Dispatches*	Music by Elizabeth Swados. Book and lyrics by Michael Herr.

Opened at the Public Theater Cabaret 4/18/79.

1981   *Marlowe*   A Rock musical based on the life of Christopher Marlowe. Music and lyrics by Jimmy Horowitz.
Book and lyrics by Leo Rost. Opened at the Rialto Theater 10/26/81.

1981   *Cotton Patch Gospel*   A musical entertainment by Tom Key and Russell Treyz, based on the Clarence Jordan book, *The Cotton Patch Version of Matthew and John.* Music by the late Harry Chapin. Opened at the Lambs Theater 10/81.

See also Rock operas.

Rock 'n' Roll   The role of disk jockey Alan Freed (1922–1965) of Cleveland and New York City in popularizing the phrase "Rock 'n' Roll" is well recognized. Freed is also generally credited with coining the phrase, although his priority in this respect has been disputed by Bill Haley (1925–1981) of the Comets and "Rock Around the Clock" fame. Haley based his contention on a song he wrote and recorded in 1952, "Rock-a-Beatin' Boogie," in which he used the lines "Rock, rock, rock, everybody/Roll, roll, roll, everybody."

But an examination of Blues literature reveals that the use of these two words without the ampersand dates back to the mid-1930s—and there is reason to believe that the word "rock" and the word "roll" were in use earlier as black slang referring to having a good time, partying, or having sex. In 1939 Buddy Jones recorded "Rockin' Rollin' Mama" (for String) and shouted, at one point, "I love the way you rock and roll!" In 1944 Arthur "Big Boy" Crudup, Presley's primary influence, recorded a song he titled "Rock Me, Mama" (for Victor). In 1947 Wild Bill Moore recorded "We're Gonna Rock, We're Gonna Roll" (for Savoy). During the 1950s there were at least three disks employing the words: "Rockin' and Rollin'" by Lil Son Jackson (for Imperial, 1950); "Sixty-Minute Man" by the Dominoes (for King, 1951), in which the lead-singing bass chanted "I rock 'em, roll 'em all night long"; and "All Night Long" by Muddy Waters (for Chess, 1952), which contained the lines: "Rock me, Baby, rock me all night long. . . . Roll me, Baby, roll your wagon wheel." In short, Haley cannot claim a priority in his use of the separated words "rock" and "roll."

But Alan Freed can claim that he coined the name by which teenage music became known, since he put the two words together and in 1952 changed the name of his program on Station KYW of Cleveland from

Record Rendezvous to *The Moondog Rock 'n' Roll House Party*. It was a step he took as the result of a visit to the record shop that sponsored his program: he discovered that Rhythm & Blues records were being bought by white teenagers. Since the white adaptation of R & B as R 'n' R did not occur until 1954–1956, Freed was of necessity spinning R & B disks on his show. In actuality, he called his program *Rock 'n' Roll House Party* because he was uncertain initially about how his listening audience would react to his spinning black records. They reacted very favorably, as sold-out concerts he ran, featuring black artists exclusively, quickly revealed.

The first national Rock 'n' Roll hit came in 1954 with the Crew Cuts' cover of "Sh-Boom (Life Could Be a Dream)" by the Chords. The Crew Cuts were a white group and the Chords were black. With the country's big 50,000-watt radio stations refusing to play R & B records, the Crew Cut cover went to No. 1 on Pop charts during the summer of '54. Bill Haley's "Rock Around the Clock," which served as the tocsin of the revolution, came in 1955. Elvis Presley arrived in 1956, scoring his biggest hit that year with "Hound Dog," a cover of Big Mama Thornton's R & B record of 1953.

Rock 'n' Roll, stemming from black Jump Blues, was an upending of Pop traditions that had prevailed from the 1920s on. It was a revolution in the following respects:

1. The guitar, the basic instrument of Blues and Country music, superseded the piano as vocal accompaniment, especially in its electrified form.
2. Small, electrified string combos superseded large orchestras with instrumental sections of strings, reeds, and brasses.
3. Control of Pop was taken out of the hands of major record companies, staff A & R executives, and Broadway or Hollywood music publishing companies, and vested in independent record producers.
4. Established song forms like the 32-bar chorus (AABA) gave way to odd-numbered formations, with shifting meters, radical stanza patterns, and changing time signatures.
5. Publication of the printed copy followed, rather than preceded, the recorded song. The record was the song, and the recording studio, the instrument.
6. This was the first song culture that was not only for the young but of and by the young.
7. The music was of native, black-American derivation, not European.

See also independent producer; Rhythm & Blues.

Rock 'n' Roll Recording, Best (NARAS Grammy Awards)

1959 Nat King Cole: "Midnight Flyer"
1960 Ray Charles: "Georgia on My Mind"

1961   Chubby Checker: "Let's Twist Again"
1962   Bent Fabric: "Alley Cat"
1963   Nino Tempo and April Stevens: "Deep Purple"
1964   Petula Clark: "Downtown"
1965   Roger Miller: "King of the Road"
1966   New Vaudeville Band: "Winchester Cathedral"
1967   The Beatles: "Sgt. Pepper's Lonely Hearts Club Band"
1968   5th Dimension: "Up, Up and Away"

Until the 1967 awards, the voting category for Rock 'n' Roll records was designated "Best Contemporary (R 'n' R) Performance." After 1967, "Contemporary" was taken to mean Rock 'n' Roll, and voting was done in four classifications: "Best Contemporary Male Performance," "Best Contemporary Female Performance," "Best Contemporary Vocal Group Performance," and "Best Contemporary Instrumental Performance."

See also National Academy of Recording Arts and Sciences.

Rock 'n' Roll revival   Periodically, attempts have been made to revive the early sounds of Rock 'n' Roll. At one point, Frank Zappa (b. 1940) renamed his Mothers of Invention and produced an album of songs reminiscent of the fifties with "Reuben & the Jets." This led a group of students at Columbia University to form a group called Sha-Na-Na, christened after the "doo-wop" syllables used on the Silhouettes' disk of "Get a Job." Specializing in a revival of fifties R 'n' R, they imitate the dress of mid-fifties youngsters in their live appearances—motorcycle pants, T-shirts, straight-leg jeans, gold lamé outfits. In the late sixties, Richard Nader, a New York promoter, mounted a "Rock 'n' Roll Revival Show" at Madison Square Garden in New York City, which thereafter played other cities. It included early rock 'n' rollers like Bill Haley (b. 1925) & the Comets, Chuck Berry (b. 1926), Bo Diddley (b. 1928), and Chubby Checker (b. 1941).

Rock Operas   To those who view Rock simply in terms of energy, spontaneity, and rebellion, the term "Rock opera" is a contradiction. But a few Rock groups have worked at creating more extended forms of expression, including operas. The most successful is the Who, with *Tommy* (1968), which dealt with the travail of an autistic child in a rapacious world and which actually was performed at the most prestigious opera site in the U.S.A., the Metropolitan Opera in New York City. *Quadrophenia* (1973), also a project of The Who, likewise started as a record album and was transferred to the screen in 1979. Like The Who's Peter Townshend (b. 1945), Ray Davies (b. 1944), who formed the British Kinks in the early 1960s, was a musical adventurer.

Arthur (1969) dealt with the problems of middle-class, middle-aged England. Presented on TV, it was more of a musical than an opera.

See also Art Rock; Avant-garde Rock; classical rock; Rock musicals and operas.

Rock Steady   *See* Reggae.

Rockys   Gold medallions featuring a winged nymph holding a guitar, they are given by the *Rock Music Awards* show as a supplement to the Grammys. At the first annual presentation in 1975, Joan Baez (b. 1941) received the Public Service Award for her support of nonviolent protest.

See also Grammy.

Jimmie Rodgers (1897–1933)   Country music, then known as ''hillbilly'' music, started with him and his blue yodeling. Known as the Singing Brakeman because he worked on southern railroads out of his native Meridian, Miss., for 14 years, he later was dubbed the Father of Country Music. Recording for the first time in 1927 at pioneer sessions that included the debut also of the Carter Family, he reportedly sold over 20 million records in the six-year stretch of his career. He died of tuberculosis in New York City two days after a final RCA session in May 1933, leaving a legacy of song that influenced many singers, including Ernest Tubb (b. 1914) and Howlin' Wolf (1910–1976). In 1963, he was the first performer—together with Hank Williams (1923–1953) and Fred Rose (1897–1954)—to be elected to the newly formed Country Music Association Hall of Fame. Though white and a superb yodeler, he was also a great Blues singer. Virtually all of his albums are Blues-titled: *Train Whistle Blues, Long Tall Mama Blues, The Brakeman's Blues, Travelin' Blues, Jimmie's Texas Blues, Mississippi Delta Blues,* et al.

See also or Country, or C & W; Country Blues.

Richard Rodgers (1902–1979)   A master show-composer whose career spanned six decades of the Broadway musical from *Poor Little Ritz Girl* of 1920 through *I Remember Mama* of 1979, Rodgers composed the music for 42 Broadway shows and wrote more than 1,000 songs, producing a larger number of hits and evergreens than any other show composer. In the opinion of composer/conductor/musicologist Alec Wilder, ''Rodgers' songs have revealed a higher degree of consistent excellence, inventiveness, and sophistication than those of any other whom I have studied.'' Wilder dealt analytically in his book *American Popular Song* with giants such as Jerome Kern (1885–1945), Irving Berlin (b. 1888), Cole Porter (1892–1964), Vincent Youmans (1898–1946), and George Gershwin (1898–1937) among those who were composing scores in the Golden Era of the American musical (1920s–1950s).

During his prolific career, Rodgers had two major collaborators: Lorenz Hart (1895-1943), the sophisticated cynic, and Oscar Hammerstein II (1895-1960), the sentimental humanitarian. Writing the music to which Hart fitted lyrics, but composing music to lyrics written by Hammerstein, Rodgers was innovative with both. He was just 17 when he began working with Hart and 40 when the collaboration ended, after 28 musicals and 9 motion picture scores, peaking in *Pal Joey* (1940). The shows written by Rodgers & Hart explored fresh topics: American history in *Dearest Enemy* (1925), Freudian psychology in *Peggy Ann* (1926), King Arthur's court in *A Connecticut Yankee* (1927), the world of ballet in *On Your Toes* (1936), political satire in *I'd Rather Be Right* (1937), Shakespearean comedy in *The Boys from Syracuse* (1938), classical antiquity in *By Jupiter* (1942), their last show. In show after show, the two moved steadily in the direction of the integrated musical, in which songs were not extraneous but were woven into the fabric of story, characters, and dances. Unquestionably, their most daring venture was *Pal Joey,* in which a sordid story by novelist John O'Hara brought the first anti-hero into the Broadway musical.

No Rodgers & Hart show was devoid of songs that sent the audience out of the theater whistling. Starting with "Manhattan" and "Mountain Greenery" in the Garrick Gaiety shows (two revues presented by the Theatre Guild in 1925-1926), the pair produced such beguiling hits as "I Could Write a Book," "Bewitched, Bothered and Bewildered" (both from *Pal Joey*), "This Can't Be Love," "Falling in Love with Love," "Where or When," "The Lady Is a Tramp," "My Funny Valentine," "There's a Small Hotel," "My Romance," "The Most Beautiful Girl in the World," "Little Girl Blue," "A Tree in the Park," "Where's the Rainbow?", "Thou Swell," and "My Heart Stood Still"—all songs whose very titles immediately conjure up unforgettable melodies.

The collaboration with Oscar Hammerstein II on *Oklahoma!* (1943) began what is sometimes known as the Rodgers & Hammerstein epoch in the Broadway theater. *Oklahoma!*, which racked up a whopping 2,212 performances, became the first musical to have its score recorded entirely by its original cast. While it was still playing, R & H wrote the score for the film *State Fair,* which put them in the enviable position in November 1945 of having three songs on *Your Hit Parade:* "It Might as Well Be Spring," which became the Academy Award song of the year; "That's for Me," and "If I Loved You." It was the first time in the *Parade*'s history that one team achieved such a record.

In the shows that followed, R & H explored many different backgrounds: New England in *Carousel* (1945); the world of medicine in *Allegro* (1947); a Pacific island during World War II in *South Pacific* (1949); Siam during the 1860s in *The King and I* (1951); Monterey, California's Cannery Row in *Pipe Dream* (1955); San Francisco's

Chinatown in *Flower Drum Song* (1958); and a singing Austrian family during the Nazi occupation in *The Sound of Music* (1959). Rodgers displayed an amazing skill in suggesting the sounds of the different eras and worlds without failing to produce top hit songs. All of these shows had the quality of musical plays in which the songs were an integral part of the story. *South Pacific* became only the second musical in Broadway history to receive a Pulitzer Prize. *The Sound of Music,* their last collaboration—Hammerstein died while the musical was running—won six Tony Awards.

Among the evergreens written by R & H are: "Oh, What a Beautiful Morning," "People Will Say We're in Love," "June is Bustin' Out All Over," "You'll Never Walk Alone," "Some Enchanted Evening," "Younger Than Springtime," "Hello, Young Lovers," and "My Favorite Things," as well as "You Have to be Carefully Taught" and "Getting to Know You," the latter two concerned with racial tolerance.

Rolling Stone   The name of the longest-lived and most influential Rock publication, it was launched in the fall of 1967 by Jann S. Wenner, a University of California student who wrote a Rock column for the *Daily Californian* and later was the entertainment editor of *Sunday Ramparts;* Michael Lydon, later the author of *Rock Folk* (1971) and *Boogie Lightning* (1974); and Ralph J. Gleason, long the Jazz columinist of the *San Francisco Chronicle* and the author of a number of books, including *The Jefferson Airplane.* Gleason died in 1975 at the peak of a distinguished writing career. Wenner is now editor and publisher.

The Rolling Stones   They broke into American charts the same year (1964) as The Beatles, whom they have outlived by ten years or more. Unlike The Beatles, who dissolved in April 1970, the Stones attracted young people by driving their parents up a wall. They were aggressive, vulgar, arrogant, outspoken, high-decibel in their music, censorable in their lyrics, and worked at being outrageous. Striking out at their middle-class origins, they attacked the hypocrisy and decadence of the upper classes. Exuding sexuality—"Let's Spend the Night Together" (1967)—they viewed women as sex objects even in their first No. 1 single, "(I Can't Get No) Satisfaction" (1963); also in their biggest single, "Honky-Tonk Women" (1969). Their onstage behavior was a reflection of their tough Hard Rock music, and was marked by surly looks and raunchy menacing conduct. Their sources and influences were basically R & B: Elmore James (1918–1963) was the idol of rhythm guitarist Brian Jones (1944–1969); Chuck Berry (b. 1926) was the favorite idol of lead guitarist/songwriter Keith Richards (b. 1943); their early albums abounded in R & B covers, songs, and sounds by Robert

Johnson (circa 1912–1938), Bo Diddley (b. 1928), Willie Dixon (b. 1915), Rufus Thomas (b. 1917), and others. They went through a psychedelic phase, producing *Their Satanic Majesties Request* (1967) in response to the Beatles' *Sgt. Pepper.* From 1966 to 1969, they were prevented from touring the U.S.A. as a result of drug busts, a phase which, perhaps, ended with the drug-associated death by drowning of Brian Jones—he had been replaced three weeks earlier by Mick Taylor, a former member of John Mayall's Bluesbreakers. Nineteen sixty-nine was also the year of the Altamont debacle, an event that caused them to stop performing one of their key songs, "Sympathy for the Devil" (they were playing it at the time that a black spectator, Meredith Hunter, was knifed to death). Although they had only eight No. 1 singles as against the Beatles' twenty, they had a No. 1 single and album, *Emotional Rescue,* in 1980. Their No. 1 singles were: "(I Can't Get No) Satisfaction" (1965); "Get Off My Cloud" (1965); "Paint It Black" (1966); "Ruby Tuesday" (1967); "Honky Tonk Women" (1969); "Brown Sugar" (1971); "Angie" (1973); and "Miss You" (1978).

Mick Jagger (b. 1944), co-writer with Keith Richards of their original songs, is the flamboyant lead singer, "all lips and no hips."

In 1981, fifteen yeras after they scored their first No. 1 single on American charts, the Stones toured the country to rack up one of the biggest box-office grosses of any Rock group. In the Readers' and Critics' year-end poll by *Rolling Stone* magazine, they swept every category. They were named Artist of the Year, with Bruce Springsteen, John Lennon, Stevie Nicks, and Tom Petty & the Heartbreakers scoring in that order, as well as Band of the Year. Their *Tattoo You* came in as Album of the Year, ahead of the Clash's *Sandinista!,* Reo Speedwagon's *Hi Infidelity,* Stevie Nicks's *Bella Donna,* and John Lennon and Yoko Ono's *Double Fantasy.* Their "Start Me Up" was Single of the Year, ahead of "Stop Draggin' My Heart Around," by Stevie Nicks with Tom Petty & the Heartbreakers, and Kim Carnes's "Bette Davis Eyes." Mick Jagger was named Male Vocalist of the Year, beating out Bruce Springsteen, Tom Petty, John Lennon, and Bob Seger, while Jagger and his co-writer, Keith Richard, won out as Songwriters of the Year, ahead of Bruce Springsteen and John Lennon. It was an amazing sweep, a testimonial to the group's long-lived appeal and artistry, but also a commentary on the failure of Rock to produce new charismatic figures.

Rolling Thunder Revue   A series of concerts organized by Bob Dylan (b. 1941) in which he headed a troupe that included Joan Baez and that traveled through 50 states and Canada, making it one of the major Rock events of 1976. Dylan used footage shot during the tour in his four-hour film *Renaldo and Clara.* He told the press that the idea for the film had developed simultaneously with plans for the tour. Despite the success of the tour, the film was less than successful.

See also Bob Dylan.

"romance"   In the music business, a gambit designed to curry favor. The line between "romance" and payola is a thin one. Both rituals aim at securing plays of a record, the recording of a song, or some related goal. To romance a contact is to wine and dine that contact, to supply theater tickets and seats at baseball, football, or boxing events, to remember birthdays, to provide an office car, etc. All of these gifts are given under the veil of friendship or conviviality. At what point "romance" becomes payola is moot, except perhaps when the gift is outright cash or when the cost of the gift is excessive.

romantic balladeers   After World War II, there emerged from the big Swing bands a group of solo singers—band vocalists during the Swing era—who specialized in romantic ballads. Included in the group were baritones like Perry Como (b. 1912), Frank Sinatra (b. 1915), Billy Eckstine (b. 1914), and Dick Haymes (b. 1916), and such female chirpers as Jo Stafford (b. 1920), Doris Day (b. 1922), Kitty Kallen (b. 1922), and Dinah Shore (b. 1922). With the advent of Rock, most of these balladeers disappeared from the record scene. But the Rock scene has not been devoid of singers who carry on the romantic ballad tradition. Although he became a teenage idol as a result of "covering" disks originally cut by black artists (Fats Domino's "Ain't That a Shame" and others), Pat Boone (b. 1934) was an early Rock balladeer. Later there was Sam Cooke (1935-1964) with "You Send Me." More recently, the tradition has found expression in the recordings of Engelbert Humperdinck (b. 1936), Barry Manilow (b. 1946), Neil Diamond (b. 1941), and even Billy Joel (b. 1949) in his award-winning disk of "Just the Way You Are" (1978). And where would one classify Barbra Streisand (b. 1942) if not in the romantic ballad tradition of slow, legato, tender melodies. These are sung even by Diana Ross (b. 1944) and Dionne Warwick (b. 1941) to driving Rock or R & B rhythms.

Roxy   In the 1930s, the premier movie palace in New York City, named after Samuel L. Rothafel ("Roxy"), its founder and managing director. Since 1974, it has been used as the name of the top showcase club in Los Angeles.

royalties   Payments made periodically on the basis of sales. In the early days of the century and into the R & B era, many recording artists, instead of being paid a royalty on the basis of the number of disks sold, were paid a flat fee. Black artists frequently preferred the flat fee because they were uneasy about the promises of future royalties. Entrepreneurs preferred the flat fee as a money-saving and bookkeeping-saving device. With the rise of the independent producer, royalties are paid today to those who function in this capacity as well as to the recording artist. A recording also involves royalty payments to songwriters and publishers based on the numbers sold.

See also copyright; Harry Fox agency.

rubato   A musical term derived from the Italian word meaning "robbed." Although the emphasis in *tempo rubato* is on rhythmic freedom, the player is actually stealing time from one note to extend another.

Rumba   A Latin dance imported from Cuba in the 1930s. It was made attractive to American dancers by Xavier Cugat (b. 1900), who simplified the 8/8 rhythm by converting it to a 4/4 meter:

The Rumba craze swept the U.S.A. in 1931 as the result of "The Peanut Vendor," a song imported from Cuba and recorded initially by Don Azpiazu as a "Rumba Fox Trot." As the craze grew, Cab Calloway recorded "Doing the Rumba."

Ryman Auditorium   The home of the *Grand Ole Opry* in Nashville, Tenn., for over 30 years (1943–1974), the Auditorium began as the Union Gospel Tabernacle. It was built by a roistering riverboat captain, who came originally to scoff and disrupt services conducted in downtown Nashville by the Rev. Sam Jones. The visit in 1885 resulted in such a thorough conversion that Captain Ryman began financing the building of the Tabernacle in 1889. After his death, the Union Gospel Tabernacle was renamed the Ryman Auditorium at the suggestion of the Rev. Jones. Recognized even today as one of the best concert halls in the South, with almost perfect acoustics, the Auditorium continues to be used by many performers for many occasions. But it remains the mother church of Country music, its well-worn stage bearing the historic footprints of all the Country music stars of the forties, fifties, sixties, and seventies. Since March 16, 1974, the *Grand Ole Opry* has been broadcast and telecast from Opryland, U.S.A., the $28 million entertainment complex in a 110-acre park setting. There are *Opry* shows each Friday and Saturday night. The Ryman Auditorium remains at 116 5th Avenue North.

See also Grand Ole Opry; Opryland.

S

SATB Acronym for a vocal arrangement for soprano, alto, tenor, and bass.

See also TTBB.

SESAC One of three performing-rights organizations in this country, SESAC (Society of European Songwriters, Authors, and Publishers) was established in 1931 by a group of copyright owners who chose not to join ASCAP, the performing-rights organization formed in 1914. Paul Heinecke (1885–1972) was the founder. For many years, SESAC was a publisher-oriented organization, noted primarily for its activity in the Gospel and Country music fields. Since 1973 SESAC has affiliated writers directly, and it now embraces a repertoire in the areas of Pop, Rock, R & B, Jazz, Disco, Latin, and Classical. The smallest of the three performing-rights societies, it makes payments to writers and publishers (as do ASCAP and BMI) four times a year. The payments are based on a quarterly review and analysis of each affiliate's catalog and performance activity. SESAC maintains offices in New York City (10 Columbus Circle), Hollywood (9000 Sunset Boulevard), and Nashville (the SESAC Building at 11 Music Circle South).

See also American Society of Composers, Authors, and Publishers; Broadcast Music, Inc.; performing rights.

SPEBSQSA Society for the Preservation and Expansion of Barber Shop Quartet Singing in America. In existence since 1938, the organization was founded by Owen C. Cash, an Oklahoma oilman. Headquartered in Detroit, the Society has thousands of members in chapters around the country. It runs a national championship each year, the first having been won by the Bartlesville Barflies from Oklahoma. The theme of the Society is the opening strain of "A Little Closer Harmony" by Geoffrey O'Hara (1882–1967), based on "Massa's in de Cold, Cold Ground" by Stephen Foster (1826–1864).

See also "Barbershop."

S.R.O. Abbreviation of a theatrical term, "standing room only." Also the title of a bestselling album (1966) by Herb Alpert & the Tijuana Brass.

Sacred Performance, Best (NARAS Grammy Award) *See* [Gospel] Sacred Performance, Best

336

Salsa   Uptempo, hot Latin dance music, originating in Cuba, that has been audible in the U.S.A. since the late 1960s. Akin to the funky style, Salsa (original meaning: ''sauce'') has been strongly crossed with Jazz. Among the exponents of Salsa are trombonist Willie Colon; conga player Ray Barretto, born in Brooklyn of Puerto Rican parents; flutist Johnny Pacheco, who came to notice with Charlie Palmieri's *charanga* (dance band); and pianist Eddie Palmieri, whose *Sun of Latin Music* album was the first winner of the Latin category Grammy. In ''Don't Worry 'Bout a Thing'' (1975), Stevie Wonder fused Soul and Salsa.
    See also ''funk(y).''

''Salt Peanuts'' triplet   So-called because the triplet appeared in a well-known piece of the same title by Dizzy Gillespie (b. 1917). Regarded as the Bop triplet, it is unlike the traditional triplet in that the accent falls on the middle syllable (''salt--nuts''), not on the first:

Salt Pea-nuts

Samba   The native dance of Brazil, it is played with a wire brush (in the left hand) and a mallet (in the right hand) on the snare drum, with the snares off. The rhythm is a fast 2/4 shuffle. The Samba was brought from Brazil by Carmen Miranda, who sang and danced it in a number of films in the 1940s, starting with *Down Argentine Way*. Fused with Jazz, it gave rise to the Bossa Nova.

''same ol', same ol'''   A teenage colloquialism for a routine time, day, or grind.

San Francisco bands   At its peak, the Haight-Ashbury district drew musicians from many areas, especially Chicago and Texas. By 1969 there were close to 50 San Franciso bands that had recording contracts:

Big Brother & The Holding Company (Columbia)

Blue Cheer (Mercury)

The Charlatans (a Kama Sutra single is unavailable; remnants of the group now record for Mercury)

Cleanliness and Godliness Skiffle Band (Vanguard)

Country Joe & The Fish (Vanguard)

Creedence Clearwater Revival (Fantasy)

The Electric Flag (Columbia)

Family Tree (RCA Victor)

Fifty Foot Hose (Limelight)

Flamin' Groovies (Epic)

Gale Garnett & The Gentle Reign (Vanguard, Columbia)

The Grateful Dead (Warner Bros.)

The Great Society (Columbia: two albums of early performances including Grace Slick's "Father Bruce")

Dan Hicks & His Hot Licks (Epic)

It's a Beautiful Day (Columbia)

Jade Muse (Vanguard)

Jefferson Airplane (RCA Victor)

Linn County (Mercury)

Loading Zone (RCA Victor)

Mad River (Capitol)

Melting Pot (Pulsar)

Lee Michaels (Buddah)

Buddy Miles Express (Mercury)

Steve Miller Blues Band (Capitol)

Mint Tattoo (Dot)

Moby Grape (Columbia)

Morning Glory (Mercury)

Mother Earth (Mercury)

Mount Rushmore (Dot)

Charlie Musselwhite (Vanguard)

Notes from the Underground (Vanguard)

Petrus (A&M)

The Quicksilver Messenger Service (Capitol)

Rejoice (Dunhill)

Salvation (ABC Paramount)

Savage Resurrection (Mercury)

Seatrain (A&M)

Serpent Power (Vanguard)

Sly & The Family Stone (Epic)

Sons of Champlin (Capitol)

Sopwith Camel (Kama Sutra)

Sweet Linda Divine (Columbia)

Tongue & Groove (Mercury)

Dino Valente (Epic)

West (Epic)

Womb (Dot)

The Youngbloods (RCA Victor)

San Franciso sound   It ran the gamut from the Blues of Steve Miller to the Protest Rock of Country Joe, from the screaming Blues of Janis Joplin to the Afro-Cuban Rock of Santana. It was the sound of the hippies, the freaks, and the Flower Children. But as Haight-Ashbury was the psychedelic center of the country, so Acid Rock—the psychedelic experience in words and music—was the core of the San Francisco Sound. It was a music of sliding notes, drone backgrounds, the absence of chord changes, the roar of feedback, and modal scales—delivered by the Jefferson Airplane, the Grateful Dead, Blue Cheer, the Quicksilver Messenger Service. It was also a music in which environment became a part of the aesthetic experience and not just a space in which to listen. Light shows became an integral part of the concerts at the Avalon Ballroom of Chet Helms and the Fillmores of Bill Graham. And these, too, were meant to recreate the visual and sensual experience of savoring LSD. Poster art was also an integral part of the scene, with the lettering stretched like rubber into acid-trip shapes. *Surrealistic Pillow,* the February 1967 album by the Jefferson Airplane, gave the group and the San Francisco sound national recognition.

See also Acid Rock; Flower Children; *Freak Out;* hippie; Protest Rock; San Francisco bands.

sarod   A complex East Indian string instrument whose great master (*ustad*) is Ali Akbar Khan. The sarod has 25 strings, set on a teak body with a stainless steel fretboard. Four of the strings are for melody, two are for rhythm, and four are retuned each time, according to the chosen raga. The other 15 strings are drones whose vibrations create a diffuse echo effect that made the instrument of great interest during the psychedelic period.
    See also Acid Rock.

"Sassy"   Nickname of jazz singer Sarah Vaughan (b. 1924).

"Satchelmouth," "Satchmo"   Nicknames of jazz trumpeter Louis Armstrong.
    See Louis Armstrong.

Savoy Ballroom   Torn down in 1958 to make way for a housing project, the famous Savoy Ballroom opened on March 12, 1926. The largest dancehall in Harlem, it occupied the second floor of a building that ran the full block from 140th to 141st streets on Lenox Avenue. It called itself "The World's Most Beautiful Ballroom," although Harlemites who frequented it regularly—in fact, every night of the week—came to know it as "The Track." Owner Moe Gale, later a well-known manager and music publisher, booked the Fletcher Henderson Band as the guest band for the opening, which drew a crowd of 5,000. Harlem businessman Charles Buchanan served as manager of the ballroom. During the 1920s, he inaugurated a feature known as "The Battle of the Bands," a tremendous crowd-getter. A battle of New York vs. Chicago on May 15, 1927, which pitted Fletcher Henderson and Chick Webb against King Oliver and Fess Williams, brought out the riot squad. In the 1930s, the Swing bands kept the joint bouncing as the ballroom changed its designation to "The Home of Happy Feet," apparently the result of a remark by actress Lana Turner. In this era, the most famous Battle of the Bands, attracting over 20,000, starred Chick Webb vs. Benny Goodman, whose playing of "Stompin' at the Savoy" from 1936 on spread the ballroom's fame. (Written by Andy Razaf and Edgar Sampson, "Stompin' at the Savoy" was recorded by Chick Webb in 1934 before publication, although Goodman made the hit record of it in 1936.) Such dances as the Lindy Hop, Suzy Q, Peckin' and Truckin' are all presumed to have originated at the Savoy.
    See also Harlem Renaissance; Lindy Hop; Peckin'; Suzy Q; Truckin'.

saxophone   Perhaps the main thing to be noted is that the sax was not part of the pioneer Jazz combos that came out of New Orleans. The front line was made up of cornet, trombone, and clarinet, the instruments that made up the marching bands from which Jazz evolved. The saxophone came into play among white Jazz combos that sprang up in the Midwest in the 1920s—the Austin High School Gang (of Chicago) and others. The tenor sax became the key instrument in Rhythm & Blues of the 1940s and 1950s. But the Swing bands of the 1935–45 period all had reed sections, which frequently numbered five or more saxes: alto, tenor, baritone, and bass. Charlie "Bird" Parker (1920–1955) is generally recognized as the greatest alto saxist, but one could not disregard Johnny Hodges (1906–1970), who worked with Duke Ellington, as one of the instrument's virtuosos. Among outstanding performers on the tenor sax, the following would figure: Coleman Hawkins (1904–1969), Ben Webster (1909–1973), Lester Young (1909–1959), John Coltrane (1926–1967), Sonny Rollins (b. 1929), and Stan Getz (b. 1927).

"saying something"   Body language, i.e., nonverbal communication.

scat singing   A vocal style in which a singer is imitating a freewheeling Jazz instrument through the use of nonsense syllables. "Scatting" is supposed to have had its start when Louis Armstrong (1900–1971) dropped his word-sheet during a recording of "Heebie Jeebies" in 1926 and proceeded to fill out the chorus with improvised nonsense syllables. A trio known as Lambert, Hendricks & Ross carried scat singing to a high degree of perfection. Today Ella Fitzgerald (b. 1918) is recognized as the scat singer par excellence.

Schlock Rock   A pejorative term rather than a category. Used by critics with reference to records that indulge in old-style Pop clichés, whether musical or lyrical. Although Rupert Holmes' "Escape (The Piña Colada Song)" was a No. 1 single, it was dismissed as Schlock Rock: in song structure, it followed the Tin-Pan Alley ballad, including the surprise ending. Schlock rockers claim they are resented because they are commercial.
    See also Pop Rock.

Schwann Catalog   Published in Boston, the Schwann Catalog describes itself as "a comprehensive reference guide to recorded music for the dealer in his store and the consumer in his home.'' It claims to list about 45,000 stereo LP records, 8-track cartridge tapes, and cassette tapes on about 814 record and 272 tape labels. Founded by William Schwann in 1949—he boasts an honorary doctorate from the University of Louisville's School of Music—it appears monthly in a Schwann 1 edition, which lists new records and tapes, and a Schwann 2 edition, a semiannual supplement of material that has been popular for more than two years.

score   As a verb, to arrange a work for a combination of voices and/or instruments. In the Hollywood motion picture studios, a distinction is sometimes made between the ''arranger'' and ''orchestrator''; the latter takes the score devised by the former and parcels it out to the different instruments. The copyist does the pedestrian work of extracting the parts from the score and writing a separate part for each instrument. Many Hollywood composers not only compose the background music for a film but arrange and score this music.

Score from an Original Cast Album, Best—Composer's Award (NARAS Grammy Awards)

1958	Meredith Willson: *The Music Man*
1959	Jule Styne, Stephen Sondheim: *Gypsy* Albert Hague, Dorothy Fields: *Redhead*
1960	Richard Rodgers, Oscar Hammerstein: *The Sound of Music*
1961	Frank Loesser: *How to Succeed in Business Without Really Trying*
1962	Richard Rodgers: *No Strings*
1963	Jerry Bock, Sheldon Harnick: *She Loves Me*
1964	Jule Styne, Bob Merrill: *Funny Girl*
1965	Alan Lerner, Burton Lane: *On a Clear Day*
1966	Jerry Herman: *Mame*
1967*	John Kander and Fred Ebb: *Cabaret.* A & R producer: Goddard Lieberson
1968	Galt McDermot, Gerome Ragni, James Rado: *Hair.* A & R producer: Andy Wiswell
1969	Burt Bacharach and Hal David: *Promises, Promises.* A & R producers: Henry Jerome, Phil Ramone
1970	Stephen Sondheim: *Company.* A & R producer: Thomas Z. Shepard
1971	Stephen Schwartz: *Godspell.* A & R producer: Stephen Schwartz

*From 1967 on, Grammys were awarded to the A & R producers as well as the composers.

1972   Micki Grant: *Don't Bother Me, I Can't Cope.* A & R producer: Jerry Ragavoy

1973   Stephen Sondheim: *A Little Night Music.* A & R producer: Goddard Lieberson

1974   Judd Woldin and Robert Brittan: *Raisin.* A & R producer: Thomas Z. Shepard

1975   Charlie Smalls: *The Wiz.* A & R producer: Jerry Wexler

1976   Various Composers: *Bubbling Brown Sugar.* A & R producers: Hugo & Luigi

1977   Charles Strouse and Martin Charnin: *Annie.* A & R producer: Larry Morton and Charles Strouse

1978   ——*Ain't Misbehavin'.* A & R producer: Thomas Z. Shepard

1979   Stephen Sondheim: *Sweeney Todd.* A & R producer: Thomas Z. Shepard

1980   Andrew Lloyd Webber and Tim Rice: *Evita—Premier American Recording.* A & R producer: Andrew Lloyd Webber, Tim Rice.

1981   Various Composers and Lyricists: *Lena Horne: The Lady and Her Music Live on Broadway.* A & R producer: Quincy Jones

See also National Academy of Recording Arts and Sciences.

Scoring, Academy Award for Best Musical   In the years since the Academy of Motion Picture Arts and Sciences has been giving Oscars for ''Best Musical Scoring''—the first was awarded in 1934—one man has outdistanced his competitors by a wide margin. Alfred Newman (1901–1970) collected nine Oscars from 1938 through 1967, whereas his nearest competitor, Johnny Green (b. 1908), garnered only four. Quite a number of film composers (11) have won three Oscars. The list of Oscar winners for ''Best Musical Scoring'' follows:

1934   Victor Schertzinger and Gus Kahn: *One Night of Love* (Columbia). Award presented to Columbia Music Dept., Lou Silvers, Head.

1935   Max Steiner: *The Informer* (RKO Radio). Award presented to RKO Radio Studio Music Dept., Max Steiner, Head.

1936   Erich Wolfgang Korngold: *Anthony Adverse* (Warner Bros.). Award presented to Warner Bros. Studio Dept., Leo Forbstein, Head.

1937   Universal Studio Music Dept., Charles Previn, head: *One Hundred Men and a Girl* (Universal)

1938   Alfred Newman: *Alexander's Ragtime Band* (20th Century Fox); Erich Wolfgang Korngold: *The Adventures of Robin Hood* (Warner Bros.)

1939   Richard Hageman, Frank Harling, John Leipold and Leo Shuken: *Stagecoach* (Walter Wanger–United Artists) Herbert Stothart: *The Wizrd of Oz* (Metro-Goldwyn-Mayer)

1940   Alfred Newman: *Tin Pan Alley* (20th Century Fox); Leigh Harline, Paul J. Smith, and Ned Washington: *Pinocchio* (Disney—RKO Radio)

1941   Bernard Herrmann: *All That Money Can Buy* (RKO Radio); Frank Churchill and Oliver Wallace: *Dumbo* (Disney–RKO Radio)

1942   Max Steiner: *Now, Voyager* (Warner Bros.); Ray Heindorf and Heinz Roemheld: *Yankee Doodle Dandy* (Warner Bros.)

1943   Alfred Newman: *The Song of Bernadette* (20th Century Fox); Ray Heindorf: *This Is the Army* (Warner Bros.)

1944   Max Steiner: *Since You Went Away* (Selznick-United Artists); Carmen Dragon and Morris Stoloff: *Cover Girl* (Columbia)

1945   Miklos Rozsa: *Spellbound* (Selznick-United Artists); Georgie Stoll: *Anchors Aweigh* (Metro-Goldwyn-Mayer)

1946   Hugo Friedhofer: *The Best Years of Our Lives* (Goldwyn-RKO Radio); Morris Stoloff: *The Jolson Story* (Columbia)

1947   Miklos Rozsa: *A Double Life* (Kanin-U-I); Alfred Newman: *Mother Wore Tights* (20th Century Fox)

1948   Brian Easdale: *The Red Shoes* (Rank-Archers-Eagle-Lion); Johnny Green and Roger Edens: *Easter Parade* (Metro-Goldwyn-Mayer)

1949   Aaron Copland: *The Heiress* (Paramount); Roger Edens and Lennie Hayton: *On The Town* (Metro-Goldwyn-Mayer)

1950   Franz Waxman: *Sunset Boulevard* (Paramount); Adolph Deutsch and Roger Edens: *Annie Get Your Gun* (Metro-Goldwyn-Mayer)

1951   Franz Waxman: *A Place in the Sun* (Paramount); Johnny Green and Saul Chaplin: *An American in Paris* (Metro-Goldwyn-Mayer)

1952   Dimitri Tiomkin: *High Noon* (Kramer-United Artists); Alfred Newman: *With a Song in My Heart* (20th Century Fox)

1953   Bronislau Kaper: *Lili* (Metro-Goldwyn-Mayer); Alfred Newman: *Call Me Madam* (20th Century Fox)

1954   Dimitri Tiomkin: *The High and the Mighty* (Wayne-Fellows Prod.-Warner Bros.); Adolph Deutsch and Saul Chaplin: *Seven Brides for Seven Brothers* (Metro-Goldwyn-Mayer)

1955   Alfred Newman: *Love Is a Many-Splendored Thing* (20th Century Fox); Robert Russell Bennett, Jay Blackton, and Adolph Deutsch: *Oklahoma!* (Rodgers & Hammerstein Pictures, Inc.-Magna Theatre Corp.)

1956   Victor Young: *Around the World in 80 Days* (Michael Todd Co.-United Artists); Alfred Newman and Ken Darby: *The King and I* (20th Century Fox)

1957   Malcolm Arnold: *The Bridge on the River Kwai* (Horizon Pictures-Columbia)

1958   Dimitri Tiomkin: *The Old Man and the Sea* (Leland Hayward-Warner Bros.); Andre Previn: *Gigi* (Arthur Freed Prod.-MGM)

1959 Miklos Rozsa: *Ben-Hur* (Metro-Goldwyn-Mayer); Andre Previn and Ken Darby: *Porgy and Bess* (Samuel Goldwyn Prod.)

1960 Ernest Gold: *Exodus* (Carlyle-Alpina, S.A., Prod.-United Artists); Morris Stoloff and Harry Sukman, *Song without End (The Story of Franz Liszt)* (Goetz-Vidor Pictures Prod.-Columbia)

1961 Henry Mancini: *Breakfast at Tiffany's* (Jurow-Shepherd Prod.-Paramount); Saul Chaplin, Johnny Green, Sid Ramin and Irwin Kostal: *West Side Story* (Mirisch Pictures, Inc., and B and P Enterprises, Inc.-United Artists)

1962 Maurice Jarre: *Lawrence of Arabia* (Horizon Pictures, Ltd.-Sam Spiegel/David Lean Prod.-Columbia); Ray Heindorf: *The Music Man* (Warner Bros.)

1963 John Addison: *Tom Jones* (Woodfall Prod.-United Artists-Lopert Pictures); Andre Previn: *Irma La Douce* (Mirisch-Phalanx Prod.-United Artists)

1964 Richard M. Sherman and Robert B. Sherman: *Mary Poppins* (Walt Disney Prod.); Andre Previn: *My Fair Lady* (Warner Bros.)

1965 Maurice Jarre: *Doctor Zhivago* (Sostar, S.A.-Metro-Goldwyn-Mayer British Studios, Ltd. Prod.-MGM); Irwin Kostal: *The Sound of Music* (Argyle Enterprises Prod.-20th Century Fox)

1966 John Barry: *Born Free* (Open Road Films, Ltd—Atlas Films, Ltd., Prod.-Columbia); Ken Thorne: *A Funny Thing Happened on the Way to the Forum* (Melvin Frank Prod.-United Artists)

1967 Elmer Bernstein: *Thoroughly Modern Millie* (Ross Hunter-Universal); Alfred Newman and Ken Darby: *Camelot* (Warner Bros-7 Arts)

1968 John Barry: *The Lion in Winter* (Haworth Prod.-Avco Embassy); John Green: *Oliver!* (Romulus Films-Columbia)

1969 Burt Bacharach: *Butch Cassidy and the Sundance Kid* (George Roy Hill-Paul Monash Prod.-20th Century Fox); Lennie Hayton and Lionel Newman: *Hello, Dolly!* (Chenault Prod.-20th Century Fox)

1970 Francis Lai: *Love Story* (The Love Story Company Prod.-Paramount); Beatles: *Let It Be* (Beatles-Apple Prod.-United Artists)

1971 Michel Legrand: *Summer of '42* (Robert Mulligan-Richard Alan Roth Prod.-Warner Bros.); John Williams: *Fiddler on the Roof* (Mirisch-Cartier Prod.-United Artists)

1972 Charles Chaplin, Raymond Rasch and Larry Russell: *Limelight* (Charles Chaplin Prod.-Columbia); Ralph Burns: *Cabaret* (ABC Pictures Prod.-Allied Artists)

1973 Marvin Hamlisch: *The Way We Were* (Rastar Prod.-Columbia); Marvin Hamlisch: *The Sting* (Universal-Bill Phillips-George Roy Hill Film Prod., Zanuck/Brown Presentation-Universal)

1974 Nino Rota and Carmine Coppola: *The Godfather, Part II* (Coppola Company Prod.-Paramount); Nelson Riddle: *The Great Gatsby* (David Merrick Prod.-Paramount)

1975   John Williams: *Jaws* (Universal-Zanuck/Brown Production-Universal); Leonard Rosenman: *Barry Lyndon* (Hawk Films, Ltd., Prod.-Warner Bros.)

1976   Jerry Goldsmith: *The Omen* (20th Century Fox); Leonard Rosenman: *Bound for Glory* (Bound for Glory Company Prod.-United Artists)

1977   John Williams: *Star Wars* (Lucasfilm, Ltd., Prod.-20th Century Fox); Jonathan Tunick: *A Little Night Music* (Sascha-Wien Film Prod. in association with Elliott Kastner-New World Pictures)

1978   Giorgio Moroder: *Midnight Express* (Casablanca Filmworks Prod.-Columbia); Joe Renzetti: *The Buddy Holly Story* (Innovisions-ECA Prod.-Columbia)

1979   George Dekerue: *A Little Romance* (Pan Arts Assoc. Prod.); Ralph Burns: *All That Jazz* (Columbia-20th Cent.-Fox)

1980   Michael Gore: *Fame* (MGM)

1981   Vangelis: *Chariots of Fire* (Enigma Prod. Ltd.)

second ending   The second ending of a song or instrumental, unlike the first, which involves a return to the beginning of a chorus or section, generally takes the piece to a new strain, theme, or segment, or even the end of the piece.

Pete Seeger (b. 1919)   Blacklisted for 17 years so that he could not appear even on *Hootenanny,* a TV show that took its name from a term he popularized, Pete Seeger has nevertheless enjoyed a distinguished career as songwriter, performer, and folk artist—a man who willingly made sacrifices in an effort to rid the world of poverty and injustice. Among his best-known songs are "If I Had a Hammer," "Where Have All the Flowers Gone?", "The Big Muddy," and "Turn, Turn, Turn," the last-mentioned a hit for the Byrds in 1965. In the late 1940s, he assisted Alan Lomax (b. 1915) in collecting and recording for the Archives of Folk Song at the Library of Congress. In 1940 he organized the Almanac Singers, together with Woody Guthrie (1912–1967), Lee Hays (1914–1981), and Millard Lampell. In 1949 he formed a very popular and successful Urban Folk group, The Weavers, whose recordings crossed over into Pop ("Good Night, Irene," 1950; "On Top of Old Smoky," 1951; "Tzena, Tzena, Tzena," 1950, and others). He assisted in the reorganization of the Newport Folk Festival and was on its original board of directors. In the late 1960s, his concern with the pollution of the Hudson River led to his becoming an important figure in the ecological movement. He is the author of a number of books, some autobiographical, on folk singing. The celebrated American poet Carl Sandburg dubbed him "America's tuning fork."

See also Woody Guthrie; Huddie Ledbetter; The Weavers.

segue   A direction to proceed without interruption to the next segment of a piece.

self-destruct groups   Groups or artists who make a stage-bit of destroying their instruments.
    See also The Who.

semitone   The tone at a half-step. On the piano, the interval between two adjacent notes, regardless of whether they are black or white, up or down. The interval from b to c is a semitone, as is the interval from e to f. All the other semitones on the keyboard involve a white and a black key. The semitone is traditionally the smallest interval in European music. But in music of some of the countries of the East, smaller intervals are used. At least two American avant-garde composer/musicians devised scales with smaller intervals than the semitone. They were Harry Partch (1901–1974) and John Cage (b. 1912). The former used metal and glass objects to achieve smaller intervals than the semitone while the latter employed tin cans, electric buzzers, and oscillators in his works as well as devising the "prepared piano." In bending, stretching, and "worryin'" notes, Blues singers frequently sing smaller intervals than the semitone.
    See also prepared piano; Raga Rock.

"send"   To thrill, excite, overwhelm, as in Sam Cooke's disk of "You Send Me" (1957).

"sepia"   Before black records came to be designated as Rhythm & Blues, "sepia" was used in trade papers and by record companies as a less pejorative term than "race" in designating black artists and their recordings.

serial technique   Relates to the 12-tone system of Arnold Shoenberg (1874–1951), in which the order of notes selected as a theme for a composition must be preserved, and all 12 notes of the scale must be used. Even when the notes are played backwards or upside-down, the sequence of the "note row" must be maintained in the new pattern: i.e., a–b–c–d must in retrograde become d–c–b–a; upside-down it must become c–b–a–g; and backwards, the upside-down sequence becomes g–a–b–c.

seventh chord   A chord traditionally consists of three notes, each a third a part. When a fourth note, a third above the fifth of a major or minor chord, is added, the chord becomes a seventh:

shake   Refers to a musical effect as well as a dance. A shake is a note produced with a pronounced vibrato, almost like a trill, by brass instruments. As a dance, the Shake was current from the turn of the century through the dizzy twenties; it was an exhibitionistic performance by women involving a suggestive shaking of the body. Sam Cooke (1937–1964) wrote a song called "Shake," which he recorded, and which later was used by Otis Redding (1941–1967) in almost all of his public performances as a tribute to Cooke. The "turn," another form of ornamentation, is less frequently used than the shake; it involves the two notes below the written note and a return to the written note:

"sham"   R & B jargon for the body movements of a singer while vocalizing—the hip swiveling, foot stomping, etc. Domingo Samudio (b. circa 1940), of Sam the Sham and the Pharoahs, a group that specialized in nonsense songs and dressed in mock-Arabian costumes, took his stage name from the word.

shanty   A sailor's work-song, originating in the days when ships were driven entirely by wind power or oars. Sometimes it is spelled "chantey." Typical themes include yearning for home and loved ones left behind, famous ships, and tough skippers. Unlike "forecastle songs," sung and played for pleasure in the evening in the sailors' quarters, or "fo'c'sle," chanteys were designed to make labor more pleasant. Depending on the task being performed, there were three categories: short drag ("Haul Away, Joe"), halliard ("Blow, Boys, Blow"), and capstan ("Santy Anno").
   See also Folk music.

The Sheet   In the era of *Your Hit Parade* and the No. 1 plug, The Sheet was a mimeographed report appearing daily, which listed all the songs performed the previous evening (6:00 P.M. to 1:00 A.M.) on the four major networks. This was superseded by two sheets. The Peatman, produced by a professor at City College in New York, evaluated each performance on the basis of listening-audience size. The Himber, produced by a former bandleader, weighted each plug on the basis employed in estimating fees for film uses of a song—whether it was vocal or instrumental, commercial or sustaining.

See also No. 1 plug; Peatman; *Your Hit Parade.*

"Sheik of the Shake"   Cognomen for R & B balladeer Chuck Willis (1928–1958), who was also known as "King of the Stroll."

shekere   *See* Latin rhythm instruments.

shindig   A gathering, party, event—sometimes used in a pejorative sense.

Shindig   An ABC–TV network Rock show of the 1960s (*Hullabaloo* was on NBC-TV). Bobby Sherman (b. circa 1944), king of the bubble-gum crowd, was a regular. Freddie & the Dreamers, an English group, introduced the Freddie on the show in 1965. When Bonnie & Delaney were part of the Shindogs, together with arranger/instrumentalist Leon Russell (b. 1941), they appeared on *Shindig*.

"shit"   Performers' term for a hit single. Also a term for heroin and other illegal narcotics.

Shock Rock   A number of Rock groups go beyond spectacle into displays of violence and sex, with the intent of shocking the spectators. Consider Iggy Pop raking his chest with a drumstick until he bleeds, or diving head-first into an audience; Alice Cooper, a man dressed in pantyhose and black leotard, dancing with a boa constrictor, mock-slaughtering toy dolls, killing rabbits and skewering chickens, and having himself "electrocuted"; The Who, smashing microphones, destroying amplifiers, shattering their guitars; the Move, demolishing TV sets; the Velvet Underground, who toured with Andy Warhol's Total Environment Show, revelling in whippings; the Nice, resorting to whipping, burning, and stabbing, with Keith Emerson attacking his organ, beating it, kicking it, and finally ripping its insides out. Many viewers found these displays infantile attempts at showmanship. By 1980 Alice

Cooper had given up his onstage shock theatrics for a more musical presentation. But by then a New York group, The Plasmatics, featured a topless singer who bumped and ground her way around the stage until she erotically dismembered a guitar with a chainsaw and smashed a TV set with a sledgehammer. As the climax to this show of sex and violence, the Plasmatics blew up a Cadillac.

See also Glitter Rock; Theater Rock.

shout   One of two types of spirituals. There were sorrow songs, elegiac lamentations over the lot of the slaves, and shouts, songs of religious jubilation. In the R & B years, the forties and fifties, "shout" became a verb and referred to the style of singing that departed from the moaning, sighing, and crying of Country Blues. Singers like Joe Turner (b. 1911), Big Mama Thornton (b. 1926), and Wynonie Harris (1915-1969) "shouted" the Blues.

See also Blues; Classic Blues; Country Blues.

show tune   In 1952, a young, big-voiced baritone, Eddie Fisher (b. 1928), recorded a romantic ballad entitled "Wish You Were Here." The title song of a faltering musical with a score by Harold J. Rome (b. 1908), it became a million-record seller. Its impact on disk was so great that the show, which had been in danger of closing, went on to run for 598 performances.

There are not too many instances of a hit song saving a musical. But the "Wish You Were Here" incident points up a characteristic of musicals from the 1920s into the 1950s that disappeared with the rise of the so-called integrated musical. During those years, what a show composer was expected to contribute to a musical was at least one big hit song—one whose appeal was so immediate that an audience would leave the theater humming or whistling it and forthwith rush to music and record stores to purchase it. The top group of show composers of those years—Richard Rodgers (1902-1979), Cole Porter (1891-1964), George Gershwin (1898-1937), Vincent Youmans (1898-1946), Jerome Kern (1885-1945), Rudolf Friml (1879-1972), Sigmund Romberg (1887-1951), Frederick Loewe (b. 1901), Frank Loesser (1910-1969), Kurt Weill (1900-1950)—seldom failed. So strong was the demand for a hit song that on occasion songs by outside composers were interpolated, and sometimes songs were introduced that had little or nothing to do with a show's plot, characters, or situation.

The top show tunes of the 1920s to 1950s remain today a repository of evergreen melodies, having supplied the Big Baritones, the Big Bands, and, through the years, Jazz artists with a rich repertoire whose appeal has not diminished with time. Show writers like Rodgers & Hart (*A Connecticut Yankee*), Rodgers & Hammerstein (*Oklahoma!* and *The King and I*), Jerome Kern (*Showboat*), Cole Porter (*Kiss Me, Kate*), George Gershwin (*Of Thee I Sing* and *Funny Face*), and Frank Loesser (*Guys and Dolls*) occasionally created a score in which virtually every song, not only the romantic ballads but the comedy material and group songs, were gems of hit caliber.

Since the development of the musical play, as distinguished from the musical comedy, songs are considered vehicles that must relate and contribute to the development of character, situation, theme, and story line. Accordingly, it has become more and more difficult for even the most talented composers to produce hits, and many of the shows of the sixties and seventies, traditional as well as Rock, are without a single memorable melody. Even so gifted, versatile, and prolific a tunesman as Stephen Sondheim (b. 1930), with an impressive list of award-winning musicals, can claim only one real hit song, "Send in the Clowns."

See also George Gershwin; Musical, Tony Awards for Best; Richard Rodgers.

"shuck"   *See* "jive."

Shuffle   A type of black dance. Also, a rhythm pattern related to eight-to-the-bar Boogie-Woogie. There are still eight notes, but instead of being of equal duration, half are longer and half are shorter, producing a limping or hopping kind of rhythm. This results from short 16th notes alternating with dotted 8ths (three 16th notes). Musically, it takes the following shape:

sideman   A musician can be in the front line of a combo. But if he is not the leader, he is a "sideman."

signature   A song or instrumental used to identify a show; it is played at the beginning and end of the program. Occasionally the song is sung, as on *Happy Days;* most frequently, it is heard as an instrumental. In the era of the Big Bands, each had its own identifying signature. Opening and closing signatures are today generally called "themes."

"signify"   From the Blues, to brag or boast, as in the well-known "Signifying Monkey" song.

"The Silver Fox"   Singer/pianist Charlie Rich (b. 1932), winner in 1973 of three awards of the Country Music Association: Best Song, Best Record, and Best Male Artist, all for the song "Behind Closed Doors."

Frank Sinatra (1915–   )   There have been three Pop Explosions in our time: one when the Beatles emerged in 1964; another with the rise of Elvis Presley in 1956; and the earliest, the appearance as a solo singer of Sinatra in 1944. In each instance, what started as a musical event immediately turned into a cultural, psychological, generational upheaval. Of these charismatic figures, Sinatra has been able to sustain his career longer than the others, and longer than any singer in Pop music. While this is partly the result of one of the keenest senses of publicity in the business, it is basically the product of an enormous talent as an actor and singer. Sinatra brought to Pop singing three qualities: a feeling of involvement; a respect and a nose for good lyrics; and a deep-seated romanticism. Selecting songs that were expressive of his frame of mind, he was the autobiographical singer long before it became fashionable. A master of exquisite phrasing, he was also virtually the only Pop singer who sang consonants, especially terminal consonants. Although he announced his retirement in 1971, he returned as a performer on TV in mid-'73. Since then he has pursued an unabating career of personal appearances, record making, filmmaking, and performances at charity events. In 1980 he was even able to put a single record on the charts, his toast to "New York, New York." He remains a giant figure on the entertainment scene.

singer-songwriter   There were no "chirper-cleffers," to use *Variety*'s colorful term, during the Tin-Pan Alley eras of Al Jolson (1886–1950), Bing Crosby (1904–1977), Perry Como (b. 1913), and Frank Sinatra (b. 1915). The songwriter wrote and the performer sang. The Rock era largely destroyed the division of labor, eventually producing self-contained units in which writing, publishing, recording, managing talent, and booking appearances were all embraced within a single setup like Motown Records, Philadelphia International, or all the artist-owned publishing companies and record labels.

The major development of singer-songwriters occurred in the 1960s after the appearance of Bob Dylan (b. 1941) and the Beatles, the former motivating followers to explore song lyrics as poetry and the latter arousing a spirit of innovation and experimentation in Rock groups. Among the singer-songwriters who appeared in the wake of the two, there were Paul Simon (b. 1941), Janis Ian (b. 1950), Joni Mitchell (b. 1943), Jackson Browne (b. 1940s), Laura Nyro (b. 1947), Randy Newman (b. 1943), Neil Young (b. 1945), and others. Although all of these recorded their own songs, and occasionally produced a hit record, many of these (except for Paul Simon and Neil Young) achieved hit singles through other recording artists. Even Bob Dylan's biggest hits came through Peter, Paul & Mary ("Blowin' in the Wind") and the Byrds ("Mr. Tambourine Man"). Laura Nyro's hit singles were produced by the Fifth Dimension ("Stoned Soul Picnic") and Barbra Streisand ("Stoney End"). With the exception of Randy Newman, who was a superb satirist, most of the singer-songwriters used their songs as vehicles of personal expression and self-exploration.

Although the singer-songwriter category is viewed as a development of the 1960s, there were singer-songwriters in the early days of Rock 'n' Roll. Carl Perkins (b. 1932) wrote the songs he recorded ("Blue Suede Shoes," "Matchbox," etc.). So did Paul Anka (b. 1941), starting with his first record release ("Diana"). Neil Sedaka (b. 1939) and his co-writer, Howard Greenfield (b. 1938), began by writing songs for others ("Stupid Cupid" for Connie Francis), and Sedaka went on to record only his own songs. The poet laureate of the Rock 'n' Roll generation, Chuck Berry (b. 1926), was a singer-songwriter from his first hit, "Maybellene."

"The Singing Brakeman"   *See* Jimmie Rodgers.

Singing Cowboys   A genre of male singers of the thirties and forties who dressed in cowboy outfits, carried six-shooters, sang frequently while riding on horseback, and appeared in what were known in Hollywood as "horse operas." The best-known were Gene Autry (b. 1907) and Roy Rogers (b. 1912). Autry, the first cowboy singing star in films, starred in almost 100 motion pictures and scored with such "western" songs as "Tumbling Tumble Weeds," which was also the title of his first starring feature film; "Deep in the Heart of Texas"; and "Don't Fence Me In." Roy Rogers, who worked originally with the California-based Sons of the Pioneers, became known as the King of the Cowboys. His white horse, Trigger, rose to renown with him, as he also appeared in about 100 films and popularized a long list of western ballads, including "Along the Navajo Trail," "A Gay Ranchero," and others.

Two country styles that evolved in the wake of the Singing Cowboys were Western Swing, as performed by Bob Wills and His Texas Playboys, and Spade Cooley; also the Texas honky-tonk dance music of Lefty Frizzell. In a new album issued in the Spring of 1982, Rex Allen, Jr., nostalgically celebrates the genre of The Singing Cowboy, as his album is titled.

See also honky tonk; Western Swing.

"The Singing Fisherman"   Nickname of country singer/guitarist Johnny Horton (1926–1960), who earned the title because of his dedication to fishing, and whose career was cut short after an auto accident soon after his disk of "Battle of New Orleans" became a worldwide hit.

"The Singing Ranger"   That was the way Hank Snow (b. 1914) was billed on his first radio show over Station CHNS of Halifax, Nova Scotia, and on one of his first RCA Victor hits ("Marriage Vows" in 1949). A regular of the *Grand Ole Opry* from 1950 on, he produced hit Country records into the 1960s, and is remembered for "I'm Moving On" (1950) and "Rhumba Boogie" (1951), among other No. 1 disks.

Sing Out!   A New Left journal, which, along with *Broadside,* published the topical and protest songwriters of the 1960s. Among those whose songs appeared in its pages: Bob Dylan (b. 1941), Phil Ochs (1940–1976), Tom Paxton (b. 1937), Peter La Farge (1931–1965), Eric Andersen (b. 1943), Buffy Sainte-Marie (b. 1941), Len Chandler (b. 1935), and others.
See also message songs.

sitar   Played with a wire plectrum, worn on the performer's right forefinger, the sitar is a long-necked lute with resonators on each end of dried gourds, a wide fretboard, and 16 to 20 movable frets, which are adjusted to the varying arrangement of notes within a given raga, or mode. Although the instrument may have four to seven strings, the melody is played on one, with the others serving to provide a sympathetic drone accompaniment. As in the case of the sarod, the vibration of the drones produces an attractive, almost hypnotic effect—which is what made it so popular at the height of the psychedelic craze in 1966–1967. In its native habitat, sitar music is wholly improvised, with concerts lasting for many hours. The most popular instrument of northern India, its great master is Ravi Shankar, who had a dozen popular albums selling in America, including one with Classical violinist Yehudi Menuhin. At the height of the sitar craze, Shankar gave a course in the instrument at New York's City University; Ali Akbar Khan gave a course at the University of California in Berkeley, which was taken by Jerry Miller of Moby Grape; and guitarist Vincent Bell developed an electric sitar. The electric instrument looks like an ordinary electric guitar and is tuned like one; it has the sitar's typical high-pitched whine and its drone effects, and was used by the Animals (*Monterey*), Richie Havens (b. 1941) on "Run Shaker Life" (1968), and others.
    The interest of Rock performers in the sitar began with the Byrds, who used it on their '66 hit "Eight Miles High," and who introduced it to George Harrison (b. 1943). Harrison anticipated the Byrds in actually employing the sitar on a recording (the Beatles' 1965 rendition of

"Norwegian Wood" in *Rubber Soul*). The Rolling Stones were quick to jump on the bandwagon in their record of "Paint It Black" (1966). Traffic used in on records in which Dave Mason (b. 1946) is on guitar.

See also Indian influence on Rock; Raga Rock.

"sitting in"   During the thirties and forties, it was commonplace for Jazz musicians to "sit in" with groups of which they were not a part. This was especially true of New York City's Swing Street (52nd Street), where musicians playing in one club would cross the street and play with another combo. Once when trombonist Jack Teagarden (1905–1964) was taken to task by a club owner for sitting in across the street more frequently than he was playing at the club where he was starred, he replied: "Jes' bein' neighborly." "Sitting in" differed from the "jam session" in that the latter involved musicians coming together for an evening of improvisation, while the former involved musicians playing for part of an evening with a resident group. The interloper's improvisational skill was tried in this situation. The difference was in one additional player interacting with a group versus many interacting with each other. The practice of sitting in disappeared partly because of developments in Jazz, which split the performers into different if not warring schools, and partly because of the opposition of the New York Musicians Union to providing free talent.

The practice of sitting in was revived to a degree in the San Francisco area when groups were interested in adding players. In 1970, for example, keyboard performer/songwriter Merl Saunders sat in with a trio playing at the Matrix and became part of the group. When multi-instrumentalist Tom Fogerty (b. 1941) was becoming disaffected with Creedence Clearwater Revival, he began sitting in with the Matrix group, and after leaving the Revival in 1971, he joined it.

See also 52nd St.; jam session.

Ska   An adaptation of New Orleans R & B: horns riffing on the off-beat of R & B shuffle. Earliest example: "My Boy Lollipop" by Millie Small, a hit in 1964. More recent: *Too Much Pressure* by the Selecters.

See also Reggae.

Skiffle   It has been variously described as British Rockabilly, a fusion of R & B and Country music, British Bluegrass, and a tame brand of Pop Folk. It had its vogue in England in the years when the Beatles were in secondary school; in fact, the Quarrymen, an early group that John Lennon (1940–1980) played with, was a Skiffle group. The vogue has been traced to the spread of coffee shops in London, which provided a locale for performances by groups employing homemade instruments like jugs, washboards, banjos, and even combs. The incentive was to play Blues and Jazz as they had been performed by poor American blacks in the early days. The word "skiffle" was, in fact, a black American term that was used as far back as the 1920s: Country Blues singer Charlie Spanel recorded "Hometown Skiffle" in 1929 for Paramount, employing homemade instruments.

The Skiffle craze in England is traced to the Ken Colyer Band, with whom Lonnie Donegan (b. 1931) played banjo. In 1953 Lonnie & His Skiffle Group played a concert at the Royal Festival Hall in London. Included in the program was an adaptation of Leadbelly's tune "Rock Island Line," which, when released as a single in the U.S.A. in 1955, became an American as well as a British hit. A second Skiffle hit climbed American charts in 1957 with an adaptation of Elizabeth Cotten's "Freight Train" by the Charles McDevitt Skiffle Group, vocal by Nancy Whiskey. This disk was quickly covered by such American artists as Margie Rayburn, Dick Jacobs, and Rusty Draper. The following year, Johnny Otis (b. 1921) wrote "Willie and the Hand Jive" in an effort to capitalize on England's Skiffle craze. The song muffed in England but became a hit in the U.S.A.

Skiffle was to British rockers what R & B became to American rockers. Members of the Rolling Stones, Shadows, Freddie & the Dreamers, Gerry & the Pacemakers, Incredible String Band, Kinks, and other British groups started out by playing in Skiffle bands. Skiffle possessed a cheerful, uptempo quality, a light Country sound, and a fast shuffle beat.

See also Bluegrass; Blues, British; jug band; Shuffle; spasm band; washboard band.

Skinhead haircut   A hairdo favored by Punk Rock fans. When alto saxist Eddie Vinson (b. 1917) shaved his head, they called it and him Cleanhead.

See also Mohawk haircut; Punk Rock.

Skinheads   "Punk Rock groups don't shock anymore," said a member of Blitz. "Skinhead is more powerful." Easily identified by their clean-shaven heads or close-cropped hair, skinheads are known for "Paki bashing," i.e., beating up Asians. Skinhead lyrics, as in the Clash's "White Riot" of 1977, reflect the racial tension: "Black people gotta lot a problems/But they don't mind throwing a brick. . . . Wanna riot, white riot, riot of me own." The Oi groups appear to represent the most aggressive fringe of the Skinheads. Meaning "hey" in London cockney, Oi has its racist, heavy, work-boot adherents in angry groups like Blitz, 4-Skins, and Infa-Riot. With a following in unemployed, white, working-class youngsters, they express an Us-against-the-world outlook.

Riots and violence are not unusual accompaniment to concerts by such groups, usually as a result of conflict between whites and Asians (or blacks). Among the songs, replete with images of violence, expressive of Oi attitudes, are "Someone's Gonna Die," "Riot, Riot," and "Nation on Fire" (Blitz). An appearance of the 4-Skins in '81 at the Hambrough Tavern in a London suburb sent 61 policemen to the hospital and left the Tavern a pile of smoldering ashes. The so-called Two-Tone movement, made up of bands that are racially mixed (The Specials, English Beats, et al.), represents an effort to reduce racial tensions. But all groups, including local Reggae bands, are united in their opposition to the government and their resentment against police harassment and brutality. "Do Nothing" by the Specials, "Sonny's Lettah" by Linton Kwesi Johnson, "Police and Thieves" by Junior Murvin—all voice angry feelings against the police. The Clash, who revived "Police and Thieves" in '77, have even advocated rebellion in "White Riot" as a response to the poverty, unemployment, and inner-city decay out of which all these groups spring.

See also Oi; Two-Tone movement.

Slack-Key   A style originating in Hawaii, audible on some of Ry Cooder's recordings.

Slam Dancing (Slamming)   An aggressive form of dancing that originated in connection with the Punk Rock movement in Los Angeles. "You bounce up and down, nice and light/You move to the left and you move to the right/Then smash the guy near you with all your might." A variation, after you have done some up-and-down bouncing, is suddenly to lunge full-tilt across the floor and knock other dancers off their feet.

See also Mohawk haircut; Punk Rock; Skinhead haircut; Skinheads.

slave songs   *See* arhoolie; spirituals.

"sleeper"   Whether it started in the music business or not, "sleeper" is now used generally to mean a song, record, film, play, book, or even a political candidate that unexpectedly develops into a hit or winner.

slide guitar   Duane Allman (1946–1971) was known for his skill as a slide guitarist, evidence of which is provided by his playing on Eric Clapton's "Layla" in the album of the same title by the short-lived group Derek & the Dominoes, of which Clapton (b. 1945) was then a member.

See also bottleneck guitar.

slip horn   Swing term for the trombone.

"Slowhand"   An early nickname for guitarist Eric Clapton (b. 1945), who worked with the Yardbirds, John Mayall's Bluesbreakers, Cream, Blind Faith, Delaney & Bonnie, and Derek & the Dominoes—and scored a hit on his own with a Reggae-inspired song, "I Shot the Sheriff" in 1974. He called himself "Slowhand" because he imitated B. B. King's technique of holding a note, bending and shaking it before sliding to the next note—a technique that involved little hand motion.

"smack"   Slang for heroin.

Ed Smalls' Paradise   Located at 2294 1/2 Seventh Avenue in New York City, the club lasted from October 26, 1925, into the 1960s, making it the longest-operating night spot in Harlem. In the early years, it featured singing and dancing waiters. Throughout the twenties, thirties, and forties, its talent included an array of the most accomplished jazzmen of the day. In the fifties, after the advent of Rock 'n' Roll, Red Prysock led an aggregation, and in the sixties, after Ed Smalls sold the Paradise to basketball star Wilt Chamberlain, Arthur Prysock (b. 1929) and Ray Charles (b. 1930) made appearances. In the seventies, when one of the owners was Charles Huggins, the husband of singer Melba Moore, it was the scene of Disco dancing. After being closed for a year, it was bought by Carl Yearwood, a West Indian who has been a New Yorker since 1951 and who is trying to make it a community-oriented spot, including community theater. In the heyday of the Harlem Rush, or Renaissance, Smalls' Paradise was one of the three hottest uptown spots, competing with Connie's Inn and the Cotton Club.
    See also Connie's Inn; Cotton Club; Harlem.

Bessie Smith (1894–1937)   She called herself the Empress of the Blues; others called her the greatest of all female Blues singers, and Columbia Records issued a four-volume anthology titled *The World's Greatest Blues Singer*. Singing on the streets of her native Chattanooga, Tenn., as a child of eight, she paid her dues working in minstrel shows, especially Ma Rainey's Rabbit Foot Minstrels. She began recording in 1923 after the success of "Crazy Blues," a record by Mamie Smith (1890–1946, no relation), prompted Columbia's recording director, Frank Walker, to seek out an authentic Country Blues singer in contrast to Mamie Smith's Urban blues. From 1923 to 1933, Bessie Smith recorded 180 songs, which, with the exception of the soundtrack of a 1929 two-reeler film, *St. Louis Blues,* constitute her entire record output.

Although these were the years when all the record labels were issuing disks by the outstanding Blues singers of the day, no one received the renown of the Empress. Adulation was showered upon her not only for the richness of her voice but for the depth of feeling which she imparted to her renditions. The Great Depression brought an end to the vogue of the Blues, a situation which Bessie's addiction to alcohol did not improve. Although in her heyday she commanded as much as a thousand dollars a record date, in 1933, when producer John Hammond arranged a session to assist her, "she was virtually penniless and completely depressed," Hammond has said; the company would pay her only a flat $50 a side.

Most of her recordings were made with the piano accompaniment of Jazz/Blues greats like Fletcher Henderson (1898–1952), Clarence Williams (1893–1965), and James P. Johnson (1891–1955)—later abetted by small combos. But in what turned out to be her final session in 1933, she was accompanied by an all-star Swing group, including Benny Goodman (b. 1909). Four years later she was dead, dying in an auto crash that prompted the first play written by Pulitzer Prize-winning playwright Edward Albee, *The Death of Bessie Smith*. For many years, it was believed that Bessie had died needlessly as the result of being refused admission by a white Mississippi hospital; but recent investigation has established that she was given first-aid by a passing physician and that her injuries were so severe she could not be saved.

"Smoky Mountain Boys"   *See* Roy Acuff.

Sob Rock   An invented category; really just a descriptive term for records on which the wailing of the Blues verges on tears. On the Dominoes' 1952 disk of "Have Mercy, Baby," Clyde McPhatter (1931–1972) reportedly broke into tears at the end of the disk. He also seemingly wept his way through the group's follow-up disk, "The Bells."

society band   An orchestra, varying in size, that plays for society dances, weddings, bar mitzvahs, debutante's coming-out parties, and other social affairs. The lead instrument always is the tenor sax. The band usually plays 20- or 30-minute segments, segueing from chorus to chorus of well-known Pop standards, show tunes, and film songs. Tempo and volume are designed to appeal to middle-aged dancers, generally doing the Fox-Trot. If there is no relief band to play Rock or Latin, society bands interpolate an occasional number addressed to the younger members of the crowd. In New York City, for many years, bandleader Meyer Davis was among a small group that monopolized the society band business; he had numerous units working for him under the emblem of a Meyer Davis band.

See also Fox-Trot; tenor sax.

Society of European Songwriters, Authors, and Composers   *See* SESAC.

sock cymbal   *See* high hat cymbal.

"Sock It to Me"   Title of a record by Syl Johnson in 1967 and the basis of a craze started by Frank Crocker, program director of WBLS-FM in New York City.

Soft Rock   Just as R & B had a "shout" strain (Big Mama Thornton, b. 1926; Joe Turner, b. 1911; Little Richard, b. 1935) and a ballad strain (Dinah Washington, 1924–1963; Bull Moose Jackson, b. 1919; Charles Brown, b. 1920), so Rock 'n' Roll had Hard and Soft strains. Johnny Ace (1929–1954) was an early proponent of Soft Rock 'n' Roll, as was Chuck Willis (1928–1958). The advent of the Beatles, as well as the turn to Rock of folk artists like Bob Dylan (b. 1941) and the Byrds, undoubtedly gave impetus to the rise of Soft Rock. In 1965–1966 a number of solo artists and groups emerged, all offering a gentler, more melodious type of Rock. Among these were Simon & Garfunkel ("The Sounds of Silence"), The Lovin' Spoonful ("Do You Believe in Magic?" and "Summer in the City"), The Mamas and the Papas ("California Dreaming," and "Monday, Monday"), Donovan (b. 1946, "Sunshine Superman" and "Mellow Yellow"), and Tim Hardin (b. 1940). Soon there were others: Scott McKenzie, ("San Francisco: Be Sure to Wear Some Flowers in Your Hair"), Procol Harum ("A Whiter Shade of Pale") Bread ("Make It with You," "If," "Baby, I'm-a Want You"), Loggins & Messina ("Your Mama Don't Dance"), Carole King (b. 1942, *Tapestry*), Brewer and Shipley ("One Toke Over the Line"), James Taylor (b. 1948, *Sweet Baby James*), and Three Dog Night ("One").

To some critics, this mild variety, lacking the energy, drive, amplified vitality, and aggressiveness of Hard Rock, is no Rock at all. Nevertheless, it has the big beat of the more raucous variety. And as the seventies moved into the eighties, Soft Rock seemed in the ascendancy. Among its many adherents, some verging on Schlock Rock, were the Eagles, Supertramp, Dr. Hook, Styx, Cheap Trick, Christopher Cross, Billy Joel, Bob Seger & the Silver Bullet Band, and Knack, not to mention Paul McCartney & Wings.

See also Pop Rock.

SoHo   An area on Manhattan's lower East Side, which has, since the advent of Rock, become the scene of a hip community of experimental artists from all disciplines; also of clubs like the Mudd and galleries that showcase works created by these artists. In the recent past, The Kitchen has become the most important alternative space for experimental music, including No Wave Rock.

SoHo, an acronym for *So*uth of *Ho*uston Street, is an associative reference to the similarly named, bohemian district in London.

See also No Wave; Punk Rock.

Solovox   An electronic instrument, mounted on or under a piano and capable of producing one note at a time on a keyboard like that of a piano. Stops or settings, as on an organ, whose tone it resembles, make it possible to alter the tonal quality.

Song of the Year, Best (NARAS Grammy Awards)

1958	"Nel Blu Dipinto Di Blu" (Volare): Domenico Modugno
1959	"The Battle of New Orleans": Jimmy Driftwood
1960	"Theme from *Exodus*": Ernest Gold
1961	"Moon River": Henry Mancini, Johnny Mercer
1962	"What Kind of Fool Am I?": Leslie Bricusse, Anthony Newley
1963	"The Days of Wine and Roses": Henry Mancini, Johnny Mercer
1964	"Hello, Dolly!": Jerry Herman
1965	"The Shadow of Your Smile" (Love Theme from *The Sandpiper*): Johnny Mandel, Paul Francis Webster
1966	"Michelle": Paul McCartney, John Lennon
1967	"Up, Up and Away": Jimmy Webb
1968	"Little Green Apples": Bobby Russell
1969	"Game People Play": Joe South
1970	"Bridge over Troubled Water": Paul Simon
1971	"You've Got a Friend": Carole King
1972	"The First Time Ever I Saw Your Face": Ewan MacColl
1973	"Killing Me Softly with His Song": Charles Fox, Norman Gimbel
1974	"The Way We Were": Marvin Hamlisch, Marilyn and Alan Bergman
1975	"Send in the Clowns": Stephen Sondheim
1976	"I Write the Songs": Bruce Johnston
1977	"Love Theme from *A Star Is Born*": Barbra Streisand and Paul Williams
1978	"You Light Up My Life": Joe Brooks
	"Just the Way You Are": Billy Joel
1979	"What a Fool Believes": Kenny Loggins, Michael McDonald

1980 "Sailing": Christopher Cross
1981 "Bette Davis Eyes": Donna Weiss and Jackie DeShannon

See also National Academy of Recording Arts and Sciences.

Song of the Year Awards (NMPA) Operating on the principle that the song is the foundation of the music business—publishing, recording, and performing—the National Music Publishers Association (NMPA) has established a series of annual awards in eight categories plus a Song of the Year winner. The honored songs are chosen in a three-step secret ballot process by members of the NMPA. Winners of the first annual balloting, held in 1980, were as follows:

1979	*Song of the Year*	"The Gambler" by Don Schlitz (Writers Night Music); tied with "You Needed Me" by Randy Goodrum (Chappell & Co. and Ironside Music).
	Broadway Song of the Year	"Don't Cry for Me, Argentina" (*Evita*) by Andrew Lloyd Webber and Tim Rice (Leeds Music Corp., MCA).
	Country Song of the Year	"The Gambler" by Don Schlitz (Writers Night Music).
	Disco Song of the Year	"I Will Survive" by Dino Fekaris and Freddie Perren (Perren-Vibes Music).
	Easy Listening Song of the Year	"You Don't Bring Me Flowers" by Neil Diamond and Alan and Marilyn Bergman (Stonebridge Music and Threesome Music Co.).
	Gospel Song of the Year	"Will the Circle Be Unbroken?" by A. P. Carter (Peer International Corp.).
	Latin Song of the Year	"Si, Pero No" by Moncada and Paco Cepero (Ediciones April Music, SRL, Spain).
	Movie Song of the Year	"Last Dance" (*Thank God It's Friday*) by Paul Jabara (Primus Artists Music, Olga Music, and Rick's Music).
1980	*Song of the Year*	"The Rose" by Amanda McBroom (Copyright in dispute)
	Broadway Song of the Year	"The Colors of My Life" (*Barnum*) by Cy Coleman and Michael Stewart (Notable Music).

	Country Song of the Year	"Looking for Love" by Wanda Mallett, Patti Ryan, and Bob Morrison (Southern Nights Music).
	Easy Listening Song of the Year	"Woman in Love" by Barry and Robin Gibb (Stigwood Organization/Unichappell Music).
	Gospel Song of the Year	"How Great Thou Art" by Stuart K. Hine (Manna Music).
	Latin Song of the Year	"No Me Lo Digan" by Bobby Capo (Peer International Corp.).
	Movie Song of the Year	"The Rose" by Amanda McBroom (Copyright in dispute).
	Pop Song of the Year	"Lady" by Lionel B. Richie, Jr. (Brockman Music).
	R & B Song of the Year	"Give Me the Night" by Rod Temperton (Rodsongs).
1981	*Song of the Year*	"Bette Davis Eyes" by Donna Weiss and Jackie DeShannon (Plain & Simple Music Corp./Donna Weiss Music).
	Broadway Song of the Year	"Any Dream Will Do" (*Joseph and the Amazing Technicolor Dream Coat*) by Andrew Lloyd Webber and Tim Rice (Novello & Co. Ltd.)
	Country Song of the Year	"9 to 5" by Dolly Parton (Velvet Apple Music/Fox Fanfare Music).
	Easy Listening Song of the Year	"Lady" by Lionel B. Richie, Jr. (Brockman Music).
	Gospel Song of the Year	"How Great Thou Art" by Stuart K. Hine (Manna Music).
	Latin Song of the Year	"De Nina a Mujer" by Tony Renis, Julio Iglesias, Ramon Arcusa, and Carlos Enterria (Sunny Pops Songs/April Music Holland B.V./Tony Renis Music)
	Movie Song of the Year	"Arthur's Theme (Best That You Can Do)" (*Arthur*) by Peter Allen, Burt Bacharach, Christopher Cross, and Carol Bayer Sager (Irving Music/Woolnough Music/Unichappell Music/Begonia Melodies/New Hidden Valley Music/WB Music Corp./Pop 'N' Roll Music).
	Pop Song of the Year	"Bette Davis Eyes" by Donna Weiss and Jackie DeShannon (Plain

| | & Simple Music Corp./Donna Weiss Music) |
| R & B Song of the Year | "Just the Two of Us" by Bill Withers, William Salter and Ralph McDonald (Antisia Music). |

See also National Music Publishers Association.

song-plugger   A man or woman whose job it was to interest singers and bandleaders in performing a song in a theater or nightclub, and especially over the radio. The heyday of the song-plugger as such was in the 1930s and 1940s, the era of the Big Bands and the Big Baritones, which was also the era of the No. 1 plug in music business. The chief of a music publisher's song-plugging staff was the professional manager. When recordings became the sine qua non of Pop music with the rise of the disk jockey, top man was the general professional manager. His job was mainly to get recordings of new songs, but he also was the executive head of the song-plugging operation.

See also general professional manager; No. 1 plug; professional man; Tin-Pan Alley; *Your Hit Parade.*

songwriters' contract   Many different types of contracts are used in the music business. The contract recommended and used by the American Guild of Authors and Composers (AGAC) for songwriters, and regarded as one that gives songwriters all the benefits and protection to which they are entitled, covers the following matters (among others):

1. After 40 years from the date of contract or 35 years from the date of first release (as provided by the copright law of 1976), publishing rights revert to the songwriter, who may then publish the song himself, renegotiate new terms with the original publisher, or sell the rights to a new publisher.
2. If a publisher fails to get a record released on a contracted song within one year, he must pay the songwriter $250 to retain rights for an additional six-month period. If he has not secured a recording at the end of that time, the songwriter can terminate the contract.
3. Ownership of a song reverts to a songwriter in the event that a publisher fails to fulfill any of the following conditions: (a) to pay earned royalties on schedule and to provide a comprehensive explanation of the royalties; (b) to consent to an audit requested by the songwriter or AGAC; (c) to secure the songwriter's consent if he wishes to assign a given song to a third party (except on the sale of his entire catalog).
4. Inclusion of a provision that the songwriter will receive half of whatever the publisher collects from any source not presently provided for (such as CATV, pay TV, cartridge TV, and other new media).
5. Sources of royalties are to include: (a) sheet music and other printed ar-

rangements; (b) song folios; (c) mechanical licenses; (d) synchronization licenses; (e) songs used as commercials.

See also American Guild of Authors and Composers; mechanicals;
synchronization.

Songwriters' Hall of Fame   *See* Hall of Fame, Songwriters'.

Son-Montuno   A Cuban dance, written in 2/4 or 4/4 time, it consists
of two strains, the first employing a Bolero-Mambo accompaniment
with accents on the first, fifth, and seventh beats of eight notes, and the
second, a faster strain generally using a Guaracha rhythm.

See also Bolero; Guaracha; Mambo.

sostenuto   As a mark indicating dynamics, it means "sustained." In
pianos, it refers to the center pedal, which makes it possible to sustain
given notes. When it is depressed, the pedal lifts dampers from the piano
strings, allowing them to vibrate.

Soul   In the 1960s, the word "soul" became a symbol of black identification, so that storekeepers in black ghettos plastered their windows
with the words "Soul Brother" in an effort to avoid the wrath of black
rioters. Also in the sixties, black music became blacker than it had ever
been, more Gospel-oriented than it had ever been. The development
came with an intensification of the struggle for equality, the rise of black
nationalism, the growth of black pride—"Black is Beautiful"—and the
emergence of a black-power movement. Out of the heightened feelings
accompanying these social and political movements came the intensity,
the drive, the fierce expressiveness of Soul music. It did not matter
whether a particular singer was a participant. The feelings of anger,
resentment, bitterness, pride, and determination were in the black community and found expression in the music of the day.

Ray Charles (b. 1930) anticipated the development of Soul when he
took a number of Gospel songs and wedded them to R & B in the late
1950s: "This Little Light of Mine" became "This Little Girl of Mine"
and a paean to Jesus became "Hallelujah, I Love Her So." It was an in-
trepid move, this fusing of the two genres of song, long regarded as alternative extremes of the life of the spirit: Blues were the songs of the devil
as Gospel was the music of the Lord. The fusion resulted in an intensification of feeling, rare in black recordings.

The rise of Soul was the work of a number of black artists. Aretha
Franklin (b. 1942) became Lady Soul with such emotionally raw records
as "I Never Loved a Man" and "A Natural Woman." Otis Redding
(1941–1967) spelled out his feelings in his *Dictionary of Soul* and a demand
for "Respect," quickly seconded by Aretha. Starting with an over-

powering cry of "Please, Please, Please," James Brown (b. 1928) unleashed a more raucous expression of feeling, replete with caterwauling screeches, that climaxed in his two-sided shout "Say It Loud—I'm Black and Proud" (1968). Jimi Hendrix (1942–1970) turned his guitar into an instrument of fury. Jazz singer/pianist Nina Simone (b. 1933) spit out her anger in "Mississippi Goddamn." The limping hop of R & B Shuffle turned with James Brown and Otis Redding into a driving stomp beat, punctuated with slashing brass figures.

Other proponents of Soul included Jackie Wilson (b. 1934), Wilson Pickett (b. 1941), preacher Solomon Burke (b. 1935), Percy Sledge (b. 1940), Don Covay (b. 1940). Add songs like "Soul Man" (1967) by Sam & Dave; Isaac Hayes's "Hot Buttered Soul" (1969); Willie Mitchell's "Soul Serenade" (1968); King Curtis's "Memphis Soul Stew" (1967); the Bar-Keys' "Soul Finger" (1967); the Ramsey Lewis Trio's "Soul Man" (1967); the Box Tops' "Soul Deep" (1968); "Soul Sister (You're Brown Sugar)" by Sam & Dave (1969); and "Soul-limbo" by Booker T. & the MG's (1968).

Soul has almost as many strains in it as there are artists. Sharing a common line of development from church choir to Gospel group, performers run the gamut from sweet romanticism (Sam Cooke 1935–1964), Al Green (b. 1946), Joe Tex (b. early 1940s), Arthur Conley (b. 1946) to Muslim anger (Last Poets). The Chambers Brothers and their wailing "harp" project Folk Soul. The Delfonics sing sexy Soul. The Impressions frequently deal in tolerance Soul. Lou Rawls (b. 1936) and his monologues moves from the Soul of deprivation to *Silk and Soul,* as he titled one of his albums. The Fifth Dimension has been typed as Champagne Soul and the group was accused of singing white. Joe Tex offered Country Soul. Otis Redding encompassed the demanding stridency of "Respect" and the soft soulfulness of his posthumous hit "(Sitting on) The Dock of the Bay."

Many record companies contributed to the prevalence of Soul. The most prolific were Atlantic Records of Harlem, Motown of Detroit, Stax of Memphis, and later, Philadelphia International. It would be difficult to type the Soul produced by each of these labels. But as the locus of their operation moved further south, the sound seemed less Pop and more ethnically black and Gospel-rooted.

See also Memphis sound; Motown sound; Philadelphia International.

Soul Brother No. 1   James Brown's billing. *See* Soul.

Soul Clan   An ephemeral group organized by songwriter/singer Don Covay (p. 1940). It found expression in a single Atlantic Record session participated in by Covay, Joe Tex (b. early 1940s), Solomon Burke (b. 1935), Arthur Conley (b. 1946), and Ben E. King (b. 1938).

Soul to Soul   The title of a film of a 1971 concert in the African nation of Ghana, attended by over 100,000 people. Among the performers, there were the Staple Singers, Ike & Tina Turner, Wilson Pickett, and Santana.

"to sound"   To question, but it can also mean to insult. "To sound off" is to lose one's temper.

soundboard   Made from solid, straight-grained Sitka spruce—at least in the higher-priced pianos—the soundboard amplifies and converts the vibrations of the strings into what we know as piano tone.

Sound System Ska   With the rise of Ska in Jamaica, an industry developed in the late fifties in which disk jockeys with a library of 45-rpm disks would mount PA speakers on a pickup truck and tour the island playing records. "Stay and Ketch It Again" was the rallying slogan of what became known as Sound System Ska.
See also Reggae; Ska; Skinheads.

Southern Rock   Blues and Country Rock as performed by southern bands, especially the Allman Brothers Band and Lynyrd Skynyrd. *Ramblin' Man* (1973) by the former and *Sweet Home Alabama* (1974) by the latter suggest the sound. Both groups lost members in accidents. Duane Allman (b. 1946) who founded the six-man group with his brother Gregg (b. 1947) died in an accident in 1971. Lead-singer Ronnie Van Zant (1949–1977), guitarist Steve Gaines (1949–1977), and backup singer Cassie Gaines (d. 1977) all perished in an air crash in 1977. Other exponents of the sound include the Marshall Tucker Band, the Charlie Daniels Band, and, most recently, Alabama.

Space Rock   A genre based on a concept, the exploration of space. It was science fiction in music, with an attendant use of sounds suggestive of outer space. The subject was anticipated by the Grateful Dead in "Dead Star" (1968) and by the Byrds in "Space Odyssey" in *The Notorious Byrd Brothers* (1968). Elton John (b. 1947) touched the matter in "Rocket Man" (1972). But it was David Bowie (b. 1947) who gave the genre substance with *Space Oddity* (1973); also Pink Floyd, with their million-copy *Dark Side of the Moon* (1973), premiered at the London Planetarium. Other groups that have been interested in space are Hawkwind (*In Search of Space*), Tangerine, Dreams, and Asia.

"spacey"   Weird, far-out, or spaced-out on drugs. Used to describe music in which an atmosphere of desolation is suggested, as in the sound of the group Moody Blues.

spasm band A band at the turn of the century, made up of homemade, junkpile instruments like the cheese-box banjo, suitcase drums, soap-box guitar, wine-jug tuba, washboard, bones, and Brownie (washtub) bass. One of the best-known spasm bands was led by Emile "Stale Bread" Lacoume of New Orleans. Known as the Razzy Dazzy Spasm Band, its personnel included Lacoume, who played a homemade cigar-box fiddle; Charley Stein, who played rattles, gourds, a cowbell, and a kettle; and Chinee, who played a bull-fiddle made from a half-barrel.

See also Brownie bass; jug band; skiffle.

speaksinging A style inaugurated by folk poet/singer Woody Guthrie (1912–1967) and imitated by young Bob Dylan (b. 1941). The words are half-spoken, half-sung, tending to follow the shape and direction of the melody rather than voicing the actual notes.

"Speed Kills" A slogan of the 1960s, now replaced by "Don't Meth Around," which refers to the avoidance of amphetamines, especially methedrine.

spinet *See* upright.

spirituals Folk songs, mainly of a religious nature, that grew out of the contact of black slaves with Christianity and European musical idiom. Maintaining call-and-response patterns, variations of meter and intonation, and the flattening of the third and seventh notes of the scale—all characteristics of African song—the spirituals manifested feelings of identification with Jesus and of empathy with the plight of the Jews under Egyptian slavery. Thus they were songs of yearning but also of protest ("Go Down, Moses, Let My People Go").

There were at least two types of Spirituals: (1) Sorrow songs like "Nobody Knows the Trouble I've Seen" and (2) Shouts like "Give me Dat Ole Time Religion" and "All God's Chillun Got Wings." The first spiritual in print was "Roll, Jordan, Roll," published in Philadelphia in 1862. Five years later the first collection, *Slave Songs of the United States*, made its appearance. But not until 1871 when the Fisk Jubilee Singers toured the country did the white world really become acquainted with the spirituals.

According to the Fisk University *Quarterly*, the spirituals should "more accurately be called *slave songs*, for the slave made no real distinction between his secular songs and his religious music. . . . He sang these songs in the fields where he worked, as well as in church and at revival meetings."

See also jubilee.

splice   To join together two pieces of recording tape or film. Used as a noun as well as a verb.

"split"   In Jazz and Rock jargon, to leave.

split time   Split or "cut" time is to Pop and Jazz musicians what *alla breve* is to the longhairs, or concert musicians. 4/4 time is split, or cut, so that it has the uptempo effect of 2/4 time.

"Splitsville"   A Frank Sinatra coinage, stemming from the practice of song-pluggers in the Tin-Pan Alley era to make places out of situations and states of mind by adding the suffix *ville*. "Bombsville" meant it missed, it failed, it's a bust; "Feelsville," let's give it a run-through; "Splitsville," let's move, let's leave.

spoons   A homemade percussion instrument consisting simply of two tableware spoons held belly to belly. Not only are beats possible by banging them together, but proficient performers can achieve rolls and trills. Dusty Springfield (b. Hampstead, London, 1939) is a skilled spoon-player ("but only Woolworth spoons," she says).

Bruce Springsteen (b. 1949)   An unknown, he was the first Rock or Pop artist—and the only one—to appear simultaneously during the same week on the covers of *Newsweek* and *Time*. The year was 1975, and *Born to Run,* his third album, seemed to establish him as the "artist of the decade." The co-producer of that album, Jon Landau, was an editor of *Rolling Stone* when he first heard Springsteen. "I have seen the future of Rock-and-Roll," he wrote, and resigned from his position with the Rock paper to become associated with Springsteen.

"square," or "L 7"   Originated in the Big Band era as a putdown of those who did not like or understand Swing. After a time, the term was applied to anyone in any field who resisted or opposed or was negative about what was "in." If you put an L and a 7 together, graphically, they make a square.

stage band   Colleges today tend to have three types of bands: marching bands to play athletic events; a concert band to perform at assemblies and at special events like a graduation ceremony; and a stage band to play at dances and functions that would not accommodate or do not require the large complement of musicians in both the concert and marching bands. The makeup of the stage band it very much like that of the Big Bands of the Swing era: a rhythm group of four or five (piano, bass, drums, guitar); a brass section (trumpets and trombones); and a reed section (saxes, clarinets, and flutes).

standard   A song which, having been a hit, has become part of the accepted repertoire of Pop music.

Stax/Volt Review   A group of artists on the Memphis labels of Stax and Volt that toured Europe in 1967, including, among others, Otis Redding (1941–1967), Carla Thomas (b. 1942), and Booker T. & the MG's.

steel band   A post–World War II Caribbean development. Oil drums left behind by the armed forces were cut down and the bottom lid was tempered so that something resembling a scale could be sounded when different segments were struck with the fingertips or with a rubber-tipped mallet. The sound had a gentle Marimba timbre, but with notes that were slightly flat or sharp. The smallest of the drums was called a "ping pong." There were also "tune booms" (sounding like celli), guitar pans, bongos, and basses. For rhythm, the bands used "chit-chats" (maracas), scratch sticks, and a "cutter" (the brake drum from a Model-T Ford). The assorted drums had a range of four octaves. Steel bands may be heard on a number of Decca records: e.g., *Steel Band, Jump Up* and *Pan. Demonia* by the 10th Naval District Steel Band.

steel guitar   An instrument that was and is quite popular among C & W artists, the steel guitar elicited only limited interest among Rock performers. Sneeky Pete Kleinow (b. circa 1935) of the Flying Burrito Brothers was an accomplished performer. Supposedly transported by Portuguese and Spanish seamen to the Hawaiian Islands, the steel guitar became popular in this country as a result of Hawaiian performers who played in American vaudeville in the years after World War I. The Hawaiians held the instrument in a horizontal position, fretting it with a piece of bone or metal, which is the way it is played by C & W artists. Bluesmen attempted to achieve the whining, ringing sound of the steel guitar by sliding a knife blade or the broken top of a bottle along the strings of their metal-stringed acoustic guitar. Apparently, the steel guitar was electrified before the standard one.
   See also bottleneck guitar.

Steel National   A guitar that was popular among street-singing bluesmen because of a circular diaphragm that acted as a resonating amplifier. The other guitar that street singers favored, also because of its volume, was the dobro.
   See also dobro.

stereo disk   First introduced in 1958 by Audio Fidelity Records and its founder, the late Sidney Frey.

stock   An orchestration issued by publishers and designed so that it can be played by average musicians. Its vogue was in the era of the No. 1 plug.

Karlheinz Stockhausen (b. 1938)   Regarded as the foremost exponent of electronic music, his sounds and techniques have attracted the more adventuresome and experimental of Rock groups. He is credited as the composer of the first published score for electronic music. In 1964 Stockhausen conducted performances of some of his works in the U.S.A. and Canada. Among his more than 70 compositions: "*Kontakte* for Electronic Sounds, Piano, and Percussion" (1959-1960); "*Mixtus* for Orchestra and Electronic Modulators" (1964); and "*Microphonie* I" (1964). He was director of the Electronic Studio at Cologne, Germany.

Stomp   A number of well-known Jazz and Swing pieces bear the word "stomp" in their titles: "King Porter Stomp" of Jelly Roll Morton (1885-1941), "Sugar Foot Stomp," and the famous "Stomping at the Savoy," popularized by Benny Goodman (b. 1909). The Stomp was presumably adapted from the old Ring-Shout, an ecstatic dance of spiritual jubilation. As developed during the Soul era by James Brown (b. 1928) and Otis Redding (1941-1967), it was a propulsive rhythm involving a hard-driving 4-to-the-bar beat and stinging brass repeating a rhythmic figure in riff pattern. Redding felt that the Shuffle, which he himself used on his disk of "Shake" by Sam Cooke (1935-1964), was out-of-date. Soul required the powerhouse drive of the Stomp.
    See also James Brown; Shuffle; Soul.

"stoned"   Originally, it meant someone who had had too much to drink and had lost contact with reality. The drug culture took it over to mean someone whom a drug has temporarily sent out of this world.

stop chorus, or stop-time   Supposedly pioneered by Louis Armstrong (1900-1971) on "Cornet Chop Suey" (1925-1927); a device in which the accompanying combo, band, or piano plays only the first chord of each measure or every other measure while the instrumental soloist fills in the open spaces.

Storyville   The red-light district of New Orleans, bounded by Canal and Basin streets, where prostitution and Jazz flourished from 1896 to 1917. Storyville got its name from Alderman Sidney Story, who was responsible for a measure setting aside a section of the French Quarter as an area where prostitution was to be tolerated but not legalized. Here there were "cribs" for the low-paying customers and the most elegant of bordellos for the affluent and mighty. Storyville was shut down during

World War I, apparently as a reaction to a wartime wave of super-morality, sending the Jazz musicians up the Mississippi River in search of employment and spreading Jazz to cities on the river and to Chicago and New York.

See also New Orleans Jazz.

Win Stracke   *See* "Chicago's Minstrel."

"The Street"   Between 1934 and 1950, musicians and even New York City cabdrivers knew that "The Street" meant 52nd Street between 5th and 6th avenues. It was the Mecca of Jazz fans.

See also 52nd Street; Jazzwalk; Swing Street.

street-corner groups   *See also* doo-wop.

Stride piano   A piano style that developed in the 1920s as an offshoot of Ragtime, which had actually developed the left-hand pattern that became the basis of the Stride school. In motion, the hand described an arc like a swinging pendulum, as it struck, first, a tonic octave or tenth chord, then a two- or three-finger chord, followed by the fifth of the chord (always below the octave) and, again, the two- or three-finger chord. The left hand thus operated as a two-beat or four-beat timekeeper.

Among the outstanding Stride pianists were James P. Johnson (1891–1955), Willie "The Lion" Smith (1897–1973), young Duke Ellington (1899–1974), Fats Waller (1904–1943), and Art Tatum (1910–1956), of whom it was said "No one can imitatum."

String Rhythm & Blues   The traditional R & B combo consisted of a hot tenor sax and a rhythm section, which was sometimes augmented with another reed and/or brass instrument. In 1959, when Leiber & Stoller undertook the production of the Drifters, they added a string section to the usual R & B combo and employed studio arrangers to prepare charts. It was a new sound for R & B, one that increased the crossover potential of the group. With Ben E. King (b. 1938) as lead and co-writer, "There Goes My Baby" became the second million-seller for the Drifters. Latin rhythms and flavoring were also added to the R & B drive in such other disks by the Drifters as "Dance with Me" (1959), "This Magic Moment," "I Count the Tears," and "Save the Last

Dance for Me'' (all three in 1960). The last-mentioned went to No. 1 on the Pop charts.

strobe light   A computer-speed, on-and-off flashing light, it gives the illusion of arrested motion; used in some Rock shows and discos.

The Stroll   A teenage dance of the late 1950s that gave rise to a hit song and record of the same name by the Diamonds. Songwriter/singer Chuck Willis (1928–1958) accidentally became the King of the Stroll when a recording he made of an old Blues, ''C. C. Rider,'' proved just right for strollers.

''strung out''   The state of being under the influence of drugs.

studio piano   *See* upright.

Studio Pop   Another designation for the Teenage Rock 'n' Roll that emerged when the major record companies decided that Presley was here to stay and began manufacturing a hothouse product in their studios. The development occurred between 1957 and the rise of Bob Dylan in 1962–63. It involved artists like Paul Anka (b. 1941), Neil Sedaka (b. 1939), Connie Francis (b. 1938) and others.
    See also Teenage Rock.

Studio Rock   A type of Rock that developed after the Beatles' *Sgt. Pepper* album (1967), in which the technical elements of the recording studio entered actively into the creative process—the writing and arranging as well as the final mix. Amplification, sonorities, timbres, textures, densities, tape speeds, and various types of synthesizers—all were capable of manipulation. The record was the song.
    See also Art Rock; Avant-garde Rock; Experimental Rock.

''Summer of Love''   Used with reference to San Francisco's hippie development, which peaked in 1967 and which promulgated the hope that the world and society could be changed through Flower Power and Love. The hippies were for honesty, altruism, and nonviolence, believing in the mystical power of flowers, bells, and beads. The Monterey Pop Festival of '67, when even the police were persuaded to wear flowers on their helmets, was a heightened expression of the feeling communicated by the hippies. ''San Francisco (Be Sure to Wear Some Flowers in Your Hair)'' captured the sentiment. Written by John Phillips (b. 1941), leader of The Mamas and the Papas, it was a million-copy hit for Scott McKenzie (b. 1944) in the summer of '67.
    See also ''Be-in''; Flower Children; ''Love-in.''

Sun Records   An oft-reprinted photograph, subtitled "The Million Dollar Quartet" shows four young singers rehearsing in the studio of Sun Records in Memphis, Tenn., in the early fifties. Elvis Presley (1935–1977) is seated at the piano, Carl Perkins (b. 1932) is playing guitar, and the two are joined in song by Jerry Lee Lewis (b. 1935) and Johnny Cash (b. 1932). All four initially recorded for Sun Records, entitling the label to credit, if any one label is to be so credited, for launching the Rock revolution.

At the outset, founder-owner Sam Phillips, an ex-radio engineer and announcer from Florence, Ala., set out to record R & B artists like Little Junior Parker (1932–1971), Howlin' Wolf (1915–1976), and B. B. King (b. 1925). He leased or sold the disks he cut with these bluesmen to Modern/RPM in Los Angeles and Chess Records in Chicago, accounting for such bestsellers as Jackie Brenston's "Rocket 88" on Chess. After he launched Sun as an independent venture, he scored an R & B hit with "Bear Cat" (1953), recorded by Rufus Thomas (b. 1917), a WDIA disk jockey.

Between August 1954 and August 1955, he released five records by Elvis Presley, backing a country song with an R & B song. The playing of these disks by a Cleveland disk jockey, Bill Randle, created such a furor that several New York companies began bidding for Elvis' services and Phillips sold his contract to RCA Victor. Elvis' rise to national prominence brought scores of budding Presley's to Phillips' studio. In addition to Johnny Cash, Jerry Lee Lewis, and Carl Perkins (who wrote and recorded "Blue Suede Shoes" on Sun before Elvis popularized it), Phillips recorded Roy Orbison (b. 1936), Conway Twitty (b. mid-1940s), and Charlie Rich (b. 1932). In short, Sun Records was the major source of the initial rock 'n' roll style known as rockabilly.

See also Elvis Presley; Rockabilly.

supergroups   Used with reference to groups formed when key musicians of other groups coalesce into a new group. Cream, formed from virtuosos in John Mayall's Bluesbreakers, Manfred Mann, and the Graham Bond Organization, did not hesitate to label their group the cream of British Rock: it consisted of Eric Clapton (b. 1945), guitar; Jack Bruce (b. 1943), bass; and Ginger Baker (b. 1940), drums. Initially an underground group, they became trend setters, provoking interest in the bass guitar as a lead instrument, in soloing by Rock drummers, and in jamming. Crosby, Stills, Nash & Young were also graduates of other groups: David Crosby (b. 1941) from the Byrds; Graham Nash (b. 1942) from the Hollies; and Stephen Stills (b. 1945) and Neil Young (b. 1945) from the Buffalo Springfield. (The supergroup also included drummer Dallas Taylor, who had worked with Crosby, Stills & Nash, and bassist Greg Reeves.) Advance orders for the initial disk by C, S, N

& Y, *Déjà Vu,* reportedly totaled $2 million, so that the album became Gold on release and then sold over 2 million copies in two weeks; No. 1 for 4 weeks, it remained a bestseller for 65 weeks. Emerson, Lake & Palmer were a third supergroup. Organist/pianist/composer Keith Emerson (b. 1944) came from the group Nice; bassist/vocalist Greg Lake (b. 1948) came from King Crimson; and drummer Carl Palmer (b. 1947) came from Atomic Rooster. The sophistication and depth of Emerson's music moved the supergroup in a Classical Rock direction, with every one of six albums they produced between 1971 and 1974 selling over a million each.

Among groups that aspired to supergroup status but did not quite make it were Electric Flag, Rhinocerous, Traffic, and Triumvirate.

superstar   Although the word is frequently used loosely, it does refer to a special category of stardom, which few stars attain. While record sales are the basis of superstardom, charisma, notoriety, and publicity play a vital role in making a record star into a superstar celebrity. Presley (1935–1977) was a superstar, but Chuck Berry (b. 1926) is not. The Beatles and Rolling Stones achieved superstardom, but the Who has not.

superstudio   An independently owned studio that provides not only the best and most sophisticated recording equipment and acoustics but "perks" such as 24-hour hostesses, sauna, Jacuzzi, spacious lounges, sundeck, and bar. All these are available, for example, at Kendun Studios in Burbank, Calif., which reports a billing of over $3 million a year. The Village Recorder in Los Angeles, where Fleetwood Mac records, built a "super" room for the group's use. Seven-sided, the studio houses a moveable wall with wooden shutters to reduce or increase resonance. All this and state-of-the-art equipment cost $1.5 million to install. Rental of the studio is $20,000 to $30,000 a week.

See also recording studio.

Surfing music   In their first homemade record, a quintet from Hawthorne, a Los Angeles suburb, celebrated a local California craze, surfing—a sport in which they could indulge, Hawthorne being five miles from the Pacific Ocean. "Surfin'," made at a small local studio, came out on a local label, Candix, and led the three Wilson brothers plus a neighbor and an LA cousin to adopt the name Beach Boys. By June 1962 they had their first release on Capitol—"Surfin' Safari"—which became a hit single and the title of a bestselling album. Although Surfing music attracted only another duo, Jan & Dean, it exercised a far-reaching necromancy. While the songs celebrated the excitement and fun of surfing, the appeal was much broader. It had to do with the sense of freedom, exhilaration, and relaxation of time spent on a sunny beach. It was a matter of sunshine, summer, and romance—and escape from the harsh and boring realities of life. During the height of the craze, it was reported that youngsters in the Midwest, a thousand miles removed from any ocean, drove around with surfboards strapped to the roofs of their cars.

Musically, Surfing songs had no real identity. Although the Beach boys said "We're white and we sing white," they took the melody and rhythm of "Surfin' USA" from Chuck Berry's "Sweet Little Sixteen." A typical 12-bar Blues with a walking Boogie bass, it used a gentle afterbeat, sounded with hand claps: rest, clap-clap, rest, clap/rest, clap-clap, rest, clap. Short-lived though the craze was (1962–1963), the feeling for the outdoor life, and the fast motion it embodied, quickly found expression in Hot-Rod music. Both the Beach Boys and Jan & Dean, who started a three-year run on the charts with their version of Brian Wilson's "Surf City," switched to songs about fast cars. Jan & Dean's "Dead Man's Curve" (1964) was an almost prophetic presage of Jan Berry's near-fatal accident of April 1966.

Surf Punks   A local Los Angeles phenomenon involving a number of musical groups: Dick Dale & the Del-Tones, Surf Punks, and Jon & the Nightriders. The Surf Punks are described as just an attitude by Dennis Dragon, who operates a Malibu recording studio: "Work is not just necessary for life. If there's waves, we're on the water. If there's sun, we're at the beach. And if there's nothing at all, we go cruise for chicks at the Topanga Mall . . . anything under 17 and over 14." Surf Punk songs involve jargon that requires a glossary. "Honkers," for example, are the favorite part of the female anatomy and "kooks" are guys who can't surf.

See also Surfing music.

Surrealism   Originally a movement in art, literature, and the theater, Surrealism exploited the incongruity and irrationality of the dreamlike state through fantastic images and startling juxtapositions. In Rock, Dylan's lyrics are not infrequently surrealistic. So are John Lennon's in *Sgt. Pepper* and in an earlier song, "Norwegian Wood," among others. "A Whiter Shade of Pale" by Procol Harum offers another interesting instance.

Suzy-Q   A dance of the Swing era (1935–1945).

Sweetheart Pop   A limited category involving the romantic balladry of duos like The Captain & Tenille, the brother-and-sister Carpenters, and Neil Sedaka with his daughter Dara in the song "Should've Never Let You Go."

"Sweet Mama Stringbean"   An early nickname of Ethel Waters (1900–1977) because she was so tall and thin. Starting on the TOBA circuit (the Theatre Owners Booking Association was known by black artists as Tough on Black Asses), Ethel sang her way to the top of the entertainment world, as Blues singer, record star, film star, and dramatic actress. Among the songs that are permanently associated with her are: "St. Louis Blues"—she was the first woman and the second performer to sing it; "Stormy Weather," which she introduced in a Cotton Club show in 1933; "Am I Blue," which she introduced in the film *On with the Show;* "Happiness Is Just a Thing Called Joe," which she sang in the film version of her Broadway musical hit, *Cabin in the Sky* (1943), nominated for an Academy Award; "Dinah," which she introduced in vaudeville in 1925; and "Supper Time," a song about lynching, which she sang in the Irving Berlin show *As Thousands Cheer* (1933). She later wrote: "If one song can tell the whole tragic history of a race, 'Supper Time' was that song." The statement appeared in her autobiography, *His Eye Is on the Sparrow,* a title that reflected her own great religious fervor. She spent the latter years of her life working with Billy Graham's evangelistic crusades.

Swing   Jelly Roll Morton (1885–1941) used the term in a 1928 composition, "Georgia Swing," and in 1932 Duke Ellington (1899–1974) wrote "It Don't Mean a Thing If It Ain't Got That Swing." In 1934 Red Norvo (b. 1908) led a group he called his Swing Septet. But as a style and an era, Swing did not fully emerge until 1935, when the Benny Goodman Band played a now-historic stand, first at the Palomar Ballroom in Los Angeles, and then at the Congress Hotel in Chicago, Goodman's hometown. The Swing era lasted until the end of World War II, when Goodman's band and several other Big Bands folded—destroyed by wartime stringencies and shortages of musicians, dancers, and transportation, as well as by the introduction of electronic instruments, three of which could achieve the sound and volume of a fifteen-piece aggregation.

During the Swing era, there were hundreds of Big Bands touring the country and keeping dancers happy in a chain of ballrooms. Numbering 12 to 15 and more musicians, they consisted of a rhythm section (piano, bass, drums, guitar), a brass section (trumpets and trombones), and a reed section (saxes, clarinets, flutes). Some bands also included a string section, two vocalists (male and female), and a singing group like the Pied Pipers of Tommy Dorsey (1905–1956). All these bands played a four-to-the-bar chugging type of rhythm, with the sections indulging in a call-and-response gambit, and individual soloists improvising against written riffs by the band. Syncopated choruses by the brasses or reeds, or both, were fully written out.

The leading Swing bands, some hot and some sweet, included those of Goodman, Artie Shaw, Tommy Dorsey, Glenn Miller, Jimmie Lunceford, Duke Ellington, Gene Krupa, Harry James, Lionel Hampton, Chick Webb, Buddy Rich, Charlie Barnet, Benny Carter, Fletcher Henderson, Casa Loma, and Count Basie. It was actually arrangements written by Fletcher Henderson (1898–1952) in the early thirties for his own Big Band that became the basis of the Goodman library. In its origins, Swing was a black musical phenomenon, evolved by bands like those of Benny Moten, Count Basie, Jay McShann, and others in the Southwest, especially Kansas City. But when Swing became a national craze, it was the white bands that were heard on the sponsored network radio shows like the *Camel Caravan* and others.

The Swing era was the only era when a form of Jazz became the country's popular music, with the hit songs of the day being presented, nurtured, and developed by the Big Bands whose leaders were then the darlings of the music business.

"Swing Street"   Few Big Bands appeared on 52nd St., which, between 5th and 6th avenues, early became known as "Swing Street." But "The Street,' as it was also known, blossomed as the haven of Jazz in the Swing era, and many of the artists and small combos that played the clubs did indeed swing. In June 1979, in a Jazzwalk ceremony, the City of New York gave official recognition to The Street's legendary status and placed signs on the lampposts at 5th and 6th avenues officially rechristening the block as Swing Street.

See also 52nd Street; Jazzwalk; The Street.

synchronization   Refers to the process of recording or videotaping a musical selection for future broadcasting or televising. A fee must be paid to the copyright owner, based on the nature of the usage: whether background or featured and whether sung or just played instrumentally. The development of video cassettes and disks has raised a number of new problems, which the industry is currently in the process of exploring. Film producers now want the fee for synchronization to include video cassettes. Although the final determination of fees and the licensing agreement is in the hands of the copyright owner (generally a music publisher), negotiations are handled by the Harry Fox Agency.

See also Harry Fox Agency.

syncopation   Accenting a beat that is normally unaccented. In R & B and R 'n' R, the most obvious syncopation is the stress placed on the afterbeat or backbeat:

Other forms of syncopation involve anticipating a note or delaying it, each of which also involves a displacement of accents or the normal metrical pulse.

synthesizer   Once musical sounds were produced by blowing (brass and reed instruments), scraping (strings), striking (piano, guitar), or beating (drums). Then along came the Theremin, an electronic instrument whose sound was produced by waving one's hands in the air. Then we had the Moog (1964). And now we have a number of different kinds of synthesizers including the ARP—complex devices that use modular-linked oscillators and other waveform constrictors to shape sound waves and thereby produce different sounds. Among Rock groups and artists that have experimented with and used synthesizers, we find Keith Emerson of Emerson, Lake & Palmer; Rick Wakeman of Yes; Brian Eno of Roxy Music; Jon Lord of Deep Purple; Stevie Wonder; Gary Numan; Peter Townshend of The Who; David Bowie; and, of course, the Beatles. Since the mid-1970s, the use of synthesizers has become a commonplace since few topnotch recording studios are without them. Vangelis, who won an Oscar in 1982 for his synthesized soundtrack of *Chariots of Fire,* has said: "Today, there are synthesizers that require the same level of technique it takes to play a violin or flute."

Synth-Rock   Abbreviation of "Synthesizer Rock," a New Wave trend in which all members of a group play some type of synthesizer, including even the drummer. Warren Cann of Ultravox, one of the leading Synth-Rock groups, switched between drums and drum synthesizer in the group's album *Systems of Romance.* Although the British group began with a guitar/bass/drums format, by the time it cut *Systems,* its third album, it was moving toward the all-out synthesizer orientation evident in its *Slow Motion* LP. Among artists and groups that indulge in ultra-synth explorations, one finds Gary Numan, the Cars, and gifted Stevie Wonder (b. 1951), who has become a synthesizer devotee. In *Hotter Than July* (1980), he plays Vocoder, flute synthesizer, Fender Rhodes, ARP, bass synthesizer, bass Melodian synthesizer, and Fairlight synthesizer.

    See also Aleatory Rock; Electronic Rock; Electro Pop; New Wave; synthesizer.

T

TOBA   *See* Theatre Owners Booking Association.

TTBB   Acronym of Tenor, Tenor, Baritone, and Bass, the four voices of the standard male quartet, and the name of the arrangement written for such a quartet.
See also SATB.

"tag"   In Classical music, they call it a "coda." It's an extension of the closing segment of a selection, designed to give the ending more impact and finality. In Jazz, Pop, and Rock, it's known as a "tag"—something that's tacked onto the end.

tailgate   A term relating to the trombone that dates back to the early days of Jazz. When bands played on horse-drawn wagons in New Orleans, either for advertising or entertainment, the trombonist sat at the back of the wagon, with the tailgate turned down. Thus he could extend the slide without fear of striking another player or tangling with another instrument. The term "tailgate" tended to refer to the lowest notes of the instrument when the slide was most extended.

"take"   A noun referring to the cut of a tune at a recording session.

"Take Five"   The title of a well-known Jazz instrumental by Paul Desmond (1924–1977), alto saxist of the Dave Brubeck Quartet, it refers to the coffee breaks that musicians take between sets during an evening's playing for dancers. The "five" is not to be taken literally as meaning five minutes.

Talent Scouts   A TV show of the 1950s, emceed by Arthur Godfrey (b. 1903), which, along with *Ted Mack's Original Amateur Hour,* opened the door to new performers, R & B as well as Pop. It was a springboard for Pat Boone (b. 1934), the Orioles, and others.

Talking Blues   A type of Blues and a style of delivery developed by folk singer/songwriter Woody Guthrie (1912–1967). Perhaps its most celebrated exponent was Bob Dylan (b. 1941), whose debut album included original selections titled "Talking Woody Guthrie" and "Talking New York." Leadbelly (1885-1949), with whom Guthrie sang at various times, has written a number of Talking Blues—"Good Morning, Blues," among others.
See also Woody Guthrie; speaksinging.

tamboura   An Indian instrument held upright, with its body of wood or a spherical gourd resting on the player's right thigh, the tamboura has a long unfretted neck and four metal strings. Three are tuned to octave unisons, while the fourth is tuned to the dominant or subdominant. A drone lute, similar to the sitar, its strings are gently plucked with the player's right forefinger, never with a plectrum. Since it is used to accompany the singing of ragas, a movable bridge of ivory allows for adjustment to the range of the singer's voice. The instrument can be heard on an early album of the Devil's Anvil: *Hard Rock from the Middle East.*

tambourine   A percussion instrument, made of a small, circular, wooden hoop into which small metal disks have been inserted. When the instrument is shaken by hand, the metal disks tinkle or rattle. Of Arab origin, the tambourine was used extensively by American slaves. In the minstrel show, one of the endmen was called Tambo and played the tambourine. Associated with Gospel singing in recent years, the instrument was used extensively by Motown Records on disks by the Supremes and other groups. It continues to be used widely by black gospeleers and others.
See also Gospel music; Motown sound.

Tango   A distinctive Latin dance, imported from Havana, Cuba, and originally known as the Habanera. The first Latin dance to become an American craze, it became popular in the pre–World War I era of the Dancing Castles. Its distinctive rhythm was used by W. C. Handy (1873–1958) in his famous "St. Louis Blues" (1914). The dance enjoyed a brief revival in the twenties as a result of Rudolph Valentino's dancing in *The Four Horsemen of the Apocalypse.*

tape cartridge   It became big as a means of listening to recorded music in cars around 1966. Herb Alpert's record of "What Now, My Love?" received the first Gold Cartridge Award (from the ITCC) for record-breaking retail sales that year.

tape loop   By attaching or looping the ends of a piece of magnetic tape together, a given selection can be played over and over without interruption or rolling the tape back to the beginning. A time- and labor-saving device, it makes it possible for an artist to overdub a number of times without losing the feel or tempo of what is being recorded. The device is also used in machines that play canned music in elevators, banks, restaurants, and other public places.

tape reverb   Based on the principle of all echo devices—namely, the time lapse between the original sound and its reflection back from a natural or electronic barrier—tape reverb produces an echo effect by exploiting the time interval as tape passes between the recording and playback heads of a tape machine. The resulting echo possesses a kind of *owowowowow* sound.

See also reverb.

"tea"   Slang for marijuana.

Teddy Boys   British counterparts of American juvenile delinquents in the early 1960s. Greasing their hair, they combed it down in a version of the American "Waterfall" hairstyle and called it "the elephant's trunk."

Teenage Rock   A stage, not a style, in the evolution of Rock 'n' Roll, it lasted for about five years—roughly from 1957, after Presley emerged, until the appearance of Bob Dylan (b. 1941) and the Beatles, when R 'n' R developed sophistication in the form of Folk Rock, Protest Rock, Poetic Rock, Psychedelic Rock, and so on. The rise of Teenage Rock was engineered by the major record companies (who had allowed small independents to dominate the R & B market), assisted by Dick Clark and the *American Bandstand.* Whereas Rockabilly as the first stage of R 'n' R was a spontaneous development, Teenage Rock was a manufactured, market-oriented development. It was also largely a white northern development, as Rockabilly was a white southern style. As studio arrangers, employed by the major companies, copied some of the aspects of R & B—the afterbeat, the use of triplets as in Boogie piano, and a raucous tenor sax—adolescent singers like Paul Anka (b. 1941), Leslie Gore (b. 1946), George Hamilton IV (b. 1937), Connie Francis (b. 1938), Neil Sedaka (b. 1939), Bobby Rydell (b. 1942), Fabian (b. 1943), Frankie Avalon (b. 1940), Ricky Nelson (b. 1940), Bobby Vee (b. 1943), Richie Valens (1941–1959), and Johnny Tillotson (b. circa 1939) made records that dealt with teenage subjects and emotions. Music publishers participated in the process, with Aldon Music proving most successful in a search for teenage songwriters: Sedaka & Greenfield, Goffin & King, Mann & Weil, among others. Songwriters/record producers Leiber & Stoller contributed songs to Presley's repertoire and added Pop overtones to their work as producers of records by the Drifters and others. Other songwriters who were part of the Teenage Rock development included Pomus & Shuman, Barry & Greenwich, and Otis Blackwell, the gifted black creator of such classics as Presley's "I'm All Shook Up" and "Don't Be Cruel."

The Teenage Rock scene included black artists like the Platters, the Shirelles, the Drifters, Little Anthony & the Imperials, Frankie Lymon & the Teenagers, Fats Domino, Chubby Checker, and the Coasters (with teenage classics like "Charlie Brown," "Young Blood," and "Yakety Yak"). These artists produced a more raucous, Boogie-driven, and R & B–oriented sound. The poet laureate of Teenage Rock, Chuck Berry (b. 1926), hardly a teenager, displayed a rare understanding of the teenage mind and feelings, and produced a driving, Country Blues–oriented sound that linked him with the Rockabilly school.

See also *American Bandstand;* Brill Building Rock; Fats Domino; independent producer; Rockabilly.

teenyboppers   The pre-teenage audience for Rock 'n' Roll, which responded to the younger-voiced singers like Frankie Avalon (b. 1940), Paul Anka (b. 1941), Ricky Nelson (b. 1940), David Cassidy (b. 1950), the Monkees, Bobby Sherman (b. 1944), and others.

See also Bubble-Gum Rock

temple block   Of Chinese and Korean origin, it is made of hollowed-out wood and shaped like a human head. When it is struck with a drumstick, it emits a hollow sound. Although the blocks are never tuned, different sizes allow for different pitches.

"tenay dee jay"   Disk jockeys on Top 40 radio stations are compelled to program from a list compiled by station management. Such lists usually contain 40 titles, not 10. However, the absence of creative control and the boredom of playing the same records over and over are suggested in the phrase "tenay dee jay." Sometimes the phrase is applied to any dull, monotonous job in the music business.

tenor band   *See* society band.

"Tennessee Plowboy"   Early billing for country singer Eddy Arnold (b. 1918), who was elected to the Country Music Hall of Fame in 1966. From the late 1940s into the mid-sixties, he had a steady flow of bestsellers, some of which crossed over into Pop. Among the songs for which he is remembered: "Any Time" (1948), "Bouquet of Roses" (1948), "Don't Rob Another Man's Castle" (1949), "Kentucky Waltz" (1951), "I Really Don't Want to Know" (1954), "Cattle Call" (1955), "You Don't Know Me" (1956), "Tennessee Stud" (1959), "Make the World Go Away" (1965), "What's He Doing in My World?" (1965), and "The Last Word in Lonesome Is Me" (1966). As the first of the Pop Country singers, he aroused such opposition that Country purists opposed his election to the Country Music Hall of Fame.

tenor sax   Of all the saxophones, the tenor has exercised the widest appeal. Its hot, raucous sound made it the basic instrument of Rhythm

& Blues, and its mellow, lyrical sound, the anchor of the so-called society bands. Although the man who is regarded as the greatest jazzman of our time, Charlie "Bird" Parker (1920–1955), played the alto sax, the tenor has challenged a larger complement of the most inspired improvisers and innovators in Jazz. Among the hornmen who have favored the instrument, there are Lester "Prez" Young (1909–1959), Ben Webster (1909–1973), John Coltrane (1926–1967), Ornette Coleman (b. 1930), Coleman Hawkins (1904–1969), Illinois Jacquet (b. 1922), and Stan Getz (b. 1927).

See also Coleman Hawkins; Rhythm & Blues; society band; Lester Young.

tenth   An interval of ten notes, two more than an octave, from C to E above octave C. A basic chord in Stride piano, it is a stretch that some small hands cannot transact. Thus, the tenth is rolled instead of just struck.

See also Stride piano.

tent shows   A southern tradition, particularly in rural areas lacking theaters. Tents could accommodate much larger audiences than those that might crowd into a school auditorium, Elks Hall, or similar indoor "theater."

Texas Blues   Blind Lemon Jefferson (1897–1929), a pioneer Blues singer, came from Texas, as did Henry Thomas, known as "Ragtime Texas" (1874–?), and "Texas" Alexander (1880–1955). Later, Johnny Winter (b. 1944) became a proponent of white Blues out of Texas. Next to Mississippi, Texas was the most important source of Blues singers.

See also Blues; Country Blues.

"Texas Troubadour"   A reference to Ernest Tubb (b. 1914), who was elected to the Country Music Hall of Fame in 1965. A dedicated devotee of Jimmie Rodgers (1897–1933), known as the Father of Country Music, he is remembered for such Country hits as "Walking the Floor Over You" (1941), "Don't Rob Another Man's Castle" (1949), and "I'm Bitin' My Fingernails and Thinking of You" (1949). Both of the latter were collaborations with the Andrews Sisters, and the first-mentioned was his own composition. He continued making records into the mid-1960s.

Tex-Mex   Buddy Holly (1938–1959), who came from Texas and recorded in New Mexico, was the prime exponent of the so-called Tex-Mex sound. Like Presley, Holly was a southern lad who had a feeling for black music and thereby developed a style that was close to the Rockabilly sound. His style was influenced by Presley, whom he heard in

Lubbock, Tex., before Elvis became nationally known, and whose animal vitality triggered his own turn from Country music to the R & B–derived sound that became known as Rock 'n' Roll. Holly's own driving exuberance was in part a product of his powerhouse guitar style, which derived from a Tex-Mex manner of playing, known locally as "brush and broom." A note was struck and a chord brushed on top of it, giving the instrument a loud ringing sound. The year (1957) that brought the rise of Holly and his backup group, The Crickets, also saw the explosion of two other Texas rockers with million-selling records: Buddy Knox (b. 1933) with "Party Doll" and Jimmy Bowen (b. 1937) with "I'm Stickin' with You." Tex-Mex could be viewed as the Southwest's stylization of Rockabilly. In 1981 a new Tex-Mex sound—as much Mex as Tex—was being explored by Joe (King) Carrasco & the Crowns.

See also Buddy Holly; Rockabilly.

Theatre Owners Booking Association   An association of theater owners that booked black artists in black vaudeville houses around the country circa 1910–1930. Among the theaters in the chain: Howard in Washington, D.C.; Apollo in Harlem; "81" in Atlanta; Palace in Memphis; Liberty in Chattanooga; Globe in Cleveland; Koppin in Detroit; Frolic in Birmingham; Elmore in Pittsburgh; Lincoln in Louisville; Walker in Indianapolis; Booker T. Washington in St. Louis; Roosevelt in Cincinnati; Ogden in Columbus; Lincoln in Winston-Salem; Bijou in Nashville; Star in Shreveport; Lincoln in Dallas; Gem in Hot Springs. Because some of the owners were so hard in their treatment and cheap in their compensation of artists, the group was known among black performers as Tough on Black Artists or Tough on Black Asses.

Theater Rock   The reference is not to the music, the songs, or the musical quality but to the onstage dress, manner, antics, and/or gimmickry. In pre-Rock days, the word was "showmanship" and referred to costume, conduct, and/or presentation whose attractiveness, oddity, or zaniness surprised, amused, and entertained an audience. The appeal to the eye through spectacle was practiced by some rock groups. Kiss, a quartet that made its debut in 1974, used heavy makeup to appear as a whiskered cat, a silver-eyed spaceman, a pouting-lipped sex figure, and a vampire. The New York Dolls and David Bowie (b. 1947) dressed in drag. The flutist of Jethro Tull performed jumping up and down, lying on the stage, or standing on one foot so that he looked like a deranged flamingo. Elton John (b. 1947), wearing huge, oversized spectacles, would kick the piano bench away, jump up and down as he pounded the keys, and at moments fling his feet out so that he became a horizontal extension of the grand piano. Devo performs in yellow space suits and 3D glasses, with flowerpots on their heads. In 1980, while Pink Floyd performed selections from their new album, *The Wall,* a crew erected, brick by brick, a giant cardboard wall measuring 35 ft. × 210 ft. between the group and the unsuspecting audience. Grace Jones startled audiences in '81 by roaring onstage on a motorcycle or entering accompanied by a tiger—after which her shaved head, except for a rectangular area on the crown, added a theatrical tingle. Theater Rock embraces all these arresting visual antics and elements, including acts of violence and morbidity designed to shock and not just entertain.

See also Glitter Rock; Shock Rock.

Theremin   An electronic instrument, devised in 1924 and named after its inventor, Leon Theremin, a Russian. Producing only one note at a time, it consists of a rectangular box from which juts an upright metallic rod. A continuous squeal is emitted when a performer waves his hands near, above, and below the rod. The position and motion of the hands determine the pitch and duration of the squeal. Americans first heard the Theremin in the Alfred Hitchcock film *Spellbound* (1945). Brian Wilson (b. 1942) of the Beach Boys used the instrument in his arrangement of "Good Vibrations" (1966).

See also Durrell synthesizer; synthesizer.

Third Stream   Gunther Schuller (b. 1925), French horn player, composer, and president of the New England Conservatory of Music, claims credit for coining the term. He conceived of Third Stream as a merging of two tributaries, one flowing from Jazz and the other from Classical music. Among the Jazz composers who experimented with this mix were Schuller himself, John Lewis (b. 1920) of the Modern Jazz Quartet, and bassist/composer Charles Mingus (1922–1979).

"threads"   Black lingo, now Rock lingo, for clothes.

three-chord structure   The basic chords of the diatonic system of Western music are those built on the first note (I), fourth note (IV), and fifth note (V). A selection that uses only these chords, as, for example, the Blues, is known as a three-chord structure. Much of early Rock 'n' Roll, stemming as it did from R & B, was built on these three chords.

See also Blues.

360-degree sound system   A setup used by Pink Floyd in which speakers are placed around a hall so that the sound is all around the audience. The group perfected the setup in 1969. The member most responsible for the innovation is lead-singer/composer Roger Waters (b.

mid-1940s), who pursued electronics as a sideline while attending college. His aim was to dispense with the traditional format of a group performing on a stage at one end of a hall. By putting the sound all around the audience, he felt that a more theatrical effect was achieved.

See also Electronic Rock.

tie-in, tie-up   An arrangement into which two firms enter in order to promote, publicize, advertise, and sell their wares. The arrangement generally involves a commodity and a medium of expression: a lipstick and a song; a brand of coffee and a book; a car and a film; a T-shirt and an artist or a group. On occasion, a firm with the medium of expression will use the product as a giveaway; the goal is to advertise both the product and the song, film, book, show, or record. In recent years, the tie-in has yielded enormous revenues both to the commodity manufacturer and, generally, an artist or a group whose popularity is so great as to promote sales.

timbales   *See* Latin rhythm instruments.

Tin-Pan Alley   A symbol of popular music. A closelyknit microcosm of publishers, song-pluggers, songwriters, and record companies engaged in producing and promoting popular music. Also, a specific place or area that houses many music publishing companies. Tin-Pan Alley acquired its name when a New York City block between 5th Avenue and Broadway on 29th Street was the locale of the main music publishers of the day. A songwriter named Monroe H. Rosenfeld, who was also a journalist, used the colorful cognomen in a newspaper article around 1911. The sound of many pianos being played at the same time by rehearsal pianists for different artists made him think of many tin pans being struck simultaneously.

When radio superseded vaudeville as the major means of bringing songs to the ears of the public, NYC's Tin-Pan Alley moved uptown into buildings on Broadway between 42nd and 49th streets. During the 1930s, 1940s, and 1950s, the Brill Building on the northwest corner of 49th Street and Broadway, housing as many as 100 music publishers, became the center of Tin-Pan Alley. Beginning songwriters hung out in a restaurant on the street-level of the building, while the more established cleffers lunched at the old Lindy's across the avenue near 50th Street, and the cream of the ASCAP crowd dined at the Paddock between 51st and 52nd streets, also on the east side of Broadway.

The rise of Rock 'n' Roll brought two other Broadway buildings into prominence: No. 1650, which fronted on 51st Street and extended from Broadway to 7th Avenue, and No. 1697, on the West Side of Broadway between 52nd and 53rd streets. In the late fifties, a dispersal of music publishers began, which in the time had some located on 5th Avenue (Shapiro-Bernstein), on West 54th Street (Edwin H. Morris), or at Columbus Circle (TRO). Moreover, so many new publishers came into the business that Tin-Pan Alley, never an alley, is now spread across the map of the country, with large publishing complexes being located in Atlanta, Detroit, Chicago, Cincinnati, Memphis, Nashville, and many smaller towns as well. In the years when the Brill was the center of the Alley, the NYC publishers had regional offices both in Chicago and Los Angeles, the former in the Woods Theatre Building near the Loop, and the latter on Sunset and Hollywood boulevards, within walking distance of Vine Street.

"Tiny Tim"   Professional name of Herbert Khoury (b. circa 1930), a singer and ukelele player who attained nationwide notoriety as a result of appearances on the Johnny Carson *Tonight* show. His forte was singing oldtime ballads of the thirties and forties (like "Tiptoe Through the Tulips"), in a nasal falsetto. His apparent appeal to teenagers, as well as middle-agers, led Rock groups to include him on their programs. The year before he was married on the Johnny Carson show, he garnered a recording contract and made a number of albums.

tipple   A small member of the plucked-string family, closer to a ukulele than a guitar. In 1933 an instrumental group called the Spirits of Rhythm—headed by scat singer Leo Watson (1898–1950)—drew New York City crowds to the Onyx on 52 Street by performing with a paper-wrapped suitcase (that served as a drum) and three tipples.
See also 52nd Street.

Titanium Album   A record industry term for an album that sells 3 million or more copies. The term came into vogue in the late 1970s.

"tithit"   Acronym for a "turntable hit," a record that garners substantial disk jockey spins but fails to become a bestseller.

TK Studio   Located in Hialeah, Fla., this studio became the premier southern Soul label of the seventies with its hard-core Funk. It included a family of record labels: Alston, Cat, Glades.
See also independent producer; recording studio.

Tom & Jerry   The name under which Simon and Garfunkel had their first record release while they were still going to secondary school in Queens, N.Y. Titled "Hey, Schoolgirl," it led to their appearing on *American Bandstand* in 1957.

tom-tom   A small Oriental drum, frequently used in pairs in dance orchestras. They may be tuned.

tonality   Although the term covers the relationship between all possible scales in the acoustical range, it has come to mean the tempered, diatonic major/minor system of European and American music. Accordingly, atonality means a departure from that traditional system.
See also acoustics; atonal.

tonic   The first note of a scale.

Tony Awards   *See* Musical, Tony Awards for Best.

"toomler"   Derived from tumult-maker, a Yiddish word for a fool or noisemaker or comic who does everything to entertain the customers. It originated in the Borscht Belt.
See also Borscht Belt.

"too much"   Depending on the intonation, it can have a positive or negative connotation. In either instance, it refers to something out of the ordinary range of expectation.

Top 40   A format for disk jockey shows devised and pioneered by Station KOWH in Omaha, Neb., in 1949. A Storz station, it was concerned with building maximum advertising revenues and a maximum audience. The Storz chain took up the format—saturation programming of a limited group of records, identification jingles, limited dee jay palaver, and hourly news-breaks. In time, other chains like Gordon McClendon, Gerald Bartell, and Plough all adopted the format for its profitability, enthusiastically supported by station managers, resentful of the earnings and celebrity status of name disk jockeys. Formula Radio, as it became known in the late 1950s, eliminated the name dee jay who made up his own programs, converting him into an announcer who programmed from a set list prepared by management and who briefly announced titles and read ticker-tape news bulletins. During the late fifties, the radio industry was the center of considerable controversy as name dee jays resigned in protest against the Top 40 format. But the format triumphed, since the exclusion of chatter by personality dee jays increased the number of advertising spots that could be introduced during an hour. And the kids seemed to like the frequent repetition of the top songs of the moment.

Curiously, a four-hour radio program currently being heard on stations around the country on Saturday morning and titled *American Top 40,* or *The Countdown,* represents a return to the type of program that was discarded in the fifties with the rise of the Top 40 format. Emcee'd by a dee jay named Casey Casum and presenting the most popular disks of the week, from No. 40 at 8:00 A.M. to No. 1 at noon, it is replete with anecdotes, stories behind the song and/or artist, and other colorful information.

topical songs   The tradition of songs commenting on current problems, protesting injustice, or inspiring people fighting a common cause is as old at least as the American Revolution. William Billings (1746–1800), regarded as this country's first professional songwriter, composed "Chester" (1778), a song that vied in popularity with "Yankee Doodle" as the *Marseillaise* of the Revolution. Although the Negro spirituals are viewed as songs of religious jubilation or sorrow, many of them were really veiled topical songs: e.g., "Go Down, Moses" and "Joshua Fit the Battle of Jericho." Some like "Oh Freedom" and "No More Auction Block for Me" were outspoken protest songs.

Leaping to World War I, we had not only "Over There" but the songs of the Wobblies, which sprang from the economically depressed lives of workers. During the Depression years, the deprivations of textile and garment workers yielded protest songs. And what about "Brother, Can You Spare a Dime?" There were also the *Dust Bowl Ballads* of Woody Guthrie and the songs inspired by the organizing drive of the CIO. In the 1930s, the Broadway theater began to sing songs of social significance, with the 1937–1938 season accounting for four political musicals. Rodgers and Hart's *I'd Rather Be Right* dealt with President Franklin Delano Roosevelt and his administration; Marc Blitzstein's pungent *The Cradle Will Rock,* with the evils of the capitalist system; Harold Arlen and E. Y. Harburg's *Hooray for What!,* with the need for international disarmament; and Harold Rome's *Pins and Needles,* produced by the International Ladies Garment Workers Union, with labor and the union problem. In this period, the Federal Theatre Project produced a number of topical revues, with *Sing for Your Supper* yielding Earl Robinson and John La Touche's notable work *Ballad for Americans.* Later, in the early 1940s, Robinson and Lewis Allen, the writer of "Strange Fruit," wrote, "The House I Live In (That's America to Me')" for a short-lived Broadway revue; the song became the theme of a film short starring Frank Sinatra, who received a Special Oscar for it in 1946. In 1972, Robinson collaborated on "Black and White," a song of brotherhood that became a Gold Record for Three Dog Night.

In 1981 the British Specials scored a No. 1 hit with "Ghost Town," a song that commented on the country's racial riots in terms of "the fighting on the dance floor" which closed down all the clubs.

See also message songs; protest songs.

torch song   A song of unrequited love or lost love, with the singer carrying a torch for one who no longer shares, or perhaps, has never shared the other person's feelings. Also, songs of slavish submissiveness in the face of mistreatment. Sometimes, the torch song is described as a white Blues. Among the most famous songs in the genre: "Can't Help Lovin' Dat Man" (1927); "Body and Soul" (1930); "The End of a Love Affair" (1950); "My Man" (1921); "The Man That Got Away" (1954); "Nevertheless (I'm In Love with You)" (1931); "Mean to Me" (1929); "I'll Remember April" (1941); "I'll Be Seeing You" (1943); "What Wouldn't I Do for That Man" (1929); "Love Me or Leave Me" (1928); "It's a Blue World" (1940); "I've Got You Under My Skin" (1936). Among the most famous exponents of the form; Ruth Etting (b. 1897), Helen Morgan (1900–1941), Libby Holman (1905–1971), Dinah Shore (b. 1917), Judy Garland (1922–1969), Billie Holiday (1915–1959), and Frank Sinatra (b. 1915).

Recent examples of the lovelorn genre, seldom identified as torch ballads, would include Kris Kristofferson's "For the Good Times," Jacques Brel's "If You Go Away," Melissa Manchester's "Don't Cry Out Loud," Crystal Gale's "Don't It Make My Brown Eyes Blue," Jimmy Webb's "By the Time I Get to Phoenix," "We Wanted It All" by Carole Bayer Sager and Peter Allen, and Stephen Sondheim's "Not a Day Goes By" and "We Had a Good Thing Going."

In 1981 Carly Simon (b. 1945) recorded an album titled *Torch,* consisting entirely of songs of lost love and bleeding and broken hearts. It was part of a development in which Rock and Country singers began dipping into the Tin-Pan Alley well of ballads of the thirties and forties. In 1978 Willie Nelson (b. 1933) recorded *Stardust,* an album containing not only that classic ballad but Irving Berlin's "Blue Skies," Kurt Weill's "September Song," and the Gershwins' "Someone to Watch over Me," among other oldtime ballads. In the year of *Torch,* Nelson titled an album *Somewhere over the Rainbow,* once again recording pre-World War II ballads, and Linda Ronstadt (b. 1946) cut an unreleased album of ballads of the same vintage. Carly Simon's album included Alec Wilder's "I'll Be Around," Hoagy Carmichael's "I Get Along Without You Very Well," Rodgers & Hart's "Spring Is Here," Duke Ellington's "I Got It Bad and That Ain't Good," and the classic "Body and Soul."

Sinatra's most recent album, *She Shot Me Down* (1981), was likewise a collection of torch songs. He described them as "saloon songs—tear-jerkers and cry-in-your-beer kinds of things." Titled after a Sonny Bono (b. 1935) ballad, "Bang, Bang (My Baby Shot Me Down)," the album included a number of new lost-love songs: "I Loved Her" by Gordon Jenkins, "Monday Morning Quarterback" by Don Costa and Pamela

Phillips, and "Good Thing Going" by Stephen Sondheim from the show *Merrily We Roll Along*.

See also No. 1 plug; Tin-Pan Alley.

Total Sonic Concept   The Byrds, especially 12-string guitarist Jim (later Roger) McGuinn (b. 1942), pioneered a new mode in Rock: the creative manipulation of sound. McGuinn's involvement was not accidental, as his liner notes on the group's first album, *Mr. Tambourine Man*, reveal. Contending that the musical sounds of any time reflect the sounds in the outside world, he stated that propeller planes determined the sounds of the forties, while jets were the sonic determinants of the sixties. "The sound of the airplane in the forties," he wrote, "was a rrrrrrrrooooaaaaaaaahhhhhhhhh sound and Sinatra and other people sang like that with that sort of overtones. Now we've got the krrr-riiiiisssssssshhhhhhhhhh jet sound, and the kids are singing up there now." This was the basis of his choice of the name Byrds, an eye-catching way of spelling "birds." The "jet-age drone" that McGuinn sought to capture was presumably realized in *The Notorious Byrd Brothers*, their group's '68 album, in which he employed the most advanced electronic gadgetry of the day.

touch dancing   Teenagers of the 1950s, and into the present, have danced apart in no-touch dances like the Bugaloo, Mashed Potato, Monkey, Hitch Hike, Frug, Skate, and Disco. To these generations, dances like the Fox-Trot, Waltz, or Cha-Cha, in which the man and woman hold each other, were "touch dancing."

See also Fox-Trot.

Trad   A British term standing for "Traditional Jazz" and referring to an imitative New Orleans style. Popular in the late 1950s and early 1960s, it may be heard in *Stranger on the Shore* by Acker Bilk (b. 1929), a bestselling album in 1961.

See also New Orleans Jazz.

"trades"   Short for "trade papers." Refers mainly to *Billboard, Cash Box,* and *Record World*. Although *Variety* includes a music and record section, which in the 1930s and 1940s was the most influential, it is today viewed largely as a film and TV trade paper.

Transcendental Rock   A limited category that had its beginnings when George Harrison (b. 1943), concerned with the inner life, traveled east to the Maharishi Mahesh Yogi to study Transcendental Meditation. Traveling with him were the other three Beatles, Mick Jagger (b.

1944) of the Rolling Stones, and Marianne Faithfull (b. circa 1946), then Jagger's girlfriend. Soon the Maharishi received visits from Donovan (b. 1946), the Doors, and the Beach Boys. Musically, TM found expression in Harrison's "My Sweet Lord" (1970) and other selections in the album *All Things Must Pass.*

transistor   Refers to the battery-operated radio in which transistors are used instead of electron tubes for amplification. The transistor was developed by a research team of the Bell Telephone Laboratories, who discovered in 1947 that germanium crystals could amplify sound as much as 40 times. The discovery led engineers from Zenith to substitute transistors for vacuum tubes in a portable radio in the late 1940s. By the 1960s, the transistor had revolutionized tape recording as well as radio. The car radio and the beach radio became important in the listening habits of the public and in the launching of record hits.

transpose   To move a pattern or sequence of notes from one register to another, i.e., to move it from one key to another. In a higher key, c–d–f–g (key of F) becomes d–e–g–a (key of G), or b♭–c–e♭–f in a lower key (E♭). The relationship of intervals between the four notes has remained the same, but one sequence is in a higher register, and the other in a lower register.

traps   The entire complement of drums, including snare and bass drums, and such auxiliary percussive items as cymbals, woodblock, and cowbell.

tremolo   The rapid repetition of a note, achieved on string instruments by fast back-and-forth strokes of the bow.

"trip"   It has nothing to do with a journey, but refers to what one experiences after taking LSD. It's a "trip" in the sense that one's perceptions of time and space are distorted.

The Trip   A Rock nightclub in Los Angeles—one in which dancing was permitted at a time when only listening was the vogue. The Byrds and the Lovin' Spoonful, among others, performed there in the early sixties.

Triple Crown   An outdated tradepaper concept that referred to a disk that made No. 1 on three different charts.

triplet   A three-note unit in which the accent is traditionally on the first note and the three notes have a duration of two. Ordinarily, three eighth notes equal a dotted quarter; but in a triplet, their duration is equal just to a quarter note. Three quarter notes in a triplet equal a half note instead of a dotted half:

Truckin'   A song and a dance that were introduced in 1935 in the twenty-sixth edition of the *Cotton Club Parade*. The lyric by Ted Koehler, to music by Rube Bloom, contains no description of the dance, except that it was something new in Harlem. It apparently was little more than a version of the Shuffle. In contemporary jargon, "keep on truckin'" signifies "keep on trying'," "keep moving ahead in life."

See also Shuffle.

"turkey"   It started out as an equivalent for a song or record that did not "happen," i.e., a "bomb." But it is now part of general usage, meaning a person one does not like.

turn.   *See* Shake.

"turn-on"   Derived from the impact of drugs, it has come into general usage as a term for "thrill," or, as Sam Cooke (1935–1964) sang in 1956, "You Send Me."

"twangy" guitar   Developed by Duane Eddy (b. 1938), who gave the guitar a raunchy, bluesy sound with a roaring vibrato and scored a flock of million sellers. The first was "Rebel Rouser" (1958), followed by "Because They're Young," title tune of the film in which he appeared and played in 1960, and "Dance with the Guitar Man" (1962). While he was working with a band in Phoenix in 1955, he discovered the unique sound that made him a guitar notable. It was a matter of playing the melody on the bass string instead of the other five, as was normally done. Skillful record production by Lee Hazelwood, who collaborated with him on "Rebel Rouser" and other instrumentals, enhanced the sound he elicited from his instrument. Eddy's success was in part the result of great exposure on Dick Clark's *American Bandstand*. Clark had a managerial interest in the guitarist as well as owning stock in Jamie Records, for whom Eddy & His Rebels recorded. Other titles that he popularized: "Cannonball" and "Ramrod," both in '58, and "Boss Guitar" in '63.

Among other guitarists and all-instrumental groups that exploited the sound, there were Link Wray (b. 1935), whose "Rumble" was a hit in '58; Johnny & the Hurricanes, who produced bestsellers in

"Crossfire" and "Red River Rock" in '59; and the Ventures, three guitarists and a drummer, who hit in '60 with "Walk, Don't Run." Although the Ventures were consistently popular in Japan all through the sixties and seventies, they made no personal appearances in the U.S.A. until 1980 when there was renewed interest in all-instrumental groups. The Raybeats were among new non-vocal groups that surfaced in the 1980s.

twelve-bar blues   The classic form of the Blues, consisting of 3 segments of 4 bars each, with a chord sequence as follows: C (4 bars); F (2 bars) C (2 bars); G (2 bars) C (2 bars). The lyric pattern is AAB.
    See also Classic Blues.

twelve-string guitar   The instrument of which Leadbelly (1885–1949) claimed to be the King. Composed of twice as many strings as the traditional acoustic guitar, it is a demanding instrument of limited popularity among Rock performers. Performers who have mastered it include Stuart John Wolstenholme (b.1947) of Barclay James Harvest and songwriter Fred Neil (b. circa 1938), whose song "Everybody's Talkin'" was used as the theme of the film *Midnight Cowboy*.

"Twentieth-century Minstrel"   That's what Richard Dyer-Bennet (b. 1913 in Leicester, England) called himself. Concerned with reviving the art of minstrelsy as it was practiced in ancient Europe, he established the first School of Minstrelsy at Aspen, Colo., in the late 1940s.

The Twist   A black dance that became a nationwide craze in 1960–62, largely as the result of a recording by Chubby Checker (b. 1941) of the tune of the same name by Hank Ballard (b. early 1930s). Although Ballard & the Midnighters made the first recording of "The Twist" in 1959, it was not until this record was re-released 15 months later in June 1960 that it stirred enough interest to prompt the Chubby Checker cover. Apart from the fact that Chubby was a sensational dancer, he had an ace-in-the-hole in the exposure he received on *American Bandstand* through the association of his record label with Dick Clark. The dance caught on partly because it was relatively easy to do, the older generation latching onto it almost as quickly as the teenagers. A nondescript bar on Manhattan's West 47th Street, the Peppermint Lounge, suddenly became the hangout of the jet set, who spent the night twisting away. Soon celebrities from every walk of life—the theater, politics, high society, corporate business, and Hollywood films—were climbing all over each other to get into the Lounge. And the general public gawked, as they did more recently at Studio 54, also in Manhattan, at the height of the Disco craze. (Although Hank Ballard is credited with writing "The Twist," the same melody was used six years earlier on a 1953 record by the Drifters of a song titled "What'cha Gonna Do?" written by Ahmet Ertegun.)

The popularity of the dance inevitably prompted a flock of Twist records: e.g., "Twist and Shout" by the Isley Brothers and "Twistin' U.S.A." by Danny & the Juniors (1960); "Twist, Twist, Señora" by Gary "U.S." Bonds and "Twistin' the Night Away" by Sam Cooke (both 1962); "Twisting Matilda" by Jimmy Soul (1963). These do not begin to exhaust the list of the numerous Twist recordings.

See also Peppermint Lounge.

Two-Beat Jazz   Refers to Dixieland Jazz, which has a two-beat feeling because of the accents on the second and fourth beats of a four-beat measure. By contrast, New Orleans Jazz tends to be an even-flowing four-beat sound in which the accents on beats one and three of March music do not obtain. To complete the picture, Swing rides on a steady, pronounced four-to-the-bar sound.

See also Dixieland Jazz.

Two-Tone movement   A group of loosely allied, racially mixed British Rock bands that surfaced in the 1970s, the Two-Tone movement represents a nonracist fringe of the anti-Establishment groups. Rooted like other skinhead combos in the poverty and unemployment of inner-city decay, they attack the present British government and the brutality of its police force. Among Two-Tone groups, there are the Specials, Selector, and the English Beat, the last of whom recorded "Step Down, Margaret," which was addressed, of course, to Prime Minister Margaret Thatcher. A 2-Tone label was founded in 1979 by Jerry Dammers, the leader of the Specials.

See also Oi; Skinheads.

two-track tape   No matter how many separate tracks are made in a recording session, they are eventually mixed down to two tracks from which the master tape is made.

U

una corda   Literally, "one chord." It refers to early pianos in which the left pedal caused the hammer to strike one string of a note instead of two, thereby softening the sound. Today it is a misnomer, since each note is the product of three strings, instead of two, and the left pedal, operating still to reduce the sound, causes the hammer to strike two strings, not one.

underground radio   It used to refer to FM radio and was apparently born with dee jay Tom Donahue, originally of KYA of San Francisco, a producer of Cow Palace shows and of recordings by the Grateful Dead, Great Society, and others. In the late 1960s, he took over a small FM station, KMPX, in San Francisco and broke a number of "underground" hits, including the Youngblood's "Get Together" and the Chambers Brothers' "Time." A strike led by Donahue caused the station's entire personnel to switch in mid-'68 from KMPX to KSAN, a larger FM station owned by Metromedia. In those days, underground radio sought out offbeat material disregarded by the Top 40 stations because of the length of a track, or the esoteric nature of the material, or the complexity of the sound.
See also Top 40.

underground Rock   The Fugs, a New York City group led by Tuli Kupferberg and Ed Sanders, are generally regarded as the first underground group. Political and pornographic, they wrote poetry and created music for it, antedating Leonard Cohen (b. 1935). They worked at shocking and repelling, but used language skillfully in satire and parody: "in the great bowling alley of your mind, I will be your pin-boy." They received virtually no airplay, since disk jockeys worried that the pronunciation of their name would be offensive. Although appearances frequently prompted people to walk out on them, they did secure a recording contract and produced four albums between 1968 and 1970: *It Crawled into My Hand, Honest* and *Golden Filth* were two of the titles. While the West Coast Mothers of Invention dealt with similar materials in a similar satiric vein and worked at making audiences uncomfortable and angry, they lost their underground status when their double-record debut album, *Freak Out,* surfaced in 1966.

With a name taken from a pornographic paperback, the Velvet Underground helped make underground Rock largely a New York phenomenon. Led by Lou Reed (b. early 1940), the group became part of Andy Warhol's Exploding Plastic Inevitable, a multimedia show, in 1966. The subject matter of Reed's songs eliminated airplay for the records they made: heroin, in "I'm Waiting for the Man"; cocaine, in "Run, Run, Run"; sado-masochism, in "Venus in Furs"; and transvestitism, lesbianism, and homosexuality in other songs. Although the group splintered in 1970, Lou Reed made it as a solo star in 1972 with an album, *Transformer,* and a single, "Walk on the Wild Side," produced by a similarly oriented performer, the androgynous David Bowie (b. 1947).

Another underground figure on the New York scene, Patti Smith (b. 1946), published several volumes of poetry before she made her debut in a Manhattan club in 1973, reciting her poetry to Rock accompaniment by writer/guitarist Lenny Kaye. Although she has recorded four albums, *Horses* and *Wave* among them, neither her sound nor her subject matter has perceptibly widened a strong in-group following. Together with Lou Reed, Patti is regarded as one of the galvanizing forces of British Punk Rock; her impact came from a tour of England.

Other groups that are considered part of the New York vanguard are Talking Heads, Television, and the B-52s.

See also Avant-garde Rock; Punk Rock.

unison   Refers to singing or instrumental playing of the same note by all the members of a group. Since instruments and/or voices of different quality and texture are striking the same note, unison performance changes the fabric of the sound even though the pitch is not changed. By contrast, harmony involves different members of the group singing or playing different notes.

"Uncle Tom"   Refers to a black person who knuckles under to whites merely because of differences in skin coloration.

Univibe   A distortion device to simulate a rotating speaker. Used by Jimi Hendrix.

"uppers"   Drugs that give one a lift, e.g., the amphetamines. Also known as "boosters," "jolly beans," "peps," "speed," "wake ups," "zooms," and "Whities."

upright   A piano, unlike the grands, constructed with the strings in a vertical position. Contemporary uprights vary according to their height: spinets, 36 or 37 inches in height; consoles, 40 to 42 inches in height; and studios, made especially for use in schools and universities, 44 to 51 inches in height.

Urban Blues   The Depression of the early 1930s prompted a large migration of blacks from the agricultural South to the industrial North. Among the migrants were Country bluesmen like Big Bill Broonzy (1893-1958), who settled in Chicago, then the recording center of the U.S.A. for blacks. As these bluesmen sought to adjust to life in a big, northern city, the sound of the Blues, its subject matter and outlook, all changed—and became urbanized. One quick change was the use of the piano for accompaniment; Country Blues had been accompanied exclusively by guitar and harmonica. Other bluesmen who are comprehended under the designation Urban Blues include Roosevelt Sykes (b. 1906); Albert Laundrew (Sunnyland Slim, b. 1907); Little Brother Montgomery (b. 1906); Champion Jack Dupree (b. 1910); Jazz Gillum (1904–1966); Speckled Red (Rufus Perryman, 1892–1973); and Leroy Carr (1905–1935). Together with Lonnie Johnson (1889–1970) and Jazz Gillum (1904–1966), Carr added Jazz and Pop inflections to the Blues.

See also Rhythm & Blues.

Urban Cowboy   In 1980 the big broad-brimmed Stetson worn by cowboys suddenly became a commonplace on the heads of young people in cities around the country, girls as well as fellers. The nostalgic movement was given impetus by a film titled *Urban Cowboy* in which 14 Country Rock artists and groups appeared. Among others: Kenny Rogers, the Charlie Daniels Band, Jimmy Buffet, Linda Ronstadt/J. D. Souther, and newcomers Johnny Lee, Mickey Gilley, and Gilley's "Urban Cowboy" Band. But to many, the real Urban Cowboy was Willie Nelson, the Country Outlaw, who did not appear in the film and who was able to revive the older generation's nostalgic idealization of the cowboy.

See also Nashville Outlaws.

Urban Folk   In 1958 the Kingston Trio, who had come together at the Purple Onion in San Francisco, recorded a folk song of the Civil War era about a man (Tom Dula) who killed his girlfriend and was hanged for the murder. Arranged by Dave Guard (b. 1934), who formed the group, "Tom Dooley" (as they called their version) climbed to No. 1 on Pop charts, sold over 3.5 million records, projected the trio into star status, and ignited the Folk development of the late fifties and early sixties. Soon the airwaves were echoing with sounds of traditional folk songs, adaptations of such songs, new Folk-oriented songs, and groups like the Brothers Four, Gateway Singers, Greenbriar Boys, Highwaymen, Journeymen, Lettermen, Limeliters, Chad Mitchell Trio, New Christy Minstrels, New Lost City Ramblers, Rooftop Singers, and Seekers—some of whom had been performing on the coffeehouse circuit before "Tom Dooley" caused the Folk explosion. In addition to the groups, there was a long list of individual artists with a Folk orientation: Joan Baez (b. 1941), Judy Collins (b. 1939), Ramblin' Jack Elliott (b. 1931), Terry Gilkyson (b. 1919), Burl Ives (b. 1909), Harry Belafonte (b. 1927), Theodore Bikel (b. 1924), Leon Bibb (b. 1935), Ed McCurdy (b. 1919), Erik Darling (b. 1933), Guy Carawan (b. 1927), Pete Seeger (b. 1919), Odetta (b. 1930), and others.

The climax of the Urban Folk development came in 1963 with the arrival of Bob Dylan (b. 1941), the emergence of Peter, Paul & Mary, and the impact of Dylan's topical song "Blowin' in the Wind." Together with Joan Baez, then the regnant Queen of Folk Music (who embraced Dylan), Peter, Paul & Mary gave new impetus to Urban Folk, which also grew with the growth of the civil rights movement and the mounting opposition to the war in Vietnam. A new group of folk writers and artists emerged who made protest and message songs the basis of their work—songwriter/singers like Phil Ochs (1940-1976), Tom Paxton (b. 1937), Malvina Reynolds (1900-1978), Peter LaFarge (1931-1965), and others.

All through the fifties and sixties, the Urban Folk development was a source of considerable controversy among Folk aficionados. There were some who adhered strongly to the traditional concept of Folk and rejected the young newcomers as upstarts; Urban Folk was a contradiction in terms to them. Some were willing to accept those urban artists whose effort was to retain the feeling and sound of authentic, ethnic material: i.e., the so-called interpreters. It was the popularizers like Peter, Paul & Mary and the Kingston Trio who faced the strongest criticism. But it was the popularizers who helped make Folk music a major Pop trend of the fifties and sixties.

Many of the Rock groups and performers who came to the fore in the sixties started with an interest in Folk material. Among these are the Byrds, Lovin' Spoonful, Jefferson Airplane, Tim Hardin, Linda Ronstadt, Harry Chapin, Janis Ian, Arlo Guthrie, Sonny & Cher, the Mamas and the Papas, and, of course, Bob Dylan.

See also the Byrds; Bob Dylan; Folk Rock.

vamp   Introductory bars of music, played by piano, band, or orchestra—repeated several times if necessary—until the singer or soloist enters. Also, a short passage connecting through modulation two sections of music. When no modulation is involved, the vamp simply consists of a repeated chord pattern.

Edgard Varèse (1883-1965)   The revolutionary composer and theorist whose work, in Joan Peyser's words, "pointed the way to a pitchless music, with an emphasis on pure sound and rhythm, and thus led the move toward the current preoccupation of serious composers with electronic music." Shortly after World War II, when he received his first tape recorder, Varèse interpolated taped sounds into *Déserts,* an orchestral work. *Amériques,* completed in 1922, was written for 142 instruments, including 21 percussion instruments and 2 sirens. His works continued to be marked by a concern with volumes and densities of sound rather than melodies or harmonies. *Ionisation,* his most familiar work and reportedly played at Oak Ridge, Tenn., while workers were constructing the atom bomb, was written for 37 percussive instruments, some with definite pitch (piano, celesta, tubular chimes) and others with indeterminate pitch (gongs, cymbals, triangles, sleighbells, guiro, maracas, claves, and cencerro). A later work, *Ecuatorial,* was scored for two Theremins in addition to percussion, brass, piano, organ, and voice. Varèse obviously anticipated the later concern of Rock with synthesizers and other electronic devices. The Mothers of Invention revealed the influence of Varèse in their *Freak Out* album.

See also Avant-garde Rock; John Cage; Classical Rock; Electronic Rock.

variety   When the minstrel show modulated into vaudeville, "variety" was an early term for vaudeville. The period is suggested by the fact that the publication called *Variety* was founded in 1905.

See also minstrel show; vaudeville.

vaudeville   It derived from the olio segment of the minstrel show in which each member of the cast performed his own specialty. That's precisely what vaudeville was: a miscellaneous collection of acts, beginning usually with acrobatics and including performers who sang, danced, told jokes, and sometimes played dramatic sketches. "Vaude was socko," in *Variety* lingo, from 1905 to 1913 and through the 1920s. Theaters across the country were aligned in circuits like the Keith-Orpheum Circuit and the Marcus Loew Circuit, with performers traveling from city to city and appearing in theaters for a week generally. In this era, music publishers romanced singers like Belle Baker (1895–1957) and Fanny Brice (1891–1951), who could in a cross-country tour convert an unknown song into a hit. The diadem of the bigtime Keith-Orpheum Circuit was the Palace Theatre in New York City, which was also the Taj Mahal of vaudeville. The emergence of "talking pictures" saw vaudeville theaters switching from a two-a-day pattern to continuous performance, with each complete bill capped by the showing of a film. By 1928, there were only four theaters in the entire country offering vaudeville without films. Radio dealt vaudeville a mortal blow. In the fall of 1932, even the Palace threw in films with its vaudeville bills. But by November 1932, the Palace had turned into a straight picture-house, a quiet admission that the vaudeville era was over. In 1916 vaudeville had room for 20,000 full-week acts and there were 1,700 theaters around the country booking acts. By 1932, the number had dwindled to a bare handful. However, live stage shows were a feature into the forties of such giant movie palaces, showing first-run films, as the Capitol Theatre, Paramount, Roxy, and Radio City Music Hall in NYC. Later, the variety or vaudeville format found nostalgic expression, including even tumbling and juggling acts, in the popular *Ed Sullivan Show* on TV.

See also payola; Radio City Music Hall.

"The Verified Legend"   The billing of Slim Whitman (b. 1924), a "Country" singer who hit in 1952 with versions of Broadway show songs like "Indian Love Call" and "Rose Marie"; who has 60 albums (19 of them Gold); and who was back in the limelight in 1980 as the result of a commercial that has sold over 2 million copies of his album *All My Best* by mail-order.

vibes   Short for vibraphone and vibraharp, instruments that were advanced forms of the xylophone. Taj Mahal (b. 1942) could play them.

"Vibes" is also a shortened form of "vibrations," currently meaning reaction, feeling, response; someone gives you "good vibes" or "bad vibes."

vibrato   Rapid vibration of a string, of the vocal cords, or of a horn tone to give luster and expressiveness to a note. In playing string instruments, different tonal qualities are achieved, depending on whether use is made of a finger, hand, or wrist vibrato. Among Pop singers, Billy Eckstine (b. 1914) was regarded as having a "wide vibrato," meaning a low, nondetached repetition of a note, a type of vibrato exemplified by Sarah Vaughan (b. 1924) in the Jazz field. It is the overtones produced by the wavering, or oscillation, of a tone that enrich it; a nonvibrato tone, i.e., one without overtones, is known as a "white" tone.

video cassette   A small plastic cartridge containing magnetic tape on which a TV show or film has been recorded. As recently as 1980 video cassettes were such a novelty that the music industry had not yet worked out a rate structure covering the recording of music on such video devices.

The Village Vanguard   Located in a labyrinthine basement at 7th Avenue South and 11th Street in Manhattan, the Village Vanguard was opened by softspoken Max Gordon on February 26, 1934. It has been in continuous operation under Gordon, who still owns and runs it, for over 47 years, making it the longest-lived club in Greenwich Village. Basically a Jazz club, the Vanguard has also presented folk singers like

Leadbelly (1885–1949), Woody Guthrie (1912–1967), Pete Seeger (b. 1919), and The Weavers; R & B/Pop artists like Dinah Washington (1924–1963); and Rock/Soul artists like Aretha Franklin (b. 1942). Proprietor Gordon has described the life and times of the club in *Live at The Village Vanguard* (1980).

See also Greenwich Village.

viña   An Indian instrument which, like the sarod and sitar, uses drone effects. Three of the seven strings are drones. A gourd resonator attached to its upper end rests against the player's left side. During the psychedelic era, the delayed echo effect resulting from the vibrations of the drones accounted for its appeal.

See also Acid Rock; sarod, sitar.

"vines"   Black lingo for clothes. "Threads" is another colloquialism for the same.

"viper"   A term used in the 1920s and 1930s for a marijuana user. In 1934 Fats Waller (1904–1943) wrote a solo Jazz composition titled "Viper's Drag." One of the most popular numbers of Jazz fiddler Stuff Smith (b. 1909) in the days he played at the 52nd Street Onyx club in Manhattan was a number he wrote titled "You'se a Viper." A Vocalion record of the tune contained a rare vocal by trumpeter Jonah Jones (b. 1909).

visual instrumental   On film and the TV tube, when the instrumentalist is seen performing the selection, it's a visual instrumental. This contrasts with a background instrumental, when the performer is not seen.

See also synchronization.

visual vocal   When the singer is on camera in a film or on TV, it's a visual vocal. If the singer is heard but not seen, e.g., a phonograph is playing, it's a background vocal.

Vocal Performance, Best—Pop Female (NARAS Grammy Awards)

1958	Ella Fitzgerald: *Ella Fitzgerald Sings the Irving Berlin Songbook*
1959	Ella Fitzgerald: "But Not for Me"
1960	Ella Fitzgerald: "Mack the Knife" (single); *Ella in Berlin* (album)
1961	Judy Garland: *Judy at Carnegie Hall*
1962	Ella Fitzgerald: *Ella Swings Brightly with Nelson Riddle*
1963	Barbra Streisand: *The Barbra Streisand Album*
1964	Barbra Streisand: "People"

1965   Barbra Streisand: *My Name Is Barbra;* Petula Clark: "I Know a Place"

1966   Eydie Gorme: "If He Walked into My Life"

1967   Bobbie Gentry: "Ode to Billie Joe"

1968   Dionne Warwick: "Do You Know the Way to San Jose?"

1969   Peggy Lee: "Is That All There Is?"

1970   Dionne Warwick: "I'll Never Fall in Love Again" from *Promises, Promises*

1971   Carole King: "Tapestry"

1972   Helen Reddy: "I Am Woman"

1973   Roberta Flack: "Killing Me Softly with His Song"

1974   Olivia Newton-John: "I Honestly Love You"

1975   Janis Ian: "At Seventeen"

1976   Linda Ronstadt: "Hasten Down the Wind"

1977   Barbra Streisand: "Love Theme from *A Star is Born*"

1978   Anne Murray: "You Needed Me"

1979   Donna Summer: "Hot Stuff"

1980   Bette Midler: "The Rose"

1981   Lena Horne: *The Lady and Her Music Live on Broadway*

See also National Academy of Recording Arts and Sciences.

Vocal Performance, Best—Pop Group or Duo (NARAS Grammy Awards)

1965   The Statler Brothers: "Flowers on the Wall"

1966   The Mamas & the Papas: "Monday, Monday"

1967   5th Dimension: "Up, Up and Away"

1968   Simon & Garfunkel: "Mrs. Robinson"

1969   5th Dimension: "Aquarius/Let the Sunshine In"

1970   The Carpenters: "Close to You"

1971   The Carpenters: *The Carpenters*

1972   Roberta Flack/Donny Hathaway: "Where Is the Love"

1973   Gladys Knight & the Pips: "Neither One of Us"

1974   Paul McCartney and Wings: "Band on the Run"

1975   Eagles: "Lyin' Eyes"

1976   Chicago: "If You Leave Me Now"

1977   Bee Gees: "How Deep Is Your Love"

1978   Bee Gees: *Saturday Night Fever*

1979   Eagles: "Heartache Tonight"

1980   Bob Seger and the Silver Bullet Band: *Against the Wind*

1981   The Manhattan Transfer: "Boy from New York City"

See also National Academy of Recording Arts and Sciences.

Vocal Performance, Best—Pop Male (NARAS Grammy Awards)

1958   Perry Como: "Catch a Falling Star"

1959   Frank Sinatra: *Come Dance With Me*

1960   Ray Charles: "Georgia on My Mind" (single); *Genuis of Ray Charles* (album)

1961   Jack Jones: "Lollipops and Roses"

1962   Tony Bennett: "I Left My Heart in San Francisco"

1963   Jack Jones: "Wives and Lovers"

1964   Louis Armstrong: "Hello, Dolly!"

1965   Frank Sinatra: "It Was a Very Good Year"
        Roger Miller: "King of the Road"

1966   Paul McCartney: "Eleanor Rigby"

1967   Glen Campbell: "By the Time I Get to Phoenix"

1968   Jose Feliciano: "Light My Fire"

1969   Nilsson: "Everybody's Talkin'"

1970   Ray Stevens: "Everything Is Beautiful"

1971   James Taylor: "You've Got a Friend"

1972   Nilsson: "Without You"

1973   Stevie Wonder: "You Are the Sunshine of My Life"

1974   Stevie Wonder: *Fulfillingness' First Finale*

1975   Paul Simon: *Still Crazy After All These Years*

1976   Stevie Wonder: *Songs in the Key of Life*

1977   James Taylor: "Handy Man"

1978   Barry Manilow: "Copacabana"

1979   Billy Joel: "52nd Street"

1980   Kenny Loggins: "This Is It"

1981   Al Jarreau: *Breakin' Away*

See also National Academy of Recording Arts and Sciences.

"The Voice"   *See* Frank Sinatra.

voice-over   The technique of first recording the instrumental background on a record and then overlaying or overdubbing a voice or a group of voices. Today this is standard practice. In the Tin-Pan Alley era, it was a rarity.

Voodoo Rock   It's the sole province of a New Orleans–born singer/songwriter/bassist named Malcolm John Rebennack (b. circa 1940), who made a number of records as "Dr. John the Night Tripper," combining Soul and voodoo. His first album was titled *Gris Gris* (1968) after charms and amulets used in voodoo ceremonies. Rebennack, who had by then established a reputation in Hollywood as a studio musician, enlarged the voodoo image by appearing in-person in the costume of a medicine man: ornate silver robes, weird-looking head-dresses, and odd necklaces. Two other voodoo-oriented albums followed: *Sun, Moon and Herbs* (1971) and *Gumbo* (1972). The latter yielded a chart single in "Iko, Iko." Dr. John hardly pretends that he is using authentic voodoo material and actually combines Cajun sounds with Haitian voodoo concepts. One of Dr. John's influences was the famous "Professor Longhair," the New Orleans creator of a piano style that also influenced Fats Domino (b. 1928), Allen Toussaint (b. 1938), James Booker, and Huey Smith (b. 1934). Dr. John played guitar on a number of Professor Longhair's recordings, including the perennial "Mardi Gras in New Orleans" (1956) and a posthumous collection, *Crawfish Fiesta* (1980).

See also "Professor Longhair."

wah-wah pedal   In the old days, trumpet players produced the wah-wah sound by waving their hand or a hat over the bell of a horn. Later, a mute inserted in the bell produced the baby cry. Now a foot pedal used by guitarists sends an electric signal up and down, from treble to bass and back. Eric Clapton (b. 1945) and Jimi Hendrix (1942–1970) popularized the sound in the 1968–1969 period.

See also echo; feedback; fuzztone; reverb.

"wail"   To wail, among jazzmen, meant to give an outstanding performance—especially, to play with deep feeling. The use of the word has been extended to mean to perform superbly in any area—fixing a car, playing cards, making one's way with the ladies. In current usage, it can also mean having a great time.

walkaround   That part of the minstrel show in which the troupe marched in and walked around the semicircle of chairs before it seated itself at the Interlocutor's command "Gentlemen, be seated." Many songs were written for this segment, the most famous being "I Wish I Was in Dixie's Land," written and composed expressly for Bryant's Minstrels in 1859 by Dan D. Emmett (1815–1904). The song eventually became known as "Dixie" and was one of the South's great rallying songs in the Civil War.

See also minstrel show.

walking bass   An eighth note figure played by the string bass in which the ascending notes of a chord are sounded. Each note is sounded twice, or, when this is performed on the piano, octave intervals are used. Boogie-Woogie basses are used, as is Shuffle rhythm. The figure may involve a descending sequence as well as an ascending one.
See also Boogie-Woogie; Shuffle.

Walkway of the Stars   Country entertainers who have contributed $1,000 or more to the Country Music Hall of Fame have their names imbedded in an area of the Nashville building housing the Country Museum and the Hall of Fame.

Wall-of-Sound   A sound-style pioneered by Phil Spector (b. 1940), involving heavy echo and tympani bombs, but most of all, a continuous flow of sound. Spector's idea was to surround the listener, enveloping him or her in a curtain of sound.

Andy Warhol's Exploding Plastic Inevitable   A touring avant-garde show devised by artist Warhol, which included a Rock band (Velvet Underground), some singers (including a whip girl), a light show, and gigantic projection of films on a huge screen. Warhol's concept was to overwhelm the audience's senses to such a degree that spectators *experienced* instead of just watching the proceedings.

washboard   In the early days of the Blues, country bluesmen used an ordinary washboard as an accompanying instrument. To produce the scraping sound, an ordinary thimble was drawn across the metal ridges. Bluesman Robert Brown (1910–1966), who called himself ''Washboard Sam,'' made many records using a washboard. To enhance and vary the sound, he attached a cowbell and a metal turntable to the washboard.
See also jug band; spasm band.

washboard band   With the corrugated washboard used by washerwomen to provide the rhythm, this type of old-style Folk band was composed of fiddle, mandolin, guitar, and sometimes even a piano. During the 1930s, guitarist Brownie McGhee (b. 1915) organized a Washboard Band which included Robert Young (known as ''Washboard Slim'') and Leroy Dallas (b. 1920), who played guitar and washboard.
See also jug band; spasm band.

washtub bass   *See* Brownie bass.

Watkins Glen ''Summer Jam''   Staged by Bill Graham (b. 1931), the San Francisco promoter, the ''Summer Jam'' at Watkins Glen in upstate New York was a one-day event on July 28, 1973. Reportedly 600,000 came to hear the Allman Brothers Band, The Grateful Dead, The Band, and other Rock luminaries. In comparing it with the celebrated Woodstock Festival, which seemed to portend "a great explosion breeding in the land," a reviewer for the *Los Angeles Time* wrote: "Watkins Glen was positively somnolent. It lacked political overtones. It possessed little counterculture vitality. Only the powerful amplified music [was vital]. Barbiturates, not hallucinogenics, were the favored drugs. To sleep, perchance, but not to dream."

See also Altamont; festivals; *Woodstock Nation.*

Wattstax (1972)   A live-recorded concert album. On the seventh anniversary of the Watts (Los Angeles) riots of 1965, the Memphis sound came to the Los Angeles Memorial Coliseum, transforming it (according to the liner note) "from a sporting arena into a soulful expression of the Living Word." For seven hours, a preponderantly black audience of over 100,000 listened to a parade of artists that included the Staple Singers, Bar-Kays, Soul Children, Kim Weston, Eddie Floyd, Rufus Thomas, Carla Thomas, and Albert King. High point of the proceedings was the arrival of Academy Award winner Isaac Hayes with two Harley Davidsons, the lights flashing and sirens screaming full blast. Resplendent in a gold-chain vest and metallic orange pants, his bald head gleaming as he performed his Oscar-winning *Shaft* theme, the "Black Moses," as folks greeted him, was "the true black sex symbol–idol." An affirmation of black power and pride, the seven-hour concert benefited the Sickle Cell Anemia Foundation, the Martin Luther King Hospital in Watts, and future Watts summer festivals. *Wattstax* became a feature film as well as a record album.

See also Memphis sound.

The Weathermen   They considered themselves the moral elite of the youth counterculture groups and offended nearly everyone who they thought lacked their resolution and depth of feeling. The most violent wing of the counterculture, they operated as terrorists, some perishing in their efforts to make homemade bombs. Curiously, they took their name from a Bob Dylan song, "Subterranean Homesick Blues," in which he renounced his former concern with social issues. "Don't follow leaders," he sang, "watch parking meters; you don't need a weatherman to tell which way the wind blows."

The Weavers   Made up of Lee Hays, Fred Hellerman, Ronnie Gilbert, and Pete Seeger—"two low baritones, one brilliant alto and a split tenor," in Seeger's words, which results in an extraordinary blend of voices—the Weavers sparked the urban folk song revival of the 1950s and later served as the inspiration for the protest songwriter/singers of the sixties. Stemming from the Country-rooted Almanac Singers—a loosely knit group that included Lee Hays, Millard Lampell, Woody Guthrie, Burl Ives, and Pete Seeger—they paved the way for such urban revivalists as the Kingston Trio, Peter, Paul & Mary, and others. Formed in 1948 for the fun of singing together, the Weavers performed for fun at union meetings, near picket lines and in hootenannies until they persuaded Max Gordon, owner of the Village Vanguard, to book them for a farewell stint.

A two-week gig at Christmas time in '49, which stretched to a six-month booking, led to a Decca contract and the release in 1950 of their debut disk, "Tzena, Tzena" b/w Leadbelly's "Goodnight, Irene," which was arranged and conducted by Gordon Jenkins. "Goodnight, Irene" became the longest-tenured No. 1 song in Top 100 charts between 1948 and 1975, while "Tzena Tzena" climbed to No. 2. Both became bestsellers just about the time that the group was attacked as subversive by *Red Channels* (a red-baiting publication). By 1952 the impact of the McCarthy-era blacklist was such that the group disbanded. Three years later, when New York City's Town Hall would not rent to them, they performed at Carnegie Hall, an event that opened the door to select bookings and the reunion of the group, which finally disbanded in 1963. Through the years, Pete Seeger performed solo annually at Carnegie Hall around Thanksgiving. In 1980 the Weavers joined Seeger, reuniting for a twenty-fifth anniversary concert and singing "On Top of Old Smoky," Woody Guthrie's "So Long, It's Been Good to Know You," and other folk songs that they had brought into the Pop mainstream in the fifties.

See also Woody Guthrie; message songs; Pete Seeger; The Village Vanguard.

West Coast Jazz   A small-combo style of the 1950s developed by such western groups as the pianoless quintet of Gerry Mulligan (b. 1927), the Sonny Stitt (b. 1924) quartet, the George Shearing (b. 1919) quintet, and the quartet of Dave Brubeck (b. 1920), with astringent altoist Paul Desmond (1924–1977). It involved such cool jazzmen as tenor saxist Stan Getz (b. 1927), vibraphonist Terry Gibbs (b. 1924), guitarist Billy Bauer (b. 1915), and alto saxist Lee Konitz (b. 1927). The school derived in part from the cool style of Lester "Prez" Young (1909–1959) and was regarded as a reaction to Bop. Like Bop, it emphasized listening rather than a dance beat. Experimental to a degree, it has been characterized as "thinking man's Jazz."

See also Bop; Cool Jazz; Lester Young.

Western Swing   In the late 1930s, as Swing was sweeping the country with Benny Goodman (b. 1909) as its kingpin, a country fiddler from

Texas named Bob Wills (1905–1975) developed a Western brand of the sound. He wedded Bluegrass to the Big Band sound, introducing drums, horns, and the electric guitar into C & W music. The Texas Playboys, as he called his band, were organized in 1932, and with Wills and his fiddle providing what Goodman and his clarinet did, produced at least one million-seller in "San Antonio Rose" (1940), which Wills wrote. Other well-known samples of Western Swing include "Mexicali Rose," "Take Me Back to Tulsa," and "Texas Playboy Rag." Other proponents of Western Swing include Milton Brown's Musical Brownies and also Spade Cooley (1910–1969), who died after spending years in jail for the murder of his wife. Composer/author of "Shame on You" (1944), which he recorded on Columbia, Spade is remembered for recordings of "The Last Round-Up" b/w "Wagon Wheels," "Oklahoma Stomp," and "Cowbell Polka." He was known as the King of Western Swing although he did not achieve the renown of Bob Wills, who was elected to the C & W Hall of Fame in 1968. Many hear the sound of Western Swing in the work of Bill Haley (1925–1981), even though his most immediate debt is to Louis Jordan (1908-1975).

See also Bluegrass; Swing.

"wheels"   Black and teenage slang for an automobile.

Where the Action Is   An ABC–TV show produced by Dick Clark (b. 1929) of *American Bandstand* in the mid-1960s. Paul Revere (b. 1942) and the Raiders were among the regulars on the show.

Whisky-à-Go-Go   A showcase of Rock talent on Sunset Boulevard in Hollywood, it was opened in 1963 by Elmer Valentine, a former Chicago policeman, and remains today one of the best and longest-lived Rock clubs in the country.

"whispering-fashion-model voice"   A French characterization (*une voix chuchotante mannequinée*) for singer Olivia Newton-John (b. 1949), whose first American hit was "Let Me Be There" (1973), followed by "If You Love Me Let Me Know" and "I Honestly Love You" (both in 1974), and "Have You Never Been Mellow?" and "Please Mr. Please" (both in 1975). Winner of many Grammy Awards, she starred in the film version of *Grease* (1978).

white Blues revival   The Blues revival of 1968 is often credited to the work of Cream, the white British supergroup that included drummer Ginger Baker, bass/harmonica player Jack Bruce, and guitarist Eric Clapton, who had been part of John Mayall's Bluesbreakers, the British daddy of white Blues groups. In the wake of Cream's American splash, the John Mayall combo toured the U.S.A., along with Ten Years After, Fleetwood Mac, and other white English Blues groups. (The strong influence of America's R & B artists on Britain's Rock groups had previously been evident in the sound and recordings of the Animals, Yardbirds, and Rolling Stones, all of whom were part of the mid-sixties British invasion of American radio.)

The U.S.A. also had its own coterie of blue-eyed bluesmen, with a main base in Chicago. As Muddy Waters (b. 1915), Howlin' Wolf (1910–1976), Bo Diddley (b. 1928), and other exponents of electrified, ensemble Chicago Blues performed in South Side and West Side black ghetto clubs, there would be a few white faces in the audience: harmonica-player Paul Butterfield (b. 1942), guitarist Mike Bloomfield (1943–1981), and organist Barry Goldberg. (They also dug the recordings of earlier bluesmen like Lightnin' Hopkins, 1912–1982, and John Lee Hooker, b. 1917.) By 1965 the Paul Butterfield Blues Band was in operation, with Mike Bloomfield playing Blues guitar. The Beatles were then the rage, while Bob Dylan and the California Byrds were electrifying Folk music to develop Folk Rock. But Butterfield worked to spread the sound of Chicago's electrified Blues. So did organist Goldberg, who was originally part of the Butterfield group; guitarist/vocalist Steve Miller (b. circa 1945), originally with Goldberg's own Blues band; and the Electric Flag, which was formed by Mike Bloomfield and made its debut at the 1967 Monterey Pop Festival. By 1968 all of these operations jelled in the Blues revival, which peaked in putting Canned Heat and their bluesy "Let's Work Together" on the charts in 1970.

See also Blue-eyed Soul; Blues; Chicago Blues style; Rhythm & Blues.

white buckskins   In his TV appearances, Pat Boone (b. 1934) always wore white buckskins. Whether or not he intended these to symbolize his own brand of soft, gentle Rock, they were so taken by the "blue suede" crowd. Some critics began using "white buckskins" as a derisive reference to the type of Pop Rock 'n' Roll that Boone represented.

See also Pop Rock; Teenage Rock.

white Country harmony   It was the sound heard in the singing of such Country duos as the Delmore Brothers (Alton: 1908–1964; Rabon: 1910–1952), the Louvin Brothers (Ira:1924–1965; Charlie, b. 1927), and the Everly Brothers (Don: b. 1937; Phil: b. 1939). The notes were just a third apart.

Paul Whiteman (1890–1967)   He was known as the King of Jazz, a misnomer, but one that was perpetuated in a Universal film with that title (1930). But he should be remembered for his contribution to "symphonic Jazz," symphonic orchestration of popular songs, and jazzing the classics. His very first platter was a 12-inch disk of "Avalon" b/w "Dance of the Hours" from the opera *La Gioconda*. That same year (1920), his recording of "Whispering" b/w "Japanese Sandman" was a million-plus seller. In 1924 he sponsored a historic concert at Aeolian Hall in Manhattan. "An Experiment in Modern Music" it was called, and it introduced to the world George Gershwin and his *Rhapsody in Blue*. The arrangement for the Whiteman Orchestra was by Ferde Grofe (1892-1972), whose scoring genius gave the orchestra its distinctive symphonic sound.

Although the title King of Jazz, fixed on Whiteman largely because of the 1924 concert, is misleading, he is warmly remembered in Jazz circles for his role in employing many of the great jazzmen of the day. A very incomplete list of such performers would include: Bix Beiderbecke (1903-1931), Frankie Trumbauer (1901-1956), Red Nichols (1905-1965), Jimmy Dorsey (1904-1957), Tommy Dorsey (1905-1956), fiddler Joe Venuti (1898-1978), and Eddie Lang (1902-1933). In the late twenties, the Whiteman Orchestra featured a vocal group known as The Rhythm Boys, one of whose members was Bing Crosby (1904-1977). Whiteman also used some of the great Jazz singers of the day: Mildred Bailey (1907-1951), Johnny Mercer (1909-1976), Lee Wiley (1915-1975), and others. In the early days of Rock 'n' Roll, Robert Louis Ridarelli (b. 1940) appeared on a teenage TV show, sponsored by Paul Whiteman, who suggested that the youngster change his name to Bobby Rydell, which he did.

white noise   A hissing sound produced when every frequency in the audible spectrum is heard at the same intensity. The analogue is the color white, produced when every hue in the visible spectrum is seen at the same intensity. In both instances, audible or visible, white implies the absence of color (tone color in the former case). White noise can be electrically generated.

The Who   One of the most creative of Rock groups, The Who was formed in London in 1964, consisting of Peter Townshend (b. 1944), lead guitar; Keith Moon (1947-1978), drums; John Entwistle (b. 1945), bass guitar, trumpet, French horn, and piano; and Roger Daltrey (b. 1945), lead singer, guitar, and harp. On their first appearance at the prestigious Marquee Club in London, they indulged in such shenanigans—Moon breaking drumsticks, Daltrey smashing the microphone against the floor and Townshend ramming his guitar into the amplifier—that they seemed to pioneer such developments as Glitter Rock, Shock Rock, and Theatrical Rock. In fact, when they made their

American debut at the Monterey Pop Festival in 1967, they scored a sensation by their destructive tactics.

By then, they had already been on tour with The Beatles and achieved a No. 1 bestseller in England with "My Generation." Title song of an album, "My Generation" was one of several songs that expressed the antagonism of young people toward their parents' morals and values. Moreover, it enunciated a basic, if unfortunately prophetic, idea of all too many rockers: "Hope I die before I get old." Stylistically, "My Generation" embodied such an extreme use of distortion that Decca believed they had a defective master when it arrived for release in this country. It was, perhaps, the first contact of American record executives with a new esthetic concept: distortion through feedback, reverb, etc., as a form of expression.

In April 1969 *Tommy,* a double LP, was on release. It was the first Rock opera, a work of innovative originality. Although Tommy, the leading character, was described as a "deaf, dumb and blind kid," he was really an autistic child who had separated himself from reality as the result of a traumatic experience that inhibited the use of these senses. A much-publicized problem of today's world, child abuse, was explored in the work as Peter Townshend, the major author/composer of *Tommy,* described the older generation's mistreatment—psychological, physical and sexual—of the boy. Apart from yielding a bestseller in "Pinball Wizard" for Elton John (b. 1947), the work was performed by the prestigious Metropolitan Opera Company in New York City, produced as a ballet, and made into a film. By 1972 the album had sold over 3 million copies and an American record company had produced a new, elegant LP, replete with an illustrated libretto, performed by the grand London Symphony Orchestra, a large choir, and such rock stars as Ringo Starr and Rod Stewart, and actor/singer Richard Harris (of "MacArthur Park" fame) in leading roles.

In the Fall of 1973, The Who produced what has been characterized as their masterpiece. *Quadrophenia,* a double album with all songs by Peter Townshend, dealt with a young Londoner's search for identity and fulfillment, and sensitively explored his alternating moods of aggression and frustration.

See also Glitter Rock; Heavy Metal; Theatrical Rock.

The Whole Earth Catalogue   Compiled by Stewart Brand of the Hog Farm commune in California, it became the Bible of the commune-minded because of its concern with health foods and vegetarianism.

whole-tone scale   A scale made up entirely of whole tones; each note is a full step, or two half-tones, away from its predecessor: c–d–e–f♯–g♯–a♯–c. Only two whole-tone scales are possible in the diatonic system: one on the note c and the other on the note c♯: c♯–d♯–f–g–a–b–c♯. If you take any note on the piano keyboard and proceed with a series of whole tone steps, any series of eight notes will contain the notes of the whole-tone scale either on c or c♯.

"wig"   As a verb, current slang for: to think, analyze, evaluate.

Hank Williams (1923–1953)   An unschooled but superlative songwriter—nicknamed "the Hillbilly Shakespeare"—he wrote songs of such wide appeal that he could reach rural southerners, and Pop artists could make mainstream hits of them: Jo Stafford (b. 1920) with his "Jambalaya," Tony Bennett (b. 1926) with "Cold, Cold Heart," and Rosemary Clooney (b. 1928) with "Half as Much." In this way, he was largely responsible for the early 1950s infiltration of Country music into the mainstream. In addition to the songs mentioned, he wrote such classics as "Your Cheatin' Heart" (1952), "Ramblin' Man" (1951), "Lost Highway" (1949), "I'm So Lonesome I Could Cry" (1949), "Hey, Good Lookin'" (1951), "Honky-Tonkin'" (1948), and "Lovesick Blues" (1949), which was his debut disk. He also wrote such deeply moving religious songs as "Mansion on the Hill" (1948) and "I Saw the Light" (1948). Like Jimmie Rodgers (1897–1933), he is one of Country music's legendary figures. He was one of the first three men elected to the Country Music Hall of Fame in 1961, together with Rodgers and his publisher, Fred Rose (1897–1954).

Mary Lou Williams (1910–1981)   The first woman in Jazz history to compose and arrange for a large Jazz orchestra, Mary Lou Williams set the style of Andy Kirk & His 12 Clouds of Joy and dominated the band's playing with her power and artistry at the keyboard. The Kirk association lasted from 1929 until 1942 and yielded such Jazz standards as "Froggy Bottom," "Little Joe from Chicago," "Walkin' and Swinging'," "Lotta Sax Appeal," and "Mary's Idea." Her Jazz compositions were to be found also in the libraries of the Louis Armstrong band, Bob Crosby, Tommy Dorsey, Earl Hines, Glen Gray, and Benny Goodman, for whom she wrote "Camel Hop" and "Roll 'Em." In 1945 at a Town Hall concert, she introduced her extended work, *The Zodiac Suite,* which was performed the following year by the New York Philharmonic Orchestra. As the sound of Jazz changed with the rise of Bop, she became associated with Thelonious Monk (b. 1920) and Bud Powell (b. 1924), pianists who influenced a style that originally was molded by Earl Hines (b. 1903) and Boogie-Woogie. She reacted to the new sounds with *In the Land of Oo-Bla-Dee,* described as a "Bop Fairy Tale." Converting to Catholicism in the mid-1950s, she produced such liturgical works as "Mary Lou's Mass" and "St. Martin de Porres."

At the time of her death from cancer, she was artist-in-residence at Duke University, where she taught Jazz history and conducted a student orchestra.

"Willie the Lion"   Everything about William Henry Joseph Berthol Bonaparte Bertholoff Smith (1897–1973), Jazz pianist and teacher, was colorful, starting with his name. An outstanding Stride pianist of Jewish/Negro parentage, he early acquired the cognomen "Willie the Lion" because of his regal manner and bombastic speaking style. During the late 1920s and early 1930s, he was featured pianist at Pod's and Jerry's, a famous Harlem nightspot. In New York he also played at the original Onyx Club on 52nd Street while it was a musicians' hangout in the speakeasy days. His students include such outstanding jazzmen as pianist Joe Bushkin (b. 1916), pianist Mel Powell (b. 1923), and clarinetist Artie Shaw (b. 1910). Duke Ellington (1899–1974), who was one of the Lion's great admirers, dedicated *Portrait of the Lion* to him.
    See also Stride piano.

Windjammer   Cajun accordion played by Leadbelly. *See* Huddie Ledbetter.

"The Wonder-Boy Preacher"   Singer/songwriter Solomon Burke (b. circa 1940) had his own church in Philadelphia before he was 13. It was known as Solomon's Temple. Breaking into the record market in 1961, he quickly became a major exponent of Soul.
    See also Soul.

"woodshed"   As a verb, to practice in private intensely and for long periods.

Woodstock Nation   In *Woodstock Nation* (1970), Abbie Hoffman sought to make a legend of the three-day Rock festival held at Woodstock, N.Y. But so did *Life* magazine, which published a special issue on it. What gave the event the proportions of a legend were the abysmally trying conditions under which it was held. For the three days of the festival (in August 1969) it rained, so that the ground on which the audience sat, ate, and slept was turned into a quagmire. Add a shortage of food, inadequate sanitary facilities, being drenched to the skin—and you have the basis for discord, anger, frustration, violence. Instead, the 500,000 youngsters who existed through these conditions lived in harmony, peace, and love. It truly had the makings of a legend—and so the "Woodstock Nation" emerged. It was a short-lived nation, rent asunder by the dismal and tragic proceedings at Altamont, only four months later.

Joni Mitchell memorialized the festival in "Woodstock," a song that included the stirring lines: "By the time we got to Woodstock/We were half a million strong/And everywhere was song and celebration/I dreamed I saw the bombers/Riding shotgun in the sky/Turning into butterflies above our nation. . . ." Recorded by Crosby, Stills, Nash & Young, the disk climbed to No. 11 on 1970's Pop charts. About the same time, Mountain, who had appeared at the festival, placed "On Yasgur's Farm" on the charts.

Although it was known as the Woodstock Festival, it actually took place at a site about 55 miles from Woodstock. Turned down by the town's authorities, the festival accepted the hospitality of Max Yasgur, a dairy farmer who offered a sloping hillside for the event. Despite the incessant rain, the show went on day and night, and yielded a triple LP, *Woodstock,* that became a Gold Record even before its release and that went on to sell over 2 million copies. Not all who performed appear in the album; but the following are represented: John B. Sebastian, Canned Heat, Richie Havens, Country Joe & the Fish, Arlo Guthrie, Sha-Na-Na, Joan Baez, Crosby, Stills, Nash & Young, The Who, Santana, Ten Years After, Jefferson Airplane, Sly & the Family Stone, the Butterfield Blues Band, and Jimi Hendrix. In addition, the proceedings, which also yielded a film, included appearances by Melanie, The Band, Creedence Clearwater Revival, Blood, Sweat & Tears, the Grateful Dead, Tim Hardin, Johnny Winter, the Incredible String Band, and Ravi Shankar.

See also Altamont; festivals.

"worryin' a word"   *See* melisma.

xylophone   Introduced from Eastern Europe in the mid-nineteenth century; a percussion instrument made of tuned wooden slats, arranged as on a piano keyboard, and played with small wooden sticks. The range is from middle C upwards for three octaves. The vibraphone is similar except that it uses metal bars instead of wood, has electrically operated resonators under the bars to give a vibrant sound, and has a range from F below middle C for three octaves.

Y

Jimmy Yancey (1894–1951)   When John Hammond (b. 1910) produced his famous "Spirituals to Swing" concert at Carnegie Hall in 1938, Jimmy Yancey was working as a grounds-keeper at Comiskey Park in Chicago, a job he had held since 1925. He had actually left the entertainment field in June 1913 after having toured Europe and appeared before King George V at Buckingham Palace. When the "Spirituals to Swing" concert aroused interest in Boogie-Woogie as a result of performances by two other Chicago pianists, Albert Ammons (1907–1949) and Meade Lux Lewis (1905–1964), a search began for Jimmy Yancey. The interest in Yancey was partly the result of a 1936 recording by Lewis of "Yancey Special," a number that was also recorded in 1938 by Bob Crosby (b. 1913) & His Bob Cats. By then, it became evident that the Father of the Chicago school of Boogie-Woogie was, indeed, Yancey. Although his friends and disciples—"Cripple" Clarence Lofton (1887–1957), Cow Cow Davenport (1894–1955), Pinetop Smith (1904–1929), and others—had been making Boogie records during the twenties and thirties, he did not record until 1939—and then it was evident who the master was. Before his death from diabetes, he recorded for Solo Art, Victor, Session, and Atlantic. Jerry Wexler, now a Warner Bros. producer and long a producer at Atlantic, has indicated that Yancey's bass-lines, "six- and eight-beat Boogies, in Shuffle as well as Rumba time, were used on countless records: Ruth Brown's 'Daddy, Daddy,' Guitar Slim's 'The Things I Used to Do,' and Pee Wee Crayton's 'After Hours,' among others."

"Yardbird"   *See* Charlie Parker.

yodel   A style of singing, practiced originally in the Austrian Tyrol, in which the voice alternates between projecting naturally and the use of falsetto. A number of American Country singers, especially Jimmie Rodgers (1897–1933), known as the Father of Country Music, were yodelers. Rodgers recorded a series of what he called "Blue yodels," as many as nine. Howlin' Wolf (1910–1976), the R & B singer who idolized Rodgers, turned to howling when he found he could not yodel like Rodgers. To put it differently, he yodeled but it came out a howl.

Lester "Prez" Young (1909–1959)   Together with Coleman Hawkins (1904–1969), he was a pivotal influence in shaping the sound of the tenor sax. As "Bean" Hawkins represented the big-toned tenor and driving dotted-eighth-and-sixteenth-note phrasing, "Prez" Young spoke for a cool type of Jazz, a sweeter, mellower sound, and a lag-along style of phrasing. During his years with Count Basie, he composed a number of evergreen Jazz instrumentals, including "Tickle Toe" and "Jumpin' with Symphony Sid." He acquired his cognomen through Billie Holiday (1915–1959) in the era of Franklin Delano Roosevelt. As a performer who was tops in his field, he was the Prez to her. The Prez Awards, given to Jazz performers whose names are to be imbedded in the Jazzwalk on 52nd Street in New York City, are named after him.

See also Cool Jazz; Jazzwalk; West Coast Jazz.

Your Hit Parade   Subtitled "America's Taste in Popular Music," *Your Hit Parade* was a brassy Saturday night show on network radio, later on TV, that bowed on April 20, 1935, and ran for 24 years until April 24, 1959. Launched with the rise of the Big Bands of Swing, its popularity peaked in the era of the Big Baritones (Sinatra, Como, Nat "King" Cole) and waned as the Big Belters (Frankie Laine, Eddie Fisher, Rosemary Clooney, etc.) moved into the Pop music scene. The *Parade*'s impact was weakened by the rise of Top 40 programming, which provided an hourly hit parade for listeners. Part of the *Parade*'s appeal had been the element of surprise: What songs would make the Top 10 on Saturday night? Its death knell was sounded when the record superseded the song in the hit-making process, for then listeners wanted to hear *the* singer who made the hit disk and not an interpreter, i.e., one of the regulars on the *Hit Parade.*

Sponsored by Lucky Strike cigarettes, *Your Hit Parade* used a tobacco auctioneer's singsong mumbo-jumbo of calling prices and the clicking of a telegrapher's key in the opening commercial, "L–S–M–F–T, Lucky Strike Means Fine Tobacco." Until it went on TV in 1950—one of the earliest shows to tackle the then-new medium—the *Parade* was the crux of the music business. The aim of every music publisher was to get his song on the *Parade,* and every publisher maneuvered to get advance information on the songs to be honored each Saturday night. (The reflection of a song's progress as a hit, being on the *Parade* led to more performances on key shows, increased sheet-music sales, and secured higher prices for foreign placements of a song.) A closely guarded secret, the list was prepared each week at the offices of the American Tobacco Co., makers of Lucky Strike, which never revealed the yardstick or statistical process used in selecting the chosen songs.

Television presented serious problems to the show, partly in the staging of songs repeated from week to week as they climbed in popularity, but especially in the contrast in age and appearance between the regular performers and the songs they had to sing when Rock 'n' Roll arrived on the scene. In 1956 a Rock critic wrote: "The creepiest of the four (regulars), Snooky Lanson, stood up in front of the cardboard set, and sang, 'You ain't nothin' but a hound dog,' with a shit-eating Lucky Strike grin on his face.''

Your Hit Parade struggled heroically to recapture the audience and appeal it had commanded when Sinatra was starred in the mid 1940s. It changed formats; it reduced the number of songs in the weekly survey; it brought on younger singers. But it was trapped in an insoluble contradiction: it needed an adult audience in order to sell its product, but the music scene was teenage. Although the cast sang, in the spring of 1958, "So long for a while. . . . So long to *Your Hit Parade*. . . and the tunes you picked to be played," it did not return in the fall of 1959.

A victim of the Rock Revolution, it left one curious fact behind. The song that remained longest in the No. 1 position of any song in the show's 24 years was *Too Young*. Popularized by Nat "King" Cole in 1951, *Too Young* presaged a favorite theme of Rock music: the older generation's failure to understand the teenager.

See also Big Ballad era; No. 1 plug; Tin-Pan Alley.

Z

Zoetrope   A variant version of the 19th-century equivalent of today's movie projector: an optical toy in which figures, painted inside a slitted drum, appeared to move when the drum was illuminated and spun. Variants of this device have been used by various Rock groups in light shows.

See also light show.

"zonked"   When a drug user or drinker has taken too much and is in a kind of stupor, that person is "zonked out."

zoot suit   A suit popular in the Swing era among blacks and Chicanos, involving a jacket that reached down to the knees and ballooning pants that narrowed at the shoe line. *Zoot Suit* is the title of a play/musical/film that was commissioned for the Mark Taper Forum in 1977 and ran for 38 weeks in Los Angeles. It deals with the life of the Chicano in the U.S.A. and with the era when Mexican-American youths dressed in the suits as a symbol of their life-style. In that era, Los Angeles passed an ordinance forbidding the wearing of zoot suits.

Zydeco   A rhythmic dance music, it emanated from the French-speaking blacks of Louisiana and east Texas. Made up of accordion, violin, and guitar, combos play a lively fusion of Blues and Cajun music. Clifton Chenier (b. 1925), who came from Opelousas, La., and settled in Oakland, Calif., is the best-known exponent of the style. The origin of the word ''Zydeco'' is not clear. It is said to be a corruption of *les haricots,* the French word for snap beans.

Index

421